Business Systems

WILLOUGHBY AND SENN

ASSOCIATION FOR SYSTEMS MANAGEMENT

Library of Congress Cataloging in Publication Data

Willoughby, Theodore C
    Business systems.

    Previous editions by the Association for Systems
Management.

    Includes bibliographies and index.

    1. Electronic data processing—Business.
2. Management information systems. 3. System
analysis. I. Senn, James, joint author. II. Association
for Systems Management. Business systems.
III. Title.
HF5548.2.W468   658'.05'4   75-14121

Printed in the United States of America

FOREWORD

This text is designed specifically for the college student who has had introductory courses in data processing, computer technology, or management and is now taking his first course in systems analysis. This textbook is intended to be used both by students pursuing a career in business systems and by those students desiring some exposure to systems analysis techniques as part of their general background. This book is designed to provide the foundation for both the systems professional and those who will pursue other disciplines, yet will interact with the analysis in the functioning of the business system. We believe that the study of this book will benefit all those participating in business management. The principles in this text will help them understand their roles in the design of new and improved business systems.

First, *Business Systems* is a textbook. It is not light reading but rather a book to study in order to gain insight into the design of better systems. In writing this text, the authors examined not only the content but also the sequence and plan for the presentation of the material. The text was purposefully divided into 30 chapters to match the teaching schedules of most Universities and Junior Colleges. All of the material presented has been class-tested for its teachability.

Overall, the text has been divided into six major sections. Each section is prefaced with a description of its contents and is designed to be taught as a separate unit, laying the foundation for the next section. Each chapter concludes with a summary which captures the main points presented. The Review Questions and Discussion Questions at the end of each chapter are for reinforcing the material that has been covered. In an effort to create "real world" class discussion, the questions presented have been reviewed and added to by professional analysts. Many are actual case situations which will give the student the feel of an actual system problem. The reviewers also input many fine examples and case histories that have been inserted into the body of the text to enhance the principles being taught.

The original *Business Systems* text published by the Association for Systems Management in 1963, pioneered the field. In those days, the need was for a basic text to unite the many individual systems curricula being taught in colleges and in-company training courses throughout North America. The demand for the original text and its subsequent revisions was very gratifying to the members of ASM who are dedicated to the continuing education of systems professionals.

This text has been written to supplant that original text. It is a response to the demand for a new text that details the systems approach to management for the "age of systems". We believe this book to be an up-to-date, integrated treatment of the entire systems function that will replace the original text as the "unabridged authority on systems". Our ultimate aim was to produce a text that would become the basic one for teaching systems and at the same time a reference for systems practitioners. We believe we have done it.

ABOUT THE AUTHORS

The authors for *Business Systems* were chosen because of their unusual blend of academic and practical experience. This unusual combination has produced a text as professional as the people it will serve.

Theodore C. Willoughby, Ph.D., is a professor at the School of Management, State University of New York at Binghamton. His doctorate was in management information systems at the University of Minnesota. However, he adds to his academic achievements 18 years of systems analysis experience with several of North America's large corporations. He has been a systems analyst, project manager, and consultant as well as an educator.

He is the author of many professional papers, an active conference speaker, a member of the CDP certification council, edits the publications of the Special Interest Group on Computer Personnel Research of ACM, a member of the Editorial Review Board of the *Journal of Systems Management* and is a member of several professional associations including the Association for Systems Management.

James A. Senn, Ph.D., is also a graduate of the University of Minnesota's Management Information Systems course and now teaching in the School of Management at SUNY—Binghamton. He brings to this text a thorough background in teaching systems management plus the experience of publishing several books and many articles in the systems field.

He has extensive background in consulting on "real world" systems problems which have added an extra dimension to this text and has class-tested much of the material contained herein.

ACKNOWLEDGMENTS

We are grateful for the input of the many colleagues, reviewers and students who contributed to the completion of this book. Special indebtedness is due the reviewers who read the manuscript and offered many helpful suggestions—

D. Richard Allen
Frank C. Ardsley
James Baldwin
Burte J. Banks, Jr.
Paul S. Benoit
Laurence Carey
John V. Chow
Albert F. Collard
A. K. Dekom
William R. Flury
Dr. Harvey S. Gellman
Donald L. Gerber
Dr. James R. Gunderman
Clyde W. Jackson
George A. Khtaian
Hank E. Koehn
Richard Masimore
Dr. Gibbs Myers
Carl Osteen
Curtis Rice
Adelmo Romagnoli
Dr. Kenton E. Ross
William S. Scott
N. L. Senensieb
Jan Snyders
Robert I. Stevens
Anderson H. Vaughan
Harvey M. Weiss

plus the many others whose specific contributions are recognized throughout this book. A special gratitude is also due to A. James Andrews, ASM Director of Publications, for his organization of the original content outline, the endless editing of several drafts, his helpful criticisms and general cheerful attitude in the frustrating delays that accompany a publishing project.

CONTENTS

PART IV—Systems Design 305

PART V—Systems Implementation 439

PART VI—Systems Control and Minor
Maintenance....................553

Epilogue 649

Index 651

Information Systems in Organizations

Many information systems projects fail to satisfy all the planned objectives. Projects can be late, over budget, or unsatisfactory to the user. Some just do not accomplish the objectives. This book was written under the assumption that knowing about the project development process is part of the solution to the problem.

Part I describes the environment in which the information system project operates. It is assumed that most of the readers have some knowledge of business management, programming and quantitative techniques. Chapters 1 and 2 introduce some general systems ideas and their relationship to modern organizations. The effect of the computer on those systems is described in some detail.

Chapter 3 shows why the systems designer cannot ignore the human dimensions of analysis and design. It covers, in some detail, the ways in which people resist change, and the ways to overcome this resistance.

Chapter 4 introduces and interprets some economic and analytic ideas that relate to systems analysis and design. Some ability to work with quantitative concepts is a necessary skill for the systems analyst.

Together, Chapters 1, 2, 3 and 4 prepare the reader for the systems life cycle description and the analysis and design tools that follow.

CHAPTER 1

SYSTEMS THEORY

The management of today's business organization is ordered by many complex theories, philosophies, and scientific methods. However, the base on which these lofty management techniques have been constructed is that all business must have an operational system which allows it to function effectively. This system is the circulatory tract of business transactions which allows the organization to function in fulfilling its purposes.

BUSINESS SYSTEMS DEFINED

The word system implies that the manager of a business organization orders his job to enable him to cope in his diverse operating environment. Every manager attempts to organize the work elements (customers, suppliers, workers, inventory, regulations, competition, etc.) that are his business environment. A business system is a set of actions which have a relationship to each other. The actions have variables of input, process, output, feedback and restriction. The action relationships may be complementary (necessary to each other) or contradictory (inhibiting each other).

A business system is not abstract or conceptual. It contains actual elements (rather than ideas) which operate in relation to the other elements for accomplishment of a common business goal. Examples of three business systems are:

Computer System	The collection of hardware and software elements which work interdependently under some means of control to process data and produce output reports.
Communication System	A collection of components capable of representing and transmitting bits of information from one point to another.
Marketing System	The collection of people, equipment, and procedures which sell, promote, and distribute commodities, ideas, and entities to a consumer or user.

SYSTEM ENVIRONMENT

All business systems operate within an environment. The environment surrounds the system, and both affects and is affected by it. The environment relates to the system's goals, needs, activities and individuals interacting with the system.

A business system is separated from its environment by a known boundary. That boundary is set by the systems designer based upon the goals and purposes of the business.

The system interacts with its environment as input and output cross the boundaries of the system. Boundaries serve to regulate the flow of information to and from the system, and to protect it from destructive or damaging agents in the environment. For example, in an inventory control system the boundary regulators would limit *which* materials would enter the inventory and *how much* of an item would be accepted.

Input to the system often must be filtered or encoded (Figure 1.1) before it will be accepted by the system. A card reader in a computer system, for example, transfers punched card information

The Boundary and Input Control

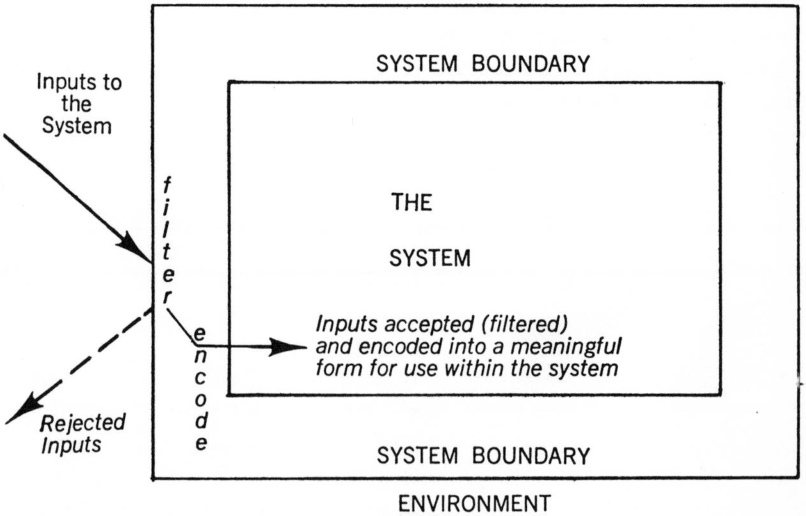

FIGURE 1.1

into electrical pulses for the computer processing unit of the system. Without the encoding process of the card reader, the punched cards would be useless to the computer system.

The two main types of input to systems are energizing input and maintenance input. *Energizing input* is data and information to be acted on by the system to generate output. A file of accounts re-

Energizing Input for the System

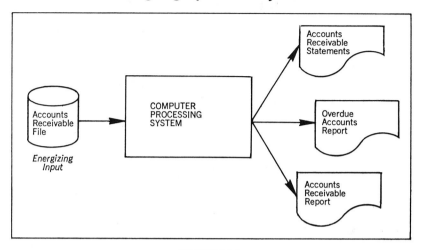

FIGURE 1.2

ceivable serves to energize a computer system to update and produce current account statements as output (Figure 1.2).

Maintenance input improves and controls the system. Output information is often fed back to the system (Figure 1.3) to check the processes occurring within the system. Feedback will be discussed in more detail later in this chapter.

Regulation of Activities and Processes

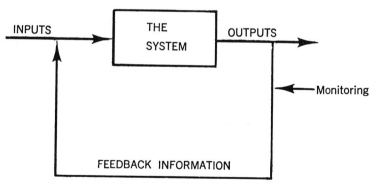

FIGURE 1.3

Output is produced from the actions of the system components on input. The output of one system may become input to another system, as shown in Figure 1.4.

Relation Among Systems

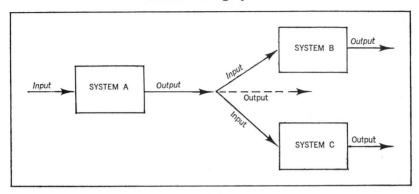

FIGURE 1.4

OPEN/CLOSED SYSTEMS

An open system is one which exchanges information, material, and energy with its environment. An open system adjusts continually to changes in input, feedback and environment. A closed system is one which does not receive input from nor output to its environment, and thus does not require these adaptive properties.

A system may be a single component or many components, but it is a functioning unit working with other subsystems to accomplish a specific purpose. Subsystems transfer information among each other through an interface. Interfaces are connections at the system or component boundaries which transfer information across that boundary (Figure 1.5). The interface provides an information encoding or decoding mechanism to make it acceptable to the system receiving it. In a computer system, for example, a data channel serves as an interface between the central processing unit and the input devices.

Physical System Interfaces

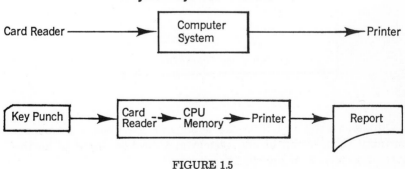

FIGURE 1.5

FEEDBACK

Feedback, both negative and positive, is important to the control of systems. The purpose of negative feedback (Figure 1.3) is to assist in maintaining the system within the critical operating range and reduce performance fluctuations. In a feedback loop a sensor detects the effect of the output on the environment and inputs this effect to the system to activate any adjustments in accordance with predetermined goals. The automatic sensing mechanism in a missile system operates on the basis of negative feedback to ensure that the missile is on an exact course to the prescribed target. If the missile is traveling at either too high or too low an angle, a signal to the control mechanism would result in a course adjustment.

In contrast, positive feedback reinforces the management of a system and causes it to continue its performance and activities without change. A production system receiving an input from management to continue production of mousetraps at the same rate as last week would be receiving positive feedback.

SYSTEMS CONTROL

Control can be defined as the process which measures current performance and guides it toward some predetermined goal. Feedback is one type of control that has already been mentioned.

Control Elements

In any process being controlled, the essential elements are:

1. A predetermined goal, purpose, objective, or standard.
Every business system has a desired result, called the goal, purpose, standard, performance or objective. For example, the objective of a marketing system may be to produce sales of 50 million dollars in a year, while a quality control system in manufacturing might have dual goals of keeping the defect rate for manufactured items under two percent and removing all defective items from the final production line.

2. A means for measuring performance.
Any controlled system must have the means for measuring performance. This measurement is often the most difficult one to develop in a man-designed system. The degree of accuracy with which a goal is accomplished will vary from system to system. The measurement of achievement must be in units which are similar to those stated in the predetermined goals.

3. A means for comparison to detect divergence from the goal.

Comparison of performance against a predetermined goal (allowing for some variation) is another step in a control operation. The critical step is in determining the degree of variation allowed.

4. A means for correction and adjustment.

Finally, the system should be able to take corrective action when a significant variance in the process is detected. System adjustments should be made only when necessary. Many adjustments indicate a need for a better designed system.

The principles of systems theory and systems control have many applications in the management of organizations. A corporate entity is an open system as it continually interacts with its environment of markets, suppliers, personnel and restrictions. Within the organization are subsystems which are complete systems in themselves, e.g., the accounting system, the production system, and the information system. These systems in turn interact with the other systems in the total organization. The accounting system, for example, produces information on operations and activities for all parts of the organization, as does the information system.

Although most organization systems are open systems, automated production has made closed systems desirable in the production and processing functions. For example, a monitor placed on a liquid flow line to make the necessary adjustments to valves for a steady rate of flow, or constant pressure, is a relatively closed system. However, most automated systems are not totally closed because human intervention is required for unanticipated conditions or when the system fails. Such occurrences are bound to happen in man-made control systems.

Many inventory systems are designed as closed loop control systems. For example, a reorder quantity might be built into the inventory control mechanism so that when the inventory reaches a specified minimum level, a standard order would be computer generated. This continual monitoring of inventory levels, adjusting of order quantities, and automatic printing of the purchase order (and in some cases communicating the order directly to the vendor's computer) is a closed system. However, managers will still intervene in the inventory control on special occasions such as special sales and when unusual quantities must be ordered. When an item is marked down for purposes of closing out stock, the closed ordering system must be interrupted. Few closed systems are completely automated.

BUSINESS INFORMATION SYSTEMS

Information is valuable input and output for any on-going system.

Information is also the central factor in a feedback loop which controls the entire set of activities of a firm. The business system of an organization cannot survive without information. Information can be defined as knowledge (narrative or numbers) which is not previously known. It is valuable to the extent that it is accurate, timely, objective and relevant.

Management in any organizational system operates on the basis of the information available to it. Information is the decision-maker's basis for actions concerning the present and future activities of the organization. Forrester (1961) has identified management to be the process of converting information into action. Since managing any part of the organizational system is a process of conversion, the information base for a management decision can have a significant impact on the organization's future.

In formulating decisions, the decision-maker must be concerned with three critical factors. He must know to the greatest degree possible, (1) the state of the system in its environment, (2) the possible changes in the state, and (3) what effects his decisions could have on the system. These three areas encompass an entire business organization's information processing operation.

Since an organization's need for information is constant, subsystems for supplying management with accurate information for them to function in a competitive environment must be developed.

Formal information supply channels exist in every organization's business system. One type of formal channel is the marketing information system, which is a structured complex of persons, equipment and procedures designed to maintain an orderly flow of information on marketing activities.

Many organizations are using the computer as an essential part of their information system. This is not to be confused with using the computer for data processing of routine clerical functions. A computerized information system assists in establishing a network linking all business systems and subsystems of the firm together. The flexibility and speed of the computer enables the information system to sense, classify, transmit, store, retrieve, transform and display information. This text is largely limited to computer-based business information systems, since this is the direction in which organizations are moving and because computer systems appear to be the most effective type of information systems for large organizations.

A single information system cannot provide all the information management needs. An organization's business information system is composed of a collection of functional area information systems

Physical System Interfaces

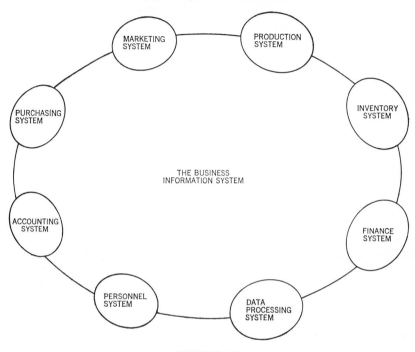

FIGURE 1.6

(Figure 1.6), each integrated through a central data storage area or data base. These functional systems serve the control and decision-making needs of department managers just as the marketing information system serves the needs of the marketing personnel. Top management depends upon certain types of summary information which is made available to it from the data input by each department to the data base. The operating principle is that marketing personnel do the best job of collecting and processing marketing information, accountants are most proficient at collecting accounting information, production personnel are most effective for collection of production information, etc. The organization's information system is ideally a collection of functional information systems, integrated by a central storage or data facility.

SUMMARY

This first chapter is background for an extensive examination of the problems, procedures and methods of developing and implementing business systems in a modern organization. Part II, The

Systems Project, introduces the methods and techniques which are important in systems development. The life cycle of a system, the origin of information system projects, and tools and techniques for systems analysis and design are the major themes.

Parts III and IV are devoted to the activities of information analysis and systems design. Key issues presented include investigation of operating procedures, analysis of information flows, and development of system proposals. The design section provides a critical analysis of the problems and procedures of such wide-ranging topics as development of forms and reports used in the newly designed system, development of documentation and operating procedures, and selection of hardware and software systems for support of the information system.

The last two sections, Systems Implementation and System Control and Modification, are perhaps the most important in this book. A well designed system may be a failure if it is installed improperly or if it is not continually maintained and modified to meet the changing needs of management. Because of their importance, extensive discussion is devoted to the critical areas of personnel selection, project management, system conversion, maintenance of the system and system security.

This book is organized around the life cycle of the business system. The authors feel that by following the logical sequence of steps in development and implementation of systems in an organization, the reader will readily grasp the most important principles. The many examples, problems, and case history discussions provide a realistic approach to systems design and development.

Centralized functional information systems appear to be the most effective and efficient means of supporting decision-making activities in the modern organization. Perhaps the greatest detriment to the proper functioning of a management information system is inconsistent human behavior. Few systems can operate without people, and people are unpredictable. This text will also examine aspects of human behavior in systems before looking into the system development process.

REVIEW QUESTIONS

1. Explain the relationship between computer, communications, and marketing systems in terms of general systems theory.
2. What is a feedback loop and what is its relation to control in systems?
3. Explain the control elements in a business system.
4. What is the distinction between information and data?
5. What are the information systems you would normally find used in a large business firm? In a non-profit institution? In government?
6. What is a systems specialist? A user? How do the activities and responsibilities of each relate to a business system?
7. Distinguish between an open and closed system. Give examples of each in the business community.

DISCUSSION QUESTIONS

1. A top-level manager explains during an interview with the systems specialist that when he reads a report or memo that has an error in it, primarily a grammatical or spelling error, he throws the report into his wastebasket. How should the systems specialist use this feedback in working with such a manager?
2. Using the information in this chapter, explain how you would develop a new management consulting business. Also, how would you develop a new internal management consulting business in an established business?
3. A manager has stated to you: "All of this systems junk is just a bunch of theory with no practical meaning behind it. There is no way in which it can be used to change our way of operating our business, especially when we are making a healthy profit already." Explain why he might feel this is a valid viewpoint for his business. Develop a counter-argument to this statement.
4. Discuss why or why not it is possible to develop a totally closed system in business and industry.
5. Develop a general control model for the marketing operation of a small corporation. How would you change your model for a large corporation? For a government institution? What steps would you take to insure that the model would be adjusted as changes became apparent?

BIBLIOGRAPHY

Anthony, Robert N., *Planning and Control Systems: A Framework for Analysis*, Boston: Division of Research, Graduate School of Business Administration, Harvard University, 1965.

Berrien, F. Kenneth, *General and Social Systems*, New Brunswick, N.J.: Rutgers University Press, 1968.

Bertalanffy, Ludwig Von, *General Systems Theory*, New York: George Braziller, Inc., 1968.

Boulding, Kenneth, "General Systems Theory—The Skeleton of Science," *Management Science*, April 1956.

Boulding, Kenneth, *The Image*, Ann Arbor: University of Michigan Press, 1956.

Churchman, C. West, *The Systems Approach*, New York: Dell Publishing Co., Inc., 1968.

Emery, James C., *Organizational Planning and Control Systems*, New York: The Macmillan Company, 1969.

Forrester, Jay W., *Industrial Dynamics*, Cambridge, Mass.: M.I.T. Press, 1961.

Leavitt, Harold J., and Whistler, Thomas L., "Management in the 1980's," *Harvard Business Review*, November/December, 1958.

Sippl, Charles J., *Computer Dictionary*, Indianapolis, Ind.: Howard W. Samms & Co., Inc., 1966.

CHAPTER 2

SYSTEMS AND MANAGEMENT

For the most part, business prior to the Industrial Revolution consisted of a few employees and a single owner/manager. Of course, even today this is not an uncommon arrangement, particularly in agricultural, professional and small business organizations. In this type of environment, the few people involved become intimately aware of the reactions of other members in the organization. The need for an orderly process for making decisions is important, but the need for detailed, written procedures may not be critical. While a systematic approach is required in almost any organization, the need for formal systems does not become necessary until the organization becomes relatively complex. As the business units grew larger, and personnel turnover became significantly higher, the need for the development of detailed procedures to handle routine activities became more important.

A significant effect of the Industrial Revolution was "automation," a process wherein some of the skills of the workers were transferred to machines to reduce costs and errors. Automation also reduced the monotony and drudgery of routine work. From management's viewpoint, automation was desirable since it lowered the unit costs of production, increasing the market which could be served or the unit profit.

Systems, as a management tool, became more and more significant as automation gradually reduced the skill requirements and the judgment decisions of many jobs. As work was broken down into job elements as contrasted with the "whole job," these job elements lent themselves to analysis of the most efficient ways of doing the job, the length of time required to do the job and the job environment desirable for optimum performance. This systems analysis held that each time a specific task was performed, that it be performed in precisely the same manner. Exceptions were permitted only when analysts or supervisors felt that changes would further increase productivity.

Analysis classified similar elements of different jobs so that the benefits of specialization could be realized and expected norms of reasonable accuracy could be quickly and economically developed. They also classified and standardized the way instructions were prepared and passed on to subordinates so that the same end results would be obtained in each of the many segments of the organization when similar or identical work was performed. In these early days of systems analysis, prior to World War II, it was generally recognized that written communications were desirable, but few attempts were made to organize this body of knowledge into a network reaching throughout the organization in a systematic attempt to improve business operations.

After the Second World War, a definite trend toward profession-alization in management developed. More of the better managed companies became aware of the fact that good managers did not just happen. They also realized that the better managers were not just the best technicians. It was found, for example, that the man best trained and able to apply general management principles would make a better machine shop foreman than would the best mechanic, unless the mechanic also had managerial qualifications.

With the advent of the professional manager, systems became identified with top management. Management saw the importance of integrating all company systems, rather than concentrating only on accounting systems. Systems was accorded the relatively high status required to function effectively in any organizational seg-ment of the organization. The recognition of the need to integrate all company systems brought a realization of greater dependence on information. Information was necessary for integrating systems and evaluating the integration. As companies continued to grow, it be-came increasingly difficult to monitor and control activities taking place in remote areas of the firm. It became even more difficult for top management to have a broad view of the company, its problems and its directions. Consequently, there was a much greater need for information.

The introduction of the electronic computer in the 1950's made information available to management quickly and in useful forms.

Today, top management accepts systems responsibility and recog-nizes personnel specializing in systems work as valuable members of the management team. This chapter will focus on modern manage-ment and the role of the information system in serving management.

TECHNOLOGY IMPACT ON MANAGEMENT OF ORGANIZATIONS

The increase in the amount of information available to managers as a result of improved information processing technology dramatically altered the course of activities in many firms. In this vortex of change was the computer. Computer-based systems provided man-agers with new techniques for structuring problems and developing solutions. The capability for collecting, storing, manipulating, trans-mitting and using information is an important one for any firm, and the assistance of computer-based systems has improved the effectiveness with which these tasks are performed. More specifically, the use of automated information processing systems, centered around the computer, made possible storage of large amounts of information from throughout the firm, centralization of information resources, rapid processing of information, ease in performance of complex calculations, and the rapid retrieval of required information.

MANAGEMENT FUNCTIONS

One of the most common means of examining managerial activities is in terms of the decision-making role of officials in the firm. Planning and control are important activities in this respect. In an in-depth examination of these activities, Anthony (1965) separates planning and control into three separate, but closely related processes:

- STRATEGIC PLANNING — The process of deciding on objectives of the organization, on changes in these objectives, on the resources used to obtain these objectives, and on the policies that are to govern the acquisition, use and disposition of these resources.

- MANAGEMENT CONTROL — The process by which managers assure that resources are obtained and used effectively and efficiently in the accomplishment of the organization's activities.

- OPERATIONAL CONTROL — The process of assuring that specific tasks are carried out effectively and efficiently.

Two basic characteristics distinguish operational control from management control. First, operational control focuses on specific tasks or transactions, whereas management control focuses on the flowing stream of on-going operations. Second, operational control is essentially objective, whereas management control is essentially subjective. Operational control is objective in the sense that it has to do primarily with activities for which the correct decisions can be objectively determined. Management control is essentially subjective in that decisions in this process inherently involve management judgment, and there is no objective or "scientific" way of determining the best course of action for a given set of circumstances.

The decision-making function of the manager is an important one. For our purposes, the overall managerial functions may be examined through five specific processes:

- PLANNING   Establishment of goals and development of policies, procedures, and programs for their achievement.

- ORGANIZING   Grouping of activities to be performed and establishing organizational structures and procedures to ensure that the activities are performed.

- STAFFING   Obtaining and training personnel to work in the organization for the purpose of achieving goals and objectives.

- CONTROLLING   Measuring performance against goals and objectives, and the development of procedures for adjustment of goals, procedures or activities.

- COMMUNICATING   Transferring information on goals, objectives and performance to personnel throughout the organization and the environment.

Each function must be performed by management in an effective and efficient organization; however, the new technology of information processing is altering the way in which these functions are performed.

Since the computer makes possible the storage of large volumes of information on many varied activities in the firm, management potentially has a greater base of facts on which to draw for planning and control activities. Regularly collected data on standards, performance against standards, funds flow and the like are accessible to key personnel for planning purposes. At the same time, maintenance of on-line files of information, which are easily accessed by decision-makers at all levels of the organization, improves communication of goals, standards and performance measures to personnel. Computer-based systems also make possible the development of management decision models for planning and operation which previously would have been too cumbersome for manual use. Such models permit the "testing" of alternative strategies and further reduce time lags between perception of problems and development of proper solutions.

The rapid response capability of computer-based systems may also free managers at all levels from seemingly endless planning tasks, and enable them to make more effective use of their time. Managers can cope with problems in less time and devote attention to other issues affecting the firm, such as employee satisfaction and community relations. Rapid response and extensive storage capabilities, coupled with quick retrieval of stored information permits the transmission of important knowledge between a corporate headquarters and its decentralized locations throughout the world. The result again is an increased potential for more informed management, improved company performance and personnel satisfaction.

While the above advances in information technology are certainly significant, they are not the only ones responsible for changes in management of organizations. The entire structure of the organization and the duties of individual managers have been greatly changed.

IMPACT OF SYSTEMS ON THE ORGANIZATION

The introduction of computers into the business community has brought with it a myriad of questions concerning the effect such a change will have on the structure of organizations. The questions seem to focus on the primary issue of the effect of automation on centralization of authority and decision-making in the organization.

The center for decision-making authority determines whether an organization is considered to be centralized or decentralized. When one speaks of centralized authority, the term generally is used in the sense that the responsibility for formulating decisions and operating strategies is retained within a small group of people, and little authority is delegated outside of the "select" group. Typically the authority resides with the top management group (Figure 2.1). Under the philosophy of centralized authority all major decisions in the organization must be "passed up the line" for action by the management decision group. All necessary information must then be made available to the decision group.

Decentralized authority (Figure 2.2) implies that limited attempts are made to separate the types of decisions in assigning authority. In other words, decentralization enables decisions to be related to work purpose, such that selection of alternatives is made at the lowest point in the organization where necessary skills and information can be brought together.

Which philosophy is the most meaningful and advantageous for

Centralized Authority

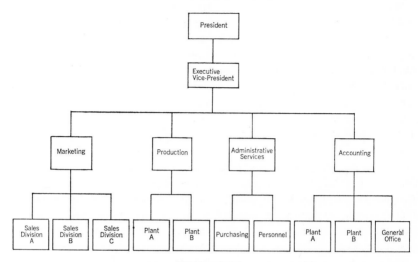

FIGURE 2.1

Decentralized Authority

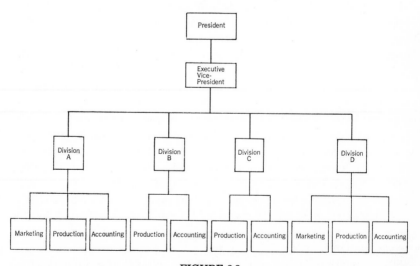

FIGURE 2.2

the modern organization is a question that is being debated continually. At the present time, there does not appear to be a conclusive trend in either direction, nor is it possible to state that one approach is better than the other. The relation between computer-based information systems and the rationale behind which of the two organizational philosophies is to be preferred is important enough to warrant a brief discussion.

Since the computer has the innate capability for storage and processing of large volumes of information, the proponents of centralization argue that it is most effective and efficient to have the decision authority rest primarily with top management. The new information technology permits more information to be organized more readily and processed in a shorter time frame. In effect, it extends the decision and thinking capability of its top level users. The technology further enables the top level of management intelligently to categorize, digest and act on a wider range of problems. Additionally, by quantifying more information, computer-based systems assist in extending top management's control over the decision process of subordinates (Leavitt and Whistler, 1958). The new technology also makes it possible, proponents of centralization argue, to design and maintain the complex communication systems necessary for operation of large centralized organizations. More information will therefore be available to top level decision makers, removing some of the need for art and judgment in the decision process.

Those individuals who argue in favor of decentralized authority in many respects employ the same arguments as their counterparts. In other words, by relating all decisions to the work task and having them made at the operating level, judgment may be removed from the process. Since the decision-maker at this level is faced with the problem directly and is familiar with the immediate circumstances surrounding a particular problem, he should be able to most accurately diagnose the problem. Information on activities in other parts of the organization which could affect his decision can be made available to him. This is possible, claim supporters of decentralization, because of the ability of a computer-based system to make necessary information available at the operating level.

IMPACT OF INFORMATION TECHNOLOGY ON MANAGERS

Modern business institutions have a mixture of managerial types in residence. On the one hand, there is the traditional manager who frequently is viewed as a manipulator of people and as one who operates on the basis of his authority. This type of manager may be characterized further as an experience-oriented person who believes that his training must come from on-the-job activities and experiences. He makes decisions judging from past experiences. He visualizes current situations within the framework of previous events. History and experience are key factors in the success of the traditional manager. Subordinates who do not have the same past experiences frequently disagree with decisions of the traditional manager. As a result, he must rely on his authority and position in the firm's hierarchy to ensure implementation of his decisions and recommendations.

The other type of manager who does not necessarily rely on authority, experience and on-the-job training is described as an information-oriented person. This manager is aware of the importance of informal relationships in effective performance of activities in the firm, and often indicates that a formal and rigid framework is not essential for effective decision making. Information processing procedures are used as an appropriate means of achieving goals and reaching objectives. Historical data and experience are not sufficient for this person who is prone to use models and analytical methods to examine historical information and "test" alternate strategies.

The information-oriented manager is not satisfied with profit as a sole measure of an organization's performance. New methods are used to investigate other performance indicators. He manages by participation rather than mere authority. Frequently his mode of operation is a result of training in colleges and universities in contrast to the traditional manager who has worked his way through the organizational hierarchy. The manager has often entered the firm at a managerial level, bringing with him the training he has had in information processing.

There is not a clear-cut distinction between the existence of traditional or information-oriented managers in a single firm. Both types of persons are active in most organizations. However, traditional managers will become less and less common and be replaced by the information-oriented manager.

IMPORTANCE OF THE INFORMATION PROCESSING SPECIALISTS

The emergence of the new technology for information processing in organizations has created a need for people who are trained in implementing information processing. These specialists are known as systems analysts, systems designers, programmer analysts and similar titles. Since they are becoming increasingly important in the business community, it is appropriate to examine the characteristics of this information processing specialist.

The use of computers for business information processing mobilized armies of programmers to translate the routine tasks of the firm into instructions which were processible by the computer system. Each programmer established a domain in his own right, developing programs which only he understood and which were neat, concise packages. The increasing size of the computer programs often reduced their neatness and conciseness. Also, since programmers were technicians and lacked managerial background, communication problems developed. Management, although adept at running various activities in the firm, lacked training in computer technology. This communication difficulty resulted in a limited number of managerial uses of the computer. The applications developed were only automated versions of traditional manual tasks and did not take advantage of the inherent power of the computer. Often applications developed for the decision-making personnel in the firm were not well received because they were not in useable form. To break this communication standoff the need for the information processing specialist emerged. The information processing specialist provides the link between managers and computer systems personnel by serving as a liaison to communicate understanding of problems and difficulties between the two. Typically, the specialist has both an understanding of the technical side of the computer *and* a knowledge of the management side of the organization, and is able to see both sides of an application issue.

RESPONSIBILITIES OF THE INFORMATION PROCESSING SPECIALIST

The information processing specialist performs a wide range of activities in promoting and assisting in development of computer applications programs for management. Among his most important responsibilities are:

INVESTIGATION — Systematic examination of existing systems and procedures for the purpose of detecting problems and inefficiencies.

ANALYSIS — Examination of data and records obtained during the investigation in order to develop new procedures and methods for operation.

DESIGN — Development of new systems, normally involving the use of computers, which assist in meeting management's goals and objectives.

IMPLEMENTATION   Development of operating systems for-
                  mulated during the design process. Im-
                  plementation includes complete docu-
                  mentation of the new system and con-
                  tinual maintenance and modification of
                  procedures throughout the life of the
                  system.

The exact nature of the specialist's duties will vary from organization to organization. However, the above responsibilities, in one
form or another, must always be present.

In many cases, specialists may work in teams for particularly
large applications or long-term projects. In such situations, the responsibilities and analysis tasks may be segmented so that the skills
of one person may be used most effectively. Again, as in the situation where a single specialist is working on a project, the four responsibilities are shared by all members of the project team. The
activities of the project team will be detailed later in this book.

LOCATION OF THE SYSTEMS STAFF
IN THE ORGANIZATION

One of the requirements for an effective systems program is that a
definite organizational responsibility must be established for the
systems staff. There is no single answer on the placement of the
systems function within the organization structure that is applicable
to every organization.

All staff functions would like the prestige and implied backing
that reporting to the chief executive of an organization gives them.
Past surveys have indicated that approximately 25% of systems
staffs surveyed reported to the President or Vice-President. Never-
theless, this is not always practical. The chief executive frequently
cannot devote adequate time to personally direct and control all
the various staff functions and, at the same time, effectively carry
out the total responsibility to direct and coordinate the major function of an organization.

Many management authorities, as well as those in the systems
field itself, stress the need for the systems function to report to a
member of top management. The systems function should be independent of pressure from particular groups in the firm. These pressures will be fewer and less violent the higher up in the organization
the function is placed.

One study similarly concludes: "For the systems staff to reflect
the corporate viewpoint, it must report to a person whose function

and viewpoint are also corporate. This may not be the company president, but it should certainly be someone in the upper management circle" (DeLuca, 1961). This study goes on to recommend against placing the systems department under a functional department executive. Where no other arrangement is possible, however, the study advocates that "management should clearly state that such a relationship is a matter of administrative convenience, and that the activities of the systems department are for the benefit of the company as a whole."

CENTRALIZED SYSTEMS STAFF

A centralized systems staff serving the whole organization is the most common organizational type. In a smaller organization especially, such a staff can view objectively the organization as a single entity.

When an organization becomes more complex, with multiple operating divisions in separate locations, or when it becomes highly diversified, a single central systems staff may not be able to maintain adequate service for all of the individual operating groups. The requests for service may also be so varied and of such a magnitude that a compact central system staff may tend to be understaffed to effectively handle them.

DECENTRALIZED SYSTEMS STAFFS

Decentralized systems staffs are frequently found in divisions of larger or more complex organizations. In effect, such divisions may be separate and distinct operating entities. Geographic locations alone may make this arrangement a necessity.

Decentralized systems staffs are closer to the operating personnel of their divisions and should be more effective in dealing with their divisions' problems than a distant central staff. However, there is a potential danger that decentralized staffs may vary in approach, duplicate each other's efforts, or lose perspective on organization-wide problems they may face. This danger can be alleviated where a centralized system staff maintains functional authority over the approaches and methods of operations of such decentralized staffs, and coordinates their efforts with those of its own for organization-wide systems projects.

A variation of the decentralized systems staff is that of a departmental systems staff which is associated with the systems work of a specific functional department, such as accounting, personnel, purchasing, production control. Such a staff usually is an integral part of the departmental function concerned. The main advantage here is that of detailed knowledge resulting from close association. However, there is again the possibility of loss of total perspective through bias resulting from loyalties to the departmental managers.

COMBINATION SYSTEMS STAFF

To overcome the lack of close association in the single centralized systems staff, and to overcome the potential bias of decentralized staffs, some combination of both may be required. One proposed solution is that of a central systems function reporting to a member of top management, with all systems personnel reporting to the central systems manager. The central systems department would provide analysts for organization-wide systems and also assign analysts on a rotating basis to specific departments. The central systems staff might also have specialists to provide special technical assistance to all systems analysts.

The above approach may not be acceptable to the divisional managements concerned and may also tend to revive some of the handicaps of the single centralized systems staff. A more practical arrangement would be to provide for separate decentralized systems staffs, which would report to their respective division managers. Such staffs would be responsible for the systems work internal to their separate divisions, but subject to the functional guidance of a central systems department on matters of systems methodology, equipment standardization, systems personnel selection criteria, etc. The central systems function would be responsible for all company-wide systems work, systems education and research, as well as providing specialized technical guidance to and coordinating efforts between divisional staffs.

SUMMARY

At one time businesses were predominately single owner/manager operations. In the period following the Industrial Revolution, organizations grew into multilevel, complex enterprises. This made the effective performance of the primary managerial functions of planning, organizing, staffing, controlling and communicating more difficult; increased the lines of authority and required the need for coordinated efforts throughout the enterprise. Strategic planning became more difficult because of the many activities of the company which were impacted by a single policy change or growth decision.

The introduction of the computer into business has affected the way in which the functions of management are performed. The tremendous storage capacity of the computer, coupled with its rapid processing capability, gave managers a greater base of facts upon which to make planning and control decisions. Computers and information systems have raised new questions on the centralization of authority and the training and experience required for managers. It is currently debated that the traditional training for managers through experience is not fully sufficient today.

The introduction of the new information technology into business resulted in the need for staff persons to assist in integrating the new technology into problem-solving processes. Information processing specialists perform a wide range of activities in promoting and assisting in development of computer applications programs for management. Their responsibilities include investigation, analysis, design, and implementation of systems to assist management.

The full impact of computers and information processing is yet to come; however, the information processing specialists are here to stay and their importance is increasing at a rapid rate.

REVIEW QUESTIONS

1. Distinguish between strategic planning, management control, and operational control. Give examples of each in the finance function for a manufacturing firm listed on the New York Stock Exchange, for a utility, for a large city government, and for a hospital.
2. What are the functions of management? How is each one related to the others?
3. Distinguish between decentralized and centralized management. What impact has automation of information processing had on each of these "styles" of management?
4. Compare and contrast the traditional and modern manager.
5. What is an information processing specialist? What are his responsibilities?
6. Distinguish between a centralized and a decentralized systems staff. What factors should be considered in choosing a centralized rather than a decentralized staff?

DISCUSSION QUESTIONS

1. Should the manager or the information specialist determine which managerial activities merit first attention in terms of developing computer-based support systems for them? Discuss the reasons for your answer.
2. The only way an information specialist can be aware of the problems of management is to come from a management background. Agree or disagree? Why?
3. With the growing use of computers in management, it is often said that organizations will recentralize, with top management taking over many of the functions previously performed by middle management. On what basis can this argument be made? Do you agree? Why or why not?
4. Planning is typically thought of as a top management responsibility. However, in actuality this activity takes place throughout a business. What are some examples of planning at lower levels in a manufacturing company? In a service company? In government? What impact might computer-based information systems have on planning at these levels?

BIBLIOGRAPHY

1. Anthony, R. N., *Planning and Control Systems: A Framework For Analysis*, Boston: Division of Research, Graduate School of Business Administration, Harvard University, 1965.
2. Anshen, M., "The Manager and the Black Box," *Harvard Business Review*, Volume 38, November-December, 1960.
3. Dantzig, G. B., "Management Science in the World of Today and Tomorrow," *Management Science*, Volume 13, February, 1967.
4. DeLuca, R. A., "Placing the Systems and Procedures Function in the Organization," *Systems and Procedures Journal*, May-June, 1961.
5. Hage, J., "Relationship of Centralization to Other Structural Properties," *Administrative Science Quarterly*, Volume 12, June, 1967.
6. Lazarus, H., *The Progress of Management*, Englewood Cliffs, N. J.: Prentice-Hall, Inc., 1968.
7. Leavitt, H. S., and Whistler, T. L., "Management in the 1980's," *Harvard Business Review*, Volume 36, November-December, 1958.
8. Miller, E. J., *Systems of Organization*, New York: Barnes and Noble Book Company, 1967.
9. Morris, W. T., *Decentralization in Management Systems*, Columbus, OH: Ohio State University Press, 1968.
10. Radner, M., "Integration and Utilization of Management Science Activities In Organization," *Operations Research Quarterly*, Volume 10, June, 1968.
11. Rosengren, W. R., "Structure, Policy and Style: Strategies of Organizational Controls," *Administrative Science Quarterly*, Volume 12, June, 1967.
12. Simon, H. A., *The New Science of Management Decision*, New York: Harper Brothers Publishers, 1960.
13. Stieglitz, H., "Organization Structures—What's Been Happening," *Conference Board Record*, Volume 5, June, 1968.
14. Tannenbaum, A. S., *Control In Organizations*, New York: McGraw-Hill Book Company, Inc., 1968.

CHAPTER 3

BEHAVIORAL ASPECTS OF SYSTEMS CHANGE

The introduction of computer-based information systems into the operation of organizations has resulted in technical, economic and behavioral changes. The technical changes were discussed in Chapters 1 and 2. They can be summarized as new techniques and methods for handling problems and decision-making situations within the firm. Today, the speed and power of the computer is challenging new frontiers in information processing within organizations. Computer-based systems are continually improving the effectiveness and efficiency of business operations by, (1) automating clerical tasks resulting in time savings and increased accuracy, (2) collecting more meaningful data on more activities to provide insight into the effects actions will have on the total firm and (3) supplying a flow of vital information to all parts of the firm, thus providing potential for higher levels of profitability and productivity.

As important as the technical and economic issues of computer-based systems are to an organization, the systems designer must also consider the behavioral aspects of technological changes. Changes may be ideal in both a technical and an economic mode, but the system will fail if they are not accepted by the users. This chapter deals with the behavioral aspects of system change in the development and implementation of computer-based systems in organizations.

Change has become a way of life in business activities. Any aspect of a firm's operation must be considered as a logical "target" for modification, with the assumption that such alterations are designed for the purpose of *improvement*. Change, once limited only to production or manufacturing processes, now may occur at any point in the organizational system of people and procedures to improve effectiveness and efficiency of the total operation.

The way an individual person accepts a change will determine success or failure. Not all changes are readily accepted. Therefore, the systems designer must consider the important variables that surround any change (Figure 3.1). Concern must be given to the reason for implementing a change, such as the introduction of an information system project into the operation of a functional department. The reason might be economic, or just to improve the general work situation. The reason for suggesting a change is an important variable affecting the success or failure of the change.

Emotional barriers are another important change variable. It is important to be aware of either potential or known fears and biases involved in a job change. Closely related to emotion is the variable of the cultural background of the worker.

Another variable important in any change is the way in which a person perceives a change. All changes require training for the new job. The manner in which this training is handled directly affects the success or failure of the change.

Important Variables in Organizational Change

● ECONOMIC	Reduction in overhead and/or operating costs
	Improved operating efficiency
	Improved operating effectiveness
● WORK SITUATION	New job tasks
	New job description
	Elimination of undesirable aspects of job
	Streamlining job activities
● EMOTIONAL	Biases concerning why the change is necessary
	Fears of what the change may mean for an individual or group
● CULTURAL	Ethnic, racial or national norms & standards
● PERCEPTUAL	Time and training requirements thought to be imposed by the change
	Individual explanation or rationalization for the change

FIGURE 3.1

CHANGES TO FORMAL STRUCTURE

Organizations can be studied in terms of their formal or informal structures for implementing activities. The formal structure of an organization has established lines of responsibility and authority. These lines of authority have departmental boundaries, divisions of labor and specialization.

A formal structure results in an explicit definition of line and staff relationships for the conduct of business activities. In a manufacturing firm, for example, a certain group of employees is responsible for the production of material goods and/or assembled products. Their task involves conversion of raw materials and parts into products which are marketed. Persons involved directly in the production work, including both the individuals on the assembly line and their supervisors, are referred to as the *line* group of the firm.

The other group of persons in an organization is the *staff* group. The functions and activities of this group are oriented toward support of the line group. The Purchasing Department is responsible for procurement of raw materials, fabricated parts and supplies used in the production process. The Accounting Department, another staff group, supports the line group by monitoring expenses and income resulting from the manufacture and sale of goods. The Systems Department provides further support by examining work methods, process flows and machine productivity. The results of their support efforts may be used to design new processes for the line which might improve output rates or increase quality levels. The type of activity for each of these three departments is support oriented.

Altering any of these existing relationships constitutes a change in the formal structure of the organization. The acceptance of the alteration by company personnel will determine the success of the change. In studying business systems, we are interested in the effect information systems projects will have on the formal structure of the firm.

Changes in the formal structure resulting from the introduction of a new information system are summarized in Figure 3.2. The introduction and acceptance of any change determines whether it is successful. Since the basic purpose of an information system project is to provide past, present and projected information of operations, it is possible that formal boundaries and responsibilities may be modified for both line and staff groups. The automatic data collection for one phase of an information system project may, for example, eliminate a sizeable amount of the line supervisor's paperwork. In this case, assuming that the information systems function is recognized as a support activity, the change results in shifting a reporting activity from a line to a staff procedure.

Automatic data collection on a large scale can result in changing departmental boundaries. If the computer is used for statistical production monitoring and eliminates the need for a majority of the clerks in a tabulating department, the clerks may be moved into some other department. The organization chart would be altered to show the elimination of one department and the expansion of another, changing department boundaries. Introduction of a computer-based information system can alter formal communication channels. Middle management may no longer need to rely on per-

Examples of Changes in Formal Structure

• FORMAL BOUNDARIES	Addition of an Information Systems Department
	Reorganization of departments: some eliminated, some added, or some combined with others
• FORMAL RESPONSIBILITIES	Elimination of report preparation by line supervisors (automated data collection and report preparation)
	Addition of new product lines to job responsibility of marketing manager
• FORMAL COMMUNICATION CHANNELS	Centralized information files may eliminate need for periodic reports from line managers
	New channels open due to constant monitoring of performance and activities

FIGURE 3.2

formance reports from operating managers. By using a terminal in his office, the manager can access large files of stored data in an instant and review the operating manager's work. Further, this type of performance evaluation can take place while operating managers are totally unaware of its occurrence. The result is that one type of information transmission is eliminated in the first communication channel and an entirely new channel is opened between middle management and stored data files, through the office terminal.

These examples indicate how a single change resulting from an information processing activity can alter the formal structure of an organization. The success of such a change will be discussed after we examine the impact of the same changes on the informal structure.

CHANGES TO INFORMAL STRUCTURE

An organization with an informal structure will also be affected by the introduction of a computer-based information system. Figure 3.3 shows examples of changes which can occur in an informal organization structure.

In any modern organization many relationships are not shown on the organization chart. In fact, the success or failure of an information systems project often hinges on acceptance by informal social and/or work groups within the organization. When working relations are changed or if group norms are violated, and status of persons or groups is diminished due to a new information system project, problems will result.

The changes that come with the introduction of information systems in an organization frequently violate group norms. For example, if a work group has a standard which states that particular types of information and data are not to be given to management, and a new information system makes it impossible for group members to continue concealing that data, the new system violates the learned structure.

Loss of an individual's status is one of the prime factors in resistance to change in the informal structure. Altering the responsibilities associated with a particular job assignment increases or decreases the status of the person performing that job in the eyes of his associates. For example, if the information system activity eliminates a sizeable amount of the line supervisor's paperwork chores, it may be resisted by the supervisor because preparing reports was a symbol of his supervisory status. Therefore, this

Examples of Changes in Informal Structure

• WORK RELATIONS	Reorganization of job tasks and work activities result in alteration of social work groups
	New persons enter a work group
	Persons leave the work group
• WORK GROUP NORMS	Information previously withheld from managers is now automatically collected and reported
	Productivity standards may be altered to conflict with informal norms established within a group
• STATUS	New work activities may be a factor in reduced or increased status of a group or an individual
	New work activities may be a factor in perceived reduction or increased status of a group or an individual

FIGURE 3.3

change infers that his status has been reduced, or management's dissatisfaction with his reports. At the same time, the line group may feel that it is losing control over the reporting of their activities because the systems staff group now does the data collection. These changes are in an informal structure, but reflect resistance to change in the firm's line of responsibility and authority.

Each type of change will have a positive or a negative (sometimes both) effect on the operating efficiency of the firm. A major reason for the success or lack of success associated with systems change is the way in which it is introduced.

INTRODUCING SYSTEMS CHANGES

In the business world change is an expected phenomenon, not an unusual occurrence. This is due to the many rapid advancements in technology, which are bringing a certain amount of change to every person in every organization. However, the way in which information systems are introduced in an organization is an important factor in determining their acceptance and success. The systems designer should anticipate resistance to change and take steps to lessen it.

The environment that accompanies the introduction of an information system is a major factor in decreasing resistance from both management and the users. The systems designer is understandably enthusiastic about the newly developed system and expects that users will be equally as enthusiastic about its installation. After all, top management has given its approval of the system's value to the firm by allocating funds for it.

Faced with the problem of gaining user acceptance of the system, the systems designer presents the same arguments which were responsible to get top management's approval. But logic that the project will result in reduced operating costs, decreased decision time, job streamlining, and more accurate information on activities does not have the same appeal to users. Logic is not a sufficient "motivator" for the acceptance of change.

Each manager has his own perception of his job and the tasks associated with it. When the introduction of an information system alters his perceived job tasks, resistance develops. Usually, the systems analyst is aware of possible resistance, and typically plans to overcome it by convincing managers early in the design stage of the need for these changes. The analyst wishes to lessen the trauma of changed working relationships, modifications to perceived status, and violation of work group norms.

Most managers resent a computer being substituted for their past reasoning processes no matter how routine. Job attitudes are not formed in a logical manner but are emotionally formed. The emotional attitudes of managers must be considered in changing a system.

TYPES OF RESISTANCE TO CHANGE

When an information system is implemented in a firm, resistance to the change may develop in many forms (Figure 3.4). Resistant and dysfunctional behavior may be grouped under the headings of aggression, projection and avoidance (Dickson and Simmons, 1970).

Aggression

If an information system is forced upon a department, aggressive behavior toward the system may come as an attack upon the system to make it either physically inoperative or ineffective. This sabotage or destruction of system components may be accomplished by dumping liquids into card readers, demagnetizing reels of tape, or scratching magnetic disk plates. Each act in some way prevents the system from functioning. A less spectacular form of aggression called "beating the system" does not lead to physical damage, but renders its output ineffective through inputs of error-laden data.

Potential Dysfunctional Behavior

• AGGRESSION	Physical or nonphysical attack on the information system in an attempt to make it either inoperative or ineffective
	Sabotage *Equipment destruction* *Beat the system*
• PROJECTION	A means by which persons can "energize" their resistance to the introduction of an information system
	The damn system caused my error
• AVOIDANCE	Withdrawing from or avoiding interaction with the information system, often as a result of frustration
	Ignore outputs and reports from the system
	Fail to provide inputs

FIGURE 3.4

Projection

Although many persons may not be willing to risk their jobs by committing aggressive acts against an information system, they may find continuous faults in the system's poor design and difficulty of operation. The introduction and training stages of a new system are particularly difficult times and if the users are projecting their resistance, it is much harder to implement the system. The incompetence of the system user in making a poor decision even with the best information available may result in projection of blame on the system for the error. This also constitutes resistance to the new system.

Avoidance

A third form of resistance is caused by frustration and avoids interaction with the information system. In this form of behavior, reports and information generated by the system are ignored in favor of using the previous manual information gathering system because "the new system can't be trusted."

Dysfunctional Behavior at Levels in the Organization

ORGANIZATIONAL SUBGROUP	RELATION TO MIS	MOST LIKELY DYSFUNCTIONAL BEHAVIOR
Operating Personnel		
• Clerical	Particularly affected by clerical systems. Job eliminated, job patterns changed.	Projection
• Nonclerical	Provide system inputs	Aggression
Operating Management	Controlled from above by information systems. Job modified by information—decision systems and programmed systems	Aggression Avoidance Projection
Technical Staff	Systems designers and agents of systems change	None
Top Management	Generally unaffected and unconcerned with systems	Avoidance

FIGURE 3.5

Each manager and user level has its own form of resistance as shown in Figure 3.5. If the new information system is to function, this resistance must be dealt with, and it is not an easy task. It is much more sensible to develop a system in cooperation with the users so that resistance is overcome in the system design.

AVOIDING RESISTANCE TO SYSTEMS

Avoiding resistance to the introduction of information systems is by no means a trivial problem. Some of the greatest difficulties in information systems are not technical, but behavioral. While there are fairly well established procedures for eliminating technical problems, there appears to be no simple remedies to resistance and behavioral difficulties. Important factors to be considered in minimizing resistance are summarized in Figure 3.6.

Factors for Minimizing Resistance

- CONSIDER PAST HISTORY OF ORGANIZATION'S OPERATING SUCCESS

- CONSIDER HOW PREVIOUS CHANGES WERE IMPLEMENTED

- DISCUSSION OF THE SYSTEM WITH MANAGERS AFFECTED

- DIRECT INVOLVEMENT OF PERSONS WHO WILL USE OR BE AFFECTED BY THE INFORMATION SYSTEM

- SET REALISTIC GOALS

- STATE OBJECTIVES CLEARLY

- DESIGN A SYSTEM WHICH IS EASY TO USE FOR ALL PERSONS

- DESIGN A SYSTEM WHICH WILL DO WHAT MANAGEMENT WAS PROMISED

- DEVELOP A SYSTEM WHICH IS RELIABLE

FIGURE 3.6

The acceptance/resistance factor for an information system begins long before the date of implementation. When there is a realization of a need for change, by either the information systems specialist or by management, the development process begins. It is important at this stage that the eventual users also feel the need for a system change. If normal operating procedures have not proven effective or if difficulties exist in sustaining adequate profit or production levels, a change may be suggested and welcomed by managers. However, if acceptable performance is being realized, it may be hard to convince operating personnel that new procedures should be introduced.

In either of the above cases, it is important that the information specialist thoroughly discuss and analyze the procedure problems with management. This discussion provides the specialist with the opportunity to know each person's true feelings about the problems of the current system and attitudes toward a new information system. If individuals are strongly against the use of computers, it will be discovered at this stage. Likewise, status priorities or important peer relations may be detected early enough to be included in the systems design. When we speak of discussion, we are referring to several hours of meetings in which the systems analyst gets to know the personality of the user group. However, before a user will "open up" to the analyst, he must respect him for his confidentiality and approval by top management.

A second reason for the conduct of repeated informal discussions is to provide the eventual user with a sense of both participation and responsibility for development of the system. When a functional area manager is directly involved in the development process, he will have a sense of pride and possession for the system. The system is no longer "their system" but something in which part of himself has been invested. This feeling of responsibility contributes to the success or failure of implementation. The pride of success and the disappointment of failure are felt by the functional manager.

Other factors which may be important in avoiding resistance to information systems include the specification of realistic goals and clear objectives as defined by the users. Setting goals at an attainable level is essential for acceptance of change. For example, if a systems designer involved in development of a purchasing information system sets a goal of eliminating the need for human intervention in the materials ordering cycle, the chances for systems success are at best minimal. Consideration must be given to unanticipated situations such as discontinued lines or sudden product shortages. Goals must be realistic, otherwise, resistance will develop because of the failure to meet them.

The systems objectives must be clearly stated so that users know precisely what the system will do and will not do. Objectives which are open to misinterpretation lead to dissatisfaction and resistance by users. The goal-setting language should be non-technical so that all may understand. Elegant terminology may impress systems colleagues, but it can easily confuse and frustrate those not familiar with it. Extra effort at this stage of the system development can markedly effect the success or failure of an information system.

Successful systems are user-oriented. The user must find the system easy to use. Avoid complex technical features that save machine time but increase management's time in interacting with the information system. Also, a system which is complex to use can lead to inaccurate inputs and poor decisions based on inaccurate output reports. Ease of use is a prerequisite for an accepted and effective information system.

It is conceivable that all of the above recommendations may be followed and the system still not be successful. To be successful, the system must be operative. If managers are enthusiastic about an information system because of its design features, the system had better function in the manner promised. When the operation of the information system is plagued by faulty input/output mechanisms or unreliability, it is very easy for the user to become disenchanted and not trust it. Errors in certain sections of the computer-related activity infer that there are other undetected errors in the system. If the system fails the user in a critical moment, he may reject it. Although it is important that development be completed by the scheduled date, a delay to ensure technical accuracy of the system is acceptable.

Avoiding or overcoming resistance to change is important in the introduction of information systems in an organization. Because the appropriate steps are both time consuming and expensive, they are sometimes skipped in order to have the system up and running at an earlier date. Such a decision is a risky one and may lead to resistance. When resistance is encountered it must be resolved. Attempts to introduce the system over user objections will not be successful. The way in which an information system is introduced will build acceptance and credibility for future efforts of the systems analyst within the organization.

SUMMARY

Information systems provide the capability to improve managerial effectiveness and efficiency. However, there is more to the problem than just developing a "good system." It is necessary to consider the behavioral side of the introduction of these systems, for if a system is not accepted by the people who are supposed to use it, it will fail.

A computer-based system effects both the formal and the informal side of the organization. In other words, a MIS may result in adjustment of department boundaries and job descriptions on the one hand, and changes in social and group relations on the other. If those factors are not considered and dealt with as a system is being developed, resistance may build up. Resistance occurs in the form of aggression, projection, or avoidance.

In dealing with potential resistance to MIS projects, a number of factors should be considered. The system should be viewed as important and necessary both by the designer and the users. This requires user involvement in the analysis and design activities. It also requires development of a system which is both easy to use and which will do what was promised. The system must be reliable.

The behavioral side of MIS is important to successful system development and operation. The most elegant project can fail if the people who are to use it are not included in the design effort. Failure to include the users in the development activities may result in failure of the system when it is implemented.

REVIEW QUESTIONS

1. What is resistance to change? What are the probable causes of resistance?
2. What variables are important in studying organizational change?
3. Why is the introduction of an information system often the source of much personnel resistance? Is this resistance usually justified?
4. What effect does logic have on avoiding resistance to information system introduction?
5. What forms of behavior might resistance to an information system take? Give examples of each.
6. Why does the operating level management seem to offer the greatest resistance to introduction of information systems?
7. What factors should be addressed in minimizing resistance?

DISCUSSION QUESTIONS

1. You as a system specialist suspect that the manager of the Marketing Department is not using the expensive reports prepared through the information system. What steps would you take to help the situation? What would you do if your actions didn't help the situation?
2. What steps would you follow to minimize resistance in the design and implementation of an automatic inventory system? What sources of resistance should you anticipate?

BIBLIOGRAPHY

Argyris, C., "Management Information Systems: The Challenge to Reality and Emotionality," *Management Science,* Volume 17, No. 6, February, 1971, pp. B275-B292.

Argyris, C., "Resistance to Rational Management Systems," *Innovation,* Issue 10, 1969, pp. 28-42.

Balk, Walter L., "The Human Dilemmas of MIS," *Journal of Systems Management,* Vol. 22, No. 8, August 1971.

Bangel, Arthur B., "Human Relations and the Management Analyst," *Systems and Procedures Journal,* Vol. 18, No. 6, November/December 1967.

Bennis, W. G., *Organization Development: Its Nature, Origins, and Prospects,* Reading, Mass.: Addison-Wesley Publishing, 1969.

Coleman, Raymond T. and M. J. Riley, "The Organizational Impact of MIS," *Journal of Systems Management,* Vol. 23, No. 3, March 1972.

Dickson, G. W. and Simmons, J. K., "The Behavioral Side of MIS," *Business Horizons,* Volume 13, August 1970, pp. 59-71.

Diebold, J., "Bad Decisions on Computer Use," *Harvard Business Review,* Volume 47, January-February, pp. 14-28.

Fried, Louis, "Hostility in Organization Change," *Journal of Systems Management,* Vol. 23, No. 6, June 1972.

Gomberg, William, "People-Sensitive Issues for Information Systems," *Wharton Quarterly,* Vol. 5, No. 1, Fall 1970.

Hall, D. M., *Management of Human Systems,* Cleveland, Ohio: Association for Systems Management, 1971.

Head, R. V., "Management Information Systems: A Critical Appraisal," *Datamation,* May 1967.

Hersey, Paul, and Kenneth H. Blanchard, "The Management of Change," *Training and Development Journal,* Vol. 26, No. 1, January 1972, Vol. 26, No. 2, February 1972, and Vol. 26, No. 3, March 1972.

Hertz, D. B., *Unlocking the Computer's Profit Potential,* New York: McKinsey and Company, 1968.

Mason, R. O. and Mitroff, I. I., "A Program For Research On Management Information Systems," *Management Science,* Volume 19, No. 5, January 1972, pp. 475-487.

Morgan, John, "Coping With Resistance to Change," *Ideas for Management, 1971,* Cleveland, Ohio: Association for Systems Management.

Wold, S., "Resistance to EDP: An Employee-Management Dilemma," *Data Management,* September 1968.

CHAPTER 4

ECONOMIC AND ANALYTIC
PRINCIPLES OF SYSTEM CHANGE

Certain analytic tools of systems analysis are covered in this chapter. Those chosen are a small part from the entire field of analytic methods of analysis, but they represent methods not usually presented in the business curriculum. The methods described in this chapter and their importance to systems analysis are the law of diminishing returns, labor versus capital intensive systems, Paretian distributions, demand elasticity, input/output analysis, queuing theory and information theory. References for more detailed study of each of these methods is included in the bibliography at the end of the chapter.

The analytical techniques of algebra, calculus, financial accounting, managerial accounting, mathematics of finance, statistics and binary arithmetic are left to be taught in other courses in a standard business curriculum. Simulation and modeling are described in Chapter 14. Other techniques such as linear programming, dynamic programming and statistical analysis are introduced in the addendum at the end of the chapter but are expected to be taught in a more advanced course.

LAW OF DIMINISHING RETURNS

"The law of diminishing returns refers to the amount of extra output that we get when we successfully add equal extra units of varying input to a fixed amount of some other output" (Samuelson, 1964).

A large number of economic variables have curves similar to the one shown in Figure 4.1. Such curves are negatively accelerating; they have a negative first differential. The usual discussion of such curves is in economic texts and the emphasis is on the use of capital as in Figure 4.1. This curve shows that the earlier uses of capital to improve productivity have more impact than later capital uses. One could also understand the curve to show that at the later stages more capital is needed to get the same percentage increase in output as at the beginning.

An example of the use of this curve is in the historical production record of some paper-making machines. Although the number of machine operators remained constant, the output of the machines increased from 600 to 1200 feet per minute, finally achieving 3600 feet per minute. The first increase was 100% while the last increase from 3000 to 3600 fpm was only 20%, although both increases were 600 feet per minute. Continuing increases in productivity became

Law of Diminishing Returns

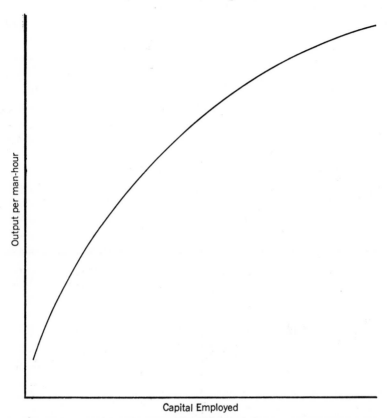

FIGURE 4.1

increasingly more difficult to achieve and represent the law of
diminishing returns.

Importance for Systems Design

The development of systems is a continuing process. Clerical systems
were first automated with punch card (unit record) equipment.
Later they were computerized on first, second and third generation
equipment. The law of diminishing returns suggests that the economic return from each successive change is probably smaller
with each conversion. For example, on a manual payroll system
operated at an original cost of 50 cents per processed check, the conversion to punched cards resulted in a cost of 20 cents per processed
check. Computerization of the system further reduced the cost per
processed check to 12 cents. Conversion of the system to second and

third generation computers reduced the check processing costs to 10 cents per check. Each change resulted in a savings, but the savings had diminishing returns against the prior cost.

A second implication for systems analysts of the law of diminishing returns is that unexplored areas may have better improvement prospects than areas previously studied. As business conditions change, systems become obsolete and need improvement, but improving a current system will have less return on the effort than the design of a completely new system.

A third implication of the law of diminishing returns is that it also applies to time expended in a system study. Major systems improvements are uncovered in the early stages of a project. For example, a one-hour system study cut the cost of the system by 50%. Later computerization of that particular system resulted in only small further improvements. Diminishing returns warn that extremely complex and sophisticated systems may not be economic to design. System improvements beyond a point may only be achieved by inordinate expenditures.

In summary, if the analyst has a choice of projects, he should choose the larger volume projects involving large groups of people and large input and output because the potential (and dramatic) return is likely to be greater. This suggests that a management information system for Sales Managers should have a higher return than one for the President simply because there are so many more Sales Managers.

The law of diminishing returns has been shown as a general tendency rather than an exact physical law. One can find exceptions to the law; however, the systems analyst who manages his activities with consideration of the law of diminishing returns is likely to design more productive systems.

LABOR OR CAPITAL INTENSIVE SYSTEMS

The general trend of industrialization and automation has been to substitute machines for people and capital for labor. The computer is the first major step in capital intensive systems which allows the manager to improve his own and his staff's work. The effects of such changes upon a system have been to increase fixed costs and to decrease marginal costs. Figure 4.2 shows how fixed and variable costs have changed with successive levels of office automation.

The wise systems designer will use fixed and variable cost relationships in his selection of systems to automate. Consider the choice between a life insurance billing system and a stock brokerage bill-

Capital Intensive Systems

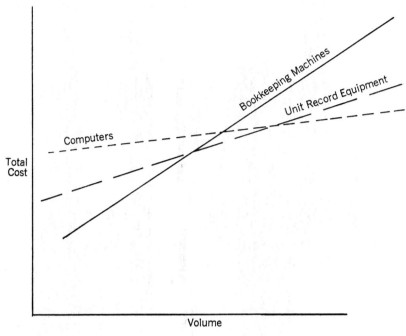

FIGURE 4.2

ing system. The volume of the former is highly predictable while the volume of the latter is highly variable. One would be much more certain of staying above the breakeven point in the life insurance company system. In fact, there were failures of brokerage houses in 1970 when the computer imposed higher breakeven points for the firms and the trading volume decreased.

Grosch's Law (Knight, 1966) suggests that the power of a computer is a function of the square of its cost. The systems designer must consider that the installation of a larger computer will lower the marginal cost but increase the fixed cost of the installation. Due consideration of both factors should result in selection of equipment with the most appropriate risk/cost relationship.

PARETIAN DISTRIBUTIONS

A Paretian distribution curve is shown in Figure 4.3, illustrating the distribution of income. Business information systems follow this 80%/20% ratio in which 20% of inventory items have 80% of the activity; 80% of workers are in 20% of the plants, mills or offices; 20% of the customers represent 80% of the sales. Not a precise measurement, this ratio is so reliable that the analyst can use it as a rule in systems design.

For example, the analyst, in gathering information, measures the time the worker takes to perform each task involved in the system. He would expect 20% of the tasks to encompass 80% of the work performed and to concentrate his improvement efforts on the 20% of the tasks which affect the majority of the work.

Similarly the analyst examines the decision points of a system. Usually only 20% of the decisions are important, as are the factors effecting a decision. The analyst should concentrate his time on the important decisions and important variables which represent cost-effective behavior.

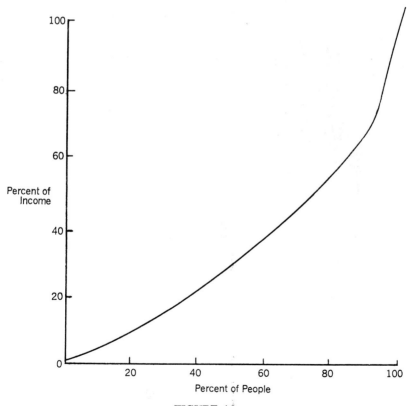

Paretian Distribution Curve for Income

FIGURE 4.3

Size Determines Type of System

The ABC method of inventory control is commonly used. This method applies a different control system to items of different activity and value. Usually three distinct modules (A, B, C) of systems are required to provide the appropriate amount of control. Applying the controls and order procedures used for spare motor generator sets (A) to fasteners (C) is as wasteful as the reverse. Similarly if one designs a payroll system for a large plant, it will rarely fit a small plant. Generally organizations find it necessary to develop separate systems, or at least a separate processing step for the high and low activity elements in the organization or system.

A systems designer using Paretian distributions in an order entry system would first find the relatively small group of products that generates most of the orders. The data for these items should then be made easier to locate and process. They might be stored in core during order processing while all other items were stored on a disk. Second, he would locate the customers that generate a large portion of the sales and special on-line arrangements would be made for such valued customers. Statistics would be kept for some customers but not for others. Individual file folders would be provided for the more active accounts with the inactive gathered in alphabetical groups. Third, he would set up a different order entry system for the small branch offices as opposed to the large offices. These examples show that Paretian concepts are universal in the work of the systems analyst.

ELASTICITY OF DEMAND

Consideration of elasticity is important to the systems analyst. Companies have found that installing Wide Area Telephone Service (WATS) without some pricing mechanism results in doubling the demand for the service within three months. Placing controls or costs on the WATS service tends to limit the use of it.

Demand curves for two products are shown in Figure 4.4. Product A has elastic demand. When the price is reduced slightly the demand increases greatly. Product B is inelastic, with changes in price having little affect on the demand (Samuelson, 1964). Before a systems analyst changes a system involving a product, he will want to know that product's elasticity of demand.

Many computer centers either do not charge for services or make only a bookkeeping charge. A result of such practices is a sharp increase in the demand for computer time. An in-house computer

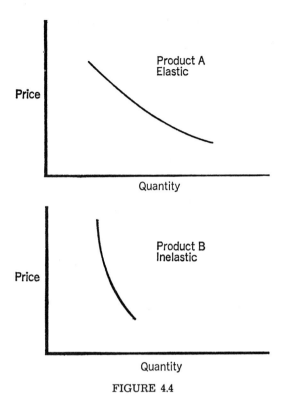

FIGURE 4.4

center director who wishes to build an empire should then fight off all attempts to institute a pricing schedule for computer time.

These illustrations show that the control function of a system serves to ration the use of a resource and that elasticity must be included in the system design. The systems designer must learn the shape of the demand curve.

INPUT/OUTPUT ANALYSIS

Leontif suggested that economic systems could be studied quite well by examining a matrix of the inputs and outputs of a system (Miernyk, 1965). Business information systems can be studied from an input/output point of view. For a large part of the information gathering, analysis and design, the internal workings of the system do not need to be known; however, the output requires that certain conditions be met by the system. Matching input against output shows areas of redundancy, missing data and other system deficiencies. This subject is described in more detail in Chapter 13.

QUEUING THEORY

Queuing theory (or "waiting line" theory) can be illustrated with the example of an airport with one runway and a control tower operation capable of handling one landing or one take-off per minute. Assume that this airport had 60 arrivals or departures in a given hour and that there was no plane waiting to land or take-off at the beginning of the hour. If the planes arrived precisely at one minute intervals (arrival rate) and if it takes the same amount of time for each plane to use the runway (service time) then the result would be 60 landings or departures and no planes lined up (queue) to land or depart at the end of the hour. Unfortunately, precision of this sort is rarely possible. Variability in either the service or arrival rates in this situation would result in an ever-lengthening queue.

Queuing Theory in Business Systems

The probability of the airplane in the illustration arriving in a given time period is expressed by the *Uniform Distribution*. That is, the probability of arrival is a function of the length of the time period chosen but independent of the period chosen. The probability of n arrivals in a given time period is expressed by the Poisson Distribution. The probability that the time between the two events (inter-arrival times) will be less than a given number is given by the Exponential Distribution. These three distributions are shown in Figure 4.5.

When transactions arrive at a facility in a manner described by the above distributions and the facility takes time to process the transactions then queues develop. For example, airplanes circle the airport, people wait in a cafeteria line, and jobs wait in a computer for processing. The responsiveness of the system depends upon the average length of the queues. The heavier the utilization of the facility the longer the queue. In business systems, facility utilization is defined as

$$\frac{\text{the time the facility is occupied.}}{\text{the time available}}$$

For instance, if a telephone is covered eight hours per day and is in use six hours the facility utilization is 75%.

Single Server Queuing Formulas

The object of queuing theory is to calculate the approximate size of queues and the average waiting time in a transaction. Figures 4.6 and 4.7 illustrate these distributions.

Let:

s = service time of a transaction

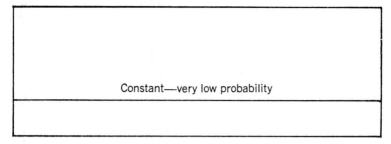

Constant—very low probability

UNIFORM DISTRIBUTION

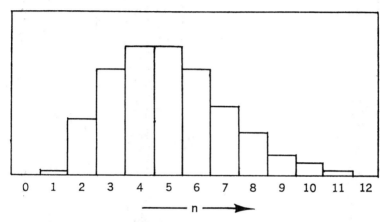

POISSON DISTRIBUTION

$$P(n) = \frac{e^{-\bar{n}} \times \bar{n}^n}{n!}$$

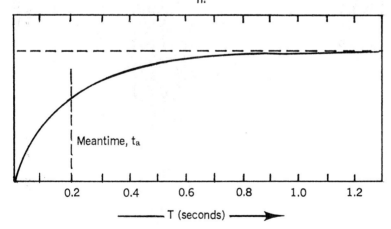

Meantime, t_a

EXPONENTIAL DISTRIBUTION

$$P(t_a \leqslant T) = 1 - e^{-T/\bar{t}_a}$$

FIGURE 4.5

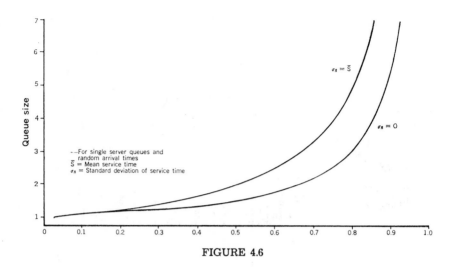

FIGURE 4.6

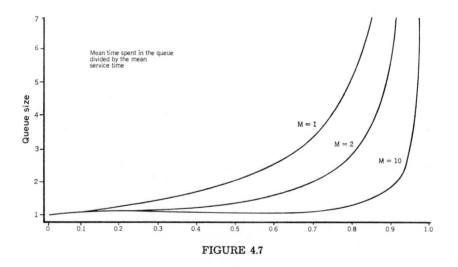

FIGURE 4.7

j_s = standard deviation of service time

w = number of transactions awaiting service

q = number of transactions awaiting service or being served

t_w = time a transaction waits for service

t_q = time a transaction waits plus time being served

Mean values are expressed by $\bar{w}$, $\bar{q}$, $\bar{t}_w$, $\bar{t}_q$

n = mean number of arrivals in a unit of time

p = facility utilization

Then:

$$t_q = t_w + s$$
$$\overline{t_q} = \overline{t_w} + \overline{s}$$

If we have a steady state condition then:

$$\overline{w} = \overline{n} \cdot \overline{t_w}$$
$$\overline{q} = \overline{n} \cdot \overline{t_q}$$
$$\overline{p} = \overline{s} \cdot \overline{n}$$
$$\overline{q} = \overline{n} \cdot \overline{t_q} = \overline{n} \cdot \overline{t_w} + \overline{n} \cdot \overline{s} = \overline{t_w} + \overline{p}$$

The assumption of steady state conditions is essential. If arrivals exceed service ability then q, w, t_w and t_q become arbitrarily large (infinite).

The basic single server queuing theory formula developed by Khintchine and Polloczek is $\overline{w} = p^2[1 - (js/\overline{s})^2]/(1 - p)$ (2).

This formula applies to exponential interarrival times (worst case), any distribution of service times and any dispatching discipline (first in, first out; last in, first out) that does not depend on service time. When service times are constant, $j = o$, then the equation becomes: $\overline{w} = p^2/2(1 - p)$. When service times are exponentially distributed (generally the worst case), $j_s = \overline{s}$, then the equation becomes: $\overline{w} = p^2/(1 - p)$. Note that the worst case formula gives a mean number of transactions awaiting service twice that of the "best case" formula. Most service times found by systems analysts fall somewhere between these two cases. A drum access has both a constant element (reading time) and a random element (positioning time).

Implications of Queuing Theory for Systems Analysis

An examination of Figure 4.6 shows that when facility utilization is greater than .8, queues grow alarmingly. In a single server queuing situation, 80% utilization of the facility is the practical design limit. Even 80% will usually be too great a utilization since most systems grow. Telephone toll calls between a city in Wisconsin and Chicago over a private line indicated a facility utilization of 50%. Three months later investigation showed the utilization of the line to be 75% and there were complaints about service. The service level later reached 80% where it leveled off. At that level, the users dropped out of the queue (aborted) or placed their calls initially over the Bell network. As a facility becomes crowded, queues develop and users abort or bypass the facility.

Systems design must anticipate growth within a system. If 100% growth is anticipated, then an initial facility utilization of 40%

should be considered. With slack defined as the complement of facility utilization, Figure 4.6 shows that with any modest level of service goals there must be considerable slack in the system. However, Figure 4.7 shows that less slack is needed as the number of servers increases. The argument that the systems analyst should deliberately design slack (inefficiency) into the system sounds strange, yet the argument is a good one.

Typical of the single server queue situation is the receptionist. Her slack time is very obvious to both visitors and management. The typical solution is to assign other duties to the receptionist when not serving visitors. Systems designers should solve slack problems not by forcing increases in facility utilization but by providing alternative uses for the facility during slack times. This alternative work must be of a type that can be easily put aside for priority work.

Multiserver Queues

One can develop similar formulas for multiserver queues. The interested reader should read one of the queuing references at the end of this chapter for further details. The restrictions on the use of the equations for multiserver queues are greater than in single server situations. Figure 4.7 showed that facility utilization can be higher without undue service delays. Multiserver facilities served by one queue can provide better service than multiserver facilities each served by its own queue. Still some slack is required. An example is the consolidation of facilities into one—e.g. a steno or motor pool. Such a strategy is effective whenever the increased utilization of the facilities exceeds the organization and communications required by the consolidated facilities.

INFORMATION THEORY

There are at least three different information theories: (1) quantity of information, (2) semantic information and (3) value of information. This section discusses only one, the quantity of information. References for the other concepts are listed at the end of the chapter. More complete discussions of the quantity theory of information are also available in the references.

The communications process is illustrated in Figure 4.8. Theories about information quantity have been closely identified with this communications process. Communication can begin with a person or a machine but the output from the information source is a transmitted message.

Communication Process

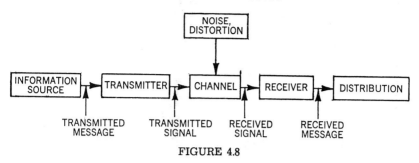

FIGURE 4.8

The transmitter transforms the message so that it can be sent over a channel. The output from the transmitter is the transmitted signal. The telephone transmitter performs this function by transforming the pressure of sound waves on the mouthpiece into an electrical current.

Channels can be wires, microwaves, or sound waves. Channels receive the transmitted signal and output the received signal. The two signals may not be identical because of noise or distortion. Noise and distortion also influence the behavior of the other elements of a communication system. Noise is random and is not completely removable from the channel. Distortion is a fixed perturbation and is therefore removable or correctable.

The receiver operates from the received signal to output the received message. The message may be written, oral, visual or an electrical impulse. The form of the transmitted and received messages need not be the same. The distribution may be people reading, listening, watching or a business machine.

What Is Information?

This chapter defines information as *most efficient coding*. Coding is the process of changing a message from one form to another. The Morse code of dashes and dots substitutes for letters; account numbers substitute for account descriptions, etc. This context does not directly apply to programming in COBOL, BAL, etc. This divorces the concept from semantics, syntax, cost and value concepts of information. In the most efficient coding sense, information can be defined as:

$$H(x) = \sum_{i=1}^{n} - p_i \log_2 p_i$$

Where p_i is the relative frequency of the ith outcome, H(x) (the amount of information) is sometimes called the entropy function since the formula is the same as that used in statistical mechanics. It will be noted that the p_i are all probabilities and thus are less than or equal to 1. The log of a fraction is negative, thus log p_i is less than or equal to 0. This explains the minus sign. The absolute value of the log of a number close to zero is very large. Thus, the formula weights the infrequent (surprise) events much more heavily than the frequent ones.

The maximum of the entropy function occurs when all p_i are equally likely. In a two output situation:

p_1	p_2	H
.5	.5	1.0 — Maximum
.2	.8	.7
.1	.9	.5
.01	.99	.1

This shows that the maximum of the entropy function is not sharp. The systems designer then need not go to a great amount of effort to develop the most efficient coding structure.

An example of this quantity of information concept in a communication that had four events of equal likelihood of occurrence would be as follows:

$$H = 4 \ (-p \ \mathrm{Log} \ p)$$
$$H = 4 \ (-1/4 \ \mathrm{Log} \ 1/4)$$
$$H = - \ \mathrm{Log} \ 1/4$$
$$H = \mathrm{Log} \ 4$$
$$H = 2$$

Suppose one tossed a coin three times and described the results in the eight equally likely outcomes as heads, heads, heads, or heads, heads, tails, etc. In this case $H(x) = \mathrm{Log} \ 8 = 3$. The H/T binary coding structure is then the most efficient code for describing the coin tossing since it is composed of three binary codes.

The best known coding systems for the English alphabet are the Morse code and the Baudot code, which are used for telegraphic transmission. The Baudot code uses five binary codes to describe each letter of the alphabet and is not the most efficient. The Morse code (Figure 4.9) takes advantage of the fact that certain letters are more frequently used than others. The difference between the number of bits transmitted using the Baudot and Morse codes for messages can be large. For example, I LOVE YOU is 50 bits in Baudot but 26 bits in Morse.

If all the letters in the English alphabet were equally likely to be used, the information represented by a random letter would be

Log 26 or approximately 4.6. The Baudot code uses the next highest integer, 5, to organize the coding structure. This neglects the relative frequency of the several letters. Thus, the Baudot code is inefficient. The Morse code is not the most efficient either, but that is of more importance to cryptanalysts than systems analysts (Gaines, 1956).

CODING STRUCTURES

In developing a customer coding structure some knowledge of the quantity of information would be helpful. With a total file consisting of 100 customers, one could use the customer names directly using about 30 characters or a 150 bit code. Knowing that the total list was 100 and assuming equal amounts of activity, a coding structure of seven bits could be developed. Knowledge that the activity was Paretian would reduce the average code level used to less than six bits.

CODING ACCURACY

Efficiency of coding is not the only important issue in the design of coding structures. While efficiency is important, accuracy is also of great significance. Figure 4.8 shows that communication is a multistep procedure with error potential at each step. Greater accuracy can be attained by increasing the fidelity (and the cost) of the components of the system. Greater accuracy can be attained by decreasing the efficiency (increasing the redundancy) of the coding structure. Such a strategy reduces the thruput of the system and increases the operating cost of communicating data. The communications engineer is greatly concerned about balancing efficiency and accuracy costs.

As an example of the problem of balancing efficiency and accuracy, consider the problem of transposition errors in handling numbers. A number like 48 is sometimes transposed to 84 by the system. If one developed a coding structure that required the units digit to always be less than or equal to the tens digit then only 55 of the 100 codes possible with two digits would be useable. Accuracy would be improved by flagging as errors all transpositions but at the cost of 45% of possible codes.

Another accuracy improvement method is to append a check digit to a number. The check digit is some function of the other digits of the number. The most used functions would catch 99% of the errors or more at a cost of one extra digit. The function usually

International Morse Code

Letter	Morse representation	Letter rank by frequency
1. E	•	1
2. T	–	2
3. I	• •	6
4. A	• –	3
5. N	– •	5
6. M	– –	16
7. S	• • •	7
8. R	• – •	8
9. D	– • •	11
10. U	• • –	13
11. W	• – –	17
12. G	– – •	20
13. K	– • –	22
14. O	– – –	4
15. H	• • • •	9
16. L	• – • •	10
17. F	• • – •	15
18. B	– • • •	19
19. V	• • • –	21
20. C	– • – •	12
21. P	• – – •	14
22. X	– • • –	24
23. Z	– – • •	26
24. Y	– • – –	18
25. Q	– – • –	23
26. J	• – – –	25

FIGURE 4.9

used is a weight for each digit plus a modulus for the sum. For instance, consider a five digit number with weights of 6, 5, 4, 3 and 2 and modulus 11. The check digit for the number 15423 is $6 \times 1 + 5 \times 5 + 4 \times 4 + 3 \times 2 + 2 \times 3 = 59$. $59 \div 11 = 4/11$. Check digit is 4. The number used in this system is 15423④. Such a check digit allows less than one error in 1,000 to enter the system at costs of 20% more digits to process, plus a code checking mechanism in the system.

The Social Security number assigned to most U.S. citizens is a 9 digit number without a check digit. There is some inefficiency built into the number system since there are now somewhat more than 200,000,000 people eligible to have a number. Eight digits would be adequate. The nine digits without a check digit do not provide very high levels of accuracy. Large companies still receive quarterly a list of mismatching names and numbers from the Social Security Administration. A substantial portion of these "errors" are number errors. This lack of a check digit is a major criticism by technicians of the widespread use of the Social Security number as a universal identification code.

SUMMARY

This chapter has focused upon some quantitative concepts of importance to the systems analyst. The law of diminishing returns was shown to influence the choice of system projects, time spent on a project by the analyst and the extent of the new system. Ideas about labor or capital intensive systems were shown to influence the amount and type of systems designed. Paretian distributions were shown to be helpful to the analyst. Paretian considerations led to the consideration of separate modules for the high and low activity segments of a system. Paretian plus diminishing return considerations lead the analyst to cut his information gathering activities short of 100% coverage. Demand elasticity was shown to be important in the design of some systems. Input-output analysis was proposed as a method of analysis for certain types of systems.

Queuing theory was described in some detail because of its importance in the design of stochastic systems. Queuing formulas and queuing theory were shown to call into question certain efficiency or maximum use concepts of analysts and managers. Multiserver facilities were shown to be capable of more efficient use than single server facilities.

Some elementary ideas about quantitative information theory were developed and related to the design of coding systems. Accuracy and efficiency demands on coding systems were contrasted. Two accuracy improvement methods were described.

These techniques were described to assist the systems analyst to better relate to the remaining sections of the book. Chapter 3 and this chapter make the point that systems analysis and design are behavioral and analytic, quantitative, and qualitative and generally among the more complex of management activities.

ADDENDUM

STATISTICAL ANALYSIS

Statistical analysis can be described as the technique of using statistical methods to squeeze the maximum information from available data. Expressed in another way, statistical analysis is a method of obtaining the same information from less data. Where data are costly to obtain, important economies may result. The computer's ability to extract the maximum information from data means that small and inexpensive trials can often provide all the answers required by management. Pilot trials can be run to determine the effect of a particular change before that change is applied throughout the organization.

Sampling

The best known application of statistical analysis is quality control. Statistical quality control is based on techniques for determining precisely when manufacturing tolerances start to drift out of control so that corrective action can be taken. Since the cost of inspecting a mass-produced finished item often approaches or exceeds the cost of manufacturing, sample inspection offers the most economical solution. Statistical theory provides the information for designing the sample, i.e., its size and the manner in which it should be taken. It furthermore aids in the analysis of the sample and indicates the size of the risk that is associated with the acceptance or rejection of the lot on basis of sample information.* An operations analyst, when designing a quality control system of this type, would take into consideration such factors as the cost of inspection, the cost of sampling and the cost associated with the shipment of a defective item. He would, in short, not just limit himself to the statistical aspect of the inspection problem, but would consider the whole cost structure that would be influenced by his particular plan.

Forecasting

A few other uses of statistics in analytical research are the design of inventory systems and the planning of production and employment. An essential component of these activities is the capability of forecasting future demand, for which statistical theory provides some techniques. A manufacturer of thermostats may have a hunch that his sales are lagging behind the issuance of building permits by about six months. Statistical theory can assist in testing his hunch and, furthermore, will indicate how much his sales variations are likely to be, given the variations in the issuance of building permits. Computations would be increased significantly if the manufacturer wanted to refine his forecast by basing it not only on building permits but also on lumber and brick sales in his area or on aggregate income statistics. While very simple problems can be handled by desk calculators within a reasonable time period, more complicated problems require the services of a computer.

In the area of forecasting a whole host of statistical techniques abound to aid in projecting for the future. These include the use

---

*uses "probability (inferential) statistics," beyond the purview of this book. In essence, the theory of Probability furnishes a means for expressing the "degree of doubt" in mathematical terms.

of such esoteric words as extrapolation, regression techniques, interpolation, Monte Carlo simulation, transformations, etc., accompanied by techniques to help assure consistency and validity of the data by way of moving averages, seasonal analysis, marginal analysis, correlation analysis, etc. Perhaps the one single technique that should be singled out for more definitive mention is the much-used exponential smoothing technique. Exponential smoothing is a technique for projecting values from past values measured at regular intervals of time. If historical values are available, it is possible to make simple forecasts for successive periods into the future. The formula for new values is a weighted sum of the last actual value and the last new (forecasted) value:

new value (forecast) = (weight × last actual) +
(1 − weight) × last forecast

with weight running between 0 and 1. The best value or weight in the formula can be found by testing how much the forecasts deviate from actuals for various settings of the weight. Some variants of exponential smoothing automatically adjust the weight if the time series suddenly changes its fundamental nature. More general exponential smoothing methods handle data with seasonal factors.

Regression Techniques for Forecasting

The basic intent is to create future forecasts from historical data by "fitting a trend line" to the intrinsic pattern contained in the raw data, e.g.:

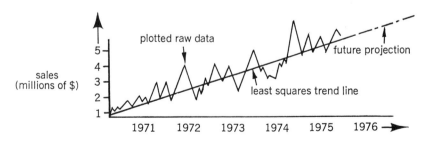

The results may be either a straight line (linear trend), as shown, or a curved line (non-linear trend). The basic linear line plot form is:

$$Y = a + bt$$

The values for the coefficients "a" and "b" are calculated by using the "least squares" (regression) equations. The resultant plotted line is referred to as the least squares line, also called the "regression line."

A variant of this process occurs when, instead of an x-axis time-series as shown, it is desired to forecast sales against other explanatory data such as groups of customers, products, etc. The regression technique is used to develop an *explanation of differences* (the "causation") in the values of these explanatory variables. The values of the explanatory variables in future periods are predicted. Those values are then inserted in the regression equation to calculate the corresponding level of sales. The regression approach takes many forms. Instead of relating total sales to total values of the explanatory variables, the analyst may relate *absolute or percentage changes* in the sales to absolute or percentage changes in the values of the explanatory variables.

LINEAR PROGRAMMING

Linear programming is a mathematical technique whereby the *best allocation of limited resources* may be determined by manipulation of a series of linear equations. Each factor in the problem is evaluated against all other factors and in relation to the long-range goals, yielding optimum paths of action for management consideration.

All of us use informal linear equations to solve even our simplest personal allocations, whether planning our day (time) or our household budget (money). As system specialists, we would construct our problem in terms of a "criterion function," an algebraic linear equation which is to be maximized or minimized, and a set of constraints, linear equations representing factors which act upon the criterion function. In terms of planning our day, our criterion might be happiness, which would be a function of leisure time and earned income. Two constraints are involved: the amount of time available (24 hours) and the minimum amount of money we can afford to earn. We assign values to money and leisure time, and, by running through a series of linear equations, arrive at the combination of both that will bring us the most happiness. This is often a fast, unconscious procedure. It is also relatively simple, unlike the operational problems to which linear programming is applied.

Linear Programming Example

The problem is to slit standard-sized rolls of steel into various widths and quantities for delivery to customers. The objective is to minimize trimming waste, or, putting it in terms of our previous definition, find the most economic allocation (slitting arrangement) of a limited resource (steel rolls) to competing demands (different widths). Naturally, as the variety of desired widths becomes greater the number of possible slitting combinations increases, and the problem becomes more complex. In determining these combinations, we have to consider the width of the original roll, the maximum number of slit widths in one roll, the specific widths on order, and the maximum allowable trim loss. These combinations can easily run into the hundreds. Then, once they are determined, the combinations that will best satisfy the quantities ordered and minimum trim loss must be established. Generating all possible combinations, and then proceeding to find the best, could require several manhours or even days. Or, all of these factors can be reduced to mathematical equations, incorporated into a linear programming program, and run off on a computer in a matter of minutes.

Following are just a few more problems to which linear programming has been successfully applied:

TRANSPORTATION

Given a large number of warehouses with limited capacities and a large number of distributors with known demands, linear programming enables the design of a shipping schedule that will minimize total costs.

PRODUCT MIX

Given a set of raw materials with given characteristics and a set of market prices for finished products, linear programming will indicate how these raw materials should be combined to produce the highest possible profits for the company. Blending of gasolines is an example of this type of application.

ADVERTISING BUDGETS

Given a restricted advertising budget and estimates about the effectiveness of an advertising dollar when applied to a particular medium, linear programming aids in the design of a total advertising program that will maximize advertising effectiveness.

DYNAMIC PROGRAMMING

The essence of dynamic programming is that an optimum decision must be made at every stage of a multi-stage problem. When considering only a single stage, there may appear to be a number of different decisions of equal merit. Only when the effect of each decision at every stage on the overall goal is determined can the final choice be made. This integration of the cumulative effect of a path of decisions through each stage of the network is the real essence of dynamic programming.

Dynamic programming can be simply illustrated by the problem of finding the best route between two points. A motorist normally solves this problem in stages. First he decides that there are, in this instance, four possible intermediate places at which he may lunch. He determines the optimum routes from his starting point to each intermediate place. He next establishes the optimum route from each possible lunch stop to his destination. The shortest total length (or time) of a journey then determines which is the best intermediate point to choose.

Many problems encountered in business life are of the multi-stage type for which dynamic programming and the computer are finding ever-increasing application. One such is the problem of investment replacement and maintenance of equipment, where decisions on capital equipment must be made at regular (often annual) intervals.

The general problem of investment is to decide whether or not it is economic to expend capital on carrying out a process cheaper and/or better. The general approach is to compare savings in running cost given by a new machine against the amortization cost of the necessary capital expenditure. As a machine wears out and decreases in efficiency, its running costs go up and the advantages of replacement increase. In general, a new machine should be purchased when current maintenance and depreciation costs for the old machine exceed the minimum annual cost for the new machine (taking into account production savings where appropriate). All these things and sundry others must be considered in the decision.

It is easy to see that complex multi-stage problems require dynamic programming to be accomplished with the aid of a computer.

GAME THEORY

Game theory is a mathematical theory dealing with decision making in a competitive situation and therefore has definite possibilities in the business area. The theory assumes a competitive situation in which both parties are active and have an effect on the final outcome. The object is to arrive at an optimal course of action by consideration of all possible moves and chance happenings.

For example, game theory provides a guide to the price level at which a bid for a contract should be submitted to achieve the maximum probable profit. If accepted, a high bid yields a high profit, but the chance of acceptance is low, so that a very high bid offers little hope of profit. Similarly, a very low bid ensures a high probability of securing the contract—and of taking a loss. Somewhere between these extremes lies the optimum bid as predicted by the theory of games. Knowledge of your competition, his resources and his bidding pattern is extremely helpful.

It should be noted that game theory is, as yet, a new and comparatively academic technique that serves primarily as a "guide in thinking" about competitive situations rather than as a tool for arriving at specific courses of action.

REVIEW QUESTIONS

1. What impact does rapid industrial change have upon the cost effectiveness of computer-based information systems?
2. An analysis of stockholders records shows that 15% of the shares are held by brokers as nominees for their customers who are the true owners. Should this fact influence the design of a stockholder record system? If so, how?
3. Describe the concept of elasticity in relation to the design of control systems.
4. Describe elasticity and queuing theory.
5. In the book *Up the Organization* Townsend recommends the elimination of individual secretaries for executives in favor of an "executive service group." What concepts in this chapter relate to that recommendation?

DISCUSSION QUESTIONS

1. Some firms have had difficulty in economically justifying the design of a true management information system. Discuss how the law of diminishing returns relates to this problem.
2. Discuss alternatives to replacing the Morse code using only three characters, a dot, a dash and a long dash. Would this be better?
3. An accounting system has 128 accounts. Sixteen of these are equally used and have 80% of the activity. The others are also equally used and account for the rest of the activity. How much information is represented by the account numbers? Design a binary coding structure that minimizes the transmission of account numbers.

BIBLIOGRAPHY

"Analysis of Some Queuing Models in Real-Time Systems," IBM Manual, F 20-0007-0, Poughkeepsie, NY: IBM, 1965.

Bar-Hillel, Yehoshua, Language and Information, Reading, MA: Addison-Wesley, 1965.

Cox, D. R. and W. L. Smith, Queues, New York: Wiley, 1961.

Gaines, Helen Fouche, Cryptanalysis: A Study of Ciphers and Their Solutions, New York: Dover Publications, 1956.

Knight, K. E., "Changes in Computer Performance," Datamation, Vol. 12, No. 9, Sept. 1966.

Martin, James, Design of Real-Time Computer Systems, Englewood Cliffs, NJ: Prentice Hall, 1967.

Miernyk, William H., The Elements of Input-Output Analysis, New York: Random House, 1965.

Raisbeck, Gordon, Information Theory, Cambridge, MA: MIT Press, 1963.

Samuelson, Paul A., Economics, An Introductory Analysis (sixth edition), New York: McGraw-Hill, 1964.

Slaybaugh, C. Jay, "Pareto's Law and Modern Management," Management Services, Vol. 4, No. 2, March-April 1967.

part II

The Systems Project

Various investigators have determined that development of new projects accounts for perhaps 30% of the budget of the information systems function. The remainder of the budget is spent for hardware, operations personnel, data entry, forms and supplies, maintenance of equipment and software, and management. This book is largely aimed at the development functions, although some attention is paid to maintenance problems in Part VI.

The development function is largely project oriented. Groups of people are selected to study a particular area of the business, propose revisions and implement the revised systems. Project teams usually include user personnel, systems analysts and programmers. The role of the systems analyst in the project is primarily that of analysis and design. The analyst is expected to apply his professional expertise to the task of building a new or revised bureaucracy for the organization.

The term bureaucracy is used advisedly. What is a bureaucracy but a formalized set of job related roles and rules promulgated to accomplish the goals of the organization. An information system can be defined as a bureaucracy. This part of the book examines in more detail the ten steps involved in the life cycle of a systems project. Sources of information systems ideas, the initial investigation and systems project organization, the first three of the ten steps of an information systems project, are here described in some detail as well as the tools necessary to accomplish them. The tools included in this part are interviewing, listening, flowcharts, decision tables, Gantt charts, and PERT charts.

One would normally expect about 5% of the total project man-hours to be expended in the first three phases of the project. While the amount of the effort is relatively small, it is critical and the value is large. At the end of these three steps one has an organization and a plan to accomplish the objectives of the project.

CHAPTER 5

THE SYSTEMS' LIFE CYCLE

PHASES OF AN INFORMATION SYSTEMS PROJECT

There is very little agreement between the many writers who have described the systems' life cycle as to the number or composition of the phases. The number of phases range from five to seventeen. This book uses the following ten phases:

Phase 1—Ideas for Information Systems Changes
Phase 2—Initial Information Systems Investigation
Phase 3—Information Systems Project Organization and Planning
Phase 4—Information Systems Investigation
Phase 5—Information Systems Analysis
Phase 6—Information Systems Design
Phase 7—Information Systems Development
Phase 8—Information Systems Installation
Phase 9—Information Systems Evaluation
Phase 10—Information Systems Maintenance

Within each of the ten phases a series of six steps are suggested. These are: (1) define objectives, (2) plan, (3) analyze, (4) design, (5) implement and (6) evaluate. A grid showing the steps within the phases is shown in Figure 5.1. Accomplishing the information

Information Systems Project Phases

Life Cycle Phases		SIX SYSTEMS DEVELOPMENT STEPS				
1.	Ideas	Define Objectives	Plan	Analyze	Design	Implement	Evaluate
2.	Initial Investigation	Define Objectives	Plan	Analyze	Design	Implement	Evaluate
3.	Project Plan	Define Objectives	Plan	Analyze	Design	Implement	Evaluate
4.	Investigate	Define Objectives	Plan	Analyze	Design	Implement	Evaluate
5.	Analysis	Define Objectives	Plan	Analyze	Design	Implement	Evaluate
6.	Design	Define Objectives	Plan	Analyze	Design	Implement	Evaluate
7.	Develop	Define Objectives	Plan	Analyze	Design	Implement	Evaluate
8.	Install	Define Objectives	Plan	Analyze	Design	Implement	Evaluate
9.	Evaluate	Define Objectives	Plan	Analyze	Design	Implement	Evaluate
10.	Maintain	Define Objectives	Plan	Analyze	Design	Implement	Evaluate

FIGURE 5.1

systems evaluation (Phase 9) involves defining the evaluation objective, planning the evaluation, analyzing the project development evaluation, designing the project development evaluation, implementing the project development evaluation and evaluating the evaluation. Some of the steps in the various phases are of less importance than others. Visualizing the process in this manner helps one to gain insight into the entire system process.

The tools of the systems analyst and where they are used in the various phases are shown in Figure 5.2. This text introduces each tool at the point where it first sees extensive use.

System Tools Used in Each Phase

Systems Analysis Tools	Idea	Initial Invest.	Plan	Investi-gate	Analysis	Design	Develop-ment	Install	Evaluate	Maintain
Flowchart	–	2	–	–	2	1	2	–	–	2
Decision Table	–	–	–	–	3	1	1	–	–	2
Interview	–	1	–	1	–	–	–	–	2	2
PERT	–	4	1	3	3	3	2	3	–	–
Return on Investment	–	1	–	–	1	–	–	–	2	–
Forms, Reports Collection	–	3	–	1	–	–	–	–	–	3
Work Measurement	–	4	–	1	2	2	–	–	4	–
Forms Design	–	–	–	–	–	1	–	–	–	2
Documentation	2	2	2	2	2	1	1	1	1	2
Procedures	–	–	–	–	–	1	1	–	–	3
Forms Control	–	–	–	–	–	–	–	–	–	1
Work Simplification	–	–	–	–	–	–	–	–	–	1
Records Management	–	–	–	–	–	3	–	–	–	1
Data Base	–	–	–	2	–	1	1	1	–	2

1 = Most used   2 = Frequently used   3 = Occasionally used   4 = Infrequently used

FIGURE 5.2

The description that follows is an overview of the phases. Details of each phase are described in later chapters.

PHASE 1—IDEAS FOR INFORMATION SYSTEMS CHANGE

Ideas come from individuals, whether or not the ideas are expressed as a function of the personal and work environmental factors shown in Figure 5.3. These are described in further detail in Chapter 6.

Figure 5.3 suggests that not all ideas generated are expressed. This can be illustrated by mentioning a cardinal principle of man-

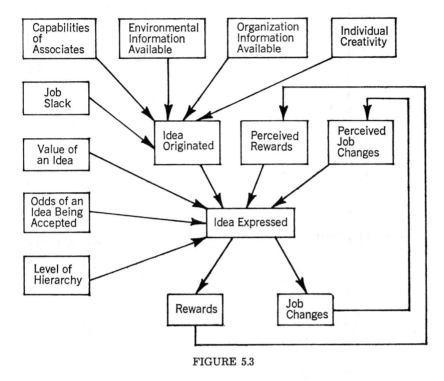

FIGURE 5.3

agement consulting: *The solution to most management problems is available within the organization.* The consultant usually finds that the solution known at lower levels in the organization is not known by the decision-maker. The consultant's role then is that of a communicator or communications link unclogger. In terms of the elements of Figure 5.3 the consultant's role is to make the ideas originated identical with the ideas expressed.

Idea generation is a complex process. The process often becomes constricted and lets too few ideas flow to the project selection process. Some suggestions for removing the constrictions are given in Chapter 6.

Usually, the output of the idea generation phase is first expressed orally as a suggestion. Next, it is documented and evaluated. Organizations differ on the evaluation process. Some use a steering committee for evaluation, others require that a preliminary systems investigation take place before the evaluation. In the former case, the steering committee would see most project proposals both before and after the preliminary systems investigation. Figure 5.4 shows a form used by one organization to record the idea and the investigation assignment.

```
┌──────────────────────────────────────────────────────────────────┐
│                                                                    │
│                   REQUEST FOR SYSTEMS CHANGE                       │
│                                                                    │
│                              Date:_____                 │
├───────────────────────────────┬─────────────────┬─────────────────┤
│ REQUESTED BY:                  │ ORGANIZATION    │ EXTENSION       │
├───────────────────────────────┴─────────────────┴─────────────────┤
│ PROBLEM/IDEA                                                       │
│                                                                    │
│                                                                    │
│                                                                    │
│                                                                    │
│                                                                    │
├────────────────────────────────────────────────────────────────── │
│ REASON FOR REQUEST                                                 │
│                                                                    │
│                                                                    │
│                                                                    │
├────────────────────────────────────────────────────────────────── │
│ BENEFITS EXPECTED                                                  │
│                                                                    │
│                                                                    │
│                                                                    │
├──────────────────────────────────────────────────┬─────────────── │
│ APPROVAL                                           │ DATE          │
└────────────────────────────────────────────────────────────────── ┘
```

FIGURE 5.4

PHASE 2—INITIAL INFORMATION SYSTEMS INVESTIGATION

The purpose of the initial investigation is to develop enough information so that the steering committee can determine whether or not to authorize a complete information systems investigation. A flowchart of the process is shown in Figure 5.5.

The initial investigation is often conducted by a single experienced systems analyst. Since the purpose is to determine whether

Initial Information Systems Investigation Process

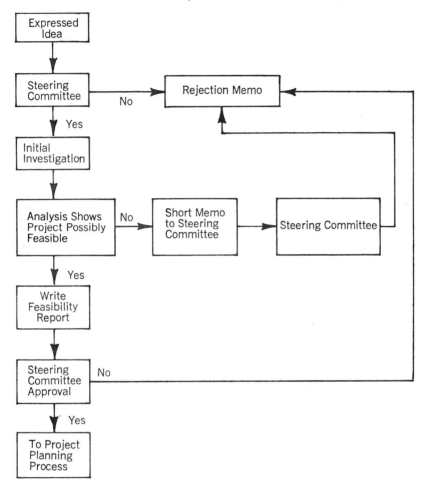

FIGURE 5.5

or not to implement a complete project, the analyst develops only enough information to determine the outcome resulting from a complete investigation. The initial investigation then is a first approximation of the complete study. This requires that the investigation include comments on all of the important aspects of the system being studied, such as:

Benefits achievable by the new system
Operating costs of the new system
Project development costs
Overview of proposed systems design

The output from the initial systems investigation is a feasibility report. The report is usually written by the systems analyst on behalf of the user department, with the user department being responsible for the content. The report contains the user's statements that if the prescribed systems changes are made certain benefits will be achieved. Too often the breaching of this report responsibility principle by the user has resulted in fewer successful projects. The benefits and costs shown in the report are an "order of magnitude" and should not be considered final or definite.

The initial systems investigation report is reviewed by a steering committee or some less formal group. The review considers each project in terms of resources available and results achievable. A favorable decision allocates funds and personnel to do the complete information systems investigation. The steering committee approval process is an interesting exercise in both quantitative and behavioral analysis. Return on investment and risk analysis are juxtaposed with power blocs, individual persuasiveness, and other interpersonal behavior.

PHASE 3—INFORMATION SYSTEMS PROJECT ORGANIZATION AND PLANNING

At this stage in an information systems project, the approval has been given for an information systems investigation. The formal investigation is substantially more detailed and requires more planning than the preliminary investigation. The objective of the project plan is to establish the project organization, determine the project reporting arrangements, select the staff, and detail the areas to be studied and the time required to study each of them. The project organization and plan is usually proposed by the same systems analyst who handled the initial investigation. The analyst obtains information from the Director of Information Systems, the Information Systems Development Manager, the Programming Manager and the executives responsible for the managers who supervise the activities being reviewed.

Staffing Considerations

The skills needed on the project staff include systems analysis and design capabilities, programming capability and functional area knowledge. Often additional skills such as communications equipment knowledge, computation equipment knowledge, operations research capabilities, etc., are required. The McKinsey study (1968) developed the principle of "diversified staffing." By staffing information systems organizations and its projects with people with a variety of skills the entire systems group was more successful.

Planning Activity

This includes determining whether functional or project organization is the more appropriate for this project. There are projects that require substantial amounts of information gathering and analysis together with significant amounts of programming. These projects tend to suggest the need for a project team. Projects with very small contributions needed from all areas save one may be best handled by that function.

Time Phasing of the Project

The planners develop detailed lists of the activities required to complete the project. The task lists are kept small (less than two weeks) so that control is more easily exercised. The tasks are then time phased on a Gantt Chart for the smaller project or on a PERT Chart for larger projects involving considerable coordination and many tasks. Both charts are shown in Chapter 9.

Project Plan Approval and Responsibility

The completed project plan is subject to the approval of both the Information Systems Director and the user organization executive. The ultimate responsibility for the plan rests with the executive to whom the project team reports. This person may be the user or the information systems executive. An inadequate proposal often results from an inadequate systems plan. The user executive must have responsibility for the proposal that results from the project plan.

PHASE 4—INFORMATION SYSTEMS INVESTIGATION

The information systems investigation phase of a project is primarily focused upon information gathering. The objective is to gather the data needed to determine whether a new system is required and to design a new system if one is required.

Ideally, if the investigation is done thoroughly the systems analysis and design phases will progress rapidly. In practice, however, one often has to go back to get missing information and the information system investigation phase is repeated.

This investigation is considerably more detailed than the initial one. To get the needed information, virtually all of the information gathering techniques described later must be used. Interviews with job incumbents are most important. The path of each form used in the system is traced. The factors involved in each decision are documented. Work diaries, work sampling and related techniques are used to measure the time expended on tasks and the production achieved. Report surveys are conducted to locate all the system output and to determine the value of the various reports. (Where necessary progress of information through the system is timed so that sources of delay can be discovered and corrected within the new system.)

As a general rule, each employee involved in the system being studied should be interviewed. Exceptions can be made whenever several people work on identical jobs. However, supposedly identical jobs are rarely identical in practice. The individual abilities of certain employees to handle particular work tends to differentiate the jobs. Also, failure to interview an employee often reduces that employee's sense of participation in the project. Loss of a sense of participation can seriously increase the employee's resistance to the changes proposed by the project group.

The project group should search externally for information as well. The external search seeks information from:

Library references
Salesmen
Other firms
Other systems professionals
Educators
Consultants

The output from the information system investigation is a file or notebook of information which is used to analyze all alternative system designs.

PHASE 5—INFORMATION SYSTEMS ANALYSIS

Information systems analysis starts with the information gathered in the investigation phase. From that information one or more alternative systems are outlined. The alternative systems are evaluated against the existing system and against each other. The best system is then chosen and a report written. This statement of the process makes it sound simpler than it is. The analysis phase can become very complex with the interactions involved.

Information systems analysis is an active process involving the entire project group. Differences in experience and values effect the perceptions of the participants in the process. Conflict is an expected and normal part of the process.

Then when a design is chosen, the project team confers informally with the user group. Key aspects of the proposed system are critiqued by those most affected by the new system. Many proposals which seemed beautiful in the system sanctum are found to be fatally flawed when exposed by the practical user.

In most of the steps in a systems' life cycle, analysis is iterative. Bad designs are thrown out. Good aspects of two designs are grafted together to form a better design. Minor flaws are corrected. Feedback and consultation are essential parts of the analysis process.

Eventually a design is selected. At this stage the design exists at the level of a systems flowchart. It is not prepared at the more detailed flow diagram or procedure level. This design in flowchart form is presented to the decision-makers in a systems proposal. The proposal includes the design, advantages and disadvantages of the proposed system, details of the costs and economics of the new system, and an implementation plan. The proposal is usually prepared by the project team but should be the responsibility of the user. The user and the project team then present the project to the steering committee. In a situation where a potential system improvement project exceeds the organization's resources, which is rather frequent, the presentation may be a rather elaborate selling process involving extensive visual aids and dramatization. In other cases, a rather short written report may be adequate.

PHASE 6—INFORMATION SYSTEMS DESIGN

After approval of a systems proposal, the detailed systems design stage occurs. Output includes detailed specifications of equipment, programs, forms, reports and the written procedures. This part of the project is directed toward installation of the approved system.

In the process of detailing the specifications, the project team frequently finds that the information they gathered needs more specific detail. They then go back to the source to get more information, thus iterating the investigation and analysis phases of the project.

As in the systems analysis phase there is also much interaction in the systems design phase. The interaction occurs both among the project team and between the project team and the users.

The volume of work needed to be done in this stage requires the necessity for careful planning. Planning results in a division of work into sub-systems which are handled by individuals or smaller teams within the project. The total project team may be augmented at this stage to get the specialized people needed.

The modularizing of the system requires careful consideration.

To be most effective the modules must have clearly defined boundaries, otherwise one quickly gets back to the entire group being involved in each design decision. Each sub-group must accept the limits of its role. Weinberg (1971), has an excellent description of an attempt to modularize a particular program. One member refused to accept the inputs as specified and repeated a previous step in his program. When the system changed, as it inevitably does, the previous module was modified and the system blew up. Investigators, after considerable difficulty, found the problem and cut out the duplicated program.

As the above example shows, it is important and necessary that well defined roles be established and *accepted* by the project team in the design phase. Details of the design process and descriptions of the outputs are given in Chapters 16 through 20.

PHASE 7—INFORMATION SYSTEMS DEVELOPMENT

To this point systems have been discussed in general. Systems implemented with computers have been indistinguishable from manual systems. We have included programming, program testing and systems testing in information systems development. While system testing is a part of all systems, programming is, of course, not applicable to manual systems.

Programming is usually described as a process which includes steps very similar to the ten we have used. The differences are more those of nomenclature than of substance. The coding part of the programming process is estimated to be as small as $\frac{1}{6}$ of the total programming effort (Brooks, 1971).

The objective of the program development phase is to produce sets of programs which accomplish the program specifications prepared by the designers. This implies that the designers prepare the specifications. It also implies that the designers prepare sets of testing specifications and data. Certainly no output from the development stage is acceptable until it has been tested. The development is again modular with careful attention to module boundaries for the reasons given previously.

The project plan prepared earlier may have scheduled the programmers to begin work on the project at the analysis and design phases or it may have enlarged the team to include programmers only at this stage of the process. There exists considerable controversy as to which is the better procedure. Bringing programmers in at a later date requires that communications be well managed when they are made a part of the team. The motivation of the programmers is reduced if they are always in the position of programming to a predetermined specification with no part in determining that specification. On the other hand, if the programmer is in the project earlier, the particular talents of the programmer are used for only a small part of the total job. This results in some dissatisfaction among dedicated programmers. Also a programmer doing analysis and design may not be working at his highest skill.

Testing of the system occurs in at least three stages. Each program is usually broken into modules for coding with the programmer testing the adherence of the module to the specifications. Modules are then put together into programs with the programmer again testing adherence to specifications. Finally, the system as a whole is tested against data prepared by the designers. This last step is often performed once with users absent and again after debugging with the users present. The test with users present is usually called an acceptance test.

PHASE 8—INFORMATION SYSTEMS INSTALLATION

The previous steps in the systems' life cycle were largely sequential with coordination needed primarily to avoid duplication, assure that parts fit together and keep the common goal paramount. The installation step encompasses the myriad of preparations for, and the actual conversion to, the new system. Previously only large tasks were performed. Now many small tasks are the responsibility of the project team such as:

Selecting forms vendor
Forms ordering, checking proofs
Delivery and acceptance testing of forms
Equipment selection
Equipment ordering, scheduling and acceptance checks
Site preparation
Supply procurement
Personnel planning
Personnel recruiting
Personnel training
Parallel operations planning
Management of parallel operations
Notification to unions, customers and vendors impacted by the
new system

Disposal of obsolete equipment

Attrition planning, placement of displaced employees

Extend some of the above to multiple vendors or sites and a complex logistical process occurs. This is one point in the process where Gantt or PERT Charts are extremely valuable to the project leader.

As coding is a small part of the total programming task, so systems analysis and design are a small part of the job of the systems analyst. The follow-up of installation details makes this apparent. The installation phase can represent over 80% of the total project time. In eight years with one organization the senior author was involved with just eight systems projects. The largest portion of the time spent on each project was in the installation phase. Installation management is very important and requires different talents than analysis and design.

Also the job of the project team is not completed with the successful operation of the new system. In the early post-conversion period the analyst knows the system better than either the user supervisors or user operating personnel. The analyst must serve as the right hand of the user supervisor during this period. If the system has few bugs and the users were well trained, then the analyst may more quickly go on to other responsibilities. If not, the debugging and implementation may take a long time. Consequently, the analyst's objective is to remove himself as a "crutch" as soon as possible.

PHASE 9—INFORMATION SYSTEMS EVALUATION

Upon its completion the project should be evaluated by two groups— the project team and the internal or external auditors. The evaluators should look only at the project and not expand their audit to the entire information systems function or the user organization. This is in no sense a management audit.

At the close of the project the Project Manager should write a final report on the project. The final report is an evaluation of the extent to which the project met the objectives planned for it. If the project was expected to reduce costs, then the report should indicate the extent to which the costs were reduced. If the project was expected to reduce inventory by a specific number of dollars, then the report should show the amount of the change in inventory.

The report comparing systems performance to objectives should detail any systems deficiencies and any instances in which the system is causing unexpected gains or losses. For instance, if customer complaints increase or decrease after installation of a new billing system, this fact should be mentioned.

People intimately involved in a systems change may not be totally objective in their evaluation. Their evaluation may be or seem to be self-serving. For these reasons it is advisable to have an audit made by either the organization's internal auditing staff, its external auditors or a consultant with expertise in the particular area. Such audits have long been standard procedure for capital appropriations projects. While systems projects may never be capitalized they represent a comparable expenditure of the organization's resources. Rationally, the systems project should be subject to the same audit requirements as other capital appropriations.

The auditor's report covers the same area as the evaluation by the project leader. Primary sources of information to be audited are the project reports, project controls, organization financial records and user interviews. By comparing the results against those expected, the auditor can make conclusions regarding the effectiveness of the project.

PHASE 10—INFORMATION SYSTEMS MAINTENANCE

Systems maintenance often looks like Figure 5.6. The problems at start-up call for large maintenance efforts. The system operating maintenance gradually rises until patching the system seems no longer appropriate and a new systems study is begun. Figure 5.6 was descriptive before the era of data base technology. It may not be as descriptive of future maintenance efforts. In any event, systems maintenance is an important part of the systems cycle and must be made a part of any attempt to describe the entire cycle.

Information systems maintenance tasks are usually quite small. There is some doubt that the typical systems project organization should be used for small projects in general and maintenance projects in particular. Some of the ways proposed for handling such projects are:

1. Design the system so that the user can be trained to maintain it. This implies a modular design and a simple modification language.
2. Train users in work simplification, especially in manual systems.
3. Use maintenance projects as training assignments for new staff personnel.

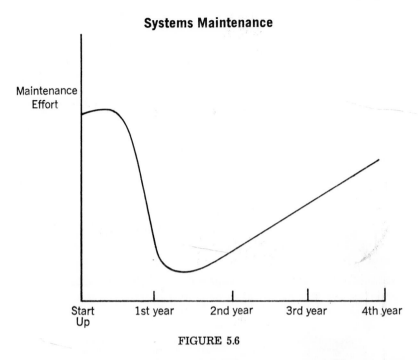

FIGURE 5.6

4. Train operations, clerical and other personnel to handle such jobs in their spare time.
5. Develop a separate staff to handle maintenance of existing systems.
6. Assign systems people to functional areas and have them maintain existing systems in that area while they are developing new ones.

Analysis will be made of these options for maintenance in Chapter 27. Forms control, records management and security, which are more appropriately thought of as related to all existing paperwork systems rather than to a single system, are discussed in Chapters 28, 29 and 30. Taken with Chapter 27 they complete the systems cycle.

SUMMARY

We have used ten phases to describe the work that is normally included in the systems development functions within an information systems organization. As indicated the function of the systems group is to institute and manage change in that part of the organization within their purview. The ten phases have been described in just a few paragraphs; more elaboration will come in future chapters.

REVIEW QUESTIONS

1. Generation of ideas is a complex process. What are some techniques that may be used to permit easy flow of ideas?
2. Why do you think "environmental" factors play such an important part in idea generation? What are some ways to overcome adverse factors?
3. The initial investigation should have as its objective the feasibility of the project. Is this true? If so, how much time should be spent on this step of the project?
4. One of the purposes of the organization and planning step is to show time required to complete the areas to be studied. Why do you think use of a charting or network method is desirable in portraying the plan?
5. What is the degree of detail difference between the initial investigation (Phase 2) and the investigation described in Phase 4?
6. What degree of importance would you assign to the user group in their review of the system specifications?
7. What are some of the advantages and disadvantages of having programmers participate in initial phases of the systems' project? Can programmers and systems analysts be merged into one function?
8. Should the maintenance of a completed system be completely divorced from the project organization? If so, why? Can you name any advantages to retaining it under the responsibility of the project organization?

DISCUSSION PROBLEM

The E-Z Construction Company is a general building contractor specializing in office and warehouse buildings. It handles about 200 contracts per year ranging in the $50,000 to $200,000 cost bracket. It presently uses an automated payroll system and manual cost collection system for each contract. The data collection system appears to be adequate in recording cost, but a time delay in getting postings completed lags several months. A new system is being considered to automate cost-keeping. Outline a system investigation plan. One important aspect of the system is to provide a mechanism to project contract expenditure on a monthly basis in order to predict final costs; one method suggested is to extrapolate cost based on observed physical per cent complete of each contract element.

BIBLIOGRAPHY

Benjamin, Robert I., *Control of the Information System Development Cycle,* New York: Wiley-Interscience, 1971.

Brooks, F. P., Jr., "Why Is the Software Late?" *Data Management,* Vol. 9, No. 8, August 1971.

Shaw, John C. and William Atkins, *Managing Computer Systems Projects,* New York: McGraw Hill Book Company, 1970.

Unblocking the Computer's Profit Potential, New York, New York: McKinsey and Co., Inc., 1968.

Weinberg, Gerald M., *Psychology of Computer Programming,* New York: Van Nostrand Reinhold Company, 1971.

CHAPTER 6

ORIGINS OF SYSTEMS PROJECTS

Three aspects of the project origination process are described in this chapter:

> Ideas for systems change
> Initial information systems investigation
> Information systems project selection

Idea generation must precede an initial investigation which again must precede project selection. The three aspects are then separate phases, yet they are all a part of the process of getting a project started.

IDEAS FOR SYSTEMS CHANGE

The selection of information systems projects to implement assumes that there are many more ideas for change than the organization has resources to implement (Schwartz, 1969). This chapter will examine the sources of ideas and relate them to the selection process. For our purposes we will assume that the selection is being done by a top-level Steering Committee. The members of the committee are selected from the top two levels of the organization.

FACTORS INFLUENCING ORIGINATION OF IDEAS

Ideas for change are usually generated by one individual and are not the product of group innovation. The ideas for changing a system presented by individuals are the function of the nine personal and organization factors discussed here. (See Figure 5.3)

1. *Individual creativity.* Writers on the subject of creativity view it as a distinct cognitive ability correlated with general intelligence in the lower half of the intelligence scale but not the upper half. Some researchers have developed tests to measure some types of creativity. There is some indication that biographic variables may be the best predictors of creative behavior. There is a large variation in the creative ability of individuals. In most organizations 90% of the ideas for change come from 10% of the members.

2. *Availability of environmental information.* Included in this category is a variety of extra-organizational influences such as trade and professional journals and books, interaction within professional organizations, communication with customers, communication with various governmental agencies, and vendor information. The num-

95

ber of ideas generated is an increasing function of the number of stimuli in one's personal environment.

3. *Availability of organizational information.* This includes stimuli within the working environment such as significant cost or budget variances, quality problems, grievances, turnover and accident incidents. Organizations vary considerably in their dissemination of such information to employees; therefore the stimuli also vary. The number of ideas developed by the employee is directly related to the intra-organizational stimuli available to him.

4. *Job slack.* March and Simon (1958) postulated a Gresham's Law of Planning. They said routine drives out planning. Idea creation is a planning activity. A routine job generates few ideas for change. Because their routine activities tend to increase, we can expect long term job incumbents to have fewer ideas for change. Periodic renovation of job structures to eliminate routine and create some slack is the prescribed way to handle this problem.

If the organization has a need to inhibit ideas for change (certain military units, for example) then it is appropriate to encourage routine and discourage slack.

5. *Capabilities of associates.* Conversations with associates can trigger ideas for systems change. The original concept of operations research was to get together competent people from several disciplines, assuming that their interaction would accomplish more than each could do separately. The Human Asset model proposed by Flamholz (1971) has in it an interaction variable.

6. *Perceived chances of an idea being accepted.* Several years ago the editors of the *Harvard Business Review* studied the manuscripts submitted to them and found no instance where a prospective author who had been twice rejected submitted a third manuscript. Salesmen typically receive several "no sales" to every successful sale. The evidence is strong that a previous history of rejected ideas inhibits new ones. Thus a neutral, non-evaluative mode encourages idea generation by employees.

7. *Perceived rewards.* Suggestion award systems show the value of positive reinforcement. For example, a new vice president of personnel found he had inherited excessive turnover and decided to tackle the problem. He received permission to make awards for good suggestions for reducing turnover. The problem of turnover was discussed during the next weekly meeting of the personnel managers from each division. The vice president asked for ideas to solve the problem. Rewards were not mentioned. At the next meeting one of the managers made a suggestion and was rewarded with a crisp, new $100 bill. The following meeting generated several excellent

ideas. Within a short time each of the managers had received the same reward, the turnover problem decreased and the group turned to the other personnel problems of the organization with enthusiasm and success.

Compensation research has shown the efficacy of irregular rewards such as the one described above.

8. *Perceived effects of the change on the job.* It was suggested recently that each government employee be allowed to retire immediately at normal retirement pay if he could figure out how to eliminate his own job. This combines the idea of reward and the reluctance to drastically change one's own job. The fact that fewer jobs will exist after a change decreasing chances for advancement retards the suggestion of ideas. It has taken years to prove that automation in an economy increases jobs and skills.

9. *Level in hierarchy.* An analogy to the hierarchical communication chain is an electrical circuit with the various levels being represented by resistors. The greater the number of resistors (levels) the less the proportion of current (ideas) gets through. Just as the existence of the many links in the communication chain reduces the possibility that the idea will be accepted, each level also acts to influence the perceived chances of the idea being accepted.

SOURCES OF IDEAS

For our purposes we will consider that the impetus for change can come from any one of four sources: outside the organization, the department directly involved, top management, or the information systems group. We will consider the types of changes coming from these areas, the potential for acceptance of ideas from each source, and the relationship of idea source to successful completion of the change.

Sources Outside the Organization

Systems changes are often required by government or regulatory bodies or industry standards. Examples of these necessary changes would be income tax withholding changes, tax regulations, audit requirements, trade association standards and government agency regulations.

User Department Originated Projects

Changes suggested by a user department are more likely to be restricted to that department. Some of the factors the Steering Committee must consider are:

1. Project payoff
2. Project risk
3. Payoff from previous projects from this department
4. Department's share of previous projects
5. Persuasive ability of department representative
6. Bias of Chairman of Steering Committee toward a particular department
7. Bias of top management toward a particular department
8. Position of department representation with respect to majority coalition
9. Other projects proposed at same time
10. Ability of Steering Committee to understand the technology involved in the project
11. Relative power of department representative vis-a-vis other committee members
12. Availability of implementers with the needed skills
13. Amount of systems design and implementation resources involved

Many of these are considered by one or more levels of management in the user area. The process of sequential review by higher levels of authority often eliminates many projects before they ever get to the Steering Committee.

Powers (1973) showed that user originated projects were the most likely to succeed when success was measured by user satisfaction. Such results are of no surprise to the adherents of a "human relations" school of management thought.

Top Management Originated Projects

There are two types of project proposals in this group. The first are certain projects which result in mandated changes such as mergers, construction of new production facilities, etc. The second group are projects such as the construction of a corporate model or the design and installation of a new budget system and typify top management originated projects.

Needless to say, the probability of a project from this latter source being accepted is very high. However, research data suggest that they are not as likely to succeed as user developed projects. The reasons for this are not known. One possible reason may be the inability of top management to devote enough attention to the development of their projects, which results in substantial differences between the developed project and the original idea. Consequently, the original ideas are implemented without being improved and tested in several design iterations.

Top management originated projects are likely to involve many departments. The resulting coordination problems may be a substantial cause of less successful projects.

Information Systems Group Projects

These projects can cover a wide range. Some will be organization-wide, others will relate to just one function and others will involve only the information systems group.

The top computer executive's involvement makes the project more likely to be accepted. First he has control of the people and equipment resources that often restrict others in implementing projects. Second, he knows the acceptance criteria and is able to structure the project to meet those criteria. Third, his technical expertise should be sufficient to prepare a project proposal with technical, economic and operational feasibility.

Research data show that information systems projects were also less likely to be satisfactory to the users (Powers, 1973; Willoughby, 1975). For example, in one project the information systems organization had in the past reacted to suggestions from users rather than originating its own. The information systems department saw that one of the major needs of the organization was for a new project cost/planning system. It sold the project and proceeded to implement it. Later evaluation showed the information systems group to be extremely happy but the users very unhappy. Subsequently, the information systems manager was demoted.

Summary

Research by behavioral scientists makes it clear that more and better ideas come from organizations which are open to suggestions rather than judging all ideas. Good information systems projects come from those organizations which have some slack.

The acceptance of information systems projects is shown to be a function of many variables. User originated projects were expected to be less likely to be approved than projects from top management or from the information systems staff, but more likely to be successful in the eyes of the user. A typical request form for a systems study is shown in Figure 6.1.

INITIAL INFORMATION SYSTEMS SURVEY

The initial systems survey is much like a complete systems study although much shorter in time. Its purpose is not to develop a new systems design in *all* of its details but to provide enough informa-

---

REQUEST FOR SYSTEMS STUDY

Date:_____

Requested by:_____ Department:_____

Problem Study Requested:

  A computer generated set of personnel reports.

Reason for Request:

  Too many requests from line departments for this information which must be looked up manually.

Expected Benefits from Request:

  Less work load for department.
  More timely information for line departments.
  Fewer phone calls between departments.

Approval:_____   Date:_____

FIGURE 6.1

tion so that a decision can be made whether or not a complete systems study should be implemented. The initial systems survey ends with the second "go, no-go" decision in the project life cycle. The first "go, no-go" decision related to whether or not the idea for change was good enough to justify the initial systems survey. Thus, the survey is focused upon a particular idea for systems change.

Initial surveys are often conducted by one person. The selection of that person is very important, even more important than selection of a project team later on in the project cycle. One reason for this is that the initial survey is a short investigation. There is not time to check all of the details of the system. Thus, the analyst must use judgment in picking out the most important areas to analyze. A second reason is that the analysis in certain areas has to be superficial. Thus, the analyst's judgment of what to expect from a more complete analysis is an important ingredient in the investigation. Third, first impressions are as significant in systems work as they are in other areas of human communication. The impressions created by the analyst in his initial study may greatly influence the success or lack of success of the ongoing project.

The skills and attributes particularly needed by the analyst in the initial study include:

Experience—preferably with the same or a similar system in another location.

Quick intelligence—since good insights are needed quickly.

Social intelligence—since many cues useful in systems analysis are to be found in the work environment and since the study will set the future relationships between the systems group and the user.

Personal authority—since the analyst must gain the confidence of the user group.

The following description of an initial systems investigation assumes that a systems analyst has been selected to investigate a particular situation or problem and that arrangements have been made to start the investigation at a particular time and place.

The aspects of the initial systems investigation which we shall examine are:

Preparations for the study
Initial meeting with responsible executive
Data gathering
Systems analysis
Systems design
Presentation of informal report
Formal report/systems proposal

Preparations for the Study

The initial systems study starts with preparations for the study by the people involved. The two groups of people of primary importance are the analysts and the users.

User Preparations

The primary preparatory activity of the user is to announce the investigation to *all* of the people involved. The form of the announcement can be a memo to those involved or an oral explanation at a meeting of the people involved in the system. This meeting should not involve the analyst because of the inhibiting effect of his presence.

User management must be prepared to respond to questions about job change and job security. These and other effects of systems change on the people in the organization were discussed in Chapter 3. Generally, the possible negative aspects of systems change are severe enough to warrant considerable care in announcing the forth-coming investigation.

Office space and telephone service may be made available at this time for the analyst within the user's department.

Preparation by the Systems Analyst

The systems analyst also prepares for the study. The details of the data the analyst gathers will be different for each organization. Table 6.2 shows the data to be gathered for a public business organization and the uses for that data.

Initial Meeting with Responsible Executive

In a meeting of the principals involved (the executive, his assistants, and the analyst) an agreement is made as to the work to be done, the general methods to be used, the people it is appropriate to contact, what can or cannot be stated about the purpose of the project and the possible results of the investigation. During the discussion of the system to be investigated, the analyst should determine whether the executive has any unstated reasons for asking for assistance. There are often some unstated reasons involved. One analyst was asked by a financial vice-president to assist his data processing manager by reviewing plans of proposed systems. The analyst did not recognize it initially, but he soon found that the real job was to evaluate the data processing manager. The vice-president took the analyst's recommendation that the manager be fired. Hidden motives for systems studies are frequent and should be uncovered by the analyst.

The executive should personally introduce the analyst to his key people. This establishes authority. Without the indication from the executive that the investigation is important and that he wants the study made, the role of the analyst becomes ambiguous and makes success more difficult.

During both the initial study and the complete systems study later, there may be pressures for the analyst to deviate from the original objective. If the pressure is from the responsible executive the changes should be seriously considered. If they are inconsistent with good systems practice then the analyst should try to persuade the executive to remain on course. If that appeal fails then reinforc-ing help should be sought from the systems analyst's manager.

If the pressure to change or enlarge the study comes from the sys-tems manager, they should be resisted. Nothing can endanger the success of a systems study more quickly than an analyst going off in an unplanned direction. User managers have been known to put

INFORMATION NEEDED
BEFORE ON-SITE SYSTEMS INVESTIGATION

Source	Data	Use
Corporate listing in financial reporting services	Corporate history Products Locations Financial statements Profit margins Inventories Cash	General introduction Attempt to identify problems and opportunities
Most recent annual report	Same as above	Attempt to identify problems and opportunities
Literature	Other designs for similar systems	Use as models for tryout in design phase. Use as guide to gather appropriate information.
Corporate organization chart	Reporting relationships Where the power lies Missing functions	Get feeling of possible constraints
Departmental organization chart	Names Reporting relationships Functions	Relate to corporate to see how department fits into whole Identify potential problems and opportunities
Others in own organization who know user organization	People data	Eliminate social blunders. Sell ideas that user is likely to accept.

TABLE 6.2

those systems analysts on the next plane back to the corporate headquarters.

Even in the initial investigation it is important to study the existing system to reveal its adequate and inadequate capabilities. A careful study will avoid designing a new system that does not satisfy present needs overlooked by the user. These needs usually surface after the system installation and can cause great panic.

Data Gathering

The focus of the information gathering phase of the initial systems investigation is on potential areas for profit improvement. Some of the areas for improvement are:

Better management decisions
Increased sales
Decreased production costs

Lower inventories
Better use of human assets
Better use of physical assets
Better use of cash
Decreased clerical costs

It will be noted that decreased clerical costs are listed last. This is not because such gains are impossible to achieve or insignificant, for clerical cost reductions can total many millions of dollars. It is because the opportunities in other areas may be considerably greater. For example, a project decreased accounts receivables by over $1,000,000 and increased accounts payables by a similar amount. Clerical cost reduction on that job was about $40,000/year; obviously the better use of cash was the more significant gain in that project.

Techniques Used

The data gathering techniques described in Chapters 7, 8, 10, 11, and 12 are all candidates for use in the preliminary study. The interview tends to be used almost to the exclusion of the others in actual practice. Some attempts will be made to validate interview data by examining reports, control forms, procedures and other documents. Report surveys, forms collections, and work measurement techniques are rarely used at this stage because their level of detail is inappropriate.

Accuracy and Completeness of the Data

In the formal systems study the analyst insures closure by interviewing all user personnel about all aspects of the system. In the preliminary study, short-cuts are taken. The analyst in this case is not attempting to reach a 99% confidence level that his judgment on a particular item is correct; an 80% confidence level is sufficient. There are typically dozens of judgments made by the analyst in surveys of this kind. Assuming no bias by the analyst, the central limit theorem indicates that the net of all the errors of estimation should be close to zero.

Bias is a part of the analyst's set of behaviors. Experience has shown the bias to be toward over-optimism. The characteristic set of the analyst can, of course, be corrected by the analyst himself or by a supervisor when such sets are known. When the judgments of the analyst vary substantially from optimism to pessimism over the course of the project, correction may be difficult.

One tendency of certain analysts (some of those trained in accounting or engineering fit this description) is to select the conservative view of each data item they see. Deliberate choice of conservative evaluations has a compounding effect. Many facts get multiplied several times in the calculations relative to a new system. This point will be discussed in more detail in Chapter 10.

Influence of Analyst's Experience on Data Gathering

Where the analyst has had considerable experience designing and installing systems similar to the one being considered, the information search activities will differ. The experience of the analyst is represented by one or more conceptual systems models in his memory. He examines the present system in the context of those models and carefully observes those areas he believes to be critical design factors. His objective is to find out whether a previously designed system fits this situation. If the fit is not perfect (and it usually is not) he considers whether a new system is necessary or whether minor modifications can be made to an existing system to make it fit this situation.

In our experience the first installation of a new system is usually more successful than subsequent ones. The most likely explanations for this are the lack of participation in the systems design by the subsequent installations and the fact that changes tend to reduce the effectiveness of a systems design.

The Systems Analysis Phase

The analysis phase of the initial survey is different from the same phase in the more formal study mainly in the time involved. For that reason the description of the information analysis and data analysis are deferred to Part III. Time constraints tend to eliminate the use of certain analytical techniques such as document analysis, matrix charting and flow charting.

The Systems Design Phase

As was the case for information analysis, the systems design aspect of the preliminary systems study is similar to the formal design process. Obviously, such design tools as automated systems design are out of place. The major tools used are economic analysis and report writing skills. The output of the design phase is an overall model of the proposed system, the advantages and disadvantages accruing to the organization from its use and the economic impact of the design and use of a new system.

The nature of the investigation usually precludes serious examination of alternative systems. The proposed systems design should then be viewed as one likely prospect for an improved system. The results are greatly influenced by the experience of the analyst and the analyst's willingness to propose a workable, rather than optimal system.

It is at this stage that systems projects are most likely to be iterative rather than sequential. The information gathered may not be adequate to evaluate a possible design. In this case a repeat of the data gathering and information analysis phases may be necessary.

Presentation of Informal Report

The user executive is responsible for all changes in his systems. His approval is needed to present a proposal to the Steering Committee. His efforts are needed to sell the proposal to the Steering Committee. His participation is needed to design and implement a new system. His commitment is needed if the economic objectives of the new system are to be achieved. Thus, the analyst's report must reflect the views of the user executive, contain no surprises and be primarily the user's view of the situation. The report can contain all of these things as well as be a responsible evaluation of the systems proposal if there is meaningful dialogue between the user executive and the analyst in the report preparation process. The report to the user executive is the means by which the dialogue takes place.

The analyst should spend about 20% of the time on the project in preparing the draft of this report. This time is immediately prior to the oral or informal presentation of the findings and recommendations. It will, of course, involve some looping back into the information gathering, information analysis and systems design phases as the report writing process uncovers holes in the previous work.

The informal report should be a handwritten draft prepared for the meeting with the findings and proposals presented orally and certain key charts or financial data copied for distribution.

Discussing the conclusions of the analyst gives the executive a clear picture of the major points of the report. Feedback at this stage is essential. Points of misinformation are cleared up. Situations calling for delicate handling are considered and appropriate language drafted to cover the problem. If the review requires a re-study of some aspect of the system, this is done following the meeting and any report modifications required are communicated to the responsible executive.

The meeting usually closes with a discussion of how many copies of the formal report are needed, who gets them and how they are to be delivered. The executive whose secretary opens all of his mail may prefer hand delivery or special envelope marking.

The Formal Systems Investigation Report

After oral presentation to the responsible executive, the initial systems investigation report is revised, edited, typed and distributed. One such report is presented at the end of this chapter.

Some firms have prescribed forms for these reports to assure uniform project evaluation.

While report writing styles differ, our preference is for the following format:

Introduction and problem statement
Summary of findings
Summary of recommendations
Detailed findings
Proposed systems design (if any)
Economic impact of proposed system (if any)
Acknowledgments
Appendices

The content of the report should include at least the following information:

a. A statement of the problem.
b. Alternatives and recommended solutions.
c. Information flowcharts (not detailed flowcharts).
d. Volumes, sequences and frequencies.
e. Categories of data to be included or excluded.
f. Nonrecurring and recurring costs.
g. Gross and net savings.
h. Intangible benefits, advantages and *disadvantages*.
i. Types of personnel required including user support.
j. Elapsed time of project after approval.
k. Target date for completion.

The material in the report is a function of the particular system being described. The general principles involved are the rules for writing good reports which are taught in such books as Douglass (1957). The findings section and its summary lists the advantages and disadvantages of the proposed action. These should be assigned values wherever possible, the values indicated and the valuation methods stated.

Also in the findings section should be a discussion of whatever warnings the analyst believes important to state. These may include the information search limitations, the not necessarily optimal systems design and assumptions of similarity to other systems. The external consultant finds these necessary to protect his assets. While they may serve that purpose, reviewing such listing of assumptions is an important part of the management decision-making process.

Summary

We have shown the initial systems investigation to be a miniature of the more formal systems investigation process. It does have some peculiarities of its own which include the limited search, the willingness to propose a workable design and the need for systems experience and behavioral expertise in the analyst.

PROJECT SELECTION

To recapitulate, at this state of the information systems project it is assumed that, in response to some idea or stimulus, an initial project investigation has been completed. We shall also assume that the project selection is done by a Steering Committee. There are some projects that are mandated either by top management or by an outside agency. These are approved regardless of return on investment, risk, etc. While Steering Committees are frequently used, they are not always organized as such. In those organizations without Steering Committees, the project selection is usually a less formal process. The process when a Steering Committee is not involved is described later in this chapter. The pressures for project approval are felt by the executive involved rather than by a larger steering group.

Some of the factors which are important in the decision as to which information systems projects to implement are these:

Economic Feasibility
Internal return on investment
Risk
Technical Feasibility
Required skills of systems group
Return on manpower
Status of other projects
Operational Feasibility
Relationships with user department

Return on Investment

The internal rate of return on investment (ROI) calculation is shown in Figure 6.3. These calculations should be made for virtually every information systems project. To make the calculation requires that the cash flow of the project be known. The cash flow is a function of the project costs, profit increases, cost reductions, equipment costs, depreciation rates, tax rates and systems operation costs for the current year and for several years in the future. Any error in any of the cash flow figures effects the ROI calculation. The approximate nature of the initial study suggests that the calculated ROI is not likely to be precisely accurate. Its value is in being compared with

ROI's calculated in a similar fashion. One should expect that projects with similar returns will often be given the wrong order. That is, the greater will be shown to be the lesser and vice versa. The Steering Committee then should use the calculated ROI as an indication of order of magnitude of return and not as a precise prediction.

Internal Rate of Return Calculation

Year	Cash Outflow	Cash Inflow	Depreciation	Tax	Net Cash Flow	Present Value 15%	Present Value 20%
0	6,000	0	0	0	−6,000	−6,000	−6,000
1	0	200	1,000	−400	600	522	498
2	0	1,400	1,000	200	1,200	912	828
3	0	2,600	1,000	800	1,800	1,188	1,044
4	0	3,800	1,000	1,400	2,400	1,368	1,152
5	0	5,000	1,000	2,000	3,000	1,500	1,200
6	0	6,200	1,000	2,600	3,600	1,548	1,188
						1,038	−90

By linear interpolation the interest rate of return is approximately 19.6%

FIGURE 6.3

Since money is a scarce and costly commodity in most organizations, it is important that savings and profit improvement projects of all types be evaluated carefully. Not all projects will yield an ROI which exceeds the organization's cost of capital. Lower return projects rarely go to the Steering Committee for the automatic turndown.

Many organizations set a minimum rate of return for approval of all projects. We have seen 20 per cent used as a minimum in several organizations. Banks, insurance companies and public organizations generally have lower costs of capital, lower minimum rates of return and therefore are more likely to approve all capital budgeting projects including information systems.

Experience has shown many projects examined by the Steering Committee have calculated ROI's just over the minimums. Paretian considerations would account for many of them. Others probably were initially calculated below the minimum, had the assumption and cash flow changed and then were recalculated. There are generally enough error potential in the estimation process and enough motivation to alter estimates for the Steering Committee to examine the ROI calculation for true savings.

Risk Analysis

A sample risk analysis calculation is shown in Figure 6.4. These tend to be calculated only in relatively sophisticated organizations and then only for a minority of projects. Risk analysis is probably of less importance in information systems projects than in new product projects or many other types of organizational projects. Calculations certainly should be made on major projects involving new or untried technology.

Calculation of Expected Value of Cash Flows with Risk

1 Estimate	2 Cash Flow	3 Probability*	4 (2) X (3)
Optimistic estimate	5,000	.2	1,000
Best guess	4,000	.6	2,400
Pessimistic estimate	2,000	.2	400
		Expected Value	3,800

*as estimated by the analyst

FIGURE 6.4

Required Skills of Systems Group

The systems unit of any company is composed of individuals with diverse skills. At any given time these people will be working on projects requiring their specific skills. Matching the skills to projects is always necessary. Often projects may be delayed or canceled because the skilled people are unavailable.

An alternative to canceling a project is to hire people to implement it, either as regular employees or as consultants. If the project is important enough to the organization, one of these alternatives will be chosen. The considerations involved in employing consulting services are described in the information system administration literature and are beyond the scope of this book.

Return on Manpower

Holtsberry (1970) commented that organizations often had more money than talented people. He then suggested that projects be selected to maximize the use of people rather than use of money. If one assumes that the organization indeed has a limited availability of analytical talent, then the suggestion is solid. Under such conditions the organization should choose the least analyst-intensive projects. Even with manpower limits, ROI is still of significance.

Required Equipment and Software

Because of a lack of particular assets, an organization may not be able to consider a feasible project. For example, a project may require only a small fraction of an on-site computer. If a computer were installed and no other projects were available to use up the computer time, then that project would not be an appropriate one. Another project might require limited use of a data base management system. If no other applications were available to share the cost, the project would not be feasible.

Both of the prior examples could have been considered in the cash flow by allocating 100% of the unused facility to the project. This problem of cost of facility apportionment is considered in Chapter 15.

Status of Other Projects

Status is of importance in project selection since it affects the availability of people with specific skills. The skilled teleprocessing programmer may find it impossible to handle an on-line, real-time purchasing system while he is developing a customer order entry system. Certain projects presume that another project is complete. Failure to select or failure to complete another project on time may cause the Steering Committee to not select or to defer a particular project.

Relationships with User Departments

This selection criterion includes more behavioral issues than can be enumerated here. Figure 6.5 shows a sample of the types of items involved. Needless to say, all of these issues assume all else to be equal, which in practice is never true. There is little evidence to support the assertions in Figure 6.5. At this time they should be regarded as testable hypotheses.

Certainly the skills of the user personnel, their previous history of success and their degree of information systems sophistication are often overlooked and underemphasized.

BEHAVIORAL ISSUES IN PROJECT SELECTION

1. If the previous projects implemented in the user department have been successful, it is more likely that the present project will be approved.
2. If no projects have been implemented in the user department, it is more likely that the present project will be approved.
3. If projects planned by an analyst have been successful, it is more likely that the present project will be approved.
4. If previous projects using this technology have been successful, then it is more likely that this project will be approved.
5. If the user departments representation on the steering committee is particularly persuasive, regarded as a comer, nephew of the president, trusted or familiar with the technology, then the project is more likely to be approved.

FIGURE 6.5

Project Selection Criteria

The selection of one information systems project out of those proposed to the Steering Committee is then a complex task. The task involves some calculations such as ROI and risk. It also involves some resource constraints such as people, equipment and software and the many behavioral issues.

SUMMARY

In this chapter we have examined the project origination process in three parts. Ideas were generated from many organizational sources. They percolated or failed to percolate through the levels of the organization. The idea was then formulated into a project and an initial investigation conducted. Those projects deemed by the analyst most likely to be profitable were written up and presented to the Steering Committee. Some of the latter are approved and the rest disapproved, tabled or returned for more information. With the judgment involved at each step it is no surprise that many good projects are never implemented. This complex process also results in each organization having a unique set of implemented projects.

Formal Systems Investigation Report

A. PROBLEM

A requirement exists for the reporting and controlling parts from the time they are rejected on the shop floor until a disposition is determined (accept, rework or scrap) and completed.

B. SOLUTION

Develop and implement a Material Review Board Manual Procedure to identify rejected parts, utilizing the attached new form and their disposition as acceptable, reworkable or scrap.
1. Implement the procedure and form at the Berea plant.
2. Make selective improvements and implement at Strongsville and Olmsted Falls plants.
3. Report parts scrapped, quantities and costs via an automated Scrap Reporting System from the data recorded on a source document (preferably the attached new form F152) generated in the procedure noted in B.1.

C. CONCEPT

1. *Material Review Procedure*
   a. Attached is a flowchart outlining the general require-

ments of the manual procedure and the use of the new Rejected Parts Form (F152).

2. *Scrap Reporting*

    a. Also attached is a system flowchart illustrating the flow within the automated scrap reporting system and the report layout.

    b. The system has been designed so as to capture data relating to rework activity, should the need arise to record and report such activity.

D. JEOPARDIES

1. The automated scrap reporting system utilizes the Part/Operation Cost File as maintained by the Cost Accounting Department for product cost build-up and subsequent pricing of inventory. The Part/Operation Cost File will be replaced by the Routing File when implemented, thus necessitating modification to the proposed system.

2. The Rejected Parts Form is the new source document that provides the data for entry into the system and must be properly completed and submitted.

E. COSTS

The following is a breakdown of the estimated costs incurred to implement the procedure and scrap reporting segments of the Material Review System:

One Time Costs:

Systems & Programming (535 hrs. @ $12.50/hr.)	$6,690.00

Recurring Costs:

Keypunching (4 hrs. per mo. @ $6.50/hr.)	26.00
Processing (2 hrs. per mo. @ $100/hr.)	200.00
TOTAL RECURRING EXPENSE PER MONTH	$ 226.00

F. BENEFITS

1. Replace current EAM card procedures.

G. SCHEDULE

1. Estimated date for completion of procedure is two weeks after go-ahead.

2. Systems and programming completion dates will be scheduled six weeks beyond your acceptance and approval date of this memo.

Therefore, your approval is requested by July 25 in order that Management Systems may proceed with the procedure and programming based on the functional specifications previously obtained from the user.

REVIEW QUESTIONS

1. What are some of the factors that influence the origination of ideas for projects?
2. Why is the selection of the analyst who performs the initial survey important?
3. Why should the analyst review the survey results with the user executive before submission of results to the Steering Committee?

DISCUSSION QUESTIONS

1. Discuss the process by which a new project "bubbles up" through various organization levels.
2. Discuss how an analyst's previous experience can affect the outcome of an initial systems survey of a new project.
3. Discuss the factors that are important in considering which projects should be implemented and why they are important.

BIBLIOGRAPHY

Douglass, Paul, *Communication Through Reports,* Englewood Cliffs, N.J.: Prentice Hall, 1957.

Flamholz, Eric, "Model for Human Resource Accounting: A Stochastic Model with Service Rewards," *The Accounting Review,* Vol. 46 No. 2, April 1971.

Holtsberry, A. W., "You Probably Have More Money Than Brains," *Journal of Systems Management,* Vol. 21 No. 8, August 1970.

March, James G. & Herbert A. Simon, *Organizations,* New York: Wiley, 1958.

Powers, Richard F. & G. W. Dickson, "MIS Project Management: Myths, Opinion and Reality," *California Management Review,* Spring 1973.

Schwartz, M. H., "Project Selection," *Journal of Accountancy,* April 1969.

Willoughby, Theodore C., "Project Success Correlates," Paper presented at the 1975 International Institute of Management Science meeting.

CHAPTER 7

INTERVIEWING AND LISTENING

Probably the most used and useful systems investigation tool is the interview. The interview is important because it is able to gather more complete information than other methods. Two other methods for gathering information have been tried and found to be less efficient than the interview. Rockart (1970) used a model for directed search of information in a medical clinic and missed information that he would have gathered through an interview. Nadler (1970) proposed that the ideal system could be constructed from the stated objectives of the system rather than depth interviews with users. In using the ideals approach to systems design the system designer found the objectives are rarely stated in the detail needed without personal interviews.

As stated in Chapter 6, users are more likely to consider a project successful when they have actively participated in the project. The interview, properly conducted, involves active user participation and, even with superior information gathering techniques, some type of personal interview is necessary to achieve a feeling of participation.

Many besides the information systems analyst use interview techniques. The doctor-patient, lawyer-client, reporter-source, and recruiter-prospective employee interview situations are common. Recently the recruiter-prospective employee interview has been researched in detail. In examining that research we shall see techniques that will aid the information gathering interview conducted by the systems analyst.

THE SELECTION INTERVIEW

Ulrich and Trumbo (1965) researched the recruiter-prospective employee interview as an information gathering technique. In the selection interview, they found the interviewer was able to gain information about the interviewee's social intelligence and long-term career motivation but was a poor source for most other information. To obtain more reliable data they suggested systematic interviews.

Mayfield and Carlson (1966) found that each interviewer had a specific but different stereotype for each job to be filled. Raters varied greatly in the weight applied to certain information supplied by the prospective employees. Generally greater weight was given to negative information than positive. More recent research by Hollman (1972) found that negative information was evaluated properly but positive information was weighted too low.

Webster (1964) tape recorded interviews and was able to observe that the interviewer spoke about twice as much as the interviewees; that a "go, no-go" decision was made early in the interview and the rest of the interview was spent gathering data to support that decision; and that stereotypes were important in the interviewer's decisions.

THE INFORMATION GATHERING INTERVIEW

There has been considerable advice written about information gathering interview techniques. The following is a brief summary of the many authorities in the field.

Conducting the Interview

Interviews can fail because of the interviewer. Generally, it is preferred that the interviewer have high social intelligence, be well adjusted, non-authoritarian, and have somewhat similar social status to that of the interviewee (Hartman, 1968). Social intelligence is needed to interpret the non-verbal language evident in an interview situation. Things which might be expressed verbally in a more casual situation will not be spoken but will be signaled in a non-verbal fashion.

Perhaps the best example of this is the lie detector. Large numbers of people show a more rapid pulse rate, increased blood pressure, etc., when they tell lies. These physiological changes can be observed. The best poker players soon learn to recognize when someone is running a bluff. Helen Sobel, one of the best bridge players of all time, tells of when she was playing a crucial hand and had a choice of which opponent to finesse for a missing Queen. As she thought about the choice she inched up her skirt. One opponent studiously avoided looking at her leg while the other got an eyeful. She took the finesse through the one who avoided looking at her leg.

The authoritarian person is not as likely to stimulate a free flow of information from the interviewee. Apparent differences in social status can likewise inhibit the information flow. Good interviewing can be done by a substantial portion of those not having the above characteristics if they are well-trained, but it will be more difficult for them.

Comprehension Rates

The average person speaks at about 125 words per minute. The interviewer comprehends oral information at a rate of 500 words per minute and has a tendency to use the time lag to frame a rebuttal or let the mind wander. It is suggested that Kipling's Who, What, When, Where, Why and How questions are an appropriate way to use this difference between spoken and comprehension rates. The interviewer can silently question himself as follows:

Do I really understand what is being said?
How often does this occur?
What facts might be available to support this statement?
How complete is the information?
Did this happen recently, or is it history?
Are there any exceptions to the described procedure?
Is this important or is it a side issue?

There is nothing more important than to have the interviewer listen carefully so that the information is gathered accurately and completely.

Who to Interview

It is tempting for the systems analyst to interview only the supervisors of the project areas. Experience has proven this not to be adequate for the following reasons. First, participation is important at all levels of the user organization. Second, the supervisor rarely knows all aspects of every job. Employees change their job without consulting the supervisor, or informal arrangements are made between employees which modify the written procedures. Third, the supervisor is at least one step away from the detail and may communicate only those things that are perceived to be important in the supervisory job.

Participation considerations should lead the analyst to interview all of the employees even if many of them have identical jobs. In doing this the analyst quickly learns that so-called identical jobs are rarely identical. Minor differences will be found which can often break a new system. Consider, for example, timekeepers for different departments. If one timekeeper is missed, the analyst may learn later (to his sorrow) that this was the only timekeeper who was involved with incentives.

It is also necessary for the analyst to interview the responsible people above those immediately involved in the project. The primary questions to this level are related to whether there are any plans to change the organization which would affect the project, and whether the information coming from the system is adequate to support top management decisions.

The best interviewing practice is to interview all personnel involved in the system. One analyst reports that on one occasion he was told that a particular form went to a department "just for information." When he checked he found six people processing the form in a major duplication of effort. It is then important to interview everyone and to follow up on every detail. The analyst should take nothing for granted and should verify the information whenever possible.

Interview Preparation

First, the interviewer should develop an organization chart for the area to be interviewed. The relationship of each manager and employee should be determined. If the analyst is not familiar with the vocabulary of that department or organization, a glossary of terms should be developed. An understanding of the purpose of the area is needed.

It is preferable for the supervisor to introduce the analyst to the employees at a meeting in which the supervisor describes the task the systems group is to perform. As was stated in the previous chapter, the meeting with the analyst should have been preceded by a meeting of just the unit, at which time the organization plans should be freely discussed and the employees should be told that they will not suffer because of any organizational changes. The interviewer should then explain his job and schedule interviews at slack times if at all possible. The worst times for interviews are just before coffee breaks, lunch or the end of the day. Interviews should be scheduled several days in advance to allow employees to complete task lists, gather forms and reports, etc.

Start of the Interview

The interview should start with an introduction of all present. Names are important and should be clearly understood. Next, the general nature of the job should be covered and job details elicited.

Point of Intimacy in Interviewing

One of the most interesting prescriptions for interviews is that of Denis Mayer (1969) as described in the following comments.

Employee Relationships

Besides the effective use of time, what can the analyst do to assure himself that significant findings are not being overlooked? One answer lies in the analyst's relationship with the employees he interviews. Much has been written about the interviews; however, there is a certain critical relationship, a "point of intimacy," to be established between analyst and employee which can be the key to effective systems investigations. The "point of intimacy" is reached in the analyst-employee relationship when the analyst has gained rapport with the employee to the point that the employee is enthusiastic about revealing his problems (personal and otherwise) and the problems in the business system that affect his job. The employee should not be made to feel that he is confiding in the analyst but rather that he is a channel to improve the system without the threat of reprisal. Certainly the employee should never be quoted or put into an undesirable situation as a result of his communication. He should know that his statements will be kept confidential.

How is this intimacy established? By the analyst effectively communicating to the employee that he will assist him with his workflow problems. The analyst must demonstrate friendliness and sincerity. Friendly, non-business oriented conversation with the employee can be most helpful toward gaining the employee's confidence. In the first encounter the analyst must show genuine interest, rather than the role of an interrogator.

The danger of an analyst being too intimate in his relationship with the employee is, of course, a reality. Any disclosures made to the employee must be made with discretion. Gossip is taboo, for once the systems analyst loses the respect of the employee being interviewed he has endangered the staff's prestige and future working relationships with all employees.

Developing the Point of Intimacy

One of the more successful uses of this technique occurred when this author/analyst was involved in a routine examination of a small manufacturing operation. The bookkeeper for the business had been at that position for a long time and was obviously quite defensive and resentful of any "meddling" from outsiders. In order to gain her cooperation, on the analyst's second visit to the area he devoted over a half-hour getting her to talk about her family and her interests. Once she had realized that the analyst was interested in her as a person and what she had to say, she volunteered to show him an "analysis sheet" which he had no idea existed. On her analysis sheet, she would allocate labor and material costs according to the wishes of one of the plant supervisors, who was interested in making those jobs for which he was responsible look like the best managed. The bookkeeper would then change the original labor and material tickets to correspond to her work sheet. In this situation, there was no audit trail which would reveal the faulty charging procedures since original documentation was tied into the accounting records. The results of this investigation would have consisted of only minor procedural changes had not a "point of intimacy" been established with the bookkeeper.

Successful approaches toward developing the point of intimacy usually begin with the analyst making a comment to the interviewee designed to channel the conversation from the business topic to one of personal interest. Some introductory remarks might revolve around vacations, sports, families, etc. Even a comment on a mundane topic such as the weather will often help. Another approach is for the analyst to make a remark about one of his own activities, which might invite a comment. It is often more effective to remark on a subject which has been giving the analyst a problem, such as the lawn, automobile, illness, in-laws, golf game—any topic that would seem to be appropriate for the moment and to which the interviewee will be able to identify. Common ground will then be established between the analyst and employee.

The Purpose of Confidence

An example of a poor technique is that of a general auditor of a large manufacturing firm who when an employee begins to confide in him, informs the employee that it's his (the auditor's) responsibility to repeat to management anything he knows and that the employee shouldn't tell him anything he wouldn't want repeated to management. The general auditor's philosophy is that he is a representative of management in the role of fact-finder and reporter. His attitude of aloofness is correct for financial auditing but certainly not for a systems analyst or operational auditor. The auditor has missed the critical relationship that can be established with the employee— a "point of intimacy" where the employee has no hesitancy about revealing his feeling or ideas relative to his job without fear of job jeopardy.

The employee's comments are weighed and tested in relation to the entire system's operation and may or may not direct the analyst to a solution that might have been missed. The "point of intimacy" technique can also be helpful to the systems analyst when systems changes are about to be implemented. If he has developed rapport with employees much of the fear and natural resistance to change will be alleviated.

Conclusion

Not all analysts have the ability to develop a "point of intimacy." It is a talent that systems and audit managers should look for when recruiting analysts. To be effective in interviewing, the analyst must be competent, personable and sincere. He must have the ability and sensitivity to deal effectively with all types of personalities. Education does not produce these qualities, but exposure to the behavioral sciences in college curricula can give students possessing the required qualities an awareness of the dynamics of the human personality.

The systems analyst can be more effective in his job if he is able to develop a certain critical relationship with the interviewee. Development of this optimum relationship or "point of intimacy" will result in maximum cooperation from the employees being interviewed. All analysts do not innately have the ability to develop this relationship, but it is something for which to strive.

Rules for Conducting Interviews

Hartman, (1968) has an excellent section on rules for conducting interviews. The following rules were in part chosen from that source and personal experience.

Conversation should be kept to pertinent subjects as employees are quickly turned off by long discussions of irrelevant topics. Yes or no questions should be avoided because more information can be gathered by open ended questions and the sense of participation is greater. Do no criticize current practices. This is extremely difficult for the analyst to do since the analyst's concern is improvement through change. However, criticism, even non-verbal cues such as the raised eyebrow or a frown, will hinder communication with the interviewee.

It is usually not advisable to have a third person present during the interview, particularly the boss of the person being interviewed. The presence of the boss can inhibit the discussion and intimacy.

A few short interviews are better than one long one. Three, two-hour talks are better than one, six-hour interview.

It is also usually best if the analyst follows the main channel of the process being studied. This usually involves following the paper flow. There is a danger of missing some important element this way that could have been obtained by an in-depth interview with each person. Thus, it is important that during the investigation process enough time is taken to check that the information is complete.

The employee should be allowed time to think about each response; this will often result in recalling an important fact that might otherwise have been missed. The responder should have adequate opportunity to respond to questions. The answers should not be interrupted or cut short with comments or additional questions. One of the better examples of interviewers was Jack Webb of "Dragnet" fame. "All I want is the facts, ma'am" should be the attitude of the systems interviewer, with the emphasis upon facts rather than opinion. While opinion is of significance in understanding a situation, it is necessary that fact and opinion be clearly labeled.

Obviously distractions of all sorts should be avoided. The interview should be conducted at the work station because the forms and reports are all readily available there. However, if the job has frequent distractions such as a switchboard operator or receptionist, a quieter location would be advisable. The analyst should be aware of his own distracting mannerisms, such as playing with his glass case, fidgeting with his coins, etc. Sarcasm and humor are generally inappropriate.

The interviewer should respond to questions regarding the information gathering but should avoid stating any future systems improvements. The analyst should always remember that the job incumbent is the expert and the analyst a humble learner. On occasion there will be disagreement between the analyst and the respondent which can result in a useful exchange of ideas. If the disagreement develops into a clash of personalities, the interview should be terminated, rescheduled for another day with another analyst, who will complete the interview. If the analyst never forgets that (s)he is a guest, it will solve a lot of problems.

Note Taking

Recording information is an essential task for the analyst, yet excessive, extensive note taking during the interview is distracting. The solution is to take short, cryptic notes during the interview and then expand them to narrative form or flowcharts later in the day while the interview is still fresh. This is another reason for not scheduling interviews at the end of the work day. The final narrative or flowchart should be read by the interviewee to pick up errors and obvious omissions.

Closing of the Interview

Do not end the interview abruptly. As a final question, the analyst should ask who else should be interviewed, and what other documents should be examined.

In general, the analyst should not believe everything he hears. Experience has indicated a 70% reliability factor. To reduce the risks of designing a system from interview data, all basic or major facts should be double-checked against documents, other interviews, work measurement studies and other investigative tools. The frequency of infrequent events is often overestimated so particular care should be taken with this kind of data. The analyst should also examine any systems restrictions. If unneeded restrictions are carried over to the new system the result will be less than satisfying.

Follow Up

It is important that the information gained in the interview be validated. With accuracy rates as low as 50% on some types of responses, cross-checking is necessary. It is also highly appropriate to show the procedures, flowcharts, decision tables and other documentation to the interviewee for corrections and feedback.

LISTENING

To interview well, one must be a good listener. Nichols (1957) wrote one of the best descriptions of the skills needed in listening. The following presents some of his comments on listening.

1. Find areas of interest.

    Good listeners are interested in what is being said. Poor listeners are bored or find the subject dry. In the systems context, this suggests that the analysts have the expectation of learning something in interviews and meetings.

2. Judge content—not delivery.

    Inept delivery or expression does not imply that the speaker has no useful ideas. The good listener looks beneath the surface to find the useful information. Similarly, the analyst finds valuable ideas in the most unlikely places. These ideas for improvement usually exist within the organization, and finding them by listening is a major function of the systems analyst.

3. Hold your fire.

    The over-stimulated listener is in almost as bad shape as the under-stimulated. Nichols calls these "the twin evils of inefficient listening." By getting over-excited by one point, the listener misses subsequent points. The analyst is subject to similar stresses. A good idea needs consideration, a bad one needs refutation, but too much attention to either is distracting.

4. Listen for ideas.

    The analyst needs facts to design the system but he must

listen for both ideas and facts because in some cases ideas are more important and offer the keys to the new system.

5. Be flexible in note taking.

Note taking is not the same as outlining. Information gathering is usually unorganized with the notes reworked shortly after the interview.

6. Work at listening.

Poor listeners are lazy. Good listening is hard work. The analyst must believe the interview is important and schedule interviews for his best working hours.

7. Resist distractions.

Earlier we discussed distractions that reduce the attention of the interviewee. Research indicates that good listeners can concentrate enough to shut out distractions but interviews should be held in locations conducive to listening.

8. Exercise your mind.

Good listening habits come from experience and training. The systems analyst should become proficient in listening.

9. Keep your mind open.

Certain words trigger solutions to problems but the analyst should reject hasty, premature solutions. We commented earlier about recruitment interviewers and their tendency to reach decisions early in the interview. The tendency is a natural one, yet the systems analyst must not make decisions before all the facts are accumulated. The job requires a tolerance for ambiguity and an ability to withhold judgment.

10. Capitalize on thought speed.

Since most people speak slower than most listeners can understand, Nichols suggests one anticipate the speaker's words, and that non-verbal messages be observed.

COMMUNICATIONS

Communications is an important province of the systems analyst. Figure 7.1 shows the steps in communication where the sending instrument is the human voice and the receiver the human ear. All are familiar with the childhood game of whispering a message around a circle and comparing the last transmission with the first. That game shows there is considerable error in the communications process. These errors also thwart interviewing and listening. We shall examine two sources of error: language/meaning and noise; and one error reducing factor, redundancy.

Language/Meaning

An oral communication starts with a message in the mind of the sender. It is then translated by the sender into language. Some of the factors influencing the accuracy of the translation are the experiences, values, attitudes and beliefs of the sender; the richness of the language; and the synonyms (words with different sounds but the same meaning) and homonyms (words with the same sound but different meanings) of the words chosen. A language is said to be rich if the number of ideas expressible in that language is large.

These influences result in an oral message that may differ from the intended message. Similarly, on the other end, the message received may differ from the message that is understood. Differences again result from the experiences, values, attitudes and beliefs of the receiver. For example, the word *systems* has quite different meanings to the engineer and the reader of this text.

Communication Process

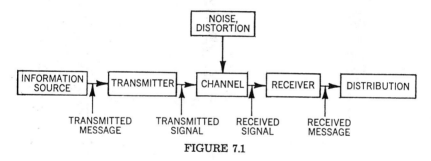

FIGURE 7.1

Noise

In interviewing and listening, noise is all distractions that reduce the fidelity of the transmission.

Redundancy

With language and noise decreasing transmission accuracy, redundancy is a tool to increase accuracy. The amount of redundancy varies in each message, but it tends to be large in most oral messages. Redundancy tends to decrease for messages between people with large amounts of shared experiences, such as members of a profession or a family. Teachers of technical writing suggest that one write not just to be understood but also not to be misunderstood. This implies redundancy.

SUMMARY

This chapter has shown the important role of interviewing in data gathering. Interviewing is a learned skill but not everyone is able to do it. Good experience with adequate coaching can assist considerably in learning. Beyond the rules and techniques mentioned for good interviewers is the prime ingredient of the ability to gain the confidence of the interviewee. The fundamental concepts of good listening can contribute as much valuable data as direct probing. Finally, the analyst is warned to keep his information gathering separate from his data analysis. Interpreting and analyzing data in the presence of the interviewee is a sure route to interview failure.

REVIEW QUESTIONS

1. What characteristics should a good interviewer possess?
2. What steps should be taken in preparation for an interview?
3. What types of body language should an interviewer avoid to prevent distraction during the interview?
4. List some characteristics of good listening techniques.
5. List the five steps of the basic communication process.
6. What is the point of opinion gathering in data collection?
7. Write five open-ended questions for an interview with an employee.
8. How may an analyst extract information through observation?
9. What are some formal records, available in most companies, from which an analyst may extract data?
10. How would you attempt to develop a point of intimacy during an interview?

DISCUSSION QUESTIONS

1. The ABC Company has a problem in the Order Entry Department. Management thinks it is due to an outmoded procedure and has asked you to investigate. Discuss the points to consider in conducting interviews to establish the facts.
2. Employee Jones does not want to discuss her activities with you as she fears her job will be eliminated. What action should be taken to accomplish a meaningful interview?
3. Why should a top management executive discuss the reasons for your assignment at a joint meeting of affected employees?

BIBLIOGRAPHY

Baskett, H. K., "Is Anyone Listening," *Ideas for Management*, 1973, pp. 18-24.

Berne, Eric, *Games People Play*, Grove Press, 1964.

Bingham, W. V. D., B. V. Moore & J. W. Gustad, *How to Interview*, New York: Harper, 1959.

Harris, Thomas A., *I'm OK, You're OK*, New York: Harper & Row, 1969.

Hartman, W., H. Matthes & A. Proeme, *Management Information Systems Handbook*, New York: McGraw-Hill Book Co., 1968.

Hollman, Thomas D., "Employment Interviewer Errors in Processing Positive and Negative Information," *Journal of Applied Psychology*, Vol. 56 No. 2, April 1972, pp. 130-134.

Mayer, Denis R., "The Point of Intimacy in Employee Interviewing," *Journal of Systems Management*, Vol. 20 No. 9, September 1969, pp. 40-41.

Mayfield, Eugene and Robert E. Carlson, "Selection Interview Decisions: First Results from a Long Term Research Project," *Personnel Psychology*, Vol. 19 No. 1, Spring 1966, pp. 41-53.

Nadler, Gerald, *Work Design: A Systems Approach*, Homewood, Illinois: Richard D. Irwin, Inc., 1970.

Nichols, Ralph G., "Listening Is a Ten-Part Skill," *Nation's Business*, 1957.

Rockart, John F., "Model Based Systems Analysis: A Methodology and Case Study," *Industrial Management Review*, Vol. 11 No. 2, Winter 1970, pp. 1-15.

Shearring, H. A., "First, Understand Yourself," *Journal of Systems Management*, Vol. 25, No. 7, July 1974, pp. 14-17.

Ulrich, Lynn and Don Trumbo, "The Selection Interview Since 1949," *Psychological Bulletin*, Vol. 63, 1965, pp. 100-116.

Webster, E. C., *Decision Making in the Employment Interview*, Montreal: McGill University, 1964.

CHAPTER 8

FLOWCHARTS AND DECISION TABLES

Two of the useful tools of systems analysis and design are flowcharts and decision tables. Couger (1973) describes flowcharts as a first generation system technique and decision tables as a second generation technique. While more sophisticated techniques are currently available for parts of the information system's life cycle, these earlier tools are still very useful. In systems investigation, both flowcharts and decision tables are used by the analyst to make certain that the operations of the current system are clearly understood. Their use in information systems analysis is to show possible alternative systems and to document the new system in the design phase. Decision tables have an additional use in the implementation phase enabling programmers to directly translate them into programs.

FLOWCHARTS

While computer specialists generally give Von Neumann credit for development of the flowchart, the technique was used by industrial engineers and systems and procedures analysts long before the computer was developed. Frederick W. Taylor and the Gilbreths are generally given credit for the early development of flowcharting techniques.

The industrial engineer called the charts "flow process charts." In the late 1940's John Von Neumann first used flowcharts to assist in programming. Since then the flowchart has been extensively used by the programmers.

Industry standard symbols have been developed by the American National Standards Institute (ANSI) and the International Standards Organization (ISO). The two sets are not alike. This chapter includes both the ANS symbols and written symbols developed by industrial engineers.

The ANS standard defines a flowchart as a graphical representation for the definition, analysis, or solution of a problem, in which symbols are used to represent operations, data, flow and equipment. It will be noted that delay and file, two of the more important symbols in flow process charts, do not easily fit this definition. The ■ symbol is also used to represent operations, data, flow and equipment in the flowchart problem description. The ▲ symbol can be used for delays in the flow process chart as well as the item shown in the ANS definition.

133

THE FLOW PROCESS CHART

The basic symbols used in flow process charts are shown in Figure 8.1. The actions symbolized are those typical of a machine shop. In fact, flowcharts are most useful in describing the process of converting a piece of metal into a finished part. They become somewhat

Basic Flowchart Symbols

A.S.M.E. (AMERICAN SOCIETY OF MECHANICAL ENGINEERS) SYMBOLS

ELEMENT OR PROCESS	SYMBOL	EXAMPLE OF THE ELEMENT OR PROCESS	THE END RESULT IS:
Operation	◯	Clerk sorts and numbers invoices.	A work step, accomplishment or production.
Transportation	⇨	Invoices delivered by messenger.	A movement.
Storage	▽	Files invoice by number.	Files—keeps.
Inspection	☐	Billing supervisor verifies the total amounts on all invoices.	A verification examination.
Delay	D	Clerk waiting for messenger to pick up invoice to be delivered to billing supervisor.	An interference— waiting, or desk-top file.
An activity outside the scope of investigation	△	Any process which the investigator considers impractical to analyze.	An outside influence.

FIGURE 8.1

awkward but are still useful when describing assembly operations. Figure 8.2 shows an example of a flow process chart.

In the past, flow process charts were used to show the flow of forms through the various paperwork operations. Today it is more normal to see the use of flowchart symbols. Certain special requirements of flowcharts used in describing the flow of forms have resulted in a special type of flow process chart called a forms process chart (Figure 8.3). This chart is better suited for showing the different flows of the various copies of a single form.

Flow Process Chart

	PAGE	OF

PRESENT METHOD ☐
PROPOSED METHOD ▣
MAN ☐ MATERIAL ☐

SUMMARY		PRESENT		PROPOSED		DIFFERENCE		
		NO.	TIME	NO.	TIME	NO.	TIME	PERCENT
O	OPERATIONS	5	6.5 hr	5	6.25 hr	O	.25 hr	
⇨	TRANS.	2	–	–	–	2	–	
☐	INSPECTIONS	1	.25	–	–	1	.25	
D	DELAYS	–	–	–	–	–	–	
▽	STORAGES	4	1.25	3	.75	1	.50	
DISTANCE		15 FT.		15 FT.		15 FT.		

TASK: DOCUMENTING AND AUDITING
ACCOUNTS PAYABLE #1

QUESTION EACH DETAIL

PROCESS BEGINS: DATE:
ANALYSIS — WHY? RECEIPT OF INVOICES

PROCESS ENDS: PREPARED BY:
PREPARATION OF CHECKS   R. R.

DETAILS OF METHOD			NOTES
1	D- SORTS, DOCUMENTS & NUMBERS ALL INVOICES	● ⇨ ☐ D ▽	–	.50
2	D- SORTS ALL M/R'S, FILES M/R'S AND INVOICES IN FOLDERS	● ⇨ ☐ D ▽		.25
3	D- FILES FOLDERS	O ⇨ ☐ D ▽	5	.25
4	C- AUDITS- VERIFY RECEIVING AGAINST BILLING & CHECK MATH ACCURACY	● ⇨ ☐ D ▽	5	3.00
5	C- WRITES DISTRIBUTION & SORTS BY DISCOUNT RATE	● ⇨ ☐ D ▽		.50
6	C- FILES BY DUE DATE - GIVES CONTRACTS TO SUPV.	O ⇨ ☐ D ▽	5	.25
7	B- RE- AUDITS PRIOR TO DISCOUNT DATE	● ⇨ ☐ D ▽		2.00
8	B- FILES BY CUSTOMER FOR CHECK PREPARATION	O ⇨ ☐ D ▽		.25
9		O ⇨ ☐ D ▽		
10		O ⇨ ☐ D ▽		
11		O ⇨ ☐ D ▽		
12		O ⇨ ☐ D ▽		
13		O ⇨ ☐ D ▽		
14		O ⇨ ☐ D ▽		
15		O ⇨ ☐ D ▽		
16		O ⇨ ☐ D ▽		
17		O ⇨ ☐ D ▽		
18		O ⇨ ☐ D ▽		
19		O ⇨ ☐ D ▽		
20		O ⇨ ☐ D ▽		
21	B= SR. AUDIT CLERK	O ⇨ ☐ D ▽		
22	C= AUDIT CLERK	O ⇨ ☐ D ▽		
23	D= CLERK	O ⇨ ☐ D ▽		
24		O ⇨ ☐ D ▽		

FIGURE 8.2

The flowcharts of an information system are often drawn at three different levels. First, a flow process chart is drawn to show the flow of information prior to and after the computing operation. The computing operation is usually charted as one operation. Next, the systems chart shows the relationships between the several computer operations in a system and indicates which pieces of hardware will

Forms Chart for Order Entry System

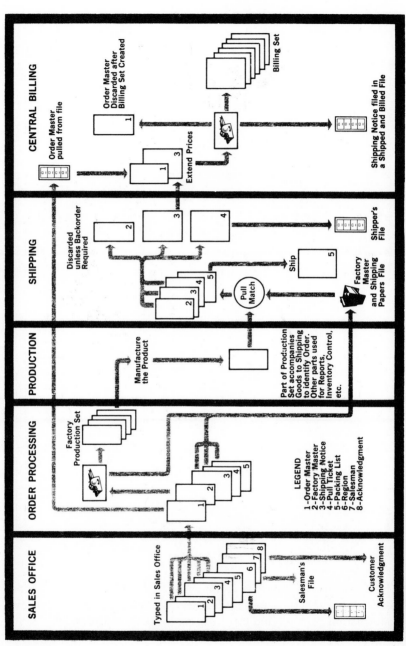

Courtesy Moore Business Forms

FIGURE 8.3

ANSI Standard Flowchart Symbols

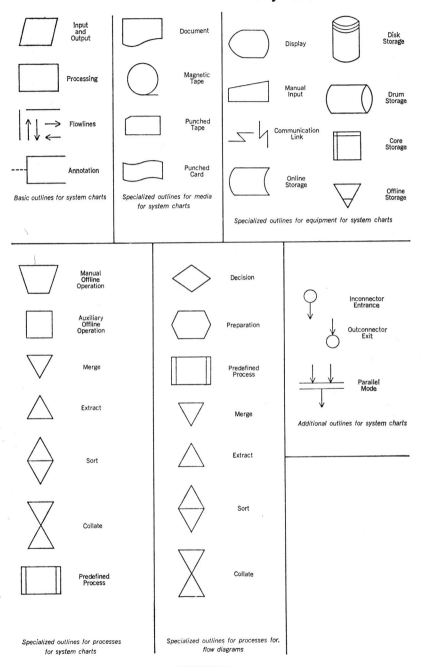

FIGURE 8.4

handle the input and produce the output. In a systems chart each computer run is expressed by a single process symbol. Finally, the flow diagram is a description of a computer program which may be drawn at several levels, from general to detailed.

Systems Chart

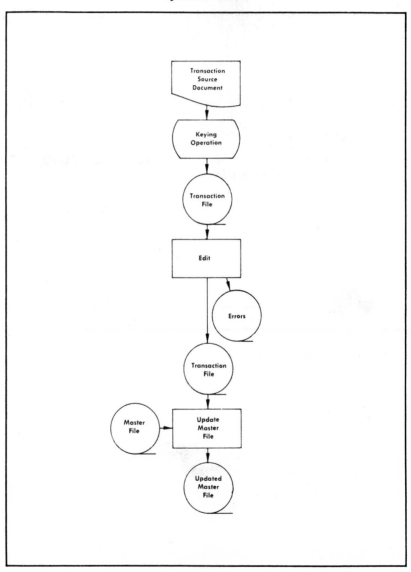

FIGURE 8.5

SYMBOLS AND THE SYSTEMS CHART

The ANS standard symbols are shown in Figure 8.4. It will be noted that the symbols are shown in two groups—basic and other. There is no flowchart which cannot be drawn with the basic symbols. However, the most sparing of symbol users usually adds the decision symbol to his own set. The connector is probably the next most frequently used symbol. These symbols, both basic and other, are used for both systems charts and flow diagrams. Figure 8.5 shows an example of a systems chart.

THE TEMPLATE

Flowcharts may be drawn freehand. For many purposes it is very adequate to take pencil or chalk and sketch the outline. Diagrams to be presented in reports or to be kept for system documentation usually require neater figures than most people can draw freehand. To speed the drawing process, templates, which are rectangles of plastic, are cut out in the desired shapes or symbols. The edges of the cut-out serve to guide the pen in the drawing of the symbol. It has been customary for computer vendors to provide free flowcharting templates to programmers in installations using their equipment. These templates have become de facto standards for flowcharting symbols.

THE FLOW DIAGRAM

The flow diagram (Figure 8.6) uses the ANS standard symbols to describe a program. Depending upon the size and complexity of the program, the flow diagram is constructed in two or more levels. The first or highest level details the modules of the program. If needed, a second level may break each module into sub-modules. The lowest level gives the detailed logic of the program.

First generation programming languages required more detailed coding; thus a detailed flow diagram was important. The use of procedural languages such as COBOL reduced the need for such detail. Now many information systems groups have standards that require only the construction of flow diagrams to the module level.

Flow diagrams are usually written by the programmer, while flow process charts and systems charts are the product of the systems analyst.

FLOWCHART SYMBOLS AND THEIR USE

The parallelogram symbol is used for an input or output operation

Flow Diagram

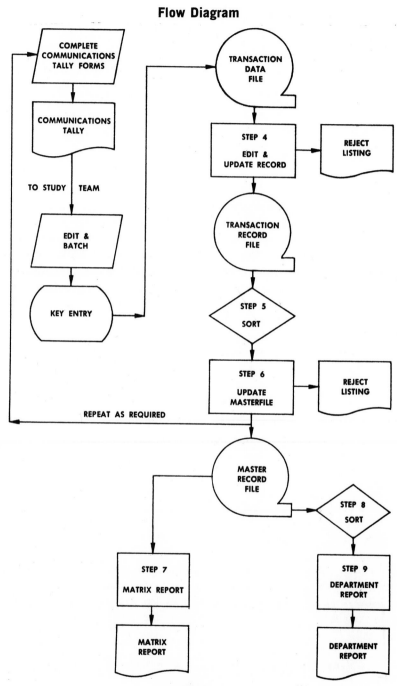

FIGURE 8.6

or input or output data. This symbol can be used for any input or output operation. However, the specialized symbols for document, magnetic tape, paper tape, punched cards and magnetic disk are often used to better define the particular type of input or output taking place.

The rectangular symbol is used for a processing operation. It is used when no other outline is appropriate. On systems charts it is often used to represent a program. On flow diagrams the process symbol is used for data movement, computation and data transformations.

The flowline must have an arrowhead to indicate direction. It is used on the systems chart to distinguish input from output and to indicate the processing flow. On the flow diagram it indicates the sequence of data manipulations.

The open rectangle symbol is used to provide comments and explanatory notes. This annotation symbol is probably the most underused of all the flowchart symbols. In good flowchart practice it is used for anything that might provide an explanation.

Typical comments which would be put into the open rectangle annotation symbol are:

> Program run annually after last payroll period.
> About 2% of transactions follow this branch.
> May be run in background mode.
> This sales tax routine applies only to residents of Maryland.
> Income tax deduction routine for percentage of federal states.
> Output tape put on rack 47 for storage.
> The age used in this routine is insurance age.

Media outline symbols are available for the various types of input and output and are used to replace the input-output symbol. Equipment outline symbols are similarly used.

There are many specialized outlines for processes. They serve to more completely define the particular process being used. As indicated in Figure 8.4 some of the special process outlines are used in systems charts and others in flow diagrams. The decision outline is a special process symbol that is used very often.

The connector outlines symbols are means of representing the convergence of several flowlines into one, or the divergence of one flowline into several and breaks in flowlines to be continued in another area. The latter use is generally discouraged for the same reason that "GO TO" instructions are discouraged in programming practice, as they add to the complexity of the procedure.

EXPERIENTIAL FLOWCHART
CONSTRUCTION RULES

1. Choose wording that will be understood by the user. The wording used in a flowchart to be published in a mathematics or computer science journal would use different wording than a flowchart for a manager or clerk. The programmer or systems analyst must always write for the user. The primary function of the flowchart is communication, and any flowchart which doesn't communicate is worthless.

The flowchart wording should be consistent with the glossary of terms developed for the system and, where possible, names should be the same as those used in the program. This is possible when programming with COBOL which has minimal restrictions on name length, but FORTRAN restricts the first character and the number of characters and may require abbreviations in the program.

2. Don't violate the standard outlines adopted. A shop may set its own standards which differ from ANS standards but should use them consistently. If the flowchart is to be published, it should meet the ANS standard.

Adherence to standards is important to the user. The combination of the words and the outline reinforce each other in the communication process. Behavioral research suggests that the number of standard outlines should not exceed twenty. Beyond twenty, there is some reduction in ability to remember the functions of the outlines.

When special outlines exist, they should be used. The general purpose outline should be used only when no special purpose one has been defined.

3. In drawing a flowchart, it is conventional to draw it from top to bottom and left to right. Entrance to each outline is on top or left, and exit is at the bottom or right. Only one entrance and one exit is preferred. Flowlines should enter and exit at the center of the outline. These conventions require the gathering of entrances above or to the left of the outline.

4. The number and size of the outlines are of some significance in the construction of flowcharts. The general rule is to retain enough space so that the flowchart is uncluttered.

5. There should be a minimum of crossing flowlines. Crossings tend to create some (even if minimal) ambiguity about the direction of the flow at the junction point. Chapin (1970) suggests that no crossings be allowed for flow diagrams and a minimum number be allowed for systems charts.

Generalizations taken from Ned Chapin.

6. Use the annotation outline extensively. This corresponds to the standard advice to use comments extensively in programming. A note will clue the reader into the thinking of the systems analyst at that point of the flowchart. The rule should be that the intended reader must be able to understand the flowchart readily and not spend effort deciphering the intentions of the writer. Weinberg's (1971) book on programming strongly recommends the reading of programs by the programmer's peers. Such a practice is also appropriate for the systems analyst and the programmer when they construct flowcharts. The flowchart should be critiqued by others, for few flowcharts are logically correct in the first draft. Checking, peer to peer, supervisor to subordinate, and subordinate to superior catches many flaws and helps create a group atmosphere of mutual assistance and trust.

7. While modular programming is in vogue with good reason, little has been written about modular flowcharting. Just as one module of a program should fit on one page of code, so also should one module be described on a one-page flowchart. The entry and exit of a module should show connectors and be cross-referenced.

8. In the flow diagram it is important that outlines related to program modification be kept separate from outlines related to data manipulation. Users find it difficult enough to keep the two separate even when the designer is meticulous in his separations. This may require that the level of detail be different for the two kinds of operations. Otherwise the level of detail should be consistent throughout a flowchart.

COMPUTER PRODUCED FLOWCHARTS

There are many software packages which produce flowcharts for a program. With rare exceptions, the software produces only flow diagrams—not systems charts. The available packages are of two types. The first requires a special input while the second uses source (or object) code. The latter appears to be the most common and is discussed in this section. Chapin (1971) provides an excellent discussion of the history, types and features of various flowcharters.

We previously suggested that drawing accurate flowcharts was a task comparable in difficulty to that of writing a program. When both flowchart and program are written, it should be no surprise to find that the two are not identical. Indeed, it would be surprising if program and flowchart showed the same logic on any large program. The maintenance programmer will often make modifications to both the flowchart and the program and then find the modifications do not work because the original programs didn't work in the way it was shown on the flowchart. This problem is solved by the flowcharter. While flowcharters have their own problems, they do accurately represent the program and ease the maintenance programmer's task.

There are three other significant reasons for using flowcharters. First, frequent changes in applications programs make it difficult to keep the flowcharts up to date. Use of the flowcharter whenever the program is changed assures that the flowchart is always current.

Second, programmers have been known to resist documentation of any type, including flowcharting. The flowcharter corrects this situation.

Third, flowcharting a program which has not yet been debugged will assist in the debugging. Some flowcharters include a cross-reference list of all the names in the program which can be of additional help.

DECISION TABLES

Decision tables, or decision logic tables as some prefer to call them, are a more recent addition to the bag of tools of the systems analyst. The principle antecedent of decision tables was the truth tables used by logicians. Their use in information systems was begun independently about 1957 by General Electric and the Sutherland Company. The Sutherland Company was able to solve a problem in 12 man-weeks using decision tables that it had struggled with for more than a year.

Sutherland used decision tables as aids to systems analysis, design and documentation. General Electric carried the work further by developing a program (TABSOL) that was capable of converting the decision table to a program. TABSOL processors were written for the IBM 305, 650 and 704 and the GE 225 by 1961. Slightly later a CODASYL group worked on a decision table processor called DETAB-X which was finished in 1962. Thus, since the early 1960's it has been possible to skip the programming step in the development of information systems.

Despite the success stories and the avoidance of programming, decision tables are not used by most systems analysts. The reasons for the lack of use include the following:

1. Decision tables are not often taught in basic courses in information systems or in programming. Flowcharts are used almost exclusively in teaching programming.
2. Third generation decision table processors were not available

until two or three years after third generation computers were available.

3. It apparently takes longer to learn the effective use of decision tables. Unlike flowcharts, it is necessary to have formal instruction to learn to use them skillfully.

4. Just as there are systems which are awkward to describe with flowcharts, so also are there systems awkward to describe using decision tables.

5. The resistance of the systems analyst to change. It may appear to be harsh to suggest the change agent may be unwilling to change, but no one is exempt from such tendencies.

6. Decision table processors are not a part of the normal software that is included in the price of a computer. Thus a deliberate decision to buy the processor is required.

Figure 8.7 shows the structure of decision tables. Figure 8.8 is a limited entry decision table and Figures 8.9 and 8.10 are extended entry decision tables. Combinations of limited and extended entry rows result in mixed tables.

DECISION TABLE STRUCTURE

A decision table is a table of all contingencies that are to be considered in the description of a problem, and the actions to be taken. The parts of a decision table are: table name, stub, condition stub, action stub, entry, condition entry, action entry, decision rule numbers and notes.

The top of a decision table has boxes for the name of the table and the numbers 1 to N for the N decision rules possible in the table. The body of the table is divided into four quadrants by double lines. Additional horizontal lines are drawn in both sections of the body. Additional vertical lines are drawn in the right half of the body of the table—one line for each rule. The individual boxes on the left are called stubs. The stubs above the double-rule are condition stubs. The stubs below are called action stubs. The boxes to the right are called rule entries. Those above the double-rule are condition entries and those below action entries. The note section at the bottom is used for any relevant comments similar to the annotation outline in a flowchart or a comment card in a program.

The structure shown is one of two major ways of drawing decision tables. The other major form is to have the rules on the left and the stub on the top. The latter form is the easier to handle with a decision table processor. However, Figure 8.7 is the more accepted way to communicate to users.

Symbols used in a limited entry decision table are:

Conditions	{	Y	Yes
		N	No
		–	Don't care
Actions	{	X	Do it
		– (or blank)	Don't do it

Decision Table Structure

TITLE	DECISION RULES					
	1	2	3	4	5	6
CONDITION STUB	CONDITION ENTRY					
ACTION STUB	ACTION ENTRY					
NOTES						

FIGURE 8.7

Limited Entry Decision Table

TABLE 14	DECISION TABLE					
CREDIT APPROVAL	1	2	3	4	5	6
ON APPROVED LIST	Y	N	N	N	N	N
PAST EXPERIENCE OK	–	Y	N	N	N	N
SPECIAL APPROVAL OBTAINED	–	–	Y	Y	N	N
APPROVED ORDER	X	X	X	X	–	–
RETURN ORDER TO SALESMAN	–	–	–	–	X	X
GO TO TABLE 15	X	X	X	X	–	–
END OF PROCEDURE	–	–	–	–	X	X

FIGURE 8.8

Extended Entry Decision Table with Else Rule

EMPLOYMENT	DECISION RULES		
	1	ELSE	
AGE	18-64	–	
PROGRAMMING EXPERIENCE	COBOL	–	
APPLICATION BLANK	GET ONE		
INTERVIEW	SCHEDULE		
DISPOSITION	?	REJECT	

FIGURE 8.9

Limited Entry Table with Else Rule

JOB DESCRIPTION	DECISION RULES		
	1	ELSE	
SALES EXPERIENCE	Y	–	
PRINT ON CANDIDATE LIST	X	–	
READ ON NEXT RECORD	–	X	

FIGURE 8.10

A decision rule is a statement that prescribes the set of conditions that must be satisfied so that a series of actions can be taken. With all of these definitions it now can be seen how decision tables are read.

Rule 4 of Figure 8.8 is read: *if not* on approved list *and* past experience is *not* OK *and* special approval is *not* obtained *then* return order to salesman and that ends the procedure. Rule 1 says that if the customer is on the approved list, then enter the order and proceed to Table 15 for further instructions.

One of the advantages of the limited entry decision table is that the number of possible decision rules is known. A total of 2^n decision rules are possible. A $(-)$ as a condition entry counts as two rules. Thus, the analyst can be certain that all possibilities have been considered. This fact is often considered to be one of the greatest advantages of decision tables. The omission of certain possible contingencies can be eliminated by checking the number of decision rules. No similar check is possible with flowcharts.

The increase in the number of decision rules as the conditions increase imposes a severe practical limit upon the number of conditions which it is reasonable to include in a table. Under normal conditions, four conditions (sixteen possible decision rules) should be the limit. When several conditions are not usually applicable, then the number of conditions can be increased somewhat. This point is a significant one. Many beginners in the use of decision tables try to build tables that are too big. The limit of human ability to perceive large tables is an additional reason to keep decision tables small.

DECISION TABLE PROCESSORS

There are presently many decision table processors being marketed. Specific processors available and the features included are too variable to be included here. Some general characteristics follow.

Some decision table processors take the source table as input and output the machine language of the particular computer, while others output the source language or another language such as COBOL or FORTRAN. Current processors take the latter approach, with COBOL the usual output. At least one FORTRAN producing processor is available.

The developers of the processors have a choice of languages in which to write. Most have chosen COBOL in the past but, as in other compiler construction, it may be more appropriate to use a language with string processing capabilities in the future.

Developers have a third choice to make. They may modify the compiler itself to incorporate decision table handling capabilities. They may arrange that the decision table be accepted as data to be interpreted during execution, or they may produce source level code for compilation in the language processor. Most developers have chosen the latter course. Thus, most decision table processors available at this writing are technically pre-processors to COBOL.

Before deciding to use a decision table pre-processor, the information systems manager should ask about the characteristics of the processor. How much compile time is used? Are the object programs compact? Are the object programs fast in execution? The developer of the processor can achieve any one of three objectives stated above at the expense of the others. There exist algorithms to optimize execution time and others to optimize core usage. The execution time algorithm requires that the frequency of the usage of a rule be included in the input. Other algorithms will not necessarily produce optimum run time or core usage but are simple to program and execute. As in all systems development tasks, the usage will dictate the particular variable to be optimized. The authors, in teaching decision tables, would prefer a processor that uses minimal compile time since the resulting program is most likely to be executed just once. The operations manager would choose running time or core usage to be optimized, depending upon which was the scarcer resource. The user would probably prefer the run time optimizer because most billing systems are more strongly a function of CPU time than of core used.

PROGRAMMING FROM DECISION TABLES

For those installations that do not have a decision table pre-processor, it is quite possible to program from decision tables. The task is similar to programming from flowcharts. Each decision rule can be quickly and easily expressed as a COBOL paragraph, however, such a program would often be inefficient. The programmer wishing to create better code would use some of the same optimization techniques built into the pre-processors. The process of converting the decision table into a program is called decomposition. Many manual and computer algorithms have been developed to do the decomposition but these are beyond the scope of this chapter.

The chart of pros and cons shows the choice to use decision tables is not entirely one sided. It is also evident that decision tables are not a systems cure-all; however, they are useful and deserve greater use than present analysts give them.

DECISION TABLE, FLOWCHART AND PROSE RESEARCH

Decision tables appeal to researchers with a strong mathematical or

DECISION TABLE PROS AND CONS

Some of the reasons for and against using decision tables follow:

Advantage	Disadvantage
1. Forces all conditions to be considered. Analyst must be thorough.	1. Learning somewhat harder than flowcharts. Necessity to train all new analysts in the technique.
2. Tables are easily updated. Area to change is evident and negative side effects usually spotted.	2. Not readily adaptable to all problems.
3. Can eliminate need for programming (coding).	3. Reluctance to change.
4. Tables easily debugged.	4. Not the best communication medium for users to understand.
5. Irrelevant tests are easily found and eliminated.	5. Cost of the decision table processor.
6. Complex problems are easily segmented in understandable parts.	
7. Efficient documentation.	

logical education. Construction of the tables is governed by a set of axioms, which can be used to prove the theorems necessary to validate some of the statements made earlier in this chapter. Those interested should read Pollack (1971).

Willoughby, together with Arnold (1972) and Johnston (1972), has done a modest amount of research involving the use of decision tables, flowcharts and prose as communication tools. The conclusions from that research are:

1. On small projects, trainee programmers trained to use flowcharts can program faster with flowcharts than with either decision tables or prose.
2. Trainee programmers on small problems, trained to use flowcharts, had equal programming errors using decision tables, flowcharts and prose.
3. Cognitive and interest factors did not correlate with ability to use decision tables, flowcharts or prose on small projects for trainee programmers trained using flowcharts.
4. Unsophisticated users can more quickly and more accurately understand small problems expressed in prose than in either flowcharts or decision tables.
5. Unsophisticated users can more quickly but *not* more accurately understand small problems expressed in flowcharts than in decision tables.

These research studies need replication to be certain that the results are accurate. However, it is our opinion that the value of the various methods is probably related more to the problem than the method and suggests that the systems analyst fit the method to the material. In communicating with users it is probably wise to describe the system in prose and use decision tables or flowcharts to further explain the process. The experts in procedure writing (Haga, 1968) suggest that a multi-media approach is often appropriate. For example, use decision tables to describe the branch points of a system, and flowcharts to show the sequential process.

❖ ❖ ❖

Magazine Decision Table Example

————————————————RULES————————————————

		1	2	3	4	5	6	7	8	9	10	11	12	13	14	15	16
Condictions	Promotional Subscription?	Y	Y	Y	Y	Y	Y	Y	Y	N	N	N	N	N	N	N	N
	For One Year?	Y	Y	Y	Y	N	N	N	N	Y	Y	Y	Y	N	N	N	N
	Payment Enclosed?	Y	Y	N	N	Y	Y	N	N	Y	Y	N	N	Y	Y	N	N
	For City Delivery?	Y	N	Y	N	Y	N	Y	N	Y	N	Y	N	Y	N	Y	N
Actions	Tag "Promotional"	X	X	X	X	X	X	X	X								
	Tag "Regular"									X	X	X	X	X	X	X	X
	Tag "One Year"	X	X	X	X					X	X	X	X				
	Tag "Two Years"					X	X	X	X					X	X	X	X
	Tag "Paid"	X	X			X	X			X	X			X	X		
	Tag "Bill"			X	X			X	X			X	X			X	X
	Tag "Bulk mail"	X		X		X		X		X		X		X		X	
	Tag "Single mail"		X		X		X		X		X		X		X		X

❖ ❖ ❖

SUMMARY

In this chapter we have described two of the most important aids to systems analysis, design and documentation. Flowcharts were shown in their several varieties as flow process charts, forms charts, systems charts and flow diagrams. The form of the flowchart varied to fit the usage. Communication was the key to usefulness. The primary purpose of the flowchart in all its varieties is to communicate systems ideas from one person to another. Similarly for decision tables. The suggestions for standardization (the use of only one form of documentation) is probably dysfunctional. The systems analyst should take an overview and use that tool that best communicates a particular systems idea. At times the analyst will draw flowcharts and later construct decision tables to describe different aspects of the same system. The analyst needs proficiency in the use of both flowcharts and decision tables. Only with proficiency in every important systems technique can the analyst choose the best to describe a particular system.

REVIEW QUESTIONS

FLOWCHARTS

1. How can one distinguish between a flow process chart and a systems chart?
2. What are the primary advantages to using standard flowcharting symbols?
3. What are the advantages of using flowcharters?
4. What situations would require the use of special outlines in flowcharts?

DECISION TABLES

1. Prepare, in skeleton form, a decision table showing all the table elements described in this chapter.
2. Assuming a limited-entry format, what is the maximum number of rules possible for a table with the following number of conditions: 3? 4? 5? 6?
3. Using the format for the most frequently used type of decision table, prepare a decision table which contains one or more examples of an irrelevant test.
4. Using your answer to Question 3 show the decision table after the irrelevant test has been eliminated.

PROBLEMS

Flowchart Problem

1. The employees of the Advanced Programming Software Corporation prepare weekly Attendance Cards. The cards are collected by Section Supervisors each Friday for validation and approval. Attendance Cards with errors are returned to the employees for correction. Corrected cards are re-submitted to the Section Supervisor. Once the Section Supervisor has approved the cards for all employees in his Section, the cards are forwarded to the company's Payroll Section. The cards are verified, control totals are prepared and the cards are forwarded to the Keypunch Section. The Attendance Card information is keypunched. The Attendance Cards are filed in a storeroom. The keypunched cards are forwarded to the Computer Room for processing. A computer program reads the cards which are matched against a Master Payroll file. The file contains personnel information such as the employee's salary, withholdings, etc. Cards not matched are re-

jected and returned to the Payroll Section along with a computer printed Error Reject Listing Report for correction. The program computes payroll information on the accepted input, prints payroll checks and a Payroll Register which are returned to the Payroll Section. Payroll checks are distributed to individual Section Supervisors for distribution to their respective Section employees.

Using the ANS symbols and flowcharting conventions described in this chapter, prepare: (1) a Flow Process Chart to describe the flow of forms; (2) a Systems Chart to describe the Payroll System; and (3) a Flow Diagram to describe the computer program logic.

Decision Table Problems

1. Application Software Corporation is expanding its operation and needs a new programmer. The new hire must meet the following minimum requirements: a college degree; two years experience working with COBOL; knowledge of FORTRAN; in good health; and willing to work at a salary of $10,000 a year.

    Using the above information prepare a decision table using the limited-entry format.

2. The Heavy Machinery Construction Company has an opening for a Data Processing Manager. The successful candidate will have the following minimum qualifications: six years of data processing experience; two years supervisory experience; a business or mathematical degree; and familiarity with production control systems. In addition, the candidate must have been interviewed and recommended by both the Personnel Manager and the Director of Management Information Systems.

    Using the above information, prepare a limited-entry, extended-entry and mixed-entry decision table.

3. Which of the three decision tables prepared in response to Question 2 is the best suited to computer applications? Why?

BIBLIOGRAPHY

ANSI, *Standard Flowchart Symbols and Their Use in Information Processing,* New York: American National Standards Institute, 20 p.

Chapin, Ned, "Introduction to Decision Tables, An," *DPMA Quarterly,* Vol. 3 No. 2, April 1967, pp. 2-22.

Chapin, Ned, "Flowcharting with the ANSI Standard: A Tutorial" *Computing Surveys,* Vol. 2 No. 2, June 1970, pp. 119-146.

Chapin, Ned, "Flowchart Packages and the ANSI Standard" *Datamation,* Vol. 18 No. 9, September 1972, pp. 48-53.

Chapin, Ned, *Flowcharts,* Philadelphia: Auerbach Publishers, 1971, 179 p.

Chapin, Ned, "Perspective on Flowcharting Packages," *Computers and Automation,* Vol. 20 No. 3, March 1971, pp. 16-19.

Chapin, Ned, "Running Time Analysis for Flowcharters," *Software Age,* February-March 1971, p. 13.

Couger, J. Daniel, "Evaluation of Business Systems Analysis Techniques," *Computing Surveys,* Vol. 5 No. 3, September 1973, pp. 167-198.

Dean, R. M., "Advantages of the Use of Decision Tables," *Computing Newsletter,* Vol. 6 No. 1, September 1972, p. 4.

Fleischauer, F. William, "Administrative Systems Design and Communication," *Journal of Systems Management,* Vol. 22 No. 8, August 1971, pp. 20-22.

Haga, Clifford I., Procedure Manuals in *Ideas for Management,* Cleveland: Association for Systems Management, 1968.

Martin, Johannes J., "Natural Set of Basic Control Structures, The," *SIGPLAN Notices,* Vol. 8 No. 12, December 1973, pp. 5-14.

Martin, Merle P., "Systems Analysis Strategy," *Journal of Systems Management,* Vol. 23 No. 5, May 1972, pp. 36-41.

McDaniel, Herman (ed.), *Applications of Decision Tables,* Philadelphia: Auerbach, 1970, 226 p.

Pollack, Solomon L. & Harry T. Hicks, Jr. & William J. Harrison, *Decision Tables: Theory and Practice,* New York: Wiley-Interscience, 1971, 179 p.

Weinberg, Gerald M., *Psychology of Computer Programming,* New York: Van Nostrand Reinhold Company, 1971.

Willoughby, T. C. and A. D. Arnold, "Communicating with Decision Tables, Flowcharts and Prose" *Data Base,* Vol. 4 No. 3, Fall 1972, pp. 13-16.

CHAPTER 9

INFORMATION SYSTEMS PROJECT ORGANIZATION AND PLANNING

Information systems projects that reach the organization and planning stage have been approved by the idea generator, the project systems analyst and the steering committee (or other project selection group). The next decision point is a review of the system proposal by the steering committee. Preceding the formal systems proposal is extensive project planning and systems investigation.

This chapter is devoted to project planning and describes the development of the master plan, the staffing of the project and tools (Gantt and PERT charts) which are used in project planning and implementation.

PROJECT PLANNING—THE MASTER PLAN

The portion of the project to be planned in detail at this stage is the systems investigation. The work to be covered by the plan is shown in Figure 9.1. All projects must have at least the components shown. Many projects break the steps shown into many smaller components. For example, an investigation that involved several departments would be likely to break the "review present system procedures" step into a separate step for each department. As a general rule no step in the plan should take longer than two man-weeks to complete.

The master plan consists of a list of tasks to be performed, an estimate of how long each task will take, an indication of the capabilities needed by the person performing the task, and a statement of any resources needed to complete the task. The resources could range from travel expense money to computer time to simulate a proposed system.

In an inventory control system, some of the elements likely to be in a master plan for the investigation and analysis of such a system are shown in Figure 9.2.

From the elements of the master plan the project leader summarizes the manpower needs by job. The manpower summary is the primary input into the staffing task, which is discussed in the next section. The elements of the master plan are also an input into the charting described later in the chapter.

INFORMATION SYSTEMS PROJECT STAFFING

The two major types of organization used in managing information

Systems Investigation Plan

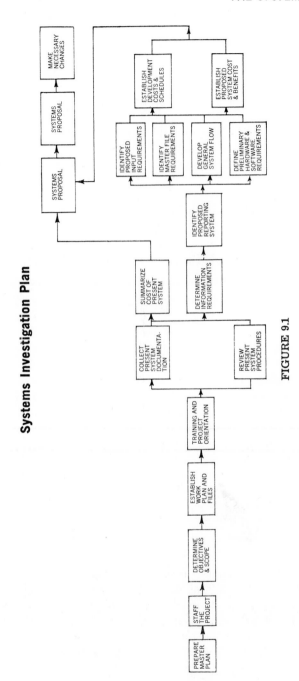

FIGURE 9.1

Project Planning Worksheet

Project Step	Performed By	Estimated Time in Hours	Expenses
Collect Present System Documentation			
Purchasing	Systems Analyst	40	
Accounting	"	20	
Receiving	"	16	
Shop Record Keeping—			
Dallas Plant	"	40	
Shop Record Keeping—			
Kansas City	"	40	Travel
Review Internal Audit Reports	Project Leader	12	
Manufacturing Vice President	"	4	
Controller	"	4	
Sales Vice President	"	4	
Shipping	Systems Analyst	40	
Identify Master File Requirements			
Product Structure	Systems Analyst	100	
Inventory Master	"	100	
Vendor	"	40	
Customer	"	8	
Prepare Systems Proposal			
	Project Leader	40	
	Systems Analyst	80	
	Typist	24	

FIGURE 9.2

systems projects are functional and project. In a functional organization all programmers report to a Programming Manager for their assignments. In the functional method of organization, work on the project is done sequentially by each functional group. Systems does the design, Programming does the programming, and Operations is responsible for the conversion.

The project organization method uses a team to plan, analyze, design, program, implement, convert and evaluate the entire project. The project team functions under a Project Manager. Few projects are organized totally under the functional or project methods, but under a combination of both.

An organization that chooses to try project organization will probably be 80% a team effort and 20% a functional method. The functions of standards, training and salary administration are often retained by a functional manager in any system organization.

The project or team organization structures are strong in control, job enlargement, morale and in knowledge for special applications. The functional organization structure yields higher technical proficiency, better personnel assignments and better training within each function.

A third, less frequently used type of project organization is called matrix organization and attempts to combine the advantages of functional and project organization. In matrix organization the project staff takes technical direction from its functional supervisors and task direction from the project leader. Matrix organization can result in high technical proficiency as well as strong control and job enlargement. However, matrix organization weakens the command structure of the organization. Multiple bosses can give conflicting assignments, causing employee confusion.

Projects are best organized and staffed to match the abilities and skills of the project personnel. In any project staffing, people are more important to the success of the project than is the organization.

Diversified Staffing. McKinsey (1968) suggests that the successful computer organizations employ a diversity of skills (mathematical, statistical, industrial engineering, computer science, systems and behavioral skills) within the organization. The original Operations Research concept, which has since turned to mathematical exercises, was to bring together people with a variety of skills to execute a systems project.

Coordination. One person can devote 100% of his time to a project, however, the addition of other personnel requires that some work time be used to coordinate the efforts of the project team and results in less work time available. Brooks (1971) stated that "adding people to a late project makes it later." The most efficient project groups are small and intact. If a project requires a large staff it should be divided into modules to minimize the time needed for coordination.

Programmer Analyst. One of the continuing debates among information systems professionals is the wisdom of combining systems analyst and programmer jobs. In combining these jobs the project gains in coordination and has fewer errors in communication but loses in the degree of analyst and programming skill applied to each task. While the two jobs have similar dimensions, there is considerable difference in their complexity and importance as well as the interests of each group. Users report that projects are more successful if the two jobs are combined (Powers, 1973). Normally, the careers are mutually exclusive in their progression to upper management positions.

Skills Needed. For this chapter's example we will assume a project involving the application of computers to a business function. The systems project example will be of the project organization type and require the following knowledge and skills:

> Project leadership
> Systems analysis and design
> Problem knowledge

> Programming
> Project records and libraries
> Audit and control
> Forms design
> Records management
> Mathematical or statistical modeling
> Behavioral science

Obviously, more people are needed with certain skills than others. Usually the project staff supplies the first five skills, with the others being supplied by consultants as needed. Forms designers and auditors are brought in only when required. A typical project might have a systems analyst as a project leader, a trainee analyst, a user representative and programmers. It would have consultants available to provide the other skills needed. Less typical, but also successful, is to have the project leader be the user representative. The project group works exclusively on the project.

Reporting hierarchy. The project group reports to the Information Systems Manager on the technical and planning aspects and the User Manager on project related matters. To be successful the project must satisfy the user, computer operations and the systems manager. The user is concerned with the usefulness of the system and its impact upon the costs and profits of his function. Computer operations wants a trouble-free system that is easily scheduled. The systems manager wants the job completed on time, within budget. Thus, in practice the project has several clients with potentially conflicting goals.

Selection of project personnel. A project can be staffed by selecting a group with the best balance of skills and personalities or by training. Selection assumes that certain personalities work better with others. Training assumes that the group can be trained to work together effectively. Those who select the project team personnel will be aware of these three behavioral principles:

1. High social intelligence improves performance.
2. High dominance variance improves performance.
3. Shared values improves performance.

Those choosing the training mode will plan some form of sensitivity training to modify the behavior of the work group.

The knowledge and skills needed are the dominant factors in the staffing for a project team. If the personnel lack any important skills, then training is necessary or a consultant used to fill that gap.

This discussion of the selection of project personnel did not consider the typical selection methods of testing and interviewing. These are not appropriate if the selection is being made from among existing systems personnel with known skills.

THE INFORMATION SYSTEMS PROJECT
AS AN OPEN SYSTEM

The systems project is an example of the open system concept described in Chapter 1. This section will consider five of the elements of open systems: input, output, throughput process, feedback and negative entropy. A partial list of the information systems project variables associated with each of the open systems elements follows.

A. Inputs

1. Individual attributes: Value system, attitudes, beliefs; Cognitive abilities; Work experience on the system being designed and in the total organization; Systems experience; Coordinating ability; Persuasive ability; Energy; Social intelligence; Dominance; Attitude toward computer and machines; Attitude toward other units involved; Attitude toward company and willingness to participate; Attitude toward company and willingness to produce; Programming experience of project personnel; Education; and Communication ability.

2. Organization variables: Reinforcers available within firm; Size; Technology; Industry; Frequency of change; Previous systems studies; Centralization; Level of project group; Audit of systems and proposals; Steering committee; Formal project selection process; Shared values; Profitability and financial strength; Span of control; Union situation; and Years of experience with computers.

3. Functional Supervisor variables: Values, attitudes, belief structure; Experience on job; Experience with projects; Level of power; Tendency to delegate; Way of applying reinforcers; Means of communicating with projects; Attitude toward other groups; and Attitude toward other technology.

4. Project variables: Number of decision points; Variables involved in decisions; Data elements; Volume of transactions; User originated; Measurable objectives; Size of project group; Length of project; Value of project; and State of art in project area.

5. Installed equipment and systems environment: Characteristics of equipment; Usage (free time available); Current time constraints; Turnabout time for programs; Languages used; Packages available; Modules available; Security; Privacy; Internal costs versus outside costs; and Reliability of operations.

6. New equipment and systems available: Characteristics; Costs; Time available; and Reliability.
7. User personnel: Satisfaction with current system; Experience with change; Attitudes toward computers and systems; Age, experience, education, cognitive abilities; and Level of job.
8. Project organization variables: Controls; Formal leader established; Power of leader; Social skills of leader; and Planning required.
9. Project dynamics and initial state: Trust; Support; Communication; Objectives; Conflict handling; Ability utilization; Shared values; and Dominance variability.

B. Outputs
1. Similar to project variables (A4).
2. Goal is a designed, installed system.

C. Feedback
1. Control mechanisms.
2. Reaction to various reports and designs.
3. Evaluation.

D. Throughput process
1. Similar to project dynamics variables (A9).
2. Information gathering.
3. Decision-making.
4. Using various systems tools.
5. Report writing.
6. Economic analysis.
7. Comparison with objectives.

E. Negative Entropy
1. Ability of group to work together.
2. Systems ability.
3. Goodwill.

This partial list of activities shows the complexity and many dimensions of an information systems project and that no two projects are alike. It also lends support to Langefors (1973) axiom that "all real systems are imperceivable."

PROJECT PLANNING TOOLS

The project group must decide how to achieve the goal of an installed system. In laying out the total plan of activities for the duration of the project, two charting methods, Gantt and PERT, are the most common for graphically displaying the project implementation stages.

Gantt Charts

Gantt charts, developed by Henry L. Gantt, are bar charts that allow management to visualize work to be scheduled and performed in relation to time. Their chief use had been primarily in job-lot manufacturing operations until applied to project planning. A typical list of activities to be completed in preparing a budget (Figure 9.3) is charted using the Gantt method with their time relationships in Figure 9.4.

Gantt charts are best for projects with a limited number of activities, as too many activities add so many lines (one line to each activity) that the charts become a confusing book. Gantt charts tend to identify only the major events and do not reveal the interdependencies between the activities. The charts are relatively inflexible and need extensive revision to meet changing requirements and tend to become outdated rapidly. They are also static representations and do not reflect the uncertainties associated with activities during the project.

The major impact of Gantt charts has been their ability to provide a method for graphically breaking a project into its component parts. Their use in business systems was a breakthrough to more effective charting methods.

Milestones

A newer method for project planning and control is the Milestone method. Milestones are key events or points in time during a project's development. For example, a project to develop a new chemical compound might be broken into these stages: research, development, testing and production. The events of interest would be the sequential completion of each of these milestones.

The major benefits of the Milestone method are that some interdependencies between the activities are revealed and the milestones are given specific completion dates. Progress is measured by comparing the status of the activities to a milestone or completion time, allowing management to keep track of the project.

The major disadvantages to the Milestone method are that time is the total criteria, and interdependencies of activities are not always apparent. Also, specific activities are not easily identified for cost allocations.

PERT

Project Evaluation and Review Technique (PERT) is perhaps the most used tool for scheduling projects. It was developed in 1958 by

Budgeting a Company Project

Job Identification	Alternate	Job Description	Department	Time To Perform Job
a	(1,2)	Forecasting Unit Sales	Sales	14 days
b	(2,4)	Pricing Sales	Sales	3 days
c	(2,3)	Preparing Production Schedules	Production	7 days
d	(3,4)	Costing the Production	Accounting	4 days
e	(4,5)	Preparing the Budget	Treasurer	10 days

FIGURE 9.3

A Gantt Chart of the Data in Figure 9.3

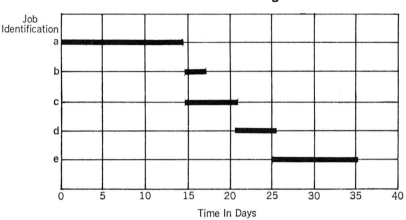

Total Project Length—35 Days

FIGURE 9.4

the U.S. Navy Special Projects Office, Bureau of Ordnance, in co-operation with Booz, Allen and Hamilton, a management consulting firm.

In developing the Polaris Weapons System the Navy needed a method to schedule and integrate thousands of industrial and scientific activities, a method for determining the project's progress, and to evaluate the effect of changes in the completion schedule. Out of these needs PERT was born. It aided the Navy in completing the Polaris Weapons System two years ahead of schedule.

PERT consists of a directed network of arcs and nodes. The arcs represent activities which must be completed during the course of a project. The nodes represent events in the network. The network (Figure 9.5) graphically answers the question, "Where are we?" To apply PERT, the project must be broken into basic sequenced tasks within a network. Looping an activity that leads into an activity preceding itself is not permitted.

Three completion times are estimated for each activity: the optimistic (A), the most likely (M), and the pessimistic (B). A and B are the upper and lower time limits for the project. The expected value of this distribution is given by $(A+4M+B)/6$, and the variance is given by $(A+B)^2/36$. Each activity in the network may be analyzed to determine early start and finish times; late start and finish times; total time; and free (slack) time. Using these times the longest path through the network, called the critical path, can be calculated. An expected duration and variance for the project may be determined by summing the estimated means and variances of the

PERT Type Network of Project in Figure 9.3

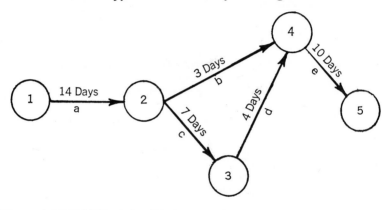

FIGURE 9.5

activities along the critical path. These calculations give the Project Manager guidelines for estimating the total project duration. The PERT network also shows activities that are critical to the project completion time and how delay will extend the project's completion.

Beyond these benefits, PERT forces the manager to divide the project into its elements, giving a logical understanding of the overall project and the interrelationships of the activities. It also tells which activities need close supervision and which ones do not. Second, it provides a network for scheduling large projects and estimating their completion. Third, it gives the Project Manager a timetable by which to judge the progress of the work. That is, by comparing the actual progress times to those given by a PERT schedule, the Manager can determine if the project is within limits.

CPM

Critical Path Method (CPM) was developed at E. I. Du Pont de Nemours by Morgan R. Walker and James E. Kelley as a method of planning, scheduling, rescheduling and progress reporting of the company's engineering department. Although PERT and CPM were developed separately and at the same time and follow the same network-based management system, CPM has certain differences.

CPM differs from PERT in that activities are given single time estimates. It is a deterministic model as compared to the probabilistic model of PERT. Going a step further, CPM assumes that all activities can be "crashed." That is, by adding more resources an activity's duration can be shortened, up to a limit.

The computational procedures in CPM are similar to those in PERT. Late and early start and finish times are computed along with slack times. A critical path is determined (Figure 9.6) and the project's activities are crashed, shortening the project's length to a specified time. The costs of crashing the various activities are recorded so that management may select the best time/cost trade-off schedule.

The benefits of using CPM are similar to those of PERT: a systemic view of the project, a project schedule and a time standard for performance. The CPM method will also give managers a choice between project schedules with their marginal costs.

Both CPM and PERT charts can be shown with the activities on the nodes giving an activity orientation stressing "What is to be done?" (Figure 9.7)

Scheduling Under Resource Constraints

PERT and CPM were developed to aid management in dealing with projects of known activities and events. The schedule and the critical path were determined solely from the integral time relationships without considering the resources that would be required to complete an activity or the competition for resources between concurrent activities.

Over the years many techniques have been developed that address themselves to this problem. These techniques may be classed into three general categories: (1) Time/Cost trade-off methods which are similar to CPM and determine alternate schedules giving the amount of resources required to meet each schedule; (2) Resource leveling methods to determine a PERT or CPM schedule using early start times and then proceeding to rearrange the activities with slack to achieve the most constant level of resource consumption; and (3) Scheduling to satisfy stated resource constraints to determine the

Critical Path Calculations for Budgeting a Company Project

Job Identi- fication	Alter- nate	Prede- cessors	Suc- cessors	Time	Early Start	Early Finish	Late Start	Late Finish	Free Slack	Total Slack
a	(1,2)	—	b,c	14	0	14	0	14	0	0*
b	(2,4)	a	e	3	14	17	22	25	8	8
c	(2,3)	a	d	7	14	21	14	21	0	0*
d	(3,4)	c	e	4	21	25	21	25	0	0*
e	(4,5)	b,d	—	10	25	35	25	35	0	0*

Critical Path— a, c, d, e
Project Length—35 Days

FIGURE 9.6

CPM Type Network of Project in Figure 9.3
Activity on Node Representation (AON)

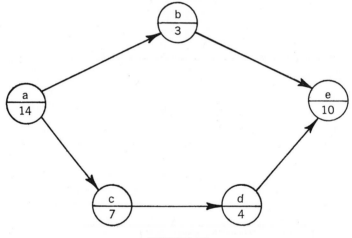

FIGURE 9.7

shortest project schedule under these constraints with a certain level of resources.

Within these three groups there is a wide variety of solution techniques from zero-one programming (a class of linear programming problems) to a quadratic programming and a computerized version of a physical model of rods and pistons. Computerized models are popular because they determine a list of activities that can be scheduled and sorted to a selected priority. This procedure then schedules activities from the list until the resources are exhausted.

The result of any of these techniques is a schedule for the start and finish times of individual activities and time estimates for the entire project length. The benefits are similar to those of PERT and CPM; however, in realistic situations the schedule will be better suited to the constraints with which the organization must work.

PERT/Cost

As seen from the previous procedures, the major emphasis in their development and use has been to reduce time and planning. Cost emphasis has dealt more with marginal costs of varying project lengths, rather than with actual operating costs, the construction of budgets or the control of a project. To compute operating costs, PERT/Cost was developed.

In 1962, the Department of Defense and the National Aeronautics and Space Administration jointly issued the DOD-NASA Guide, *A PERT/Cost Systems Design.* In mid-1963 certain military research and development projects required the use of PERT/Cost procedures and allowed their development as an expense in the contracts.

The basic differences between a PERT or CPM cost system and a traditional accounting system are stated by Weist and Levy (1969) as:

"Costs are to be measured and controlled primarily on a project basis, rather than according to the functional organization of a firm. That is to say, individual activities or groups of activities form the micro cost centers for accounting (and therefore management control) purposes, rather than organizational units (divisions, departments, sections and so forth). The rationale for the system is the entirely logical notion that responsibility for expenditures should coincide with the responsibility for managing that which gives rise to the expenditures. Under a PERT or CPM management system, project managers and sub-managers ordinarily are chosen for supervising individual activities or groups of activities. Since they are responsible for seeing that the activities are completed on schedule, it is argued, they should also be responsible for controllable costs associated with the activities."

The PERT/Cost system is based on activity accounting with activities grouped into workpackages. A workpackage is similar project activities under the responsibility of an organizational unit. By assigning account numbers to the workpackage traditional and PERT/Cost budgets can be constructed. PERT/Cost budgets are formulated by computing all of the workpackages in a particular project. The traditional budgets are formulated by grouping all of the workpackages contained in a particular organizational unit of the project.

Workpackages are the lowest level of a PERT/Cost budget. As stated in the DOD-NASA Guide: "The workpackages formed at the lowest level of breakdown constitute the basic units in the PERT/Cost system by which actual costs are (1) collected and (2) compared with estimates for purposes of cost control." Using this system, cash flows are shown as recorded expenditures of each workpackage throughout the project. The actual cost and performance data gathered helps management to answer:

1. Are the actual costs within the budgeted costs?
2. Are the workpackages on schedule?
3. What is the cost of the work to date?
4. Will there be any delay in the completion date?
5. Will there be any overrun or underrun in expenditures?
6. What workpackages are ahead of schedule?
7. What workpackages are behind schedule?

PERT and PERT/Cost have been used in a variety of different situations ranging from fairly deterministic projects to complex R&D projects where every activity is probabilistic, and from a simple planning tool to a complex on-line, real-time information system. Their effectiveness relies heavily on the accuracy of the data that is used, the manager's understanding of the inherent assumptions, and his ability to apply them to a particular situation and interpret the results.

Gantt and PERT Charting of Information Systems Projects

Project leaders use charts to visualize their plans, remind them of tasks to be done and to make certain that all activities are completed. The actual PERT or PERT/Cost chart serves as the project report and does not require other formal reports. Most project leaders recommend that no tasks take longer than two weeks to allow the project manager to have regular reporting intervals and keep abreast of any delays that may occur.

SUMMARY

The first step in project planning is preparation of the master plan itself. The elements of the plan were shown to be breakdowns of a general plan. Staffing takes the elements of the master plan and determines what people are needed to implement the plan. The choice of people and their organization were shown to be complex behavioral questions.

The charting techniques used in planning and controlling information systems projects were shown. The smallest project can make profitable use of Gantt charts. As projects become larger and more complex the more elaborate charting techniques such as PERT and PERT/Cost are appropriate. In practice, project leaders seem to use these charts more for planning than for control.

REVIEW QUESTIONS

1. How would an authoritarian, dogmatic industrial engineer who believes that employees must be prodded into work fit into a systems project?
2. Who does systems maintenance when project groups are dismantled?
3. List 15 more inputs to a project team.
4. Construct a Gantt chart for the data in Figure 9.2.
5. Construct a PERT chart for the data in Figure 9.2.
6. Why do systems practitioners suggest that project tasks take no longer than two weeks?

DISCUSSION QUESTIONS

1. Discuss how to prepare a project planning worksheet (Figure 9.2) for the remaining blocks in the inventory control system described in Figure 9.1.
2. Discuss the characteristics of projects that would require an operations researcher to be assigned full-time to the project.
3. Explain how, in the absence of PERT, it was possible to build the Empire State Building in one year and 45 days.

BIBLIOGRAPHY

Brookfield, Kenneth L., "Scale Charting," *Journal of Systems Management*, Vol. 23 No. 8, August 1972, pp. 14-17.

Brooks, Frederick P., Jr., "Why is the Software Late?", *Data Management*, Vol. 9 No. 8, August 1971, pp. 18-21.

Bruegman, Donald C., "Using Critical Path at a University," *Journal of Systems Management*, Vol. 24 No. 1, January 1973, pp. 22-25.

DOD—NASA Guide, *PERT/Cost Systems Design*, Office of Secretary of Defense and NASA, U.S. Government Printing Office, Washington, D. C. 1962.

Harris, William I., "Project Scheduling," *Data Management*, Vol. 9 No. 9, September 1971, pp. 40-43.

Hershauer, James C. & Gabriel Nabielsky, "Estimating Activity Times," *Journal of Systems Management*, Vol. 23 No. 9, September 1972, pp. 17-21.

Hollander, Gerhard L. & Elizabeth A. Tilley, "Optimize Your Project Management," *Computer Decisions*, Vol. 4 No. 11, November 1972, pp. 26-28.

Kaimann, Richard A. & Frank R. Probst, "PERT—Review Possibilities," *Journal of Systems Management*, Vol. 23 No. 6, June 1972, pp. 39-41.

Langefors, Borje, *Theoretical Analysis of Information Systems*, Philadelphia: Auerbach, 1973.

Metzger, Philip W., *Managing A Programming Project*, Englewood Cliffs, N.J.: Prentice-Hall, 1973.

Moder, Joseph J. & Cecil R. Phillips, *Project Management with CPM and PERT* (Second Edition), New York: Van Nostrand Reinhold, 1970.

Montgomery, Douglass C. & Daniel Sipper, "Probability Zones in Stochastic Project Networks," *Journal of Systems Management*, Vol. 23 No. 8, August 1972, pp. 36-42.

Nenzel, George J., "Critical Activities Network, The," *Journal of Systems Management*, Vol. 22 No. 8, August 1971, pp. 39-41.

New, Ronald, "Optical Planning Over Time," *Journal of Systems Management*, Vol. 23 No. 3, March 1972, pp. 32-34.

Powers, Richard F. & Gary W. Dickson "MIS Project Management: Myths, Opinions and Reality," *California Management Review*, Spring 1973.

Sauls, Eugene, "Use of GERT, The," *Journal of Systems Management*, Vol. 23 No. 8, August 1972, pp. 18-21.

Shaw, John C. & William Atkins, *Managing Computer Systems Projects*, New York: McGraw-Hill, 1970.

Sims, William Dale, "CPM or PERT—Tool for Motivating Data Processing Professionals," *Data Management*, Vol. 10 No. 2, February 1972, pp. 20-23.

Stern, Alan A., "Putting CPM to Work," *Journal of Systems Management*, Vol. 13 No. 6, November/December 1962.

Unblocking the Computer's Profit Potential, New York: McKinsey and Co., Inc. 1968.

Weist, J. D. and F. K. Levy, *Management Guide to PERT/CPM, A*, Englewood Cliffs, N.J.: Prentice-Hall, 1969.

Yeagle, Paul H., *Study of Time Estimation Relative to PERT, A*, Unpublished MBA Paper, Pennsylvania State University, 1971.

Yorks, Robert A., "Systems Management Relationship, The" *Data Management*, Vol. 8 No. 9, September 1970, pp. 25-26.

part ‖ |

Information
Analysis

The theme of Part III is information systems investigation and analysis. Here we show how the analyst starts with a plan and ends with a proposal. Several information gathering and analysis techniques are also described.

The systems investigation phase is particularly difficult to describe. This phase is more of an art than any of the other phases of systems analysis. The closest analogy would be that of the task of the reporter. While we can specify useful techniques, such as the interview, it is quite difficult to describe the process.

Other techniques include forms and reports surveys, work sampling, source data automation, work measurement, ideals, delphi and simulation techniques, flowcharts and discussion tables. In a particular investigation, one or many of these techniques may be used. The techniques used must fit the situation. The objective here is to lead the reader to the right tool.

Finally the information gathered is analyzed and a systems proposal is prepared. There is current work being done to automate the systems analysis and subsequent design. However, at this writing that work is not yet ready for practitioner use.

Chapter 15 includes a proposal together with a critique. The critique is rather general in its analysis. It would be a good exercise for the interested student to try to write a better proposal.

CHAPTER 10

INFORMATION SYSTEMS INVESTIGATION

INTRODUCTION TO FACT GATHERING

The scientific search for fact is through the investigative process. Investigation involves a review of what is already known, discovering unknown areas, and devising and carrying out an experiment to learn something about the unknown areas. Traditionally, systems fact gathering has explored the first step: determining what is known. However, just determining what is known is too limited for analysis purposes. Systems investigation should include model building, hypothesis generation and testing, experimentation, brainstorming and simulation. The techniques appropriate for information systems investigation go beyond the usual interview, observation, questionnaire measurement and document analysis.

The application of both the usual and the innovative techniques is to determine fact. For example, it may be a fact that a present order entry system handles all orders within two hours of receipt. However, the analyst may want to consider the consequences of hiring two more clerks. To evaluate the result of this action the analyst may want to perform the experiment in the real-world situation, or he may build a model of the system and manipulate it. In either case, added facts would be learned. Some will argue that this type of fact investigation borders on analysis. What is important is that the systems analyst have tools for ascertaining all facts.

The previous chapter focused upon the information systems plan. The first phase of the plan is an investigation to gather the data needed for the analysis and design phases of the project. This chapter explores the sources and classes of data, the plan for the investigation and the techniques that might be used in the investigation. Cataloging and validation complete the investigation process.

SOURCES OF FACTS

The sources of facts are many and vary greatly for each project. Some projects rely almost entirely upon internal data, while others involve great amounts of external facts. Some of the sources of information are:

Supervisors and executives in the user departments
Other user department personnel
Current system documentation
Company policies

Financial reports
Organization charts
Personnel department
Internal and external auditors and audit reports
Staff professionals (legal, tax, etc.)
Published system descriptions
Vendors
Friends in other organizations
Experimental data

User personnel are probably the most important source of facts for the operation of the current system. As a group, they know all the important and trivial data that one individual does not possess. The supervisor may not know all of the detailed procedures of his group. A worker may be misinformed as to the duties of another person, resulting in duplication of effort. Although important operations are well known, conflicting information about the system is frequent. The validation procedures described at the end of this chapter are an important part of the fact gathering investigation.

In practice, the analyst will find current systems documentation to be highly variable. Sometimes it is complete to the fine details but there will also be instances of no prior documentation. The documentation may exist in several forms. Places to search for systems documentation are:

Company policy, procedure and practice manuals
Department manuals (Sales, Personnel, etc.)
System descriptions written during the previous system's update
Program documentation files
Data management documentation
Letters of instruction from executives and staff
Union contracts

Financial reports of the system can be quite important. By examining the reports, the analyst learns about all of the significant areas of expense that are currently recognized. The reports also reveal the growth of costs and revenues and the variances from the budget. These facts often point toward the significant problems in the system. It is the examination of this data that often signals the need for the investigation in the first place.

Any other systems performance reports that exist should also be examined. Salesmen's call and personnel turnover reports are examples of useful reports.

The Personnel Department can be an important source of the following facts:

Job description

Job grades
Detail supporting requests for changes in grade and salary
classifications
Organization charts
Grievances
Turnover data
Satisfaction studies
Training needs, plans and recent activity
Observations of the personnel specialist serving the area

Auditors can provide information about the current system and about constraints on system modifications. If the current system has any financial implications it has probably been audited. Auditors' reports point out the error level of the current system and any weaknesses in the system. In the design of a new system, the analyst must know how much and what kind of audit trail is required by internal, external and governmental auditors. For example, the IRS has some very specific requirements for computer-based systems. These facts can have a significant influence on the design.

Other staff professionals, such as the Legal and Tax Departments, may influence systems design. For example, the systems designer may want to consider moving an order entry function from one state to another. One constraint in this decision is the method of allocation of corporate income among states for state income tax purposes. Some states use the proportion of in-state to total payroll and property. Others use sales entered as a part of the allocation scheme. Moving an order entry unit from the former to the latter increases taxes, while the reverse decreases them.

As this is written, the grocery packagers are installing a product coding system that identifies each product with a unique code. Although fine for the large retailers and large manufacturers, it creates intolerable cost burdens for the small manufacturer, if he is forced to comply. Litigation is expected to test if this is a violation of the Anti-Trust Statutes. There are current proposals for the licensing of data processing personnel, the control of data banks and taxation of software. Fact gathering on laws applicable to systems is likely to become more important in the future.

The library can be an excellent source of facts for the systems analyst. There are books that are compilations of systems. Some of these books are included in the bibliography for this chapter. The information processing periodicals frequently carry systems descriptions. These are best searched by referring to bibliographies.

One certainly should not ignore the available software packages. Even if the eventual decision is to develop the system internally, the design of the existing packages can provide important facts to the analyst.

Equipment and forms vendors often have prepared descriptions of similar systems to the one being designed. Some have data banks of applications implemented by customers which they will search. Excellent systems have been found in such searches. There are times to invent and other times to avoid re-inventing what has been done. The vendor search helps to decide which way to go.

One of the values of professional organizations such as the Association for Systems Management is the opportunity to find out what others are doing. Systems concepts are rarely considered to be proprietary at the general level. Details may be kept secret, particularly if the system is being or may be marketed. Generally, people are proud of their system inventions and are happy to describe them in considerable detail. It is our experience that the friend-to-friend communication is much more free than the formal request through the organization hierarchy.

CLASSES OF FACTS

The facts learned in the information systems investigation may be classified in several ways:

> System environment
> Degree of mechanization
> Reliability
> Organization

In any system studied the analyst defines the boundary between the system and the environment. The data related to equipment, transactions or processes of the system are called system data. All other facts relate to the environment. System data are generally used directly in the analysis and design phases, while environmental data are more likely to represent constraints.

Data may be available in manual, electro-mechanical or computer processable forms. Manual data is shown on forms and reports. Codes describing the data are kept in notebooks, procedure manuals, etc. Computer readable data is described in the system documentation and, in some cases, in the data management schema. Facts kept for each data element are described in detail in Chapter 17.

Facts should be classified by their reliability. It is well known that interview facts are less reliable than measured facts. Forecasts are less reliable than current information to the extent of the errors in the forecasting process. Weather and economic forecasts use extremely sophisticated models and have access to extensive data banks, yet their forecasts are far from perfect. The analyst assigns a probable range of values for any key facts. One system assigned customer numbers to all but the small miscellaneous sales which in total were less than one percent of sales. The coded customers were over 30,000 of the total 60,000 customers. (An automated system would need to code all customers.) This example is extreme, but it does illustrate the necessity of estimating the reliability of critical facts.

PLANNING FOR FACT GATHERING

Fact gathering is one of the areas of the project plan described in Chapter 9. The precise list of activities is a function of the particular system being studied. In a project involving the processing of expense reports some of the fact gathering tasks are shown in Figure 10.1.

FACT GATHERING TASKS FOR AN EXPENSE ACCOUNT PROJECT

1. Gather company policies re: expense reports.
2. Gather sample filled-in copies of reports and forms.
3. Discuss tax implications with Tax Department.
4. Discuss legal implications with Legal Department.
5. Discuss accounting implications with Chief Accountant.
6. Call friends in other firms to get copies of their forms, reports, procedures and policies.
7. Call forms vendors for sample forms.
8. Search systems library for information on expense account systems.
9. Select sample of organization personnel to interview.
10. Conduct interviews.
11. Develop questionnaire.
12. Distribute questionnaire.
13. Summarize results of questionnaire.
14. Flowchart flow of forms in organization.
15. Write decision table documenting approval procedures.
16. Conduct repeat interviews to fill in incomplete data and to verify correctness of flowcharts and decision tables.
17. Select organization departments for forms tracing.
18. Develop time stamp form.
19. Time stamp each step in selected departments.
20. Summarize timing of information flow.
21. Determine work measurement needs.
22. Collect work measurement data.
23. Summarize work measurement data.
24. Select sample of users of forms.
25. Interview users—both travelers and approvers.
26. Prepare user questionnaire.
27. Distribute user questionnaire.
28. Summarize user questionnaire.
29. Compare results of both questionnaires with existing corporate summary data.
30. Prepare project progress reports.
31. Prepare data for project reporting system.

FIGURE 10.1

A specific project would be very unlikely to have as complete a list of tasks as this. The list indicates the complexity of the systems investigation process. Project tasks in Fig. 10.1 are quite detailed but have good criteria for completeness. Most require less than 100 hours to complete.

FACT GATHERING TECHNIQUES

The following are some of the gathering techniques which the systems analyst might employ. Some are reviewed in this chapter and others are described in later chapters.

1. Interview (See Chapter 7)
2. Work Measurement (See Chapter 12)
3. Questionnaire
4. Observation
5. Report Survey (See Chapter 13)
6. Forms Survey (See Chapter 13)
7. Forms Tracing
8. Brainstorming
9. Delphi Technique
10. Directed Search (See Chapter 14)
11. Ideals Approach
12. Modeling and Simulation (See Chapter 14)

QUESTIONNAIRES

Many information systems involve large groups of people. The example of the expense account system is one such system. Also, many organizations are widely dispersed geographically (retail store chains) making the use of a mail questionnaire an economical fact gathering tool.

Examples of Questionnaire Use

A company considered consolidating the order processing and invoicing operations of its 17 warehouses. The warehouses were very similar in products handled and shipped. The general office had no volume information related to order processing. The systems analyst on the project devised a questionnaire to get the volume information needed.

In another firm the analyst used a questionnaire to learn the magnitude of communications expenditures at each plant and office location. This questionnaire asked for the amount of the bill for cables, telegrams, telephone switchboards, local telephone calls, long distance telephone calls, data communication equipment costs and other communications expenses for each of the three preceding months. It also asked that the toll tickets be sent into the general office with the questionnaire.

Questionnaire design is beyond the scope of this chapter; however, certain basic rules can be stated. Questionnaires should be used when small amounts of data are needed from large numbers of people or people to be surveyed are in widely scattered locations. Questionnaires can also be effective in collecting data quickly without expending a lot of the analyst's time.

Questionnaires should follow the rules in Chapter 19 for good forms design. Good questionnaires are good forms. Questionnaires are quite effective when the data requested is factual. They become less reliable when opinions are elicited. Opinion surveys are the province of the professional poll-takers. The word choices in the questions are extremely critical. For example, abortion polls get different responses to the words "fetus" and "baby."

Questionnaires should be short. The response rate to a two-page questionnaire is much lower than for one page. The number of categories of responses to each question should be from five to nine. The questions should be straight forward without complex structure and negatives. Even the best questionnaire designers find it difficult to formulate good questions. It is standard practice to try out the questions on a test group before printing questionnaires. Finally, it is good practice to address the questionnaires by personal name.

The questionnaire that follows was used by a congressional committee to learn the extent of the records kept about individuals by the Federal government.

Instructions for Subcommittee Questionnaire

General

This questionnaire is designed to obtain a systematic inventory of certain types of information currently maintained about identifiable individuals in the files of Federal agencies, together with related information on the source and legal status of the information with respect to confidentiality and compulsion in reporting. We are concerned only with those records in the physical possession of your agency. You need not answer for records which have been transferred over to the National Archives.

Please prepare a separate copy of this form for each bureau or comparable organization unit within your agency.

Use footnotes to explain any answers that do not fit into the categories outlined.

Replies should be forwarded to Mr. Benny L. Kass, Assistant Counsel of the Subcommittee, no later than October 1, 1966.

Detailed

Description of record(s) filed.—This column is to be as general as possible but with sufficient description to enable the subcommittee to analyze the rest of the form.

Column (a): Enter on a separate line the code number for each type of information held, as given in the attached appendix, entitled "Code for reporting types of information in Column (a)." However, where the data to be provided in columns (b) to (j) are the same, related items may be combined and shown on one line. (For example, the entry in column (a) might read "1, 3, 4, and 7".) Do not attempt to cover items of information other than those listed. Information on the agency's own employees as such will be obtained through the Civil Service Commission and should not be listed here.

Column (b): Indicate in a phrase the precise group of individuals covered. Examples: "all veterans"; "veterans applying for housing loan guarantee"; "individuals in current population survey sample"; "Selective Service registrants." If the coverage of distinct bodies of your records of a given type is differently defined, the covered groups may be listed on separate lines without regard to possible duplication.

Column (c): For each covered group of individuals defined in column (b) give the approximate number of individuals covered by your records *regardless of the age of the records* (going back only as far as 1900), and regardless of whether in current files or records centers. Estimates to the nearest 100,000 will be satisfactory (Use "*" to indicate less than 50,000).

Column (d): If individual records of the type listed are currently generated by a program of the agency, indicate the estimated annual rate at which new records are acquired (without regard to duplication with existing records, except that monthly or other periodic reports from the same individuals should be counted only once annually).

Column (e): Indicate in terms of the broad classes defined below the source of the information, using the following code. The first four categories refer to data obtained directly from the individuals covered.

Stat: Statistical reports or surveys.

Appl: Applications.

Tax: Tax returns.

Other: Other reports or procedures.

Co-op: Shared records of cooperating public or private agencies.

Column (f): Indicate, using the following code, whether the data were obtained from the individual on a compulsory or voluntary basis. Note that certain procedures, neither strictly voluntary nor strictly mandatory, are designated "Conditional."

Mand: Mandatory. Data obtained under express or implied compulsion.

Vol: Voluntary. Data obtained through voluntary cooperation of the respondent.

Cond: Conditional. Data required as a condition for an application, for participation in a program, for the award of a contract, etc.

Column (g): Indicate whether the data for individuals are subject to confidentiality restrictions, and the basis of confidentiality, as follows (with citation of any statute):

Statute: Confidential by specific statute.

Pledge: Confidential by reason of pledge to respondents (no specific statute).

None: No guarantee of confidentiality.

Column (h): If the data are subject to confidentiality restrictions, indicate the unit within which the data are held confidential. Explain briefly any procedures for exceptions to this rule.

Bureau: Not disclosed beyond collecting office of bureau.

Agency: Not disclosed beyond the department or agency.

Government: Not disclosed outside Government.

Other: Explain.

Column (i): Indicate the form on which the data referred to is stored. Use the following categories:

Eye: Eye readable.

Mach: Machine readable.

Either: Either.

Column (j): Indicate how the information referred to may be retrieved:

Mnly: Manually retrieved.

Cmpt: Computer retrieved.

Appendix.—Code for reporting types of information in column (a):

(Personal History)

1. Name.
2. Social security number.
3. Age.
4. Birthplace of parents.
5. Marital status.
6. Number of children.
7. Race.
8. Religious affiliation.
9. Citizenship and national origin.
10. Physical characteristics.
11. Addresses, current and past.
12. Military service.
13. Military serial number.
14. VA claim number.
15. Welfare status and history.

(Financial Information)

16. Income: total and/or by sources.
17. Assets.
18. Debts.
19. Expenditures.
20. Credit rating.
21. Checking and savings account.

(Housing)

22. Homeownership.
23. Public housing occupancy.
24. Mortgage delinquency history.
25. Condition of living quarters.

(Education)

26. Highest grade completed or degree(s) earned.
27. Grade average or class standing.
28. Knowledge of foreign languages.

(Employment and Occupation)

29. Occupation: current and/or past.
30. Employment status and history.
31. Occupational licenses and certifications held.
32. Employer.
33. Recommendations and references.

(Legal and Investigational Information)

34. Police record.
35. Security or other investigative reports.
36. Involvement in civil or criminal court action.

(Health)

37. Medical history.
38. Dental history.
39. Psychiatric history.
40. Personality inventory.
41. Alcoholism or drug addiction.

(Consumer Interest)

42. Food purchases and consumption.
43. Consumer preferences.

Senate Subcommittee on Administrative Practice and Procedure

Agency_____

Bureau_____

Inventory of information on individuals
in the records of Federal agencies

Descriptions of record(s) filed	(a) Type of information	(b) Type of individual covered	(c) Approximate number of individuals covered	(d) Annual rate of accession	(e) Source of data

Descriptions of record(s) filed	(f) Mandatory or voluntary	(g) Basis of confidentiality	(h) Limits of confidentiality	(i) Form of storage	(j) Access

OBSERVATION

An infrequently used means of factual data gathering is observation. Through this technique, a systems analyst views how documents are handled by participants in the system. He can also see how problems are handled under various conditions, detect bottlenecks in the system and recommend new systems to overcome the problems. The two types of observation are the observer being someone outside of the actual activities who does not participate in the operation and the participant observer who actually becomes involved in the work process. The first observer is most effective when objectivity is essential because he is detached from the situation. However, he may miss some of the essential factors of the situation which a participant observer will catch. The participant observer will provide the most thorough observation but is often restricted in use because of the emotions of the situation. The observer often becomes an intervening influence on the very processes being observed. Regardless of which means of observation is used, just the observation will cause the subjects to follow strictly all rules and procedures during the period rather than their deviations, making it difficult to uncover the true system.

A related problem is in the ability to view a series of activities and continually focus on the proper aspects without distortion or distraction. Concentration in observation requires special training and much practice.

FORMS TRACING

Forms tracing is a technique for determining the many steps taken in processing a form and locating any bottlenecks. Forms tracing is usually done by attaching a buck slip to each document and requiring that each recipient stamp the work station number and time received on the buck slip. The tracing information can be used to construct flowcharts and/or decision tables. The most important reason for forms tracing is that by logging time spent at each work station, workload and unnecessary delays can be learned. The facts obtained from this type of data gathering are particularly appropriate if the analyst intends to simulate the system. The data gathered make it possible to define quite accurately the service times, arrival rates and exception rates needed to program a simulation.

BRAINSTORMING

The concept of brainstorming was developed by an advertising agency as a method for improving staff creativity. Brainstorming calls for a heterogeneous group to hear a problem explained and then interact with each other for a limited period, offering any solution that comes to mind without evaluation. No negative comments are allowed to discourage the spontaneous flow of ideas in the brainstorming session.

Research studies indicate that group performance or brainstorming is not superior to individual idea generation. However, individuals have interruptions, procrastination and pre-occupations that hinder their creativity. Brainstorming is most effective when the problem being brainstormed is within the experience of the group.

Brainstorming is rarely used in information systems analysis. Once in our experience, when it was used to develop an alternative systems design, the effort failed. The failure may have resulted from the participants not having the required knowledge of the systems field. Fact gathering and planning are more appropriate areas for the application of brainstorming. In planning, brainstorming the project group would develop a list of all tasks to be performed, such as the list in Figure 10.1. Similarly, in fact gathering, brainstorming by the project group would produce results superior to a single person's plan or fact source.

DELPHI TECHNIQUE

Often data which are needed to evaluate or design alternative systems are not available. Future levels of activity, future technology and values of intangible benefits resulting from a system design are three such groups. The Delphi technique is a method for developing a consensus on the needed data.

In the Delphi technique a questionnaire is prepared for those best prepared to answer the questions, the responses summarized and fed back to the evaluator. The evaluator then gives his response in the light of the responses of others. An example of Delphi is shown in Figure 10.2.

The consensus obtained by use of the Delphi technique may be wrong. Its past use, however, indicates that the process yields better forecasts than trying to reach a consensus in an open meeting. Potential users of the Delphi techniques for information systems projects should read more detailed descriptions of these techniques, such as Helmer (1967) or Bright (1968).

A DELPHI TECHNIQUE

ROUND 1
Question 1: The company has fifteen payroll deductions at present. How many do you expect we will have in 1985?
Question 2: Some people predict that payroll checks will be replaced by an electronic funds transfer system. In what year would you expect this to happen?

ROUND 2
Question 1: The company has fifteen payroll deductions at present. How many do you expect we will have in 1985?
First Round Response:
First Quartile *17* Median *18* Third Quartile *20*
There appears to be a consensus on this question. Do you, by and large, agree with the consensus? If you disagree, briefly state your reasons.
Question 2: Some people predict that payroll checks will be replaced by an electronic funds transfer system. In what year would you expect this to happen?
First Round Response:
There was no consensus on this question. Please make another estimate. If your estimate falls below 1980 or after 1990, briefly state your reason.

ROUND 3
Question 2: Second Round Response:
First Quartile *1982* Median *1984* Third Quartile *1987*

FIGURE 10.2

DIRECTED SEARCH

Is a thorough study of a system necessary in order to redesign it? If it isn't, the savings in analyst-time is obvious. The risk is that an incomplete study will miss facts important to the design. More often than not the risks are unknown, so "complete" studies help to chart a clear course for systems success.

In conducting a directed search the analyst must know the essential aspects of the current system. The search begins as an attempt to learn the particular characteristics of the system being studied. This is like having a blueprint of a house without the dimensions. The analyst fills in the dimensions. If the blueprint contains all the rooms the final analysis will be complete. The same is true of a systems analysis. An example of a directed search by Rockart is detailed in Chapter 14.

Directed searches are often used when a successful system is being transported to another unit of the same organization. For example, one order entry system that had been operating successfully in one location required the following information to modify the design for use at another location:

Customer order pattern—Telephone, letter, his form, our form, computer entry

Products ordered

Response time needed

Plant shipping capabilities

Rail and truck facilities and schedules

Order statistics—Volume, size, variation by day of week, variation by month of year

Characteristics of market distribution—chain, co-op, independent, wholesaler

Abilities of current staff

Availability of staff needed in new system

Equipment maintenance facilities

Salary rates

Equipment prices

Responsiveness of local competition

Plant organization, physical arrangement (effected need for copies, information)

The major part of the information needed was environmental (not task) information. The search time was reduced to three weeks from six months for the original system. Post-installation review showed the system to be nearly as effective as in the first location, but the system was not as well accepted by the users because of their lack of involvement in the development.

IDEALS SYSTEM

One systems authority, Nadler (1967), suggests that the current system should be ignored when designing a new system. He stresses beginning with an ideal system, determining its cost and then trying to come as close to the ideal as possible. His point is that studying the old system makes it difficult for the analyst to conceive of revolutionary alternatives.

The typical purchasing-receiving-accounts payable system has separate purchase orders and receiving notices. The two documents can be compared when the material is received, and a check written. The objective of the system is to obtain the materials, confirm the delivery and pay for it. The Kaiser system, an alternative in which a blank check is sent with the order, accomplishes the objectives with reduced paper handling. Nadler's thesis is that knowing how a typical system operates would not have generated the Kaiser alternative.

The principal objective of a payroll system is to transfer the appropriate funds from employer to employee. Yet the system must also meet accounting and government regulations. It is doubtful that the ideals approach will identify *all* of the objectives in a payroll system. Systems improvements are too often evolutionary when they should be revolutionary. Developing a revolutionary system requires design creativity which IDEALS encourages.

A major advantage of the IDEALS approach is that the systems design team does not have detailed knowledge of the current system and must rely on user participation to build the new system. The higher level of participation should result in more acceptable systems for the user.

DATA VALIDATION

In the discussion on interview techniques it was pointed out that the facts gathered varied from 50% to 100% in reliability. This unfortunate fact of life applies to other information sources as well. It is not unusual when observing a system to see improvements that are needed which were not mentioned in any interviews.

Some readers may feel that our advice to examine, copy and improve upon a current system is to plagiarize from a successful system. True as this is, a second important piece of advice is *validate* every bit of data possible. Every systems analyst can cite horror stories about systems failures because of unvalidated data.

The principal method of validation available to the systems analyst is cross-checking. Is the information from Source A consistent with that from Source B and is Source D's information verified in the accounting records? The analyst should ask these kinds of questions related to each important piece of information. Generally, written information is more accurate than data collected in interviews, but all data should be verified. Exceptions in verification are

Criteria for Use of Fact-Gathering Techniques

Technique	Cost of Use	Data Accuracy	User Participation	Iteration Frequency	Frequency of Missing Data
Interview	High	Low to Moderate	High	Moderate	Moderate
Work Measurement					
Time Study, MTM	Very High	High	Moderate	Low	Low
Work Sampling	Moderate	Moderate to High	Low	Low	Moderate
Work Diary	Low	Moderate to High	Moderate	Moderate	Low to Moderate
Questionnaire	Low	Moderate	Low	Low	Moderate
Observation	High	Moderate	Moderate	Moderate	Moderate
Reports Survey	Low	Moderate	Low	Low	Moderate
Forms Survey	Low	Moderate	Low	Low	Moderate
Forms Tracing	Moderate	High	Moderate	Low	Low
Brainstorming	Low	Low	High	Low	High
Delphi Technique	High	Moderate	High	Low	Low
Directed Search	Low to Moderate	Low to Moderate	High	High	High
Ideals Approach	Low	Low	High	High	High
Modeling & Simulation	High	Moderate to High	Low	High	High

FIGURE 10.3

the published company policies, sales manuals and procedures. These standards are sources for checking data, e.g., expense reports against the expense report policy.

SUMMARY

The emphasis of this chapter has been on the gathering of facts for later use in analysis and design of systems. The major fact-finding techniques used by systems analysts were discussed. There are several criteria the analyst considers when choosing a technique, the most important being the cost of the search. Figure 10.3 shows how techniques vary greatly in cost. Interviewing and time study techniques are certainly very costly fact-gathering techniques when compared with questionnaires. Each fact-gathering technique has particular attributes, and the analyst must learn how and when to use each technique to best advantage.

REVIEW QUESTIONS

1. When is it appropriate for the systems analyst to go beyond the observable facts in data gathering?
2. List the ways a banker would be a source for systems fact gathering.
3. How would a questionnaire help gather facts in a student registration system?
4. Pick any cell in Figure 10.3 and justify the low, moderate or high value shown.

DISCUSSION QUESTIONS

1. Discuss some systems fact-gathering situations in which observation is the best technique.
2. Discuss how to plan an investigation phase for a student registration system.
3. Compile a list of periodicals of value to the systems analyst that are in a local library.
4. A university is considering the purchase of a computer. Future technology and future used computer prices are some of the considerations. Devise a Delphi questionnaire to provide facts for the computer center directors to analyze the situation. Suggest the types of people who might serve on the panel.

BIBLIOGRAPHY

Bower, James B., et al., *Financial Information Systems*, Boston, MA: Allyn and Bacon, Inc., 1969.

Bright, J. R. (Ed.), *Technological Forecasting for Industry and Government*, Englewood Cliffs, N.J.: Prentice Hall, Inc., 1968.

Business Systems, Cleveland, Ohio: Association for Systems Management, 1971.

Couger, J. Daniel (Ed.), "Books Useful in Teaching Business Applications of the Computer," *Computing Newsletter for Schools of Business*, Vol. 8, No. 5, January 1975.

Data Processing Yearbook, Detroit, Michigan: Gille Associates.

Government Dossier, New York, N.Y.: Arno Press, 1969.

Helmer, O., *Analysis of the Future: The Delphi Method*, Santa Monica, Cal.: Rand Corporation, March 1967.

Nadler, Gerald, *Work Systems Design: The Ideals Concept*, Homewood, Ill.: Richard A. Irwin, Inc., 1967.

Optner, Stanford L., *Systems Analysis for Business and Industrial Problem Solving*, Englewood Cliffs, N.J.: Prentice Hall, Inc. 1965.

Payne, Stanley L., *The Art of Asking Questions*, Princeton, N.J.: Princeton University Press, 1951.

Pescoe, Jerome K., *Handbook of Successful Data Processing Applications*, Englewood Cliffs, N.J.: Prentice-Hall, 1973.

CHAPTER 11

REPORTS, FORMS AND RECORDS: COLLECTION AND ANALYSIS

Kennedy (1973) stated that "reporting systems are not static. They are processes rather than products. There is no such thing as a perfect reporting system. If it were perfect today, then its very existence should be constantly educating its users to be ready for a better system tomorrow." Reporting systems designed in one time period are then usually inappropriate for another. Once-useful reports become obsolete. Needs develop without a reporting structure to satisfy them. This chapter discusses some important reports concepts and then deals with the details of the collection of records, forms and reports. The chapter concludes with a description of some of the problems of report design.

The planning process of an organization (Figure 11.1) shows features of special interest to the systems analyst to be measurement, standards, filters and significant exceptions.

MEASUREMENTS

It is accurate to say that a report can be no more reliable than the measurements upon which it is based. Reports of production counts for line management, as well as long-range forecasts for top management, are susceptible to measurement problems. The systems analyst is concerned with measurement cost-effectiveness, reliability, omission and scales. Examples are a device on an automatic screw machine that would send a signal to a computer as each screw was produced; the operator could read a counter at the end of each shift and using a data collection device, transmit the information to the computer; the operator could record the production quantity on a form. These are all ways to report production. In most organizations, the cost of the first and second methods is not commensurate with the benefits achievable from written reports. Reports should be prepared only when they contribute marginal revenue greater than their marginal cost. Report preparation should also be contingent upon a contribution greater than that return available from alternate uses of report preparation time.

Reliability can be a major problem in reports. In the Dairy Co-op case at the end of this chapter at least two measurement problems are evident: (1) the loss of milk in the process, and (2) the inventory counts. Bias of the instrument or person doing the measurement can be a problem. Project reporting often calls for frequent

Organization Planning Process

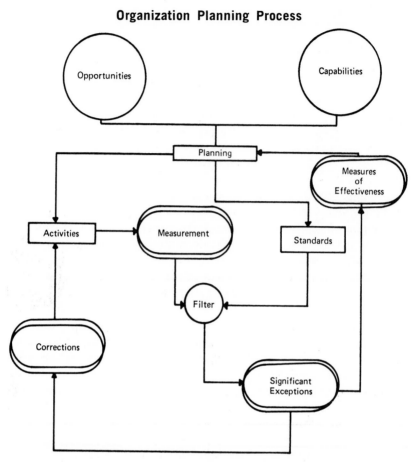

FIGURE 11.1

Source: Kennedy, 1973

reports of percent complete for each task in a project. It is common for the percent complete to reach 95% and then plateau at that level. Whether this is done deliberately to conceal lack of progress or is wishful thinking is not important. What is important is that the project leader's bias has influenced the report.

In order entry, for example, weekly totals of orders entered tend to have much less variation than daily entries. The daily totals are subject to the vagaries of the calendar, workweek and post office—factors that tend to balance out in the weekly report. Reliability and cost tend to increase or decrease together. Reliability can be increased at a cost or decreased with a cost saving. For example, productivity can be estimated roughly at low cost from work hours and total production figures. Accurate productivity calculations require standards for each task and accumulation of the production and hours worked for each task which costs considerably more.

Of the hundreds of variables that together describe a particular system, the manager chooses to control a small set that seems to be of most significance. This means that most variables are omitted. As the environment changes other variables become important but are not measured. These omissions are an important measurement issue. Also, some variables are quite difficult to measure with any accuracy, so these are often omitted. The value of the human assets and trademarks of an organization are two such variables. While perfect measures may be impossible to achieve for many (if not most) variables, it is possible to use a "quick and dirty" approach and get measures useful for decision-makers. For example, the current work force of an organization is at least worth the cost of hiring and training the replacement staff.

Finally, determining which aspect of a transaction to measure can be a problem. In a shipment of an item to a customer, there are many measures that could apply to this transaction: product identification, quantity, sales value, cost value, weight, freight cost, ship to location, ship from location, salesman involved, sales commission, product serial number, and customer end use. Some reports require certain information to be measured while others have different requirements. The systems analyst then needs to determine which characteristics to measure. One Personnel Manager once listed over 200 data items of interest for applicants. The system eventually designed used fewer than 40 of these items. Associated with what to measure is the measurement scale problem. For an applicant, is the complete birth date necessary, or just the year? Should costs be kept in dollars and cents or whole dollars? Two rules seem to generally apply:

1. The attribute measured and reported should relate to the activity involved.
2. The scale should be only as precise as the control warrants.

Standards

Data becomes information when it provides a signal that the standard situation has changed. To recognize that a change has happened one must have a norm or standard with which to compare. These standards take the form of budgets, cost standards, quality control limits, last year's comparisons, and productivity norms. The process of setting standards involves many behavioral issues beyond the scope of this chapter. The interested student will find Hofstede (1968) of considerable interest.

The setting of standards might be unimportant in small organizations where the standard is kept in the memory of the proprietor. In larger and more complex organizations, standards are distillations of prior experience and current expectations. They serve in a sense as the organization's memory and are an important element in the reports of an organization.

Filters

In comparing measured events to standards, differences or variances occur. Some of the variances are just noise in the system and should be ignored. Others are important and should result in action. The filter serves to select the significant variances from the insignificant.

Several variances are shown in Figure 11.2, but there is not enough data to determine which are significant. A guess would be that items 4 and 5 are significant from the size of the figures.

Budget Item	Variances
1	− 2,000
2	− 178
3	+ 432
4	+ 5,000
5	−40,000
6	+ 1,418

FIGURE 11.2

Adding a standard column such as in Figure 11.3 does give some help. Items 1, 2 and 5 appear to be problems. If one uses the range of the variances as a filter (Figure 11.4) items 1, 2 and 4 are considered significant. Some control items vary much more than others, so both percentages and dollar values are of dubious value alone as filters. Yet the −178 variance is probably too small to warrant much attention even if the variance is out of the normal range. Hence, both dollar value and range filters may be useful.

Budget Item	Standards	Variances
1	50,000	− 2,000
2	300	− 178
3	25,000	+ 432
4	300,000	+ 5,000
5	475,000	−40,000
6	58,000	+ 1,418

FIGURE 11.3

Budget Item	Standards	Variance	Last 12 Months Variance Range
1	50,000	− 2,000	− 1,800 to + 2,500
2	300	− 178	− 50 to + 50
3	25,000	+ 432	− 1,000 to + 1,500
4	300,000	+ 5,000	− 3,000 to + 2,000
5	475,000	−40,000	−70,000 to +50,000
6	58,000	+ 1,418	− 4,000 to + 7,000

FIGURE 11.4

Significant Exceptions

Use of a well selected set of measurements, reliably measured, compared with an appropriate standard and passed through a filter results in a set of exceptions. These are the items that belong in control reports.

The best control system has measures that account for most of the variations in the process, and shows standard costs and variances. Some reports put the figures into the appendix and make the body of the report a narrative in which the Cost Accountant describes the cause of each important variance. In this type of report the explanation is in more detail at the first level of the organization than at higher levels. This system has good measurements and standards and the Cost Accountant uses his knowledge of the system to filter out the important exceptions.

REPORTS AND FORMS COLLECTION

The systems analyst collects forms and reports in the systems investigation for several reasons. First, forms and reports are deliberately designed for particular purposes. The analyst must first learn the purposes of the form or report, and be satisfied that those purposes are considered in the analysis. Second, the distribution of copies tells the analyst who else to interview, some hints to the power structure of the organization, and the impact changes in this system will have on the environment. Third, the collection of forms and reports gives the analyst a good view of the size of the system being analyzed. This information is useful in project planning.

How Reports, Forms and Records Are Collected

The systems analyst collects reports in personal interviews with those involved in the system and by a questionnaire form. Reports involving few departments which are geographically close can usually be collected by the analyst at the time of the interview. Geographically dispersed systems or systems involving many departments usually require a questionnaire. In either event, the information collected is the same.

Use of the questionnaire technique requires the construction of questions, selection of recipients, mailing and analysis of the responses.

Analysis of Forms (Reports) Received and Prepared

Document Status	Form	Report
Incoming		
Preparer in Department		

Form (Report) Title 1		Form (Report) Number 2
Department 3	Analysis Prepared By 4	Phone 5

Frequency 6	Daily	Weekly	Monthly	Quarterly	Annually	Other
Due Date 7						

No. of Copies 8	Purpose 9

Distribution Indicate Copy No.
10

☐ _____   ☐ _____

☐ _____   ☐ _____

☐ _____ .   ☐ _____

☐ _____   ☐ _____

Method of Preparation 11
Manual ☐   Computer ☐   Machine ☐   Other ☐

Is Summary Data Available 12	13	Preparation Cost If Available

Forms (Reports) Received

Issued By 14	No. of Copies Received 15	No. Pages Per Copy 16
Major Use 17	Operations	Decisions	Information	Other	How Used

Is Its Purpose Accomplished? 18	Yes	No	If No, Explain

Value 19	On a Scale of One-Ten Indicate Its Value to Major Use									
	1	2	3	4	5	6	7	8	9	10

Can It Be Eliminated? 20	Yes	No	Is It Accurate?	Yes	No	If No, Explain

Is It Timely? 21	Yes	No	If No, Explain

Comments 22

FIGURE 11.5

The information requested in a survey of reports prepared and received is shown in Figure 11.5. *Major use* is intended to determine whether the report is used in the routine operations of the department, whether it provides information for decisions, or whether it serves primarily to keep the recipient up-to-date on organizational activities. *Purpose* is asked for to further specify the primary uses of the report.

Value is intended to elicit information about the importance and necessity of the report. Obviously, low value reports are possible candidates for elimination. The question of elimination should establish whether that particular report user finds the report to be of enough value to warrant its continuance.

Questions of *accuracy* and *timeliness* are asked to locate problems in the present report preparation routines. A *comments* area is provided to allow the respondent to explain any of his responses and to add any other information considered to be of value.

The covering letter of instructions with the questionnaire will usually ask for copies of all reports. Usual practice is to collect copies of reports from the accounting areas and from computer operations directly. Thus, copies are requested of all reports except those on a specified list. Note that comments about each report are still needed. A report from the computer may be just as good a candidate for elimination as any other report. It is important that filled-in copies of forms, records and reports be supplied. Actual usage of a document is often quite different than that indicated.

The *cost* of a report should include the cost of data collection, reproduction and distribution, as well as the direct report preparation costs. The cost quoted should be the marginal cost. That is, the cost should be the total amount of cost reduction to the organization, if the report were eliminated.

Forms Collections

The systems analyst needs a collection of forms used in the current system in order to design a new system. The forms can also be gathered as the analyst interviews the user staff or by survey questionnaire. The forms survey should gather the same material gathered for reports. Additionally, the information listed in Figure 11.6 is needed. The emphasis here is determining who does what, when and how. This is necessary because forms often flow through several people's hands before completion. Certainly, volume and cost are needed to determine the relative significance of each element of the paperwork process.

Errors are a fact of life in handling the data of an organization.

ADDITIONAL FORMS SURVEY INFORMATION

Volume
Cost
Information entered by originator
Error frequency and significance
Information added
Required signatures
Use of each datum

FIGURE 11.6

The data collected with forms is not immune from errors. In designing the system the analyst attempts to develop a system with adequate accuracy. To do this, it is necessary to know the error characteristics of the current system. In one system the handwritten entries of the Shipping Clerk were typed on the invoice by the billing typist. When errors occurred the typist said the Shipping Clerk's handwriting was illegible. The Shipping Clerk retorted that the typist was at fault. It was not important for the analyst to assess blame. It was important to know that the transcription step was an error-prone feature of the system.

Manual Record Surveys

The analyst also collects the manual records involved in the system being studied. (For description of computer files or records, see Chapter 16.) The information collected here is similar to that for reports and forms with the additions in Figure 11.7. As before, the

ADDITIONAL RECORDS INFORMATION
(NON-COMPUTER)

Volume of transactions
Volume of records
Method of accumulation
Equipment used
Sequence

FIGURE 11.7

information can be gathered by survey, but is much more often gathered as the analyst conducts interviews.

The volume of transactions posted and the number of records maintained are important again, because of the need of the analyst to determine the relative importance of the changes contemplated.

Method of accumulation refers to the way in which data in the records are accumulated for entry into the record and summarized for use in reports.

The sequence of the records indicates the normal posting or retrieval method. This is of considerable value to the analyst designing the new system. The analyst must know what data is available on the source record that can be used to select the appropriate record for update. Perhaps of more significance, the search parameter of requests for information from the new system must be known. For example, in a payroll system the analyst might find that virtually all requests relate to an individual. Thus, a simple system that allowed retrieval of an individual record would satisfy the need. If retrieval of the records of all people of a certain age, in a certain department, were frequent, the design would be different.

REPORT, FORM AND RECORD ANALYSIS

As in economics, one can speak of both macro and micro report analysis. At the macro level, the analyst focuses on the document as a part of a system. The details of a single document are equivalent to the micro level of analysis.

Macro Analysis: Upon collection of a group of documents, the analyst first organizes them by organizational unit. The documents, however, are more useful when grouped by subject. In this way, duplicates may be discarded. The responses on each document must then be tabulated. For small surveys, this can be done manually by paging through the departmental reports and recording the responses directly on the documents. For larger surveys, it is recommended that the computer be used to summarize the responses.

Given the documents, sorted by subject, and a summary of the responses, the next step is analysis. Analysis is still an art—not a science—and somewhat difficult to describe with any precision. Some of the things to look for are:

1. Reports that *all* respondents say could be eliminated, probably should be eliminated.

2. Reports that most respondents wish to eliminate should have responses of those wishing to keep the report carefully considered. Are the reasons for keeping the report strong and sound? What is the impact of decisions made by the respondent on this report? What is the respondent's political power in the organization? Is there another report containing the same information that the respondents who need that information do not get? After considering these and other points, the analyst will decide whether to recommend elimination. If this report is kept, certainly the copy distribution should be reduced.

3. Reports with substantial similarities should be combined or one eliminated.
4. Reports that do not contain the information necessary for the report to be used as indicated require revision by the analyst.
5. Accuracy problems indicated usually require a systems change or an indication on the report of the tolerances in the data.
6. Timeliness problems also may be solved by a design change; however, the change must be cost-effective.
7. Information reports are those reports considered as information by most respondents and should be evaluated for possible elimination as under item 2.
8. The cost of each report should be compared to the value and those with disproportionate costs examined carefully. One way of challenging reports is to ask for preparation costs on each report. The responses are a way of determining the cost benefit relationship.
9. Occasionally the analyst will see areas where reports are normally available in most organizations, but which do not exist in his company. An aged accounts receivable report might be an example. An aging report is usually important. If no report exists, then the analyst should call this to the attention of those responsible. Usually this proves to be an oversight on the part of the respondent.

Micro Analysis: Those reports surviving the macro analysis should be individually examined. Some of the factors considered in this analysis are:

1. Reports not designed to promote action, but to report accomplishment.
2. Design not effective in fostering "management by exception." Weak areas not spotlighted. Important facts not prominent.
3. Presentation does not enhance the use and effectiveness. Time is wasted on irrelevant and extraneous facts.
4. Creation and preparation is too expensive. Collection of feeder reports, creation costs, reproduction methods, volume and format should be considered.
5. Terminology used is confusing.
6. Data may be too highly refined.

NEW REPORTS

To this point we have considered reports as pre-existing in the organization. This is the way the analyst usually finds them. Organizations change and people request new reports. Figures 11.8, 11.9, and

REPORTS ANALYSIS RECORD-REQUIRED*

To be completed only by a reports requiring or requesting activity.

1. Title of Report				

2. Form No. or Format	3. Frequency	4. Due Date	5. Classify the Report as: ☐ Essential ☐ Informational

6. Offices or activities which are required to prepare report (identify by Title and Dept. No. where possible)

Total Activities Preparing Report: _____

7. What is your estimate of man-hours expended to receive, process, analyze this report one time? Payroll No. 1_____ Payroll No. 2_____ Payroll No. 3_____	8. Is this report a feeder to another which your office is preparing? ☐ YES ☐ NO If "yes" what is the title of the other report?
9. Is this requested report a ☐ TAB REPORT ☐ MANUAL REPORT If tab report, give tab no. _____	10A. What is the time span coverage per each report e.g., accounting month, calendar week, etc. 10B. Give inclusive period: From To

11. List or identify instructions or directives which your office has issued requiring submission of this report (if verbal, so state)

12. What is the purpose of this report, i.e., what action does it initiate or what supervisory control does it provide? List briefly the main elements of information it provides.

13. Signature (Name of supervisor having cognizance of report)	Dept. No.	Zone	Ext.	Date

* A "required" report is identified as one which a particular office requires or requests from another office or offices. The report is incoming to the office which requires it. One copy of this form will be completed for each kind of report which your office requires or requests from another office or offices.

FIGURE 11.8

REPORTS ANALYSIS RECORD–PREPARED*

To be completed only by a reports preparing activity.

1. Title of Report

2. Form No. or Format	3. Frequency	4. Due Date	5. Means of Reproduction

6. Offices or Activities to which Report is Forwarded	8. What is the average number of pages per each submission?

ORIGINAL:

9. Identify instructions or directives which direct preparation of this report (if verbal, so state and name requester)

COPIES:

10. Are any other feeder reports necessary for the preparation of this report?

☐ YES   ☐ NO

If "yes" give titles or tab tape numbers

If "no" how is the information obtained?

11. What is your estimate of the average number of man-hours expended in a one time preparation of this report?

Total Number of Copies Distributed: _____

7. Classification:

☐ Secret ☐ Confidential ☐ NAI Private
                              ☐ Unclassified

Payroll No. 1_____   Payroll No. 2_____

Payroll No. 3_____

12. Remarks or Recommendations

13. Signature (Name of supervisor having cognizance of report)	Dept. No.	Zone	Ext.	Date

* A "prepared" report is identified as one which a particular office prepares at the request of another office. The report is an outgoing report from the office which prepares it. One copy of this form will be completed for each kind of report which your office prepares at the request or requirement of another office.

FIGURE 11.9

REPORT EVALUATION

REPORT NO. _____ REPORT TITLE _____

	Check One	Indicated Action
1. Is Norair compensated for the cost of the report, by contract callout or agreement?	☐ YES ☐ NO	*RETAIN REPORT Check further
2. Is the report duplicated by a tabulated or manual report?	☐ YES ☐ NO	*CANCEL REPORT Check further

3. How is the report used?

	Check One	Indicated Action
a. In Operations?	☐ YES ☐ NO	*RETAIN REPORT Check further
b. To measure performance	☐ YES ☐ NO	Check further Check further
c. As source material for other reports	☐ YES ☐ NO	Check further Check further
d. As a basis for making decisions	☐ YES ☐ NO	*RETAIN REPORT Check further
e. For information only	☐ YES ☐ NO	*CANCEL REPORT Check further
4. Can the report be eliminated without adversely affecting productivity?	☐ YES ☐ NO	*CANCEL REPORT *RETAIN REPORT

Check One	RECOMMENDED FINAL ACTION	
☐	Cancel Report	*When any asterisk item is checked, final action has been decided.
☐	Retain Report	
☐	Further Study	_____
		Evaluator's Signature Date

FIGURE 11.10

11.10 are copies of forms used by one organization to evaluate new report proposals. Use of evaluative tools such as these should reduce the Parkinsonian tendency to add reports.

SUMMARY

By collecting current forms, reports and records the analyst learns how the current system is operating. While the current operation is unlikely to be ideal (because of the changes outside the system), the collection gives a starting point for analysis. Certainly, things currently being done should be explicitly eliminated rather than forgotten.

A good set of reports must apply the appropriate level of measurement to the right variables, be compared to a standard and use an appropriate filter to report the exceptions that need control attention.

The type of information needed about each document selected was listed. Perhaps the two most important questions to ask about each document are "Why?" and "At what cost?" Document gathering of this type does not locate areas in which controls or reports are missing. For this area, nothing completely replaces the interviews with the system users.

Report Analysis Case History

Dairy Co-op Inc. is a farmers' cooperative that was started in the early 1900's. When it was first organized it was a marketing cooperative that collected raw milk from the member dairy farmers and sold it to processors. All of the money was then pooled and divided among the members, according to how much milk they produced. As time progressed Dairy Co-op underwent a vertical expansion: they acquired processing, wholesaling and retailing facilities. They usually expanded by acquisition, building their own facilities only when suitable facilities could not be found.

Dairy Co-op is located mainly throughout New York State with some branches in Pennsylvania, Connecticut and Massachusetts. Total sales for 1970 were $335 million. The main offices are in New York City and Syracuse. A branch may consist of anywhere from a sales depot to a full production facility with a full office staff and a sales office.

The main goal stated at the organization's inception and underlying all development in the company was to "sell all of the milk that a member farmer produced and then to guarantee the best return to him." Due to the greatly fluctuating rate of production of milk throughout the year, Dairy Co-op reasoned that the best way to accomplish this goal was to move from a marketing organization to a marketing-production organization. In this position it would have better control of the distribution of the milk.

During the course of this growth and development the organizational structure that resulted is shown in Figure 11.11. The member farmers elect regional representatives to a Directors Council. This council serves in the same way as a board of directors. They meet periodically and are concerned with planning and future development. The President reports to the Directors Council and is responsible for the continuing operation of the organization. The organiza-

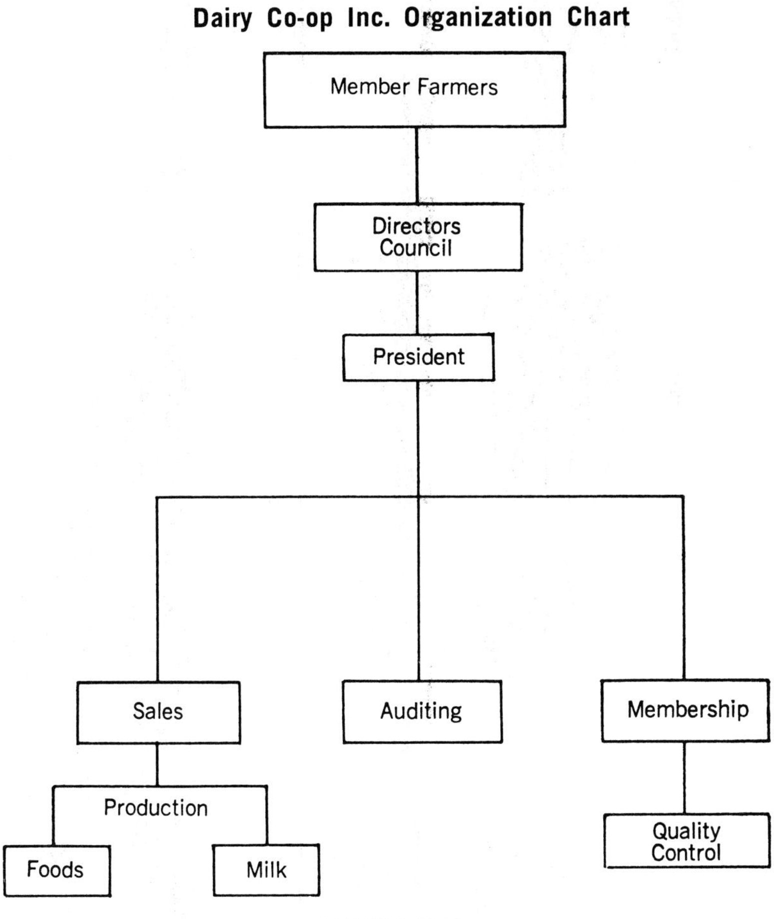

Dairy Co-op Inc. Organization Chart

```
                    ┌──────────────────┐
                    │  Member Farmers  │
                    └──────────────────┘
                    ┌──────────────────┐
                    │    Directors     │
                    │     Council      │
                    └──────────────────┘
                    ┌──────────────────┐
                    │    President     │
                    └──────────────────┘

   ┌──────────┐      ┌──────────┐      ┌──────────────┐
   │  Sales   │      │ Auditing │      │  Membership  │
   └──────────┘      └──────────┘      └──────────────┘
   ┌─────────────┐                         ┌──────────┐
   │ Production  │                         │ Quality  │
   └─────────────┘                         │ Control  │
 ┌────────┐   ┌────────┐                   └──────────┘
 │ Foods  │   │  Milk  │
 └────────┘   └────────┘
```

FIGURE 11.11

tion is then split into three sections. Membership is the division that deals directly with the farmer. They direct farm inspections, provide consulting-type aid and continuing education and organize social events for the members. They also direct the sale of raw milk to outside organizations. Auditing performs the usual internal auditing and control functions. Sales controls the flow of processed milk and also has control over production. Production is divided into two divisions. Milk Division processes raw milk into fluid milk that is sold in that form. Foods Division processes milk into such non-fluid products as cheese, ice cream, yogurt, butter and powdered milk. Each division has its own plants; however, there is some overlap in production.

Following the original goals, all revenues that are generated from the sales of the milk, minus expenses and money needed for capital budgeting, are pooled and apportioned to the member farmers. Complex Federal and State Milk Marketing Orders further complicate matters. To meet these State and Federal requirements detailed accounting procedures are required. They set limits on the prices that a farmer must receive for his milk by how it is used. For example, a farmer, by law, must receive more for his milk if it is used for fluid milk than if it is used in making butter. In each plant accurate records must be kept, showing for what products the milk was used. These requirements have necessitated the implementation of an elaborate accounting system to deal with the milk flow within the organization.

In the vertical expansion that Dairy Co-op has undergone, some problems have arisen. In acquiring milk processing plants, many of the facilities that have been purchased are old and because of new technology are inefficient. For example, when many of the plants were built, gravity feed was the best way to distribute milk throughout a plant. Therefore most plants were multi-story with the holding tanks located on the top floor. With the new more efficient pumps and automated controls, the most efficient plant layout is on one level. These inefficiencies cause many problems in the plant operation. A major dysfunction that is caused is that the accurate measuring of milk pumped to various points in the plant is impaired. This complicates the accounting system.

The Branch

One of the branches of Dairy Co-op is located in the city of Reading, Pa. There is a sales office, a membership office, production facilities (these are fluid milk processing facilities; however, a small portion of the milk is used for foods processing) and a full office staff at the branch. It serves as a retail and wholesale sales point and a distribution point for many sales depots throughout Eastern Pennsylvania. This branch has total sales of approximately $12 million a year. The office staff takes care of the billing and the regular accounting functions.

This particular branch had been built in the early 1900's and had been operated as a family business until 1956. At this time the two brothers who owned it sold out to a large national organization. It was sold twice again, before Dairy Co-op bought it in 1967. However, the internal operation of the plant remained fairly constant through all of these changes in ownership. The only change in the branch since 1956 was the addition of the membership office and its four employees.

The Branch Manager is responsible for all of the operations in the Reading area. The Plant Manager reports to the Branch Manager and is responsible for operating the plant and transferring the products to sales at the lowest possible cost. The Plant Clerk is to operate the milk accounting system that follows the flow of milk in the plant. Each of these men has been working at this branch for at least 25 years and in his particular job for 20 years.

The Production System

The plant employs 65 men and consists of three main areas: standardization-pasteurization, bottling and cooler. The men working in standardization-pasteurization start at 5 a.m. and process enough milk for that day. This station finishes for the day by 2 p.m. The bottling starts at 7 a.m. and finishes around 7 p.m. After the bottling is finished, the men on the second shift are responsible for cleanup. The cooler men start at 7 a.m. They are responsible for taking the cases of milk off the conveyor lines and putting them into inventory. They also load the 6 to 7 trailers that are shipped per day. They finish at 3:30 p.m. At this time, another person comes on the job and puts the product into inventory until the bottling is complete. A second crew starts at 11 p.m. and works loading retail and wholesale route trucks that leave early in the morning.

The Product Flow

A product flowchart is shown in Figure 11.12. The raw milk is received in large tanker trucks. It is then put into holding tanks. When it is needed it is then pumped into one of two tanks and standardized for the desired butterfat level, while the other tank is available for processing by the pasteurizer and the homogenizer. Also it can be pumped into a third tank where chocolate powder is

Dairy Co-op Production Process

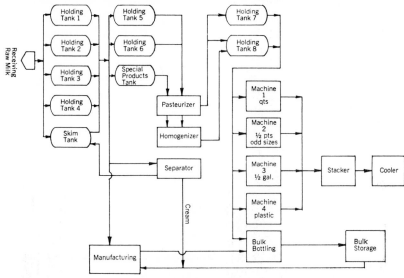

FIGURE 11.12

added and this is pasteurized at the end of the day. From the pasteurizer the milk is run into one of two tanks. From these two tanks the milk can be pumped to any or all of four bottling machines. Here it is bottled and cased. The cases of milk are then taken to the cooler via a conveyer chain, where they are stacked and put into inventory or on a waiting trailer. Milk is also sent to a manufacturing operation at the beginning of the day. Here it is made into food products such as ice cream mix, egg nog or coffee creamer. From here it is sent to a bulk bottling operation which puts the product into 20 or 40 quart cans. This operation also produces a limited amount of bulk fluid milk. Milk is also separated into cream and skim milk. The cream is stored in cans and used to make ice cream mix or sold. The skim milk is used to standardize raw milk and is stored in a separate tank until it is needed.

The Information Flow

The Plant Clerk is responsible for the daily collection of data for the milk accounting system. He produces a daily report (Figure 11.13) concerning the amount of milk bottled, in inventory, and lost. He gathers the data concerning processing, bottling, manufacturing, spoilage and loss from the men who work in the particular areas. They have the responsibility of calculating the necessary data and for the most part have the proper equipment and procedures for arriving at the correct figures. He compiles this data and enters it on a form, calculates the gain or loss and plots the flow of milk for that day.

As stated before this is an old plant and its design is far from optimal. The setup of tanks and pipes causes the measurement of the fluid flows to be inaccurate. For example, in the separating operation milk is pumped from one tank through the on-line separator. The skim milk goes into one tank and the cream into another. The measurement reveals a consistent 2% to 3% loss in butterfat. The equipment was checked and no trouble found. This loss has been attributed to an uncorrectable measurement error.

When asked what he thought about the system, the Plant Clerk said that most of the errors are small and that, except for separating, the errors tend to cancel each other out over a period of time. That is, if there is an error that causes a gain today, there tends to be an offsetting loss tomorrow. He also said that there is an expected loss for the daily production. He said, "If you pour a quart of milk into a container, you will not get a quart out of it. Some will stick to the sides and you will be short a few drops." He said that this loss is small (about 1% per day) and that "If I see something going on for a day or two that I think is strange, I'll check it out. I can usually tell what's wrong just by looking at the figures. I'll tell you a major source of the error; those counters on the bottling machines are not accurate, and there is nothing that I can do about them."

Dairy Co-op Milk Accounting Report

Raw Milk Processed		3200
To Bottling	2250	
To Manufacturing	475	
To Separating	500	3225
Gain or Loss		25
Bottling		2250
Bottled	2240	
Returns	4	2244
Gains or Loss		(6)
Separating		500
Skim	449	
Cream	48	497
Gain or Loss		(3)
Manufacturing		475
Bottled		472
Gain or Loss		(3)
Cooler Gain or Loss		(15)
Total Gain or Loss For Day		(2)

Units measured in cans (40 quart)

FIGURE 11.13

The Problem

The Auditing Department became concerned when the cooler gain and loss figures kept fluctuating. These figures are calculated by the Plant Clerk using a form given in Figure 11.14. These figures might

Product	Begin. Inv.	Sales	Spoil-age	Produc-tion	End Inv.	Units Gain	Bulk Gain
½ gal	3,600	3,400	–	3,500	3,750	50	200
gal plas.	200	175	–	200	220	(5)	(20)
½ gal plas.	1,200	1,150	–	1,200	1,340	90	180
qt.	3,800	3,400	–	3,500	3,950	50	50
⅓ qt.	1,500	1,250	–	1,500	1,780	30	10
pt.	600	500	–	600	690	(10)	(5)
½ pt.	50,000	40,000	100	40,000	50,040	(60)	(15)
					Gain or Loss (qts.)		400
					Gain or Loss (cans)		10

FIGURE 11.14

vary by 1% to 2%. This was not a great relative deviation, but it might represent one or two hundred units. The central office felt that this was too high. The figures were fluctuating from gain to loss. This tends to point to the fact that the problem was in the information system and not the production system.

When asked about this, the Plant Clerk replied "The production figures are probably wrong. Like I told you before, the counters on the machines are not accurate. Another thing is the inventory figure is probably a big cause of the error. When inventory is taken, there is still some production going on and a few sales being made that are counted in that day's sales but are not deducted from that day's inventory. Besides when you are counting that many items there are bound to be errors." When asked about the effect of these mistakes, he said that they usually balanced out in the inventory for the next day and that if they didn't he would "check them out. I can usually tell if it is a mistake in counting or a real loss, I keep my eye on it." When asked how large the error should be before he looked into it, he replied, "It depends; if we had an error of 100 units of gallons, I would look into it. That's 25 cases. If it were ½ pints, I wouldn't. That's only 2 cases and besides, the cooler gang probably drank half that much for lunch. It also depends on the number of cases that the figure is off. For example, if we were over or short 100 gallons, like I said before, that's 25 cases. They pile gallon cases 5 to the stack. That's 5 stacks. There are 5 stacks to a row in inventory. In this situation when they took inventory, they probably miscounted the number of rows in the pile, but I would keep my eye on it tomorrow."

A systems analyst from the central office came to the Reading branch and remained for two weeks. He came to see what could be done about the gain or loss in the cooler gain or loss category. After interviewing the managing personnel, he walked around the plant and the cooler for the rest of the week. He found that most of the procedures were correct considering the plant layout. He found that, despite the Plant Clerk's statement concerning the accuracy of the machine counters, the operators did turn in very accurate counts. They were very conscientious and their figures only varied by 10 units, even on lots of four or five thousand. The analyst made two recommendations concerning the inventory procedure at the end of the day. At that time the inventory was taken at 4 p.m. There was still bottling going on at this time and a few sales being made. There were only a few items to be bottled and they were counted last. The sales were supposed to be deducted from inventory but occasionally they were not. The man left working in the cooler would then add any additional bottling to these figures. Also inventory counts were recorded in units, while the inventory was being taken, on a standard sales order form. This form had about 120 items listed. The analyst recommended that the inventory be taken between 9 and 11 p.m. by a member of the night crew coming in early. The overtime cost of this would be offset by the reduction in the cost of having a day shift man stay late to do this. At this time the bottling would be complete and the sales stopped. He also suggested that there would be less chance of error if the man taking the inventory entered the number of cases on the order form, went to the office to use a calculator to determine the number of units and entered this amount on another copy of the order form, turning in both copies to the Plant Clerk. This would reduce another possible source of error and provide a possible check point for mistakes.

These procedures were implemented the following week. The analyst stayed and observed the results. The fluctuations were dampened somewhat but they were still present. He said that it was the best that could be done. "You could set up very elaborate control procedures but this would cost much more than the accuracy was worth. Some errors are still in the system, but they are small and their effect disappears over a period of time. What is the effect at the end of the month if you are short 10 units out of 5000 today and over 10 units tomorrow?" he said.

REVIEW QUESTIONS

1. Do you agree with the systems analyst's statement? Why or why not?
2. What formal controls are in the system now? Informal controls?
3. Are these controls effective?
4. Could the system be reorganized to give more effective controls at a reasonable cost?
5. What would be the value of the added accuracy of the information?
6. If there is a long run trend toward a gain or loss in the system, could this be detected using the present information system?
7. What is noise in relation to an information system?
8. Could all of this noise be accounted for in an information system design?
9. At what point should controls be set to discriminate between noise and information?

BIBLIOGRAPHY

Hofstede, G. H., *The Game of Budget Control*, London: Tavistock, 1968.

Kennedy, Miles, "Exception Reporting Systems," *Ideas For Management*, 1973, Cleveland, Ohio: Association for Systems Management, pp. 131-148.

Kenney, J. W., "Financial Reporting, RVFQ, and the Computer," *Data Management*, Vol. 10, No. 3, March 1972, pp. 17-20.

Martin, Merle P., "Making the Management Report Useful," *Journal of Systems Management*, Vol. 24, No. 5, May 1973, pp. 30-37.

CHAPTER 12

WORK SAMPLING, WORK MEASUREMENT AND WORK DIARY METHODS

"The primary objective of a work measurement program is staff reduction" (Caruth, 1971). The secondary goals most frequently mentioned are methods improvement and systems analysis. Staff reduction is of concern to the systems analyst because he heads up most work measurement projects. However, staff reduction is not the primary objective of the work measurement techniques used by the systems analyst in the majority of projects. For most projects work measurement is used as a method of gathering information about the existing system. To properly understand the present system and to devise alternative systems, the analyst needs to know what is now being done, how long the current tasks take, what might be done and how long those tasks might take.

Previous chapters listed several tools for gathering information about current tasks in a system. These data gathering techniques are good for developing what is being done but do not tell the analyst how long each task takes. The work measurement techniques described in this chapter tell how to measure work. Work measurement in this chapter will be viewed both as a control device and as a technique for gathering information for analysis.

PREDETERMINED TIME SYSTEMS AND STANDARD DATA

The most formalized approaches to work measurement are called "engineered standards." Formalized work measurement began early in the 20th century in a factory environment with the work of Frederick Taylor. Taylor originated what is known today as time-study: close observation of how long it takes to perform a given task, with an objective of finding a simpler, less time-consuming method of performing that task.

Taylor's work was followed by that of Maynard and Stegmarten, who developed Methods-Time Measurement (MTM) and Duncan & Quick, who developed Work-Factor. The former is now in the open domain; research and certification of practitioners is in the hands of the MTM Association. The latter is proprietary, owned by Science Management Corporation.

Both systems call for breaking tasks into small movements,

applying a measurement factor to each movement and totaling the time required. The total time required for the task becomes part of a "standard data" file. The technique is used today only where simple large volume tasks not involving decisions are involved. The systems analyst will rarely encounter such situations.

Both systems have versions with grosser measurements: MTM-2 and Abbreviated Work-Factor. They also have still grosser versions: MTM-3 and Ready Work-Factor. At this "3rd level" of engineered standards, they are joined by Modapts, a system originated in Australia. Modapts assumes that all human movements can be expressed in multiples of $1/7$ second. The measurement necessary to develop standards can, in all three systems, be displayed on a wallet-size card.

The method in which predetermined or standard time data are used in a measurement study, and the usual phases of such a study include:

1. *Orienting the supervisors* who will participate in the study. Supervisors will naturally be skeptical of time values not developed in their own operations. They must be convinced that time values are applicable and usable in their work operations or the essential cooperation will be missing. Most measurement studies using predetermined values rely heavily on the supervisors. They must participate in identifying work items, simplifying and improving the work, and must fully understand the method and type of measurement used. (It is very infrequent that the supervisors themselves perform the measurement.)

2. *Development of work distribution charts* showing the *estimated* distribution of employee time by major activity of the group being studied. Selection of those activities, which consume the largest portions of personnel time, usually point to the greatest potential savings. This estimated distribution of time is of considerable usefulness later in the study. The estimates will not be extremely accurate for individual activity requirements, but the balancing of the activities to the total time of the group provides for the comparison of improved times later in the project. The chart also aids in the selection of the activities to be studied and measured earliest in the study.

3. *Preparation of process charts* on the activities selected. The process charts should cover the normal flow process preparation, but must be supplemented with information as to frequency or occurrence of each step, method of performing it,

distance between steps, number of copies handled or prepared, size of documents or cards used, etc.

4. *Selection and assignment of time values* from the predetermined time tables to each of the basic steps of the flowcharts. A great deal of the accuracy of the final standards will depend on how carefully the comparisons of the work steps were verified to the table values, and calculation of variables and frequencies of occurrences.

5. *Development of a standard value.* The addition of the individual time values and the multiplication of the values by the frequencies are increased by an allowance for fatigue, personal time and unavoidable delays. The major reason for this step is to allow a final productivity measure that is emotionally acceptable to management and supervision. The standards so developed are usually converted into hours.

6. *Comparison of actual time* expended to the total "standard" time. Multiplying the standard value by the volume of work completed for the reporting period (usually monthly or weekly) results in the development of the *time earned. The ratio of effectiveness* is obtained by dividing the total time earned by the time actually expended for each activity. Figure 12.1 illustrates the development of the standard time for a simple process of work.

Advantages and Shortcomings

The use of standard data is particularly good for routine, repetitive work which is standardized as to methods. Much of the advantage stems from the fact that the standards have been developed for a normal situation and are generally accepted as sound.

They make it relatively easy to compare the efficiency of a current system with that of a proposed system not yet performed. For this reason, large organizations which see frequent systems or product changes (automobile plants, insurance companies, banks, etc.) are most likely to use predetermined times.

Use of predetermined times is probably the least disrupting to current operations of any technique of measurement. Maintenance cost is generally low and changes are easily made. Modifications to standards can usually be accomplished without interruption to work since segments of documented processes can be altered and recalculated to incorporate the changes.

Proponents of such systems claim a major advantage in that standards are set impartially. There is a high degree of acceptability to management. The original cost of using predetermined time stan-

Standard Time Calculation

OPERATIONAL TIMING SHEET			Date 4/7	Dept. Code 623	Chart No. 3	Page No. 2	of 2
DEPARTMENT (DIVISION-BUREAU-SECTION) Statistical				JOB NAME Process New Adult Cases			
Oper. No.	Work Cycle Detail MTV DESCRIPTION		Unit MTV	Frequency	Constant	Variable	
5	File Reach		13.0			13.0	
	Identify		16.0			16.0	
	Separator		37.0			37.0	
	Place		47.0			47.0	
	Insert		35.0			35.0	
6	File Tab Card A-20-S	*	188.0		188.0		
	O & C	*	55.0		55.0		
	Identify		16.0			16.0	
	Place		100.00			100.0	
	Insert		35.0			35.0	
7	Statistical list on clip board P/U board	*	96.0	3	288.0		
	Thumb—turn	*	19.5	3	58.5		
	Insert on bottom	*	54.0	3	162.0		
	Lay aside board	*	96.0	3	288.0		
					3398	1308.8	

$$\frac{(1.309)\,(1.15)}{60} = .025 \text{ hrs/occurency}$$

$$\frac{(3.398)\,(1.15)\,(20)}{60} = 1.53 \text{ hrs/month}$$

FIGURE 12.1

dards is high, for it is time consuming and should only be attempted by skilled technicians.

A major disadvantage of predetermined times is that they do not take into account environmental and other factors which may affect work performance. Temperature, lighting, interdepartment coordination and legibility of source documents will affect the performance of the work, but are difficult to incorporate into a standard developed from predetermined times. Often, practitioners of such systems are forced to incorporate arbitrary adjustment factors to make the standard consistent with that which has been attained historically. Such allowances are termed "pf&d" (personal, fatigue and delay) by the specialists.

HISTORICAL APPROACH TO
WORK MEASUREMENT

Undoubtedly, the simplest method of measuring work lies in the use of past performance records. Historical work measurement simply is the calculated correlation of data, using the records of cases (or work completed) and the time spent on its performance for as reliable a period of time in the past as is available. For example, in a payroll office, the personnel time devoted to payroll work and the number of employees on the payroll of the company might be pieced together from past records to indicate the following:

Year	Payroll Personnel	Total Employees
1975	8	1,610
1974	7	1,450
1973	6	1,108
1972	5	915

Based on this data, a requirement of one payroll clerk for each 200 employees might be assumed. Unless other requirements were introduced to influence the nature of the work, the supervisor would continue to ask for additional employees on this basis.

A simple approach to historical work measurement is shown in Figure 12.2. This form is designed to serve one work area only. In that work area, a single "key volume unit," identified with the work area's basic assignment, is identified. In a Shipping Department, it might be "carloads dispatched"; in a Purchasing Department, it might be "purchase requisitions processed"; in an Accounts Receivable Department, it might be "invoices received." Dollars should never be used, for obvious reasons.

This approach requires only the counting of the key volume unit and recording of actual hours worked. Instructions for calculating the relationships are carried on the bottom of the form. Over a period of years, a productivity trend line, and historical standard, is established.

A standard established from this type of information is often useful. Yet at best, the historical measurement lacks a great deal of helpful detail.

The primary failing with this use of background data is that work variables and difficulties, changes occurring in work processing, training of employees, types of machinery used, types of payrolls prepared and other factors are usually overlooked. Even if these variables are detected, little information would exist to permit accu-

KEY VOLUME REPORT

KEY VOLUME UNIT:_____

PLANT:_____

DEPARTMENT:_____

PERIOD FROM:_____   TO:_____

WEEK ENDING MONTH/DATE	ACTUAL HOURS WORKED			KEY VOLUME	RELATIONSHIP		
	NON EXEMPT	EXEMPT	TOTAL		THIS YR	LAST YR	DIFF. ±
/							
/							
TO DATE							
/							
TO DATE							
/							
TO DATE							
/							
TO DATE							
/							
TO DATE							
/							
TO DATE							
/							
TO DATE							
/							
TO DATE							
/							
TO DATE							
/							
TO DATE							
/							
TO DATE							
/							
TO DATE							

A   B   +C   =D   ÷E   =F   -G   =H

FIGURE 12.2

rate evaluation of their effect, or the segregation of the personnel time on the more detailed basis. Yet the effect of such changes could distort the measurement significantly, and radically up-or-down-grade the standard.

Another weakness in this type of measurement lies in the tendency to use too broad a unit of work. Although a "standard" of one employee for each 200 employees on the payroll may be a broad general yardstick, its usefulness becomes limited for more specific planning. If no more specific work standard is developed, a relatively insignificant change in work requirement might be the basis for requests for additional personnel, and no firm projection of actual need is available. Even historical measurement should be refined to provide more detail in work requirement than this example. This often can be accomplished by estimating and reconstructing work components for the more recent period of work and applying the data to past records. To illustrate:

Assume the past records of a claims office indicated:
1. That each additional 80 claims per month required the services of one additional employee.
2. That the current average of 640 claims per month required eight employees.
3. That the type of computation work for some of these claims is going to be substantially changed.
4. That new requirements will need to be developed.

The following approach could be taken to develop the necessary more detailed information:

Each employee would be required to estimate the distribution of time currently spent on the major types and components of work performed. (This could be done on either a percentage distribution or on an hours-per-week basis.) The results are simulated on Figure 12.3.

With information such as this, which is relatively simple to obtain, a fairly accurate picture of current time usage and past performance can be reconstructed with reasonable and useable accuracy. (The fact that employees must balance the time they report to the overall weekly total decreases the distortion which might be expected under other reporting conditions. Individual items are not usually distorted to any material extent under this simple estimate of major work items.)

With this information, it is an easy matter to adjust for work changes by adding or subtracting a percentage allowance to separate work items. A 30% increase in the investigation of Claims Z for increased complexity or processing would produce an approximate

Estimated Distribution of Employee Time

Employee	X Claims (400)					Z Claims (240)					Total
	Invest.	Type	Review	Misc.	Total	Invest.	Type	Review	Misc.	Total	
A	5		7½	7½	20	5		7½	7½	20	40
B	15		2½	2½	20	15		2½	2½	20	40
C	25		5		30	5			5	10	40
D	35		5		40						40
E	25				25	15				15	40
F			5		5	25	10			35	40
G		40			40						40
H		10			10	30				30	40
TOTAL	105	50	10	25	190	65	40	10	15	130	320

FIGURE 12.3

increase of 20 hours, half the time of an additional employee. Knowing the distribution of time as currently expended, the most effective placement of the additional time and the regrouping of individual employee time can now be undertaken.

This example is greatly simplified. In a real work area, there will be other activities performed which are ancillary to the assignment of the area. These activities do not occur in proportion to the basic assignments. In a Claims Department, for example: housekeeping; preparing form letters; answering subrogation letters; cross-training of personnel; and requisitioning and stocking office supplies.

In developing standards from historic time data, adjusted to reflect current distribution of employee time, it is essential to search out the key units of work most indicative of the total work effort of the group. This approach to work measurement, while lacking a great deal in detail and refinement, often provides quite adequate data. It also permits valuable experience for a more comprehensive program of developing work measurement and work standards. The steps to be taken to develop historical standards include:

1. Review the basic functions of work for which a measurement is desirable.
2. Obtain employee time records for a representative period long enough to even out work fluctuations and to spot trends and cycles.
3. Obtain production records applicable to the work units for the corresponding periods. Again, these may be difficult to obtain, but often are available in the records of the office ac-

tivities, accounting information regarding checks written, bills sent, time cards handled, etc.

4. Analyze data. This may be difficult to do in retrospect, but it is a valuable means of providing a great deal of information regarding variation in the unit times and possible means of correcting distortions in the future.

   Ask questions like:

   a. Is there a cyclical effect, either monthly or seasonally, which affects the unit times?

   b. Is there a variation in training or working experience?

   c. Have new procedures or equipment been installed?

5. Divide the hours worked by the units produced to establish the actual hours per unit. It is especially helpful to plot this information against the time period for a clear picture of work progress.

6. Determine the time per unit. (Considering the results of the analysis, select the time most representative of the work to be performed.) With an adequate amount of information and the proper statistical analysis, a very representative figure may be obtained. An average of the three lowest periods is often used as a goal.

This historical procedure has several advantages. It is fairly factual, simple to understand, and can be obtained at minimum cost and without disrupting the normal office routines. It requires little or no method work or preparation. It provides acceptable information in that it has been achieved in the past, includes all work performed and all personal allowances, and represents the entire group. It can be used as a benchmark for future programs and does provide a sound starting point.

Its principal disadvantage, of course, is that it represents what has been done, not what should be done. It builds in all the inefficiencies of methods, delays, performance, etc. It is difficult to analyze the effect of undocumented changes in methods or to adjust for them in the standards. Quality requirements are seldom reflected.

THE EMPLOYEE REPORTING APPROACH

The employee reporting approach to work measurement is a satisfactory, yet simple technique for the measurement of operations. It is particularly applicable in the office, for it is readily adaptable to various situations and relatively inexpensive. As in the development of historical measurement data, two basic kinds of data are needed —detailed time records and volume data. While in the historical measurement approach these are obtained from past performance, in this approach both are developed from current operating periods.

This approach to work measurement requires each employee in the group being measured to maintain a log or tally sheet of time spent on each work activity and, in some cases, the number of units of work completed. Although an obvious weakness of such data is the distortion which the employees might report, a certain amount of control can usually be built into the system. The usual steps in an employee reporting approach to work measurement include:

1. *Meetings should be held with all the employees involved.* It is essential that the complete understanding of employees be secured. This is an important key to the success of the technique. Make clear the reason for the program, its objectives, how the information will be used, and its effect on the workers. Emphasize the need for the study and for their cooperation. The mechanics of the program, descriptions of functions and reporting techniques should be discussed with the employees in detail, and log sheets, codes, etc., must be entirely understood.

2. *Plan the reporting.* The system for obtaining the data can range from an informal "diary" the employee keeps to an elaborate system where forms with codes for the basic activities are utilized. The use of punched cards or optical mark reading can, in some cases, be especially advantageous.

   Each job must be examined for its basic functions or activities. These activities should be related to a count taken by the employee, or related to a count made by the supervisor or some higher level. A list of these activities is used by each employee. Time spent in defining the activity will save considerable employee and analyst time. Terminology familiar to the employee should be used to describe the activity, indicating its start and finish. Key words are then established—abbreviated, if possible, or assigned codes—to describe the function. Sometimes written descriptions may be desirable for long or variable jobs, to explain key word designations.

   The minimum length of the time interval to be reported must be established. Usually, less than five or ten minutes harasses the operator unduly, complicates the analysis and is not warranted by the accuracy obtained.

   Clocks should be easily visible to all employees in the study. Special forms should be provided with headings, columns, lines, etc., for ease in reporting and analyzing material. This, with the use of a good functional breakdown and description, provides the materials which will save confusion and time.

It is especially important that a means for handling delay, personal time or idle time be established and understood, since operator cooperation for accurate results is essential in this somewhat touchy area.

Proper and accurate recording of production units is very important. Short cycle or repetitious functions should not create a problem. Longer cycles, which may mean partial or incompleted assignments, are more difficult. The use of a daily count may be necessary during the study. The use of estimates of the percentage of job completion may be used either by the employee or supervisor.

Every employee in the office being studied should maintain the reporting log. This is necessary to obtain a complete picture of all functions and relationships. More important, it provides a psychological advantage in that it eliminates any idea of favoritism or non-representative information.

3. *Make a trial run with the reporting.* Usually, a short period of trial reporting is desirable. This affords an opportunity to determine problem areas as they arise, and to give employees an opportunity to use categories, definitions and forms. It saves time later in the study. Several days or a week is generally sufficient for this trial. Where necessary, changes in the procedure for reporting are made at this time.

4. *Gather the data.* The length of time required to obtain adequate data will usually depend upon the variables in the work itself, repetitious and cyclical effects, and the operator's performance. Short cycles or repetitious work can sometimes be reported in three to four days, while variable work with cyclical aspects may require three to four weeks. Some work may require as much as six months, but this is quite exceptional. Usually, two weeks is an adequate period.

Reports should be reviewed daily. Questionable items are checked for reporting accuracy and errors; review should observe consistency and variation so that, when the analysis is started, misinterpretation of instructions or reporting data will not invalidate the entire study.

In this method of measurement, probably more than any other, the observer must be close to the operation, especially at the beginning, to answer questions, help formulate policies and make decisions regarding employee progress reports.

5. *Analyze and summarize the results.* This can be a time-consuming task depending on the length of the study, number of operators involved, job functions, etc. If the material has been

assembled by machine tabulation, considerable time can be saved.

The analysis includes developing the elemental time used in producing the number of each type of completed units. Times for each employee performing the particular units and for the entire group performing the work should be developed. In this way, range of unit time, averages, and special allowances are identified and studied.

6. *Establish the Standard Unit Time.* It should be remembered that the unit times developed are raw data. They include variations in methods, operator performance and training. Management's objectives must be considered in selecting standards with varying degrees of tightness and looseness. Average performance vs. the establishment of a high goal are always the opposing factors pertinent in this phase of the study. Averages are seldom selected. More frequently, the standard is established at the upper quartile or somewhere between the 75% and 90% achievement level.

Employee Reporting Forms

There are many forms for recording employees' time, ranging from simple columnar pads to elaborately printed forms. One of the most practical logging forms is shown in Figure 12.4. The simplicity of the form makes it very acceptable to employees, and assists materially in gaining the cooperation of the employees in this approach. Preliminary to using the form, the major categories of work are identified and numbered. They are typed or written on the worksheet itself. This assists in maintaining uniformity of reporting work categories.

A separate work sheet is used each week by each employee participating in the study, as follows:

He records the time at which he starts to work by drawing a line through the bar chart at the indicated time. He determines the code of the work he will begin and records the number in the space to the right of the time marked. When he changes the type of work he's doing, a line is drawn through the time indicated, and the number recorded for the new type of work. When he stops for a coffee break, he records the code for non-productive time. Thus, the way he spends every portion of his time is indicated simply and yet in detail.

At the end of the week, the employee's time for each type of work is summarized and put into the columns on the right of the chart. Totals are summarized for all employees for the week (or

Weekly Report of Distribution of Time

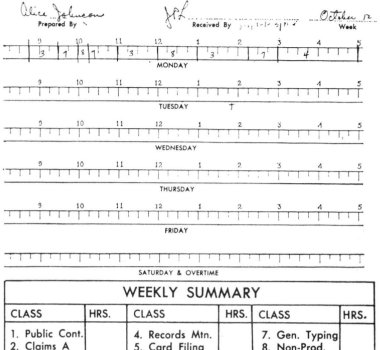

WEEKLY SUMMARY

CLASS	HRS.	CLASS	HRS.	CLASS	HRS.
1. Public Cont. 2. Claims A 3. Claims B		4. Records Mtn. 5. Card Filing 6. Form Letters		7. Gen. Typing 8. Non-Prod.	
TOTAL					

BAR CHART WORKSHEET

FIGURE 12.4

the month) and these totals are calculated against the number of each type of cases (units of work produced) during the corresponding time. Volume produced can either be obtained from separate work reports, or where these do not correspond to work items identified, can be reported by the employees directly below the time bar as they are completed. The result is a simple, yet fairly reliable, measurement of how much time each unit of work is currently taking to be completed.

Advantages and Shortcomings

The advantages of the Employee Reporting approach to measurement are many. Its cost is relatively low; it provides a large amount of current and relatively detailed information. It is generally very acceptable and easily understood. It requires relatively little training to handle once the program is established, and can be administered effectively by the supervisor. It also brings the importance of time and work to the operator and makes him conscious of its importance and of management's interest in it. It also provides a considerable amount of information as to operating methods, delays, work schedules and machine utilization. It provides an opportunity for employee participation.

This approach is applicable to a wide variety of situations, since it is an extremely flexible technique. It is especially good where there is a great variety of jobs and the work content may be highly variable. It shows job duties and frequencies of work occurrences very well. In a large and repetitive work situation, it can establish work standards with good accuracy.

This approach requires the full understanding and cooperation of the employees and the supervisor, since it can interrupt work routines (especially where the detail of the reporting unit is high) and can be annoying to the employee.

The major disadvantage of this measurement is that it gives no real indication of whether the work should take as long as reported, or whether there might be good potential to reduce the details of the operation. It simply indicates how much time is being used to accomplish the work under the current circumstances. Some indications of improvement might be developed through the comparison of several time periods or similar offices, groups or individuals, but this requires fairly continuous or frequent recording of data by the employees, supplemented by statistical volume records for the matching periods.

THE TIME STUDY MEASUREMENT

Probably the best known device for measuring work is the stop watch. In its simplest form, a time study is merely clocking the time it takes to do a particular operation. Measurement by stop watch timing can be a very precise form of measurement. It has been used in industry for many years, due largely to its low cost flexibility and potential accuracy. Time study is often used, like predetermined time systems, as a base for compiling standard data.

This technique can produce a standard in the true sense of the word, for close examination of the work measured provides an opportunity to evaluate the rate or speed at which it should be performed.

Because of the complexity of most operations and the occurrence of delay factors, it is common practice to break the operation being timed into elements of the total task. These elements are usually groups of basic motion and are long enough to be practical, usually at least .5 minutes.

Sometimes a video or movie camera is trained on the subject. The film is then later replayed and studied by the technician. This has the advantage of repeated observations.

Stop watch time studies, like MTM studies, should only be undertaken by a trained practitioner. The elements must be identified in a specific way; operating the stop watch requires learning a technique; and "leveling" the observations in order to develop a standard is something that is often done badly even by trained people. Further, stop watch studies are often deemed offensive by the employees being observed; some union contracts even forbid their use.

Direct Observation

A variation on stop watch time study, direct observation is easy to learn, provides accuracy sufficient for most office work and seems to arouse less resentment. The technique is sometimes called batch study, and is the technique most commonly used by practitioners of short-interval scheduling. It requires only a wrist watch or wall clock for timing.

1. Develop procedures based on a natural unit of work, and make sure that the operators agree with their validity. A natural unit of work has a logical beginning point and completion point, and may be completed without inherent interruption. It may be simple or complex, and the measurement unit should be at the beginning point.

2. Make direct observation. Agree with operator that the work can be performed in the described manner. Count out a "batch" of purchase requisitions for person to work.

   The operator then completes the work as described, with no interruptions that are avoidable. The observer times the operation, using either a clock on the wall or a wrist watch. Interruptions that are not part of the activity will be subtracted from the elapsed time for performance, such as coffee breaks and incoming telephone calls.

3. When complete, divide the number of units completed into the net elapsed time for an actual average time per unit. Several observations should be made, with batches of different size and different operators. Observations should take from 10 minutes to 100 minutes each.

   It will not be unusual to find different workers in an office performing apparently identical task at rates differing by more than 300%. Analysis of the differences provides insight into potential improvements.

4. Level the different observations to develop the standard. If the analyst is determining standard costs, for example, he may simply average the average times, then add a factor for delays which are avoided during direct observation.

If the analyst is trying to set performance goals, then the standard is usually set slightly below the best times achieved by the best operators.

Direct observation provides a modified historical standard. It takes into account such factors as operator skill, environmental conditions, and legibility of source documents. It is easy to understand and apply. Preparation of the procedures provides useful documentation for methods, procedures or systems analysis.

The major disadvantage is that it is impossible to measure a proposed method, procedure or system.

Direct Observation Example

Type purchase orders. Unit: purchase requisition. Using purchase requisition signed by buyer as source document, type purchase orders. Use source directory, make telephone calls, ask questions of buyer for any needed information not on requisition. Proofread purchase order for accuracy. Verify extensions. Make any corrections required. Sign with buyer's name and own initials. Address envelopes. Stuff envelopes with first two copies of purchase order. Place in outgoing mail. Post to register. Attach third copy of purchase order to purchase requisition, route to originating department. File fourth copy of purchase order in vendor file, by vendor and date. Route fifth and sixth copies to accounting.

WORK SAMPLING

The work sampling (sometimes referred to as ratio delay) technique of measuring work was first developed in the textile industry in England. It is based on the principle that, if through unbiased observation one records sufficient accurate samples of an activity, one can determine the relative time being spent in various interruptions or delays as well as in productive portions of the work. Both the sampling theories and the theory of probability on which the deductions are based have been used and developed with a high degree of efficiency and validity. Work sampling is fundamentally a technique for accurately determining the *content* of jobs and utilization of operators and equipment. It is somewhat less frequently used to develop work standards.

Work sampling is based on the premise that a carefully chosen small sample selected at random from a large number of occurrences will tend to follow the same pattern and have the same distribution as the whole. The larger the sample size, the more accurate will be the predictions of the characteristics of the whole.

The procedure devised for sampling work requires the making of observations at random times throughout the working day. A random sample is not a haphazard sample. It is one obtained when each item has an identical chance of being selected. It is essential that the observation times and sequences be randomly determined. Random number tables may be prepared by drawing numbers from a bowl, providing that the numbers are replaced in the bowl after being drawn. Tables of random numbers are available commercially, or are provided in numerous texts on work sampling and statistics.

By applying the work sampling technique to a work measurement study, we find out what percentage of the work day is spent in each of the various activities, and what percentage of the activity of each worker is spent in performing it, contrasted to what percentage of time he is idle or away from his work area. The kinds of idle time can also be categorized into such groups as waiting for the supervisor, waiting for additional work, personal time, etc. Sampling is also used to good advantage in determining downtime on equipment.

Number of Observations Required

Perhaps the key factor in the success of a work sampling measurement study is determining and obtaining the proper number of observations. Too few observations provide inaccurate and distorted results. Too many samples are costly and discouraging to those participating. There are two methods of determining the number of observations required in a work sampling study: the statistical method based on a mathematical formula, and the empirical method depending upon judgment and experience. The statistical method, based on the formula of work sampling, is influenced by two factors:

(1) how accurate the results must be, and (2) the percentage of time required by that observed item which takes the least time. Before the formula can be applied, the second of these factors must be developed. A reasonable estimate of the percentage of time devoted to each of the categories of work to be observed is therefore compiled. The lower the percentage of time of the smallest pertinent work item to be observed, the greater the sample of observations will be needed.

The statistical formulas used in work sampling are designed so that one can make the following type of statement: *The probability is 95% that the real value is within ±3% of the observed mean % of times the activity is observed.* The 95% and the 3% are parameters chosen by the sampler. Increasing the first parameter gives the system analyst greater assurance that the true value is within the range shown. Decreasing the range improves the precision of the measurement. Both increase the sample size. If there is a need to know with great assurance that the sample mean percentage is very close to the true mean, then the sample must be very large. Normally, for systems analysis purposes, neither great assurance or great precision of measurement is needed. Hence, the samples can be fairly small.

Conducting the Study

The major phases of a work sampling study are:
1. Determine the categories of work to be sampled. Rarely is it practical to observe more than six categories, even with highly trained observers. A study might consist of five categories:
   1. Typing.
   2. Reading back typed copy.
   3. Preparing work for typing.
   4. Not working.
   5. Out of sight.
2. Prepare an observation form (Figure 12.5). Its design will be based on the number of people or work stations to be studied and upon the elements established in step 1.
3. Determine the study duration. Decide how long the study should take. This step is important because the study should be of sufficient duration to be representative of the job being observed. This will require some investigation but should not be overlooked. Generally, the more repetitive the work or type of work, the shorter the required duration. Do not relate the duration of the study with the number of observations required to obtain desired accuracy; they are not the same.

Work Sampling Observation Sheet

Division: Claims · Observer · Date 4/7	Tallies of Observations										TOTAL
Categories											
1. Counter Work	₦₦ //			₦₦ /							13
2. Typing Reports	//	////		₦₦ //	//	₦₦ /	₦₦ //				30
3. Misc. Typing	/		////		₦₦						10
4. Assemble Reports		//		₦₦	///	//					13
5. Index Cards	///	/	//	/							9
6. Misc.	/	/	/								3
7. Idle	/	/	//	/	///	/					9
8. Away	//	/	/	//	/	/	/	/			10
9. Personal		//									3
10.											
11.	10	10	10	10	10	10	10	10	10	10	100
20.											

FIGURE 12.5

Example of a Study Method

In a work processing center, perhaps 65 different kinds of assignments are run through automatic typewriters. Certainly, one or two days would not give a very representative look at the work required to set up and run all those jobs. In 10 days enough variety of jobs (not every job) would be seen to establish that this would be typical of any other period of time for these operations under similar levels of production. This type of analysis determines the minimum duration of the study.

4. Determine the number of observations needed for the desired statistical reliability. This can be easily done by using the alignment chart designed by J. M. Aldrich of Eastman Kodak (Figure 12.6). This chart is based on the formula:

$$S.D. = \sqrt{\frac{P\,(1-P)}{N}}$$

S.D.—Standard Deviation
P —% Occurrence of an element
N —Total number of observations

The chart is extended to the two standard deviation limit, which assures that 95% of the time the data is within the precision interval selected. Precision interval is the plus or minus tolerance desired for a given element. Normally, one works to the desired accuracy of the largest element in terms of percentage of the whole.

Example of Determining Observations

In a study with only two elements: Element 1, Working; Element 2, Idle, the initial evaluation estimates the work element to equal 80%. The idle element equals about 20%. Desired accuracy is plus or minus 5% of the work element. This means work could be 76% to 84%. The precision interval is 4% (5% × 80% = 4%). On Figure 12.6, line up the percent activity, 80%, and precision interval 4%, and draw a line across to the number of observations (400). These are the number of observations needed to assure that the true percentage will be within plus or minus 4% of the percentage in the sample 95% of the time.

After having determined the number of observations required to obtain the desired accuracy from Figure 12.6, divide this figure (number of observations) by the number of days determined in step 3, to find the number of observations required each day. This may be more or fewer observations than the number of observers available can handle. If it is less, reduce the number of observers; if more, return to step 3 and select a longer duration for the study. Do not shorten the duration of a study once the minimum time has been established to be representative of the total.

5. Establish trip times. Determine how long it takes for an observer to make his rounds to the various observation points in order to know how many trips he can make on a random basis. It is important that trips be made on a random, not haphazard, basis. Select the starting times of each trip by use of a set of random numbers (available in any statistical reference) converted to random times. To further add or assure randomness, use another random number set to aid in assigning random starting points and routes to follow.

6. Observer consistency. Observers must be trained for meticulous, objective and consistent recording of information.

RANDOM SAMPLING ALIGNMENT CHART FOR DETERMINING SAMPLE SIZE

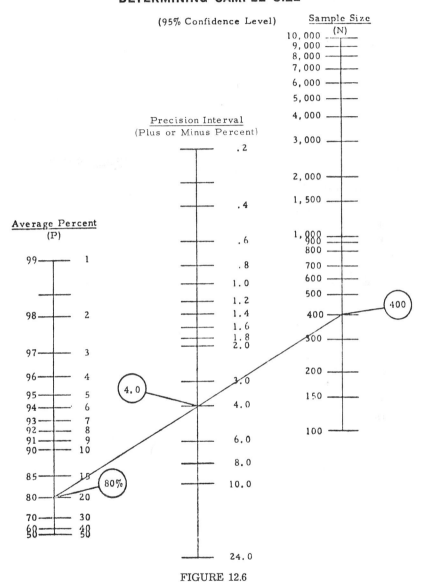

FIGURE 12.6

7. Take the study. At the predetermined starting times, the observers begin their rounds, making and recording observations in the appropriate locations on the observation form. Observations should be made at approximately the same location or same

distance from the operation or operator. This will help reduce bias on the part of the observer. It is taken for granted that the people being observed have already been informed of the fact that a study is to be conducted, the techniques employed, and the kind of information to be gathered.

8. Calculate the work time. When the required number of observations have been made, they are summarized and their percentage of the total time of the employees/operations is calculated. This percentage is extended to provide the calculated minutes of time chargeable to each of the categories of work observed, as indicated in the first four columns of Figure 12.7. Using the work volume produced during the period of the study will result in the development of unit times for each of the work categories as shown in Figure 12.7.

Table of Unit Times
Computed from Work Observations

Work Item	Number of Observations	%	Calculated Minutes	Work Volume	Unit Time
A	160	10.8	1,850	419	4.41
B	173	11.6	1,987	1,314	1.51
C	425	28.6	4,899	3,078	1.59
D	214	14.4	2,467	744	3.32
E	183	12.3	2,107	1,018	2.07
Idle	102	6.8	1,165	–	–
Personal	113	7.6	1,302	–	–
Lunch	117	7.9	1,353	–	–
Total	1,487	100.0	17,130		

FIGURE 12.7

Photography

Sometimes a video or movie camera is trained on the area to be observed. A special camera which runs continuously or makes snapshots at pre-set intervals is used. If this approach is used, steps 1, 2, 5, 6, and 7 of the study must be modified to accommodate this equipment.

Advantages and Disadvantages

A major advantage of this technique is the relatively brief time required in contrast to that required in most other approaches. Usually, one observer can observe and record a fairly large number of employees, especially if the study is extended rather than concentrated into a large number of observations per day. Another advantage lies in the practicality of using observers without lengthy technical training; a supervisor from the group is often used for the recording.

If the work is very simple, amazingly accurate work measurement data can be developed. More important, the development of separate lost time factors (ratio of delay) is of extra value to management in attempting to make improvements in utilization.

A major disadvantage is that of employee resistance. Unless employees fully trust the analytical team, they are apt to feel that they are being spied upon. Another disadvantage is that it is often difficult to attain the recording discipline required to avoid distortions in the data. Further, the observations taken and the data gathered are usually not helpful for systems, procedures or methods analysis. For example, the data might show that 10% of the time in a department is taken up with typing. The analyst must know what is being typed, from what source material, for what reason . . . and it is impractical to attempt to gather such detail through random samplings.

WORK MEASUREMENT AND PARETO'S LAW

Pareto's Law states that "the significant items in a given group normally constitute a relatively small portion of the total items in the group. A majority of the items in the total will, even in the aggregate, be of relatively minor importance."

Twenty percent of a company's products usually account for 80% of sales volume, and 20% of the employees some 90% of the tardiness.

If work measurement is to be used as the basis for a control system, it is therefore wise to identify those few tasks which represent the greatest portion of the workload, measure them with the greatest accuracy, and make the greatest effort to forecast, control and evaluate performance. The far greater number of tasks which represent the smaller portion of the workload can be much more loosely controlled without losing control of the total workload.

REVIEW QUESTIONS

1. List some of the uses of work measurement in business.
2. List some areas where work measurement cannot help in determining staffing levels.
3. List some factors which will affect how rapidly a person performs work that may not be recognized in a given set of predetermined times or standard data.
4. List some factors which will affect how rapidly a person performs work that may not be recognized when standards are set by random sampling, direct observation or time study.

DISCUSSION QUESTIONS

1. Discuss how work measurement techniques would help you determine a historical standard for how long it will take you to drive from one place to another (routes you frequently travel) in various traffic conditions.
2. Discuss how work measurement techniques can help you estimate how long it will take you to travel to a place you have never been, provided you have a map and mileage.
3. Discuss how you know when to set your alarm clock for arriving at work on time. Would a motion study help you reduce preparation times?
4. The Grunion Company is introducing a new product, the Schmeckenclip. Marketing forecasts that Company sales will rise from $10 million annually (present rate) to $20 million annually within two years. You're asked to determine how many people should be assigned to the Accounts Receivable Department by then. No major systems changes are envisioned. Discuss what steps you should go through.

BIBLIOGRAPHY

Anderson, Donald S., "Supervisors as Work Measurement Analysts," *Management Services*, Vol. 8, No. 1, January/February 1971, pp. 20-26.

Berg, Charles J. Jr., "Cutting Overhead to Increase Profits," *Journal of Systems Management*, Vol. 23, No. 2, February 1972, pp. 24-27.

Caruth, Donald L., *Guidelines for Organizing a Work Measurement Program*, Cleveland: Association for Systems Management, 1971, 52 p.

Fuhro, Wilbur J., "Five Standards for Office Control," *Journal of Systems Management*, Vol. 24, No. 2, February 1973, pp. 16-19.

Luby, Joan F., "Administrative Manager's Dilemma," *Journal of Systems Management*, Vol. 21, No. 8, August 1970, pp. 9-12.

Martin, Donald D. and Charles Johnston, "Proxemics as a Work Standard Influence," *Journal of Systems Management*, Vol. 22, No. 11, November 1971, pp. 26-29.

Radius, David A., "Clerical Work Measurement," *Journal of Systems Management*, Vol. 23, No. 5, May 1972, pp. 28-31.

Reuter, Vincent G., "Work Measurement," *Journal of Systems Management*, Vol. 22, No. 9, September 1971, pp. 10-15; Vol. 22, No. 10, October 1971, pp. 13-20.

Slaybaugh, C. J., "Pareto's Law and Modern Management," *Management Services*, Vol. 5, No. 2, March/April 1967, p. 53.

Stevens, Robert I., "Time Distribution Charts: A Technique for Job Analysis," *Journal of Systems Management*, Vol. 23, No. 10, October 1972, pp. 40-41.

Woodridge, Henry S. Jr., "Whittling Clerical Costs," *Personnel*, Vol. 49, No. 1, January/February 1972, pp. 47-52.

CHAPTER 13

INFORMATION FLOW AND ANALYSIS

In the analysis of an information system the analyst must study the flow of information through the system. The analysis is facilitated by the use of some of the tools described earlier, such as flowcharting and forms tracing. The major themes of this chapter are:

How information flows

What information flows

How information flows is considered at the general principle level. This leads to an elementary discussion of some of the results of the application of Forrester's *Industrial Dynamics* (Forrester, 1961). Another significant off-shoot from the flow discussion is the source data automation (SDA) idea which is described in some detail.

Knowledge of the flow of information gives little idea of what data is flowing. Flowcharts are less than perfect descriptions of the data available at the decision and processing points of the flowchart. Data analysis is then discussed in general followed by three concepts very much involved in studying data. These are BISAD, ARDI and Data Bases.

FLOW PRINCIPLES

When the Corps of Engineers improves the flow of water in a river it dredges, straightens, removes obstacles and by-passes meanders. These activities have analogies in the information system flow analysis and design.

The channel through which the data flows must have enough capacity to carry the data. Communication facilities are of several grades, each with a different capacity to transmit data. The analyst examining a communication system would determine whether the data flow, the channel capacity and the control needs were congruent. If not, the cost-effectiveness of greater or smaller capacity would be studied.

In an expense account approval procedure for sales personnel, it is common for all expense reports to be approved by at least the sales manager. When the sales manager is traveling, the channel capacity is zero unless other arrangements for approval are made. To keep the channel open it is obvious that the sales manager should deputize someone else to act on his behalf.

The major systems (i.e., payroll, purchasing, cash receipts and order processing) within an organization must flow if the organization is to continue to exist. These systems often are engineered with substantial capacity. It is then appropriate in the design of other systems to use the channels established for the main stream systems. As examples, personnel records systems have been designed as adjuncts to payroll systems and marketing information systems are often related to order processing systems. Developing a separate flow for the related systems is appropriate only if the main system has inadequate capacity. Even then, redesigning the main system may be a better solution.

The flow of information should be straight line. Again, using the

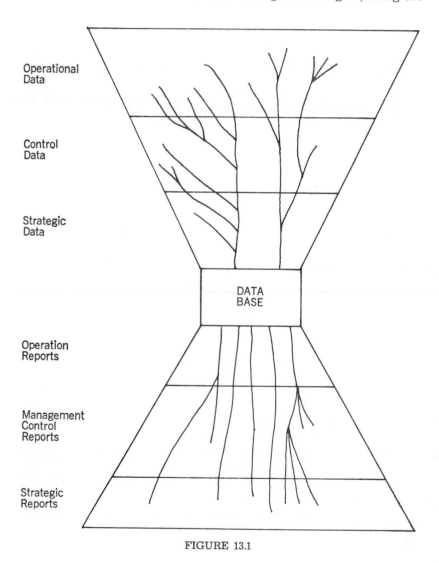

Operational
Data

Control
Data

Strategic
Data

DATA
BASE

Operation
Reports

Management
Control
Reports

Strategic
Reports

FIGURE 13.1

river analogy, the wandering of the river decreases the velocity of the flow and increases the rate of silt collecting in the channel. Similarly, detours in the information system process reduce the reaction time of the system and increase the fallout of undesirable side effects. Straight line coding is a popular subject for programming articles. The salutatory effects of straight line coding are increased readability, decreased debugging and often faster running programs.

The flow of information can be illustrated as in Figure 13.1. The use of the data base concept makes the flow look straight line. Actually, all of the cross-relationships are hidden within the data base. Later in the chapter, the data base description will show how to handle these relationships without undue loss of efficiency. This straight line flow is in reality a way of simplifying the system. If all real systems are imperceivable, then perception is only possible by segmenting the system into perceivable parts. This is the aim of designing with simple flows.

Two corollary ideas come from the simple flow idea. First, the systems analyst should avoid exceptions. Second, the data base serves as an effective decoupler, just as inventory serves that purpose in physical systems.

Exceptions should be avoided because they impede and complicate the flow of information. Generally, exceptions divide the flow as in Figure 13.2. Assume process 1 and 4 use six processing facilities, process 2 uses four, and process 3 uses two. It is then obvious from queuing considerations that the queues in front of processes 2 and 3 will exceed those for 1 and 4. Thus, the exception creates a

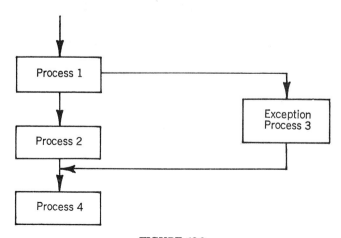

FIGURE 13.2

bottleneck in the flow of information. This is not to say that exception reports are bad. They serve the same simplification purpose and add to the perceivability of the subsystem and thus, of the system. In programs, exceptions add to the logic structure of the programs, which requires more core and running time to process. Programs secured from computer manufacturers are good illustrations. They are notorious for their extravagant use of core and slow speed. Why? In part, the inefficiencies are caused by the attempt of the designer to build in processes to handle great numbers of exceptions. It is thus no surprise to see service bureau subsidiaries of computer manufacturers develop their own operating and application software.

Certainly, some exceptions cannot be avoided and others are processed with hardly a blink in the system. The analyst must ask whether processing the exception would make a material difference and whether the exception is necessary.

The several flows of information in the organization operate at different rates. In a physical system, inventories are used to level the flows. *Data bases* perform that function in information systems. The daily flow of time cards is held in a data base for weekly payroll processing; the payroll statistics are held for annual W-2 processing, etc. Consider an inventory system where data is needed from at least production, order processing, shipping, purchasing and receiving. If each of these systems operates independently and deposits information into a data bank, then the designer of the inventory system has fewer design problems. The interfaces are simple and require little specific design effort.

INDUSTRIAL DYNAMICS

Jay Forrester, the inventor of magnetic core memories, has made a significant contribution to information systems analysis by his concepts of industrial dynamics. Forrester conceived a system as a complex of levels (inventories) with valves to regulate the complex system flows and feedback loops to monitor the flows. An example of the result of a simulation using an industrial dynamic type of flow is shown in Figure 13.3. The industrial dynamic systemology is useful to describe information systems.

As will be mentioned in Chapter 14, one purpose of building a model is to perform experiments using the model. Forrester's experiments with industrial dynamics models were quite interesting and often controversial, as reported in his book, *World Dynamics*.

Forrester's original models showed that the number of stages of processing in a system was inversely related to the stability of the system. A two-stage system was more stable than a three-stage. This suggested that minimizing steps was a valuable goal in systems design.

He also showed that modest changes in systems input could result in changes several times as large in the rest of the system before the system was stabilized. These results were contrary to the expectations of systems designers. One of the more popular devices used in the design of a system is the insertion of an inventory between two sequential processes. The two processes are said to be decoupled. That is, if clerk A does tasks a, b, and c to a record while clerk B does e and f, then it is normal to build a backlog of work (inventory) between A and B. The varying time it takes A to process the transactions is muted in its effect upon B by existence of the inventory. Also, the fact that B is working from an inventory rather than getting stochastic transactions suggests that the slack built into the job can be minimal. As was discussed in Chapter 4

Industrial Dynamics Flow

Response of a Distribution System to a Sudden 10% Increase in Retail Sales

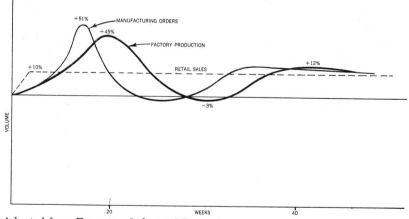

Adapted from Forrester, *Industrial Dynamics*

FIGURE 13.3

under Queuing Theory, jobs receiving stochastic input require some slack.

Forrester's work showed that such systems worked well in stable situations, but would multiply the impact of any systems changes. Unfortunately systems change generated by outside controls, can have severe side effects. These experiments proved that efficiency within a system and ability of the system to react to environmental change are inverse functions of each other.

What does all this have to say about the analysis of information flows? It suggests that the analyst must carefully examine the environment of the system in the analysis phase of a project. If the existing system, upon examination, is seen to be a complex multi-stage one, the analyst should expect it to perform badly in certain environmental conditions and very well in others.

SOURCE DATA AUTOMATION

The two assumptions behind the idea of source data automation (SDA) are:

1. Getting data into machine language can be expensive.
2. Each processing step performed by a machine is less costly than the equivalent step performed by humans.

Certainly there are situations where these two assumptions are invalid; however, there is a large number of situations where the conditions are met.

The principle of source data automation is to capture data in machine language form at the earliest possible stage in the process, and as a by-product of another required operation, if possible.

Source Data Automation Examples

A student writing test answers on a form that can be read by an Optical Mark Reader (OMR).

A meter reader marking the meter readings on an OMR Form.

A voter voting by punching holes in a card with a stylus.

A check with check number preprinted in MICR code.

The piece of paper tape in the check reorder form and its subsequent use to print more checks.

SDA also uses turnaround documents extensively. Turnaround documents are machine record outputs on which additional data is recorded for re-entry in a subsequent cycle. Examples include punched card checks, stub cards on utility bills, the paper tape used to preprint checks, meter cards and time cards.

The equipment involved in SDA includes:
Paper tape readers and punches
Optical mark readers (OMR)
Optical character readers (OCR)
Magnetic ink character recorders (MICR)
Punched tag readers
Point-of-sale recorders
Embossers
Styluses
Terminals (typewriter and cathode ray tube)

The keypunch and its derivations are not among the equipment shown because a major purpose of SDA is the elimination of keypunching. A close look at alternatives to keypunching can eliminate 80% of that activity with little or no increase in work elsewhere. Creative use of SDA equipment may well be one of the most cost-effective parts of a new information system.

In an information system, the person at the source has the value of an element of data in mind. The usual process is to write the data on a form, keypunch and key verify it. In SDA the originator creates the machine language in the process of recording the data. This saves the keypunch and key verification steps.

Not only does SDA save two of the three typical data entry steps, it also tends to reduce errors. The one-step SDA process pinpoints responsibility while the other process dilutes it. Generally, people in data origination positions respond well to the knowledge that their actions directly affect the outcomes from the system.

Precisely which SDA equipment to use in a particular situation is a subject for analysis by the systems analyst. There is a great variety of equipment designed for many situations. The major considerations will be possibilities of turnaround documents, volume of transactions generated in total and by each originator and the form in which the data becomes available to the originator.

DATA ANALYSIS

As was discussed in Chapter 11, the data used in a system is a subset of the data available. Data analysis selects that subset and then develops volume, frequency, sequence, storage and retrieval information about each element of the subset.

The selection of an appropriate subset occurs at two levels. First, at the transaction level, some transactions are important to the functioning of the system and others are not. Second, each transaction has a large number of possible descriptors. The appropriate subset of these must also be chosen. Often, some form of statistical analysis such as regression analysis is useful in reducing the overall set of descriptions and transactions to that set appropriate to use for systems control.

Considerable information is needed for that data chosen for analysis. For each transaction type, the analyst needs to know the volume of transactions per period and often the distribution or variability of the transactions. The sequence of transactions and of transaction files can be important to the file designers. The frequency of retrievals of transactions is also needed for file design. The size of files is dependent upon the length of time a transaction is stored so criteria for purging are needed.

For each data element within a transaction, the analyst needs to know its name and whether the element is always present, sometimes present as several items, or ever used as a key for retrieval. How the data is stored, accessed, used, displayed, reported, and analyzed are of significance in the analysis and design.

BISAD

BISAD, Honeywell's acronym for Business Information Systems and Design, is a complete and well-integrated concept of analysis and design. It involves the entire project from origination through installation and evaluation. BISAD includes one analysis technique, the information matrix, which is not usually found in systems analysis texts. This useful idea is worth describing in some detail.

The relationship between the data used in a system and the reports developed by the system can be described in matrix form, as in Figure 13.4. Organizing the information flow in this way can be quite useful. Note that data item 11 is not shown in any report and can be eliminated in the system's design. Report B differs from Report D only in the use of data item 13 and could possibly be merged into a single report.

Figure 13.5 shows a useful relationship between the input documents and the data items in a system. Duplication of data items on each of the report documents can be easily spotted. Duplicated items are the key to the file since they are needed on each input document. The duplication of the entry of data item 2 on document A and B

DATA ITEMS	REPORTS						
	A	B	C	D	E	F	G
1	X	X		X	X	X	X
2		X		X	X	X	
3	X	X		X			X
4	X		X				
5	X		X				
6			X			X	
7	X					X	
8			X		X	X	
9	X	X		X			
10						X	
11							
12					X		X
13		X			X		X
14					X		X

FIGURE 13.4

and data item 5 on B and E should be carefully studied from an efficiency point of view. Note that data item 14 is not entered. If data item 14 is used elsewhere, then it must be entered on some input document.

The advantages of the analyses shown in Figures 13.4 and 13.5 are completeness and elimination of excessive redundancy. Some redundancy is good and, as discussed in Chapter 26, is one of the primary tools used to assure a system's reliability.

The information matrix and flow used in BISAD (Figure 13.6) expands upon these two simple charts. This particular chart shows BISAD at the macro level with input, output and files easily described in a two-dimensional format. The information items missing from this description are the activities needed to transform the

	INPUT DOCUMENTS				
DATA ITEMS	A	B	C	D	E
1	X	X	X	X	X
2	X	X			
3			X		
4	X				
5		X			X
6	X				
7		X			
8	X				
9	X				
10		X			
11			X		
12			X		
13				X	
14					

FIGURE 13.5

input into the output. The information flow matrix with its complete descriptive narrative is a useful technique for describing a system.

ARDI

ARDI (Hartman, 1968) represents Analysis, Requirements determination, Design and development, and Implementation and evaluation. Information flow is part of Analysis (A). Some of the tools used are:

Data usage charts
Report usage charts
Form and file description sheet

Information Matrix

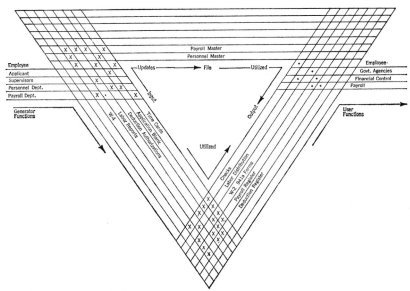

Adapted from BISAD, Honeywell

FIGURE 13.6

Field description sheet

Function worksheet

The data usage chart is a two-dimensional matrix similar to Figure 13.4. The report usage chart has information similar to that in a reports chart.

The form or file description describes for each data element the name, coded name, number of characters, usage frequency and comments. For the file or form as a whole, the information entered includes purpose, retention, sequence, labels, copies, usage volume, reporting delay, size and color.

The field description sheet gives names, size, pictures, the input, output, record layouts and programs in which the data elements appear.

The function worksheet is the documentation of a problem area or subsystem. It specifies the input, output and processing needed to describe the problem or subsystem. Data included are name, identification code, volume, frequency, medium and source.

The essence of ARDI is organization. Real systems are quite

messy but systems analysis requires that a minimal ordering of data be attempted. ARDI provides one way of ordering the mass of relevant information and irrelevant data.

THE COMPUTER IN INFORMATION FLOWS

A computerized information system combines a large number of clerical tasks into one batch of computer runs. In a batch system the transactions are combined before submission to the run thus decoupling them from the random fluctuations of the environment. On the other hand, on-line real-time systems handle each transaction as it comes and are directly coupled to the environment.

The reduction in number of stages of processing in a computerized batch or real-time system makes the system more stable in relation to environmental change. This system stability may mean more and longer batch runs; however, with many applications run on the computer the fluctuations in the volume of transactions handled tend to balance out.

In an on-line system, the computer must serve to buffer the stochastic nature of the input. Thus, on-line systems are typically designed with considerable slack so that they are still operative in times of unexpectedly high transaction volume. The computer center with several different on-line applications finds that some of these applications tend to balance each other while others aggravate peak load situations.

Generally, the use of computers will increase the fixed costs of an organization and decrease the variable costs. Thus, the costs associated with input variability will be lower in computer-based systems. This ability to handle major increases in volume is one of the most important benefits of using a computer in the information flow of an application system.

DATA BASE SYSTEMS

The information flow of computer-based information systems has often been designed as in Figure 13.7. Systems like these work well in a relatively stable batch environment but are inappropriate in the less stable environment, and won't work at all in the on-line environment.

Systems that fit into the general mold of Figure 13.8 are appropriate for less stable environmental conditions and are necessary for

Batch System

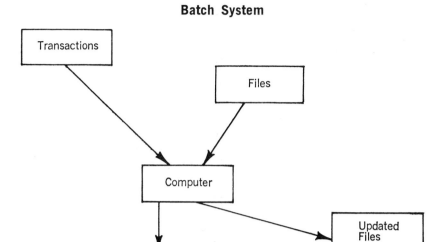

FIGURE 13.7

on-line conditions. Note the decoupling of the reports from the transactions in Figure 13.8. Here the decoupling is accomplished with a data base, making it possible to use generalized information retrieval and report preparation routines. A new changed report is quickly implemented. Systems such as those in Figure 13.7 are much more difficult to change. Thus, we have an example of one system in which decoupling or adding stages make the system more responsive to environmental change.

The gain in responsiveness from data base systems to some extent sacrifices efficiency. The recent rapid increases in computer speeds tend to minimize the efficiency losses and make data base systems more competitive. Generally, when using a moderate to large sized computer it is wise (at this writing) to use data base systems. The single step systems are more appropriate when using small computers simply because the data base handling software is not usually available with the small computer.

In a data base type of system the information flow analysis process is simplified. Figures 13.4 and 13.5 are then more adequate descriptions of the process and need not be combined as in Figure 13.6. The analysis focuses upon each data item, the potential use and the value of that item in the reports the users might request. Information flow is a secondary concern.

Transaction Based System

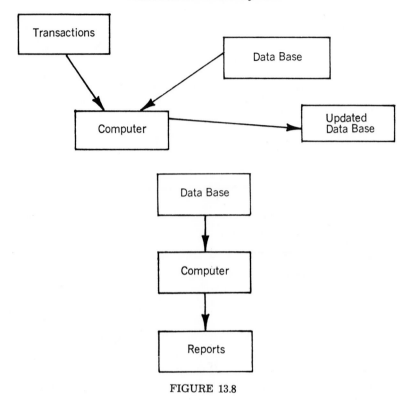

FIGURE 13.8

SUMMARY

This chapter presented the information matrix for displaying the information flows through a system. The information matrix is most useful in the analysis of non-data base systems.

The influence of ideas developed from industrial dynamics types of models was discussed. The experiments with these models were shown to suggest the effectiveness of the elegant and the single stage design.

Regardless of how complex the system is, there is a substantial need for displaying the information flow in the system proposal. Each system proposal should show the origins, flow and disposition of all data used in a system. Some of the analysis techniques used are flowcharts, decision tables, information matrices and narrative.

The following checklist from Hartman, (1968) is perhaps the

best summary of this chapter. If the information flows are well enough described so that the checklist can be answered, they are probably at least very good and perhaps excellent.

Information Flow Performance Checklist

Check on:	Examples of detail questions:
Timeliness	• Does any backlog of work exist?
	• Are personnel idle due to paper-processing delays?
	• Are reports produced too late to be of value to management?
	• Do reports come too late to permit operational feedback?
Accuracy	• Is too little or too much checking being performed?
	• Are too many corrective documents being prepared?
	• Are the figures or data presented too accurate for the intended purpose?
Usefulness	• Does the procedure provide the user with the information he requires?
	• Does the procedure contribute to profitability?
	• Does the procedure serve its intended purpose?
	• Is there an obviously better method?
	• If a computer is currently in use, does it support all functions or only a select few?
	• Does the information have decision-making value?
	• Are all copies of forms used?
	• Are exceptions or items requiring special attention buried in the normal procedures?
Efficiency	• Must a clerk look in many places to answer a question?
	• Could telephone sales, or mailing, be more economical (without substantial loss in effectiveness) than personal contacts?
	• Is information supplied too frequently on slow-moving items?

Necessity

- Is work being duplicated?
- Are different people performing tasks which because of basic similarities, could be combined advantageously?
- Are there reports which are prepared frequently but used only occasionally?

Completeness

- Are production problems, changes in customer buying habits, etc., reported?
- Is management provided with information which enables it to determine in advance the effect of decisions, or of such factors as increased sales and market campaigns, upon production facilities and inventories?

Reliability

- Does management trust the facts with which it is supplied, or does it initiate its own private investigations?
- Do sales and production forecasts reflect actual sales trends?

Responsibility

- Are responsibilities clearly defined for each decision process within the information flow?
- Are the boundaries of the responsibilities defined?

REVIEW QUESTIONS

1. Contrast the flow principles given with those of Chapter 8.
2. Chapter 11 recommends exception reports. Chapter 13 recommends having information flows with few exceptions. Are these recommendations contradictory? Explain.
3. Search the data processing literature for descriptions of five types of SDA equipment using different media.
4. Give three reasons why systems analysts use keypunches rather than SDA equipment.
5. Contrast the usefulness of flowcharts, BISAD, ARDI, and Decision Tables in describing information flows.

DISCUSSION QUESTIONS

1. In his book, *Up the Organization*, Robert Townsend recommends that when the chief executive officer leaves town someone else should take over. Discuss the effect of this on information flow.
2. Discuss how a systems analyst could decide which transactions and transaction attributes to include in a system being designed.
3. In a computer system to log and analyze the transactions from several on-line systems, discuss how each system could balance or aggravate peak load conditions.

BIBLIOGRAPHY

Forrester, Jay W., *Industrial Dynamics*, Cambridge, Mass.: MIT Press, 1961, 464 p.

Forrester, Jay W., *World Dynamics*, Cambridge, Mass: Wright-Allen Press, 1971.

Hartman, W., H. Matthes & A. Proeme, *Management Information Systems Handbook*, New York: McGraw Hill Book Company, 1968.

Langefors, Börge, *Theoretical Analysis of Information Systems*, Philadelphia, Penn.: Auerbach Publishers, 1973, 489 p.

Staff, *BISAD, Business Information Systems Analysis & Design*, Wellesley Hills, Mass.: Honeywell Information Systems, 1968.

Townsend, Robert, *Up the Organization*, Greenwich, Conn.: Fawcett, 1970.

CHAPTER 14

MODELING AND SIMULATION

An equation, a flowchart, an artist's drawing and an architect's model graphically represent a reality. Even the space modules in which astronauts train, although complete in every detail except propulsion systems, are merely three-dimensional models. Models represent a real entity.

The use of models in systems analysis is very helpful. They can be used to study the operation of a system without establishing the real system. Just as a student using a driver training simulator can learn driving practices without injuring himself, others or a vehicle, a systems model can anticipate events without disruption to the ongoing system. Also, certain events can be staged in a model which would rarely happen in an actual system operation. In a general sense, we can consider models as vehicles for experiments. Simulations are specific experiments using a model.

TYPES OF MODELS

Models can be described as *deterministic* or *stochastic*. Deterministic or fixed models provide only a single answer for a given set of input variables. Flowcharts and mathematical equations are deterministic. While corporations, as can be seen in Figure 14.1, are in reality stochastic, most of the models of the corporations to date have been deterministic. Stochastic or probabilistic models differ in that the models have generators creating variability in the model by using "random numbers." Models of the bank teller function or of airport landings are examples of stochastic models. The random number generators in these models generate customer or airplane arrivals in such a way that the model exhibits the same variability as that of the real world.

Models can also be classified as *continuous* or *discrete*. Discrete models can only take on integer values while the variables in continuous models can take on any *real* value within their range. Real value includes such numbers as 5, $\frac{1}{3}$, and pi, while the integers are 1, 2, 3, 4, etc. Continuous models are then useful for modeling certain analog, time series or dynamic phenomena. The major simulation language used for modeling continuous models is DYNAMO. DYNAMO was developed by Jay Forrester's Industrial Dynamics group at Massachusetts Institute of Technology. Discrete models will be discussed later under the GASP and GPSS families of simulation languages.

Stochastic Aspects of the Firm

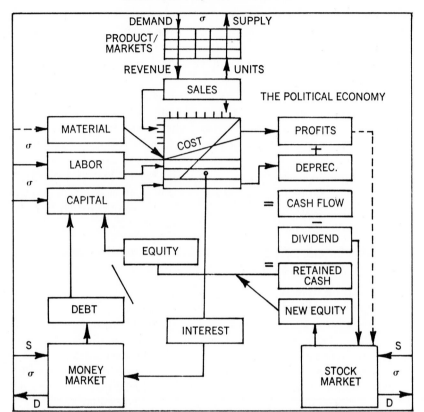

FIGURE 14.1

A third group is *computer systems simulation models* which are models of computer systems themselves and are useful in designing systems and selecting equipment.

Other Simulation Terminology

The variables used in a simulation which do not change or change only at prescribed times are called *parameters*. Variables which unpredictably change (stochastically) are called *system, state* or *endogenous* variables. The two types of variables have this meaning: *given* these parameters or conditions, *then* these states can occur.

At the beginning of a discrete simulation there are no entries in the queues (lines of events), placing the model in an unreal state. A number of events must be added to the simulation before the model is in a *steady state* condition. For purposes of analysis the analyst usually discards the pre-steady state results and works with the steady state ones. Simulation languages often provide instructions to aid in separating the two.

Example of a Model

One of the earliest models of a management system was of the finished goods transportation system for the Scott Paper Corporation. Rather than use linear programming techniques, Scott chose to develop a physical analog (an actual hydraulic network) of the system. By modifying the fluid pressures within the system to indicate demand, they could determine the changes in shipping patterns required. Increases or decreases in output were also easily simulated. However, it was difficult to simulate the best location for the Scott plant and warehouse. Location simulation is best accomplished with linear programming. Using linear programming techniques rather than analog, changes of all types can be easily simulated, but the solution for any particular simulation takes much more time, i.e., hours versus seconds.

ADVANTAGES OF MODELS AND SIMULATION

Where it is not feasible to experiment with a real system or where a real system rarely takes on the particular state one wants to analyze, it is appropriate to build a model and run simulations. The advantages of models are availability, low experiment cost, ability to simulate problems not subject to analytic solution and ability to simulate the consequences of rare events. The disadvantages of models are their simplification of the real system; they may not represent all of the relevant variables.

Simulation results are so well organized and presented by the simulation programs that the user becomes more interested in the presentation and the results than in the validity of a model. Both a valid and an invalid model have good-looking output. The old garbage in/garbage out warning is especially appropriate to simulation results.

MODELING AS A SYSTEMS INVESTIGATION TOOL

In a case history investigation of the operations of a clinic, the analyst decided that the system could be best described as a job shop scheduling system (Rockart, 1970). He then searched for the information needed to implement the model he had in mind. The results produced by the model were incomplete. A problem-oriented rather than model-oriented systems investigation would have resulted in a more complete analysis. However, the model-oriented investigation search was completed in less time than a normal systems analysis with less disruption of clinic personnel, but it reduced the employee's sense of participation in the project. The model-oriented approach gathered more detailed statistics on arrival rates and service times than would have been found in equal time devoted to a standard systems investigation.

This case history suggests that when the analyst is certain the situation being investigated fits a known model, and when search time is more important than participation, then a model-oriented search is appropriate.

Automated systems analysis and design techniques are being improved and may, in a few years, be available for general use. These techniques will make certain that all relevant information was gathered by the model. There will still be the need for human participation, resulting in some difficult behavioral problems associated with automated systems installations.

MODELING AS A SYSTEMS ANALYSIS TOOL

Models and simulation are used in the design of communications networks. In this situation the analyst gathers estimates of volumes to and from various points, prices the various levels of service between the points, and then uses this data in a model to simulate the best network.

In the selection of a computer, computer systems simulators are frequently used. The systems designers may use the simulator to get a proper combination for the central processing unit, disk drives, drums, high speed core, low speed core, channels, communications controllers and other peripheral devices. Computer systems simulators can produce a set of computer performance statistics for each design proposal. To make these estimates the simulation model must contain performance characteristics for each computer considered. SCERT and CASE are names of computer systems simulators on the market.

Many computer manufacturers use their own computer systems simulator to generate their proposals for prospective customers and the proposals they might expect the competitors to offer the customer. If the comparisons are unfavorable the manufacturer may decide not to present a bid for the contract.

After the order for a specific computer is placed the systems design group sometimes builds a simulator for that particular configuration to evaluate alternative designs. File accessing methods and trade-offs between storage media are two of the types of problems that are often simulated.

One of the statistics most examined in computer systems simulation output is the behavior of the queues. As discussed in Chapter 4, queue length and companion service time are important indicators of realtime systems performance. Therefore, it is normal to explore the performance of a proposed system using a range of simulations. This determines the *sensitivity* of the model.

SIMULATION LANGUAGES

Ira Kay (1972) classified some 38 simulation languages into three groups of families—GASP, GPSS and SIMSCRIPT. The authors of GASP type languages generally took an existing scientific language such as FORTRAN or ALGOL and appended simulation subroutines. Using these languages the programmer writes in the accustomed language calling on the subroutines for desired functions.

GPSS and similar languages use a flowchart to describe the model. Each block of the flowchart is represented by a function in the language. In the GPSS family the computer interprets the block design and produces an operational program. These languages generally provide excellent statistics, but usually use a substantial amount of computer core and time. The novice programmer can learn these languages quickly. A detailed description of GPSS is given in the next section.

The SIMSCRIPT family of languages provides syntax especially suited to the simulation task. These languages handle complex tasks with less computer core and time than the GPSS family.

The usefulness of each language to the systems analyst is relative to his experience and computer tasks. Many teachers of simulation techniques prefer GPSS languages because they can be taught quickly and the instructor can devote more time to the problem. However, simulation specialists prefer SIMSCRIPT because of its flexibility and sparing use of computing facilities.

GENERAL PURPOSE SIMULATION SYSTEM/360 (GPSS)

GPSS was developed by IBM. The version in this example was developed for the IBM 360 series of computers. GPSS has been implemented on many other computers and many similar computer languages are now available.

The language structure is essentially a flowchart processor. The simulation analyst writes a flowchart using GPSS symbols to represent each line of the program. Every flowchart symbol matches a line in the program.

GPSS is a discrete, transaction-oriented simulation language. The program instructions relate to the handling of individual transactions. The most used instructions have names such as Generate, Queue, Seize, Depart, Advance, Release, Start and Terminate. Figure 14.2 shows some of the block types available in GPSS/360 language. The letters A, B, C, etc., refer to parameters to be specified for that block.

Figures 14.3, 14.4, and 14.5 show examples of GPSS programs.

GPSS Instructions

Instruction	Use	Parameters
GENERATE	Brings transactions into existence	A. Mean intrarrival time B. Spread or function modifier
TERMINATE	Destroys transactions	A. Decrement to termination counter
SEIZE	Allows transaction to be processed by a facility	A. Number of the facility
RELEASE	Ends processing of a transaction by a facility	A. Number of the facility
ADVANCE	Corresponds to processing time	A. Mean holding time B. Spread or function modifier
QUEUE	Causes updating of waiting line statistics	A. Number of the line
DEPART	Stops accumulation of waiting time	A. Number of the line

Control Cards

START	Allows analyst to control duration of simulation	A. Initial value of termination counter
FUNCTION	Specifies attributes of any mathematical functions used	
STORAGE	Used to specify number of facilities available	

FIGURE 14.2

A Simple One-Pump Gasoline Station Model

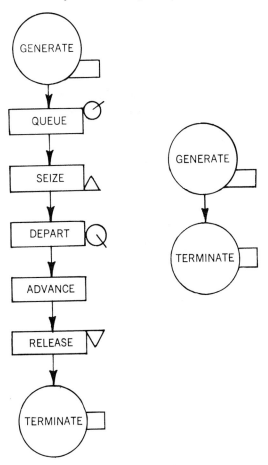

FIGURE 14.3

MODEL VALIDATION

As indicated earlier, a model is almost always a simplification of the real world including only a few variables involved in a given system. The value of the model is then dependent upon the importance of the chosen variables. One of the ways the information systems analyst might learn which variables are most important is to use multiple regression analysis. By regressing all of the variables against some performance measurement, the important variables will be found and the model built to contain only those. In practice, however, one rarely has enough data to use regression analysis.

Models must be validated. The normal validation procedure is to

Flowchart for GPSS

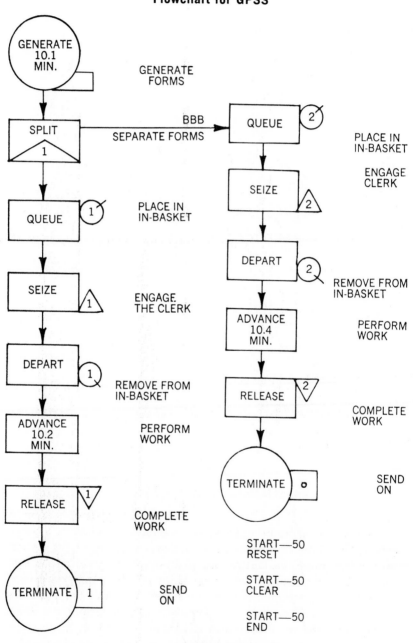

FIGURE 14.4

Statistics for GPSS

QUEUE	MAXIMUM CONTENTS	AVERAGE CONTENTS	TOTAL ENTRIES	ZERO ENTRIES	PERCENT ZEROS	AVERAGE TIME/TRANS	$ AVERAGE TIME/TRANS	CURRENT CONTENTS
1	2	.717	52	1	1.9	7.192	7.333	2
2	2	.575	52	6	11.5	5.769	6.521	2

$ AVERAGE TIME/TRANS = AVERAGE TIME/TRANS EXCLUDING ZERO ENTRIES

FACILITY	AVERAGE UTILIZATION	NUMBER ENTRIES	AVERAGE TIME/TRAN	SEIZING TRANS. NO.	PREEMPTING TRANS. NO.
1	.979	50	10.319		
2	.967	50	10.199	9	

FACILITY	AVERAGE UTILIZATION	NUMBER ENTRIES	AVERAGE TIME/TRAN	SEIZING TRANS. NO.	PREEMPTING TRANS. NO.
1	1.000	50	9.959		
2	.987	50	9.839	9	

QUEUE	MAXIMUM CONTENTS	AVERAGE CONTENTS	TOTAL ENTRIES	ZERO ENTRIES	PERCENT ZEROS	AVERAGE TIME/TRANS	$ AVERAGE TIME/TRANS	CURRENT CONTENTS
1	3	1.652	51		.0	16.137	16.137	1
2	3	1.331	51	3	5.8	13.000	13.812	2

$ AVERAGE TIME/TRANS = AVERAGE TIME/TRANS EXCLUDING ZERO ENTRIES

FACILITY	AVERAGE UTILIZATION	NUMBER ENTRIES	AVERAGE TIME/TRAN	SEIZING TRANS. NO.	PREEMPTING TRANS. NO.
1	.982	50	10.239		
2	.965	50	10.059	3	

QUEUE	MAXIMUM CONTENTS	AVERAGE CONTENTS	TOTAL ENTRIES	ZERO ENTRIES	PERCENT ZEROS	AVERAGE TIME/TRANS	$ AVERAGE TIME/TRANS	CURRENT CONTENTS
1	2	.717	52	1	1.9	7.192	7.333	2
2	2	.575	52	6	11.5	5.769	6.521	2

$ AVERAGE TIME/TRANS = AVERAGE TIME/TRANS EXCLUDING ZERO ENTRIES

FIGURE 14.5

collect data for each of the simulated variables, run a simulation with these data, and then compare the simulated results with the actual performance indicators of the systems. Since performance is almost always multi-dimensional, and the mathematical formulae for multi-criteria models are not well developed, simulation techniques are often preferred.

Stochastic simulations should be checked to be certain that the random numbers chosen have the appropriate statistical qualities. The digits of numbers chosen should fit a uniform distribution. A chi-squared test can be used to verify this. The chi-squared test is used to measure the extent of the difference between observed frequencies and those frequencies expected from the assumed distribution.

The numbers should also be checked to eliminate any auto-correlation. Correlation measures the extent to which two variables vary together. For example, the correlation between father's and son's IQs is about .50; between identical twins' IQs about .90; and between a male's height and his IQ about .10. Auto-correlation measures the relationships between values in a series and subsequent values. For numbers in a series to be random the auto-correlation should be zero. Since random numbers are often used to pick points from another distribution, those selected points can be compared with the expected distribution, again using the chi-squared test.

In many queuing models the various queue statistics can be calculated using formulae shown in Chapter 4. These calculated values should be checked statistically against the values obtained in the experiment.

These are just a few of the tests that can be used to validate a simulation. More complete validation testing is to be found in Naylor's (1966) book.

CRITERIA FOR USE OF SIMULATION

The best reason for using simulation techniques is the inability to get solutions any other way. Problems that can be stated mathematically and yet not solved mathematically are excellent candidates for simulation. Systems which have known solutions are poor candidates. Thus simulation is a technique of last resort.

Simulation is, however, more than a way to solve intractable problems. It is also a way of conducting experiments apart from the real world. If we wish to study the effects of particular war strategies, it is more appropriate to experiment in simulation than to wage war. It may be more expedient to simulate chemical experiments involving highly volatile materials than to actually use them. Similarly, rather than disrupt an organization with experimental systems it is more appropriate to simulate them.

As a note of caution to the proponents of simulation, simulation results (regardless of how impressive) must be treated cautiously until they are tested in the real world.

SUMMARY

Modeling and simulation have been shown to be important tools for information systems investigation, analysis and design. While simulation can be overdone, it is an indispensible tool of the systems analyst. Perhaps with simulation more than with any other information systems tool, the user must be extremely careful to state the assumptions, carefully describe the included variables and validate the entire process.

REVIEW QUESTIONS

1. Define the terms:
   Stochastic model   Endogenous variable
   Deterministic model   Steady state
   Parameter   Sensitivity
   Model   Random number
2. What significance are queues in a simulation model?
3. Which simulation language would you expect to have the most use? Why?
4. Draw a GPSS flowchart of a one-chair barber shop.
5. Draw a GPSS flowchart of a two-chair barber shop.
6. Why is simulation useful in computer selection?

DISCUSSION QUESTIONS

1. Discuss the advantage of digital and analog models.
2. Discuss the problems in keeping a simulator of computer systems up-to-date.
3. Survey computer centers to determine what simulation languages are used, how extensively they are used and for what applications.

BIBLIOGRAPHY

Aiso, M., "Forecasting Techniques" *IBM Systems Journal*, Vol. 12, No. 2, 1973.

Anthony, Ted F. & Hugh J. Watson, "Probabilistic Financial Planning" *Journal of Systems Management*, Vol. 23, No. 9, September 1972.

Anthony, A. L. & H. K. Watson, "Techniques for Developing Analytic Models" *IBM Systems Journal*, Vol. 11, No. 4, 1972.

Boodman, David M., "Profit Prophets: Computer Based Planning Models for Managers" *Data Processing Magazine*, Vol. 13, No. 9, Winter 1971.

Boulden, James B., "A Systems Approach to Corporate Modeling" *Journal of Systems Management*, Vol. 24, No. 6, June 1973.

Canning, Richard G., "Using Corporate Models" *EDP Analyzer*, Vol. 9, No. 1, January 1971.

Dzielinski, B. P., "A Guide to Financial Planning Tools and Techniques" *IBM Systems Journal*, Vol. 12, No. 2, 1973.

Emery, James C., "Decision Models" *Datamation*, September 1, 1970 and September 15, 1970.

Forrester, Jay W., *World Dynamics*, Cambridge, Mass: Wright-Allen Press, 1971.

Highland, Harold Joseph, "A Taxonomy of Models" *Simuletter*, Vol. 4, No. 2, January 1973.

Kay, Ira M., "An Over-the-shoulder Look at Discrete Simulation Languages" *Simuletter*, Vol. 3, No. 3, March, 1972.

Kingston, P. L., "Concepts of Financial Models" *IBM Systems Journal*, Vol. 12, No. 2, 1973.

McDougall, M. H., "Computer System Simulation: An Introduction" *Computing Surveys*, Vol. 2, No. 3, September 1970.

Nance, Richard E., "Towards a Unifying Structure for Discrete Event Simulation" *Simuletter*, Vol. 3, No. 2, January 1972.

Naylor, T. H., J. L. Balintfy, D. S. Burdick & K. Chu, *Computer Simulation Techniques*, New York: Wiley, 1966.

Poliski, Iris, "Improving the Odds in the Business Gamble" *Business Automation*, Vol. 17, No. 8, August 1970.

Pomerantz, Allan G., "Predict Your Systems Future: Use Simulation's Crystal Ball" *Computer Decisions*, Vol. 2, No. 6, June 1970.

Rechtschaffen, R. N., "Queueing Simulation Using a Random Number Generator" *IBM Systems Journal*, Vol. 11, No. 3, 1972.

Rockart, John F., "Model Based Systems Analysis: A Methodology and Case Study" *Industrial Management Review*, Vol. 11, No. 2, Winter 1970.

Schriber, Thomas J., *Simulation Using GPSS* New York: Wiley, 1974.

Stults, Fred C., "Data, Information and Decision-Making" *Journal of Systems Management*, Vol. 22, No. 6, June 1971.

Willoughby, T. C. et al., "University Student Registration Systems Design Using Simulation" *Journal of Educational Data Processing*, Vol. 7, No. 4, 1970.

Wyman, Forrest Paul, *Simulation Modeling: A Guide to Using SIMSCRIPT*, New York: Wiley, 1970.

CHAPTER 15

THE SYSTEMS PROPOSAL

The systems proposal is the report to the Steering Committee, or other responsible manager or group of managers, recommending that a particular system be designed and installed. The report must satisfy good report writing principles. The format of the report is the same as that of the preliminary report described in Chapter 6:

> Introduction
> Summary of Findings
> Summary of Recommendations
> Details of Findings
> Proposed Systems Design
> Economic Impact Details
> Acknowledgments
> Appendices

Perhaps the best way to describe a systems proposal is to include one in the text and then to criticize it. The report that follows is a report to management. It was written as a case for presentation at a conference of economists and information systems specialists. For the purpose it was written, it is a very good report. For a report which the management of an organization might use to make a decision, it has some deficiencies. The report was written by W. E. Hanna, Jr. of the U.S. Social Security Administration, and is reprinted with permission. The criticisms follow the report.

A SYSTEMS PROPOSAL

Background

As our own national data system began building massive files of socio-economic data on the population, it became a tool of economists and social researchers.

Those interested in these data include not only our own research staff and many private students but also large numbers from the academic and economic world. These data files are available for their studies but only under carefully controlled conditions. Never is a personal name or identifying number made available in connection with the social or economic data gathered from the files. Thus the privacy of the citizen is carefully preserved while the researcher is still not denied his legitimate need for statistical data to study.

This use of the social security data has grown by leaps and bounds over the years. As we become more conscious of social trends and the welfare environment of the nation, the numbers of researchers increase and the demands for statistical data grows.

Early in our development we found that the statistical uses of our data were a particular concern and could be accommodated more effectively if separated from our operational data processing stream. Accordingly, a special function was established to provide statistical services on a nationwide basis. This statistical unit does not simply release the data but provides a computer service to process the data tailored to the particular requirements of the user. We provide complete services to the extent of developing special reports, tables and analyses to fit the user's special needs.

Although we had a separate functional organization to provide these statistical services, the data processing was still performed on our central computing equipment and competed for computer time. Coupled with this conflict was the ever-present need to provide computer time for program development and testing. As time progressed these special workloads increased faster than our equipment acquisition. This forced us into contracting out much of our statistical data processing.

In 1968 these several problems prompted us to embark on a study to seek a solution to our equipment capacity dilemma that provided a more cost effective operation than buying services to meet our customers' needs.

We believe it to be of value to recount for others our own experiences in the conduct of this analysis and economic study to improve our statistical services operations.

Non-productive Workload Study

OBJECTIVE—To study non-productive workloads, and identify statistical service workloads, program development workloads and applications of the time-shared computer workloads. Also, the study analyzed these several workloads, their impact on production operations in the central computer complex and developed cost/benefit factors. Further, the study was to make appropriate recommendations to improve processing effectiveness and eliminate deteriorating impact on regular production operations.

APPROACH AND ANALYTICAL TECHNIQUES—It was decided to study these problems in three parts. First, production processing of both the large-scale and medium-scale workloads in the central computer processes was analyzed to determine possible volumes of future workloads and the characteristics of these workloads. Second, the programs development process was studied to determine standards and techniques which could be applied to improve programmer production and to provide more rapid responses to their request for data. Third, the general requirements for time-shared computer access by research personnel were analyzed in terms of both expected volumes and type of machine capacities needed.

Data were collected about the production process in two general ways. A complete picture of current machine utilization was obtained by analyzing the logs of all statistical services computer operations. This log is produced from the console log sets prepared by the computer operator during each run and includes such data as run identification, run type, data, system, start time and stop time. There were 84,000 entries representing all of statistical services processing for three months which were analyzed to illuminate such factors as average run times, frequency distribution by type of run and by day and distribution of runs by project. Along with analysis of current operations statistics were accumulated to provide an historical picture in large-scale and medium-scale utilization since the beginning of 1967. The historical data was obtained from monthly reports on machine utilization from the central computer complex operations since 1966 which included a breakdown of machine time between production and program development uses.

Data about the program development process were obtained through analysis of the computer log described above, by collecting the history of statistical services staffing and through conducting several studies concerning the programming staff. This determined numbers and types of programs being developed, program tests, turnaround times, frequency distribution of program development and machine requirements by time of day.

Time-shared access to the computer was also studied by in-depth analysis of operating reports and interview discussions with user offices concerning their requirements. Other government agencies were also consulted to gain the benefit of their experience in time-sharing computer operations. From operational records in-depth analysis was made of contract time-share operations with the several computer services contractors being employed. Charts 1 and 2 provide data which resulted from a study of time-sharing contractor operations and illustrate the depth of the analysis undertaken. Chart 3 converts this data to cost information to be later used as a part of the overall cost/benefit determination.

CURRENT OPERATIONS—Considerable time and effort was devoted to studying the current operations. The following is an abbreviated explanation of the operations as they are today using the central computer facility for production operations, statistical,

Contractor No. 1

Period	User A			User B			User C			Total		
	Term Hours	CPU Sec	Save** Storage	Term Hours	CPU Sec	Save** Storage	Term Hours	CPU Sec	Save** Storage	Term Hours	CPU Sec	Save** Storage
Jan.	28.4	7,321	64	44.3	3,190	20	20.1	1,545	2	92.8	12,056	86
Feb.	13.5	1,828	30	27.4	2,093	13	32.7	4,461	5	73.6	8,382	48
March	23.0	5,201	39	14.7	1,009	13	30.0	10,072	2	67.7	16,282	54
April	9.2	2,171	43	9.1	602	17	6.5	462	3	24.8	3,235	63
May	9.1	794	11	20.6	2,067	16	3.8	271	5	33.5	3,132	32
June	2.3	275	41	11.0	838	11	11.1	1,159	5	24.4	2,272	57
July	9.2	1,112	14	26.3	1,779	14	5.8	587	3	41.3	3,478	31
Aug.	22.7	1,576	21	15.0	1,374	13	—	—	2	37.7	2,950	36
Sept.	1.5	190.2	21	5.2	342.1	12	—	—	2	6.7	532.3	35
Oct.	1.5	154.2	11	4.1	293.2	11	—	—	2	5.6	447.4	24
Nov.	.9	148.4	6	7.5	956.3	9	.2	3.3	2	8.6	1,108	17
Dec.	.4	CR* 20.8	6	3.2	CR* 357.7	12	—	—	2	3.6	378.5	20
Total	121.7	20,790.6	307	188.4	14,901.3	161	110.2	18,560.3	35	420.3	54,252.2	503

*Computer Response Unit does not accurately reflect CPU seconds.
**Up to 1536 characters = 1 storage unit

CHART 1

Contractor 1702

Period	User A			User B			User C			Total		
	Term Hours	CPU Mins	Save** Storage	Term Hours	CPU Mins	Save** Storage	Term Hours	CPU Mins	Save** Storage	Term Hours	CPU Mins	Save** Storage
Jan.	5.1	*	6	90.8	*	18	1.7	*	1	97.6	*	25
Feb.	4.0	—	4	88.7	—	25	19.3	—	4	112.0	—	33
March	18.1	—	7	57.1	—	31	5.5	—	1	80.7	—	39
April	31.8	—	8	29.0	—	34	82.3	—	9	143.1	—	51
May	16.5	—	6	15.6	—	9	4.9	—	10	37.0	—	25
June	13.0	—	10	26.1	—	29	1.5	—	9	40.6	—	48
July	65.9	—	39	42.3	—	36	4.0	—	14	112.2	—	89
Aug.	18.5	—	38	86.3	—	62	14.3	—	33	119.1	—	133
Sept.	15.78	—	45	89.73	—	90	1.4	—	14	106.91	—	149
Oct.	25.9	—	54	82.6	—	144	15.0	—	43	123.5	—	241
Nov.	21.5	17.5	64	77.7	62.1	137	18.9	7.7	65	118.1	87.3	266
Dec.	18.1	12.3	92	55.2	39.7	192	44.3	19.6	123	117.6	71.6	407
Total	254.18	29.8	373	741.13	101.8	807	213.1	27.3	326	1,208.41	158.9	1,506

*Contractor did not charge for CPU minutes separately until November 1968.
**1024 characters = 1 storage unit

CHART 2

Funds Allocated to Time Sharing
FY 1969

	OR-OA	ORS	OACT	BDI	BDOO	Total
Begin FY						
Contractor No. 1	5,000	12,000	—	6,000	2,700	25,700
Contractor No. 2	3,500	8,000	250	1,000	—	12,750
Contractor No. 3	2,000	20,000	—	2,500	—	24,500
Total	10,500	40,000	250	9,500	2,700	62,950
End FY						
Contractor No. 1	5,000	4,859	—	200	7.50	10,066.50
Contractor No. 2	3,500	8,000	250	1,000	—	12,750
Contractor No. 3	2,000	91,500	750	8,300	2,692.50	105,242.50
Total	10,500	104,359	1,000	9,500	2,700	128,059
Increase	None	+64,359	+750	None	None	+65,109

CHART 3

and other computer services. The statistical services produce the statistical and management data required for the research and management functions of the Social Security Administration. This is accomplished by processing the social security master files through many and complex information retrieval operations. Also, the statistical services organization provides the same statistical function for "outside" customers. For these outside customers a cost reimbursement arrangement is negotiated to defray the cost of operations in the government agency.

Individual requests for data are established as projects. Each project requires the writing of several computer programs and scheduling of computer operations for program testing and production of the reports. During one quarter in the year 1968, 150 of these projects were in a stage requiring machine utilization for program development and/or production.

Machine and personnel resources required each month for the completion of these projects include approximately 1,300 large-scale computing hours, 1,300 medium-scale computer hours and 19,000 programming man-hours. Chart 4 depicts the growth of computer hours over the years 1966 to 1968. Assuming the same trends, we predict a continuing growth shown by the dashed lines. Chart 5 is the same presentation for the growth of programmer staff interposed over the computer production hours per month. Here also an extension of the general growth trend predicts considerable increased requirements for programmer staff as well as computer production time. Based on previous growth patterns machine requirements for production alone can be expected to reach 1,400 large-scale and 1,400 medium-scale hours per month by the end of 1971. These projections are indicated on Chart 6 which is a tabulation of computer hours per month by year and our projections are given a probability rating which will enable us to make a considered conservative estimate by using reasonable probability levels.

It has been considered in our investigation that machine efficiency in the central computer complex is decreasing because statistical operations are processed on the same equipment configuration as are the normal social security data file maintenance operations. With only one computer complex to serve several processes we perforce have configured the equipment to serve the social security production requirements and special statistical runs historically have been forced to run on the configuration as established. Although statistical operations processes the same data files as are processed by the file maintenance, the machine requirements differ considerably from those found most efficient for our normal social security system.

Statistical operations are usually short, one-time runs characterized by extensive computation, low input-output channel utilization, flexible file structure and the use of generalized program packages, while file maintenance operations generally are repetitive long running programs which make maximum use of machine input/output facilities to process massive sequential files. The table in Chart 7 compares the several computer runs and provides some estimates of the percentage of total run-time required by the different types of runs. Table B on the same chart gives an indication of the length of time occupied by various production runs.

A reference to Chart 5 reveals that the growth pattern in programming man-hours since 1967 has been the same as the growth pattern for machine utilization, i.e. programmer productivity in development man-hours per machine production hour has remained constant. Unless change occurs in programmer productivity the net programming man-hour requirement can be expected to reach 80,000 man-hours per quarter by the end of 1971. This is an unacceptable trend and changes must be sought to improve programmer productivity. An increase in program productivity can be obtained through modular programming in high-level language such as COBOL provided that machine facilities for rapid compilation and debugging are available. Currently a statistical services programmer works on five programs concurrently and has 2.3 programs in the testing stage at any one time. Chart 8 provides some statistics found as a result of analysis of these programming factors and also indicates the magnitude of problems in monthly man-hours and cost. Machine facilities now available to the programmer provide an average of only 3 test sessions per week. This in turn causes each project to remain in the test stage, an average of 5.1 weeks. It appears that remote terminal facilities which would permit an average of two sessions per day per programmer would reduce project turnaround time to 1.5 weeks and reduce current net programming man-hours requirements up to 3,700 hours per month.

Most of the time-shared computer access operations are obtained by a contract arrangement with outside time-share contractors. Cost of these terminals is expected to reach $250,000 during the year of 1970. The instant batch terminal in one of our central office buildings is the primary center of the time-sharing activity. The personnel who use these facilities express a preference for the instant batch mode of operation. Teletype terminals average two hours per day use while the instant batch terminals are saturated. The research organization within the Social Security Administration has a strong requirement for expanded time-sharing facility for their problem-solving activities. The potential researchers using time-sharing within the central office complex number about 400 including statisticians, actuaries, economists, and management analysts. In addition, requirements are rapidly emerging from both management and research groups for access through remote terminals to on-line data bases in such areas as continuous sampling, personnel, inventory control, finances and management information. Requirements for specific on-line capacity are not yet fixed but can be expected to include large volume direct access capacity and on-line software support for data storage and retrieval.

Conclusions

Significant economies can be obtained through providing statistical services with a computer system designed specifically for information retrieval in a job shop environment. An analysis of operations of other installations shows that a machine environment designed specifically for the information retrieval function can produce a multi-programming ratio in the neighborhood of 3 to 1. Such ratios are not obtainable in a machine environment optimized for file

Computer Utilization Growth

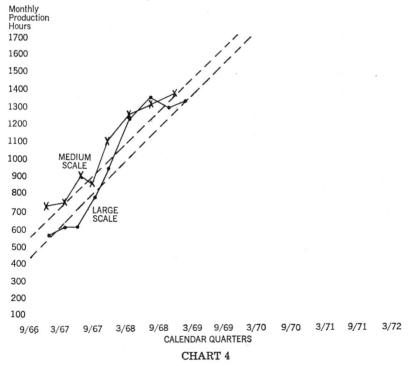

CHART 4

maintenance operations as in our complex. The growth in the demand for the data provided by statistical services indicates that an information retrieval system can produce a significant saving equivalent to at least one large-scale system.

Many user costs can be reduced by providing the capability for quick turnaround testing and compiling through remote terminals. Use of remote terminals on program development will permit a minimum of a 10% increase in programmer productivity and will reduce the average time required to complete individual statistical projects by about one month. See Chart 9. Since program development is a major cost element the productivity increase should provide savings of $25,000 to $50,000 per month in the first year of the proposed time-sharing systems operation. Additional savings will be realized due to the reduced waiting time of users.

Outside time-sharing terminal costs can be eliminated by providing in-house time-sharing savings. Contract costs for low volume instant batch terminals average about $3,100 a month while an in-house equivalent facility would cost less than $2,000 a month. In addition an in-house system would provide expanded facilities capable of

Production and Staff Growth Curves

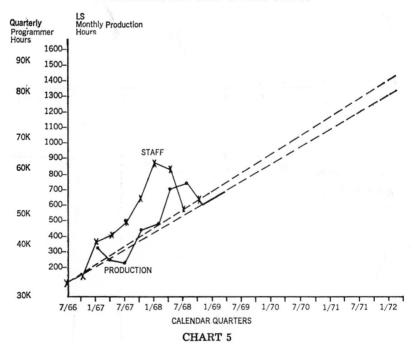

CHART 5

Projected Growth
Production Workload—Hours Per Month
(Fiscal Years)
Large Scale
360/65

Probability	1971	1972	1973	1974	1975
.0	900	1600	2300	2900	3400
.5	600	1200	1800	2300	2600
1.0	300	800	1300	1700	1900

7080

Probability	1971	1972	1973	1974	1975
.5	800	500	200	0	0

Total Large Scale

Probability	1971	1972	1973	1974	1975
.0	1700	2100	2500	2900	3400
.5	1400	1700	2000	2300	2600
1.0	1100	1300	1500	1700	1900

Medium Scale

Probability	1971	1972	1973	1974	1975
.0	1700	2100	2500	2900	3400
.5	1400	1700	2000	2300	2600
1.0	1100	1300	1500	1700	1900

CHART 6

Workload Characteristics

A. Types of Large-Scale System Production Runs

Tabling	41.6%
Sort, no added programming	8.4%
Sort with added programming	23.7%
Update Master	5.8%
Consistency Edit	2.8%
Reformat and/or Code	13.5%
Select	4.2%

B. Distribution of Production Runs by Percentage of Chargeable Time

1 to 10 minutes	3.47%
11 to 30 minutes	11.95%
31 to 60 minutes	16.12%
61 to 90 minutes	12.67%
91 to 120 minutes	15.50%
2 to 3 hours	15.41%
3 to 4 hours	8.10%
4 to 6 hours	8.87%
6 to 8 hours	3.62%
8 to 10 hours	1.76%
Over 10 hours	2.42%

CHART 7

providing researchers with computer access for problem solving. It is estimated that approximately $250,000 per year presently allocated for contract time-sharing services can be eliminated.

The tables shown on Charts 10-12 summarize the cost factors of the existing in-house system which is today attempting to provide computer functions for both production and statistical services. These charts also show the operating cost of the proposed time-sharing system on a monthly basis. The cost/benefit comparison between the two states indicate a monthly savings in the year 1971 of over $50,000.

Program Development Man-Hour Costs Summary
12/68 Quarter

1.	Monthly development man-hours	18,992.
2.	Monthly man-hour costs	$ 262,709.
3.	Concurrent programs per programmer	5.0
4.	Concurrent programs tested per programmer	2.3
5.	Turnaround time per test (hour)	23.2
6.	Projects in test status during quarter	150.0
7.	Programmers per project	1.12
8.	Concurrent programs tested per project	2.5
9.	Weekly development runs per project	3.36
10.	Quarterly development runs per project	43.0
11.	Equivalent serial development runs per project	17.2
12.	Total test turnaround per project (weeks)	5.1

CHART 8

Proposed Time-Sharing System
Program Development Objectives

Weekly test per programmer	10.0
Turnaround time per test (hour)	1 to 3
Total daily development runs	500.0
Average LS time per run (minute)	5.0
Average MS time per run (minutes)	—
Weekly test per project	11.2
Test turnaround per project	1.5 weeks
Reduction in non-productive man-hours per project	73.6
Monthly man-hour savings (12/68 quarter)	3,680.0
Monthly man-hour cost reduction	$50,710.0
Percentage increase in programmer productivity	19.4%[1]

[1] This is conservatively referred to in this study as a "minimum of 10%".

CHART 9

Current SS Operations Monthly Cost Summary

Current In-House System	1969	1971	1975
360/65 monthly production	$ 5,482.	$ 64,748.	$251,240.
360/65 monthly program development	20,556.	125,620.	216,980.
Total current LS cost	$26,038.	$194,368.	$468,220.
Multi-programming reduction	—	−129,579.	312,147.
Adjusted LS cost	$26,038.	$64,789.	$156,073.
MS production	19,222.	29,810.	46,070.
MS program development	18,292.	31,165.	47,425.
Total current MS cost	$37,514.	$60,975.	$93,495.
Multi-programming reduction	—	−40,650.	62,330.
Adjusted MS cost	$37,514.	$20,325.	$31,165.
360/65 cost	26,038.	64,789.	156,073.
MS cost	37,514.	+20,325.	31,165.
Total in-house system cost	$63,552.	$85,114.	$187,238.
Contract Time-Shared Services			
Program development man-hour cost	$262,709.	$372,035.	$550,255.
Outside terminal cost	10,000.	20,000.	20,000.
Total current systems cost	$336,261.	$477,149.	$757,493.

CHART 10

Proposed Time-Sharing System Monthly Cost Summary

Time-Sharing System	1971	1975
Hardware rental (new dedicated computer)	$ 62,400.	$150,800.
Amortized training	9,186.	9,186.
Systems programming	10,105.	18,189.
Recompile cost	6,917.	—
Operator cost	15,638.	26,139.
Total proposed systems cost	$104,246.	$204,314.
Reduced program development man-hour cost	$297,628.	$440,204.
ORS outside terminal cost	0.	—
Total proposed operational cost	$401,874.	$644,518.
Unabsorbed LS production	$34,260.	$ —
Unabsorbed MS production	29,810.	—
Total unabsorbed production	$64,070.	$ —
Multi-programming reduction	42,714.	—
Adjusted unabsorbed production	$21,356.	$ —
Total operational cost	$401,874.	$644,518.
Unabsorbed production cost	21,356.	—
Total time-sharing system cost	$423,230.	$644,518.

CHART 11

Cost/Benefit Comparison
Current Systems vs Time-Sharing System

	1971	1975
Current system	$477,149	$757,493
SSA time-sharing system	$423,230	$644,518
Monthly net savings	$ 53,919	$112,975

CHART 12

Recommendations

To satisfy the production, program development and the time-sharing requirements of statistical services the SSA should acquire a computer system tailored for and dedicated to operation in an on-line, job shop service and information retrieval environment. The system should provide for programming in COBOL and FORTRAN so as to minimize conversion problems with other systems. Great emphasis should be placed on expansibility and flexibility. The system should initially emphasize program development and time-sharing so as to facilitate conversion to the new system. A phased conversion of all operations from existing systems to the new environment should be undertaken over a five year period to minimize implementation problems.

CRITICISMS OF THE SYSTEMS PROPOSAL

ORDER OF PRESENTATION

The order of the case presented here is:

> Introduction
> Detailed findings
> Summary of findings
> Recommendations

This contrasts with the recommended order that would place the detailed findings at the end of the report. The basic reasons for this arrangement in the report are first, the busy executive would find it necessary to read the entire report to find out why the report was written and his time is well worth saving. Also, in practice, many will not be able to stand the suspense and will look ahead to the recommendations. Second, by presenting the findings and recommendations early, the reader who reads the entire report is led to consider whether the detailed evidence supports the findings and recommendations. The reader can focus upon the critical assumptions and evidence.

In the report presented, there are several assumptions that are critical to the conclusions and recommendations. One is the assumption of continued linear growth in computer utilization and programming staff. A top-level executive with budget responsibility in the computer area may very well agree with this growth as a probable fact. However that executive may have no plans to increase either hardware or staff, due to a budget crunch. Note that the projection of programming man-hours in the report was said to be unacceptable. There are then some pressures in the Social Security Administration to control the growth of programming, even though the constraints are not made explicit in the case.

It is known that order of presentation of information (Senn, 1974) can make a difference in the decision. Since the report writer usually has a bias in favor of the point of view presented, it is important for the writer to use the best order. While the evidence is not available for this example, it is believed that this order results in more favorable decisions.

FORM OF PRESENTATIONS

The systems proposal example made liberal use of figures and tables in the presentation. The writer assumed that figures and tables communicate better than text but this has not been found to be true. Text combined with figures and tables communicates better than prose alone. The best strategy is to carefully explain the figures and tabular material in the text portion of the report.

Examination of the case reveals that the text explaining the tables is quite thin. For example, Chart 1 is only referred to as "data from a time-sharing study." Chart 9 particularly needs further explanation since the relationships among the data are not obvious. The source of the "reduction in non-productive man-hours per project" datum is especially opaque.

BENEFITS OF DATA PROCESSING

The benefits possible from a new information system are many and varied. The best published list of benefits was done by Couger (1971) and is reprinted below:

1. *Lower costs.*
   a. Reduction in clerical operations.
   b. Savings in space required for personnel, desks, and files.
   c. Reduction in redundant files.
   d. Reduction in duplication of operations.
   e. Detection of problems before they become costly.

      f. Reduction in the routine, clerical elements in high caliber jobs.

      g. Reduction in amount of paperwork by utilizing exception principle.

      h. Reduction in inventory.

      i. Combination of like functions in several departments.

2. *Faster reaction.*

      a. Improved ability to react to changing external conditions.

      b. Larger reservoir of information for producing realistic operating plans and forecasting market conditions.

      c. Closer monitoring of operations and utilization of feedback principle to produce corrective actions.

      d. Assessing impact of problems of one area on the other activities of the firm.

      e. Faster turnaround time for processing jobs due to less clerical activity.

      f. Ability to compare alternative courses of action more comprehensively and rapidly.

3. *Improved accuracy.*

      a. Mechanization of operations, permitting more checks and less error possibilities.

      b. Sharing of information between files, reducing the errors resulting from manual intervention.

      c. Ability to raise confidence limits on activities due to more information for measuring performance and more information to permit more accurate forecasts.

      d. Integrity of information maintained through improved validation techniques.

4. *Improved information for management.*

      a. Higher quality information through feasibility to employ management science techniques.

      b. Capability to utilize management-by-exception principle to a greater extent.

      c. Capability of developing simulation models for inclusion of all factors in forecasting and developing alternative management plans.

      d. Improved performance indicators through more quantitative data and faster response on performance of all functions.

EVALUATION OF COSTS AND BENEFITS

The numbers in a systems proposal generally describe the costs and the benefits of the system proposed. The benefits must exceed the costs to justify the proposal. If not, a verbal or short, written report disposes of the project.

In Chapter 6 some of the hazards of ROI calculations are suggested, including the human propensity to make the figures tell the story from the project team's viewpoint. Often the temptation is to exaggerate estimates. The stress of this section is on calculating the defensible benefits and costs.

Clerical cost reduction is a frequent benefit in a systems proposal. While clerical cost reductions are among the easiest benefits to measure, they also present some problems.

First, the rates of pay can be a problem. Wherever possible, it is preferable to use a specific rate for each grade level. This rate may be the mid-point, maximum or some other point in the salary range for the grade. The point to be used is dependent upon corporate policy in progressing people through the salary range. One advantage of this policy is that specific salaries need not be sought by the analyst nor disclosed in the report. Use of a standard rate makes the proposed savings independent of the particular people involved. Thus, the groups staffed by long-time employees are just as easy or hard to automate as groups staffed by trainees.

Second, fringe benefits should be included. The usual method is to apply a percentage to the clerical costs or savings for the fringe benefits.

Third is the partial people problem. Let us assume that a project saves ½ of job A, ⅓ of job B, all of job C, ⅔ of job D and ½ of job E in Department Alpha and ½ of a job each in Departments Beta and Gamma. The proportions save a total of four jobs but only one of those jobs is completely eliminated and reasonably certain to be saved. The others may be subject to the Parkinson idea that "Work expands to fill up the time available." None of the jobs should be considered as eliminated unless the supervisor responsible agrees to operate without the person after the change. In the example above, the reduction in Department Alpha totaled three persons. It shouldn't be too difficult to combine job A with E, and B with D, to allow a reduction of three jobs in the department. The jobs in Department Beta and Gamma are a more difficult problem. Department Alpha is more involved and probably more supportive of the system gains. Beta and Gamma are on the periphery and may view the change as a nuisance. Thus, they may not agree with the analyst's conclusion that the change is equivalent to ½ a person. Even if they agree, how do they cut ½ person from the payroll? Some of the ways in which a net reduction may occur in the partial person situation are:

1. The department has had some slack and feels that it can cut one person. This happy event is unexpected but does happen occasionally. When it does, the analyst has a delicate ethical problem of whether to claim a systems gain of ½ person or one person.
2. Work can be transferred from department Beta to Gamma or some equivalent change that allows the reduction of a full person.
3. The analyst's reporting chain of command may be to the superior of Department Beta's supervisor. This communication link has been known to induce the supervisor to cooperate.

Without one of these or some other way of making a real payroll reduction, the analyst should be very reluctant to claim dollar savings. The benefit, however, should at least be claimed in the other unquantified benefits.

Reduction in assets used in the system, such as receivables or physical assets, are a somewhat easier problem to evaluate. We multiply the assets reduced by the long-term cost of capital for the organization. If the change were a short-range one, perhaps the current rate on short-term loans might be more appropriate. For longer range projects, the capital saved must be presumed to come partly from equity and partly from debt. Thus, the cost of capital would appear to be the most appropriate measurement.

Inventory reductions do result in a reduction in assets with the attendant benefit. Inventory reductions also result in lower materials handling costs, lower property taxes, lower obsolescence and lower inventory management costs. Inventory reductions often occur in corporate savings proposals, so it is quite common to have a standard percentage used for all inventory reductions. Depending upon the specific situation in the organization, the standard savings rate may range from 15% to 30% of the reduction. The most important variables in setting the savings rate are cost of capital and obsolescence.

Increases in sales are frequently proposed as benefits of new systems. A new salesman's call report system or an airline reservation system are examples. In the short-range perhaps a rate based upon revenues less cost of goods sold would give the appropriate measurement. For most projects, it is preferable to use the percentage of profit before taxes for that product line.

Forecasts and projections have to be made in the evaluation proposals. The accuracy of forecasting is such an important issue that some warnings about their use should be made. First, the accuracy of any forecast diminishes with time. A forecast of corporate sales for five years will be less accurate than a forecast for one year.

Some forecasts are more accurate than others. For example, the forecast of kindergarten school population for the next five years is more accurate than a forecast for ten years because the latter involves unborn children.

The forecast of computer hours and costs (Chart 10) for 1971 is more accurate than the 1975 forecast because of computer technology changes, federal economic restraints and other influences that create change. A technique often used to temper forecasting errors is shown in Chart 6, with optimistic, pessimistic and most likely forecasts. Ideally, these three forecasts are then carried through the rest of the evaluation.

The diminishing of future returns, because of the discounting that is used in return on investment calculations, does reduce the influence of forecasting errors. For example, the fifth year returns are discounted by 62% when discounted at a 20% rate.

Is the proposed change necessary? It is common for the project team to find that of the total improvements possible, many, perhaps half or more, could be accomplished by fine tuning the present system rather than supplanting it with a new system. The project team should claim as benefits only those improvements beyond those attainable through fine tuning the current system. Analysts will claim that the fine tuning would not be done without their intervention. There is some justification for that view, since often there is acceptance of radical change but not minor change.

An estimate of the improvements possible with alternate designs should be a part of the proposal. For example, a proposal was made to install leased telephone lines between a general office and manufacturing facilities for the acquisition of sales statistics. The figures in the proposal looked like this:

		Monthly Costs
Current Costs—Telephone Toll Calls		$6,000.
Less proposed costs:		
Leased Lines	$5,000	
Transmission Equipment	$1,000	$6,000.
	Net Gain	None

The careful reader will note that the firm could have saved $1,000 per month by just changing all telephone toll calls to the leased line. The data collection system was then costing $1,000/month.

Measurement of benefits. Of the 23 benefits suggested by Couger, only four are readily measurable. This is a normal situation. Some organizations such as the Department of Defense are reported to not consider those benefits that are not quantified. Thus, we need methods for measuring those items not easily measured.

A substantial portion of the unmeasured items can be measured if the analyst is resourceful. Couger's item 3a "improve accuracy by mechanization of operations" may reduce waste or reruns or some other measured item. A proposed change of duties by a foreman can be measured by before and after surveys. The change can then be valued according to the relative contribution of each duty toward the accomplishment of organizational objectives.

Information is quite difficult to value. There are many occasions when information in the economic sense is priceless. For example, the *Harvard Business Review* is reputed to have learned that their subscription list is relatively insensitive to price. That is, increases in subscription price reduce subscribers only slightly, and decreases in price also increase subscribers only slightly. The information in the magazine is, then, in the economic sense, priceless. The reader cannot predict the value before the magazine arrives. It is the same with a large segment of business information. The value of a report may be nil for years but suddenly a significant result may give it immense value.

One method of measurement proposed by Churchman (1968) is to take a group of measured and unmeasured benefits and rank them; if an unmeasured benefit is ranked between two measured benefits, an estimate of its value can be made.

It is generally good practice for the Steering Committee to rely primarily upon the measured benefits in projects. A way one company handles the deserving unmeasured benefits is to arbitrarily allocate 10% of the budget to such items. In this way, projects heavy in unmeasured benefits compete among themselves rather than with the measured benefits.

Should the claims for the benefits be conservative or liberal? Exaggerated claims cast suspicion upon the entire report and ultraconservative estimates are often increased in the minds of those evaluating the project. The best policy is to keep all benefit claims to a reasonable ground.

BENEFIT EVALUATION

The benefit evaluation shown in this case is missing several important items: the project development costs, details of the calculations required for checking, justification of workload increases, impact of the change upon the existing computer configuration, equipment obsolescence, use of the optimistic and pessimistic forecasts in subsequent calculations and no discount of future benefits. Each of these items is discussed below.

Project development costs are only partially shown in Chart 11 as Amortized Training and Recompile costs. The computer installation costs, costs related to the time spent by the project team, and similar items are not shown. The Steering Committee needs to know the amount of change resources involved in the project to determine how much of that resource has been committed.

Details of the calculations are not shown, making it impossible to check the accuracy of the calculations with the data shown. (This specific case was prepared for presentation at a conference, and the pages in the conference proceedings limited the details the author was able to show. Thus, this criticism is unfair since this report was prepared for a different use. However, the limitations add to the value for instructional purposes since the deficiencies are so evident to the student.)

Justification of the programming workload increases are not indicated. This proposal assumes that the additional requests for information must be met. The benefits involved in each request may or may not justify the use of the programming staff on the project. The key question is whether the additional workload needs to be undertaken.

The impact of the change upon the present computer configuration is shown to some extent in Chart 11 as Unabsorbed Production Cost. We would expect that the IBM 360/65 was justified over using several smaller machines at least in part by the statistical jobs proposed for transfer. Is a large computer still justified or would smaller machines be more cost effective? What would be the cost of converting from the present equipment to smaller computers?

The possibility of increasing the productivity of the present computer by increasing core storage, drum storage, channels or disks was not compared to the new machine proposed.

Equipment obsolescence is not mentioned in the report. A new generation of computers is announced every five years. The IBM 370 computers introduced in 1970 were more cost effective than the 360 models and should have been considered in the forecast. What happens if a future computer generation has 150% greater capacity and sells for the price of the 360/65?

The optimistic and pessimistic forecasts were not carried through to the subsequent analysis. This gives the decision maker little idea of the sensitivity of the situation. Is there any real possibility of handling even the low volume with the present equipment? If this is true, the case for the proposal becomes a very strong one.

Discounting future benefits and costs was not done in the report. The significance of a flow of costs and benefits covering several years is not readily apparent without discounting.

COST PRESENTATION

It will be noted in Charts 10 and 11 that some of the items shown are net figures of the current and the proposed system. It is better to show the complete before and after costs of each department involved. It would have been easy to show both costs in this example as they were accumulated during the study. One reason for doing this is management's familiarity with the present cost and budget reports. Using the same items as are in the budget facilitates an easy comparison. Otherwise management will consider the unorthodox report with suspicion.

Also, systems proposals are sometimes audited, and auditors are paid to be suspicious. If a report balances with known figures, the normal suspicions are quickly allayed. Otherwise, a searching investigation will occur. Even the best proposals have some figures that are more defensible than others. There seems little point in deliberately increasing the number of debatable items.

SUMMARY

A systems proposal was presented and criticized against a background of preferred standards. The principles involved are these: First, the proposal is an attempt to persuade and should be organized in the way it best accomplishes that purpose. Second, the report is one of the few parts of the analyst's work that many people in responsible positions will see, so for personal career enhancement the analyst should do this job well. Third, the proposal is really that of the user and must carry his signature or endorsement if the benefits are to have a maximum chance of occurring. Finally, the proposal must be defensible. Resistance to change is strong enough to motivate someone to search the report for any weak or unsupported data or arguments. If any weak links are found, the entire chain of argument is threatened.

REVIEW QUESTION

The Arbitrage Company has recently installed a new accounts receivable system that reduced the receivables by $1,000,000. The earnings of the company are $3.00, the dividend is $1.50, the current interest rate charged on short-term loans is 8%, the stock is priced at $36, the capital is 70% equity and 30% debt, and several acquisitions have been made in the last five years, usually at about ten times earnings. What annual benefits should the analyst claim for the reduction in receivables?

BIBLIOGRAPHY

Churchman, C. West, *The Systems Approach,* New York: Dell Publishing Company, 1968.

Couger, J. Daniel, "Benefits of Data Processing," *Journal of Systems Management,* Vol. 22 No. 11, November 1971 p. 34.

Hanna, W. E., Jr., "A Case Study in Procurement," A paper presented at the 1974 Economics of Informatics Conference.

Senn, James A. and Gary W. Dickson, "Information System Structure and Purchasing Effectiveness," *Journal of Purchasing and Materials Management,* Vol. 10, No. 3, August 1974.

part **IV**

Systems Design

This Part describes how the analyst starts with an approved proposal and ends with systems design specifications. In between, we will describe some important tools used during the design phase. They include file and data base design, forms and report design, procedure writing and hardware and software selection. Certainly, many of the tools previously described are also useful during this phase.

Systems design is still largely an art. The task is to develop a system to meet the objectives of the project at the lowest cost. It is important here that the analyst subject all parts of the proposed system to rigorous cost analysis and justification. Adding "desirable" features to a good system can turn it into a bad one. A hard-headed "show me" attitude is very appropriate for the analyst to adopt at this stage. The system is going to be evaluated by management before implementation is approved, and audited by auditors after implementation. Self-protection is the least important, but it and pride in one's work are sufficient reasons for designing good systems.

CHAPTER 16

FILE AND DATA BASE DESIGN

The human mind, like office files, retains everything but not everything can be recalled. Some of the typical office resources are:

Telephone book
Appointment calendar
Calling cards of salesmen
List of frequently used telephone numbers
List of office employees
Customer list
Vendor list
Purchase orders
Customer orders
Correspondence files

Some of these resources are well-organized for response to inquiries and some are not. If the customer list were organized by name, it would be easy to use for retrieval if one had the name, but hard if one had only the customer number. Likewise, if the calling cards of salesmen were in order by firm, a search by firm would be facilitated but a search by salesman's name would be difficult.

Files are necessary when a transaction is handled and neither the transaction nor the memory of the person handling the transaction contains adequate information. To help them search out the reason for a customer complaint, many mail order houses have to request that complaints include the shipping documents which were sent with the order. Complaints accompanied by such documentation need no file search for additional information. However, if the mail order house had retained the shipping documents in a file, then the receipt of a complaint would only require the retrieval of the shipping documents from the file. As simple as this solution seems, files are costly to maintain for the small percentage of complaints received. Files should be eliminated if possible, and many businesses tend to retain too much material.

DEFINITIONS AND STRUCTURES

The fixed length of each record in Figure 16.1 is 79 characters. If one wanted to find the balance of a particular customer and had only the customer's name, that field or key could be searched to locate the record. If the file had two customers with the same name, the search would produce two records. These are called synonyms. Another code or customer number would be required to distinguish

FILING TERMINOLOGY

Character—A number or letter.

Field—One or more characters that in total serve as a description of an entity. In an accounting transaction the account number, units and amount are three fields.

Record—All of the fields considered relevant in relation to a particular entity. A complete accounting transaction, a telephone directory listing, employee applications, and inventory summaries are records.

File—A file is a collection of related records. In a computer system, a file is called a *data set*.

Data Base—A data base is a collection of related data sets. A Data Base Management System manages a data base.

Key—A key is typically a field or several fields in a record that is used to identify the record in processing the file.

Record Length—This is the number of characters in the word structure of a particular computer that describes one record. The record length may be *fixed* (all the same) or it may be *variable* (all may be different).

Logical Record—This is the total of the characters (fixed or variable) used to describe one record.

Physical Record—This refers to the amount of data handled by the data processor as a single entity. In magnetic tape systems, physical records are separated by interrecord gaps.

Blocking Factor—This denotes the number of logical records in each physical record.

A Simplified Accounts Receivable File of Fixed Record Length

Characters	Description
5	Customer's number
20	Customer's name
20	Customer's street address
15	Customer's city
2	Customer's state
5	Customer's ZIP code
6	Balance
6	Credit limit
79 TOTAL	

FIGURE 16.1

between the two records. An important reason for assigning codes is to make fields mutually exclusive, eliminating synonyms.

Codes and identifiers also reduce *sort time*. A sort arranges the records in order (ascending, descending, alphabetical) in relation to a key. The length of time required to sort a file is to some extent a function of the number of characters in the key.

An Accounts Receivable File of Variable Record Lengths

Characters	Description
3	Record length
5	Customer's number
20	Customer's name
20	Customer's street address
15	Customer's city
2	Customer's state
5	Customer's ZIP code
5*	Invoice number
6*	Invoice date
6*	Invoice amount

*Variable number of these elements

FIGURE 16.2

The record shown in Figure 16.2 has a fixed *segment* and a variable number of additional fixed length segments.

Another example of a file containing variable length records could be the following:

Characters	Description
2	Field code
Variable	Field data

The field code would identify the number of characters to follow before reading another field code.

The key to a file in Figure 16.2 is not a function of the file itself but a function of the particular search being made. For example, to find all customers in a specific ZIP code, the key would be the ZIP code.

A processor reading a variable length record needs a signal to indicate the end of the record. This can be accomplished by a *record length field* or an *end of record indicator*. The record length field specifies the number of characters in the record and is often the first field of the record. It must be updated whenever the record is changed. In Figure 16.2, if the file contained two invoices, the file length would be 104 characters and be increased 17 more for a third invoice to 121 characters.

The end-of-record indicator is a special character at the end of the record. The programmer uses the special character instruction to modify the processing stream when this method of indicating record length is used.

CLASSIFICATION OF FILES

Files have been classified in four different ways: (1) Contents; (2) Mode of processing; (3) Mode of access and storage; and (4) Hardware device. How files may be classified in these four ways will be described. The organization of this section follows that of Clifton (1969).

Classification by Contents

The contents of files may be *transactions, transition data, master data, parameters, codes, output* or *logs.*

Transaction data in an inventory system would include such items as receipts, withdrawals, customer orders, purchase orders, new stock numbers and revisions to the data in the file. The transaction file contains a record for each event that occurred during a particular time period. The records in the file usually relate to a single system, i.e., payroll, sales analysis, etc.

The contents of the file are most useful in the updating of the master file; however, transaction files are usually kept through a complete audit cycle so that the tax and external auditors can verify the accuracy of the updating process. Many systems aggregate the transactions rather quickly in processing them. Every system requires periodic changes to the codes for sales territories, departments and other groups. To facilitate such changes it is necessary to keep the source transactions available.

Transition data is transaction data that has undergone some editing, sorting, or expansion into the multiple transactions needed to update particular files. This data is transitory in nature and need not be kept for long periods. It is usually organized to facilitate the update of the appropriate master files.

Master data files are the permanent files of each system. They reflect the current status of the system. Some important master files are the payroll, customer, inventory, accounts receivable, parts and stockholder files. Master files are subject to activities abnormal for other files. A file is *updated* if the transactions are processed against the file and the information in the file is modified as a result of the process. In this way, the master file represents the state of the system within the limitations of the *updating cycle.* Payroll files may have a weekly update cycle, sales analysis a monthly cycle, etc.

Master files are frequently *referenced.* This process is a direct analogy to the *information retrieval* operation in a library. Where a book search involves the use of an author, title or subject card index, by using the code on the index card the book can be located on the shelf. Master customer files are referenced by customer name or number which identifies the storage location to be accessed.

The transactions in an updating run or the references in a reference run access some or all of the records in a file. The proportion of records accessed is the *hit rate* or *activity rate*. This rate is useful in choosing the filing device (tape, disk or other) and the storage and indexing systems.

The *volatility* of a file is measured by the proportion of records that are changed in a given period. A Social Security name file would be much less volatile than a Social Security address file.

The hit rate focuses upon transactions per run while volatility refers to transactions per period. Thus, it is easily possible to have low hit rates and high volatility and the reverse.

Parameter files are files of data that remain constant for a particular run of a program. For example, a payroll program will have the following parameters:

> Social Security tax rate
> Social Security earnings limit
> Federal income tax table
> State income tax rates and limits
> Hospital insurance premium rates
> Life insurance premium rates
> Union dues rates
> Check date
> Payroll dates

When these parameter files are kept separate from the programs, the necessity to recompile payroll programs for each run is reduced.

Code files are similar to parameter files in that they also serve to reduce the frequency of recompiling. Code files also provide the information associated with a particular code. A price file would store price codes and prices; a state file would have state codes, state abbreviations, and state names; a ZIP code file would have ZIP codes, cities and states.

Output files are created during a run and are usually quickly used to print reports or provide off-line retrievals.

Logs are used in on-line systems to record all of the transactions done by the central processor. If several systems are being processed by the computer, then the log has a mixture of transactions relating to all of the implemented systems. In some systems, the log is used to verify each day that the on-line updates were made correctly. The log always serves as a backup source should an emergency occur. Having a file for a specific time plus the log of all transactions since that time, an operator can recreate a file if it becomes necessary. The log is then a normal security arrangement for on-line systems. The log also serves as the audit trail so necessary to the proper control of an information system.

Classification by Processing Mode

The four processing modes that will be discussed are: (1) input, (2) output, (3) reconstruction, and (4) overlay.

Input mode. Data is input from the file into the primary (core) storage unit of the computer. Transaction files are usually read in the input mode and the input mode is used in the creation of a new file.

Output mode. Data is output from core storage to the file. Report files and dumps are examples of the use of the output mode.

Reconstruction mode. This is the primary mode used with magnetic tapes. A master tape record is read in, a transaction is processed against it and a new record is written on a new master tape. In this way, the old master is preserved as a security measure and as an audit trail.

Overlay mode. Some records are read in, changed by transactions and written back into the same location, overlaying the original information. While there are a few magnetic tape and other devices that can be used in this manner, disks are the primary medium.

Reconstruction and overlay are the primary modes of updating master files. It will be noted that the overlay mode is particularly valuable when the hit rate is low. However, the security of a file updated using overlay must be assured by using logs and dumps or copying the file.

Classification by Access and Storage Method

There is a tendency to mix the way in which files are stored and the methods used to access information in the files. Records may be stored serially, sequentially or by the address of a location on a storage device.

Serial storage is typified by the records of transactions on paper tape or a log. Records are stored in the order of time. Thus, to find a record, one must start at the beginning and examine each record until it is found.

Sequential storage is storage in a logical sequence usually ascending order of a key. The file of outstanding checks might be kept on tape in ascending order of check number. Storage devices such as tapes are used mostly for sequential storage. Disks may be used for sequential storage but are most often used for other storage methods.

Random storage files are stored on a device that has an address for each storage location. There is then a predictable relationship between the key of the record and the address of the storage location.

The result is that there is no necessary order in which the file is stored. An on-line credit authorization system might make good use of random storage.

Classification by Hardware Device

Some of the hardware devices used to store files are: magnetic core, magnetic drum, magnetic tape, fixed and removable disks, and magnetic cards. These devices vary greatly in cost, access time, and transfer rates.

Magnetic tape storage devices have both advantages and disadvantages for storage. The number of characters capable of being stored on a single tape is large. A record of 200 characters, blocked ten, stored on 1600 bpi tape with a ¾" inter-record gap, is capable of storing nearly 28,800,000 characters on a 2400 foot tape and the entire tape can be read in a few minutes. Access to any single record is not easy because the entire tape may have to be read to get at the desired record. The cost of the tape itself is quite low, making a library of tapes economical.

Some files are too large to fit on a single tape reel and require multi-reel files. This causes some computer operation problems and adds complexity to the input and output modules of the program.

Figure 16.3 shows the normal method used to update tape files. For this system to work, the transactions and the master tape must be in the same order; thus sorting is often a significant factor in using tape files. There are several methods of sorting that minimize the time or resources needed. In many computer installations the systems analyst will have a choice of packaged sorting programs. This will typically include techniques such as two-way merge, cascade, polyphase and oscillating. The techniques vary in number of secondary storage units used, core used for build-up of strings, and complexity of the program. The effectiveness of the sorting technique is then a function of the computer configuration available for the system being implemented. In a multi-programming environment the effectiveness of a particular sort is also dependent upon the resources needed by the competing programs. Ideally, the choice of sorts should be made by the computer operating system in a multi-programming environment. The operating system would base the decision upon parameters specified by the programmer and competing resource requests.

Tape files can be protected against loss by keeping the previous generation tape. In Figure 16.3, the new tape can be backed up by keeping the previous master and the transaction tapes. Security is further discussed in Chapter 30.

Disk storage devices have both advantages and disadvantages. The access to an individual record is quick and the transfer rate is rapid, but the cost per unit of storage is higher than for tape, but lower than a drum. The higher cost per unit of storage for disks should be weighed against the reduction of processing time in retrieving selected records.

Updating a Master Tape File

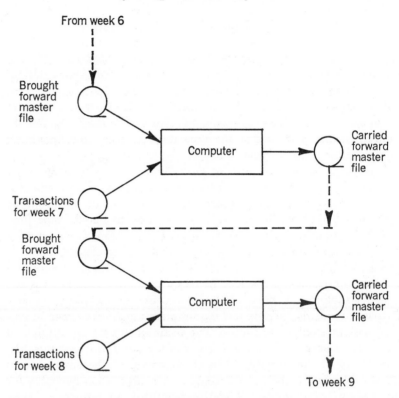

FIGURE 16.3

The ability to access individual records makes it possible to consider several different file access arrangements. This flexibility can give the systems designer many options that would not otherwise be available.

ACCESS AND RETRIEVAL METHODS

Serial Access—This is one of the least useful methods since there is no organization of the file. In using such files, the analyst must usually reorganize the file into some more useful arrangement. In one exceptional case, a file of product numbers and prices is read into core as a table. Table lookups can be minimized if the most active product numbers are at the top of the table. This type of file is a serial file.

Sequential Access—A sequential file is in a logical order of the file key. It could be in alphabetic order by name or numeric order of codes. Each record in a sequential file has a predecessor and a successor, making these two records easily accessed. When a sequential file is stored in random storage files (such as core or disk) it is possible to program other than sequential searches. The binary search technique in which the file is repeatedly halved until the record is found is one such method. Note that while a sequential file has an order in relation to a key, it has no specific order and thus is serial in relation to other fields of the record.

Sequential files are most useful when the records are usually searched for using a key or when the hit rate is high. Individual payroll records are usually kept in sequential files so they can be updated each pay period.

On the other hand, personnel file updates involve a low hit rate and often require searches in fields such as department, skills, etc. Personnel files are not usually organized sequentially unless they are combined with the payroll file.

Random Access—In one payroll program there was a need to store certain totals such as union dues, credit union deductions, hospital and surgical insurance. The program stored 70 totals in locations 3901 to 3990. It was possible to add a payroll deduction code to a partial instruction and get an instruction that added the deduction taken from an employee to the total. In this illustration, the file of deductions taken was a random file; the filing device was addressable and there was a predictable relationship between the key and the storage address, i.e., the key + 3900 = storage address. Some locations were unused with ninety locations reserved for only seventy records.

The storage of larger records in peripheral devices is similar in concept to the above example. A section of the direct access device is reserved for a particular file. A section of the storage with N addresses will have M records (M is generally less than N). The keys to the file will be many more than just 1 to M. It is common to construct employee numbers by using only one number in ten. Product codes are often even more widely dispersed through the range of acceptable numbers. One task of accessing a record in a random access file is to construct a way of reducing the M keys to numbers in a range from 1 to N. To do this, select a prime number between M and N, divide the key by the prime and use the remainder as the *search argument*. This process results in some keys that have identical search arguments (synonyms). The normal practice is to provide an overflow area at the end of the file (between prime and M) and to use that area for the synonyms that develop. The address of the relocated record is stored in the record found with the search argument. Using this method, a *chain* or *list* is developed. The search argument is at the head of the list with the other elements of the chain added as needed to store the synonyms.

Since the search time to read a storage location in a direct access file can be substantial, it is helpful if there are few synonyms and few searches occur along the chain. Experience indicates that files loaded less than 80% have few problems while files loaded over 90% have many problems.

Another method of developing a search argument from a key is to square the key and use as many digits as needed from the middle of the squared number. The best search argument develops few synonyms and few unused arguments and requires the least calculation time on the central processing unit. The best search argument for one file may not be good for another. As in the sequential file, a search using any field except the key is not effective.

Indexed Sequential Access—The indexed sequential access method provides a way of accessing both sequentially and randomly. The records are usually stored sequentially to limit the search times between accesses. These files are subject to additions and deletions which are handled by chaining or by putting a *pointer* in each record to indicate the next record in the sequence. The random access to an individual record is usually accomplished with one or more levels of indexes. The index gives the location of certain records in the file and saves search time because one can choose the closest index location as a starting point.

In practice, computer installations with disks use more index sequential files than any other because of their ability to handle both updates and inquiries with reasonable effectiveness.

List Structures—An example of the application of a list structure is the inventory file. An inventory file often contains data regarding the outstanding product purchase orders. In other file arrangements these are variable length files which require more complex retrieval and which must be updated from both the inventory and purchasing systems. By putting a pointer in the inventory file, one can locate the beginning of a list of the outstanding purchase orders and make the inventory file of fixed length. In this way, one can get independent files that can be interrogated by another system. The obvious gains are offset by the storage required for pointers and a fairly slow retrieval time for some cases.

Lists can be constructed as rings and can be organized for bi-directional searches when such techniques are appropriate.

Generally the use of lists requires the storage of indexes which are pointers to the required records. Note that with lists it is now possible to search for information using something other than the record key. For example, in a personnel file, one might store in the index the record for one person in Department 55 and have that record point to another item. This list, when traversed, would locate all of the records of the Department and would be more efficient than searching the entire file. The cost would be the added pointers associated with each field in the record on which searches were expected.

Inverted Files—The extreme list structure is the inverted file which has a list length of one. The index contains the address of each record associated with the datum. If the searcher wants to count only the number of people in Department 55, this can be done by counting the index. If one wanted all people of age 47 in Department 55, he would use the logical operation AND on the Department 55 and age 47 indexes.

Such responses require a large and complex indexing structure. The index may well occupy more storage than the file. In constructing the index, one would use substantial amounts of computer time. Changes to the file would also require large amounts of computer time to process. Inverted files work well for stable files that have irregular inquiries of unanticipated form.

CONSIDERATIONS IN FILE STRUCTURE CHOICE

Many of the considerations in the choice of the most appropriate file storage medium and structure have been mentioned earlier. Some of the major considerations relate to:

> Hit Rate
> Cost of Media
> Volume of Data
> Frequency of Change of Data
> Frequency of Inquiry Using the Key
> Other Inquiries
> Security

Hit Rate—Sequential files have a very small seek time between records, but each record must be read. Random files have a longer

seek time, but irrelevant reads can be skipped. The break point between the two considerations is a function largely of the characteristics of the computer and its peripherals. It can be a function of
the file also. If an extreme Paretian distribution should exist, such
as 90% of the activity occurring on 10% of the items, the systems
analyst would divide the file and consider the two hit rates separately. The solution might well be an index to a fast access sequential portion of the file with the remainder of the file being accessed
randomly.

Cost of Media—Certainly tapes cost less than disks and removable
disks less than fixed disks. The substantial variation that exists must
be considered in the total cost of a proposed system.

Volume of Data—The cost per unit of storage needs to be multiplied by the volume of data to determine the total cost of the operation of each proposed file design.

The several media have substantial breaks in their cost curves.
The breaks occur at the point where more storage units are used.
The cost curve is described in Figure 16.4. It is certainly possible
to have a volume of data that hits at a high point on the cost curve
for one medium but at a low point on another curve. This consideration is important only for the dominant file in an installation.
Smaller files will normally be forced into the pattern that fits the
major file.

Some of the access methods work well on small files but less well
on large ones. Inverted files have been shown to be most competitive for smaller files.

Frequency of Change of Data—Complex file structures tend to
require substantial amounts of computer time to make file updates.
Large volumes of changes favor sequential files while storage with
few changes favors inverted files. Substantial change activity affects
random access files by increasing the hit rate and by increasing the
frequency with which synonyms occur. When a large number of
synonyms exist, the file must be reorganized.

Frequency of Inquiry Using the Key—The frequency of inquiry
and the value of the information obtained from each inquiry are important in deciding whether inquiry facility should be provided.
The occasional inquiry can be answered from a sequential file.
However, the response time for sequential files is minutes compared
to a fraction of a second for random access files. The cost is high
for each inquiry from a sequential file. If there is a volume of inquiries, it pays to index the file. One alternative to providing access
to the file is to print the master on paper or microfilm.

The very frequently-referred-to-file should be put on a drum or

File Storage Cost Curve

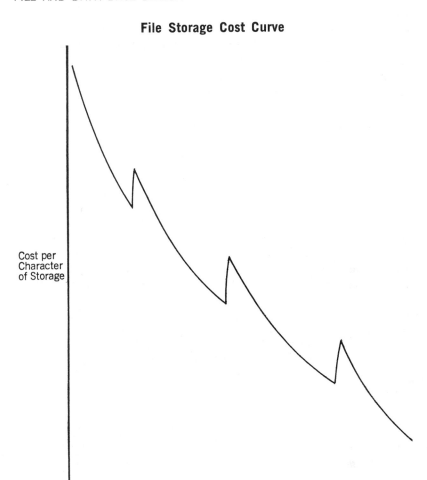

Cost per
Character
of Storage

Amount of Storage

FIGURE 16.4

in core rather than on a disk. Access time and transfer rates can dictate the use of the more responsive files.

Other Inquiries—Inquiries using the key can be effectively answered from random or indexed sequential files. Inquiries using a different field or a combination of fields cannot be answered the same way. If complex inquiries need rapid responses, then a list or inverted file may be appropriate. If overnight turnaround is adequate then batching the inquiries for a nightly run against a sequential file is likely to be a more cost effective solution unless the file is very large or the hit rate very low.

Security—Reconstruction files and overlay files require different procedures to bring them back up after a system failure. Both can be protected at the same level of security.

O⊖line files have different security problems than those that are only accessible during a batch run. If security is an important consideration, the files should be located on tape or removable disks. Security considerations are further discussed in Chapter 30.

SUMMARY

File, data set and data base design is a very complex subject. One can expect computer science researchers to be exploring the subject for as long as computer science exists. In this chapter we have given definitions of some of the terms used. The focus then turned to the variables that the systems analyst considers in making a choice of a file arrangement for an application. Our conclusion is that there is no one best file organization. The best choice is a function of least hit rate, cost of media, volume of data, frequency of change of data, inquiry frequency using the key, inquiry frequency using other descriptors and security needs.

REVIEW QUESTIONS

1. A personnel record contains, among other data, the complete educational history, job history, and salary history of each employee. Should these records be fixed or variable? Why?
2. Assume that the above personnel record is to be placed on disk. Does that change the recommendation?
3. Assume that the above personnel record is to be accessed randomly. Does that fact change your recommendation?
4. How many characters could be stored on a 1600 bpi 2400 foot tape with a physical record length of 10,000 characters?
5. Using any currently available tape and disk, what is the break-even hit rate between random and sequential organization for a 1000 character file with 20 percent synonyms?

DISCUSSION QUESTIONS

1. Discuss how you would flowchart a system to secure an overlay file containing log files and dumps.
2. Discuss the advantages and disadvantages of an inventory system designed so that the stock number was the disk address.
3. A vendor uses a census file to illustrate the advantages of an inverted file. Is this a good example? Why or why not?
4. Discuss the statement: "Given the many different data base structuring methods, no one method can handle the universe of applications satisfactorily."
5. Answer the following statement: "Many people feel that current data base approach requires entirely too much knowledge on the part of the user in terms of how the data base should be constructed and how the information should be accessed. One simply need specify the data he wants and not how it should be retrieved."

BIBLIOGRAPHY

Bachman, Charles W., "Integrated Data Store" *DPMA Quarterly*, Vol. 1, January 1965.

Bachman, Charles W., "The Evaluation of Storage Structures" *Communications of the ACM*, Vol. 15, No. 7, July 1972.

Bachman, Charles W., "The Programmer as Navigator" *Communications of the ACM*, Vol. 16, No. 11, November 1973.

Cahill, John J., "A Dictionary/Directory Method for Building a Common MIS Data Base" *Journal of Systems Management*, Vol. 21, No. 11, November 1970.

Canaday, R. H., et al., "A Back-End Computer for Data Base Management" *Communications of the ACM*, Vol. 17, No. 10, October 1974.

Canning, Richard G., (Ed.) "The Cautions Route to a Data Base" *EDP Analyzer*, Vol. 11, No. 6, June 1973.

Canning, Richard G. (Ed.), "Problem Areas in Data Management" *EDP Analyzer*, Vol. 12, No. 3, March 1974.

Canning, Richard G., (Ed.) "What's Happening with Codasyl-Type DBMS?" *EDP Analyzer*, Vol. 12, No. 10, October 1974.

Cardenas, Alfonso F., "Evaluation and Selection of File Organization—A Model and System" *Communications of the ACM*, Vol. 16, No. 9, September 1973.

Charles, William R., "Some Systems Shouldn't Use Chained File Techniques!" *Data Management*, September 1973, Vol. 11, No. 9.

Clifton, H. D., *Systems Analysis for Business Data Processing*, Princeton, NJ: Auerbach Publishers, 1969.

Dollhoff, Terry, "A Survey of Hash Techniques" *Thruput*, Vol. 3, No. 3, April/May 1972.

Everest, Gordon C. & Edgar H. Sibley, "A Critique of the Guide-Share Data Base Management Systems Requirements" *MISR-WP*, 71-02

Gildersleeve, Thomas R., *Design of Sequential File Systems*, New York, NY: Wiley, 1971.

Gosden, John A., "The Making of a Management Information Data Base" *Computer Decision*, Vol. 4, No. 5, May 1972.

Harvison, C. W. & K. J. Radford, "Creating a Common Data Base" *Journal of Systems Management*, Vol. 23, No. 6, June 1972.

Head, Robert V., "Structuring the Data Base" *Journal of Systems Management*, Vol. 21, No. 9, September 1970.

Martin, George N., "Data Dictionary/Directory System" *Journal of Systems Management*, Vol. 20, No. 12, December 1973.

Olle, T. William, "The Large Data Base, Its Organization and User Interface" *Data Base*, Vol. 1, No. 3, Fall 1969.

Rist, Karsten A., "Solving File Maintenance Problems" *Journal of Systems Management*, Vol. 23, No. 11, November 1972.

Rustin, Randall (Ed.), *Data Base Systems*, Englewood Cliffs, NJ: Prentice-Hall, 1972.

Senko, M. E., et al., "Data Structures and Accessing in Data Base Systems" *IBM Systems Journal*, Vol. 12, No. 1, 1973.

Shneiderman, Ben, "Optimal Data Base Reorganization Points" *Communications of the ACM*, Vol. 16, No. 6, June 1973.

Slamecka, Vladimir, "Requirements for a Data Base Management System" *Ideas for Management*, 1972, Cleveland, Ohio: Association for Systems Management.

Treanor, Richard G., "Data Management Fact and Fiction" *Data Base*, Vol. 3, No. 1, Spring/Summer 1974.

White, Bard F. & Michael Abbott, "Evaluation and Selection of a Data Base Management System" *Journal of Educational Data Processing*, Vol. 11, No. 3, 1974.

CHAPTER 17

FORMS AND REPORT DESIGN

Forms design is predominantly a planning activity, with the actual drawing of the form playing only a minor role in total procurement of a desired form. The actual designing effort is made considerably easier for the forms designer if he knows the Who, What, When,

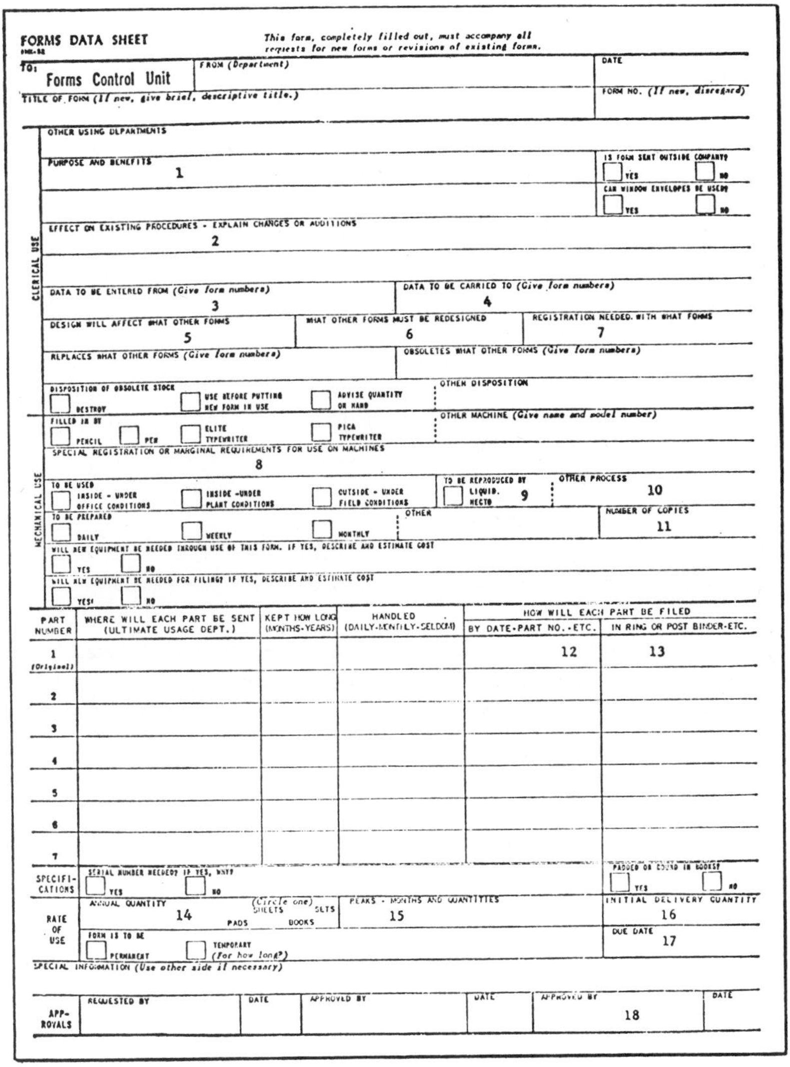

FIGURE 17.1

How, Where and Why questions concerning the desired form and the system within which it is used.

By formalizing the design function through the Forms Control unit, the attitude toward proper design, the installation of standards and an awareness of total cost are all obtainable principles of good forms design. To enhance the standardization of forms design, it is recommended that the Forms Control unit develop and institute a design check-off list (Figure 17.1).

REQUIREMENTS OF FORMS DESIGN

Since clerical and mechanical efficiencies are desired objectives in designing a form, what specifically should we look for in forms design? There are eight major requirements for a good design:

1. The form must fit into the system and meet the objectives for which it is being used. The value of the forms system analysis work is reflected in this major requirement.
2. The form must be easy to use and void of any misinterpretation where data is to be entered. Regardless of how the form is prepared there must be ample writing space, correct arrangement and sequence of data, and correctly placed instructions for filling out the form.
3. The entry of data on the form should reflect the sequence that the form travels in a given system and the source from which the form user is obtaining data. Again, forms system analysis is invaluable in determining the correct sequence of data.
4. Adequate space must be provided for manual or mechanical entries. The width and length of each data field must be analyzed and properly allotted. The problem of variable lengths for data must be given close attention by the forms designer. Figure 17.2 illustrates how good form design allowed 100% more writing space.
5. Many cases can be cited to illustrate how clerical errors due to an inadequate forms design are costing the company valuable time and dollars. Costly clerical errors can be prevented through good forms design. The factors in design that contribute to error reductions are:
   a. Completeness of data and the elimination of unnecessary data.
   b. Clear division of data items by vertical columns.
   c. Ease of following a reading line across the page.

SCRAP CARD — Section 1.

Received by Scrap Handling.   Scaleman will fill out all three sections, dating only this section, detaching it and forwarding to Scrap Record Clerk.   Attach sections 2 & 3 to scrap container.

From Dep't _____ Date Rec'd _____

Metal _____

Scrap No. _____ Weight _____

SCRAP RECORD   Section 1

RECEIVED BY SCRAP HANDLING   Scaleman will fill out all three sections dating only this section, detaching it and forwarding to Scrap Record Clerk. Attach sections 2 and 3 to scrap container.

FROM DEPT.	DATE RECEIVED
METAL	
SCRAP No.	WEIGHT

FIGURE 17.2

  d. Proper printed captions to insure that information is correctly posted.

  e. Well-designed forms that induce good mental attitude in the user.

6. The input from the forms analyst effort is required to insure that filing, storage and microfilming of a desired form is considered by the form designer.

7. The knowledge of how the form is prepared, used and handled

is required to insure that the forms designer produced the right type, construction and quality of form.

8. The user and how the form is distributed must be clearly indicated on the form to insure proper handling and on-time delivery.

TYPES OF FORMS

There are four broad categories into which forms can be classified: standard flat forms, specialty forms, computer oriented forms and miscellaneous.

Standard Flat Form

This is the most common type of form and is the easiest to design, print, reproduce and procure. Other basic characteristics of flat forms are: (1) they represent the majority of forms used by a typical enterprise; (2) they have as a rule low annual usage; and (3) they are the least expensive.

Flat forms have a single sheet construction and can be prepared by hand or machine and printed on any size and grade of paper in a variety of colors. When additional copies are required, carbon paper is inserted between copies.

The flat form is easily bootlegged (unauthorized procurement of a form) especially since the introduction of the automatic office copier. With these machines every office employee is a potential printer and supplier of forms.

The single sheet flat form can be padded by stapling or gluing of a group of forms, singly or in sets, at one end or one side with or without clipboard backing and/or cover. Linen reinforcement may be used for padding.

Specialty Forms

Any form which requires "special" equipment for its manufacture is a "specialty" form. These include carbon interleaved, perforated and die cut forms, hectograph and offset masters, unit sets (multiple unit), and continuous forms. Usually the multiple unit forms are printed on high speed rotary presses which prenumber, collate, perforate and print in one or more colors simultaneously.

The major advantages in specialty forms are elimination of: alignment and carbon insertion problems, feeding forms by hand into machines, removing of carbon sheets from forms after completion. Also utilization of equipment and hardware oriented to handling and preparing specialty forms.

Although specialty forms cost more initially than single forms, the clerical cost reductions made possible through their use far exceed any increase in their procurement cost over that of other forms. Space does not permit coverage of all of the many specialty forms now available to business, but those described here provide a good idea of the possibilities in this area (Figures 17.3, 17.4).

SPECIALTY FORMS

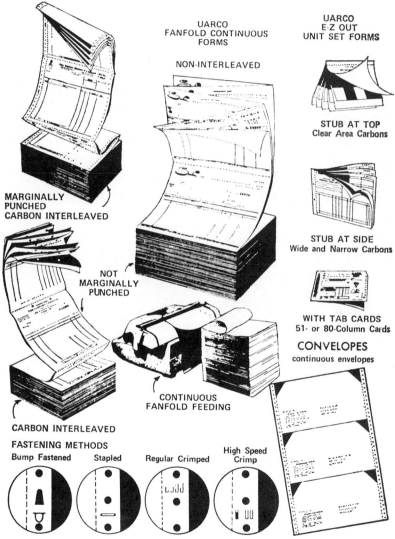

FIGURE 17.3

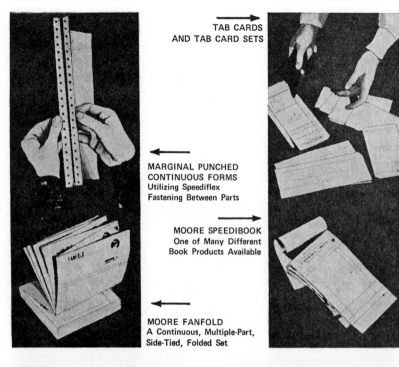

TAB CARDS
AND TAB CARD SETS

MARGINAL PUNCHED
CONTINUOUS FORMS
Utilizing Speediflex
Fastening Between Parts

MOORE SPEEDIBOOK
One of Many Different
Book Products Available

MOORE FANFOLD
A Continuous, Multiple-Part,
Side-Tied, Folded Set

REGISTER FORMS
A Continuous Handwritten Form
Utilizing a Moore Register

MOORE SPEEDISET
Multiple-Part Sets Utilizing
One-Time Carbon

FIGURE 17.4

Unit Set/Snap Out Forms

These forms are composed of several sheets of paper, fastened to-gether at the top, with carbon paper interleaved between the sheets. The sheets of paper are perforated for the tear-out but the carbon paper is not perforated. Both paper sheets and the carbon paper are glued together at the top "stub." Some of the sheets of carbon can also be perforated making it possible to tear out part of the sheets and carbon, leaving the rest of the set intact for further writing. The carbon paper is shorter than the sheets of paper, leaving a margin of paper that can be grasped in the fingers without taking hold of the carbon. After typing the form, the stub can be grasped in one hand and the bottom margins of the sheets of paper in the other hand and the set is pulled apart with the stub and carbon paper remaining in one hand and the sheets of paper in the other. The carbon paper is "one-time" usage and is discarded after the form is pulled apart.

An analysis of the flat form clerical operations as compared to a unit set follows:

Standard Flat Forms

Pick up forms.
Pick up carbon paper.
Insert a sheet of carbon between every two forms.
Jog into position to register.
Insert in typewriter.
Adjust to be sure of registration.
Roll to first typing line.
Type the form.
Remove the forms from the typewriter.
Separate the carbons from the forms.
Replace the carbons for reuse.
Dispose of the forms.

Unit Set Forms

Pick up the unit set.
Insert in typewriter.
Roll to first typing line.
Type.
Remove the unit set from typewriter.
Snap the set apart.
Throw stub and carbons away.
Dispose of the forms.

Continuous Strip/Fanfold Forms

Multiple unit forms constructed in a continuous strip or fanfold arrangement are known as continuous forms (Figure 17.3). Marginal punched continuous forms are perforated with holes or slots on each side, which fasten onto an aligning or feeding device on the writing machine. This provides accurate registration across and down each set and feeds the forms in a continuous flow through the machine, permitting faster preparation than by any other method because it eliminates time-consuming individual insertion of forms or sets.

The aligning device also permits close registration of copies so that single spacing is possible and the resulting reduced form size lowers the form's printing and processing costs.

Continuous forms can be prepared on typewriters, billing machines, addressing machines, and electronic data processing machines. They can be one-time carbon interleaved, or, by means of a special attachment on the writing machine, the carbon can be fed through the forms, permitting use of the same carbon for many forms.

When different grades, weights or colors of paper are required, continuous strip forms are best. Fanfold continuous forms are best when forms must be kept together for later insertion of data, and when all copies are of the same grade and weight of paper. Either type of continuous form is recommended only if usage is heavy for prolonged periods. For example, annual usage of 50,000 sets at one location would justify continuous forms, but multiple unit sets are more practical if annual usage is only 1,000 sets.

When forms are written in large quantities, but the forms writing machine does not have aligning or feeding devices, continuous forms without marginal perforations may be used. They have the same advantages as marginal punched continuous forms, except that close registration is not possible. Forms tend to slip during typing, so that realignment is necessary from time to time. They can be fanfold or continuous strip, with or without interleaved carbon. A carbon feeding attachment is necessary on the writing machine when the forms are not carbon interleaved. This is practical and economical when all entries are made in one session and form sets do not have to be held intact for later entries.

Carbonless Paper

Carbonless paper is chemically coated paper designed for use in continuous and multiple unit forms to eliminate the need for carbon paper. Pen, pencil, or machine-printed markings are automatically printed on other copies in the form set, without benefit of carbon paper. The imprint is the result of the reaction, on contact, of two different chemical coatings, one on the back of the top sheet and one on the front of the next sheet.

The elimination of time-consuming carbon paper insertion and disposal is the most important advantage in using carbonless paper. Elimination of carbon also means cleaner copies, no soiling of hands and clothing, no smear or smudge of paper. Copies are clear, sharp and long lasting.

Carbonless paper has many applications—in voucher checks, statements of account, inventory tickets, salesbooks, and deposit slips, to name a few. Forms may be printed on an offset press and padded into sets. Continuous forms may be "crash printed" up to six copies at a time. Carbonless paper also may be used on teleprinters and, used as the first copy on a high-speed printer, eliminates the need for a ribbon.

A disadvantage of carbonless paper is the need for a heavy backing sheet for each form set in padded forms, to keep from writing through onto copies of the next set. Tissue sheets between copies correct this problem, but the user must remember to remove the tissue before using the form set.

Price is frequently termed a disadvantage of carbonless paper. Carbonless forms usually are priced 10% or more higher than carbon interleaved forms. However, where usage is considerable they save more than this differential in clerical time and effort. This is another example of the tendency on the part of many forms procurement people to consider only the printing cost of forms.

Erasures are difficult to make on carbonless paper, and the number of copies per set is limited—6 to 8 for handwritten forms and 10 to 12 for machine-prepared forms.

COMPUTER ORIENTED FORMS

With the emergence of computer data processing a whole new array of forms has evolved. Due to the rapid change and constant innovations, the forms designer is cautioned to obtain assistance from outside suppliers in selecting, designing and procuring computer oriented forms.

Tabulating Cards

Punched cards are an important input, output and storage medium. In designing cards or card sets, the forms designer must work very closely with the Operations Manager. His knowledge of the equipment and procedure is a prime asset in the design. There are many suppliers of cards who are most cooperative in resolving design or construction problems.

A few of the many special features available in cards are:

Mark-sense cards—These are cards specially designed to permit the marking of them with special black pencils. The mark is then picked up by the machine and the punching done automatically without the intermediary manual keypunching and key verifying operation.

Aperture cards—These are cards with apertures cut in them to receive microphotographs of documents, engineering drawings, X-ray pictures, etc., to be used in record storage and retrieval. These cards are used in conjunction with other machines to blow up the image on a screen or to print an enlarged copy of the document for delivery to the user.

Continuous strip cards—Cards may be obtained in continuous strips, perforated for tearing apart after having been filled in with information. The most common use of continuous strip cards is probably in bank checks used for payroll or accounts payable. Such checks usually are not only printed on cards and prepunched with the static data representing the bank and the company, but are also preprinted with magnetic ink for electronic sorting after they have been cashed. These checks can be printed with top, bottom, or side vouchers in multiple parts with interleaved carbon paper.

Preprinted Forms

The forms to be used on the high-speed printers, 600 to 1,000 lines per minute or more, are similar to the continuous strip or fanfold form. These forms are available in a variety of sizes and range from one to eight copies. The title, heading, form number, data captions, vertical and horizontal lines, etc., are all preprinted on the form; only the variable data is added by the printer on the forms.

Since these forms are prepared on the high-speed printer, the registration and alignment factors are of prime importance to the forms designer. The specifications for pin-feed, bending, perforation, carbon, etc., are all vital factors and must be properly handled by the forms analyst and designer.

Stock Forms

These are similar in construction to the previously described pre-printed form; however, they are void of any preprinted information. The user of these forms must supply all the data that is to be printed. This type of form comes in many sizes, styles, colors and construction and is the most widely used form in the computer area.

Specialties

There are a wide variety of forms which can be prepared on the computer printer. A few are:

1. Offset Masters—These forms are used on offset printers to

produce thousands of copies. By using special ribbons on the computer printer, these masters can be prepared for use by the company's printing department.

2. Tags and labels.
3. Two-up forms—Depending on the width of a form, two or more can be prepared simultaneously on the printer. In order to achieve these economies, the analyst, designer and Operations Manager must work together to resolve any problems.

OCR, OMR, and MICR Forms

Forms to be read by an optical character reader, optical mark reader or magnetic ink character reading equipment must meet special restrictions. The design is usually restricted by equipment specifications. It is recommended that the analyst with OCR, OMR or MICR forms design problems study the equipment manuals to learn how to design these forms.

FORM LAYOUT AND CONSTRUCTION

Included under this topic are a few of the more prevalent layout and construction features associated with good forms design. The serious student and forms designer must perform in-depth research to associate himself with the many facets of forms design.

Form Title and Number

The form layout should always start with the least flexible item or area, which is most frequently the title and form number.

A. Selection of Title

The form title should be brief, but descriptive, to indicate clearly the form's purpose. It should not contain such superfluous words as "form," "card," "sheet," "blank," etc., which bear no relation to the form's function, and merely denote something which is obvious. Here are some examples of correct and incorrect titles:

CORRECT	INCORRECT
Remittance Advice or Notice	Advice or Notice of Remittance Received
Credit Application	Application for Credit
Termination Notice	Notice of Termination
Time Record	Time Sheet
Payment Request	Request for Payment
Abstract Transmittal	Transmittal of Abstract

Notice that prepositions have been eliminated; also, in each case a noun in the title describes the form's function, as:

NOUN	FUNCTION
Advice or Notice	To advise or notify
Application	To apply for
Record	To record
Request	To request or ask for
Transmittal	To transmit or route

B. Placement of Title

While the placement of the title may vary under certain circumstances, it should be placed in the upper left corner of the form whenever possible.

When filing reference or other important data must go across the top of the form, as in the case of visible records, the lower left corner may have to be used for the title. Sometimes the title may be most advantageously placed along the binding side of forms such as ledgers or journals, allowing space at the top of the form for write-in of name and address, or description of entries on the form. On oversize forms, the title may be centered across the top in larger type than that used for other titles.

C. Form Number Best under Title

The form number, like the title, is part of the form identification; therefore, the two should be grouped together. The number should be placed immediately below the title in smaller size type.

Sequence of Data

The important question to be answered in order to determine the proper sequence of data is: What other forms will be affected by the requested form?

If information is to be copied, or "posted," from another form to the requested form, the sequence of data should be the same for both forms. This also applies when data is to be posted from the requested form to another form. And the sequence of data on all of the forms involved should follow the natural sequence of the procedure.

Sometimes the entire procedure must be considered. Figure 17.5 illustrates the relationship of forms in a typical procedure.

Horizontal and Vertical Spacing

More questions! How is the form prepared? Who prepares it? How much space is required for easy insertion of data?

RELATIONSHIP OF FORMS IN A PROCEDURE

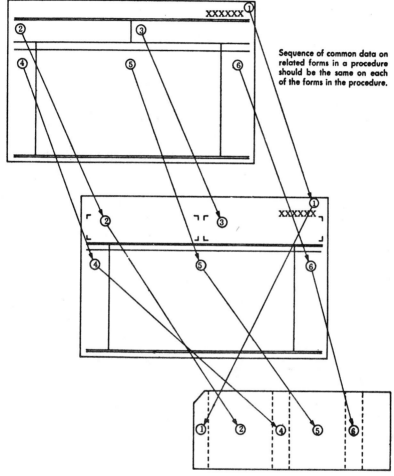

Sequence of common data on related forms in a procedure should be the same on each of the forms in the procedure.

FIGURE 17.5

The method of preparation tells us whether to allow for hand-written or machine written entries, or both. We need to know who will prepare the form, if handwritten, in order to allow sufficient space for the type of worker involved.

A. Handwritten Forms

For horizontal spacing, at least ⅛″ per character should be allowed for clerical workers and ⅙″ per character for manual workers. For vertical spacing when "box" style (upper left corner) is used, ⅓″ per line should be allowed. Otherwise, ¼″ is adequate.

B. Typewritten Forms

Elite type requires 12 characters per inch and pica type 10 characters per inch for horizontal spacing. Vertical spacing should be 6 lines per inch for single spacing and 3 lines per inch for double spacing.

C. If the form is to be filled in by either hand or machine, horizontal spacing for handwritten forms should be provided and double typewriter spacing used for vertical lines. If space permits, one way to simplify this problem is to specify 3 lines to the inch for all vertical spacing. The form can then be handwritten or typewritten. Figure 17.6 shows a method of laying out uneven lines on a form.

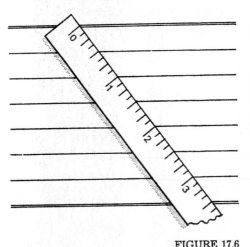

Laying out uneven line spacing

Wanted: Seven writing lines in a space measuring 2-5/8 inches.

Solution: Lay a ruler diagonally across the space so that the 3½ inch mark, equalling seven half inches, exactly spans the area. Mark off the half inch points and draw the writing lines on these marks. The result is seven exactly spaced writing lines.

Any other uneven spacing can be laid out in the same manner.

FIGURE 17.6

D. Special equipment used in the preparation of forms may necessitate completely different spacing. Therefore, it is important to investigate the spacing requirements of such equipment before starting the actual layout of the form.

Box Design

The box design, usually referred to as "ULC" (upper left corner) arrangement, provides the box heading and entry explanation or instructions in the upper left corner of the entry box or writing space. This technique reduces form size by as much as 25%, yet provides more writing space than the frequently used method of placing captions or explanations on or below the writing line (Figure 17.7).

The box design permits easy and rapid entry of data in a continuous flow from left to right. This is particularly important on machine

CAPTION-ON-LINE ARRANGEMENT VERSUS BOX DESIGN

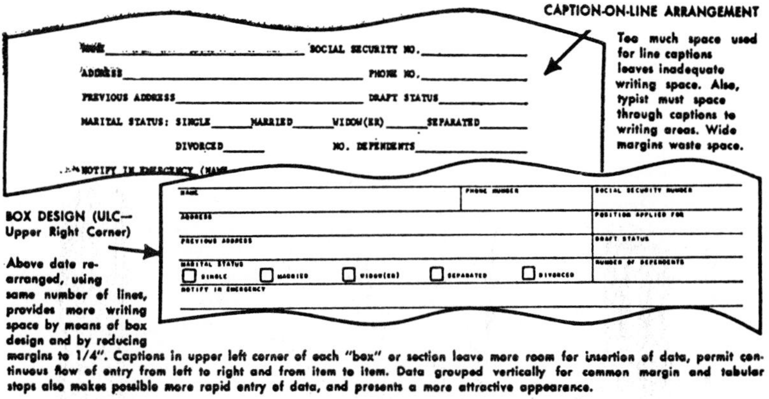

FIGURE 17.7

prepared forms, where the typist must otherwise space through the printed caption in order to reach the next fill-in space. Also, the caption and its explanation are completely visible while the entry is being made, so the typist does not have to roll up the platen to read the explanation and then roll it back again to continue typing.

Form preparation is further simplified by the alignment of vertical rules for common tabular and marginal stops on machine prepared forms, and by the distinctly outlined boxes, each with its own easily identified caption and each restricted to one entry. These features also add to the form's attractive, well-planned, uncluttered appearance.

Columnar Arrangement for Common Data Grouping

When several similar entries on a form can be grouped under one heading, a columnar arrangement is better than the box design. It eliminates repetition of the common items and conserves space (Figure 17.8).

A. Column Width

Column width should be based on the amount of data required in the column and on the method of write-in, not on the length

COLUMNAR ARRANGEMENT AND NUMBERED COLUMNS

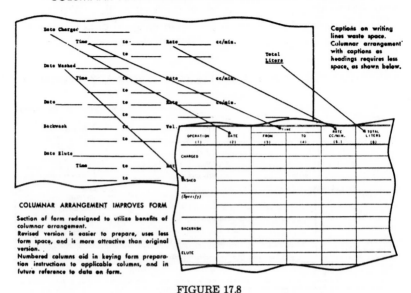

FIGURE 17.8

of the heading. To determine the amount of space required for write-in of entries, the instructions for horizontal spacing in this section should be followed.

B. Depth of Heading Sections

The main or primary heading describes the data to be entered in the column (s) to which it applies. Secondary and tertiary headings may be used to group related data under the primary heading.

The depth of the heading section is based on the length of the longest heading, which may have to be broken down into two or more lines. Long words may be divided and abbreviations used, to the extent that they are understandable.

Minimum vertical spacing requirements are:

Primary
and $\frac{2}{12}''$ for one line
Secondary $\frac{3}{12}''$ for two lines
             $\frac{4}{12}''$ for three lines

Tertiary $\frac{2}{12}''$ for one line
             $\frac{2}{12}''$ for two lines
             $\frac{3}{12}''$ for three lines

However, a little more than the minimum is desirable, if space permits.

Special attention should be given to spacing of column headings for machine-prepared forms to assure the typist will reach the first typing line without having to make a platen adjustment when spacing vertically down through the headings.

C. Writing Lines Necessary for Hand Fill-In

If entries will be handwritten, writing lines are necessary and should be spaced ³⁄₁₂″. When fill-in method is optional, ⁴⁄₁₂″ (double typewriter spacing) is suited to either hand or machine fill-in. Writing lines are unnecessary when the form will be machine prepared, unless line captions are required (see Item E).

D. Arrangements and Size of Headings

Headings should be centered across the width and from top to bottom of their sections.

Heading type sizes should be progressively smaller or larger for each degree of importance. That is, the secondary heading should be smaller than the primary heading, and the tertiary heading smaller than the secondary. Type faces also may be more condensed as the size is reduced. Crowding can be avoided by allowing ¹⁄₁₂″ on each side of the heading, whenever possible.

Numbering or using letters to identify columns simplifies reference to them in instructions. The usual practice is to place the numbers or letters in parentheses under the column heading and immediately above the heavy horizontal rule (as shown in previous Figure 17.8).

Column headings should be arranged horizontally whenever possible. However, if space is limited it may be necessary to use vertical headings (Figure 17.9), or place them at an angle (Figure 17.10). Since this is not a natural position for reading, vertical or tilted headings should be used only when there is no other way of fitting the heading into the available space.

MONTH	REMEDIES				COSMETICS				PERFUMES				MEN'S SHOP			
	ASPIRIN	COLD TABLETS	VASELINES	BANDAGES	FACE POWDERS	LIPSTICKS	DUSTING POWDERS	NAIL POLISH	PERFUMES	COLOGNES	CREAM SACHETS	PURSE FLASKS	SHAVING CREAMS	AFTER SHAVING LOTIONS	HAIR BRUSHES	HANDKERCHIEFS
JANUARY																
FEBRUARY																
MARCH																

FIGURE 17.9

REPORT NUMBER	DISTRIBUTION AND NUMBER OF COPIES														OTHER
	PRESIDENT	VICE PRESIDENT	TREASURER	CONTROLLER	CHIEF ACCT.	SALES MGR.	PRODUCTION MGR.	PURCHASING AGT.	OFFICE MGR.	BUDGET DIR.	CHIEF ENG'R.	PERSONNEL DIR.	CREDIT MGR.		
1011-A															
1012-B															
1012-H															
1013															

FIGURE 17.10

E. Caption-on-Writing-Line

When certain column headings are repeated several times, space can be saved by placing the common headings on writing lines to the left of the write-in columns (Figure 17.11). This is known as the caption-on-writing-line arrangement.

F. Vertical Side Headings

Sometimes, when a primary heading does not completely describe all of the line captions used, separate primary headings are used for each major group. This wastes a writing line for each added heading. By arranging these primary headings vertically at the

ITEM	REMEDIES					
	JANUARY	FEBRUARY	MARCH	APRIL	MAY	
ASPIRIN						
COLD TABLETS						
VASELINES						
BANDAGES AND ADHESIVES						
TOTAL						
	COSMETICS					
FACE POWDERS						
LIPSTICKS						
DUSTING POWDERS						

FIGURE 17.11

far left of each grouping, each horizontal heading so eliminated means an added writing line or a corresponding reduction in form size (Figure 17.12).

Secondary vertical side headings may be used when desired. However, each such side heading space provided reduces the available space for write-in columns. If horizontal space is inadequate and vertical space is ample, it may be more practical to

	ITEM	JANUARY	FEBRUARY	MARCH	APRIL	MAY	
R E M E D I E S	ASPIRIN						
	COLD TABLETS						
	VASELINES						
	BANDAGES AND ADHESIVES						
	TOTAL						
C O S M E T I C S	FACE POWDERS						
	LIPSTICKS						
	DUSTING POWDERS						
	NAIL POLISH						
	TOTAL						

FIGURE 17.12

use the horizontal headings. In such cases, "X's" or shadings are used to block out the resulting column spaces which are not to be filled in.

Preprinted Data

Form preparation can be further simplified and speeded by providing preprinted optional answers with ballot boxes or check-off spaces. The person preparing the form indicates the desired answer by placing an "X" in the appropriate box or space.

A. Ballot Boxes

When there is a limited number of optional answers, or where a "yes" or "no" answer is expected, ballot boxes are recommended to reduce the amount of writing required (Figure 17.13).

BALLOT BOXES

PRINT
☐ ONE SIDE. ☐ TWO SIDES ☐ HEAD TO HEAD ☐ HEAD TO FOOT

FIGURE 17.13

CHECK-OFF SPACES

CREDIT RATING	EXCEL.	GOOD	FAIR	POOR	COD	CANCEL

FIGURE 17.14

A $\frac{2}{12}$" square ballot box is best, set $\frac{1}{24}$" above the horizontal rule and in front of the preprinted answer. This size is large enough for ease of entry by hand or machine. At least $\frac{1}{12}$" should be allowed between the ballot box and its answer, and $\frac{2}{12}$" between the answer and the next ballot box; preferably more, if available.

A horizontal arrangement is better than vertical because it is easier to fill in on a typewriter and requires less space. It is especially effective for multiple choice answers. The vertical arrangement requires $\frac{2}{12}$" vertical spacing between boxes for machine fill-in and ½″ for hand fill-in. This arrangement takes up more space and presents an alignment problem when the form is machine-prepared in multiple copies.

When using ballot boxes it is important to avoid a hit-or-miss scattered arrangement. By aligning boxes with other data to the fullest extent possible, a minimum of tab stops is required for entry of data.

B. Check-off Spaces

When there are many possible answers, the ballot box approach may not be as efficient as a modified check-off arrangement.

Like ballot boxes, check-off spaces may be arranged horizontally or vertically, but the horizontal arrangement is easier to fill in, particularly by machine, and requires less space than the vertical arrangement (Figure 17.14). However, it does require 9⁄12″ rather than the 4⁄12″ line normally allowed for a row of ballot boxes. Check-off spaces also are easy to read and act upon.

C. "Yes" and "No" Arrangements

There are several arrangements for "Yes" and "No" answers, depending upon the length of the question, the number of questions involved, and the amount of space available, as shown in Figure 17.15.

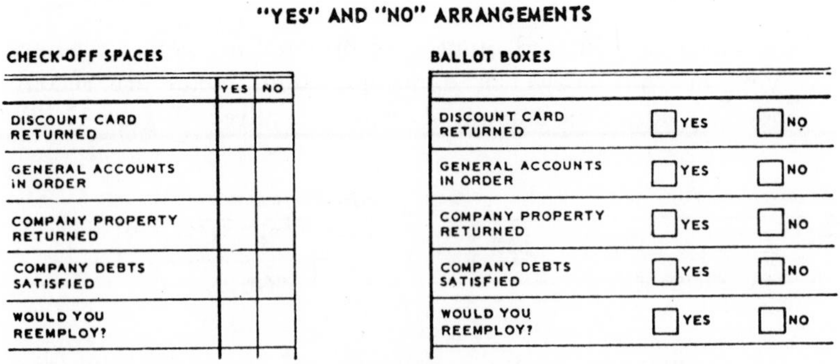

FIGURE 17.15

D. Use of Heading

Space also can be saved by printing possible answers in the heading as shown in Figure 17.16.

Form Instructions

A well-designed form needs little or no instructions for completion because its box and column captions are so clear that further ex-

ANSWERS PRINTED IN HEADING

TYPE OF BUSINESS (MFG., RETAILING, SERVICE, OTHER)

COMPARISON OF DIFFERENT ARRANGEMENTS OF SAME DATA

BALLOT BOXES - HORIZONTAL

TYPE OF FORM

☐ SINGLE ☐ SET ☐ SNAPSET ☐ TAG ☐ DITTO ☐ LABEL ☐ VISIBLE (KARDEX, ETC.) OTHER

. "Space Saved"

CHECK-OFF BOXES - HORIZONTAL

TYPE OF FORM	SINGLE	SET	SNAPSET	TAG	DITTO	LABEL	VISIBLE (KARDEX,ETC.)	OTHER	

"Space Saved"

ANSWERS PRINTED IN HEADING

TYPE OF FORM (SINGLE,SET, SNAPSET, TAG, DITTO, LABEL,
VISIBLE (KARDEX, ETC.)

BALLOT BOXES - VERTICAL

☐ SINGLE   ☐ DITTO

☐ SET   ☐ LABEL

☐ SNAPSET   ☐ VISIBLE (KARDEX, ETC.)

☐ TAG   ☐

CHECK-OFF BOXES - SINGLE AND DOUBLE TYPEWRITER SPACE

TYPE OF FORM
SINGLE
SET
SNAPSET
TAG
DITTO
LABEL
VISIBLE (KARDEX, ETC.)

TYPE OF FORM	
SINGLE	DITTO
SET	LABEL
SNAPSET	VISIBLE (KARDEX,ETC.)
TAG	

FIGURE 17.16

planation is unnecessary. But when special instructions are necessary, they should be brief and placed where most effective.

A. If the instructions are to be read before the form is prepared, they should be placed at the top of the form. For example, the instruction "Prepare in Duplicate" has little value when placed at the bottom of the form because it probably would not be noticed until the form had been prepared, single copy only, necessitating the preparation of another copy.

B. When instructions pertain to actions to be taken after the form has been completed, they are most effective placed at the bottom of the form, where they will be noticed when the action is to be taken. A typical example is the instruction covering distribution of various copies of a form.

C. Special instructions should be placed close to the items to which they pertain, so they will be noticed when the entry is being made.

D. When instructions are too long to include on the form, they can be placed on the reverse side or in separate procedure instructions. Padded forms of the salesbook type often carry instructions on the cover. In such cases, a reference to the instructions must be provided on the form.

Because lengthy instructions usually relate to preparation and/ or processing of the form, reference to these instructions should be placed at the top of the form, so they will be read before preparation is started.

E. Distribution or routing instructions usually appear at the bottom of each copy, where they will be seen as the last entry is being made on the form.

It's more economical to print the complete distribution on all copies than to place a different identification or instruction of each copy, except when there is a very large number of copies. One plate can be used for printing all copies, and each user knows who receives each of the other copies.

Filing References

Like form titles and address areas for window envelopes, the filing reference on a form, when applicable, may have to be provided for before any of the remaining areas are drawn in.

The filing reference may be a number, date, individual or company name, or a geographic location. It must always be placed where it will be seen easily and quickly in the particular type of housing used for it; e.g., filing cabinet, binder, visible file, and so on.

A. Filing Folders

When forms are filed in folders for shelf or drawer filing, the filing reference may be placed in the upper right corner of the form or across the right hand vertical border for reading ease.

B. Vertical File Cards

The most common vertical file cards are the index or tickler type card, usually 3 x 5, 4 x 6, or 5 x 8 inches. Other vertical file cards are larger and used in machine bookkeeping systems. Cards may be housed in file boxes or trays, in file drawers or on shelves.

Vertical file cards carry the filing reference across the top or in the top right corner. It should be large enough and bold enough to stand out prominently on the card, so that it can be spotted quickly. If necessary, the form title may have to be placed in the lower left corner of the form or elsewhere to provide for filing reference at the top.

C. Visible Records

Chief characteristic of visible records is their overlapping arrangement in pockets or jackets, or loosely in binders, so that only the top or bottom border is visible. This exposed area contains the filing reference.

Visible records may be cards, available in a wide variety of sizes, and housed in shallow tray-like drawers or panels in desktop or larger files. Jackets or pockets hold two cards, one on the front and one on the back, and are hinged or hooked onto the panel so they can be flipped forward or back to expose either card for reference or posting.

To permit machine insertion of data along the exposed border, a ¾″ stub must be provided to keep the card from slipping in the machine. After data is inserted, the stub is separated from the card along the stub perforations. Other visible records are loose forms with left or right borders. A ¾″ stub must be provided to keep the card from their overlapping arrangement in multiple-ring binders specially designed for the purpose.

D. Binders

Normally, forms are fastened in binders along the left margin and the filing reference should be in the upper right corner. However, forms are sometimes bound at the top and the reference is placed in the lower right corner or along the lower border of the form.

In visible record binders, the forms are arranged each overlapping the next form, so that the upper or lower border is visible. The filing reference appears along the exposed border on such forms.

CARBON PAPER

There are many grades, types and colors of carbon paper; therefore, the forms designer needs to rely on the forms supplier to assist him in selecting the proper carbon paper. When purchasing a multicopy form, the Forms Control unit should insist that the supplier submit a carbon test. This test will insure that satisfactory results will be obtained when the form is used in the system. The carbon test should be processed through each step of the system, including mailing, if applicable.

FASTENINGS FOR UNIT, FANFOLD AND CONTINUOUS SETS

Sometimes it is desirable that several or all parts of a unit set be held together, either to assist in machine processing or to hold the part together for further clerical processing. There are several methods that can be utilized to fasten forms together:

Stapling—A metal staple is put into the set at one or more places in the stub or the edge that contains the registration pin-feed holes.

Sewing—In this operation, the parts are sewn together with thread in the perforated strip, which is later torn off and thrown away.

Crimping—A small die cut is made on the set, with a small tab being cut out and folded back over and under and through a slot immediately below the die cut. It is an interlocking arrangement to hold the several parts together. Another crimping operation does not cut a tab and fold it back, but merely cuts little parallel slots and pushes the intermediate paper alternately back and forth to create a holding action.

Gluing—This is very similar to the gluing done in making unit sets, although the glue is usually applied in small spots spaced along the waste edge of the form rather than in a continuous line.

FORMS EQUIPMENT—IN-HOUSE

The first type of company forms equipment considered here is the forms producing hardware. These include offset printing presses and the myriad office duplicating machines and copiers. The offset presses produce forms via a plate or various types of masters.

The emphasis is not on the ability to produce forms via this equipment but of maintaining quality and control. Studies show that more badly designed forms are produced on office copiers and in-house print shops than from any other method of procurement.

The second type of in-house equipment is that used in handling the prepared forms. The use of this equipment has paralleled the increased usage of automated data processing equipment. The forms-handling equipment is capable of performing a wide variety of functions, either separately or together, in one operation.

Deleaving—This operation separates the parts of a multi-copy form and removes the interleave carbon.

Bursting—This operation separates the forms in the strip. It may be done in conjunction with the deleaving process. Some bursters leave the forms in complete sets, while others separate the parts into individual piles.

Slitting—This operation cuts off the pin-feed margins from the forms or separates two forms which have been printed side by side.

Imprinting—This operation prints additional information on a prepared form.

SUMMARY

Designing a good form lies in the quality of the analysis given, the skill of the forms designer, and most important, the executive management's emphasis on forms management and forms control. The results of good forms design are:

A. Total company involvement in the processing of forms.

B. Improvement of clerical attitudes toward filling and handling forms.

C. The knowledge that the forms being used are the most efficient and effective that can be designed.

D. The money savings that can be obtained by knowing that each form, copy and data item is necessary to fulfill a given system's requirements.

REVIEW QUESTIONS

1. What are business forms? What major purposes should they serve?
2. What are the visible and invisible costs associated with business forms?
3. What is a specialty form? When is a specialty form needed?
4. What are form specifications? Why are they important? Who should be responsible for developing forms specifications?
5. What are the results of good forms design?
6. Tell how check boxes can be used effectively in forms design.

DISCUSSION QUESTIONS

1. Discuss the impact of EDP on forms management and what changes in EDP mean to forms management.
2. Discuss the various forms systems analysis tools.
3. Discuss the eight major requirements for good forms design.
4. Discuss the four categories of business forms. Emphasize specialty forms.
5. Discuss the following form layout features—form title and number, sequence of data, box design and preprinted data.
6. Bring to class an example of a multipart form and discuss any inadequate instructions for completing it.

BIBLIOGRAPHY

Andrews, A. James (Ed.), *Forms Design and Control*, Cleveland, Ohio: ASM, Bookshelf Series, 1970.

Carey, L. Chester, "Quality Form, The," *Journal of Systems Management*, Vol. 23, No. 6, June 1972, pp. 28-31.

Chu, Albert L. C., "Plodding Progress of OCR, The," *Business Automation*, Vol. 17, No. 3, March 1970, pp. 48-55.

Editorial Staff, "EDP Forms and Forms Handling," *Modern Data*, Vol. 5, No. 7, July 1972, pp. 52-57.

Editorial Staff, *Engineering Your Forms System*, Niagara Falls, New York: Moore Business Forms, Inc., 1964.

Editorial Staff, "Will Business Forms Change Form?", *Modern Office Procedures*, Vol. 15, No. 11, November 1970, pp. 44-45.

Eisdorfer, Alfred, "Study of Optical Character Recognition, A," *Journal of Systems Management*, Vol. 21, No. 11, November 1970, pp. 19-22.

Evans, Hugh S., "Where to Use Optical Mark Systems," *Journal of Systems Management*, Vol. 24, No. 3, March 1973, pp. 8-13.

Hockman, J., "Checklist for Forms Design," *Management Review*, Vol. 60, No. 10, October 1971, pp. 26-30.

Kaiser, Julius B., *Forms Design and Control*, New York: American Management Association, 1969.

Kish, Joseph L., Jr., *Business Forms: Design and Control*, New York: Ronald Press, 1971.

Knox, Frank M., *Knox Standard Guide to Design and Control of Business Forms*, New York: McGraw-Hill, 1965.

Marien, Ray, *Marien on Forms Control*, Englewood Cliffs, New Jersey: Prentice-Hall, 1962.

Martin, Merle P., "Making the Management Report Useful," *Journal of Systems Management*, Vol. 24, No. 5, May 1973, pp. 30-37.

Meyers, Gibbs, "Changing the Company Name," *Journal of Systems Management*, Vol. 21, No. 12, December 1970, pp. 27-31.

Miller, F. G., "Managing Forms," *Journal of Systems Management*, Vol. 23, No. 8, August 1972, pp. 27-29.

Mulhern, T. P., "Tyranny of Forms," *Journal of Systems Management*, Vol. 25, No. 8, August 1974, pp. 32-33.

Osteen, Carl E., *Forms Analysis*, Stanford, Conn.: Office Publications, 1969.

Radow, Michael, "OCR-A Versus OCR-B," *Datamation*, Vol. 16, No. 6, June 1970, p. 43.

Schwartz, Steven J., "Paperwork—The Problem No One Can Escape," *Infosystems*, Vol. 19, No. 11, November 1972, pp. 48-49f.

Staggs, Earl W., "Maybe It's Your Forms," *Journal of Systems Management*, Vol. 23, No. 3, March 1972, pp. 8-12.

Taylor, Alan, "Single Form for All Output No Longer Justifiable," *Computerworld*, Vol. 7, No. 1, January 1973, p. 9.

CHAPTER 18

DOCUMENTATION AND PROCEDURES

Documentation is not new or unique to systems applications (Menkus, 1970). It was practiced by the earliest of systems analysts, was reflected in their procedure manuals and preceded those manuals in the form of policy manuals and standard operating procedures.

Documentation is the written description of the system being studied, proposed or designed. Jackson (1973) made an important point when he said that documentation is also communicating the facts necessary for the Steering Committee's decision to investigate and to authorize a system design or to implement a proposed design. Documentation communicates these same facts to all members of the systems project team.

Employees with long service in a company can be an informal part of the organization's memory—but employees leave. For an organization to continue, it needs formal written policies and procedures of operation called documentation. Written documentation provides job details for present and future employees and assists in the operation of any system. The familiar routine is easily remembered but the unusual transaction requires a reference to policy or procedure manuals for correct handling. Documentation of how things are done is of great value when a system revision is being considered or implemented.

Systems documentation is used for systems development, user training, systems operation, systems revision, and current reference. Each of these uses requires a different kind of documentation.

WHO SHOULD WRITE DOCUMENTATION?

It has been normal practice for the programmers and systems analysts to document the parts of the project for which each was responsible. Recently this practice has been questioned. Coughlin (1973) suggests that procedure manuals are the responsibility of a separate functional group. There is ample precedent for such specialization in the forms design, forms control, and records management area. The Chief Programmer Team concept described by Mills (1971) and Baker (1972) points in the same direction. This concept is more fully described in Chapter 23. In the Chief Programmer Team concept the documentation is created by the project personnel and maintained by the project librarian. Such specialization allows all members of the project team to work closer to their highest skills.

It is a fact that project documentation is often done as an after-thought and is done reluctantly, and poorly. Doing the documentation after the project is completed prevents important step-by-step communications as the project progresses. Assigning responsibility for maintaining project documentation to a specialist results in having the documentation build with the project. The benefits to the project team and the project librarian from a specialist in documentation for larger projects exceed the cost of the specialist. The project documentation specialist requires the same skills as those of a technical writer.

The use of a documentation specialist does not reduce the need for the systems analyst to document the work. Early in the system life cycle the documentation is almost entirely the responsibility of the analyst. The documentation of a beginning project consists largely of working papers and reports to management. As the project reaches the design and installation phases the need for more elaborate and more standardized documentation grows and with it the need for talents of a documentation specialist.

Shaw and Atkins (1970) describe project documentation as cumulative. The documentation for one stage serves as the start of the documentation for the next step.

DOCUMENTATION STYLES

An overview of the several different procedure styles is shown in Figure 18.1. The diagram is modified from Haga (1968) and does not include reports, glossaries and data descriptions.

Figure 18.2 is an illustration of a procedure written in conventional narrative or paragraph form. This form is most suitable for short procedures and policies. The user must read the document until he finds the information he is seeking. There are no references to specific information areas.

The playscript procedure (Figure 18.3) is similar to flowchart procedure in its advantages and disadvantages. It is most appropriately used in information flow situations where many people or machines have specific sequences of action. The format of the play-script procedure uses two columns—responsibility and action. The responsibility script describes who takes a particular action. The action script describes the action to be taken. Note in Figure 18.3 that each action entry begins with an action verb. Reference to a particular action is facilitated by the responsibility column. In searching for a particular instruction, the user can locate the par-

Choosing the Best Procedure Layout

Legend: XX—Most Suitable X—Suitable

KIND OF ROUTINE	LAYOUT	CONVENTIONAL NARRATIVE— PARAGRAPH	PLAYSCRIPT	FUNCTIONAL (CAPTION)	MATRIX	ILLUSTRATED (Use only to supplement others)	FLOW CHART (Use only to supplement others)
ONE JOB TITLE	Unbroken Sequence	X		XX		X	X
	Unsequenced Action	X		XX		X	
	Action Depends on Variables			X	XX		
	Mixture of Policies and Procedures			XX			
SEVERAL JOB TITLES	Unbroken Sequence		XX	X			XX
	Unsequenced Action			XX	X		
	Action Depends on Variables			X	XX		
	Mixture of Policies and Procedures			XX			
	Combination: Sequenced Action & Unsequenced Funct.		X	XX	X		X
Straight Policy		XX		X	XX when showing delegation		
Data Entry By Many Locations In Forms For IDP and EDP				X	X	XX	

FIGURE 18.1   Source: Clifford I. Haga

ticular job function among the entries. The responsibility entry serves as a pointer or index to the specific instruction sought.

The format of playscript follows the flow of documents (or work) in a system rather than focusing on the work performed by individuals. This can be a disadvantage to training procedures when the

Sample Conventional Narrative Procedure

Veterans Administration Center   Circular Number 21
Fort Snelling   December 31, 1959
St. Paul 11, Minnesota

PHYSICAL FITNESS—MOTOR VEHICLE OPERATORS

1. Public Law 766 of the 83rd Congress provides for the establishment of procedures to insure the safe operation of Government-owned vehicles on Government business. The purpose of this circular is to implement Interim Issue 11-3 which sets forth the policy of the VA in carrying out the provisions of Public Law 766.

2. Each employee whose position requires him to operate a Government-owned vehicle, and each individual operator of Government vehicles, will complete SF 47, Physical Fitness inquiry for Motor Vehicle Operators, at the time he takes the driver's examination given by the Protective Section, Engineering Division, and every three years thereafter.

3. The Chief, Engineering Division, or his designee, will be responsible for reviewing and signing the SF 47. He will also be responsible for insuring that all employees who drive Government-owned vehicles have complied with the requirements of paragraph 2 above.

4. If the Chief, Engineering Division, or his designee, determines that a physical examination is not necessary, he will sign the SF 47 and route it to the Personnel Physician, who will insure that the results are posted to VA Form 5-3831a, Employee Health Record. After posting, the SF 47 will be routed to the Personnel Division for filing in the personnel folder.

5. If the Chief, Engineering Division, or his designee, determines that a physical examination is advisable, he will check the appropriate block on the SF 47, schedule a physical examination, and route the SF 47 to the Personnel Physician. The physical examination by the Personnel Physician will be based on the physical standards set forth in section I, appendix to chapter M-2, Federal Personnel Manual, using SF 78, Certificate of Medical Examination. After completing the examination, the Personnel Physician will route the SF 78 (including his recommendations), and the SF 47 to the Chief, Engineering Division, for final determination as to whether the employee should continue to operate a Government vehicle. The chief, Engineering Division, will notify (by memorandum) (a) the Personnel Physician and (b) the Assistant Manager for Insurance, the Director, Outpatient Clinic, or the Division chief (VB or Personnel), as appropriate, as to the final determination. The Personnel Physician will insure that the necessary postings are made to VA Form 5-3831a. The Engineering Division will route the SF 47 and the SF 78 to the Personnel Division for filing in the personnel folder.

6. *References*
    Chapter M-2, Federal Personnel Manual
    Chapter 9, VA Manual MP-5
    Interim Issue 11-3

                                                             John Doe
                                                             Manager
Distribution: "C"

FIGURE 18.2

                                             Source: Clifford I. Haga

various job functions performed by individuals need to be described and related to each other.

The functional or caption procedure (Figure 18.4) is perhaps the most versatile method of writing procedures. It uses the same re-

Sample Playscript Procedure

DEBIT TRANSACTIONS

Responsibility	Action
Installment Loan Clerk	1. Completes Debit Transaction Form.
	2. Totals all of the debit transactions.
	3. Bands the debits together and attaches total tape to batch.
	4. Labels batch as "new debits" and dates the batch.
	5. Places debits total on teller shee.
	6. Forwards debit transactions to Proof.
Proof	7. Proves debit transactions.
	8. Forwards debits and totals to Data Processing Operations.
Data Processing Operations	9. Keypunches the debit transactions.
	10. Processes the debit transaction cards through Computer Operations.
	11. Balances the debits to Proof's total.
	12. Returns the debits to Installment Loan.
Installment Loan Clerk	13. Files the debit transactions.

FIGURE 18.3

sponsibility and action columns as the playscript procedures and decision tables but relaxes the requirements for the columns by allowing the use of captions other than those relating to particular jobs. It also does not have the sequential requirements of playscript. The requirements of the action column are also reduced to allow for entries that are not actions.

The structure of the functional or caption form of procedure makes it as useful as playscript for retrieval purposes. It serves well for training in that all instructions related to a particular job can be shown on a single procedure. For tasks involving flows, the functional form is inferior in project development documentation, because the analyst has difficulty in perceiving the whole. The analyst must be certain that all steps in the process are included in the procedure. Closure is more apt to occur with playscript procedures supplemented with flowcharts.

A matrix procedure (Figure 18.5) is very similar in concept to the decision tables discussed in Chapter 8. Decision tables can be defined as a precisely defined subset of matrix procedures just as playscript procedures are a subset of caption procedures. Matrix procedures are most useful for two "if" situations. In Figure 18.5, *if* a particular officer and *if* a particular task occur, *then* the action is

Sample Functional or Caption Procedure

SYSTEM: Christmas Club   Section _____
PROGRAM: CC 180   Page _____

FUNCTIONS	It calculates interest due, based on a daily compounding factor of 4½% times number of interest days earned per 50 cents.
	It generates the Christmas Club checks with date, N/A, and amount.
	It updates the master file with the check number and the check amount.
	It places packed zeros in the check number and amount fields if a check is not generated for an account.
INFORMATION	No interest is calculated for accounts that cash out early and for accounts that are not completed.
	The program deducts one dollar service charge from the balance of incomplete accounts before generating the check. On balances less than one dollar, the full amount is taken as the service charge.
	The operator can cancel and restart the program at any point in the run. See instructions below.
INPUT	Christmas Club master file.
OUTPUT	Checks Service Charges Journal Interest Paid Journal Etc.
REFERENCES	The check layout is section ___; page ___. Report layouts are section ___; page ___.
OPERATOR INSTRUCTIONS	Mount special carriage control tape and the correct check forms on the prints.
	Set the "E" in the word "DATE" on the check to print position 73; set the first print line on "Account No." (Top right corner of check)

Restart Procedure
- Reload the program.
- Answer "yes" to console message, "Is this a restart run?"
- Type in the last good assigned (used) check number.
- When asked by the program, type in the next check number. This will be the beginning number, and the program will print checks starting with that number.

FIGURE 18.4

Source: Clyde W. Jackson

suggested. When the number of ifs exceeds two, the formal decision table format is superior to the matrix chart. The number of *thens* is not a determining factor.

Both matrix charts and decision tables are good methods for showing procedures involving decisions. Their disadvantage is that they tend to be awkward for showing flows or lists of tasks.

It is usually wise to illustrate procedures. For example, when

A Matrix Procedure

TELLERS POLICY GUIDE FOR CHECK CASHING

Item Is / Presentor Is	Customer with Checking, Savings, or Certificate of Deposit who is well known to the teller	Customer with Checking, Savings, or Certificate of Deposit who is NOT well known to the teller	Customer who has Installment Loan or Christmas Saving only	Non-Customer accompanied by a well-known Customer who has endorsed the item	Non-Customer	Non-Customer Friend or Relative of the teller
Maker's own check on Us payable to cash	TC 61 on Maker CASH	TC 61 on Maker CASH*	Not Applicable	Not Applicable	Not Applicable	Not Applicable
On Us Personal Check Payable to an individual (or to cash if presentor is other than the maker)	TC 61 on Maker CASH	TC 61 on Maker CASH*	CASH* if small, REFER if large TC 61	TC 61 on Maker CASH	REFER to Officer	REFER to Officer
Personal Check Drawn on Another Bank	TC 88 on Customer	TC 88 on Customer*	REFER to Officer	TC 88 on Customer	REFUSE Politely	REFUSE Politely
On Us Payroll Check	TC 61 on Maker CASH**	TC 61 on Maker CASH**	REFER to Officer	TC 61 on Maker CASH**	Identify and CASH** TC 61 or REFER	TC 61 on Maker CASH**
Payroll Check Drawn on Another Bank	CASH	CASH, hold if Company is Unknown	REFER to Officer	CASH	REFUSE Politely	REFUSE Politely
Insurance Draft	CASH	DEPOSIT Hold	Enter as Collection Item	REFER to Officer	REFUSE Politely	Enter as Collection Item
On Us Officers, Official Cashiers, or Certified Check	CASH	CASH*	CASH if not Identified REFER	CASH	REFER to Officer	REFER to Officer
Officers, Official, Cashiers, or Certified Checks on another Bank	CASH	REFER to Officer	REFER to Officer	REFER to Officer	REFUSE Politely	REFUSE Politely
Government Checks	CASH	CASH*	REFER to Officer	CASH	REFUSE Politely	REFUSE Politely
On Us Money Orders	Call M.O. Department CASH if OK	Call M.O. Department CASH* if OK	Call M.O. Department CASH* if OK	Call M.O. Department CASH if OK	REFER to Officer	REFER to Officer
Other Money Orders	CASH	CASH*, hold if necessary	REFER to Officer	CASH	REFUSE Politely	REFUSE Politely
Travelers Cheques	CASH	CASH*	CASH*	CASH	CASH*	CASH

IMPORTANT: This sheet is a guide only. It is a statement of what you can attempt to do in given situations. It IS NOT permission to go ahead and take the action specified. It states the bank's policy on various kinds of checks and customers. It is up to you to decide if the type of account the customer has, the identification presented, and type of check presented to you justify your taking the action permitted. Do not refer to this chart in the presence of customers, and do not use its terms or classifications in conversation with customers.

"CASH, HOLD" means to cash the item only if the customer's balance is sufficient to hold the amount of the item.

*One asterisk means that you must always identify the presentor from the signature cards, or from other positive identification if no signature is available. You must make a note of the identification used on the back of item.

**Two aserisks mean that you must verify the signatures and the authority to sign on company checks.

A Well Known customer is one whose account has been open at least one year and is trouble free. He comes in regularly, and you know his name, employment, and signature from memory. You feel that he would be able to take care of the amount of the check if it is returned.

FIGURE 18.5

Source: Clyde W. Jackson

describing the flow of a form we recommend that a copy of a *filled in* form accompany the procedure. It is good practice to provide notes on the form such as shown in Figure 18.6. Flowcharts also serve as illustrations of written procedures. They are not a substitute for written procedures!

Procedure with Notes

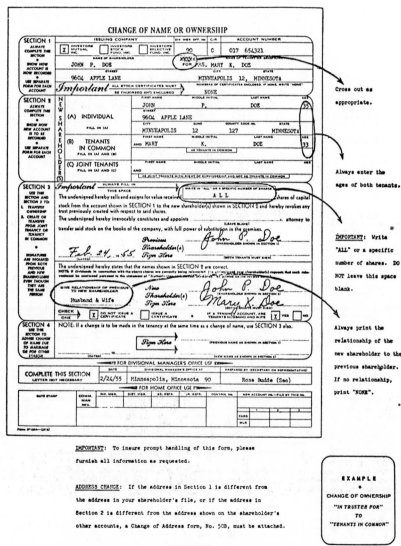

FIGURE 18.6

Source: Clifford I. Haga

Illustrations are recommended to increase the learning effects of understanding written procedures. First, people vary greatly in their preferred source of stimuli. Providing both narrative and illustrations in the procedure results in understanding by more readers. Second, showing the procedure in two forms provides redundancy which increases the probability of the message being understood.

Filled in forms are suggested because they convey more information than the blank form. Sometimes the information will be erroneous. Once a wallet manufacturer used a secretary's social security card as an example of what to put in a pocket of the wallets the company sold. The Social Security Administration is still receiving reports each quarter using that secretary's social security number. The systems analysts should also be careful with the information used to fill in forms. It certainly should be an accurate representation but not anything confidential. The solution in the wallet manufacturer's insert was to print a card with 000-00-0000 as the number and John and Jane Doe as fictitious names.

SYSTEM DEVELOPMENT DOCUMENTATION

To this point the chapter has described the ways in which an organization can write its policies, procedures and standards. We will now consider how useful such methods are for the more specialized information systems needs. The following is a list of the modules needed in a system library described by Hochschild (1971). We shall discuss the documentation requirements of each of the items on his list.

System Introduction

The system introduction describes the purpose and principle elements of the system. It is written in paragraph form and may be supplemented with a simple systems chart as an illustration.

System Requirements

This section presents the detailed specifications that the system must meet. It is usually written in conventional paragraph form with illustrations. The requirements section of the systems specifications shown in Chapter 20 is an example of the type of text that would be used.

Field Library

The field library gives a detailed description of each field in the system. The style of presentation is usually caption and would include:

Field names and codes
  Single standard name and/or code used
  COBOL name
  Assembly language name
  FORTRAN name
  Revision Date
Pictures
  Internal
  Input
  Display or report
Description
  A one paragraph description of the field, its purpose and its use in the system.
Values and Codes
  The legitimate range of values is shown. Codes are listed with the description of the item they represent. When calculated the algorithm is shown.

Segment, Record and Data Set (File) Libraries

Segments are logical groups of fields. Records are segments and fields gathered together to describe a transaction or a system entity. Data sets are groups of records. They are described using similar techniques to those employed for fields.

Processing Modules Programs

The following five modules are the usual methods used in programming documentation and include flowcharts, decision tables, comments and the written program itself.

1. Control modules show the structure of the program as a whole and the relationships of the other modules. Flowcharts or decision tables are very appropriate documentation forms here.

2. Data set modules provide for the physical transferring of data, usually to and from peripheral devices. The caption form of documentation is a possible alternative to the more often used flowchart. Blocking factors, search algorithms, overflow techniques, etc., can all be described using the caption style. These factors are hard to locate in flowcharts.

3. Interpretative modules manipulate data between work areas. Creation of report lines and error messages are examples. Flowcharts or a tabular arrangement are appropriate documentation techniques here.

4. General modules such as checkpoint or calculation routines

can be documented by flowcharts or captions depending upon the procedure.

5. Programs are the detail of the four procedural components. Information systems programs must be readable by the others on the project team, user personnel and maintenance programmers. This requires extensive use of comments. The field names should also be meaningful to the reader. Many organizations restrict modules to one page of code as a help to the reader.

Operating Modules

Hochschild defined two operating modules—job steps and jobs. These are the programs and groups of programs which process the data. These libraries are meant to be read by the computer and are in a machine language.

Operating instructions should really be included in this area, probably as a separate library. These are most often organized in caption style under the headings shown in Figure 18.7.

Support Libraries

The four remaining documentation libraries used by Hochschild are procedures, systems flow, notes and appendices. The latter lists meeting records and cross references. The procedures are the usual input/output and clerical tasks which can be described by any one of the documentation methods proposed. The systems flowchart is heavily annotated.

The Project Folder

Brotherton (1974) suggests a somewhat different and more conventional project documentation system as shown in Figure 18.8. The Hochschild libraries are automated while the Brotherton folder is not.

Training Manuals

It has been stated that training manuals differ from reference manuals. Since training usually involves training groups of people with the same job at a particular time, the need is only for a training manual that contains the material related to that particular job. Training manuals then differ in the following ways:

1. The playscript procedure is usually inappropriate since much of the procedure is not applicable. Note that it may be appropriate to include some relationships of the job to the environment to give the employee a sense of participation and to show the

Operating Instructions Manual

- Job name or function name
- Purpose of the function
- Processing description (narrative)
- Type of function
- System set-up
  - Reader
    - JCL
    - Input data (listed in required input sequence)
  - Disk
    - Drive and volume number (each pack)
  - Tape
    - Drive, label, and whether input, output, or work file
  - Punch (if required)
    - Card code, color, corner cut, etc.
- Terminal support
  - If yes, list report and terminal codes
- Console messages
  - List all program generated messages and any action or response required, or else specify 'Program does not generate any messages'
- Restart procedures
  - Narrative for each restart section
- Reports
  - Report title
  - Form and number of copies
  - Carriage tape
- Input files
  - File name
  - Disposition and retention
  - Label book name
  - Symbolic address
  - Drive
- Work files
  - File name
  - Disposition and retention
  - Label book name
  - Symbolic address
  - Drive
- Output files
  - File name
  - Disposition and retention
  - Label book name
  - Symbolic address
  - Drive

FIGURE 18.7

Source: John P. Robinson

importance of the particular job steps in the overall scheme. Caption procedures are more often appropriate.

2. A separate training manual should be prepared for each major group to be trained.
3. While there is some use of the manual in training replacements the primary use is in training the original group of employees.
4. Good training material is replete with explanations, examples

PROJECT FOLDER TABLE OF CONTENTS

BY	DATE	Section	Contents	Mod Date	Mod Date
			PROJECT NAME PROJECT NUMBER		
		10.00	Systems Approval and/or Authorization		
		11.00	Request for Systems Development		
		14.00	Evaluation of Request for Systems Development		
		18.00	Resources Sharing Statement		
		20.00	Systems Design Specifications		
		21.00	Systems Definition		
		21.10	Objectives and Requirements		
		21.20	Method of Accomplishment		
		21.30	System Description		
		21.31	System Narrative		
		21.32	System Flowchart		
		21.40	Organizational Chart		
		22.00	System Components		
		22.10	System Input		
		22.20	System Processing		
		22.30	System Output		
		22.40	Record Formats		
		23.00	System File Design		
		24.00	System Tables		
		25.00	System Controls		
		26.00	System Test and Audit		
		27.00	System Error Recovery		
		28.00	System Back-up and Recovery		
		29.00	Sources of System Information		
		29.10	List of Personnel		
		29.20	List of Literary References		
		29.50	Glossary of Nomenclature		
		30.00	Program Design Specifications		
		31.00	Program Description		
		31.10	General Program Flowchart		
		31.20	Program Narrative		
		31.30	Program Constraints		
		40.00	Detailed Program Module Specifications		
		41.00	Module Description		
		41.10	Flowchart		

FIGURE 18.8

Source: C. W. Brotherton

PROJECT FOLDER TABLE OF CONTENTS (cont.)

PROJECT NAME

PROJECT NUMBER

BY	DATE	Section	Contents	Mod Date	Mod Date
		41.20	Decision Tables		
		41.30	System Records and Files		
		41.40	Resident Module Constants		
		41.50	System Tables		
		41.60	Compiler Listing		
		41.70	Module Recovery		
		42.00	Program Controls		
		43.00	Glossary of Nomenclature		
		44.00	Glossary of Codes		
		45.00	Testing Procedures		
		46.00	Acceptance Test		
		50.00	Production Data		
		51.00	Schedules		
		51.10	Input/Output Schedules		
		51.20	Computer/Hardware Schedule		
		52.00	Data Control Instructions		
		53.00	Input Data Preparation Instructions		
		54.00	Operating Instructions		
		60.00	Systems History		
		61.00	Correspondence		
		62.00	Project Reports		
		63.00	Progress Reports		
		64.00	Miscellaneous Work Papers		
		65.00	Change Requests		
		66.00	Periodical Review		

FIGURE 18.8

Source: C. W. Brotherton

and exercises for the trainee. This type of material is less appropriate in a reference manual.

5. The training manual will often include descriptions and characteristics of the equipment used by the employee. These are often omitted in reference manuals.

Reference Manuals

Reference manuals, in contrast, use playscript, cover the entire system, are used in the on-going operation, and have fewer examples and exercises. They must be well organized with easily identified sections, indexes and cross references so that the user can quickly retrieve the required information. These features are less important in a training manual intended to be read in its entirety.

Completeness is a criterion for a good reference manual. Answers must be provided in the reference manual. On the other hand, if the training manual acquaints the user with the principle activities in the system and relies on the reference manual for details, it is an adequate manual.

User's or Operations Manual

The user's manual, like the training manual, may describe only the parts of the system seen by the particular user but must be as complete in detail as a reference manual.

The user's manual is ideally something of a hybrid between the training and reference manuals.

Criteria for content of a user's manual are:

1. All user area references must be well indexed.
2. Step-by-step operating instructions for a new system operator.
3. Overview of entire system to assist the user to locate a subsystem is included.
4. Instructions are clearly written for the user with a minimum of jargon and code.

Manual Revision

Emerson's Law states that "the better the documentation, the less likely it is current." Good documentation is voluminous and large amounts are difficult to keep current because they involve so many cross references that must also be updated. Also, the publication of frequent revisions is expensive. Facing these difficulties, many organizations have elected to keep their documentation by computer. Some of the advantages and disadvantages of computer kept documentation are as follows:

Advantages
1. Ease of change.
2. Availability of flowcharting programs and other computer directed documentation.
3. Computer built cross references and indexes are easier to maintain.
4. A system on computer tape can be mailed to another location or transmitted via telephone lines.

Disadvantages
1. Inability to reproduce certain illustrations such as Figure 18.6.
2. Offset reproducers can produce copies of documentation cheaper than computers.
3. Cost of developing the computer documentation system is expensive.

Major advantages occur mostly on large systems or ones requiring frequent changes. Organizations having such systems may well find it appropriate to acquire computerized documentation systems.

IS DOCUMENTATION REALLY IMPORTANT?

In a tragic-comic tale, Mulhern (1973) tells of a programmer who wrote a program that returned one to three million dollars to the company whenever it was run. The program was undocumented, incomprehensible and impossible for anyone else to run. In the tale Toltot Kaposztas quit when he is given only a $50 raise. The company's personnel policy would allow no more and would not allow Kaposztas to be rehired. The reader is at liberty to discover his own moral of the story.

Powers (1971) tested the hypothesis that using and enforcing documentation standards predicts project success. He found that such actions contributed to completing the project on time but had no relationship to user or computer operators' satisfaction with the system.

Good documentation is not usually as important as user participation and many other project management variables but it is still very important. It has been observed that wherever a program acceptance procedure is inserted between the project group and computer operations, one of the acceptance criteria is documentation. Without good documentation the program isn't accepted. Good documentation appears to be a necessary condition for a good system.

Shrout (1971) found that writing ability was the most important competency currently needed by systems analysts. Since writing for the systems analyst is virtually synonymous with documentation, the systems managers Shrout surveyed certainly believed documentation was highly important.

SUMMARY

It has been shown that documentation is important in the systems project. It is written by the analyst, the programmers and sometimes by documentation specialists. The documentation types described in the chapter were conventional narrative, playscript, functional or caption, matrix, and flowcharts. Each has its merits and each may be the best method to use in certain cases.

The documents needed in a system library were described in both manual and mechanized form. Mechanization was shown to be appropriate for large or frequently changed documentation.

Training manuals were distinguished from reference and user manuals. The uses of each differed enough to warrant separate manuals in many, if not all, cases of documentation.

REVIEW QUESTIONS

1. What documents are required to obtain management approval for a system investigation? For authorization to develop the system?
2. What documents are necessary to obtain user approval of a proposed system?
3. Under what circumstances would automation of documentation be justified?
4. How would you determine which documentation would be best for Question 3? What circumstances would determine the best way?
5. When is a decision table appropriate? Playscript?

DISCUSSION QUESTIONS

1. Discuss what documentation is needed for a keypunch operator. For a remote CRT terminal operator.
2. Given an undocumented program; discuss how it could be deciphered.
3. Discuss your procedures for studying for an exam and how you would document those procedures.

BIBLIOGRAPHY

Baker, F. T., "Chief Programmer Team, Management of Production Programmer," *IBM Systems Journal,* Vol. 11, No. 1, 1972, pp. 56-73.

Borgen, Fred H., et. al., "Occupational Reinforcer Patterns," *Minnesota Studies in Vocational Rehabilitation,* Vol. 24, Minneapolis: University of Minnesota Industrial Relations Center, 1968.

Brotherton, C. W., "Documentation—A Forgotten Unit," *Journal of Data Education,* Vol. 14, No. 8, May 1974, pp. 12-16.

Coughlin, Clifford W., "Need for Good Procedures, The," *Journal of Systems Management,* Vol. 24, No. 6, June 1973, pp. 30-33.

Haga, Clifford, "Procedure Manuals," *Ideas For Management,* ASM, Cleveland: pp. 127-154 1968.

Hochschild, Alan, "Disciplined Systems Development," *Data Management,* Vol. 9, No. 9, September 1971, pp. 32-37.

Jackson, Clyde W., "Documentation is Spelled Communicating," *Journal of Systems Management,* Vol. 24, No. 6, June 1973, pp. 34-35.

Jackson, Clyde W., *Verbal Information Systems,* Cleveland: Association for Systems Management, 1974.

Kendall, Raymond H., "Manual for Systems Users, A," *Journal of Systems Management,* Vol. 23, No. 10, October 1972, pp. 20-22.

Matthies, Leslie H., "Playscript Procedure, The," *Office Publications, Inc.,* Stamford, Conn., 1961.

Menkus, Belden, "Defining Adequate Systems Documentation," *Journal of Systems Management,* Vol. 21, No. 12, December 1970, pp. 16-21.

Mills, Harlan, "Chief Programmer Teams: Principles and Procedures," Gaithersburg, Md., IBM Report FSC71-5108.

Mulhern, Thomas P., "Toltot Kaposztas," *Journal of Systems Management,* Vol. 24, No. 5, May 1973, pp. 28-29.

Powers, Richard F., "Empirical Investigation of Selected Hypothesis Related to the Success of Management Information Systems Projects, An," Unpublished Doctoral Dissertation, University of Minnesota, 1971.

Robinson, John P. and James D. Graviss, *Documentation Standards Manual for Computer Systems,* Cleveland: Association for Systems Management, 1973.

Shaw, John C. and William Atkins, *Managing Computer Programming Projects,* McGraw-Hill, 1970.

Shrout, Ethel H., "Competencies and Training Requirements for Information Systems Analysts," in Willoughby, Theodore C., Proceedings of the Ninth Annual Computer Personnel Research Conference, New York, ACM, 1971.

Stephan, Richard W., "Setting Up A Manual of Policies and Procedures," *Data Management,* Vol. 8, No. 9, September 1970, pp. 93-95.

Stevens, Robert I., "Policies and Procedures: Getting Out the Word," *Management Adviser,* Vol. 10, No. 1, January/February 1973, pp. 49-54.

Walsh, Dorothy, "Guide for Software Documentation, A," New York: Advanced Computer Techniques Corporation, 1969, p. 157.

CHAPTER 19

HARDWARE AND SOFTWARE SELECTION

HARDWARE SELECTION

Many information systems projects do not involve the procurement of any new equipment. In those cases, the project is designed to fit the available equipment. If the project cannot be implemented satisfactorily without the addition of new equipment, the systems analyst is responsible for the selection of new equipment from the smallest unit to a complete computer installation. This chapter discusses general criteria for hardware selection. Readers interested in in-depth discussion of hardware selection will find Joslin (1968) and Sharpe (1969) to be excellent sources of basic information about hardware procurement.

SATISFICING OR OPTIMIZING MODE

Since equipment manufacturers offer an almost infinite range of capabilities for their equipment, the project leader must determine whether his goal is to procure the optimal equipment or satisfactory equipment. Factors in this decision to be discussed in detail are search costs, size of procurement, equipment availability, legal constraints, organizational relationships with vendors, project and personal risk.

Search costs will obviously be higher if the selection goal is to reach an optimum conclusion. Search costs involve obtaining lists of potential vendors, corresponding with vendors, conferences with vendor sales and service personnel, preparation of detailed specifications for a competitive comparison. A satisficing mode searches only the minimum time required to locate equipment that satisfies the need. Optimizing equipment comparisons can be a very expensive activity.

Size or dollar volume of the equipment to be procured is an important selection factor. An optimum choice of a thousand dollars worth of equipment is much less important than for a million dollar computer installation. The difference between satisfactory and optimum selection for a small procurement is often the cost of telephone calls to potential vendors. A small equipment procurement usually restricts the search to a satisficing mode.

The equipment available for selection provides further restrictions. Until recently the telephone companies could restrict the kinds of equipment attached to their lines. This resulted in the teletypewriter manufactured by the Teletype Corporation, a subsidiary of Western

Electric and the American Telephone and Telegraph Company, being virtually the only reasonable choice of equipment for certain jobs. In many remote locations service is restricted to one vendor which severely limits choice.

Governmental agencies are required by law to have competitive procurement procedures for all except very minor items. The selection mode is an optimizing one in theory, yet the product specifications may be so restrictive as to eliminate all except the satisficing equipment. Although reducing competitive bids is not purposely done, reducing time in search and evaluation is enough of a motive to write restrictive specifications.

The organization's relationships with vendors can be an important search restricting variable. Once the satisficing mode has been accomplished by a vendor a long and satisfactory relationship can develop, restricting the motives to search for alternative suppliers. Studies of computer procurement have shown a considerable amount of brand loyalty with users tending to stay with a specific vendor.

Some organizations choose to have all computer equipment supplied by the same vendor to simplify maintenance and training activities, although some of the vendor's equipment may cost more than that of a competitor.

Risk to the project is another influence in selecting satisficing or optimum performance. Here the analyst must consider the risks of using new untested equipment, the responsibility of the vendor if the equipment fails and the excellence of a new vendor trying to break into the market. In the final analysis the project risk must be commensurate with the potential to be gained.

Personal risk can be an important consideration in equipment selection. There is job security in choosing the most successful vendor in the field at the expense of other criteria. For some decision-makers the personal job security aspect of the decision can be important.

These are the major reasons for choosing to satisfice or to optimize the conditions of equipment selection for a project.

SATISFICING SELECTION

The information search in a satisficing selection may be the same as for the optimizing selection or it may be restricted in those situations described above, for example, where a single vendor is the only one considered. Some sources of product and vendor information are shown in Figure 19.1.

Initial evaluation of the equipment considers the basics of capa-

---

SOURCES OF EQUIPMENT INFORMATION

Evaluation Sources
    Auerbach
    Datapro
    Office Automation Reports

Trade Publications
    Modern Data
    Infosystems
    Computers and People
    The Office
    Modern Office Procedures
    Datamation
    (Most of these publish lists of equipment with
    comparison of significant features)

Purchasing Department References
    Thomas Index of Manufacturers

Peers

FIGURE 19.1

bility, cost and confidence in the vendor. The analyst then selects the most likely vendors and contacts their salesmen.

The detailed investigation of the equipment is conducted with sales representatives of vendors and includes detailed specifications, demonstrations, pricing, delivery commitments and implementation assistance.

The final evaluation eliminates equipment that will not do the job and equipment that is priced too high or too low. Too high or too low prices infer doubt that the vendor understands the situation.

From the reduced list of potential vendors, the decision-maker selects the best combination of price and service with the emphasis on service, since selection of the satisficing mode relegates price to a secondary consideration.

OPTIMIZING SELECTION

The search sources are the same as for a satisficing selection (Figure 19.1). However, the search is longer since it gathers a complete list of potential vendors.

A detailed request for proposal is then prepared for the vendors. The details of such requests are described later in this chapter.

The evaluation of proposals submitted by the vendors is against the criteria described in the formal request for proposals. The evaluation results in a "best" proposal which is selected.

REQUEST FOR PROPOSAL

The following discussion follows closely the selection procedures proposed by Joslin (1968). The items to be included in each of the five sections of the request for proposal are as follows:

SECTION 1: GROUND RULES

Who to contact
Date for discussion of ground rules
Date for proposal delivery
Date for presentation
Date for running benchmarks
Contract arrangements such as rent, third party lease, purchase
Who pays for proposal preparation (usually vendor)
Statement that proposal will be considered part of contract
Procedure for suggesting systems changes
Procedure for notification of systems changes

SECTION 2: SYSTEM REQUIREMENTS

Description of work load
Time constraints
Growth projection
Mandatory requirements such as:
  COBOL compiler
  Sort utility
  Run existing HAL programs
  Delivery schedule
  Space available
Desirable features such as:
  PERT
  Automatic flowcharter
  Decision table processor
Expansion needs
Vendor support needed
Cost restrictions

SECTION 3: EVALUATION OF DESIRABLE FEATURES

The specific value of each such feature is given.
Where gradations of service occur, gradations of value are given.

SECTION 4: BENCHMARKS

Listing of the programs
Weights for each program

Limits on running time of the mix
Source code

SECTION 5: PROPOSAL INSTRUCTIONS

Specification of what information is required in the proposal:
  Covering letter
  Summary
  Statement of required features
  System processing characteristics
  Cost data
  Contract provisions
  Housing requirements
  Answers to specific questions
  Technical literature
  Equipment characteristics

EVALUATION OF PROPOSAL

Upon receipt of the proposal the evaluators ascertain whether the proposal meets the specifications. If not, it is rejected. Those proposals meeting specifications are evaluated by assigning costs and values to each feature or deficiency included in the original Request for Proposal. The values are totaled and the proposal with the lowest cost is recommended for implementation.

The mandatory requirements of a proposal may include such items as:

Capability of handling existing COBOL programs
Capability of processing the benchmarks to the satisfaction of the selection personnel.
Capability of handling the projected workload which is expected to be 150% above the present workload in five years.

The desirable components may include:
Availability of a PERT package
On-site maintenance
Less than 5% hand changes to COBOL programs

Failure to meet any of the mandatory features would disqualify the proposal. Providing capacity beyond the requirement would be given credit according to its value to the buyer.

Additional capacity for handling the workload might be evaluated as follows:

Additional Life 20% per year expansion	Value Assigned
0	None
1	$100,000
2	$150,000
3	$180,000

While development of a PERT package might cost $100,000, its value to the buyer might be considered to be worth $25,000. This is calculated from estimates of programmer time savings in drawing flowcharts.

The equipment failure incidence rate is multiplied by the value of computer time to arrive at an estimated value of on-site maintenance.

Hand changes to COBOL are evaluated at the cost of programmer time to make the changes. The table might look like this:

Changes Required	Value
None	$40,000
Less than 2%	$20,000
From 2% to 5%	$10,000
5%	0
From 6% to 8%	−$10,000
8% to 15%	−$40,000

By totaling the equipment costs plus the values assigned to the desirable features, the systems analyst can make comparisons between the proposals.

Where it is necessary to equate differing cost values, discounted cash flow methods (described in Chapter 6) should be used.

SOFTWARE SELECTION

The expense for software can often equal the hardware purchases. The software costs include both in-house programming and software packages. The latter represent a growing percentage of the total costs. The software packages are available from computer manufacturers, user groups, universities, government organizations and software vendors.

For the over 100,000 computer installations in the U.S. there must be 50,000 specially written payroll systems. Obviously there are not that many variations in payroll operations and many organizations have wasted programmer time when they could have purchased and adapted a software package to fit their payroll situation. This is the basic reason for buying software: the development cost can be apportioned across many users.

The programs available from the several sources differ in many respects (Figure 19.2). Goetz (1972) suggested that to be saleable a software package must:

Have a useful life of three or more years.

Be priced considerably lower than development cost.

Satisfy a variety of users.

Be able to be enhanced.

Survive against competition.

SOFTWARE CHARACTERISTICS BY SOURCE

Source	Cost	Package Size	Documentation	Service
Computer Manufacturing	Some Bundled, Some Costly, Some Free	Full Range	Full Range	Generally Good
User Groups	Nominal	Usually Small	Often Poor	None
Universities	Nominal	Usually Small	Often Poor	None
Government	Nominal	Usually Small	Often Poor	None
Software Vendors	Costly	Full Range	Full Range	Covered in Contract

FIGURE 19.2

The typical program developed and written for application within an organization does not usually have the generality and flexibility to make it useful to another company. This feature has made the development of software packages a marketing speciality.

VENDOR AND PACKAGE INFORMATION

The *ICP Quarterly* publishes perhaps the largest list of software package descriptions and vendor addresses. It lists hundreds of software packages currently available for business systems. Other trade publications are also sources of advertised software packages. Datapro, Business Automation Specification Reports, and Auerbach are organizations that sell evaluation services of current software packages.

Each computer manufacturer offers a referral service among its users for the exchange of information on software programs. Perhaps the best known of such groups is SHARE, a group of scientific users of IBM hardware. The members of SHARE contribute programs to a library, which distributes the programs to interested users at cost.

The data processing and systems journals offer considerable information about software packages. *Computer Decisions, Computerworld, Datamation, Data Management, Infosystems, Journal of Systems Management,* and *Modern Data* all have regular features and/or advertisements of particular packages.

Software programs developed under government contract are considered to be public property and NASA publishes its listings in *Computer Program Abstracts.*

In 1969 IBM moved to "unbundle" or sell its various computer services separately. This action opened the door to other manufacturers to sell software packages to all computer installations. Figure 19.3 indicates the potential market software packages represent.

IBM SOFTWARE CATEGORIES—PRICES AND SUPPORT

Type of Product	Price	Support
Pre-1969 Programs	Free	Generally at a charge
Older Operating System	Free	Moving toward a charge
Newest Systems Control Programs	Monthly fee	Supported
Program Products Data base, applications	Monthly fee	Supported
Field Developed Programs	Monthly fee— 12 to 24 months Free thereafter	At a charge
Installed User Programs	"	At a charge
RPQ Programming	Usually a single fee	At a charge

FIGURE 19.3

When confronted with the need for a new program, the systems analyst has a make-or-buy software decision. Generally, it is appropriate to buy where the cost of external programs is lower than the cost of internal ones, when the programming unit is overloaded and when the programs are beyond the technical ability of the internal group.

Before attempting to evaluate vendor packages the systems analyst must estimate the cost of developing the programs in-house. Program estimation is described in some detail in Chapter 23. Also, the analyst must determine whether the programming group has the ability and the time to develop the programs. The advantages of external and internal program development will become apparent as we examine the characteristics of software evaluation.

SOFTWARE SELECTION CRITERIA

Software evaluation and selection can be a very complex task. The references at the end of this chapter provide much more information about the process and two good examples of how to make an evaluation (Chapin, 1970; and Adams and Mullarkey, 1972).

Cost

Software packages are marketed under such a variety of programs that it is difficult to arrive at cost comparisons. Some packages have an initial purchase price plus a monthly maintenance fee. Others have monthly license fees plus fees for maintenance. Others have a license fee that is renewable every 12 months.

One important consideration is whether the license restricts the software package from use elsewhere in the organization. If a package is restricted to use on one CPU, a multi-computer organization may find that package cost-prohibitive. Currently, the federal government is attempting to eliminate this restricting practice. Also as competition in the marketing of software packages develops, it will result in reduced costs and volume discounts.

The discounted cash flow method which provides an internal rate of return for a project is useful for comparing software packages.

Software Selection Example

The company needs a new production control system. Internal development would take three years, cost $50,000/year to develop and return a net benefit of $50,000 in seven subsequent years at which point the system would be obsolete. Software package A could be purchased and installed for $100,000 in three months and return a net benefit of $40,000 per year for ten years. Package B could be licensed for $3,000 per month, installed in three months and return $38,000/year in net benefits. The best package from a financial viewpoint is not obvious. Internal rates of return are needed to compare the three alternatives.

System Configuration

The system configuration under which a package will operate should be viewed in terms of both hardware and software. In the equipment configuration, the minimum configuration needed to operate the package should be determined. Such factors as the size and model of the CPU, special features required such as decimal arithmetic, memory protection and types and speeds of the I/O devices must be taken into account.

This isn't always as simple as it would seem. Many packages will run on several versions of a particular computer system with corresponding changes in throughput rate, file size limitations, etc. For instance, a package which is capable of running with a 32K bytes memory may be designed to run more efficiently if the computer has 64K bytes while in other packages this may not make a difference. In another case, magnetic tape storage can be substituted for files maintained on disk or vice versa in certain packages with little loss in efficiency while in others this may not be true. When a package supplier specifies a three disk system, he may mean exactly three disks or it may be that the system permits a reduction to two disks or an increase to four. In summary, the package may be extremely hardware sensitive or it may have considerable flexibility.

Software Environment

When it comes to the software environment, the language in which a package is programmed and the operating system under which it is designed to run can be very important considerations.

First of all, one should find out if the package is written in assembly level language or in a higher level language such as FORTRAN. If it is planned to modify or extend a package, it is better if it is written in a language in which the programming staff is proficient. In operating the system, if the package runs only under DOS and the installation is under the OS, there may be serious problems. Either the package will have to be upgraded to the larger operating system or the installation will have to contend with a package that does not fit into the system environment common to the other applications.

Operating Costs

The software packages available for purchase vary greatly in the amount of computer core, set up and running time required. A generalized software program is likely to handle all contingencies but may not be cost-effective in handling the major groups of transactions. A more limited program may be faster but require the manual handling of exceptions. These operating factors must be converted to a cost basis for evaluation purposes. The influence of the program upon other programs must also be considered.

Cost to Customize

A demand deposit system cost $300,000 to develop against a purchase price for a packaged system of $50,000 plus another $100,000 to customize it to the specific company's operation. This example clearly shows the purchase/adapt route as the best to take. Often the decision to purchase and modify an existing software package is the most economical procedure.

Cost of Maintenance

This is another significant software cost. All software programs must be maintained but maintenance costs vary widely. Often the software package developer will contract to maintain the program (for a certain number of years) for all users provided extensive modifications have not been made to the program.

Contractors also vary in the support provided to assist in the maintenance. The range is from none to support equivalent to that provided for hardware. This item, like the others, is subject to the Joslin Cost/Value analysis described previously.

Immediate Installation

An advantage of purchased software packages is that they are available for installation which can be important when schedules are tight and returns on the new system will be large. However, the installation costs of purchased software must be taken into account. Sometimes the vendor includes his installation costs as a part of the purchase price but the customer still has personnel and other installation expenses to consider.

Contract Terms

Normally the contract will specify the following important features:
1. Buyer and seller
2. Location of use
3. Restriction of conveyance by buyer to a third party
4. Time and place of delivery
5. Price
6. Patent escape clause
7. Warranty against defects
8. Liability of seller limited to sale price.

The warranty clause in the contract is particularly important because no program of any significant size is completely free of defects and the buyer wants the developer to agree to correct defects. Since the seller is reluctant to make such agreements, the result is often a compromise in which the vendor agrees to correct defects for a short time period. Errors encountered later are to be paid for by the user.

The developer will not warrant the consequential errors of the buyer. For example, if a purchased stock investment package was erroneous and the user went bankrupt because of the errors in the program, the only damages recoverable from the developer would be the cost of correcting the program.

Sale contracts are such that the buyer must quickly learn the characteristics of the program and adapt it to his own operation for it to have significant economic consequences for the organization. The purchaser should be sure to get all oral promises written into the contract. While recovery of damages may be possible without the promises in writing, the case is much better with them.

Quality Evaluation

It is important that the software be effective, efficient and reliable. Perhaps the best sources for information on the quality of a software package are the current and previous users. Inquiries to the users should be made without the presence of the software vendor. The information obtained should include type of use, error frequency, maintenance record, errors found, service, quality of documentation, ease of use and operating characteristics. If possible, the interviews should be held with operators, users, project personnel and systems programmers because a program that is satisfactory in one area may not work in others.

If the software program has had regular maintenance by the seller, then the reliability of the program is generally a function of its age, with older programs being more error free. Information systems managers have found an added risk in being the first to install new types of hardware or software.

The best evaluation of software quality is to test it thoroughly, and an acceptance test should be included in the contract. Chapter 24 describes some testing precepts that can be applied to purchased software.

Ease of Use

This is another important consideration in the purchase of a software package. For example, in choosing between one program that required programming to prepare a special report and another which required a 15 minute, hand-written request by a trained user after four hours of instruction, the second package would be the better choice because of its simplicity.

A payroll package that must be recompiled after every change in tax rates is a poorer choice than one which handles tax rates as data sets separate from the program.

Reputation of the Supplier

The reputation of the supplier as a developer of quality software packages is a vital consideration. Many software developers market what appear to be excellent products but through poor business management go out of business and fail to maintain the package they have sold. On the other hand, software packages available from hardware manufacturers have been claimed to have deliberate inefficiencies to maximize the hardware sales. As the software packaging field becomes more competitive, all suppliers will have incentive to develop more efficient packages.

Software packages may be purchased from developers who do not offer maintenance services if the buyer has programming capabilities within his organization to adapt, maintain and service the purchased program.

Documentation

Unless one can get a "signed in blood" statement that the supplier will be around throughout the useful life of the system, you had better make sure that you are going to receive complete documentation including narrative descriptions at both the system and run levels, system logic and logic flowcharts, I/O and file descriptions and layouts, operator instructions and keypunch source data preparation instructions.

The amount of documentation required can vary according to the type of package under consideration. Certain utility packages or application independent packages, such as those for program flowcharting, may not require the detailed documentation that is necessary for an accounting application such as accounts receivable. Some suppliers consider a certain package to be proprietary and agree to provide only an object deck and operating instructions in an effort to prevent outsiders from determining the way in which the package is structured.

SUMMARY

The systems analyst critically examines hardware and software comparing advantages and disadvantages, estimating risk and return on investment. The Request for Proposal (RFP) formally states the criteria to be met by the suppliers of large hardware installations.

Selection of peripheral equipment is the same in concept, yet it is usually simplified in practice because of the smaller amount of money involved and reduced complexity.

Software selection involves modest to moderate expenditures but moderate to substantial complexity. A well-done evaluation then often requires the Request for Proposal and the careful evaluation of options and alternatives suggested for hardware.

The expenditure is often too small to warrant such an effort. It is recommended that the Joslin model be considered as the ideal and approached as closely as practical in each software procurement task.

System Selection Case History

The economic feasibility of a computerized information system of accounting and financial information of clients in a dental organization was analyzed. This organization had affiliated "sites" throughout a large county; each site provided services to its own clients. Various weekly, bi-monthly and monthly reports of financial and accounting information of clients and of services provided to them were generated clerically at each site.

The central organization was considering the establishment of a centralized computer-based system to systematize the periodicity, types and formats of such reports, to improve the reliability and timeliness of information needed for proper client management (e.g., speed collection of accounts receivable), and to reduce present costs of manipulating data and of producing the present reports.

First, the types, formats, and periodicity of the new output reports and of input forms for data collection desired were established. The aggregations of data and management decision guidelines to be programmed to produce the reports were explicitly defined in writing with the aid of large and interrelated decision tables. Then average data input and data output workloads for an average site were established.

The next task was to identify and estimate the major costs of a computer-based system, to determine if savings could be achieved over the costs of the clerical system (about $1000/month for two clerical employees per site) for the present volume of transactions, and to estimate such savings (or losses) for various volumes of affiliated sites. All fixed, semi-fixed and variable costs were to be identified and estimated.

The information system was to generate a total of 16 different reports, two of them weekly, four bi-monthly and the rest monthly. Four of the monthly reports would go to each client monthly, the rest would be for other uses at the site. Each site handled an average of 5000 clients, but only about 900 of these accounts were active in any given month.

A general design of the COBOL-based programming system to accomplish the task was made. There are of course many tradeoffs involved in deciding how processing should flow in what hardware configuration. The design was made assuming the use of a small to medium size computing system of the IBM 360/30 or UNIVAC 9400 type; five tape units and five disc units were required.

Costs

The resultant economic analysis of the information system appears in Figure 19.4, showing the important cost items per month versus the number of sites, i.e., the volume of data entry. Figure 19.4 is based on the following estimates made on a per site basis:

1. *Computer costs.* Based on the general system design made and the estimate of the average workload of a site, the size of the basic data bases required (three small semi-invariant random access files, and two large sequentially organized files with about two million bytes per site) and the computer time needed to produce the reports were estimated. About 10 minutes of computer time was needed per site, using sort/merging calculations on a 64K IBM 360/40 configuration. Sort/merging operations made up the major portion of the processing effort. Assuming a cost of $100/machine-hour, it means $18 per month per site. Processing costs per site were directly proportional to the number of transactions (i.e., active accounts) per month. The lease of a computer solely to support the proposed information system was justified only for very large volumes, nearing 500 sites. An adequate computer configuration (IBM 360/30 type) would lease for about $12,000/month.

2. *Personnel costs.* An information system requires the attention of capable personnel to make it function. This is in addition to keypunching and data entry operations. Any support time spent by any employee must be charged as a cost of the information system. Too frequently some of this time is grossly underestimated or accounted as free time and charged to other sources. The step curve in Figure 19.4 accounts for needed secretarial, clerical, analysis/programming, coordinating/liaison and managerial personnel for various volumes of data entry. For example, it was estimated that nine individuals would be needed for about 100 sites. Personnel costs would be about $100 per month per site (Figure 19.4).

3. *Printing costs.* As indicated earlier, the system would generate any number of a total of 16 different reports. Based on the average number of reports needed and average number of characters per report, it was estimated that 2.1 hours of a stand-alone, 1100 lines/minute printer would be needed per month per site. If it is assumed that one such printer at about $2000/month (e.g., Mohawk Data Sciences' 2501 system with a 1250 lines/minute printer and a 9-track 1600 bpi magnetic tape unit) could be operated full time during two shifts daily (two individuals at, say, $600/month each), then a maximum of about 150 sites could be serviced per month if forms production were ideally spread throughout the month (2×158 hours per month/2.1 hours per site = 150 sites per month). Hence the minimum cost for an average site is 3200/150 = $21/month. Obviously, if the printer is not operated so fully then the cost will be higher due to amortization over fewer users; this, as with all hardware, depends on the accounting and pricing schemes used.

4. *Data entry costs.* This was the largest expense by far. Four types of forms were to be used per site. Two of these, call them type-A, were almost identical, and 90% of the input monthly information would be contained in them. An average site accounted for about 900 type-A forms (one for each active account), each form containing an average of 300 characters. Thus, about 34 hours of keypunching time per month (900 forms/month $\times$ 300 strokes/form $\times$ 1 hour/8000 strokes) per site were needed. Taking into account verification and other costs, this would mean $253 per month assuming a cost of $0.94/1000 strokes (900 forms/month $\times$ 300 strokes/form $\times$ $0.00094/stroke = $253/month). Keyboard and OCR unit alternatives were also carefully analyzed following the methodology illustrated earlier. Notice in Figure 19.4 the significant savings over keypunching. Data entry is possible at about $156 per month per site. The OCR cost curve is for two sample models.

Table 1 summarizes the costs of operation of the computer-based information system. Including an estimate of $100 per site accounting for costs of the forms, paper and mailing, and an overhead estimate of 60% of personnel costs, the cost per site would be $552, or $465 if key-to-disk or OCR systems are used. Thus, if each site is currently spending about $1000/month (two full time employees at $500/month each) to manually produce the various reports needed, then the computer-based system should be implemented if the volume of sites is large enough to amortize in a reasonable amount of time an estimated $60,000 to implement the system (in COBOL). As an example, the investment would be fully recovered by 10 sites in one year:

TABLE 1

**ESTIMATED MONTHLY COSTS PER SITE
OF THE SAMPLE COMPUTER-BASED INFORMATION SYSTEM**

Computer time (leasing time at $100/hour)	$ 18
Personnel	$100
Overhead (@ 60% of personnel)	$ 60
Printing (stand-alone printing)	$ 21
Data entry	$253 to $156 (keypunching) (OCR or key-to-disc)
Paper, forms, mailing	$100
	$552

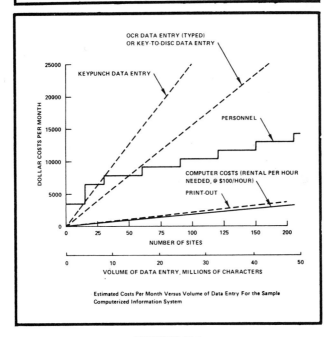

Estimated Costs Per Month Versus Volume of Data Entry For the Sample Computerized Information System

FIGURE 19.4

Savings per year per site = 12 × ($1000 − $465) = $6420.
Sites to amortize $60,000 = $60,000/$6420 = 10 sites investment in one year.
This case has illustrated the large cost of data entry and the need

to analyze the alternatives. Note that even if key-to-disk or OCR units were used, 34% of the costs per site would be due to data entry.

The methodological analysis above is of critical importance in order to establish the economic feasibility of any computerized system. Some of the cost factors involved are very difficult to estimate with a high degree of accuracy for larger systems, such as the manpower required to support the system; others are more readily quantifiable, such as data entry costs. Much analysis and detailed work are needed in order to obtain good estimates. Detailed considerations for the case above were not included.

The proper estimation of the cost of developing computerized systems, including detailed design, programming, documentation, testing and installation, is of critical importance—although it still continues to be one of the real problem areas in the computing profession. The decision of whether or not a system should be implemented is based on a consideration of both projected operational savings (and perhaps indirect benefits) and development costs.

Conclusions

Data entry continues to be the unglamorous and rather seldom-publicized cost giant of computer-based systems. This problem has been magnified by dramatic advances in technology and cost effectiveness of computers contrasted with only modest advances in data entry systems. An example based on a real case has illustrated the fact that data entry is a most expensive item in medium to large-scale information systems.

The methodological cost analysis of the various data entry alternatives and of all significant costs is of critical importance in establishing the economic feasibility of any computer-based system before launching its implementation.

REVIEW QUESTIONS

1. What sources of hardware information are available in your office or school?
2. Is it reasonable for the hardware selection people to consider the risk to their own jobs in the selection process?
3. Prepare your own list of characteristics of a saleable software package.
4. What sources of software information are available in your office or college?
5. What reaction should the systems analyst expect from programmers if a software package is purchased?

DISCUSSION QUESTIONS

1. Calculate the internal rate of return for each of the three hypothetical software procurement options shown on page 381.
2. Assume that computer A could do the planned jobs in 350 hours per month and computer B in 400. Discuss how you would determine what additional value to assign to the greater speed of computer A.
3. Speculate upon the status of packaged software today if IBM had unbundled in 1959.
4. Estimate in detail the cost of an optimizing selection of a computer equivalent in power to the IBM 370-145. What elements would be reduced or eliminated in a satisficing search?

BIBLIOGRAPHY

Adams, Donald, and John F. Mullarkey, "A Survey of Audit Software," *Journal of Accountancy*, Vol. 134, No. 3, September 1972, pp. 39-66.

Auerbach Information, Inc., 121 N. Broad Street, Philadelphia, Pennsylvania 19107.

Canning, Richard G., Application Packages Revisited, *EDP Analyzer*, Vol. 9, No. 7, July 1971.

Cardenas, Dr. Alfonso F., "Data Entry: A Cost Grant," *Journal of Systems Management*, Vol. 24, No. 8, August 1973.

Chapin, Ned, "Flowchart Packages," *Data Management*, Vol. 8, No. 10, October 1970, pp. 16-23.

Datapro Research Corp., 2204 Walnut Street, Philadelphia, Pennsylvania 19103.

Goetz, Martin, "Proprietary Software" (Four part series), *Computerworld*, Vol. 6, Nos. 4-7, June 1972 and ff. issues.

Head, Robert V., *A Guide to Packaged Systems*, New York: John Wiley and Sons, 1971, 116 p.

ICP Quarterly, International Computer Programs, Inc., 2511 East 46th Street, Indianapolis, Indiana 46205.

Joslin, Edward O., *Computer Selection*, Reading, Mass.: Addison-Wesley Publishing Company, Inc., 1968.

Sharpe, William F., *The Economics of Computers*, New York: Columbia University Press, 1969.

Smith, Robert A., "Guidelines for Software," *Journal of Systems Management*, Vol. 23, No. 4, April 1972, pp. 8-11.

Welke, Larry, "Buyer vs. Seller: Software Packages," *Datamation*, Vol. 18, No. 5, May 1972, pp. 76-79.

CHAPTER 20

SYSTEMS SPECIFICATION

STOCK STATUS SYSTEM

Table of Contents

The system description beginning below is abstracted from the complete description of 119 pages. This report is not unusually long and many detailed systems descriptions are much longer. Following the actual report is a description of the recommended format for systems descriptions and an analysis of the strengths and weaknesses of this specific system description.

This report is *not* included as an ideal which the analyst should strive to reach. In fact, it has many weaknesses, omissions and other assorted deficiencies. The report writer fell into many traps, such as the use of playscript and flowcharts to the exclusion of other documentation techniques. In an attempt to provide a complete systems description the writer missed many opportunities to modularize the system.

STOCK STATUS SYSTEM
GENERAL SYSTEMS DESCRIPTION

This general description of the stock status system is organized into four procedures: Start-Up, Year-End, Monthly and Daily. The general description describes the general flow of data through the system. The exceptions to the general rules, the details of special procedures for particular items, and the decision rules for specific items are described in the Decision Rule Section of this report.

Start-Up Procedures

To start the system, a stock status record is created using the stock status file maintenance procedure and program. The stock status record is described in Exhibit 3. The stock status record creation procedure enters all constant data and codes associated with a particular part number but it does not enter the quantity information for the item. The quantity information is entered using the same procedure and programs as are used to initialize the files at year-end. The year-end procedures are described by the general flowcharts in Exhibit 1A. Details of the year-end procedure are given below.

Year-End Procedure

The year-end stock status procedures provide for the insertion of forecast and planned ending inventory (safety stock) data into the stock status record. The programs used in the year-end procedure are the same as those used for daily and monthly processing, with control cards specifying the alternative procedures to be used.

A shipping forecast is made for each model and for certain other products. The shipping forecast is the resultant of (1) sales forecasts prepared by the sales department using both company and industry data, and (2) changes in consignment inventories. The shipping forecasts are made by product groups. The product group shipping forecast is subdivided into shipping forecasts for an item which a customer might order. In addition, the shipping forecast is subdivided by month of shipment.

The forecast program accomplishes the subdivisions described above. Similarly, the forecast program subdivides planned ending inventory into product numbers. The forecasts and planned ending inventory records make up the level 0 forecast file shown on flowchart in Exhibit 1A.

The level 0 forecast file is then exploded on a gross basis using the bill of material file and the bill of material program. The output from this explosion is a forecast file for levels 0, 1, 2 and 3.

The exploded forecast file is then used by the stock status program to initialize the stock status file for use during the year. The 12 fields reserved for shipments by month are all zeroed. The 12 monthly and one annual forecast fields are zeroed and replaced by the new forecasts. The planned ending inventory field is zeroed and replaced by the new planned ending inventory if the stock status report code equals 1 or 2. If the stock status report code equals 3, 4, 5 or 6, then the ending inventory field is left unchanged. Since the forecasts and planned ending inventory results from explosions, there will be multiple records for many items which must be totaled to arrive at the new forecast and planned ending inventory.

In addition to applying percentages to a manually prepared forecast the forecast program also calculates forecasts for all options, repair parts and other products sold. These forecasts are based upon data in the stock status file. The above forecasts are exploded by the bill of materials program and inserted into the initialized stock status record by the stock status program in the same manner as for basic products.

The initial run of the stock status program at year-end does not cause the printing of a set of reports. The second run immediately following performs that function. The initial run creates a requirements-B file, Exhibit 3, which contains the requirements of all parts leveled over the year and adjusted for the difference between planned ending inventory and inventory on hand.

The requirements-B file is then exploded into requirements by part. The second run of the stock status program performs the same functions as it does during the monthly process. The monthly

functions performed by the stock status program are described below
in the monthly procedure.

The year-end procedures are used only at the beginning of the
year. A major change of forecasts must be entered as forecast
changes rather than by reinitializing the file.

Monthly Procedure

There are two monthly procedures—one for the first month of the
year and the other for any other month. Those procedures for the
first month of the year which vary from the normal month's procedures are:

1. The forecast program is not used.
2. Requirements-B file is used rather than file A.
3. The program uses requirements data from the file rather than
   calculating it on a $\frac{1}{11}$ basis.

The procedures for normal months start with the use of the forecast program which is used to subdivide a forecast change. The forecast change is expressed as a plus or a minus to the original forecast
and is given as an annual amount. The forecast program will also
originate forecast changes for options, repair parts and other products. These changes are then handled in the same manner as a
change originated externally to the program.

The bill of materials program explodes all the above forecast
changes on a gross basis to develop requirement changes for each
finished product assembly or part affected.

The stock status program uses the requirement changes to update
the stock status file by adding algebraically the amount of the change
to the amount of the previous forecasts.

Stock status reports are prepared from records created by the
stock programs and are described in Exhibit 2. The stock status
report is a reference report and is not intended to be used to initiate
any action.

Some of the fields on the stock status report require explanation
as to their content and meaning and are described below.

Inventory on hand is the quantity physically in the plant at the
time of the latest transaction included in the report. For any period,
inventory on hand is equal to the inventory on hand for the previous
period plus receipts or production and minus shipments or production usage.

Unshipped customer orders is the quantity of an inventory item
needed to fill the customer orders received but not shipped. For any

period unshipped customer orders (backlog) is equal to unshipped customer orders for the previous period plus orders entered less shipments.

Unallotted inventory equals inventory on hand less unshipped customer orders.

Required inventory has different formulas depending upon the inventory control group code. These required inventory formulas are described in the decision rule section of this report.

The sales forecasting procedures describe the method of changing forecasts which keeps forecasted sales by major groups up-to-date. Variations occur within major groups, which tend to make the percentages in the forecast program less than completely reliable. The methods described above for calculating required inventory and over/under schedules provide for revision of the annual forecast for a particular finished product so that:

1. The total forecast for the product group is not changed, and
2. The inventory will be balanced to correspond to the overall forecast.

As noted in the specific description of the forecast program, there is a mechanism which will trace shipment history versus percentages and call attention to situations apparently out of control.

The stock status program examines each stock status record looking for conditions which would indicate an actual or potential out-of-stock condition and for conditions which indicate the need for production or purchase requisitions. The above examination results in shortage reports, expedite reports, purchase authorization reports and production authorization reports.

An item appears on the shortage report whenever inventory on hand is zero or negative, or whenever unallotted inventory is zero or negative.

An item appears on the expedite report whenever inventory on hand is less than planned ending inventory. An item which appears on the shortage report does not also appear on the expedite report.

Production and purchase authorizations are prepared whenever the purchase orders or releases, production plans, purchase authorizations and production authorizations are not equal to requirements. Thus the authorizations can be either positive or negative. If negative they would usually require the reduction of a production plan or the delayed receipt of a purchase order. Specific details of the possible decisions relating to negative authorizations are described in the procedures for each authorization report.

A part is listed on the expedite report whenever the remaining annual or current period requirements times S_i are greater than 80% of capacity, where,

$$S_i = \frac{1}{(\text{Days Remaining}) \ (1 - \text{scrap percent}) \ (\text{Utilization percent})}$$

Scrap percent and utilization percent are constants by type of machine and are entered by means of control cards or are contained in the stock status record.

Daily Procedure

The daily procedure may be used daily or less frequently as experience suggests. It is organized to update the stock status file with production, sales, customer order, purchase order and receipt data, and to examine the file for shortages and situations requiring expediting.

The order entry subsystem provides order and shipment information. The exploded shipment data reduces inventory and backlog while the exploded order information reduces available inventory while increasing backlog.

Purchase orders and releases are keypunched and entered to the stock status record individually. Cards are also punched from receipts and used to increase the on-hand inventory as well as decrease or eliminate the on-order quantity. Matching is done by purchase order number and release number. The majority of purchase requisitions will be prepared by the computer program. If the quantity and delivery date are satisfactory, it is not necessary to keypunch a card for the purchase order. The purchase order card punched as a result of the computer program is used instead of keypunching a new card. If a change is needed, the adjusted quantity or date is punched and replaces the date calculated by the computer. The above procedure also applies to production plans. The order number assigned by the computer is marked with a prefix of "R" until the purchase order or production plan is entered into the system.

From the production subsystem, production and planned production figures are keypunched and entered into the system. Production reduces production orders and increases inventory while scrap and inventory adjustments reduce the inventory figures. Production plans are prepared for a three month horizon reducing toward two months as the month progresses. The production plans are decided by production control but are based upon production requisitions created by the stock status program.

Some of the fields on the stock status activity list require explanation as to their content and are described below.

Inventory on hand is the quantity physically in the plant at the time of the latest transaction included in the report. For any period, inventory on hand is equal to the inventory on hand for the previous period plus receipts or production less shipments or production usage.

Unshipped customer orders is the required quantity of an inventory item to fill the customer orders received but not shipped. For any period unshipped customer orders (backlog) is equal to unshipped customer orders for the previous period plus orders entered less shipments.

Unallotted inventory for shipment equals inventory on hand less unshipped customer orders.

The stock status program examines each stock status record looking for conditions which would indicate an actual or potential out of stock condition, and for conditions which would indicate the need for production or purchase requisitions. The above examination results in shortage reports, expedite reports, purchase authorization reports and production authorization reports.

An item appears on the shortage report whenever inventory on hand is zero or negative, or whenever unallotted inventory is zero or negative.

An item appears on the expedite report whenever inventory on hand is less than planned ending inventory. An item which appears on the shortage report does not also appear on the expedite report.

DECISION RULES

Warehouse Goods—Level Procurement

The items with inventory control group codes 1 or 2 have certain procedures which are different from the procedures for other items.

Required inventory equals planned ending inventory plus shipping forecast for the rest of the year less the annual forecast times the production months remaining in the year divided by 11.

The stock status program calculates the over/under schedule as follows:

$$\text{Over/Under Schedule} = \text{Inventory on hand} - \text{Planned ending Inventory} + \frac{\text{Annual forecast}}{11} \times \text{production months remaining in year} - \text{Shipping forecast for rest of year.}$$

Stock status report code 1 is used for items for which any over/

under schedules are to be spread evenly through the rest of the year. Stock status report code 2 is used for items for which any over/under schedule is made in the current month.

If the stock status report code is 1 then the over/under schedule is divided by the number of production months remaining in the year. If the stock status report code is 2 there is no change made to the over/under schedule.

At the beginning there will be no use of stock status report code 1 but provision is made in the program for possible use at a later time.

The over/under schedule amount is then netted against requirements in the earliest months if the stock status report code is 2, or spread through the year if the inventory control group code is 1.

Seasonal Procurement—Finished Products—Warehouse Goods

For seasonally procured items the output of the forecast and the bill of materials programs is identical with that for those items procured on a level plan. The difference in control is in the way the data is treated by the stock status program.

In the monthly stock status program the required inventory equals the year-end inventory less the over/under schedule. The requirements for any month equal the forecast for that month. Authorizations are developed for these items using the same formulae shown in the level procurement section but with the revised data described in this section.

Planned inventory for the current month equals the actual inventory plus any receipts scheduled during the current month. Similarly planned inventory for the following month equals planned inventory for the current month plus receipts scheduled in the following month. Receipts arriving ahead of schedule will reduce the receipts scheduled in the following month.

The lead time in weeks is found in the stock status record if the lead time code is 1. If the lead time code is 2 then using the number shown as lead time as the argument the lead time is found in the lead time table which is stored from control cards. The lead time in months equals the lead time in weeks divided by 4 and rounded high.

Requirements over the lead time equal the sum of the monthly requirements over the lead time in months.

A part is listed on the purchase list or production plan list whenever the planned inventory is less than the required inventory for any of the three months for which the difference is calculated. The amount to be ordered is the order quantity if shown; otherwise the order quantity is to be calculated using an economic order quantity formula.

Parts—Requirement Basis

Parts procured on a requirement basis are controlled using the basic procedures described for finished products, except for the exceptions and explanations detailed below.

Processing the forecast data through the year-end procedure results in the calculation of an over/under schedule figure which is used in the initial monthly procedure to net the requirements.

The year-end stock status program procedure eliminates the seasonality of the forecast and instead sets the forecast requirements equal to $\frac{1}{22}$ of the annual requirements for July and December and $\frac{1}{11}$ for each other month.

The bill of materials program explodes production data one level down and codes the exploded data as production usage.

Required inventory equals safety stock for parts.

Safety stock is set on the basis of a management decision to provide a certain level of service. A high level of service requires higher safety stocks and a higher inventory while a lower level of service requirement results in lower inventories after the replenishment cycle is completed. Management can implement its decisions relating to inventories and to service levels by adjusting safety stock. There is a safety stock code in the stock status record which can be used to establish an appropriate safety stock for each item in the inventory in line with the requirements of the business.

The safety stock code specifies the method of calculating safety stock. For code 1 the safety stock equals X month's requirements where the factor X is a variable to be specified by management for each month's run. For code 2 the safety stock is the amount specified in the stock status record and may be zero. For code 3 the safety stock equals Y times the requirements over the lead time where Y is a variable to be specified by management.

Parts—Reorder Point Basis

Parts ordered on a reorder point basis are controlled using the same basic procedures as for parts ordered on a requirement basis, except for the exceptions and explanations detailed below.

The stock status record contains the reorder point quantity. When inventory on hand is less than or equal to the reorder point and there is no production or purchase requisition in the file, a production plan requisition or a purchase requisition is prepared for the current period plus lead time. Any requirement or forecast data in the stock status record is ignored. The order quantity is taken from the stock status record if possible; otherwise the order quantity is calculated using an economic order quantity formula.

The stock status record may contain a quantity in the safety stock field for use in determining need to expedite.

The bill of materials program explodes production data one level down and codes the exploded data as production usage.

Parts and Products—As Required

The "as required" basis for control of replenishment indicates a decision by Production Control to carry no inventory of these items. Whenever an order is entered a purchase order or production order must be initiated. In order to meet customer shipping dates the information is needed immediately, so suggested purchase orders for the "as required" items are printed as a result of the daily stock status program. The order quantity equals the quantity required to ship the customers' orders for the day. Each of these items appears on the exception list in the usual format.

Optional Items

Forecasts for miscellaneous items sold are made in the forecast program using the technique of exponential smoothing seasonally adjusted. The forecasts are arranged into the same format as those for major products and are exploded into forecasts for individual parts by the bill of materials program. The replenishment policy is indicated by the stock status code and can be level, seasonal, reorder point requirement, or as required.

Subsidiary and Other Plant

Subsidiary and other plant items generally are finished products procured on a level basis, but on whatever basis they are controlled the normal procedures produce requests for purchase orders. After examination and approval these purchase orders are entered back into the system and are exploded on a gross basis by the bill of materials program. Thus subsidiary and other plant parts requirements pass through the stock status program, are sorted and are printed on the report which is described in Exhibit 2.

Castings

The regular control procedures apply to castings. In addition during the monthly stock status computer run a record (described in the tape records section of the system description) is created for use in printing the molds per day report which is described in the reports section of this system description.

The quantities shown on the molds per day tape record are the totals of production orders by month increased by a factor S_i to provide for scrap and non-utilization of facilities. The factor S_i are input through control cards and vary by type of molding machine.

The quantities shown on the production plan are also increased by the factor S_i. If the scrap factor and the utilization factor are in the stock status record, then

$$S_i = \frac{1}{(1 - \text{scrap factor}) \times \text{utilization factor} \times \text{days}}.$$

PROCEDURES

The procedures that follow are intended to be used by programmers in writing the forecast and stock status programs and by systems personnel and operating personnel in making the appropriate changes to present clerical systems. The procedures show the details of the data processing steps required for the stock status system and describe their relationship to existing systems. Both the actions to be taken and the individual or department responsible for taking the action are presented.

Forecast Procedure

Responsibility	Action
1. Sales Department	Using salesmen's forecasts, economic data, sales data, anticipated company developments, competitive developments and judgement, prepare a forecast for the sales of each model and product group.
2. Sales Department	Adjust the sales forecast to reflect the anticipated changes in consignment inventory. The adjusted forecast is a shipping forecast.
3. Production Control	From the forecast data calculate the ending inventories needed and enter them on the present forecast form as separate items.
4. Data Processing	Use shipping forecast to key punch and verify forecast cards and planned inventory cards.
5. Service Bureau	Use forecast cards and planned inventory cards as input to forecast program. Pro-

Responsibility	*Action*
	gram breaks down the forecast into individual products.
6. Monthly Forecasting Meeting	Each month a meeting of sales and production personnel is held to discuss the forecast and agree upon necessary changes.
7. Production Control	Prepare change lists by entering kind of change, product code, amount of change and + or −. The amount of the change is the annual amount agreed to at the monthly forecast meeting. The excess or shortage of shipments year to date over forecast year to date is computed and used as a forecast change by the forecast program. Send change cards monthly to the Service Bureau.
8. Data Processing	Key punch, list change cards.

Percentage and Seasonal Factor Card Procedure

Responsibility	*Action*
1. Production Control	Using the forecast and sales statistics, prepare a transmittal list of product groups, part numbers, percentages and seasonal factors. Send the transmittal list to data processing.
2. Data Processing	Use the transmittal list to keypunch percentage and seasonal factor cards. See Exhibit 4 for percentage card layout.
3. Data Processing	List and total the percentage and seasonal factor cards by product forecast. If any totals differ from 100.00 recheck the accuracy of the keypunching and, if necessary, the accuracy of the percentages themselves. When the percentage and seasonal factors are accurate, send them to the service bureau.
4. Service Bureau	Use the percentage and seasonal factor cards as input to the annual and monthly runs of the forecast program. Percentages will convert forecasts by product groups into forecasts by products

Responsibility	*Action*
	which can be identified by part numbers.
5. Service Bureau	At end of year the forecast program calculates a new set of percentage and seasonal factor cards which are then used for the next year. A list is made of the computer prepared percentage and seasonal factor cards for use by production control.
6. Service Bureau	File

Percentage and Seasonal Factor Card Changes

Responsibility	*Action*
1. Production Control	The need for changes in percentages comes from changes in products, changes in customer requirements and changes becoming apparent as a result of examining the forecast exception report. As changes become necessary, prepare a transmittal form specifying that this change is a percentage and seasonal factor card change, and give the part number and the new percentage and/or seasonal factor.
2. Production Control	Changing percentages does not automatically change the forecasts previously calculated which therefore must be changed using other techniques. Changing forecast as a result of percentage or seasonal factor changes is accomplished by manually calculating the seasonal forecasts before and after the change in percentages and by preparing a forecast change for the total difference during the remaining portion of the year.
3. Data Processing	Keypunch new forecast and percentage and seasonal factor cards according to the card layouts in Exhibit 4. Initial and file the transmittal form. Send the new cards to the service bureau.
4. Service Bureau	Replace old cards with the revised percentage and seasonal factor cards and use

Responsibility	*Action*
	the revised file in the next month's processing.
5. Service Bureau	File obsolete cards.

Purchase Orders

Responsibility	*Action*
1. Service Bureau	For items on the stock status system a purchase authorization list of items requiring purchasing action, according to the decision rules incorporated into the computer program, is printed daily and monthly. A set of purchase authorization cards corresponding to the purchase authorization list in the format of purchase order cards is punched at the same time. Copies of the purchase authorization list are sent to Production Control, Purchasing and the Materials Manager. The purchase authorization cards are sent to data processing. Nonstock status system purchase requisitions are prepared by the using departments as traveling requisitions.
2. Purchasing	Use the purchase authorization list or other notification from production control to pull the traveling requisition from the file for each item requisitioned.
3. Purchasing	Examine the list for possible product changes, supplier problems, and lead time changes. Obtain approval of the Materials Manager for any resulting order quantity changes with value of more than $100. Mark the amount to order from the list (or as otherwise determined) on the traveling requisitions. Determine whether the requirement might be better satisfied by changing a previously issued purchase order. If a purchase order change is in order mark the amount of the change and the purchase order to change on the traveling requisition. Select the vendor and

Responsibility	*Action*
	mark the traveling requisition accordingly. If a release rather than a purchase order, mark the traveling requisition, pull the purchase order and record the released quantity on the purchase order. Check whether the due date is normal to supplier and, if not, expedite shipment. Mark the due date on the traveling requisition. Separate those traveling requisitions requiring a purchase order change, those requiring a purchase order and those requiring a release.
4. Purchase Order Typist	Using the traveling requisition, type purchase order changes, purchase orders and releases. Each purchase order should have a price or amount.
5. Purchasing	Separate those documents representing material in the system from others. For those in the system, compute the total quantity now ordered and the quantity previously ordered for order changes, and the quantity ordered for purchase orders and quantity released for releases. Record the totals on a transmittal form and forward one copy of all changes, purchase orders and releases together with the adding machine tapes and the transmittal form to data processing.
6. Data Processing	Use the purchase orders and releases to pull cards from the authorization file. Check that quantities match. If the quantity on the purchase order or release matches the quantity on the punched card keep the card and do not punch a card from the purchase order or release. If the quantities are not equal destroy the card and keypunch a purchase order or release card. For order changes always punch a card and

Responsibility	*Action*
	destroy any corresponding cards in the file.
7. Data Processing	Total the purchase order cards to balance to the adding machine tapes. Note the total in the control log.
8. Service Bureau	Various computer runs.
9. Data Processing	Service bureau returns cards which are filed and reports which are distributed for use as in Step 1.

Receiving Procedure

Responsibility	*Action*
1. Purchasing	A copy of the purchase order is sent to receiving to use as a receiving report.
2. Receiving	Using the purchase order and any packing slip enclosed with the goods received, enter the receiving information to the receiving report. If the receipt is partial mark the report accordingly.
3. Purchasing	For all receipts make a copy of the receiving report and send to accounts payable. For all partial receipts make a copy and return original to receiving. Pull corresponding purchase orders for all receipts. Check accuracy of purchase order number, material received and quantity received. Separate receiving reports of material on the stock status system from other receiving reports. For the non-system receiving reports, clip the receiving report to the purchase order and file. For the system receiving reports, total the quantities received, record the total on a transmittal form and send the transmittal form, tapes and receiving reports to data processing.
4. Data Processing	Use receiving reports to keypunch receipt cards.
5. Data Processing	Total quantities received for the daily batch. Total the receipt cards and reconcile any differences.
6. Data Processing	Send receiving reports to purchasing.

Responsibility	*Action*
	Send receiving cards to the service bureau.
7. Service Bureau	Use the receiving cards as an input into the stock status programs. The program uses the information to increase the inventory and reduce the purchase order quantity in the stock status file. For partial receipts, leave the remainder on order in the file. For complete receipts, delete the item but print any quantity difference on an exception report.
8. Data Processing	File the returned receipt card. Distribute the exception report.
9. Purchasing	Upon return of receiving reports from data processing, clip them to the purchase orders and file. Use this file for invoice approval as in the present accounts payable system.

Order Entry Data Procedure

The order entry system, in addition to providing information for shipping and invoicing, also provides data for use in the stock status system. For each major product order, one card is provided for the product and one additional card for each option and addition. For repair parts orders, one card is provided for each assembly or part. For other orders, one card is provided for each item ordered. The information described above is also provided for shipments.

The order data is summarized in the stock status program and is used in the forecast program. The forecast program compares the data to forecasts and initiates an exception report whenever orders vary significantly from forecasts.

Both orders and shipments are used in the daily stock status program to keep actual inventory, backlog and unallotted inventory figures.

Card formats for the order cards and shipment cards are described in Exhibit 4.

Production Procedure

The production data procedures, in addition to providing information for day-to-day control of production operations, also provide the data needed to support the stock status system. Production data is used to increase or decrease inventories kept by the stock status system. The production data procedures provide the data for stock status purposes in the form of punched cards—production cards, scrap cards, production order cards, inventory adjustment cards and requisition cards—which are all described in Exhibit 4.

The production procedures which, among other things, provide the punched cards described above are being written as a separate project and are therefore not included here.

Within the stock status system the primary use of production information is the updating of inventory figures. The quantity from production cards increases the inventory of the production item, decreases the amount of the production order quantity, decreases the inventories of parts making up the item produced, and increases production this month and year to date. The quantity from scrap cards acts as the reverse of production and in addition accumulates as scrap. Production order cards set up an order in the stock status file or, if they are validating a computer prepared requisition, remove the "R" from the production order number. Inventory adjustment cards result in an increase or decrease in inventory dependent upon the sign of the adjustment and cause the printing of an item on the inventory adjustment report—Exhibit 2. Requisition cards cause the decrease or increase of inventory.

Control Card Procedure

Some of the control information originates in production control while other information originates in data control. See types of control codes for details of which function prepares what information.

Responsibility	Action
1. Production Control or Data Control	From stock status systems specifications plus program documentation, determine control cards needed for each computer run. Determine data needed for each card and enter to transmittal form. Send transmittal form to Data Processing.
2. Data Processing	Keypunch and verify control cards; then send cards to Service Bureau with data for the period.
3. Service Bureau	Use cards in computer run. When run is complete, return the cards with the data.
4. Data Processing	File

Stock Status File Changes

Responsibility	*Action*
1. Production Control	Enter change data to transmittal form. Send transmittal forms to data processing.
2. Data Processing	Keypunch change cards. List change cards to verify keypunch accuracy. Take hash total of part number for batch control. Send change cards to service bureau.
3. Service Bureau	Use change cards and change program to update stock status file. Balance to hash total of part number.

Transmittal Form:

The transmittal form is designed with columns corresponding to the card layout following and with field numbers corresponding to those indicated on the card layout.

A new part is entered by writing part number, code 1 and the other information in the applicable columns.

A part number is deleted by entering part number and code 2.

New information is entered for any field by marking the part number code 3 and the new information for that one field.

Assignment of Lead Times Codes

Provision is made in the stock status record for lead time and lead time code. It is intended that either lead time or lead time code, but not both, be in the stock status record.

Lead time codes are used strictly as a convenience in that by changing one datum, the lead time corresponding to a given lead time code, the lead time for a whole group of items is changed. Thus there is little to be gained by assigning a lead time code to a group containing only a few items. It is suggested that a group contain at least 10 items before a lead time code be assigned to the group.

A group of items to which a lead time code should be assigned should meet these criteria:

1. The group contains at least 10 items.
2. The lead time for all the items is the same.
3. The probability is quite high that a change in the lead time of any item will be identical with the change in lead time of any other.
4. The group of items should have commodity or supplier in com-

mon so that it can be described in a exclusive way in the lead time codes.

To be most useful, lead time codes should require very little change. Since frequent changing of lead time codes is equivalent to changing lead times frequently, and since it is just as efficient and easier in concept to change lead times, then it is preferred that lead times be changed if frequent changes in groups are expected.

Lead times and lead time codes will be assigned concurrently by a knowledgeable person from the Purchasing department. Lead times and lead time codes are assigned by examining separately each part number group to see if there are any groups of items which meet the four criteria described above. If there are any such groups, lead time codes are established and these lead time codes are assigned to the items to which they correspond. Those items with no lead time codes are assigned a lead time. If no lead time codes are applicable to a part number group, then all items in the group are assigned lead times.

EXHIBIT 1

STOCK STATUS SYSTEM
FLOW CHARTS

Page

Exhibit 1B
Monthly Procedure

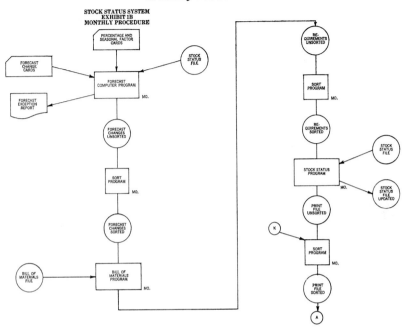

Exhibit 1C
Daily Procedure

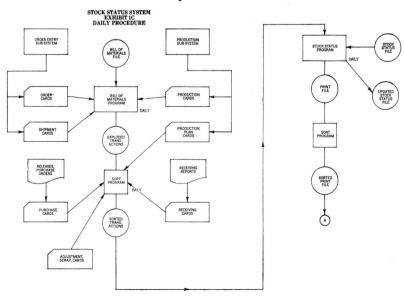

EXHIBIT 2

STOCK STATUS SYSTEM
REPORT SPECIFICATIONS

STOCK STATUS REPORT

Description	Source	Characters	A/N	Format
First Line:				
Part number	Stock status file	9	N	
Description	Stock status file	30	A	
Unit of measure	Stock status file	4	A	
Inventory control group code	Stock status file	1	N	
Manufactured or purchased code	Stock status file	1	N	
Plant and subsidiary code	Stock status file	1	N	
Safety stock code	Stock status file	1	N	
Purchase order or release code	Stock status file	1	N	
Inventory classification code	Stock status file	1	A	
LIFO inventory accounting class code	Stock status file	2	N	
Lead time code	Stock status file	2	N	
Molds per day	Stock status file	4	N	
Castings per mold	Stock status file	1	N	
Molding machine type	Stock status file	1	N	
Cores per day	Stock status file	4	N	
Packing labor (2 decimals)	Stock status file	5	N	.
Average days late	Stock status file	2	N	
Lead time	Stock status file	2	N	
Reorder point	Stock status file	6	N	,
Reorder quantity (EOQ)	Stock status file	6	N	,
Second Line:				
Planned ending inventory	Stock status file	6	N	,
Inventory on hand	Stock status file	6	N	,
Unshipped customer orders	Stock status file	6	N	,
Unallotted inventory	Inventory on hand less unshipped customer orders	6	N	,
Required inventory	Planned ending inventory plus seasonal ship-			

Second Line (Cont'd):

Description	Source	Characters	A/N	Format
	ping forecast for rest of year less require- ments rest of year. Safety stock for inven- tory control group 3, 4, 5 and 6 items.	6	N	,
Over/under schedule	Inventory on hand less re- quired inventory	6	N	,
Forecast—annual	Stock status file	6	N	,
Forecast—annual/11	Annual forecast/11	6	N	,
Forecast—current month	Stock status file	6	N	,
Forecast—following month	Stock status file	6	N	,
Forecast—second following month	Stock status file	6	N	,
Forecast—third following month plus subsequent months	Sum of rest of seasonal forecasts	6	N	,
Shipments—year to date	Sum of monthly shipments	6	N	,
Receipts—year to date	Stock status file	6	N	,
Order number	Stock status file	6	N	
Order quantity	Stock status file	6	N	,
Month order due	Stock status file	2	N	
Subsequent Lines:				
Order number	Stock status file	6	N	
Order quantity	Stock status file	6	N	,
Month order due	Stock status file	2	N	

Order of Report:
  Manufactured or purchased code
  Plant and subsidiary code
  Inventory control group code
  Part number

Stock Status Report (Cont'd)

Totals:
   Final totals only
   Count of items listed
   Inventory on hand × unit cost

Copies:
   Production control (1)

Stock Status Report

DATE XX-XX-XX   PAGE XXX

PART NUMBER	DESCRIPTION	P/M	S	SAF STK	LI FO	LEAD CODE	MOLDS DAY	C/M	M M	CORES DAY	LEAD TIME	REORDER POINT	REORDER QUANTITY
PLANNED END. INV.	INVENTORY ON HAND	UNSHIPPED CUST. ORD.	UNALLOTTED INVENTORY	REQUIRED INVENTORY	O/U SCHEDULE	ANNUAL	1/11 ANNUAL	CURRENT	FOLLOW	2nd FOLLOW	REST	SHIPMENTS YTD	RECEIPTS YTD	ORDER NUMBER	ORDER QUANTITY

(FORECAST SHIPMENTS: ANNUAL, 1/11 ANNUAL, CURRENT, FOLLOW, 2nd FOLLOW, REST)

EXHIBIT 3

STOCK STATUS SYSTEM
RECORD LAYOUTS

Exhibit 3 (Cont'd)

Past due production order report record.....................(not shown)
Error list report record.....................................(not shown)
Inventory adjustment list report record.....................(not shown)
Stock status file change report record.....................(not shown)
Purchase commitment report record.....................(not shown)
Forecast exception report record.....................(not shown)

REQUIREMENTS FILE—SEASONAL— NOT EXPLODED

Characters	*A/N*	*Description*
1	A	Record type—A
1	N	Forecast or explosion
9	N	Part number
6	N	Planned ending inventory
6	N	Shipping forecast—January
6	N	" " —February
6	N	" " —March
6	N	" " —April
6	N	" " —May
6	N	" " —June
6	N	" " —July
6	N	" " —August
6	N	" " —September
6	N	" " —October
6	N	" " —November
6	N	" " —December

Source and Formula:

Part number—Stock status record, forecast card or percentage card.

Planned ending inventory = Planned ending inventory from forecast card × percentage in matching percentage card.

Shipping forecast—January = Forecast × percentage in matching percentage card × percent of shipments shipped in January in matching percentage card.

Shipping forecast for other months is calculated in the same fashion as for January.

Forecast or explosion code is 1 for original data from the percent book program and 2 for exploded data from the bill of materials file.

The output seasonal requirements records from the percentage book program (Exhibit 1A) come from several sources and represent parts and products at various levels of the bill of materials file.

a. Product external forecasts result in records corresponding to the zero level of the bill of materials.

b. Repair part computer forecasts result in records corresponding to any level of the bill of materials.

c. Option computer forecasts result in zero level records.

The output seasonal requirement records from the bill of materials program are the result of a complete explosion. The formulae for the data are the same except that all quantity fields are multiplied by the quantity per unit field in the bill of materials file.

REQUIREMENTS FILE—LEVEL

Characters	A/N	Description
1	A	Record type—B
1	N	Forecast or explosion
9	N	Part number
6	N	
6	N	Requirements—January
6	N	" —February
6	N	" —March
6	N	" —April
6	N	" —May
6	N	" —June
6	N	" —July
6	N	" —August
6	N	" —September
6	N	" —October
6	N	" —November
6	N	" —December

Source and Formula:

This file is the output of the annual stock status program first pass (Exhibit 1A).

Part numbers come from the stock status file.

Requirements for each month are taken directly from the equivalent field in the stock status file.

A record type B is created if inventory control group code is nonzero and if forecast annual shipments is nonzero.

STOCK STATUS ACTIVITY LIST RECORD

Characters	A/N	Edit	Description
2		None	Report number (2)
1		"	Manufactured or purchased code
1		"	Plant and subsidiary code
1	N	"	
9	N	"	Part number
30	A/N	"	Description
4	A	"	Unit of measure
1	N	"	Manufactured or purchased code
1	N	"	Source code
1	N	"	Stock status report code
6	N	, CR	Receipts/production
6	N	, CR	Shipments/usage in production
6	N	, CR	Inventory on hand
6	N	,	Unshipped customer orders
6	N	, CR	Unallotted inventory
4 of these (6	N	None	Order number
(6	N	,	Order quantity
(2	N	None	Month order due
6	N	,	Production this month
6	N	,	Planned production this month

Source:

For all fields except those described below, the source of the information is the named field in the stock status record.

Report number is 2 for all records.

Receipts/production equals the sum of the receipt and production transaction records for the day.

Shipments/usage in production equals the sum of the shipment transaction records (which have been exploded to the warehouse goods level by the bill of materials program), the usage in production (which is production exploded into parts by the bill of materials program), scrap, adjustments and requisitions.

EXHIBIT 4

STOCK STATUS SYSTEM
CARD LAYOUTS

Exhibit 4 (Cont'd)

FORECAST CARD

Columns	*Description*
1	Kind of card (A)
2-3	Year
4-5	Month
6-7	
8-16	Part number Note: Use as many digits of part number as are forecast. Leave the other digits blank.
17-21	
22-26	Forecast quantity
X26	Credit
27-80	

Source: Shipping forecast. See the forecasting procedure for details.
Use: Forecast program. See Exhibits 1A, 1F and 1G for details.

EXHIBIT 5

STOCK STATUS SYSTEM CODES

Exhibit 5 (Cont'd)

SAFETY STOCK CODE...424
PURCHASE OR RELEASE CODE...............................(not shown)
INVENTORY CLASSIFICATION CODE....................(not shown)
LIFO INVENTORY GROUP CODE............................(not shown)
LEAD TIME CODE...(not shown)
KIND OF CARD CODE..(not shown)
TYPES OF CONTROL CARDS...................................(not shown)
REPORT NUMBER CODE..(not shown)
REQUIREMENTS FILE TYPE...................................(not shown)
UNIT OF MEASURE...(not shown)

CODES

INVENTORY CONTROL GROUP CODES

Code	Description
0.	Sales unit whose components are warehouse goods
1.	Warehouse Goods—Level Procurement—Level corrections
2.	Warehouse Goods—Level Procurement—Immediate correction
3.	Warehouse Goods—Seasonal Procurement
4.	Parts—Requirement Basis—Safety Stock
5.	Parts—Reorder Point—Safety Stock
6.	Items Not Stocked

MANUFACTURED OR PURCHASED CODE

1. Manufactured
2. Purchased

SAFETY STOCK CODE

1. X Months Requirements
2. Amount Specified
3. Y X Lead Time Requirements

EXHIBIT 6

RECORD RETENTION PERIOD

RECORD	RETENTION PERIOD
Reports	
Stock Status—Annual	(A)
Stock Status—Other	(B)

Exhibit 6 (cont'd)

Stock Status—Activity	(B)
Shortage	3 Months
Expedite	3 Months
Error List	(B)
Purchase Authorization	(B)
Purchase Commitment	Current Year-to-Date plus Previous Year
Subsidiary Purchase List	(B)
Production Authorization	(B)
Molds per Day	3 Months
Packing Personnel Requirements	3 Months
Past Due Order	3 Months
Inventory Adjustments	(B)
Cards	
Control	(B)
Purchase Order, Production Plan	(B)
Receipt, Production	(B)
Percentage, Seasonal Factor, Forecast	Current Year-to-Date plus Previous Three Years
Order, Shipment	Current Year-to-Date plus Previous Year
Tape or Disk Records	
Stock Status File—Year-End	3 Years
All Other Files	Grandfather, Father

(A) Until completion of audit of Federal income tax returns.
(B) Until completion of audit of financial statements by independent public accountant.

RECOMMENDED SYSTEMS SPECIFICATION FORMAT

The purpose of the systems specification is to provide the information needed by the project staff to implement the project. From the specification, the programmer should be able to program, the forms analyst should be able to design the necessary reports, and the training specialist should be able to design the training programs. The specification is not intended to persuade or to instigate action. It is intended to provide a detailed and accurate description of the project to enable the user to satisfy himself that the system, when completed, will satisfy the requirements for the system.

The recipients of the report are those people who need to know details. These recipients determine the format and style of the report, for it is important that the details of the system be accurately and completely understood by the recipients. All systems specification reports should contain the following elements:

1. A table of contents and marginal tabs for easy reference to each section.
2. A statement of the problem should begin the specification. The need for the system and the use intended by the user should be specified.
3. The flow of information should be shown in narrative with explanatory figures as flowcharts or decision tables. The narrative and figures should be on the same page, if possible.
4. All sources of input, forms and reports planned.
5. All machine language records planned for the system.
6. All codes must be described. This is often done by specifying the data set to be used. The current description of that data set is then often included with the understanding that the data set specification will be controlled by the data base manager.
7. A glossary of terms used in the description.
8. A records retention section.
9. All manual procedures should be shown in a style appropriate to the specific procedure. Playscript and caption styles will be used most commonly.
10. Job descriptions of the personnel in the user area included.
11. Control records and procedures.
12. The specification should be as complete and accurate as possible.

EVALUATION OF STOCK STATUS
SYSTEM SPECIFICATION

The report shown in this chapter meets some of the above requirements but not all. The table of contents was included but marginal tabs were not included, requiring users to hunt for the sections they wanted.

Probably the most significant problem in the specification relates to modularity. The first statement tells us that the system has four components, but the individual components are not dealt with discretely, but from the overall system level. If the specifications were turned over to a programmer group for development they, the programmers, would waste many hours looking for answers to their questions. By putting all of the information about Start-Up procedures together, then that component could be turned over to one or more programmers to develop without the need to reference and research the entire system specification.

The flow of information was shown by both flowcharts and narrative but not on the same page or referenced to each other. This arrangement would have been satisfactory if each user used only the narrative or the flowchart in each section and the flowchart or narrative did not add to the understanding of the specification. Readers often refer to both the narrative and the flowchart to gain information from seeing the data in a different form.

The specification then would have been much more useful if the flowcharts had been included in the text rather than as a separate section. The list of flowcharts does not include an overall systems chart. Second level systems charts are the only ones indicated.

The use of two monthly procedures involves the input of a different file in January. In a five-year period it is a safe bet that at least three reruns will be caused because the operator mounted the wrong file.

The Decision Rules are not nearly detailed enough but if combined with the file description they would be satisfactory. They should be combined. Again, by grouping the data for each component, this would have been accomplished.

All reports and forms were described. Note that the reports layouts are shown with the descriptions of each report field. Most of the information needed by the forms analyst is included. Volume of use and filing method are conspicuous by their absence.

Clerical and operational procedures were not shown. In the project these were the responsibility of another member of the project team, which explains their absence. They normally would have been included and should have been referenced in the specification. Similarly, references to the interface of this system with other systems should have been included.

Card and file layouts were included in the specification. The specification shows the number of characters, whether the data is alphabetic or numeric or both and the description of each field of each record. In addition, the source and calculations required for each field are shown. All of this information is necessary. Missing are the ranges of legitimate values for each field. It is preferred that the description include the internal and display pictures of each field rather than just the A/N classification. The heading to be used when the field is printed should also be shown. Volumes are not indicated.

The codes used in the system were described completely. These, to some extent, provide the legitimate values needed for each field and the need of the glossary. None of the codes has any built-in redundancy structure. Certain fields such as the part number should have such check codes.

The part numbers are not usually shown in the systems specification. A system with 10,000 parts is not unusual. At 50 items per page the stock number list would be 200 pages long, requiring a separate part number book. The Inventory Control Group code includes 0 as a legitimate value. This is not recommended as good practice.

The report contains no glossary. Here the definition of terms is contained in the specification and is not easily retrieved. The definitions should not be removed from the narrative but should be duplicated in the glossary.

A records retention section was included. The section wisely specifies an event as the end of the retention period rather than setting a time period. This arrangement tends to reduce the length of time specified. It does require that the record centers be informed when that end event occurs.

The playscript style was used to document the procedures. While this is appropriate for some of the material it is not the best for all. Caption formats would have been preferable for at least the forecast procedure. Flowcharts should have been used to illustrate the procedures.

Job descriptions for the new system were not included. This is inconvenient for the person responsible for staffing and training personnel involved in the operation of the new system.

Control records and procedures were not included. This is a very serious omission. Chapter 26 further discusses this issue.

The original systems specification was not complete and accurate. It had at least 150 changes between the first printed version and the implemented version. Some changes were suggested by users while others were typographical errors or errors made by the analyst. Errors will occur despite efforts to avoid them. The project team should organize to thoroughly check its work.

Format for Writing Specifications
for the Design of an Information System

SUBJECT:

4.3.0 Objective of Step 3—Design

The objective of the third step of the System Innovation Process is to develop a Detailed System Design based on the Conceptual Design approved in Step 2, and to develop it in accordance with the approved Development Plan.

At this stage of the project, attention is concentrated on the development of design details so that construction of the system can take place during Step 4. The technical skills of information systems personnel are then employed to develop complete Master and Component Specifications. The system users review and approve the computer specifications to ensure that the detailed design, when constructed, will enable them to fulfill their responsibilities.

SUBJECT:

4.3.1 Products & Documentation

The principal outputs from Step 3 are the Master Specification and Component Specifications. The Master Specification typically contains information which applies to the system as a whole, while the individual Component Specifications provide detailed information on each of the clerical and EDP components of the system. The Master Specification draws on elements of documentation contained in the Conceptual Design and adds further sections. The amount of detailed design information required in the Conceptual Design varies widely. This, the detailed design step, must provide all the remaining design details needed to carry out construction of the system.

The contents of the Master Specification are described in the following paragraphs:

1. *The System Description* consists of the General System Description taken from the Conceptual Design, updated and expanded as necessary to provide the additional details needed to understand how the system fulfills its functions. It is helpful to structure this information so that each component of the system is described separately. This is done by providing a Detailed System Description of each component which also serves as the first element of documentation in the Component Specifications. A further useful grouping is by batch so that the various system job

SUBJECT:

4.3.1 Products & Documentation

streams are easily recognized. This will enable similar groupings to be made in the operations specifications described later.

2. *The System Flowchart* section contains the General Flowchart which may be updated to show precise names for files, programs and procedures, and similar detailed information that is developed during the Design Step. Detailed System Flowcharts may be added to assist in understanding complex system interrelationships. The object is not to duplicate the process logic information provided in each Component Specification. On the contrary, the object is merely to ensure that the interrelationships between each component are thoroughly understood.

3. *The Data Description* aims to bring together all of the Data Item Definitions required by the system. In addition, it should provide cross references which show the data sets containing the items and the components of the system which use the data sets. This decouples the Data Item Definitions from the individual components and avoids multiple appearances of the same definitions. In the event that the organization has a data dictionary, then this is the design reference for the definitions, and they need only be named in the Data Description. Otherwise, the Data Description section of the Master Specification is the design reference for all data definitions required for the system.

4. *The System Controls* documentation is expanded from the general view given on the Conceptual Design so that all the control mechanisms are clearly shown. A combination of report references, manual and EDP routines should be provided which stipulates exactly how the overall system control is to be accomplished. This information is then distributed among the Component Specifications to ensure each part is properly integrated to provide the required continuity.

5. *The System Boundary* may require expansion of the general information given in the Conceptual Design in order to specify more precisely what organization, documents and routines interface with the system. Typically, it will be helpful to provide cross references to the documentation sections of the interfacing systems.

There are four categories of Component Specification. Each of these specifications provides the additional data needed, in conjunction with the data provided in the Master Specifications to enable

> SUBJECT:
>
> 4.3.1 Products & Documentation

a corresponding system product to be constructed. In order to provide the complete data, these four categories should contain the
data described in the following paragraphs:

1. *A Program Specification* is typically prepared for each program
   required. It provides all the data needed to construct the program. Each specification should include:

   1. Purpose
   2. Schematic
   3. Input and output files
   4. Processing

   The purpose is a copy of that described in the Master Specification. It is included to avoid reference to the master when only
   a component is being worked on. The schematic provides a diagram of the program and all of the data inputs and outputs. It
   corresponds to a specific part of the overall System Flowchart
   provided in the Master Specification. The input and output files
   section gives Record Layout Sheets and their associated files,
   as well as printer spacing charts and any other data needed to
   completely specify the various inputs and outputs required. All
   the data items are named, but they are defined in the Data
   Description contained in the Master Specification. The processing section describes how the purpose is to be met. The descriptive portion corresponds with the Detailed System Description of
   the component which is included in the Master Specification. In
   addition, a function flowchart is used to display the relationship
   between the principal modules of a program, and to name them.
   The process logic for each named module is then precisely defined.

2. *The EDP Operations Specification* describes each of the program
   groupings required to fulfill the various on-line and batch operations. The data it contains enables the EDP operations procedures to be constructed and properly tied back to the individual
   component programs. It is presumed that the EDP operation
   should be optimized so that service is economical and directed
   towards those jobs requiring the highest priorities. It is also
   assumed that the EDP operating organization has a standard
   set of information requirements which must be provided in
   order that a system will be accepted for production. The data
   contained in the EDP operating specification brings together the

SUBJECT:

4.3.1 Products & Documentation

key facts needed to construct the standard information. The data required includes such things as clearly identified operation names, the programs involved, timing, frequency, volume, sources of inputs, disposal of outputs, forms and files needed and file backup requirements.

3. *The Clerical Operations Specifications* provide the data needed to prepare the various clerical procedures carried out in support of the EDP jobs. As a result, they are usually organized to show how they interact with the corresponding EDP portions of the system. When the clerical procedures are written during the construction step, this grouping may be less evident since some of the clerical procedures may be supporting several EDP jobs and the procedures may be combined to obtain economies. The contents of the user operations specifications are similar to those of the programming specifications. These are purpose, schematic, input & outputs and processing. The purpose of the routine is taken from the Master Specification. The schematic shows what inputs and outputs enter and leave the routine being specified. The inputs and outputs are named and, where possible, cross-referenced to the EDP routine generating or using them. When they cannot be cross-referenced to a definition elsewhere, they are defined in terms of format and content in this section. The processing section should provide a flowchart of the main routines together with a compact statement of the logic associated with each of them, as well as a description as to how the purpose is fulfilled.

4. *The System Test Specification* describes the overall test strategy to be developed and used in order to ensure the system can safely be implemented when construction is completed. It is desirable to have a standard approach to the testing of all systems; however, these will always be special requirements and test sequences which must be determined and specified at various levels of detail. These include the testing of parts of all of the clerical and EDP components, their relationships within a routine and the relationships between routines. The system test specification is required before construction starts to ensure that a system approach is taken to testing and the preparation of the various elements of test data.

SUBJECT:

4.3.2 Process

This aspect describes the system activities which are usually performed during the third innovation step. In essence, there are six principal system activities which tend to be highly interactive:

1. Define the data items, records and files.

    The definition of the data items, records and files consists of many tasks. Typical of these are the definitions of:
    1. Forms used as input to the system
    2. Source documents generated in the system
    3. EDP transaction inputs
    4. Clerical references and tables
    5. EDP references and tables
    6. Output documents from EDP processes
    7. Clerical outputs
    8. Clerical master files updated by the system
    9. EDP master files updated by the system

    An increasingly important aspect of data definition is the use of a data base or preparation for its future use. To this end, a great deal of attention has to be paid to the consistent definition of data items and their structural relationships to each other. Whether the data definitions are for items used in clerical procedures or EDP ones, it is highly desirable to maintain consistency in such matters as size, format and allowed values. Furthermore, it is important to note that definition of a data item and its relation to others automatically defines the validating rules which must be applied to ensure that a system is protected against invalid data. This key principle allows data to be defined once in terms of the validation tests it must meet in order to be data processable, instead of generating diverse clerical and EDP validating rules throughout the system, which tend to be either redundent or contradictory. It is not the role of this report to explore data items, records, documents, reports or file layouts. However, it is appropriate to recommend strongly the adoption of a standard means of defining data for use throughout an information systems organization. By its nature data interacts with many systems. The use of a unique data name for each definition will do a great deal to simplify detailed design. Under these conditions, the first step in data definition is to see whether the definition already exists as a result of previous systems work. If it does,

SUBJECT:

4.3.2 Process

then the data names are adopted. If the data items have been linked by a specific data base structure, is the structure one that can readily be used for the system under design? This question was asked, of course, at the Conceptual Design stage. Now it is asked again in terms of each data item required. If the data base has been designed with future systems work in mind, basic structural changes should not be required, though new linkages may need to be added. In the case of items not previously defined, it is essential to consider what other system may later use the data and in what manner. In this way, the definitions will not require frequent costly updating. Throughout the data defining process, as items are assembled into documents and reports, it is essential to work closely with those who will prepare or use them. It is essential that the users understand and approve what will be provided when the system is implemented.

2. Define the process logic, sequence and components for each routine.

The definition of the process logic, sequence and components for each routine seeks to establish the precise interrelationships between the various system components needed to carry out a routine. During the Conceptual Design stage, it was stressed that each function had to be considered separately before its individual information flows were lost in the overall system design. Now, during the Detailed Design stage, it is essential to see precisely how each function is fulfilled. All of the clerical and EDP components must be clearly recognized in terms of who is responsible, when they are needed, what volume of data must be handled, the conditions which determine when the components should be used. Once again, these key timings and interrelationships must be worked out with those who will be responsible for operating the clerical and EDP portions of the system. Their approval must be obtained before the logic design of the components can be completed. The decisions made during these systems activities provide most of the data required for the EDP and user operations specifications.

3. Determine detailed design logic for each component.

The detailed design logic of each component is prepared by

SUBJECT:

4.3.2 Process

analyzing precisely what routines it supports, what logic is required to provide the support and how it may be most effectively arranged, and factors such as the relative amounts of the various transactions to be handled. Their sequence, priority and complexity are considered in order to specify a component design which will give the optimum overall performance. Particular care should be taken to ensure that exceptions and summary controls are handled in a manner consistent with the routine as a whole. Once again, the users of the system should be involved not so much to define the precise design logic, but to ensure that the module accomplishes what is required. These activities provide the data needed to prepare the component specifications for the EDP and manual parts of the system.

4. Prepare and obtain approval for the master and operations specifications.
5. Prepare and obtain approval for the component specifications.
6. Prepare the system test specifications.

   The preparation of the system test specification depends on defining an overall test structure for each routine and the linkages between them. The specification is then extended to include the test criteria which each component should meet in order for it to be acceptable. The specification may also include test criteria for specific logic modules within a given component of the system. The data in the system test specification is intended primarily to indicate to those who will construct the system exactly what tests must be made before implementation. Test data and a test plan will later be constructed to carry out the tests.

SUBJECT:

4.3.3 Skills

The skills required in the Design Step of system development are those typically associated with systems analysis. During this step, the Conceptual Design is translated into a level of detail that will permit system construction to take place. Thus the main skills needed are the technical skills required for such things as logic development, data file and element definition and the preparation of specifications for a wide range of construction activities.

SUBJECT:

4.3.3 Skills

In addition to the primary technical skills, there is a need for a wide range of secondary technical skills. These include such things as the ability to read computer programs, analyze and optimize detailed design solutions, blend clerical and EDP routines, prepare appropriate control and security features as well as specifying the detailed conversion procedures needed to switch from existing routines to the new system.

A further skill is the ability to handle fine detail at a highly complex level over a lengthy period of time. This ability must include not only working as an individual but also communicating in a very precise, unambiguous manner with a wide range of personnel both within and outside the information systems organization.

SUBJECT:

4.3.4 Tools & Techniques

Since the purpose of the third step is to prepare the detailed design for the solution chosen, the principal tools and techniques required are those which enable a detailed analysis and presentation of design specifications to be made.

Typical tools and techniques required to present the EDP and clerical aspects of the system logic and data requirements include:

Data Definition Conventions
Logic Diagramming
Decision Tables
Ionic Modeling
Local Practices and Standards
File and Record Definition
Operating Requirements
Specification Writing
Forms Design
Internal Control Techniques

The third step is concerned with many levels of detail. On the one hand the overall design must be kept in perspective, while on the other hand every last logic and data detail must be settled. The tools used must be versatile enough to cover this range completely and economically. In addition, it is important to make use of design control techniques which enable changes to be controlled and applied throughout the whole design.

SUBJECT:

4.3.5 Process Management

Concurrent with the system activities the following process management activities are required to manage the system activities carried out during Innovative Step 3:

1. Review and maintain the plan and allocation of resources required for the development phase
2. Maintain up-to-date schedules and cost estimates
3. Assign resources to activities
4. Review individual assignment planning
5. Monitor progress of activities
6. Propose and implement corrective action when needed
7. Accumulate and report cost and time data
8. Approve completed assignments
9. Issue Step 3 progress and project status reports
10. Obtain approval of master and component specifications
11. Update the documentation control sheet.

SUBJECT:

4.3.6 Personnel Preparedness

In addition to the general background stipulated in 4.0.4, the personnel involved in this step require training or experience in the following:

Data Base and File Organization
Systems Analysis
Teleprocessing Concepts
Operating Systems Concepts
Project Management
Programming Languages
Report Writing
Iconic Modeling
Decision Theory
Logic
Cost Estimates
Parametric and Non-parametric Statistics
Modeling and Gaming
Data Acquisition and Control

REVIEW QUESTIONS

Review the Stock Status System described in this chapter and:
1. Rewrite the general system description in modular form.
2. Rewrite the procedures changing the appropriate ones to other forms such as caption.
3. Prepare a glossary.
4. Rewrite the file description.
5. Write a Stock Status Record File description.

BIBLIOGRAPHY

Collard, Albert F., "Format for Writing Specifications for the Design of an Information System," paper presented at GUIDE Conference, Miami, Fla., March 1972.

part V

Systems
Implementation

After the system design is completed and approved the project team focuses upon the implementation tasks. The management tasks of the project leader are quite different. The leader usually must manage a larger number of people and must organize so that the myriad details of the project are all done correctly and on time. Previously, the need was for creativity and selling ability. Now the need is for coordination. Part V describes some of the tasks that come to the fore during the implementation, conversion and evaluation phases of a project.

Chapter 21 describes people aspects of the project. Included in the chapter are descriptions of staffing of the project and the training of the users.

Next, the space requirements for the system are described. The context is deliberately made to be the entire office and computer center. The specific needs for space planning for a particular project are a subset of that environment described.

As this is written, programming management is rapidly becoming more systematized. Top-down programs using well defined structures may well substantially reduce programming. Error-free programs may become a thinkable objective.

Conversion also is changing. Fewer projects convert from manual operations to machine ones. Thus, the analyst will more often focus upon file and program conversion in the future.

Finally, there is an evaluation phase for the project. The successes and failures are listed. Hopefully, they provide lessons that enable the organization to develop more effective systems in future projects.

CHAPTER 21

STAFFING AND TRAINING

The systems project must concern itself with two groups of people. The first is the project staff. There are many important considerations involved in the staffing and training of the project itself. Of equal importance are the issues involved in the staffing and training of the organizations using the new system.

This chapter assumes that several activities mentioned previously have been completed such as the preparation of a project plan and that the plan specifies the number of people and skills needed to develop the project. A typical plan is shown in Figure 21.1. This

ACME Distribution Center Teleprocessing System Cost/Time Estimate

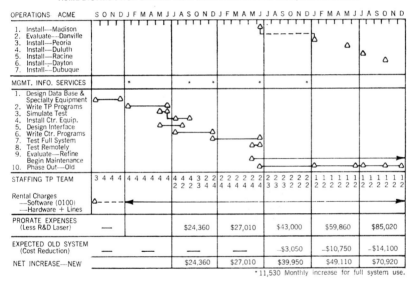

ACME DISTRIBUTION CENTER TELEPROCESSING SYSTEM COST/TIME ESTIMATE

OPERATIONS ACME — S O N D J F M A M J J A S O N D J F M A M J J A S O N D J F M A M J J A S O N D

1. Install—Madison
2. Evaluate—Danville
3. Install—Peoria
4. Install—Duluth
5. Install—Racine
6. Install—Dayton
7. Install—Dubuque

MGMT. INFO. SERVICES

1. Design Data Base & Specialty Equipment
2. Write TP Programs
3. Simulate Test
4. Install Ctr. Equip.
5. Design Interface
6. Write Ctr. Programs
7. Test Full System
8. Test Remotely
9. Evaluate—Refine Begin Maintenance
10. Phase Out—Old

STAFFING TP TEAM: 3 4 4 4 | 4 4 4 4 4 4 | 4 4 4 3 2 2 | 2 2 2 2 2 2 | 2 2 2 2 2 2 | 1 1 1 1 1 1 | 1 1 1 1 1 1
2 2 2 3 4 4 | 4 4 4 4 4 4 | 3 3 3 2 2 2 | 2 2 2 2 2 2 | 2 2 2 2 2 2

Rental Charges
—Software (0100)
—Hardware + Lines

		PRORATE EXPENSES (Less R&D Laser)	EXPECTED OLD SYSTEM (Cost Reduction)	NET INCREASE—NEW
PRORATE EXPENSES (Less R&D Laser)	—	$24,360	$27,010	$43,000	$59,860	$85,020
EXPECTED OLD SYSTEM (Cost Reduction)	—	—	—	—	−$3,050	−$10,750	−$14,100
NET INCREASE—NEW			$24,360	$27,010	$39,950	$49,110	$70,920

*11,530 Monthly increase for full system use.

FIGURE 21.1

chapter also assumes that the installation plan has been developed so that the people and skills needed for the operational system are known. These plans must be implemented by the people in the project group and in the user organization. This chapter is also concerned with the selection and training of people to perform the project and system tasks.

STAFFING THE PROJECT

Project groups vary greatly in size. Some projects are small enough

443

to be handled by one person; others may require a small army of people. The various phases of a project require particular skills. Thus projects often involve adding and deleting people as the project progresses.

The level of skill needed also varies by project. For example, the project leader may have the official job title of systems project leader, senior systems analyst, systems analyst, trainee systems analyst, programmer/analyst or programmer depending upon the size and type of project. The information systems project includes the functions of programming and systems analysis. Also included in the project staff may be user representatives, auditors, operations research analysts and clerical personnel. This chapter will consider the staffing requirements for the three major areas of programmers, systems analysts, and other personnel used in a project team.

Programmers

Programmers have been the most studied of the whole range of data processing personnel. Thanks to the work of a number of researchers, there is a great deal known about this occupational group. The most recent and elaborate study was done by Berger (1974). Previous work of considerable value has been done by Lothridge (1964), Berger (1963), and Willoughby (1971). The list of tasks examined by these researchers caused them to hypothesize that certain aptitudes are involved and that certain tests are appropriate predictors of the aptitudes. Since the hypothesized aptitudes predated the task information, the research is somewhat suspect. However, it is apparent that there are several dimensions in programming that require different abilities. It is unlikely that any single ability or any single attribute test is sufficient to predict programming ability. The tests uncovered the following criteria for successful programmer selection:

1. Success in programmer training is related to intelligence as measured by most intelligence tests.
2. Highly intelligent and above-average subjects perform about the same.
3. Currently used tests predict training success better than job performance (Willoughby, 1972).
4. Reasoning, letter series, number series, and diagramming have been shown to be predictors of programming success. Verbal abilities do not usually correlate (Palarmo, 1967).
5. Tests deliberately designed to test coding ability have correlated highly with coding performance (Wolfe, 1970, and Seiner, 1971).

6. Programmers have interests different from men and women in general (Perry, 1967 and 1968).

7. Those employees with interests like other programmers tend to be better performers (Sweetland, 1962, Willoughby, 1971, and Mussio & Wahlstrom, 1971).

8. The difference in performance between the best and the average programmer is perhaps ten to one, a ratio much higher than in most jobs.

In addition, good selection practice indicates that any personnel selection system must be validated in the environment concerned. Also, the various selection devices vary in effectiveness with work samples, knowledge tests, aptitude tests, interest inventories, psychological inventories and interviews generally being rated in order of decreasing effectiveness. These factors should be considered when staffing a project with programmers.

The preferred sources of programmers in order of rank are:

1. Programmers within the organization are known quantities with low risk of failure.

2. Programmers from outside the organization selected by using a work sample to test their ability to program. Previously trained people are preferred because of the cost of training and because evaluation can be more certain.

3. Trainees. The little evidence available indicates that selection of trainees from inside the organization is neither more nor less effective than selection from outside. Training a programmer may take up to a year and cost as much as $15,000 so the trainee option can be a costly one. The training option requires the selection of a particular group of trainees from among the applicants. When the group to be trained is fairly large, a test validation study is recommended. Included in the tests should be one to test cognitive abilities in reasoning, diagram reading and coding ability.

Equal employment opportunity laws make it necessary to validate the selection devices separately for non-whites and females. Lack of separate validation in the past has often resulted in employment quotas by sex and color.

The single most used test of programming aptitude has been IBM's Programmer Aptitude Test (PAT) in its many versions. Distribution of the test has now been discontinued. We would not have recommended its use because many prospective employees have taken the test in the past and scores on the PAT tend to improve each time it is taken. Willoughby (1972) lists some of the other tests that might be considered.

Systems Analysts

Much less is known about the systems analysts' job. The requirements described by Shrout (1971) are certainly different from and much more extensive than a comparable programmer list, yet Hoyle and Arvey (1972) found that programmers and systems analysts should be evaluated by the same scales, only using different values for the criteria.

There is some evidence that programmers and systems analysts are different psychological groups. Willoughby (1971) found each to have different interests while Dauw (1967) found differences in creative ability with analysts being broader while programmers' creative outputs were fewer but deeper.

In practice organizations seem to choose their analysts from the programmer ranks, new college graduates and the user areas. The typical analyst has at least a bachelors degree. This is partly due to the fact that the department heads with whom he deals are usually college graduates.

Selection of an analyst for a project should ideally be from among the organization's analysts. Other choices would be to promote a programmer and allow a year of training or hire a business school graduate and train for two years, or promote a current employee and train for one or more years. The relative effectiveness of these three strategies is not known.

Other Project Staff

While there may be other personnel assigned to a systems project, the focus here is upon the representatives of the department(s) involved in the project. Unlike systems analysts and programmers, these people will always be current employees of the organization. The first law of selecting a user representative is that *the person most available is not the best person for the project*. Competence seems *to vary inversely with availability*. The project leader then should pay particular attention to this assignment. One frequently successful tactic is to select an employee who is about due for a promotion. This staff type assignment can then be a broadening experience that better prepares the employee for the next job.

The special talents needed by the user representative are knowledge of the user functions, an open mind and personal authority. The reason for the first is obvious. The second is a necessity if change is to occur. The person unable to seriously consider alternatives to the present system can completely stymie the project. The user representative must have a good reputation in the using department. Not everything done is going to be possible to explain completely to all involved. Thus, an element of trust and confidence (personal authority) is necessary. As mentioned previously it may be appropriate for the user representative to be the project leader. The choice of a leader is more dependent upon perceived leadership skills than upon task skills.

General Considerations

To this point we have focused upon the skills and personality attributes of the potential staff. Other considerations include experience with the type of system being designed, the equipment used and familiarity in the organization. The evidence to date does indicate somewhat greater user satisfaction with an experienced crew. However, the projects manned by the more experienced personnel tend to run over their time estimates.

Availability is important. Organizations have more system projects than they can implement. When one project is completed another awaits. With some projects taking years to complete, the systems manager is often faced with dilemmas like these:

Jay Davis is the best man for the job but he won't be available for eight months.

Robert Wood has less experience with that type of project but will be available in two weeks.

The project should return about $100,000/year and be completed in 6 months if Davis does it.

Results are not very predictable if Wood does it.

Project turnover of personnel can be disruptive. Assignments should consider possible promotions and expected staff changes. Some consider this so important that they equate leaving the firm in the middle of a project with unprofessional conduct.

A particular project requires a specific set of skills. Everything else being equal, one would like to staff the project so as to minimize the training needed to develop the required skills.

Small, medium and large project staffs are shown in Figure 21.2, 21.3 and 21.4.

PROJECT STAFF TRAINING

One of the groups of tasks in the project is the training plan for the project staff. An assessment of the training needs is made and the required training scheduled. The systems analyst will need additional training in a minimum of areas. Depending upon the nature of the project and the education of the analyst, it may be necessary

Small Project Staff

```
┌─────────────────────────────┐
│      Programmer/Analyst      │
└─────────────────────────────┘
```

FIGURE 21.2

Medium Sized Project Staff

```
┌──────────────────────────────────┐
│          Systems Analyst          │
│  User Representative (½ time)      │
│            Programmer              │
│            Programmer              │
└──────────────────────────────────┘
```

FIGURE 21.3

Large Project Staff

```
┌──────────────────────────────────┐
│          Project Manager          │
│    Manager Analysis and Design    │
│             Analysts              │
│  Manager—Programming Group A      │
│           Programmers             │
│  Manager—Programming Group B      │
│           Programmers             │
│  Manager—Programming Group C      │
│           Programmers             │
│      Manager—Integration          │
│              Staff                │
│        Manager—Test               │
│              Staff                │
│       Manager—Staff               │
│          Accountant               │
│          Clerks, etc.             │
└──────────────────────────────────┘
```

FIGURE 21.4

for an analyst to be trained in such things as simulation techniques, teleprocessing, linear programming, and data management systems. The programmer may need special training in a simulation language, advanced file techniques, and teleprocessing access methods. The user will frequently need training in basic data processing techniques, basic systems analysis and systems design.

Training courses are offered by manufacturers, consultants, and universities. These courses are available at fixed times which may be inconvenient for the project team. Ideally, the project team should complete its training in the early part of the project. The need to fit training to different schedules and small groups has led to the development of video tape, audio tape, film, programmed learning, and correspondence courses. These courses are generally available for the basic training needs.

The training of the programmer and the systems analyst must bring them to the level of skillful use of the knowledge and techniques available. Lectures alone are insufficient. Skillful use requires hands-on practice and the experience gained from immediate feedback. For example, Weinberg (1971) found that lecturing about JCL did not reduce the JCL errors his students were making. Some of the most successful programming courses are taught at the Uni-

Staffing Plan before Systems Project
Total personnel—82

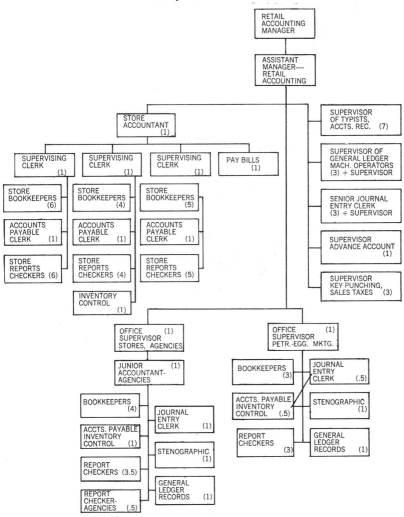

FIGURE 21.5

Staffing Plan after Systems Project
Total personnel—48

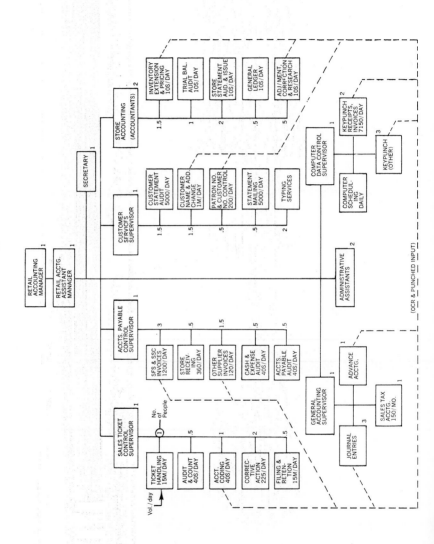

FIGURE 21.6

versity of Minnesota using self-paced material and the teacher in a coaching role. Willoughby (1972) found extremely negative attitudes associated with the normal lecture course in programming.

The training of the user representative need not reach a technical skill level. A knowledge level for the user representative is usually adequate. The more usual lecture and reading techniques of teaching are adequate for this purpose. Basic data processing and systems courses are taught by many community colleges and universities, hardware vendors, correspondence schools, and a large number of training specialists so that they will fit into most project schedules.

STAFFING FOR THE NEW SYSTEM

The new system may need more or fewer people than the old system. Figures 21.5 and 21.6 show the before and after staffing for one project. Aside from timing considerations, additions are neither more nor less of a problem than the normal hiring problems of the organization. Redundancies may well be difficult to manage and are certainly worth considering.

Example of a system conversion

The Memphis plant of the Kappa Corporation planned to make a systems change. The change was a major one involving about 40 of the 70 clerical employees. As a result of the change it was expected that the clerical force would total 55 employees. The change was planned one year in advance of the target date for completion, with sub-systems set for installation at the six, nine and twelve month points. Turnover among clerical personnel had averaged about 18 employees per year. Immediately after the change was approved the office manager made his staffing plan. He announced the plans for the new system and the staffing plan concurrently.

The staffing plan was to allow attrition to reduce the clerical staff. The policies established were:

1. When a current employee quit, he would decide whether the work could be done by the remaining staff for the next few months. If so, the position was left vacant. If not, but if modest amounts of overtime or a temporary employee would solve the problem, he would use those methods.

2. The temporary employee was to be told upon hiring that the job might not exist at the end of the year. The employee was to be told further that if employment was not possible after

the end of the year, the company would search for a new employer for that person.

As the conversion time approached, the services of people from temporary help agencies were used. The first conversion reduced the total needs for staff, thus soaking up some of the vacant positions. Two people made redundant in the first change filled positions that had become vacant elsewhere in the organization. Similar results occurred during the second conversion. Attrition occurred at about the expected rate for the usual reasons. There appeared to be no evidences of insecurity among the clerical staff.

The final conversion was accomplished on schedule. One month after the final conversion date, the new systems were operating with the planned staff. At that time two of the temporary people were redundant. The Personnel Department called some of the local firms, and gave the employees excellent references. Jobs were offered immediately (at higher salaries) for the two people who were not needed for the new staff.

The bills for overtime and for workers from the temporary help agencies were high, but were only half the cost of the full-time employees. The productivity of the staff that year was well above previous levels, and the office manager kept the respect of the employees.

The lessons learned from this case are the need for making detailed personnel plans, that attrition does help solve redundancy problems, that insecurity can be alleviated by communication where there is good will, and that the use of overtime and temporary employees can contribute to good redundancy planning.

TRAINING FOR THE NEW SYSTEM

The training elements in a project plan are:
1. Determine the amount and type of training needed for each new job and for each changed job.
2. Determine the training materials needed for each training element.
3. Determine the training schedule.
4. Communicate the training plans to employees.
5. Produce training materials.
6. Train all personnel involved in conversion.
7. Provide materials and plans for training employees added to the system later on.

The following discusses some of these training elements in detail.

Training Schedule

The rate at which people forget is high. This makes it necessary to schedule the training sessions as close to conversion as possible. The extra work required during conversion may impact this decision. Certainly an employee already working long hours to handle the conversion is not likely to accept training gracefully. Generally, the best compromise is to train about two or three weeks before conversion date.

FIGURE 21.7

Training Materials

The documentation produced during systems design is *not* adequate for training. Materials should be especially prepared for the training sessions that include a short overview of the new system and a detailed step-by-step description of each new job task. Worked-out

How an IBM Optical Reader Works

When a document is fed into the Optical Reader, it passes across a tube similar to the picture tube in your TV set. Then, a small spot of light begins to scan (read) the document.   When this spot of light comes to a hand-printed character, it begins to trace around the edges of the character. When the spot has finished going around the character, it sends the outline of what it has just "seen" to a part of the machine that decides which (1234567890XCTZS) of the possible characters has been traced.

The IBM Optical Reader makes this kind of contour analysis of every character you print. It happens very fast—over 300 times per second.

Beginning on the next page, you will learn to shape each character properly. Then, by practicing, you will be able to make digits and symbols consistently acceptable to the IBM Optical Reader.

FIGURE 21.8

WRITE LIKE THIS

FOLLOW THESE RULES	THE RIGHT WAY	THE WRONG WAY
1. Write Big—Fill the Blocks.	2 8 4 7 9 1 0	2 8 4 7 9 1 0
2. Close the Loops.	0 6 8 8 9 9 6	0 6 8 8 9 9 6
3. Use Simple Shapes. No Loops.	0 2 3 7 5 4 1	0 2 3 7 5 4 1
4. Do Not Link Characters.	0 0 2 8 0 0 7	0 0 2 8 0 0 7
5. Connect Lines.	4 5 T 4 5 5 4	4 5 T 4 5 5 4
6. Block Print All Special Characters.	C S T X Z T X	C S T X Z T X

7. *Handwritten characters to be read by SSC's Optical Reader must be written with a black-lead pencil or a black fine-line lead.* The pencilled characters should be as dark as possible without smudging. *Standard no. 2 pencils and grade HB fine-line leads* give best results.
Erasures are acceptable as long as the original character is completely erased.

FIGURE 21.9

1. KEEP YOUR #2 PENCIL SHARP.

2. ALWAYS WRITE YOUR NUMBERS LIKE THIS:

3. KEEP ALL NUMBERS TALL, DARK, AND HANDSOME,
    AND WITHIN THE BOX.

4. USE NO LEADING ZEROES.

5. ALWAYS COMPLETE THE 8 NECESSARY BOXES.
    patron number, producer or non-producer,
    quantity, inventory code, amount, total,
    transaction and clerk number

6. DO NOT PUNCH, FOLD, SPINDLE, OR MUTILATE
    THE SALES TICKET.

*WHEN YOU DO ALL THIS, YOU HAVE COMPLETED YOUR PORTION OF THE
PATRONAGE REFUND REPORT, THE MONTHLY STATEMENTS, THE ACCOUNTS
RECEIVABLE REPORT, THE MONTHLY STATEMENT OF OPERATIONS, AND
STATE SALES TAX REPORTS.

*after testing is complete, and we have shown that OCR can be used.

FIGURE 21.10

examples, filled-in forms and test data to use on a terminal are
most helpful.

The training materials should introduce the employee to the systems documentation if they will be using it. One must remember
that the best training material is not a good reference material and
vice versa. Assuming that the system documentation is well organized as a reference then the training sessions should introduce the
employee to the documentation. Examples of special training materials developed for one application are shown in Figures 21.7, 21.8,
21.9 and 21.10.

Training

Training is teaching a skill. Acquiring a skill generally takes practice. Therefore, training sessions should include practice opportunities.

Some systems practitioners have had poor success using optical mark or character reading. The bane of such systems is the marks that cannot be read. The systems analyst should not expect the employee to have the ability to make readable marks. Skill development is needed. Perhaps the best way of developing the marking skill is for the employee to go to the reader, mark some documents, have the operator pass the documents through the reader and observe the result. In this way, the employee can experiment with heavy, light, long and short marks. The sensitivity of the reader is then apparent.

Systems using the organization's message communication system often require training of the operator. Untrained operators can foul up a tape conversion process. New skills must be developed even when the changes seem very minor. The process of forgetting the old systems is called extinction and is difficult to achieve when the new skill closely resembles the old one.

SUMMARY

This chapter examined the manpower part of the systems plan and discussed the staffing and training requirements that result from the plan.

Substantial research concerning programmers has been performed so that the job dimensions, attitudes and abilities related to successful programming are known. Systems analysts' characteristics are less well known but are known to be different from programmers'. Sources of training for programmers, systems analysts and users were described.

The major problem within the user area is the handling of staff reductions. Some ways of minimizing the impact of such changes were described. User training requires specially designed training materials together with considerable planning. The staffing and training areas of a project are stated in the old proverb "Plan your work and work your plan."

REVIEW QUESTIONS

1. Describe several sources for COBOL training and the advantages and disadvantages of each.
2. Why does it take two years to train a graduate of a college of business to be a systems analyst?
3. List the advantages and disadvantages of training a current employee versus hiring a programmer.
4. List the advantages of using a systems analyst as a project leader.
5. List the advantages of using a user as a project leader.

DISCUSSION QUESTIONS

1. Develop a linear organization chart for Figures 21.5 and 21.6.
2. Prepare a project staff plan for the project described in Chapter 15 or Chapter 20.
3. Assume a clerical staff of 200 people and that all typewriter keys will be changed to OCR type fonts. Discuss a training program for the conversion.

BIBLIOGRAPHY

Ashenhurst, R. L., "Curriculum Recommendations for Graduate Programs in Information Systems," *Communications of the ACM*, Vol. 15, No. 5, May 1972, p. 364-398.

Berger, R. M. and Rigney, Joseph W., *Computer Personnel Selection and Criterion Development: Description and Classification of Computer Programming and Analyst Jobs*, NR 153-093, AD 432-020, 1963.

Berger, R. M., *Computer Programmer Job Analysis*, Montvale, N.J.: AFIPS, 1974.

Computing Newsletter for Schools of Business, College of Business Administration, University of Colorado, Colorado Springs, Colorado.

Couger, J. Daniel, "Curriculum Recommendations for Undergraduate Programs in Information Systems," *Communications of the ACM*, Vol. 16, No. 12, Dec. 1973, p. 727-749.

Dauw, Dean C., "Creativity in Organizations," *Personnel Journal*, Vol. 45, No. 8, Sept. 1966, p. 465-474.

Dearden, John, "MIS is a Mirage," *Harvard Business Review*, Vol. 50, No. 1, Jan.-Feb., 1972, p. 90-99.

Hoyle, Joseph C. and Richard D. Arvey, "Development of Behaviorally Based Rating Scales," *Proceedings of the 10th Annual Computer Personnel Research Conference*, New York: ACM, 1972, p. 85-103.

Lawshe, C. H. and Balma, Michael J., *Principles of Personnel Testing (2nd Edition)*, New York: McGraw-Hill, 1966.

Lothridge, Charles D., "Levels of Programming Jobs," *Proceedings of the 2nd Annual Computer Personnel Research Conference*, New York: ACM, 1964.

Mussio, Jerry J. and Wahlstrom, Merlin W., "Predicting Performance of Programmer Trainees in a Post High School Setting," *Proceedings of the 9th Annual Computer Personnel Research Conference*, New York: ACM, 1971, p. 26-46.

Palarmo, Jean, *Computer Programmer Test Battery Manual*, Chicago, Illinois: Science Research Associates, 1967.

Perry, Dallis K. and Cannon, W. M., "Vocational Interests of Female Computer Programmers," *Journal of Applied Psychology*, Vol. 52, No. 1, 1968, p. 31-35.

Perry, Dallis K. and Cannon, W. M., "Vocational Interests of Computer Programmers," *Journal of Applied Psychology*, Vol. 51, No. 1, 1967, p. 28-34.

Seiner, J. P., "Programming Aptitude and Competence Test Systems (PACTS)," *Proceedings of the 9th Annual Computer Personnel Research Conference*, New York: ACM, 1971, p. 3-25.

Shrout, Ethel, "Competencies and Training Requirements for Intermation Systems Analysts," *Proceedings of the 9th Annual Computer Personnel Research Conference*, New York: ACM, 1971, p. 75-100.

Sweetland, Anders, *Factors in Selecting and Training Programmers*, Santa Monica, Ca.: Systems Development Corp., RM 3245-PR, 1962.

Weinberg, Gerald M., *The Psychology of Computer Programming*, New York: Van Nostrand-Reinhold, 1971.

Willoughby, T. C., "Computer Attitudes of Business Students," *SIGCSE Bulletin*, Vol. 3, No. 1, Feb. 1973, p. 145-148.

Willoughby, T. C., "Staffing the MIS Function," *Computing Surveys*, Vol. 4, No. 4, Dec. 1972, p. 241-259.

Willoughby, T. C., "Needs, Interests, Reinforcer Preferences and Satisfaction of Data Processing Personnel," Unpublished Ph.D. Dissertation, University of Minnesota, 1971.

Wolfe, Jack M., "A New Look at Programming Aptitudes," *Business Automation*, Vol. 17, No. 8, Aug. 1970, p. 36-45.

CHAPTER 22

SPACE PLANNING AND FACILITIES

Terry (1970) defines office space planning as "the arrangement of all physical components within the available floor space to provide maximum effectiveness and the coordination of these components into an efficient and attractive unity." He assumes the floor space as fixed, but in good office layout and design the specific operations to be performed should precede the floor space allotment. This requires that the organization and the information system be designed before the building. This is standard procedure in a production facility. Before deciding how space should be planned, one must first analyze the needs of both the organization and the individual.

NEEDS OF THE ORGANIZATION

Flexibility

The organization must be able to respond quickly to change, rearrange people and work places, disband old groups, form new groups and relocate quickly and cheaply. Industry experts have estimated that 50% of the space utilized within a company changes every five years, at costs running from $2 to $17 per square foot in offices with fixed partitions. A reasonable average is, perhaps, 25% of space changing each year at $5 per square foot.

Economy

Maximum economy is needed in four areas: 1. Initial construction—cost of designing, furnishing and installing. 2. Physical maintenance—cost of keeping up the physical installation. 3. Rearrangements—moves of people covered above. 4. Space use—ratio of people to square feet. None of these items should be considered in isolation. The net result of costing out all four areas should be the economic criterion.

Efficiency

The office layout should be conducive to a high level of productivity, both clerical and managerial. Work flow, communication patterns and information storage and retrieval methods must be the key determinants of space use. Special attention must also be given to the placement of functional furniture and equipment.

Substantial portions of this chapter are quoted from Rice (1972) with permission. Also the chapter owes much to the ideas presented by Terry (1970).

461

De-emphasis of Status

Perhaps the greatest friction encountered in space planning is undue emphasis on rank and status expressed through demands for private offices and partitioned work places. Meeting these demands is the main cause of inflexible layouts. Status is important but it can be recognized in more functional and less expensive ways.

NEEDS OF THE INDIVIDUAL

Privacy

This need not mean seclusion behind walls. It does mean freedom from visual distractions, freedom from interference from passers-by, and freedom from one's conversation being overheard. Special provision is necessary for privacy in confidential interviews and meetings.

Territory

Everyone needs space of his own. This is part of privacy; but beyond this, everyone needs to feel a part of a work group whose larger space is identified. Space planning must satisfactorily define the space of the individual and the space of the larger group of which the individual's space is a part.

Comfort

Everyone needs an attractive and inviting environment to perform well. This means proper attention to lighting (particularly natural window lighting), color, floor covering, wall and window coverings, heating, air conditioning, sound control, and the design of workplace furniture and equipment.

Status

Recognition of status is a genuine social need that cannot be ignored. What is important is to find an appropriate, flexible, and inexpensive expression of status that is conducive to the morale of the individual and the group. Status should grow out of and express the needs of the job, rather than be an arbitrary embellishment to it.

SPACE PLANNING CONCEPTS

Several space planning concepts exist which should be evaluated with reference to the space planning objectives stated above. These concepts are:

Cellular

This concept emphasizes individual private offices or partitioned areas, rectilinearly placed, with a minimum of open space, e.g. engineering offices and cubicles; data processing work station layouts.

Openness

Here there are large open areas with very few or no private offices or partitioned areas, laid out in a strict rectilinear format, e.g. the traditional "large insurance company" type of layout.

Traditional

This is a combination of the above two with large open rectilinear areas, but also a fair number of private offices or partitioned areas (perhaps the most commonly employed concept).

Office Landscape

This concept, which originated in Germany and has been widely adopted in Scandinavia, Britain, and North America, rejects the cellular approach with its emphasis on private offices, and the "open-plan" office with its regimented rows of desks. It rather takes a large open area, lays it out on the basis of work flow and communication patterns, and provides for privacy by a combination of moveable partitions, indoor planters and furniture groupings. It does this in the context of a carefully designed total environment emphasizing openness and airiness and paying special attention to acoustics, light, and color. It favors curvilinear rather than rectilinear layout, reserving a complete freedom to create whatever shaped space is functionally advantageous.

A systems analysis of work flow and communication patterns must underlie all space planning. This analysis can be best translated into actual layout using office landscaping concepts. It can be applied to the open and, within limits, the traditional concepts.

The cellular concept has some merits in certain cases, particularly where the emphasis is on individual thinking and individual production, e.g. engineering and programming, and not on a main stream of work flow. Even so, this concept is continually being modified in the direction of group modules storing central resources, e.g. conventional files, microfilm-fiche files and readers, terminals, calculators and other equipment. There is no reason why properly designed work places should not provide the positive values of the cellular concept within a landscaped office while escaping the undesirable "egg crate" effect of so many cellular layouts.

EVALUATION OF THE
OFFICE LANDSCAPE CONCEPT

The office landscape-type layout achieves maximum flexibility. There are no fixed partitions. Relocation is easy and cheap. Without doubt, rearranging is the largest area of cost savings in an open layout as compared to the traditional layout.

In addition to savings in moving costs, there are savings in initial construction. For example, the Port of New York Authority estimated construction costs for a private office at $800 ($1,000 with engineering overhead) compared with costs for office landscaped work stations of $360, including screens, acoustical baffles, and planters. Maintenance savings were estimated at 3.9 cents per square foot for landscaped offices by the U.S. Department of Labor in Federal office buildings. Also, office landscaping cuts down on the amount of space needed.

Improved communication and work efficiency result from layouts based on communications and work flow analyses. The office landscape concept offers maximum freedom and minimum restraints to the effective translation of communication and work flow patterns into physical space. In a landscaped office, privacy is achieved in two ways: visual privacy by the placement of moveable screens in conjunction with arrangements of furniture and plants; conversation privacy by baffles, and sound absorbent ceiling, wall, window, and furniture surface coverings, and by maintaining a background of sound between 50 and 55 decibels, with no disturbing peaks of intensity. The result should be freedom from visual distraction and a guarantee that normal conversation will not be understood beyond 18 feet.

ROLE OF SYSTEMS ANALYSIS

Once planning concepts have been agreed upon, the systems person and the interior design consultant must work together to translate the plan into a practical and aesthetically pleasing design for the total office environment. The systems person is responsible for determining, on the basis of communications and work flow analysis, how departments and people within departments relate to one another, and where they should be functionally placed. The interior designer is responsible for expressing these relationships in layouts that are aesthetically pleasing in the context of a total environment of color, light, sound, texture and spatial relationships.

The two roles overlap and require a genuine partnership to

achieve the best results. This is particularly necessary in applying ergonomic principles to individual workplace design—relating working surfaces, seating, files, etc., to the human frame and its needs; and also in the design and placement of services such as food services, mail, and reproduction.

SPACE PLANNING REQUIREMENTS

Assuming that the information flow design precedes the architectual design, the following requirements must form a basis for office space planning:

1. Organization and manning charts.
2. Flowcharts of all operating information systems.
3. Analysis of common files and equipment.
4. Communication analysis.
    a. Between units
    b. Within units
    c. With visitors
    d. With specific production units
5. Job descriptions.
6. Growth plans and predictions.
7. Equipment specifications.

The information is gathered in the same way as the information gathering phase of a systems investigation. Space planning is a systems project different only in that the analyst is working with a physical system instead of an information system.

TOP-DOWN VERSUS BOTTOM-UP

Space planning can be done by asking each department to prepare a design, with the analyst then assembling the designs. This is equivalent to the bottom-up design of an information system. The drawbacks to this approach are more obvious in space planning than in information systems.

For example, one new building planned using the bottom-up system had double doors on the computer room to allow entry of the equipment but only a single door to the loading dock which would not permit the equipment to enter the building. Also, the walls of the safe were fire-resistant but the floors were not.

The top-down approach considers departmental interrelationships before developing the space layout. If the Payroll and Personnel sections are to share employee files, then these two sections should abut. Personnel and Purchasing departments should be close to the receptionist because of visitor traffic. The designer should first develop a layout of the various organization units and the work flow among them. The design of new units should be based upon these flow considerations. The individual work stations within the units should be designed so that the effectiveness of each employee is maximized.

WHO AND WHAT GOES WHERE

Only a small part of the total communication within an organization follows the formal lines of the organization chart. The majority of communications takes place among peers in the same department and between departments. Similarly, paper flows in non-hierarchical patterns. The space designer must develop data that shows true patterns of communication (telephone calls, walking traffic and mail circulation) in the organization. This data is gathered by the questionnaires, work measurement and work diary methods discussed in Chapter 12.

In addition to direct work flow analysis there are two well documented techniques that can be used to determine who should be close to whom. These are: "Activity Relationship Analysis," based upon completing a written Relationship Recording Sheet as advocated by Richard Muther and documented in "Systematic Layout Planning"; and "Communications Tally" as advocated by the Quickborner Team, and used by them in their office landscape planning. There is a place for both techniques, and in some projects it may even be desirable to use both. We are dealing with space planning and layout at two levels: the general layout of all departments over total available space, and the detailed layout of people and equipment within departments. Let us call these levels "general" and "detail" for convenience and simplicity.

Begin with an Activity Relationship Recording Sheet as shown in Figure 22.1. The sheet is filled in simply by inserting in the appropriate columns the value letter for closeness priority and the number code(s) for reason (there may be more than one). The information may be requested in one of two ways: by sending out the sheet to departments with a request for its return by a given date; or by arranging personal interviews with departments and having the sheet completed on the spot. The main advantages of the interview method are: a greater sense of department involvement with the design team is achieved; questions departments want to ask can be quickly and immediately dealt with; and the job is done right then, on the spot.

Activity—Relationship Recording Sheet

Activity No_____ Name _____ Date _____

Val	Code	#	Activity	Val	Code	#	Activity
		1	Personnel Records			21	Purchasing
		2	Employment Office			22	Custom Engineering
		3	Accounts Payable			23	Mtce. Engineering
		4	Accounts Receivable			24	Building Service
		5	General Accounting			25	Admin. Services

Value	Relationship	Code	Reason
A	Closeness absolutely necessary	1	Use common equipment
E	Closeness especially important	2	Use common records
I	Closeness important	3	Share same personnel
O	Ordinary closeness OK	4	Degree of personal contact
U	Unimportant to be close	5	Paperwork contact
X	Closeness not desirable	6	Sequence of work flow
Example: E/1,5 indicates especially important relationship because of equipment common to both activities and because of frequent personal contact.		7	Perform similar work
		8	Noise, vibration, fumes and hazards
		9	Other (explain)

FIGURE 22.1

For the general departmental layout the meetings would be with representative departmental supervisors. "Departments" should be small working groups to make analysis meaningful, even counting 2 or 3 people as a group if this is functionally warranted. For the detail layout a series of group meetings should be arranged with all personnel concerned. The more that people know what is going on and the more involved they are in the very early stages, the smoother and more successful will be implementation.

The next stage is to post the data from the Activity Relationship Recording Sheets to a Relationship Chart or matrix that will consolidate the relationships in one display as shown in Figure 22.2. In

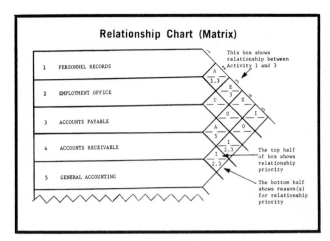

FIGURE 22.2

practice, the unimportant relationships (U) need not be posted. Also note that two relationship values are posted in each box—one from each activity whose relationship is represented in that box. Ideally, they should agree. Where they do not, the difference must be resolved—by reference back to the departments or individuals if necessary.

The procedures described are exactly the same, whether applied to the general departmental level or to the detailed individual level.

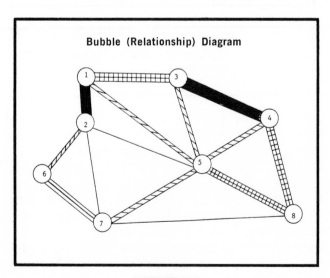

FIGURE 22.3

A department can be an "activity"; a person can be an "activity." It is just a question of scale.

From the Relationship Chart a bubble diagram is drawn as shown in Figure 22.3. This is simply a schematic arrangement of activities designed to optimize locations in relation to closeness priorities. The procedure is to take the 'A' values from the Relationship Chart and draw these first, connecting each 'A' pair with four lines; then to take the 'E' values and join each 'E' pair with three lines; then the 'I' values, connecting pairs with two lines; and finally 'O' values, connecting pairs with one line. The first attempt will be far from perfect. The object is to have as few crossing lines as possible. The sketch will need to go through several iterations before the best arrangement is determined.

COMMUNICATION TALLY

The Communication Tally is a ten-day study of all communications between departments—telephone calls, paperwork, personal visits.

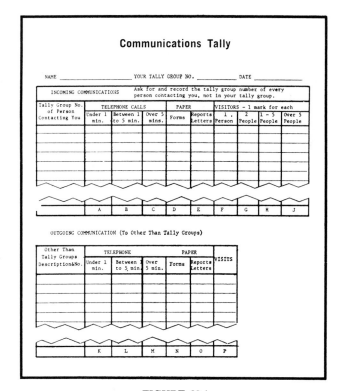

FIGURE 22.4

Each employee is asked to complete each day a Communication Tally form as illustrated in Figure 22.4. Tally groups must be established in the same way as for Activity Relationship Analysis. They will be basically those people who functionally work together in a group—whether two or 20. The groups are assigned numbers. Only incoming communication from tally groups needs to be tallied. All that is necessary is for each person in the tally to ask the tally group number of each incoming communication and put it on the form, and keep the same line for all communications from any one tally group for the day. Outgoing communication need be recorded only to other than tally groups, e.g., senior management, suppliers, customers, etc.

The Communication Tally is designed for groups, not individuals. A Communication Tally at the individual level could be devised, but for other than a small staff it becomes extremely cumbersome, and unless it is for a specific purpose such as telephone traffic analysis, it is of doubtful value. Relationships between individuals for purposes of detailed layout are best derived from Activity Relationship Analysis as already described, combined with work flow analysis.

After the ten days of the study the Communication Tally forms are tabulated and expressed in a matrix format (Figure 22.5) similar to the Activity Relationship Chart. Instead of letter values the actual number of measured communications appears in the matrix. By inspection it is easy to see where communication is high and low and thus establish a scale of priority for closeness similar to the letter value scale in the Activity Relationship Chart. From this data the same type of Activity Relationship Diagram can be drawn as is shown in Figure 22.4.

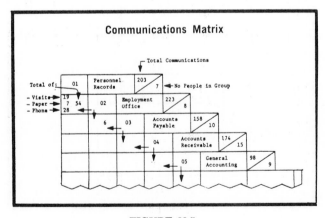

FIGURE 22.5

COMPARISON OF TECHNIQUES

There are advantages and disadvantages to both of the above methods. Activity Relationship Analysis is less demanding of both team and departmental time. For example, if there are 50 groups and 500 people, Activity Relationship Analysis will result in 50 returns which can be posted directly to the matrix; a Communication Tally will result in 5,000 tally returns which must be properly co-ordinated and controlled and then consolidated before posting to the matrix. Some time, however, is needed in activity relationship to resolve differences of rating between pairs; and a computer program can simplify the consolidation and analysis of returns in the Communication Tally. The tally represents a much larger paperwork procedure.

The Activity Relationship Recording Sheets reflect informed judgment; the Communication Tallies reflect observed fact. This would seem to favor the Communication Tally approach. However, what is happening is not necessarily what should happen, particularly in the case of communication by paperwork with the visits and telephone calls associated with it. It is easy to cite examples of forms routed through several sections unnecessarily when they could go direct from point of origin to final destination. This means that interpretation of the Communication Tally results should be weighted by independent work flow analysis. This is an essential phase of the pure office landscape approach—the Communication Tally, although a major factor, should not be the sole factor in space planning. On the other hand, the Activity Relationship Recording Sheet, though based on judgment, takes into account other than communication factors, e.g., sharing of equipment, security, etc., and thus has a broader base. The results of Activity Relationship Analysis, also, should be weighted by independent work flow analysis.

A good case can be made for using both approaches: get Activity Relationship Recording Sheets completed first, using the group interview method; follow up immediately with a Communication Tally; compare the two matrices and adjust as required. Any choice between one method and the other must depend upon circumstances. A Communication Tally is most appropriately used when a large number of existing departments are being moved to a new location. Activity Relationship Analysis is equally appropriate in a large move and can be more easily used for smaller moves, such as locating a newly formed section or moving a limited number of sections to a new location. Both methods are systems tools. The systems man must decide how to use them.

The Communication Tally is normally used only for general departmental layout, not for the detailed layout of space for individuals within a department. Activity Relationship Analysis is, therefore, the method to use, in any case, for the detailed layout. Both methods need checking and adjusting from the results of work flow analysis. Even more important, both methods need checking and adjusting by an informed layout team combining the expertise of the systems analyst and the experience of departmental representatives.

Both techniques are only useful where there is an existing organization. Developing a new office is a different problem. The data equivalent to that obtained from the Activity Relationships and

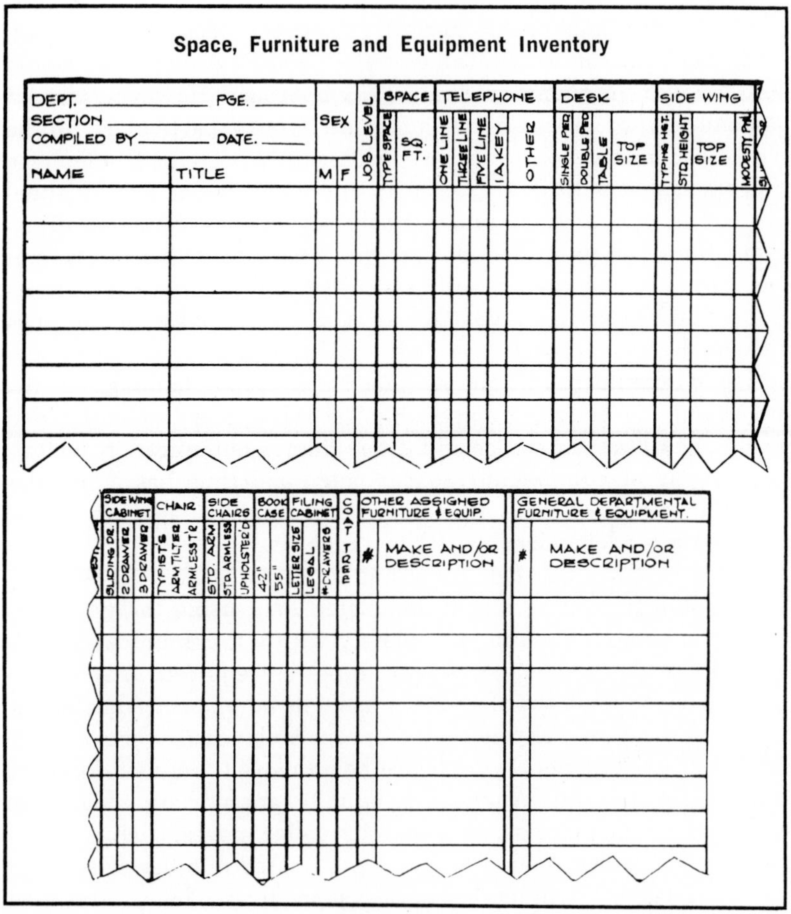
Space, Furniture and Equipment Inventory

DEPT. ______ PGE. ______
SECTION ______
COMPILED BY ______ DATE. ______
NAME | TITLE | SEX (M, F) | JOB LEVEL | SPACE (TYPE SPACE, SQ. FT.) | TELEPHONE (ONE LINE, THREE LINE, FIVE LINE, 1 A KEY, OTHER) | DESK (SINGLE PED, DOUBLE PED, TABLE, TOP SIZE) | SIDE WING (TYPING HGT., STD HEIGHT, TOP SIZE, MODESTY PNL)

SIDE WING CABINET (SLIDING DR., 2 DRAWER, 3 DRAWER) | CHAIR (TYPIST'S, ARM TILTER, ARMLESS STR) | SIDE CHAIRS (STD. ARM, STD ARMLESS, UPHOLSTER'D) | BOOK CASE (42", 55") | FILING CABINET (LETTER SIZE, LEGAL, # DRAWERS) | COAT TREE | OTHER ASSIGNED FURNITURE & EQUIP. (#, MAKE AND/OR DESCRIPTION) | GENERAL DEPARTMENTAL FURNITURE & EQUIPMENT (#, MAKE AND/OR DESCRIPTION)

FIGURE 22.6

from the Communication Tally must be synthetically developed. Systems and organization planners can develop expected communication levels from their proposals.

PREPARING THE OFFICE LAYOUT

The place to start in making the office layout is with a blueprint of the area involved. Lacking a blueprint, measure the space and make a scale drawing showing the location of all doors, windows, electric outlets, telephone ducts, pipes, heating and ventilating equipment and columns. From the communications data analysis already described, the traffic patterns to and from the areas can be determined as well as the traffic patterns within the unit.

Departments should be asked to submit lists of all personnel plus planned additions using a form such as Figure 22.6.

LAYOUT TECHNIQUES

Templates (Figure 22.7) can be made from cardboard or purchased for all furniture and equipment units in the area. A scale of $\frac{1}{4}'' = 1'$ is convenient for most purposes.

Each template should be identified by the type of unit and occupant's name if possible. By mounting the blueprint on a solid backing, thumbtacks can be used to move the templates of the furnishings into various arrangements. Also, a plastic overlay can be put over the drawing and marked upon with grease pencil.

The systems analyst usually works with the unit supervisor in developing the first draft of a floor plan. The layout is then left with the supervisor for review and any changes. Total space required per office employee ranges between 60 and 125 ft. including all aisles, conference rooms, coffee areas and other public space.

The following list represents some general considerations to take into account during a space planning project:

1. A large area is better than several small ones for lighting and for acoustics provided proper treatment is given to ventilating and communicating.
2. A two-drawer file uses as much floor space as a five drawer with only 40% of the capacity.
3. Files can be effective organizational unit dividers.
4. Files should be put back to back. Lateral files are more efficient than conventional filing units. They require less space between them when arranged in rows, are easier to access and all space is utilized, with no hard-to-reach areas at back of drawer.

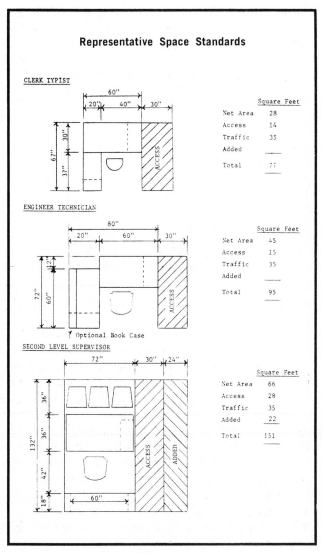

Representative Space Standards

CLERK TYPIST

	Square Feet
Net Area	28
Access	14
Traffic	35
Added	____
Total	77

ENGINEER TECHNICIAN

	Square Feet
Net Area	45
Access	15
Traffic	35
Added	____
Total	95

SECOND LEVEL SUPERVISOR

	Square Feet
Net Area	66
Access	28
Traffic	35
Added	22
Total	151

FIGURE 22.7

5. Work flows and communications are extremely important and should dominate the design.
6. Organize all work to flow to the employee—not the reverse.
7. Arrange office furniture so that separate organizational units can use the same files.
8. Locate units with people or information flows to the outside,

on the periphery of the layout. For example, Purchasing and Personnel should be near an entrance.

9. Keep the layout flexible. Avoid fixed partitions and built-in fixtures.
10. Don't let private offices cut off natural light.
11. Arrange desks so that natural light comes from the left rear.
12. Provide sufficient phone and electrical outlets.
13. Place noisy equipment in separate soundproofed areas.
14. Locate supervisors so that they can see and be seen.
15. Solicit employee participation, as creativity isn't the sole property of the systems analyst. Disruption of the informal work group is poor design.

All changes in layout, even minor ones, should be reflected in permanent space records, a detailed layout drawing being maintained for each floor. This should not only show how the space is allocated to departments and groups, but also identify furniture and equipment by type and tag number. It becomes a convenient and visual form of property record, providing both the detailed backing for the accounting department's furniture and equipment accounts, and a base for physical inventory and audit verification. Telephone placement, numbers and layout also may be shown on these drawings.

COMPUTER ASSISTED LAYOUT

Some work has been done in developing computerized layout planning, but it must still be regarded as in a developmental stage. There appears to be no substitute yet to the manual design processes already described. A useful summary of four computer aided layout planning programs was made by Muther and McPherson (1970). The programs described are CRAFT (available through the SHARE Program Library), CORELAP (available from Engineering Management Associates at Northeastern University, Boston), ALDEP (available through IBM sales offices), and RMA Comp 1 (available through Richard Muther and Associates, Kansas City, Missouri). CORELAP and RMA produce schematic layouts, RMA producing the type illustrated in Figure 22.8, but limited to one iteration based upon the placement of the first activity selected. CRAFT and AL-DEP produce floorplan layouts but cannot be relied upon to find the optimum solution. CRAFT has the disadvantage of requiring an initial solution as part of the input. It is an optimization, not a developmental program.

Significant advances have been made in the interactive version of

CORELAP, described by James M. Moore (1971). This version works on a man-machine basis by allowing interruptions and adjustments in an on-line mode. It is designed for compatibility with Muther's Systematic Layout Planning procedure. It requires as input the activity relationships from the Relationship Chart (Figure 22.2) and the space requirements. It develops internally the relationship diagram (Figure 22.3) and the space relationship diagram (Figure 22.8), and outputs a number of alternatives which may be scored,

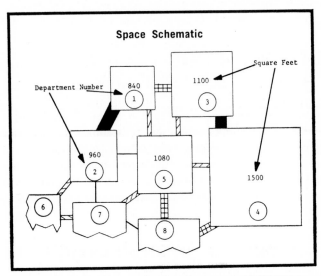

FIGURE 22.8

adjusted, and rescored. Scoring is based upon the factor common to all of these programs, the distance between all pairs of activities, weighted by closeness ratings.

No computer program now available or likely to be available in the immediate future, will unaided do as good a job as can be done manually. In all cases manual adjustment to the output is required. The most promising approach would seem to be along the lines of interactive CORELAP, where the computer is used to assist with the designer in control, interrupting, adjusting, and seeking optimization on the basis of his skill and knowledge working on the information and display generated by the computer program.

ENVIRONMENTAL CONSIDERATIONS

Color
It is well established that color influences behavior and that warm

colors (yellow, orange and red) are cheerful and stimulating. Blues and violets are subduing and even depressing. Certain tints of buff, ivory and beige are moderately stimulating. These are only general reactions to colors and everyone is affected differently by intensity of color. Color is important in office design and becomes a very personal choice for private offices. Color schemes are often selected to reflect the nature of the company and then varied by departments within the building (strong colors for Sales and Production; tints for Research and Personnel).

Lighting

The needs for an office design vary from 200 footcandles for a forms drafting area to 100 footcandles for a general office to 30 footcandles for halls and stairs. The productivity of people has been shown to be improved by 10% to 15% by properly lighting an area. The fluorescent fixture has become the predominant lighting source for offices because it costs less to operate for long periods of time.

Music

Music in the office is controversial. There is some indication that music and productivity are positively correlated for certain routine clerical tasks such as keypunching; however, some find music disruptive. Some offices have used music for ten minute periods each hour.

Temperature

Differences in physical tasks plus individual preferences account for a wide range of temperatures. The best is to strike a compromise with the thermostat set and not able to be changed by the employees.

Humidity

In an office environment, humidity is best kept in the range from 40% to 60% with good ventilation. Stagnant air absorbs the body heat of the workers and loses its oxygen. Two thousand cubic feet of air per hour per employee is the recommended ventilation standard.

Noise

Noise can reduce office productivity and cause irritability. The low hum of air conditioners or other quiet equipment has been termed "white noise" because it masks the sounds of speech coming from adjacent areas. Some of the ways to control noise are:

Place hoods over office equipment.
Use felt pads under typewriters and calculators.
Use drapes and rugs.
Install acoustic ceiling tile.
Install acoustically treated partitions.

WORK STATIONS

The desk, table, file, bookcase and chair were for a long time virtually the only building blocks of a work station. A business office at the turn of the 20th century (Figure 22.9) was resplendent with all

FIGURE 22.9

wood furniture, gas lights, spittoons, a clock for all to see and a coffee maker. Today there is a wide variety of office furniture for work stations. Figure 22.10 illustrates a modern working environment for a secretary.

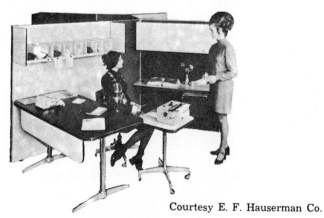

Courtesy E. F. Hauserman Co.

FIGURE 22.10

The programmer work station, (Figure 22.11) has ample work space for flowcharts, reference manuals, listings and coding forms. The storage areas will accommodate the 14⅞" x 11" forms rather than the standard 8½" x 11" forms. The bookshelves are built for reference manuals and the dividers allow privacy for concentration.

Courtesy Wright Line

FIGURE 22.11

Unfortunately, work stations are not always designed for the work to be performed. Systems analysts include these factors in good work station design:

1. Minimum hand and body movements needed.
2. Storage area for incoming and outgoing work.
3. An uncluttered work area large enough to accommodate the normal papers and tools used.
4. Storage space for paper and supplies outside the working surfaces.
5. Storage area for reference materials.
6. Rapid access to individual records needed. A visible index is important since this search is generally random.

The typical office desk does not generally meet the specifications for most work stations.

ADMINISTRATIVE SERVICE UNITS

Queuing and paper cycles (Figure 22.12) often suggest that certain functions should be combined into single units. Typical examples

The Paper Cycle

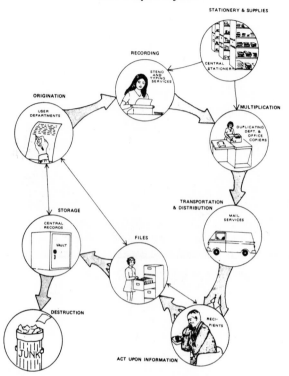

FIGURE 22.12

are the secretarial pool, office copying and filing. These work units are designed to accomplish limited tasks. They are particularly susceptible to good work space design which results in better utilization of people and equipment, and greater efficiency. Two disadvantages to establishing them are the increased communication necessary between the user and the work station and the loss of involvement of the user in these functions.

COMPUTER ROOM LAYOUT

The design of computer installations is a task of the systems analyst requiring special considerations, i.e. security, noise elimination and cleanliness.

The following analysis by Dinan (1974) should be used as the primary basis for computer room equipment layout before trade-offs (cable lengths, switches, power requirements, etc.) must be considered.

PROCEDURE

1. Establish the following:
    A. What kind of operation will be performed (Batch, Communications, etc.) on each shift?
    B. What is the probable equipment complement?
    C. What is the probable per-shift manloading and what duties will each operator have (sequentially listed)?
2. Prepare a scale layout of available floor space and scale models of the computer equipment and tape, disk, and forms supply cabinets.
3. Attach a plexiglass overlay to one end of the floor sketch so it can easily be lifted and replaced (while moving the scale models).
4. At this point make a preliminary floor layout (using the layout aids) and trace on the plexiglass overlay (with grease pencil) operator-equipment and operator-operator task links.
5. Using the layout aids, modify the basic layout to satisfy each of the following items:
    A. Isolate the operator from main frame units (CPU-Memory-IOC).
    B. Does daily use require the (console) operator to monitor the maintenance panel? If not, the operator console can be moved up to 10 feet from this point.
    C. Isolate the operator from the air conditioner. Place the CPU racks between the operator and the air conditioning unit if possible.
    D. In order to insure equal usage and visibility of tape stations, all tape stations should be an equal distance from the console, and within the operator's field of vision when seated (or standing) at the console.
    E. Batch operators require physical access to card readers, tape stations, printers, and card punches. Unfortunately, these produce much noise. Where trade-offs exist in equipment layout, consideration would be given to providing a reasonable separation between the operator's console and these noise-producing units.
    F. Disk units are used less frequently and therefore do not have to be close to the operator's console. If two operators are to use disks, they should be separated and laid out for expected use.
    G. In laying out time sharing and communications systems, prime space consideration should be given to operational use of non-computer equipment (data phones, ASR's, RO's, etc.).

H. In batch operations especially, operator fatigue can be significantly reduced by locating forms supply cabinets near the
input/output devices they support.

I. Disk and tape storage cabinets should be located near the
devices they support.

J. Input/output job tables should be located near the computer
room door (to keep non-computer room personnel out of the
area) and near the input devices (tape stations, card reader).

K. The need and use of work tables must be established to speed
the flow of work to and from the computer room and within
the computer room.

L. Where two or more operators work on the floor, care should
be taken so that the following objectives are met:

a. Equipment that is task-shared is equally accessible to all
user-operators.

b. Equipment that is not task-shared is laid out so that non-
user operators do not have to pass through the area surrounding this equipment.

c. Where communication is required between operators, the
computer room layout should enhance this requirement.
This need should be positively established, however, as
the exchange of instructions is probably the only valid
communication. There are more team activities (where
task performance is dependent upon the interaction of
two or more operators) in the zone type operation, i.e.,
operator assigned to devices rather than following a job
from beginning to end.

M. Environmental displays (Temperature-Humidity) should be
visible from the operator's primary work position.

N. The console operator's work surface must be sufficient to
support his writing tasks (usually a job log).

O. If sit and stand versions of the operator's console are available from the computer manufacturer, the need should be
determined as follows:

a. Establish the number of tasks to be performed for an
average eight-hour period.

b. Establish the duration of each of these tasks.

c. If 80% or more of the operator's time is spent away from
the console or if the duration of time spent at the console
is almost always limited to the time required to give brief
commands to the Executive, the sit-stand console configuration should be chosen.

P. Where feasible, sequential task-equipment operations shall be located adjacent to each other to reduce personnel and equipment travel time, enhance communications, and promote orderly traffic flow.

Q. The equipment complement should not expand to fit the floor space available. This results in unnecessary operator walking. Minimize equipment separation, but not to the point where crowding would result (two or more operators).

R. The user's off-floor activities that have a relation to computer room activities should be considered in laying out the computer room, i.e., job flow to and from the computer room.

S. Multiprogramming—Its Effect On Site Layout.

This type of system will require a full-time console commander who will monitor the job stream and handle problem situations (flush out jobs, 'hold' jobs with missing files, etc.).

Some multiprogramming operations have more than one console. A remote console is sometimes used exclusively to signal the input/output device operator to load a tape or disk, to remove a job, etc.

The multiprogrammed system will generally have heavy (and more frequent) input/output device activity, and consequently more computer room personnel activity.

T. Multiprocessing—Its Effect On Site Layout. The multiprocessor layout will present the same layout problems as the Multiprogramming Operating System. One additional factor that must be considered is the use of the second processor as a back-up. In this case, equipment must be laid out to be operated efficiently regardless of which processor is active. The floor layout should enhance the identification of equipment tied to a device such as RCA's 310 switch, which places peripherals on or removes them from on-line status.

U. If the equipment is tied to such a switch and is to be used by two operators, the layout should permit equal operator access (assuming equal use).

V. The use, and therefore location, of telephones should be evaluated. Except in a small one-operator system, it is desirable to have someone other than the console operator handle phone calls.

W. Work tables should be provided at points where the operator must handle large card decks, tape reels and card decks, etc., and should be as close as possible to the device to be loaded/unloaded to minimize carrying.

X. If the operator has to monitor the printer paper stacker, the

layout should permit visual access without the use of overhead mirrors.

Y. Are CCM rack displays visible to the responsible (console)
    operator?

Z. Card carts should not be pushed near main frame racks be-
    cause of possible damage to the main frame elements.

6. Review the layout against the following:

A. Can floor space between input/output devices be reduced
    (thereby reducing operator walking) without creating
    crowding problems?

B. Is the flow of operator activity sequential?

C. If the equipment is used for two types of operations over two
    shifts, does the layout reflect a stated priority? (The batch
    usage should establish the layout basis unless the user has
    some peculiar requirements.)

D. Are site-peculiar control/display enhancements necessary
    (such as a service representative call button on the console)?

E. Have off-floor activities related to computer room activities
    been considered in the layout?

F. Has the growth of the site equipment complement been esti-
    mated and reflected in site layout drawings?

G. Are there any customer safety or security requirements that
    impact equipment layout?

H. Does the customer prefer zone (operator stationed at unit)
    or job (operator follows job) assignments? Does the layout
    reflect this preference?

I. Can two (or more) operators perform without interfering
    with one another?

7. Repeat this process to achieve three floor layouts and use the
    guide as a checklist to tally the number of positive features in
    each layout (layout features can be given 3-2-1 value weights de-
    pendent upon local needs and objectives). Measure operator-
    equipment and operator-operator links and rate the three layouts
    for operator efficiency. Involving as many of the computer opera-
    tors as possible in the layout design process will prevent the
    rejection of a design.

SUMMARY

This chapter described the process and tools of office space planning.
The reader will have noted the several suggestions for employee
involvement in the planning process. The employer and employee
needs must be reconciled into the most efficient acceptable plan.

Space planning projects can be very large and complex. For example, Rice recently completed one such project that took two years. Great savings and efficiency can be achieved by doing space planning well.

REVIEW QUESTIONS

1. List four typical space planning concepts.
2. What does Activity Relationship Analysis determine? What are the main steps in this procedure?
3. What is the purpose of a Communications Tally? What types of communication does it measure?
4. What is the difference between a schematic layout and the working drawing of an office layout?
5. What information do you need to prepare the working drawing?
6. Describe an easy method to 'mark up' the working drawing.
7. List six environmental considerations.
8. What steps can be taken to improve office acoustics?
9. List factors to be taken into account in work station design.
10. What functions can be brought together in administrative service units?

DISCUSSION QUESTIONS

1. Discuss the main characteristics of the 'landscaped' office.
2. In space planning what are:
    (a) The needs of the company?
    (b) The needs of the individual?
3. Discuss the roles of:
    (a) systems analyst.
    (b) interior designer.
4. Describe three computer programs to assist in office layout.
5. Discuss special considerations necessary in computer room layout.
6. A corporation has a Head Office with a staff of 1500 decentralized about equally in five separate downtown buildings. It plans to bring all head office departments together in a new 15 floor headquarters building. At present all departments are responsible for their own typing, duplicating, filing and stationery supplies (drawn from an out-of-town purchasing and stores department). A centrally controlled mail service is provided by the Personnel Department. Make recommendations for carrying out these administrative functions in the new building, considering problems of both location and organization, and give reasons for changes you suggest.

BIBLIOGRAPHY

Armstrong, Regina Belz, *The Office Industry*, Cambridge: MIT Press, 1972.

Buffa, E. S., G. C. Armour, and T. E. Vollmann, "Allocating Facilities with CRAFT," *Harvard Business Review*, March/April 1964.

Churchman, C. West, *The Systems Approach*, New York: Delta, 1968.

Dinan, John A., "A Guide to Computer Room Layout," *Journal of Systems Management*, Vol. 25, No. 3, March 1974, pp. 28-30.

Maguire, Laurence K., "Housing the Hardware," *Journal of Systems Management*, Vol. 25, No. 1, January 1974, pp. 13-15.

Moguleseu, Maurice, *Profit through Design: Rx for Effective Office Space Planning*, New York: American Management Association, 1970.

Moore, James M., "Computer Program Evaluates Plant Layout Alternatives," *Industrial Engineering*, Vol. 3, No. 8, August 1971, pp. 19-25.

Muther, Richard, and Kenneth McPherson, "Four Approaches to Computerized Layout Planning," Industrial Engineering, Vol. 2, No. 2, February 1970, pp. 39-42.

Muther, Richard, "Systematic Layout Planning," *Management and Industrial Research Publications*, P.O. Box 7133, Kansas City, Missouri, 64113, 1961.

Office Landscapers, Second Edition 1972, Willow Grove, Pennsylvania: Administrative Management Society.

Raymond, Morton M., "The Office Work Station," *Information and Records Management*, Vol. 6, No. 7, July/August 1972, pp. 16-21.

Rice, Curtis, "Planning a New Building," *Journal of Systems Management*, Vol. 23, No. 8, August 1972, pp. 8-15, *Journal of Systems Management*, Vol. 23, No. 9, September 1972, pp. 24-30.

Terry, George R., *Office Management and Control*, Sixth Edition, Homewood, Illinois: Richard D. Irwin, Inc., 1970.

CHAPTER 23

PROGRAMMING MANAGEMENT

Development of programs and software which enable the implementation of a system design is an expensive, difficult, and important activity for any organization involved with computer-based systems. Billions of dollars are spent on programming each year. Even though large sums of money are invested in computer programming, there are few guidelines or techniques available to assist in the management of this activity. Programming management is far too often *ad hoc*—being treated as an art rather than a procedure based on clearly specified guidelines and techniques.

In this chapter, we will examine the process and concept of programming management. The most important problems to be discussed in this respect include programming scheduling and control, interfacing with managers and users, and development of standards. These aspects can be grouped into three categories: environmental, technical, and human aspects of programming management. Each will be discussed in detail.

ORGANIZING THE PROGRAMMING FUNCTION

The environment in which the programming activity occurs is a key factor in meeting deadlines, minimizing costs, achieving acceptable levels of standards, and maximizing personnel satisfaction. In order to more fully understand the environmental implications, it is important to examine the relation of programmers to systems analysts, user and management groups, and the interface with computer operations.

Programmers and Systems Analysts

Frequently the terms programmer and systems analyst are used interchangeably. However, precise job specifications are attached to each title. A key factor in a successful programming department is the identification of the above roles, responsibilities, and authority lines. When this is not the case, inefficiency, substandard software, tense personnel relations, and lowered productivity may result. If one person is obliged to fulfill both the responsibilities of a programmer and analyst, he should be so advised and aware of his job activities in either case.

User and Management Groups

The relation among members within the programming group and to the users and management groups frequently is a sensitive issue. The relation between the systems and programming group and the management and user groups in an organization should be similar. In normal line and staff activities, there is a hierarchy of authority and responsibility which persons must follow for decision-making, operating, and grievance purposes. When a problem situation arises calling for a change in operating procedures, the issue is "passed up the chain of command" for action by the appropriate authority.

When a programmer encounters a situation in the coding process which he either does not understand or for which he is not able to develop the logic, the tendency may be for him to contact the user for which the system is being developed. When this occurs, even greater problems may result if the user is not able to understand the programmer's question. Often the programmer, who is accustomed to thinking and speaking in technical terms associated with the computer system, may not be able to communicate to the user or management representative. The result may be frustration on the part of the programmer, mistrust of the programmer by the user, or a feeling of the manager that a programmer who cannot understand the manager's job cannot develop a system for him. Mistrust and resistance for the developing system could arise from a single question by the programmer.

If the above communication failure does not occur and the programmer has all his questions answered by the user, there may still be difficulties. When one program is part of a larger system, it is conceivable that neither the programmer nor the user group may know all the processes involved. An answer from the user may solve his segment of the problem but create a more significant problem to the overall system design.

When a programmer goes directly to the management group, particularly in the case of a large-scale system development effort, difficulties may arise. This potential source of problems is present also if a user communicates directly with a programmer. A line of communication between the two parties could easily result in a suboptimal design which satisfies neither the user group nor the system design specifications. To avoid such difficulties, both parties should follow the formally established communication procedures. The problem is somewhat different in instances where the programming and systems development is on a relatively small-scale, and therefore, some of the communication procedures may be relaxed. Chapter 27 focuses on management of the "small" programming project.

Questions raised by the programmer should be directed to the systems analyst responsible for the project. Since he has a broad view of the overall system development process, he should be able to provide solutions and answers based on the goals, purposes, and procedures of the system. In the event that he does not have the answer, he may contact the user's representative on the project team who also has a broader perspective of the system and design processes. The same procedure should be followed when a member of the management group has a question.

At some point in the system development process, a lock-in date should be established, after which modifications to the design or the supporting software should not be possible without review and approval by the entire project team. This procedure minimizes the tendency of both the programmer and the user to make "one small change" or add "just one more item" to the system. The review procedure ensures that meaningful changes are included but creates a definite package of specifications from which the programmer may work and encourages logical progression toward the project's goals.

Interface with Computer Operations

The relation between programmer and manager is a sensitive and difficult issue. However, an equally important and difficult relation is between the programmer and the computer operations personnel in the system testing and debugging stages. Since several projects will probably be under development in the programming department at any one time, it is necessary to have guidelines which determine use of the computer time. Rights and privileges of computer use must be defined, priorities established, and schedules prepared for on-site and remote testing.

There is no specific set of procedures which are applicable for all programming departments. Rather, one must ask a series of questions to determine the important variables which should be considered in preparing guidelines for computer use.

When a particular program or application project is nearing completion or when a project deadline is approaching, it is wise to assign it a high computer use priority. The anticipation of a successful "final test run" or the fear of not completing a project may cause programmers to work faster and more efficiently. However, if such activities are frustrated by the inability to access the computer, productivity may decrease. Since such situations could occur, it is important that programming managers have rules and procedures for computer use defined in advance and communicated to the programmers.

Consideration must be allowed for special demands on the computer. For example, when an application requires the loading of a new operating system, provision must be made for the scheduling of such a computer activity. Procedures as to when this should be permitted and who must authorize it should be determined before the situation arises. Likewise, when disk drives must be dedicated to testing a program, resulting in a dedicated system, what rules govern this occurrence? Also, who should supervise operation of the system during the testing period—the normal operator or the programmers involved in the project?

Many times before a system goes "on-line" the intended users will be interacting with it, either on site or from a remote site. There should be procedures to govern this activity. Does system testing involving management ever take priority over the normal job stream? Are definite time segments scheduled for such activities as a matter of procedure, or is it the result of a special request authorized by supervising personnel?

To suggest a standard set of rules for computer use is impossible because of the many variables at each installation. The above issues are just a few examples to show the importance for consideration in examining the interface between the programmer and the computer operator. Every programming department operates under a unique set of constraints, goals, and objectives.

HUMAN RELATIONS AND MOTIVATION

The prior section examined the significance of the environment in a successful programming department. Equally important is how to maintain the interest and productivity of a programmer in a long-term systems project. A programmer who is not self-motivated in his job cannot be expected to produce at maximum levels of effectiveness and efficiency.

Few theories about motivating persons in work situations are backed up with enough empirical evidence to prove their validity. The outstanding contributions of Maslow, Vroom, and Hertzberg will be discussed in this section.

Need Theory

The need theory, postulated by A. H. Maslow (1954), is based on the premise that man has a basic and fundamental set of needs which guide his activities. These needs are arranged in an order of hierarchy. Essentially, man is a wanting animal caught in the middle of a never ending process of need development. As soon as one need is satisfied, another need in the hierarchy triggers the emergence of a more abstract one. So, man is constantly working to satisfy his needs.

At the lowest level in the hierarchy are the physiological needs (food, rest, exercise, shelter) which are of extreme importance when not met. These are the needs which are essential to survival. When man's basic and economic needs are not fulfilled, all other needs are inoperative. When they are met, these needs cease to become significant motivators. A satisfied need is not a motivator of behavior.

When man's physiological needs are reasonably satisfied, the next level of safety needs begins to serve as a behavior motivator. Safety needs include protection against danger, threat, deprivation, or attack by external forces. Since every person employed by an organization is in at least a partially dependent relationship, safety needs are represented by the need for equal opportunity and fair treatment. Arbitrary, unethical, or unfair actions by management are threats to safety needs. Thus, it is important that an employee's authority, responsibilities, obligations, and expectations be clearly defined.

The need to be accepted, and for giving and receiving friendship, is the social need that occupies the next higher niche in Maslow's hierarchy. Although management is aware of social needs, they are often poorly planned for and even misinterpreted. The histories of organizations clearly indicate that members of cohesive work groups often perform much more effectively than if working alone. Yet, managers often discourage such team activities, thwarting social needs and causing resistance, antagonism, and lack of co-operation.

Ego needs (self-esteem, self-confidence, achievement, competence, and knowledge) do not become motivators until the previous needs are reasonably well satisfied. Reputation, status, recognition, appreciation, and respect of associates are also important ego needs with individuals continually seeking higher levels of satisfaction. Organizations can offer only limited opportunities to satisfy ego needs, particularly at the lower levels in the firm.

The highest level in Maslow's hierarchy is the need for realizing one's own potential. He believes each individual has a constant striving within to continue personal development and reach his greatest potential. This need is seldom met and rarely even considered by management.

Preference-Expectation Theory

Vroom (1964) advanced a theory that combines a person's preferences for outcomes from a set of actions with the means of, and expectation for, their outcomes. His theory proposes that persons have notions about the expected outcomes of various courses of actions.

Therefore, when a person decides to pursue a certain activity, he does so not only on the desirability of its outcome, but also because of the perceived probability that it will actually occur.

This preference/expectation theory also suggests that behavior explanation must consider not just the outcome being sought by an individual, but also the perceived significance of their efforts in bringing about the preferred result. The level of a person's performance is due to both motivation and ability. For example, if one can see a high value for a certain outcome and/or a result from a set of actions, but does not believe that any action he can offer will affect the outcome, he will not be inclined to act. The greater the perception of his actions as being a cause agent for a desired outcome, the more likely he will be to take those actions. To use this theory as a means of motivation, one must understand the individual being motivated.

Two-Factor Theory

Hertzberg's two-factor theory (1959) focuses on satisfiers and dissatisfiers in work situations. Satisfiers are factors which are associated with the work itself. When they are present, they lead to increased satisfaction, but when they are absent they do not cause dissatisfaction. The most significant of these factors are those which encourage a sense of self-fulfillment and personal growth, including:

Perceived opportunity for achievement
A feeling of performing work which is interesting
A feeling of performing work which is important
Recognition
Advancement
Responsibility

Dissatisfiers do not relate directly to the work itself, but rather are concerned with the work situation. They are factors which, when absent, lead to satisfaction on the job, but when present cause dissatisfaction. The most important factors in this category include:

Poor operating policies and procedures
Power struggles within the organization
Incompetent supervision
Touchy interpersonal relations
Poor working conditions
Inadequate pay

Human Relations and Motivation in Programming

Programmers do not typically work in isolation nor are they unaffected by their environment or their personal needs. As indicated in the preceding section, each person has a set of factors which influence the way he performs his job and which are, in turn, influenced and/or modified by the job. The programming manager should be aware of these factors and should be able to develop procedures which maximize benefits to the individual and to the department.

As Maslow pointed out, individuals have social, ego and self-fulfillment needs. How well these needs are met on the job is a significant element in determining productivity and efficiency. Weinberg (1971) examines programming in terms of its classification as a human activity and a social activity. In other words, a programming task is not something which can be performed in isolation and without contact with other persons on the project team or facing similar programming problems. This is true because of the nature of the persons involved and due to the nature of the task. Since a programmer has a need to affiliate with other persons, to be accepted by associates, and to give and receive friendship, it is unreasonable to place him in a secluded corner and expect him to do nothing but code. Such expectations are contrary to human nature.

Development of a computer program to support a systems project is one activity in a set of several interrelated activities and procedures. The features of one design or programming activity will be of importance to each of the other activities. Programmers must work together in order to complete a project task efficiently and effectively. One of the most meaningful ways to accomplish this goal, and at the same time to assist in satisfying social and self-fulfillment needs, is through the establishment of programming teams. This team concept is discussed in detail in the last section of this chapter.

Programmers are motivated both by their assigned job and by the environment in which they work. A task which appears meaningless or which is poorly organized can easily detract from employee satisfaction (Hertzberg, 1959). An employee wants to be aware of what his specific responsibilities are, and where his task fits into the overall systems project. Similarly, supervisors and programming managers should be able to communicate this information clearly to the persons in their area. If supervision is inadequate or incompetent, or if changes are made continually by supervisors due to poor policies or power struggles, job dissatisfaction may result.

This is closely related to Vroom's preference/expectation theory (1964). One cannot expect that a programmer will apply himself to a job completely and enthusiastically if the chances are high for changes in program specifications and personnel are continually reassigned from one programming project to another. If a programmer is able to begin a job with a clear specification of what the program should do, and with relative certainty that he will complete the task, his interest and effort will be sustained at high levels. In summary, the programmer must be able to perceive his efforts as being an im-

The Managerial Grid for Programming Management

9,1
I am the programmer's friend.
I want to understand him and
respond to his feelings so that
he will like me. It is the
personal bond which leads him
to work for me.

9,9
I consult with the
programmer so as
to inform myself of
all the needs in his
situation that my
help can satisfy.

5,5
I have a tried-and-true method
of getting a programmer to work
for me. It motivates him through
a blend of "personality" and job
emphasis.

We work toward a
solid piece of work
on his part which
yields him the benefits
he expects from it.

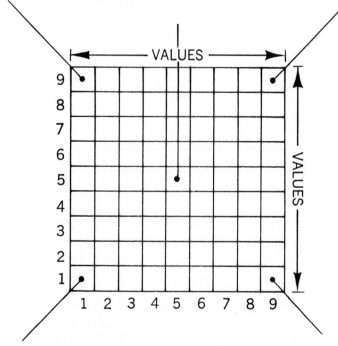

1,1
I place the job task before the
person and it sells itself.

1,9
I take charge of the
programmer and hard-sell
him, piling on all the
pressure it takes to get
him to work.

FIGURE 23.1

Adapted from Blake, Moulton and Bidwell, 1962.

portant and necessary part of a larger effort. When this is not the case, motivation will be minimal, and results inadequate.

The programming manager is faced with the dual task of supervising completion of a relatively large-scale program and assisting in fulfillment of programmer needs. These should not be construed as two individual tasks, but rather one task which has two parts. To emphasize one or the other too heavily (Figure 23.1) detracts from goal achievement. Programming management includes both an orientation to the job and a concern for persons performing the job.

The project manager has needs which should be met also. Among those to be considered are the capability to maximize personal and personnel satisfaction, to increase productivity while reducing error rates, and to reduce grievances and transfer rates among personnel. These issues will be addressed when we examine the team programming concept later in the chapter.

PROGRAMMING ESTIMATION

Estimating time requirements for programming activity is an important factor in allocation of human and financial resources during the software development stage of the system life cycle. Most delays in the preparation of software are not because the programs are for unique systems requiring exorbitant amounts of time, but rather that the program development time was inaccurately estimated and used ineffectively. Although exact time estimations are virtually impossible to develop, there are guidelines to help minimize the differences between estimated and actual programming times.

Detail and Accuracy in Estimation

Attention to detail is essential in formulation of programming estimates. Often the analyst is too concerned with *total time* required for software development. It is more valuable to formulate accurate estimates for every function and phase within the development cycle. The total time estimate will then be the sum total of the time for each detailed step in the program development.

The logic of this method is simple. It is less difficult to estimate accurate time requirements for a set of small tasks and then total them, than to estimate the time to create a major program set. Using this method, the analyst might first identify the time needed for algorithm formulation. Then the analyst should estimate times for each of the separate modules of various computer programs. The module and the interface between module development should be estimated carefully. Finally, linking and testing time estimates should be computed. The total of these steps would provide a useful *first estimate* of programming time.

It is important to point out that each of the above steps should be performed sequentially. The tendency is to have several persons doing time estimations at once. Since there are so many interdependencies between each module, it is better to examine each step in sequence, so that all assumptions and interdependencies can be taken into account. This method requires more effort to estimate, but the results are more accurate and useful to the project manager.

Re-estimation

A single estimate which is developed on the basis of the above guidelines is not sufficient. Re-estimations must be performed to improve the accuracy of the time estimation. In the above method it is important to document all assumptions on which the estimate was based; otherwise the estimate is meaningless. As development of the programs progresses, there will be fewer assumptions, improving the accuracy of the estimate. New estimations should be formulated periodically during the development cycle, incorporating greater detail into the product. The series of estimates is not complete until the final product is complete.

Program estimation is an important but difficult task. The effectiveness with which it is performed relates closely to whether or not a program will be completed on time with the allocated resources. The following section on production programming provides a framework in which the estimation process might occur.

TEAM MANAGEMENT OF
PRODUCTION PROGRAMMING

The management of the actual programming activity determines if the project will be completed on time and within cost constraints. Beyond the limits of time, one of the most serious problems which the programming manager faces is the availability of suitable and trained personnel. Currently, there is a serious shortage of competent programmers, largely because of the inability of training programs to keep pace with the rapid growth of computer and information systems installations. As a result, systems departments may not always have the necessary personnel available for assignment to new projects. A solution to this problem is to use team management of programming projects.

Chief Programming Team

Because skilled programmers are not available, programming projects are often staffed by junior personnel whose experience is limited. The top programming personnel have been moved up to management positions and are not involved in the necessary detailed programming. The junior personnel, because they lack experience, frequently produce results which are below the desired levels of effectiveness and efficiency in terms of design, coding, and testing. This is particularly a problem where a set of subsystems must be developed in conjunction with a large-scale project. When various subsystems are assigned to different junior programmers, problems may result in integrating the code sets and in their testing and documentation, resulting in an overall reduction of effectiveness (Baker, 1972).

One solution to this problem is the formulation of chief programmer teams. The teams consist of a chief programmer, who is a senior person in the area, a backup programmer, who is also a senior person, and a programming librarian, who is either a programming technician or a clerical person with some technical training. The concept of chief programmer team is analogous to a skilled surgical team in medicine, consisting of a chief surgeon supported by specialists in different areas or techniques. As the size and importance of the operation or activity grows, more persons may be added to the team.

The chief programmer team is responsible for the central part of the system, but may be supported by other programmers developing complex algorithms or large logic sections. The team must then insure that each functional capability produced outside of the team is properly integrated into the total project. Almost invariably the team prepares or constructs the data management subsystem, the driver (executive) module, and the control card language sets.

Libraries Under Team Programming

Two different types of libraries, internal and external, are desirable in the development of a large-scale program or system project. Both are necessary and strategic to the development of a successful system. Each is handled in a different way by the chief programmer team.

External Program Library

Development of an external program library makes it possible to separate production activity from support activity through the documentation stage. The programmer team works with an external library consisting of a series of data sets. Included in the library are source code sets, object modules, temporary drivers, test data, and control card sets. The actual visible library consists of sets of binders containing the most recent versions of each of the data sets. The library also contains various machine procedures, and the sets of computer steps for:

1. Updating libraries
2. Retrieving modules for compilation and storing results
3. Linkage editing of jobs and test runs
4. Backing up and restoring libraries
5. Producing library status listings (Baker, 1972).

The programmer works only with the external library.

Internal Documentation Library

To free the programmer from the time consuming task of maintaining listings, documentation, decks, and keypunching corrections, a librarian may be added to the programming team. The task of the librarian is to maintain an archive for use in the event that the external library would be damaged or destroyed. When a change is to be made to the external library, the programmer need only mark it in the binder. The librarian is then responsible for changes to be made or work to be done. In essence, the librarian is involved with the following "office procedures":

1. Accepting directions marked in the external library
2. Using machine procedures
3. Filing updated status listings in the external library
4. Filing and replacing pages in the archives

By performing the above activities, the librarian frees the programmers to make more efficient and productive use of their time.

Chief Programmer Team: An Example

Perhaps the most highly publicized example of application of the team programming concept involved development of an information bank system for *The New York Times*. The purpose of the system is to make the extensive clipping file available to the newspaper's editorial staff through terminals both on site and at remote locations. The system was designed to include 64 local terminals and up to 120 remote lines with either display or typewriter terminals. Accessible are abstracts of all articles which are stored on-line as well as texts of full articles stored on microfiche. Information can be accessed by input of such descriptors as date or date range of publication, publication in which the articles appeared, or type of article. An extensive and comprehensive searching and storage system was developed to support these desires (Baker, 1972).

Development of the information bank was performed as a test activity using the chief programmer team concept. A selected team designed and developed the system, which involved more than 83,000 lines of code (written in a higher level language) assembled in a 22 month period. Eleven man-years of time were involved, an amount which is substantially lower than what would have been required under traditional programming procedures. The time factor was decreased significantly, but so was the error rate in the production effort:

> For example, the file processing system (delivered one week after unit coding was completed) passed a week of acceptance tests without error, and ran 20 months until the first error was detected. In the first 13 months of operation of the on-line retrieval system, only one program error was detected that resulted in system failure. The chief and backup programmers produced code that had one detected error per man-year of effort (Baker and Mills, 1973).

Team programming efforts appear to be a particularly meaningful and effective way of increasing programming productivity while reducing substantially error incidence. It is expected that this approach will be generally accepted in large-scale project efforts. It is an important factor to consider when selecting programming methods for system development.

Top-Down Versus Bottom-Up Programming

The most common approach to programming is the bottom-up method. Under this approach, separate, relatively small-scale modules of code are written and tested separately. That is, large sub-programs or overlays can be coded to perform a task or specific function. In order to test the module, a driver must be written and a test data deck formulated for input by the driver. The driver executes control transfers and generally "runs" the module being tested. For a large systems project, the process must be repeated many times necessitating the development of many test drivers for one-time use. When each lower level module is completed, tested, and debugged, it is linked to a higher level module, and the process is repeated. Although the process is effective in many cases for pro-

Structured Programming Progressions

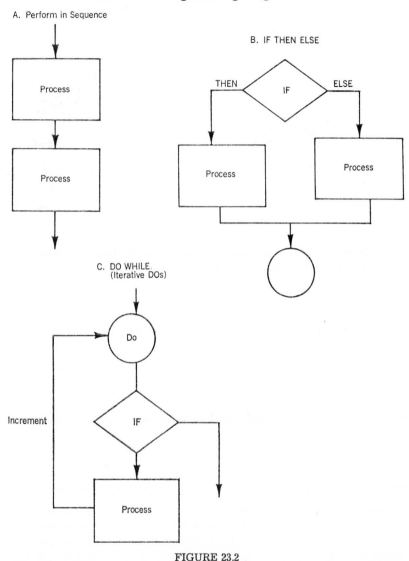

A. Perform in Sequence

B. IF THEN ELSE

C. DO WHILE.
(Iterative DOs)

FIGURE 23.2

gram development, it is not efficient due to the extra coding activities.

The top-down approach reverses the process just described. Rather than focusing on the lowest level modules first, one following the top-down method for programming begins by establishing the necessary control language set, i.e., the highest instruction level.

Subsequently, the main driver, executive, or calling routine is written with dummy calls and files of test data. In essence, the functional code is added section by section, moving from the highest level to the lowest level, incrementally. This method is effective in testing the program and at the same time is efficient since temporary drivers and one-time test data files need not be written. The concept also fits well with chief programmer team activities.

Structured Programming

The idea of structured programming centers around a set of rules employed in the coding process which makes a program easier to both read and maintain (Bohm and Jacopini, 1966 and Baker, 1972). Under the rules of structured programming, a program with one entry and one exit can be written using only three progressions:

1. Sequence
2. IF THEN ELSE
3. DO WHILE

This method (Figure 23.2) eliminates the many GO TO statements typically found in a source listing so that one examining a listing can readily follow the logic or modify the instruction sequence. It also makes top-down programming easier since one can write control statements first and subsequently insert functional code. Compilation and debugging can also begin at an earlier stage in the program development process through dummy statements and sub-program calls.

READING PROGRAMS

In a typical programming department, there is a diversity of skills among the various persons. No two persons have the same level of competency and effectiveness. Yet, it is expected that all individuals should be able to work as a team in developing system software and application programs. Programming teams of the type discussed in the last section provide a means of integrating the diversity of skills into a functional working body. But, the problem remains of finding a viable means of maintaining acceptable quality levels and at the same time increasing the skills level as team members. One of the ways which this may be done is through reading programs.

The Concept of Program Reading

Program reading as an activity was proposed by Weinberg (1971). The reading was proposed as a training aid and as an error reduction tool. It was intended to be done by peers rather than supervisors.

As a training aid it is appropriate for the programmer to read substantial numbers of programs of many applications. The intent is to have programmers gather techniques and style from peers. Since programming is a form of writing it is appropriate to learn in the same ways that writers learn. This certainly includes reading the writings of others as well as having one's own programs read.

Reading programs is also an appropriate error reduction technique. (It serves the same function as the reading of a manuscript. The page you are now reading was read by six different people before printing. Few programs get such scrutiny although perhaps many should.) The person who never makes errors is rare. Few people can find their own errors as well as they can find errors of another.

Also knowledge that one's program is to be read by others influences writing style. The program structure tends to be less involved. The comments are much more frequent. These are both good programming practices. Thus, reading results in better quality programs in the initial writing.

With the rapid growth of computer technology and the advent of terminals, programmers often do not see their complete code set on a regular basis. Often they only receive regular statements containing errors or statement changes. Similarly, the rapid throughput and fast turnaround capabilities of computer equipment have caused many programmers to become so enamored with correcting an error and resubmitting the program for "one more run" that they don't take time to examine the complete set of code.

Program Reading and Programmer Teams

Through the programmer team concept, program reading is an easily implemented activity that contributes to efficient software development. Individuals can readily examine the written code produced by other members of the team to assure fulfillment of design requirements. The true purpose of reading programs is not to increase efficiency and foster learning, although these are important peripheral benefits, but to produce the programs needed for system development.

Another concept of program reading in the context of programmer teams is to determine whether or not the code compensates for machine and implementation limitations, and if such modifications are clearly shown. Allocation of storage and its relation to imposed limitations should also become evident through reading programs. Each of these issues is important in determining how functional the application software will be and how well it meets design specifications.

Not all programmers have comparable skill levels and not all will have full mastery of the computer language being used. Consequently, algorithms and processing techniques used in the coding process may be less efficient than those which an individual with a greater capability in a given language would have used. Reading programs can reveal these situations, leading to improved software and again closer adherence to design specifications.

Reading programs is a valuable technique in assuring quality software on which to base an information system application. When it is used in conjunction with the chief programmer team concept and structured programming, it has even further value. With the new computer techniques and modern technology, we find less of this type of activity taking place today when it would have more value than ever.

SUMMARY

Management of the programming phase of system development is an important but difficult task. Even though large sums of money are involved in software development activities, there are few guidelines to assist in control of the process. A number of important factors should be considered, however, including a clear specification of duties and responsibilities for the various kinds of personnel involved in software development. Likewise, the relation between programming and project personnel should be specified clearly, including acceptable communication and reporting procedures. This is particularly necessary for large-scale projects.

Human relations and motivation are significant factors also in the conduct of project development activities. Individuals have a variety of needs and wants over and above a suitable salary. Each of these needs should be met in one way or another to assist in the assurance of effectiveness and efficiency on the part of personnel involved in the project. A number of theories are relevant here, including need theory, preference-expectation theory, the two-factor theory, and the managerial grid.

Programming estimation is important in the allocation of human and financial resources during the software development stage of the system life cycle. Therefore, attention to detail is essential in formulation of programming time estimates. Consideration of time estimates should not focus on the total time required, but rather on the sum total of time required for each step in the process.

Further, re-estimation should occur at various points in the process to ensure that realistic appraisals serve as working guidelines.

The way in which the actual programming activity is managed significantly impacts completion of the project on time and within cost constraints. Several important concepts are of significance in this respect, including chief programmer teams, structured programming, and program reading. Important also is an understanding of the top-down and the bottom-up approaches to system development, either of which could be combined with the above considerations.

Programming management is a difficult task, and one where few clear guidelines have been developed. Yet, it is an important factor in successful completion of project assignments. The concepts and considerations addressed in this chapter deal with some of the more difficult and unwieldy problems.

REVIEW QUESTIONS

1. What is the basic assumption of the following human relations and motivation theories: need theory, preference-expectation theory, the two-factor theory?
2. Of what significance is the consideration of human relations and motivation in programming activities?
3. How would you characterize a 1,1 manager; a 5,5 manager, a 9,9 manager?
4. What is programming estimation? Why is re-estimation necessary?
5. Discuss the meaning of Chief Programming Team. What assumptions underlie the use of team programming?
6. What is contained in an internal documentation library?
7. Compare and contrast top-down, bottom-up, and structured programming.
8. Is there a relation between program reading and team programming? If so, what?

DISCUSSION QUESTIONS

1. Programming management is often handled on an "ad hoc" basis with few guidelines or techniques available to assist in supervision of the activity. What controls, procedures, and standards are appropriate for consideration in overseeing a large-scale software development project?
2. The Department of Defense has requested that you serve as project leader for design and development of a planning information system to support budget preparation and monitoring for each fiscal year. Discuss the procedures you would follow to ensure successful completion of the task. What security precautions would you take? What steps would you deem necessary to ensure that the programs developed would meet the needs of the Department of Defense? Consider this problem in both a team programming and in a non-team programming situation.
3. In a recent software development project for a large multinational firm, a senior programmer and the head of the Accounting Department worked closely to develop a sophisticated and intricate cost management program for their firm. Normal communication procedures through the project team leader were not followed. As a result, although the program developed was a "good" one, it did not conform to original design specifications. What would you do as the team leader?

4. The amount of turnover among programming personnel in industrial organizations is often claimed to be relatively high. What steps would you take to ensure that such turnover is held to a minimum?

5. In *The New York Times* example, both performance standards and programming productivity were at very high levels. In other words, the job was done quickly and with a very low number of errors. These results were attributable to use of a chief programmer team. Do you feel that consistent results of this nature could be obtained in all instances where teams are used for production programming? Why or why not? Discuss the implications of the team approach for small-scale projects.

BIBLIOGRAPHY

Baker, F. T., "Chief Programmer Team Management Of Production Programming," *IBM Systems Journal*, Volume 11, Number 1, 1972, pages 56-73.

Baker, F. T., and H. D. Mills, "Chief Programmer Teams," *Datamation*, Volume 19, Number 12, December 1973, pages 58-61.

Blake, R. R., J. S. Mouton, and A. C. Bidwell, "The Managerial Grid: A Comparison of Eight Theories of Management," *Advanced Management Journal*, 1962.

Dahl, O. J., E. W. Dijkstra, and C. A. R. Hoare, *Structured Programming*, New York: Academic Press, 1972.

Hartman, W., H. Matthes, and A. Proeme, *Management Information Systems Handbook*, New York: McGraw Hill Book Co., 1968.

Hertzberg, F., B. Mausner, and B. Snyderman, *The Motivation To Work*, New York: John Wiley and Sons, 1959.

Maslow, A. H., *Motivation and Personality*, New York: Harper and Row, 1954.

Vroom, V. H., *Work and Motivation*, New York: John Wiley and Sons, 1964.

Weinberg, G., *The Psychology of Computer Programming*, New York: Van Nostrand Reinhold Company, 1971.

Weinwurm, G. F. (editor), *On the Management of Computer Programming*, New York: Auerbach Publishers, Inc., 1970.

CHAPTER 24

SYSTEM AND APPLICATION TESTING

Before an information system or information system application is brought into use and made an integral part of an organization's operating management system, steps must be taken to ensure accuracy and correctness of the supporting software and procedures. In many respects, the testing procedures are actually subsets of the larger *programming phase* of systems development. However, due to the importance of the testing activity and because it takes place as a separate phase of the development process, it is discussed here as a specific entity.

This chapter examines in detail the broad range of issues that fall under the heading of testing. The meaning and importance of this activity will be reviewed candidly in terms of its technical, economic, and behavioral implications for information systems development with procedures recommended for the pre-test and testing phases. The problems of generating good test data will be discussed. Finally, procedures will be explained which are necessary to convert an application from a test machine to the target system on which the application will be run permanently.

The implied meaning of program testing is to locate coding errors, logic problems in the source code, conditions that cannot be defined by the system and inoperative file designs. Testing of an information system is much broader than this.

INFORMATION SYSTEM TESTING

To ensure the development of a successful information system, each application series must be examined carefully to remove all difficulties which might infringe on its successful and meaningful use. Consequently, by program testing, one must examine not just the software system around which the application is constructed, but also the information system in general and the procedures which support and link together the various activities contained within the overall information processing system schema.

Generally, there are two types of errors which can occur during formulation of the information system software. *Syntax errors* refer to program statements which violate one or more rules of the programming language's instruction set. Improperly defined field lengths, omitted key words, undefined variables, and no-path statements are typical examples of syntax errors. As a general rule, these errors are detected first and are most readily evident due to diagnostics generated by the compiler, assembler, or other translator being used.

The second type of programming error, a *logic error,* is somewhat more subtle and difficult to detect. Logic errors occur when syntactically correct program statements result in incorrect output after execution. Logic errors may be the result of such problems as omissions, improper transfers of control, and faulty data fields. A diagnostic or error message is not provided, and thus examination of the system output is necessary to detect the occurrence of the error.

System Testing

Neither program testing nor module testing (discussed in Chapter 23) are sufficient means of validating a new information system application. A program free of syntax and logic errors does not ensure a correct application. Rather, more serious errors can develop due to problems inherent in the use of the overall information system.

An information system application usually consists of several different programs, a series of distinct program runs, and use of an integrated set of files or data bases. Therefore, it is essential that these individual entities be examined in terms of their effect on the system as a whole. Interesting problems which we will examine focus on file sizes, data base accessing and potential run-time conflicts.

Procedure Testing

A correct and effectively operating information system is not possible without proper running procedures. The way in which computer operators carry out their duties and responsibilities directly determines whether a system will be functional. Consequently, during the testing stage it is imperative that the run procedures be carefully followed by the computer personnel.

Similarly, the information system application must be able to accommodate the demands which will be made upon it by its many users. This phase of the testing process is particularly difficult because it is virtually impossible to predict the various inputs which users will develop. Procedures must be developed and tested to account for virtually all situations created by the system's users.

THE IMPORTANCE OF TESTING

Testing an application can be a tedious and tiring task, but it is an extremely necessary and vital one. The many interdependencies between programs, hardware, operating systems, and the diversity of users and personnel require that testing be performed thoroughly to minimize technical, economic, and behavioral difficulties. All types of potential software and system problems must be taken into consideration during the "debugging" process.

The amount of time devoted to this phase of system development may be disproportionate to the size of the overall system. However, if the application involves important financial material or personnel transactions, it is essential that the program run correctly. Examinations of articles and stories in many of the trade journals and magazines will reveal an astoundingly high number of cases where large amounts of money were lost or improperly recorded due to an error in a system program. Organizations have had to spend large amounts of resources to correct errors that cost money through incorrect systems. In many instances these financial losses could have been avoided or reduced significantly with more thorough and carefully planned testing procedures.

The behavioral issue (examined in Chapter 3) is directly affected by testing procedures. It is important to know how users will react to the introduction of an information system into their daily activities and how users will attempt to interface with the new system.

When data is entered into an on-line system through a terminal, there may be a brief delay in its acceptance by the system. Even though users are told repeatedly of the reason and need for the delay, there is a tendency to *re-enter* the data under the apparent assumption that some error has occurred during the original entry, and the data was not accepted. Re-entry of data may cause problems in the use of the system and its data/information reliability. The user's re-entry tendency should be detected during a testing procedure and steps taken to prohibit it when the system reaches operating status.

The ultimate responsibility for the testing activities lies with the analyst or system specialist in charge of the development process. He must ensure that the system will operate in accordance with the design specifications. His responsibility is a large and important one, which should not be minimized or overlooked.

Pre-Test Procedures

Before any testing of application programs begins, specific procedures should be developed to minimize the difficulty of the task and maximize the effectiveness and efficiency of the process. Some of the pre-test procedures may appear obvious and perhaps even trivial. However, failure to use these procedures can result in unreliable installations.

Prior to initiation of any testing procedures, it is important to have a complete and detailed *program description* on hand. Included in the written program description should be a statement of the purpose of the program, its users, the equipment required to run it, the routines of which it is made, the programmer(s), and an estimation of the time to run it. Additionally, input and output files should be described to indicate how input and output images will appear. A detailed flowchart of each program routine, as well as a brief systems flowchart of the entire program, should be available before testing begins. Particularly difficult or intricate logic sections should be detailed in narrative form or decision tables to avoid any possible misunderstanding of symbols or confusion on the part of those conducting the testing. Having this information available should not be any particular problem, as it is the type of description that should be prepared continuously as the software is being written.

Desk checking of source code should have been performed prior to initiation of testing. Careful perusal of the code and listings can reveal problems which might occur when long execution runs begin. This particular type of checking is relatively low cost, since computer time and resources are not needed, but the payoff can be substantial if errors or omissions are detected and corrected.

It is very important to formalize *test schemes and run order schedules* prior to beginning the test phase. A test scheme specifies the way to go about checking the program software. For example, a top-down approach may be followed where the control card language is first tested, followed by the sequential addition of drivers (main calling programs) and sub-programs or lower level modules. A bottom-up approach in contrast would imply that individual sub-programs and modules are tested first, followed by addition of higher level calling programs, and finally the "real" control card language to be used during the live operation. (These approaches are presented in an expanded form in Chapter 23).

The run order schedule, which is closely related to the test scheme, details the kinds of transactions to be tested and the order in which they will be tested. Different transactions, of course make various demands on the programs and therefore can cause unique problems for the tester. The run order schedule is necessary to ensure that the transaction types which are of highest priority and value to the organization are tested, debugged, and ready for implementation first.

Certain *test aids*, such as flowcharting routines, trace programs, before and after looks, file and memory dumps, and loader and core maps are available at most test centers. It is worthwhile to specify beforehand what aids are available for use, under what conditions they should be used, and how they are to be employed. A few minutes spent in listing this information can minimize time loss later.

APPLICATION TESTING

Once pre-test procedures have been prepared and a definite test plan developed, the first stage of application testing can begin. We will examine the three phases of application testing—program testing, system testing, and procedure testing—in terms of what activities should take place during each phase, and which persons should have primary responsibility for each.

Program Testing Guidelines

Program testing is the first and most basic phase in the overall process of application testing. Assuming that any well-written program is going to be "segmented" into a set of integrated but logically distinct modules (Figure 24.1), it may be most efficient to test individual modules in a program separately, followed by subsequent "linking" together of all modules in order to test the complete program as a whole. By focusing attention first on the separate and distinct modules, coding or logic difficulties can be isolated more rapidly and problems that may arise due to connections between modules can be avoided.

Program testing involves the search for and correction of both syntax and logic errors. We will not discuss syntax errors as they are easily detected by diagnostics provided by compilers, interpret-

Levels of Testing

MODULE TESTING	Testing of individual components and/or subsystems of an application. Temporary drivers and files are created to simulate the main program in the application, enabling testing of logic and syntax.
PROGRAM TESTING	Search for and correction of syntax and logic errors in the assembled modules. Interfaces and calling sequences for linking the program modules together are examined.
SYSTEM TESTING	Testing the programs which make up the system application, including file compatability, existence of data sets, and fulfillment of physical requirements.
PROCEDURE TESTING	Testing of operating training, formal run procedures, run sequences, and emergency procedures.

FIGURE 24.1

ers, and assemblers, and are rapidly corrected by comparing the coded instructions to the instruction set of the language.

Logic errors are a much greater problem during program testing. They are often difficult to detect and may require relatively complex corrections. These types of errors comprise the greatest time and resource expenditure during this phase of the testing process. To aid the programmer and analyst, a number of tools and techniques have been developed by equipment vendors, software houses, and service centers for dealing with logic errors.

When performing any test of logic, it is imperative to know the desired or predicted results for a particular run *before* the test is actually made. It is not sufficient to run a set of data past a program and then check to see if the results are correct. Since the output from the program typically *appears* to be correct, it is easy to overlook hidden logic errors. The testing must state explicitly the *expected* output and then compare it with the *actual* output.

Trace programs offer one very helpful means of following data flow in a coded instruction format. The result of these programs, which are mostly supplied by the computer manufacturer, is realized when an application program fails to produce the desired results even after all mechanical errors have been eliminated, but logic errors cannot be detected. This testing and debugging aid enables one to trace the sequence of executed instructions to determine where control is transferred at various points in the program and what the specific data values are at a given moment. The trace program prints out data values and information on control operations at the end of each computer run. Careful use should be made of these programs because they are expensive to run due to their numerous internal tests and extensive output.

Core or memory dumps are also useful in this particular phase of system development. Their particular value is realized in situations where one needs to know the contents of the various internal registers and large blocks of internal memory. Printing out this information, which constitutes a core dump, provides one with exact information on internally stored data values. While these lengthy printouts may prove highly valuable in program testing, they are also expensive, and so should be used judiciously.

Loader and core maps are of particular usefulness in determining how specific data sets and storage blocks appear in memory. In large application programs it is not unusual for storage to be allocated in a fashion which is different from that anticipated by the programmer. Unless the core is mapped, data may be written over or erased by another programmer and cause erroneous output.

Loader and core maps give the locations of data and comparisons made between actual and expected locations of the data.

Each of the above techniques produces somewhat lengthy output. (The size of the output does not determine its usefulness.) Many cases arise where it is necessary only to examine changes in a few variables or data values. In these situations, it is probably inappropriate to generate the long strings of output associated with trace routines or memory dumps. Use of *beforelooks* and *afterlooks* is an effective alternative. Beforelooks are samples of the value contained in a particular storage location before a certain processing action takes place. Similarly, afterlooks are outputs of values of interest after certain actions have taken place. By comparing the two values, one is able to see exactly what changes have occurred and minimize the output burden on the system.

A variety of other very simple tests can be used to aid in detection of logic errors during program testing. Among these are such simple checks for negative numbers, division by zero, invalid combinations, incorrect formats, out of range items, and sequence and edit checks. While each of these tests are low cost and very easily performed, they may assist in locating many hard to find logic difficulties.

Detection of logic errors is one of the most difficult parts of software development. The more complex the program, the higher the level of difficulty in error detection. Consequently, in very complex programs where there are seemingly infinite paths through the instruction sequences, it may not be possible to completely debug all execution options. In these cases, rather than correcting all errors, it may be possible only to provide instructions which will repair their effect and enable the program to continue execution. While this is less than the ideal, it may be the only alternative open to a programmer if he is to make the system useful.

The conduct of program testing commonly is performed by the programmer who developed the code, since no one knows the program better than that person. It can be a disadvantage to have one test his own production. There is a tendency to pass only trivial test data past the program to check for deficiencies and never truly test the program. One sensible alternative is to establish a testing group which does virtually all program testing for software developed in a programming department. By specializing in this activity, persons are able to more thoroughly and accurately evaluate software for introduction into the information system.

System Testing Guidelines

When test procedures have rendered individual applications functional and sufficiently error-free, attention shifts to testing the software systems as a whole. While it is important to insure that each individual application is correct, testing cannot cease at this point. The interdependency between the separate and distinct programs making up an application has the effect of creating difficulties not anticipated during the programming stage of system development. Most important are problems which might occur with run linkage, data storage and timing factors. Each must be tested by the system analyst in charge of the project.

If a system application consists of a series of separate programs, which is the most common situation in information system applications, chances are high that several programmers will have been involved in their development; a single programmer probably will not have performed all of the coding work. In these cases, communication between programs and programmers may have left differences in the software such that certain incompatibilities exist. Compatibility of files, data sets, and overall physical requirements may not be at a functional level. Therefore, it is essential that one aspect of system testing examine the linkage between separate program runs so that the set of runs does link smoothly. These tests should uncover and make possible correction of any problems which would prevent the output from one run from being acceptable input for a following run.

An equally important test in this phase of the system development focuses on storage areas allocated to files, tables, indices, and data arrays. During program testing, full size data sets may not be passed past the programs. Consequently, situations may have gone undetected where adequate storage space may not have been provided for "live" runs. One must insure that the allocated space on storage devices or in main memory is sufficient to handle the size of transaction sets to be used when the system goes into operation. Additionally, provisions for handling of overflow of files and storage areas should be tested during this stage. A separate set of test data will probably be needed here merely to extend the application to a representative size run.

One test often omitted during system testing is that of examining stored data existing after an application run has been completed. In stored files, what one thinks is on the tape or disk after processing may not be the same as what actually exists. For example, a programmer may have thought he had stored all data in coded form, when the software and control card language used actually resulted in creation of binary files and data sets. Many persons assume that this test is made implicitly when the newly created and stored output becomes input for a subsequent run. This is not a sufficient test, and it is almost always necessary to dump the file to the printer and manually check what has been written on a storage medium.

The system testing activities are the most efficient ways to verify anticipated program run times. The calculated or *estimated* execution times may not be the same as *actual* amount of time that will be expended during a "full-blown" run. Causes for the variations may be related to how data is physically stored on magnetic medium, the size of input buffers, or variances in access times in general. To avoid later difficulties in run scheduling and timing, execution time must be tested during system testing. Results found for this factor carry over into the third type of application test—procedure testing.

Procedure Testing Guidelines

When application programs have successfully passed all the tests conducted during the above stages, one can be reasonably certain that the most evident software problems have been found and corrected. However, this does not exclude failure later in the system. Difficulties which are procedural in nature can crash the most elegant and sophisticated software that an organization's programming staff can develop.

It is necessary to verify that the physical equipment necessary to run the system application is actually available for use. Important considerations here are the number of tape and disk drives available, the standard memory partition available, and sufficient printer time to complete the output. All too often, programmers and analysts will conduct system tests at times when the job stream is below the normal level, i.e., non-peak time. Under these conditions, it is very possible that below normal equipment usage demands are being made on the system. That is, disk packs and certain tapes containing system oriented software (compilers, assemblers, interpreters, operating systems, file management packages, etc.) may not be mounted. The tester may be able to make use of the idle equipment that will not be available in the normal job stream/job load. Testing run procedures during normal load conditions should pinpoint these problems.

A related issue is that of determining run procedures when a particular piece of equipment is temporarily down or unavailable for use. For example, if one disk drive in the configuration has failed and is down, is it still possible for the application being tested to run? If so, there probably will be no difficulty. If not, one must decide what alternative actions are appropriate in the live situation. It must be determined if the application is of such importance that postponing the run for a short time will not cause severe problems for the user. In the case of on-line, real-time systems where a relatively rapid response is necessary, any down-time could cause severe operational difficulties. The procedure testing phase of application testing is the time when these difficulties should be anticipated.

Conflicts and important interdependencies often exist between several programs in an application set. As mentioned above, the output of a given computer run frequently serves as input for a subsequent program. However, when a large application is being developed by several programmers, a *double dependency* may exist such that both programs depend on output from each other, and neither one can produce the other's output. Such a situation can occur only through very poor programming practices and extremely poor communications between programmer and analyst. These situations should be detected and corrected during system testing; however, when dummy files are being used in the testing process, these problems can slip in. They must then be detected and corrected during procedure testing, which is usually the last step before conversion to the live operation.

Frequently, operation problems can surface which involve the computer center personnel directly. Run manuals, procedure policies and plans are designed to explain in detail all actions to be taken by operators in running a given program. This documentation identifies the files to be loaded, disks to be mounted, operating systems to be resident, and forms to be loaded on the printer. Sometimes the operators do not understand the written guidelines. The procedures must be clear for each step to be performed by the operator. The steps to be taken during emergency situations or times of equipment failure should also be clear. The operator must know what *not to do* in an emergency situation. Procedure testing instructions should provide these answers. A series of "dry runs" which create the above circumstances will provide answers for the analyst.

Procedure testing offers the analyst in charge of the project the last opportunity to debug the system prior to initiation of the steps to convert the system from a "prototype" operation into a live operation. Should omissions occur here, a good deal of correction cost and user disappointment is certain to be produced. Therefore, the procedure testing activities must be planned carefully and executed expertly.

NATURE OF THE TEST DATA

The procedures to be followed in system testing are, of course, important to the success of the entire process. However, the data chosen for the process is equally, if not more, important to the system's success. The most carefully designed testing process can be rendered worthless by poorly chosen test data.

Meaning of Test Data

The ideal situation is to have a basic set of data which can be used for testing all programs in a system. Such an arrangement is seldom possible. Consequently, most have separate test data for each specific program.

Test data comes from many sources. It may consist of artificial data created solely for test purposes, or selected live data. Either would be of value in testing a system; however, if the extreme situations are to be tested, it is not sufficient to count on live data to contain the extreme values. Also, live data may not contain all combinations of formats or values which will test all logic/control paths in the program. Live data is often biased toward typical values which are of the least danger to the system and receive the most programmer attention. It is the extreme values which were not tested for during the data passing process that cause the system to fail or crash. These are best checked by generating special test data (Figure 24.2).

Sources of Test Data

ARTIFICIAL DATA   —created solely for test purposes
                           —higher probability of containing all combinations of formats and values if properly created
                           —makes possible testing of all logic/control paths
                           —may be developed by a data generating program

LIVE DATA   —extracted from actual organizational files
                           —low probability of containing all combinations of formats and values
                           —biased toward typical values
                           —may ignore the most dangerous extreme values
                           —difficult to obtain in sufficient amounts

FIGURE 24.2

Creation of Test Data

When an application designed to deal with large files is ready for testing, the problem of having *sufficient* amounts of data available arises. Not only must test data be available which will make it possible to examine all conditions covered in the program, but a large amount of test data must be accessible. Acquiring sufficient amounts of live test data is difficult. One alternative is to manually develop artificial test data. In this situation, the tester is obliged to develop items which will meet program requirements and yet make it possible to examine processing results under all situations which could occur within the program design. Often a computer program can perform the task of test data generation. Such a program must of necessity be written in a very general fashion, so that it has broad application for all programs in the system.

A typical data generating program has to specify parameters pertaining to such factors as formats, size maximums and minimums, and file organizations (random, sequential, etc.). The data generating program subsequently creates fields within a record one at a time, on the basis of generated pseudo random numbers. Each random number is checked to see if it falls within the parameter constraints and accordingly is moved into the record field or is discarded in favor of a new number. This process is repeated until records are created in sufficient quantity to fill a file of the size specified as an input parameter. The data generating program should also be able to generate data for the key fields in such a way that high to low, or low to high sequential files can also be created.

Wide-use data generating programs can save large amounts of time for the programmer and the testing process, and if properly designed, can ensure more thorough testing than would be the case with live data. Careful selection of parameters for input to the data generating program can ensure testing for all conditions. Finally, when both analyst and programmer are responsible for conducting separate tests, the data generating program can result in multiple time and cost savings.

Testing the System in Operation

To this point, we have discussed a variety of methods and techniques for information system testing. Each has been concerned with test activity which *precedes* actual implementation of the newly developed information system application. Such tests, when taken together, are referred to as system *testing in the abstract*. All of the steps are essential to ensure that an effective system has been developed and that it will perform as designed. However, the testing does not stop at that point. An additional step is necessary, called *testing in operation*. The following case study points out the need for and importance of testing the system in operation.

The Ripley Paper Company: A Case Study

Ripley Paper had one old, small mill located in Ripley, North Dakota. The mill produced a wide variety of fine papers ranging from 25 to 100 percent rag content and from onionskin to ledger stock in weight with several different kinds of finishes and packaging. Sales per year had averaged about $10,000,000 for several years. Sales were stock items to independent paper distributors who warehoused the product and sold it to the consumer and other items which were manufactured to order by the mill.

The major raw materials used by the mill were pulp and textiles. The major pieces of manufacturing equipment were the paper machines which produced rolls of paper of the required rag content and weight. The width of the paper off the machine was fixed. The widths wanted by the consumer were obtained by slitting the rolls. Thus, the production planning problem involved solution of the classic trim-fill linear (or integer) programming problem. The mill had some sales of rolls of paper from this production stage. Next, the rolls were cut into sheets and the sheets trimmed. The sheets were stocked on skids for another group of customers. The remaining paper was ream wrapped or packaged. This paper was stored in the warehouse awaiting orders for shipment.

The order department received an average of 100 orders per day. About 80 of these were from distributors and 20 from direct customers.

When the Ripley Paper Company was purchased by the Clark Kent Corporation, the field salesmen were merged with the field sales units of the parent corporation, but kept the same product and customer responsibilities. The Ripley sales manager was made a product manager and transferred to the home office of the Clark Kent Corporation.

The Clark Kent Corporation had two other fine paper mills at Munsing, Michigan and at West Overshoe, Ohio. The three mills were put under common management. This new management found that there was some overlap in products for the three mills. The separate order entry system resulted in shorter production runs and other inefficiencies which suggested that a consolidated order entry system was appropriate. A system project to develop a coordinated order entry system for the three mills was implemented.

Analysis of the systems problems resulted in a recommendation for a centralized computerized order entry system located at West Overshoe. Communication facilities to Ripley and Munsing were part of the proposal. The proposed system was accepted and implemented.

One of the time consuming tasks during the implementation was programming the Ripley Paper pricing structure. In addition to the type of paper, weight, packaging and order size variables, there were many special manufacturing processes which the mill would undertake at a price. The analysts spent considerable effort understanding the pricing manual and converting the pricing instructions to a program. They conferred frequently with the product manager to check their understanding of the pricing structure. In the testing stage they constructed a test desk which checked each of the possible customer order specifications. The results of the test were checked by the product manager and found to be correct.

Much to the surprise and dismay of the analysts, the first day of operation found half of the Ripley Paper orders incorrectly priced, even though they had been calculated according to the manual. However, the product manager had never told the analysts, his sales management or corporate management that Ripley Paper had special deals with certain customers. Doubting that the discounts could be justified by cost differences or competition, he feared that the discounts might be in violation of the Robinson-Patman Act, and had kept this secret until the first day of computer operation. Needless to say, the implementation team was forced to scramble. They had provided a bypass (or manual entry of price) for certain very unusual price combinations. This bypass was used temporarily for half the orders. A later systems patch provided for a specific customer discount branch in the pricing program.

Questions

1. Would you fault the analysts for not checking whether current orders were being priced according to the pricing manual?
2. Why didn't the product manager reveal the discounting practice?
3. To what extent should analysts go to crosscheck system data?

THE CONVERSION PLAN

Testing the system begins as soon as the implementation or conversion process is initiated, i.e., at the point where operational use of the system starts. Obviously, this is one of the most critical activities in the entire system development life cycle, and it should be planned carefully. The conversion plan should detail explicitly the series of activities which will take place as the system is phased into operation.

Organizing the systems and the user personnel for the conversion testing and the implementation phase is important to insure a smooth cutover to a live operation. Training programs must be conducted so that all affected users are familiar with the procedures to be followed in the use of and interaction with the information system. The training sessions should include not only those persons who will interact directly with the system through a terminal or other communication device, but also individuals who will use the generated outputs and reports. It is not sufficient for users to know what information is on a report. Each one must understand how the information is derived or calculated. Such knowledge is essential if a user is to have confidence in system output and not offer resistance to it (see Chapter 3). Moreover, training programs offer feedback to systems personnel in terms of providing information on whether the information provided is prepared correctly. The training program, therefore, is a significant part of the testing that takes place at the time of conversion. (A more detailed discussion of the overall conversion process is presented in Chapter 25).

During the conversion process, it is advantageous to form a short term "fire-fighting" team of system personnel. The primary purpose of such a group is to handle the problems which develop as the live system begins to replace the old system. Members of this special team may have responsibilities varying from guiding the users through the first several iterations of the system to repairing errors in the software or problems in the hardware. Each member of the team should have a special skill and be totally familiar with his duties and responsibilities during conversion testing.

Cutover to the New System

As the users are trained and become familiar with operation and use of the application software, greater dependency on it builds and the complete cutover begins. The permanent data files must be constructed and tested for accuracy and reliability. Backup files must be constructed to prevent data or information loss during initial operations. Minor modifications to output and report layout may be necessary also to meet the desires (and whims) of the users, all of which will require large quantities of time.

Operators and users may still be unsure of procedures to be followed or may take unanticipated actions which could jeopardize reliability of outputs or assurance of continued system operation. Although these eventualities should have been provided for during system and procedures testing, certain cases may have been undetected. Consequently, they must be taken care of during the cutover and the conversion testing.

It is extremely important that systems personnel detect problem areas and bugs in the application during this final testing phase. The user should not be the one to discover debugging errors. As we mentioned in Chapter 3, one of the most significant problems in system development is that of gaining user acceptance of a new system. The way in which the development proceeds and the amount of user involvement in the analysis and design process are important factors in gaining user acceptance. However, it is equally important to deliver a product that functions according to design and that is not full of errors. This is the reason behind both the extensive testing procedures outlined earlier and the availability of the fire-fighting team during the conversion process. Problem areas must be caught and corrected quickly, before user acceptance is degraded.

When the cutover process is completed and the new system is installed, there is a tendency on the part of analysts and project teams to feel that their work has been completed and that the system is finished. However, improvements need to be made continually as more efficient operation methods may be discovered and new user demands formulated. There will be constant maintenance and modification for the system application to meet the growing needs of management. We will examine both the conversion and the maintenance and system modification issues in detail in subsequent chapters.

SUMMARY

System and application testing is an integral part of the system development process. In its broadest sense, the term includes not just examination of the software system, but the overall system in general. This involves the procedures and considerations which link together the various activities contained within the overall system. Complete system testing includes not just the modules and programs, but also such factors as file compatability, existence of data sets, formal run procedures, and emergency procedures.

A number of tools exist which can assist in this evaluation process, including file dumps, loader and core maps, and trace programs. However, considerable attention should be given also to the data which is passed through the programs. Incomplete test data which does not foster checking of all conditions can lead to system failure after live operations begin. In many instances, a more thorough test of the programs and the system can be achieved through the use of artificial data rather than with live data drawn from the organization's files.

Testing does not cease when all of the identifiable "bugs" are removed from the software. Rather, close scrutiny of activities as the system is cutover into operation is required. The complete testing process anticipates questions and deals with difficulties before they develop into major problems.

REVIEW QUESTIONS

1. How is program testing accomplished? Why is repeated testing necessary? What pre-test procedures are necessary?
2. Distinguish between system and program testing; between module and program testing.
3. With whom does ultimate responsibility for system testing lie? Why?
4. What aids are available for assistance in system testing?
5. What factors are important to keep in mind when creating test data? How might such data be developed?
6. What considerations are important in cutover to the new system?

DISCUSSION QUESTIONS

1. Should programmers test their own programs or should all programs be tested by an independent group? Why?
2. There are advantages and disadvantages to desk checking versus "bulling through" on the machine. Discuss.
3. Develop a system testing procedure to be used in a team programming operation. Include specifications of duties at various levels and a time table for a large scale system test such as *The New York Times* case in Chapter 23.
4. Discuss the membership and responsibilities for a "fire-fighting" team of systems personnel.
5. Compare and contrast the problems and requirements for testing and installing an on-line system with remote terminals versus a resident batch system.

BIBLIOGRAPHY

Bohm, C., and G. Jacopini, "Flow Diagrams, Turning Machines and Languages with Only Two-Formation Rules," *Communications of the ACM,* Vol. 9, No. 5, May 1966.

Clifton, H. D., *Systems Analysis For Business Data Processing*, Princeton, N.J.: Auerbach Publishers, 1969.

Hartman, W., H. Matthes, and A. Proeme, *Management Information Systems Handbook*, New York: McGraw-Hill Book Company, 1968.

Joslin, F., *Analysis, Design and Selection of Computer Systems*, Arlington, VA: College Readings, Inc., 1971.

Keelan, C., "Controlling Computer Programming," *Journal of Systems Management*, Volume 20, Number 1, January 1969.

Langefors, B., *Theoretical Analysis of Information Systems*, Lund, Sweden: Studentlitteratur, 1968.

Maclean, J., "Caution: Crash Computer Conversion," *Journal of Systems Management*, Volume 18, Number 1, January, 1967.

McKinsey and Company, Inc., Unlocking the Computer's Profit Potential, *The McKinsey Quarterly*, Fall 1968.

Orlicky, J., *The Successful Computer System*, New York: McGraw-Hill Book Company, 1969.

CHAPTER 25

INFORMATION SYSTEMS
CONVERSION AND EVALUATION

This chapter is concerned with the change from one information system to another. Conversion is often from a manual system to a computer-based one. When changing from one computer to another, systems programs and hardware are affected as well as many existing computer-based systems. Program conversion is the only aspect of the change from one computer to another to be discussed in this chapter. Chapter 24 covered program and system testing.

The objectives of a conversion effort are to switch to the new system accurately, with minimum risk, with the least cost and with minimum personnel irritation. These objectives frequently conflict with each other.

Where risk is great, it is important to install the new system *parallel* to the old so that both systems are running together until the new system is operating correctly. Where cost is to be held to a minimum it may be acceptable to convert without running parallel systems. Where accuracy is important, a verification or audit function should be done for each conversion task. Where user satisfaction is primary, the user should participate in the planning, conversion, and training for the new system.

The usual conversion plan compromises. Some such compromises are:

Some conversion tasks are completely verified but others are not.

Training would be better with the latest in audio-visual equipment, but the cost of the equipment is too high.

Not enough manpower is available to run everything in parallel, so some operations are tested as they are developed.

CONVERSION PLANNING

As soon as the systems design is firm, work begins on the elements of a conversion plan.

Master Files Creation

If new master files must be created from non-machine language sources, the data must be keypunched or otherwise converted into machine language form. As soon as the conversion begins, a change procedure must be activated to keep the new master file up-to-date. If revised master files are required but contain no new fields, only a conversion program is required. If the revised master files contain new fields from manual record sources, then input must be created with the key field and the new field and this conversion file maintained until the program to create the new file from the conversion file and the old file is implemented. An alternative to use with existing files is to modify existing programs to accept new file arrangements and to install the updating and change procedures before the major conversion date. In this way, the conversion effort is done in modules.

Auditing the creation of the master files is most often done by manually comparing a listing of new records with the input documents. One of the best methods for checking the accuracy of a new master file is to create the file through the change procedure. Then, each old record is processed as if it were a new addition to the master file and the change program is throroughly proven.

Special Conversion Programs

Conversion programs are often a large part of the total programming task because of the needs for reformatting files. Other conversion program needs include listing and totaling programs, programs to recode the history files, programs to recreate the history files, and other special one-time programs. For example, in a sales or inventory forecasting system it is necessary that considerable history be processed to establish the initial forecast values. This often requires a special conversion program.

Project leaders try to organize projects so that large modules of the programs for the new system can be used in the conversion, thus reducing the total programming task. They also try to use utility programs wherever possible. Since conversion programs are generally run only once, it makes sense to minimize programming time for these programs.

Manpower Plan

If parallel operations are needed, the manpower plan must include staff for both the old system and the new. The details of what will become of the extra personnel once the new system is operative should be worked out with the Industrial Relations and user departments prior to the hiring of extra people. Systems designers find their most realistic estimates of the manpower needs are sometimes cut drastically. Manpower solutions for these heavy load periods are to use temporary help or to pay regular employees overtime. The disadvantages are that temporary help is not familiar with the system and employees working overtime make more errors. The result is that it is common for the project group to work long hours during a conversion, often doing the clerical conversion tasks themselves.

Many information systems projects result in a net reduction of personnel as shown in Figure 25.1. Knowledge that fewer jobs will be available after the conversion can lead to employee turnover before the conversion takes place. To prevent an exodus of valuable personnel some firms have paid bonuses to those who stay to the end of conversion or borrowed employees from other departments to meet the high temporary manpower needs.

Manpower Needs

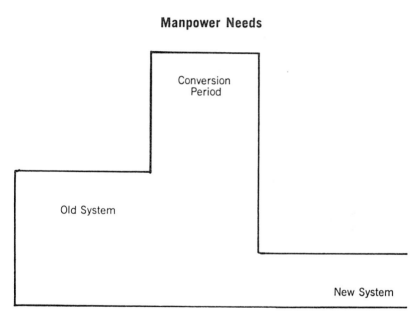

FIGURE 25.1

Any conversion staffing plan requires careful planning and a strong spirit of goodwill within the group. The rapport built up between the system designer and the user during the information gathering helps to make the conversion smoother. If a prior commitment to reduce staff is not made, the staff rarely gets reduced. Work is found to fill up the time available. Besides, it is easier to operate with a surplus of staff than to run a lean operation.

Staffing Case History

A company made a systems change which involved starting an order processing department in each of its manufacturing plants. All order processing had previously been done at the sales offices. The change was complicated by other systems being redesigned. The office management in one sales office was very authoritarian. This sales office was to convert to the new order processing system and after six months the department was to move to a new plant in New England. The conversion went well, but the staff was decimated by resignations. They knew their jobs were to end in six months and were given no incentive to stay through the complete conversion process. Two clerks were sent out from the general office to hold things together temporarily. Meanwhile, a quick search found a storefront available at the new location. New people were hired in the new location, brought to the old sales office for a fast training course, and then sent back to the storefront sales office until the new plant began operations. A good recovery occurred, but the whole exercise could have been avoided if adequate staff planning had been followed.

Trial Run

This is the final test of the new system. The conversion plan should organize tasks so that the actual files can be used. Chapter 24 covers the many aspects of testing procedures.

Timing of Conversion

Most systems have a natural point where the installation of a new system is easiest. Payroll systems are easiest to convert at the beginning of the year because no year-to-date information needs to be converted from the old system to the new system. Similarly, accounting systems are converted easiest at the end of the fiscal year. Order entry systems are usually easiest to convert at the low point in the seasonal activity. The end of the year is typically a busy time for systems analysts.

The conversion should ideally take place at the point at which conversion costs are lowest, regardless of the inconvenience to the personnel involved in the change.

Equipment and Forms

Most system changes require new forms and new or modified equipment. The purchasing department usually handles the scheduling and expediting of the purchase orders for these forms and equipment. However, some changes in the systems require quick equipment modifications such as changing time clocks during a shift or installing a new on-line computer overnight. These changes demand critical planning.

Physical Facilities

The physical facility aspects of changes required by a systems project are described in detail in Chapter 22 except for timing. It is best to be extremely conservative in allowing for time to make physical facility changes in the conversion plan. The best plans are often delayed by unanticipated snags.

PUBLIC RELATIONS

The conversion process must embrace all of the publics concerned with the system. If the system impacts the union in any respect, the union officers must be informed and the earlier the better to assist in acceptance of the system.

Customers are affected by order entry, invoicing and accounts receivable systems. It is good practice to put together a description of the planned system that the sales personnel can pre-test with customers for any negative reactions they may have.

Vendors are touched by purchasing and receiving systems. They will need the new system explained to them by the buyer. Again, the systems designer should be receptive to any inputs that will make the proposed system function more smoothly.

New systems may involve changes in banking arrangements. The corporate treasurer's office will usually want to handle these explanations personally.

The introduction of a new system should not be a surprise to anyone. Since not being informed (accidental or not) is the same as being ignored, the omission can have serious repercussions for the success of the project.

USER TRAINING

The training of the user is perhaps the most important step in conversion activity. Written procedures for the system design and for reference during the operation are rarely appropriate as training materials. Students of programming are most aware of this. The reference manual is usually a poor text, and the best of texts is usually a poor reference manual. User training materials must be designed.

It is not enough to provide materials and expect the system operators to read them and learn the system, nor is a lecture sufficient. Real learning takes place in an exchange of information between the teacher and student. For example, if one wishes to train users to operate a new copier, it is best to take the user to the machine. With a variety of documents the user can then explore the machine settings and handling required to get good copies.

Similarly, by actually using a CRT terminal, most of the mystery disappears. Terminal systems often reserve at least one terminal for training purposes or may have a training mode available on each terminal.

PROGRAM CONVERSION

In the second generation of computers, a large portion of the programs were written in assembly language. To use these programs on third generation equipment required hardware or software emulators. The former were expensive and the latter were inefficient and restrictive. The solution was to rewrite the program. Upon being told that a program to convert from IBM 1410 Autocoder to IBM 360 BAL was impossible, two young men from Boise set out to prove IBM wrong, and wrote a program (EXODUS) that converted 95-98% of the lines of codes. One organization using the EXODUS conversion program found that a programmer could convert one program per day. The fewer programming tricks used, the easier the conversion. The resulting programs were more efficient than emulation but somewhat less efficient than programs written directly for the new equipment.

Many firms spent millions of dollars converting programs. In hopes of reducing this expenditure the next time around, ANSI COBOL was usually chosen as the programming language in third generation computer shops. With COBOL the conversion task was reduced and the resulting programs had an acceptable efficiency level.

Paul Strassman (1974) of Xerox stated that his firm had $50,000,-000 invested in application programs of which 85% were in COBOL. Consider the large cost of rewriting those programs.

Dr. Grace Hopper, USNR, has in recent years, headed a group which developed a program to test whether COBOL programs meet the specifications set by the CODASYL committee. The goal was to use this program as a test for compilers being considered for acceptance by the Department of Defense. Large variations were found, including outright errors. This effort, if successful, will simplify future conversions from one computing system to another.

One nagging conversion problem is the lack of industry standards in many areas. For example, the collating sequence has been different for IBM and Honeywell machines. This lack of standards unnecessarily complicates the conversion task.

CONVERSION SUMMARY

Conversion is a complex management task involving good planning, communication and task performance. All these detailed tasks must be performed and carefully scheduled with the other conversion tasks. The details of the tasks must be communicated to all involved when they are planned and as the project schedule progresses. Finally, each task must be performed on schedule so that the entire project can be installed on time and within the budget.

INFORMATION SYSTEMS PROJECT EVALUATION

There are often two evaluations in the post-conversion review of an information systems project. One is a final report by the project group and the other is an audit of the project by an internal or external audit group. The first will be done in most organizations, while the latter is done in few organizations. Both are described in this chapter and an actual audit report for a completed project is included at the end of the chapter. The final project report is usually written one to two months after the conversion. The audit usually occurs from three to twelve months after conversion.

FINAL PROJECT REPORT

The major points of the system proposal are a listing of the benefits and costs of the proposed system. The final report should begin by restating those objectives. The second section should summarize the outcome for each of the objectives, unplanned benefits and unplanned costs. The third section should provide a detailed explanation of each of the elements in the summary. Expressed in these terms, the whole process seems simple but the following are some pitfalls to avoid.

Who Is the Report for?

Any systems project is done for the user by the project work group, with the user bearing ultimate responsibility for the project because he knows what the project should achieve and must live with the result. With these objectives in mind, the final project report should be written by the project leader assisted by his group and signed by the project leader and the user manager. The signature of the user attests to the accomplishment of the project objectives. There are many occasions when the accomplishments of the system are discretionary to the user manager. He may decide to operate with the planned staff, more people or fewer people; the planned reports or extra ones; the planned record sizes or larger ones. For example, a systems project ordered by corporate headquarters for its 25 locations had only two of the 25 locations achieve the anticipated gains because of a lack of user commitment to the objectives.

Qualitative Benefits

The most debatable items in the report are likely to be the intangible benefits. Some organizations make substantial attempts to quantify everything by assigning dollar values (see Chapter 15). All project benefits should be listed.

The manner in which partial reductions of personnel are evaluated is also debatable. A few hypothetical cases will show the problems and proposed solutions.

Partial Reductions of People and Equipment

A systems project that was expected to save one hour per day for each of 40 widget operators actually reduced the staff to 36 widget operators. Therefore, the project should be credited with saving four jobs against an expected five.

$$\frac{40 \text{ people} \times 1 \text{ hour/day}}{8 \text{ hours/day}} = 5 \text{ people}$$

A systems project was designed to save four hours per day of the time of an overworked clerk. At the end of the project the clerk was still working eight hours per day but was no longer working overtime. The project would take credit for the overtime reduction.

A new system was expected to save three hours for Sally and five hours for Dick. At the end of the project Sally was promoted to a new job in another department while Dick took over the remainder of her duties. The system would take credit for the maximum rate for Sally's job.

In a systems project for Department A the expected result was a reduction of four hours per day in a job in Department B. At the end of the project the supervisor of Department B claimed no reduction. If the systems project leader and the supervisor of Department A are still convinced that the benefit was real, it would be listed as a benefit with no gain, although the tasks were reduced.

A systems project had the objective of reducing four hours per day on one job. It eliminated the job by transferring the remaining tasks to another department which was able to handle the increased workload with no increase in staff. The system would take credit for ½ person.

While the above cases all involved people, the same principles apply for equipment. For most projects that use minor portions of the computing resource, the normal charge-out rate should be used. Major changes require the same type of analysis as described above.

Cost Techniques

As indicated in Chapter 15, the final report should use the maximum rate for each job and a standard percentage for fringe benefits rather than the actual salary paid to avoid the security classification for the report.

Reductions in inventory are a frequent savings in systems projects. Most large organizations have a standard percentage to apply to the reduced inventory to represent the savings.

Changes in cash available or of investment should be priced out at the long-term cost of capital, not at the current borrowing rate or the current return of short-term investments. This way all projects are evaluated on the same basis.

The value of better information provided through the new system is shown by comparing decisions made without the information with those made with the better information. This may be difficult to evaluate, but if a certain operation has been 95% efficient and the new system results in 96% efficiency, the value is obvious.

In evaluating benefits, the project group should be allowed to brag a little about the results of their work. However, the report should be accurate and defensible. Overstated claims may turn off the users and the post-conversion auditors.

AUDIT REPORT

Auditors are paid to be suspicious. They believe that managers may so desire certain capital and systems projects that they will exaggerate the benefits to be achieved from a systems project. An audit verifies that the actual benefits were achieved. The technique of the auditor's review is the same as that used for the final project report.

The auditor's written review, however, has a different format. It states the objective, the project reported result and the calculated result. Differences between the reported and calculated results are then itemized with appropriate comments.

The auditors gather information for their report from several different sources within the organization. They read all of the reports of the project team. They independently gather the data from the Personnel and Payroll Departments, Budget or Cost Accounting Department and computer operations to establish the before and after conditions. They interview the users involved with the new system to determine the benefits claimed. They also attempt to find errors not previously reported in the results of the project. Any negative cost impacts will have been uncovered by the cost or budget people but often not the people problems. Certainly it is appropriate to report that the people don't like their new jobs or that this terminal doesn't perform as expected or computer operations hasn't provided the expected turnaround. The auditor then verifies that the negative (or positive) consequence exists and writes it up in his report.

The initial draft of the auditor's report is usually shown to the user manager and to the project leader for correction. If the auditor is convinced that the report is wrong then the report is changed. If the auditor will not change his report, it is standard for the user to prepare a rebuttal which is attached to the report. If the systems project group is convinced of errors uncovered by the auditor, they should indicate how they plan to correct the errors. The auditors do not usually review the entire system design at this point. A detailed review is usually only made of the troublesome parts of the system. As indicated earlier, auditors are an important part of those projects involving the internal control of the organization.

Internal Audit Report Example

INTRODUCTION

In examining Law Enforcement Assistance Administration (LEAA), Department of Justice, grants for criminal justice information systems, the General Accounting Office (GAO) reviewed the prototype System for Electronic Analysis and Retrieval of Criminal Histories (Project SEARCH). Project SEARCH was largely an experiment in the interstate exchange of criminal histories of offenders; it was funded under title I, part C, of the Omnibus Crime Control and Safe Streets Act of 1968, as amended (42 U.S.C. 3701).

Development of the System

As of June 30, 1972, LEAA had awarded about $4 million to Project SEARCH for developing a prototype criminal history exchange system and to enable 20 states to participate when the system became operational. Substantial additional funds will be required by federal, state and local governments before the system can become fully operational in all 50 states.

Project SEARCH began in July 1969 as a 14-month project to (1) establish and demonstrate the feasibility of a computerized system for the interstate exchange of criminal histories and (2) design and demonstrate a computerized statistics system. At the time the fieldwork was completed, 15 states were participating in the criminal history exchange project.

The criminal history exchange system, as envisioned by Project SEARCH, was to enable criminal justice agencies—law enforcement agencies, courts, and correctional institutions—to obtain, in seconds, information about offenders. The criminal justice agency would obtain information by making an inquiry on a "user terminal." The inquiry would be transmitted through the state computer to a central computer index. The central index, to be maintained by a designated agency and containing a brief index of all persons in the system, would then electronically tell the inquiring agency whether a criminal record existed for the individual in question and, if so, from what state detailed information could be obtained. Without such a system, it would take days or weeks to obtain this data, if it could be obtained at all.

The system was to have been demonstrated during July and August 1970; however, to gain more experience and to give states which had recently joined the project a chance to participate, the demonstration period was continued until June 30, 1971.

The system adopted by the SEARCH project group and tested during the demonstration period used detailed criminal history records maintained and controlled by the individual participating states and certain identification and summary data maintained in a central index accessible by all states. When an inquiry was received, the central index (temporarily maintained by Michigan) responded with (1) personal descriptors and identifying numbers, (2) an abbreviated criminal profile, and (3) the name of the state holding the full criminal record. The inquiring agency then had direct access through its state computer and the central index to the desired file in the state holding the record. The information in this file was then electronically transmitted to the inquiring agency through the central index and the inquiring agency's state computer.

Operation of the System

The National Crime Information Center (NCIC) of the Federal Bureau of Investigation (FBI) has maintained, since 1967, computerized national files of wanted persons and certain stolen articles. The NCIC network consists of 102 law enforcement control terminals, which make information in the files available to all 50 states within seconds.

In 1967 NCIC recognized that a computerized criminal history file would be a logical part of a nationwide criminal justice information system. NCIC's stated goal was to provide a national index of criminal justice information and communication lines linking NCIC and the national index with a central state computer in each state. However, NCIC initially emphasized developing and implementing a system that would provide information only on wanted persons and certain stolen articles. After the SEARCH project group demonstrated the feasibility of a criminal history exchange system, the Attorney General in December 1970 authorized the FBI to manage the exchange system. In November 1971 the FBI began operating, through NCIC, a limited version of this system.

Since the FBI assumed management responsibility, LEAA has continued to assist states to participate in the system. Under NCIC, the system has also been changed, at least temporarily, from a system of state maintained and controlled files linked by a central index to a system in which the NCIC central index maintains all information provided by the states. According to an NCIC official, this change was necessary because the present NCIC communication lines could not handle the requirements of transmitting detailed criminal histories from one state to another.

NCIC, under its criminal history exchange system, maintains a central index containing more detailed information than would have been contained in the central index under the system adopted by the SEARCH project group. Except as noted below, NCIC will maintain all criminal history information and answer all inquiries directly.

NCIC maintains detailed history records of all federal, multi-state, and single-state offenders whose records have been placed in the system. According to FBI officials, when the system is fully developed, NCIC will maintain detailed history records of multi-state and federal offenders but only a summary record of single-state offenders.

The summary records will contain personal identification and descriptive data for an arrested individual; the number of times arrested and the number of charges and convictions for each type of offense; and the last arrest, court, and custody status. The detailed criminal history records will include (1) personal identification and descriptive data, (2) complete information on each arrest, the charges for each arrest, and the disposition of each charge, (3) complete information on each count entered in court, the disposition of each count, and any appeal, and (4) information on the custody status of an individual and any change in that status, such as parole.

Under NCIC's system, all record entries, clearances, and modifications, other than for federal offenders, are to be made through the states; hence the states will control all input to the system, other than for federal offenders. Each entry must be supported by a criminal fingerprint card processed by the state making the entry. Processing involves an analysis of the card to come up with a 20-character fingerprint profile of the offender. Therefore a state will not be able to enter criminal records into the system until it has an identification unit capable of processing such cards.

Scope of Review

Our review was made at Project SEARCH headquarters in California and at FBI and LEAA headquarters in Washington, D.C. We reviewed documentation developed by the Project SEARCH group, LEAA and the FBI on developing the criminal history exchange system. We also interviewed officials of LEAA, the FBI, Project SEARCH, and several states.

After work to develop the system began, additional tasks were assigned to the Project SEARCH group. These included determining the feasibility of transmitting fingerprint images and other information by communications satellite, enhancing the development of automatic fingerprint comparison, analyzing the requirements of state identification bureaus, initiating the development of a standardized crime-reporting system, and developing a prototype system for the interstate exchange of organized crime intelligence information. Our review concentrated on the project's major task—developing a computerized criminal history exchange system.

NEED FOR COST INFORMATION
AND IMPROVED INPUT TO SYSTEM

The cost to develop and operate the criminal history exchange system has not been determined and problems related to the system's operational effectiveness have not been resolved. No one has determined what a fully operational system will cost. Therefore the participants cannot determine whether they will be able, or willing, to meet the financial requirements of developing and operating the system. Although the reporting of arrest and disposition data within the states is known to be incomplete, neither LEAA nor the FBI has insured that all information entered into the system is complete. About half the states do not have laws requiring that arrests and dispositions be reported to central state identification units.

Without an accurate forecast of all system costs and a plan for insuring the completeness of reporting, the federal government is entering into an open-end commitment; it has no assurance that the participants will be able to meet the financial requirements of the system or that the system will provide complete and accurate criminal history information.

Need for Estimate of Total Cost

As of June 30, 1972, LEAA had awarded to Project SEARCH grants totaling about $4 million for developing a prototype criminal history exchange system and to enable 20 states to participate when the system became operational. For fiscal year 1972, the FBI budgeted $1.3 million and LEAA budgeted $3 million for expanding the system during 1972.

Despite the substantial federal funds already committed to this system and a greater funding commitment expected in the future, LEAA and NCIC officials told us that neither agency had estimated the total cost of a fully operational system. According to statements by LEAA and state officials, a fully operational system could cost at least $100 million.

To participate, each state will need the necessary hardware, software, personnel, and intrastate communication lines, as well as the ability to convert arrest and disposition data to the standardized NCIC format and to identify fingerprints and maintain fingerprint cards for offenders whose records will be included. The states, assisted by LEAA, will pay these costs. Law enforcement agencies, courts, and correctional institutions within each state will also incur costs to obtain and maintain user terminals for querying the system. About 6,500 user terminals are on the NCIC network and have access to NCIC data. NCIC estimates that about 45,000 user terminals will be added to the system when it is fully operational. Although LEAA and NCIC have already spent several million dollars on developing and operating the system, only four states had entered records in the system as of September 1972.

An NCIC official told us that most of NCIC's future costs will be incurred in upgrading communication lines that link NCIC with the states in the system. Accordingly, NCIC has started a study to determine these costs.

LEAA expects to provide funds to enable the states to participate in the system through block and discretionary grants. LEAA block grants, awarded under title I, part C, of the Omnibus Crime Control and Safe Streets Act of 1968, as amended, are allocated among the states according to their respective populations. The individual states decide how much of their block grants to use for a given purpose, such as the criminal history exchange system. Under the act LEAA also awards discretionary grants in response to specific state applications.

In May 1972 LEAA allocated about $12 million of fiscal year 1972 discretionary grant funds to initiate a comprehensive data systems program intended to finance the development of criminal justice statistics programs in the states. To receive funding under the comprehensive data systems program, a state must submit a plan for implementing a five-part program. One of these parts is the establishment of a criminal information system that will track offenders passing through the criminal justice system and also provide criminal history exchange capability. Each state will decide whether to participate in the comprehensive data systems program.

According to an LEAA official, because the FBI manages the criminal history exchange system, it, in conjunction with the states, should make any analysis of the total cost of developing and operating the system.

In a paper delivered at a national symposium on criminal justice information systems, the Commissioner of Florida's Department of Law Enforcement said that he was:

". . . not sure that we are in a position to justify the cost involved to implement a criminal history exchange system on an operational basis."

"We must determine the value of criminal history information in relation to the cost."

He acknowledged the limitations in performing a meaningful in-depth, cost-benefit analysis but recommended that LEAA develop a "white paper" to serve as the first phase of such an analysis.

A cost-benefit analysis, an LEAA official told us, would be inappropriate because of the many intangible benefits to be derived from the system. We believe, however, that sound financial management of a project of this magnitude requires at least an estimate of the costs of the project. Otherwise neither the sponsoring federal agencies nor the Congress can determine whether they will be able or willing to meet the financial requirements of the system. Further, the intent of title I of the Omnibus Crime Control and Safe Streets Act of 1968, as amended, is that state and local governments will assume project costs after a reasonable period of federal assistance. For this reason it is vital that state and local governments have the information necessary to determine whether they can finance the development and continued operation of the system.

Need for Improved Reporting of Arrest and Disposition Data

A criminal history exchange system is valuable because it provides criminal justice agencies—law inforcement agencies, courts, and correctional institutions—with complete, accurate, and timely information on all offenders. Under the NCIC system, criminal justice agencies must report arrests and dispositions within each state to the state's central identification unit which maintains and controls state criminal records and supplies the data for the national files. According to the department, only 24 states had laws requiring that criminal justice agencies report arrests and dispositions to a central identification unit.

An August 1969 to July 1970 LEAA survey showed that many arrests and their dispositions were not reported by criminal justice agencies to their state identification units, as shown below:

	Number of states by percent of completeness of arrest and disposition reporting to state identification units (note a)		
Transaction	More than 90 percent	65 to 90 percent	Less than 65 percent
Arrests	11	20	18
Dispositions	7	11	31

a One state did not provide information on arrests; another state did not provide information on dispositions.

Only four states had achieved more than 90 percent reporting for both arrests and dispositions which means that, in each of these four states, over 90 percent of the arrests and over 90 percent of the dispositions were reported to a state identification unit. Of the 15 states participating in Project SEARCH at the time our fieldwork was completed, only five had more than 90 percent arrest reporting and only four had more than 90 percent disposition reporting. According to our July and August 1971 survey of the 15 states participating in Project SEARCH, although some improvements had been made, reporting was still incompleted.

Until such reporting is improved, the exchange system cannot be fully effective. System users must be certain that they are aware of all of an offender's prior arrests and their dispositions. Otherwise, the users may face time-consuming investigations to determine whether all prior arrests have been reported and the outcome of arrests reported.

An LEAA official agreed that the system would not be fully effective if reporting was incomplete. He told us, however, that the system should be put into operation and that arrest and disposition reporting problems could be worked out later. He said that the Project SEARCH group had developed a model state act which, if adopted by individual state legislatures, would improve reporting in those states.

An NCIC official made essentially the same comments. He said that, when the criminal history exchange system was in full operation, NCIC would be able to provide participating states with periodic lists showing reported arrests for which disposition data was missing. These lists would make the states aware of deficiencies in disposition reporting and would encourage improvements.

To put a system into operation without first insuring that the information it will process is complete will result in a system that maintains and provides incomplete data to system users. The value of the system to law enforcement or court officials will be diminished if they cannot rely on the completeness of the record they are using. When decisions are being made to set bail, impose sentence, or grant parole, the offender's record should present an accurate and complete history of arrests and dispositions.

The model state legislation formulated by the Project SEARCH group is a step in the right direction. The model act, however, deals primarily with security and privacy. Although it may enhance state efficiency in maintaining offender records, it does not specifically address the problem of arrest and disposition reporting.

Our survey and that of LEAA show that the states are well aware of their reporting problems. An NCIC list would aid the states in improving the completeness of records, but it is no solution because it will not insure that the file is accurate or complete at all times and will have no effect on preventing the dissemination of information on an arrest for which a disposition has not been obtained. The failure to restrict dissemination of data on an arrest for which a disposition has not been obtained is a serious system deficiency because it permits dissemination of arrest information without showing whether a person was convicted or found innocent. According to the department, NCIC did not have procedures to remove an arrest entry which was not followed by a related disposition entry. The department recognized that restricting the dissemination of such data may be required by future legislation or other mandate but said that NCIC had no definite plans along this line.

CONCLUSIONS AND RECOMMENDATIONS

The computerized criminal history exchange system may provide intangible benefits which would make a cost-benefit analysis difficult. We believe, however, that sound financial management of a project of this magnitude requires at least an estimate of total project costs. Otherwise the participants cannot determine whether they will be able or willing to meet the financial requirements of developing and operating the system.

The incompleteness of arrest and disposition reporting is also a system deficiency. Until all criminal justice agencies are providing the required data on arrests and their dispositions, system users will have no assurance that the criminal history data they receive is complete or accurate.

Recommendations to the Attorney General

We recommend that, before authorizing any substantial additional expenditures for the system, the Attorney General require that:
—Either the FBI or LEAA determine the total cost of developing and operating the criminal history exchange system so that the participants can decide whether they are able, or willing, to meet the system's financial requirements.
—The FBI and LEAA implement a program for improving the reporting of arrests and dispositions by law enforcement agencies, courts, and correctional institutions to state agencies which enter such data into the national system.

Agency Comments and GAO Evaluation

The Department of Justice agreed with GAO's recommendations

and said that it was taking action to accomplish their objectives. According to the Department:

—LEAA has started a program which requires each state to submit a comprehensive data system plan to LEAA as a prerequisite to LEAA funding of data systems under the program. The states are required to estimate in the plan the total cost of their criminal history systems plus the required incremental cost to be supported by the federal government.

—LEAA, under its comprehensive data system program, will not fund data systems in states which do not require mandatory reporting when the states' systems become operational.

—The FBI is continuing to encourage prompt and complete reporting of arrest and disposition data by law enforcement agencies.

—The Attorney General, on July 18, 1972, proposed legislation that would place the burden upon the agencies submitting criminal record information to insure accurate, complete, and current information. Present law does not require the states or other governmental entities to report arrest and disposition data.

The department's actions, if effectively implemented, should provide cost data and should improve arrest and disposition reporting.

It is questionable, however, whether the comprehensive data systems plans will provide an estimate of the total funding that will be required to make the criminal history exchange system fully operational or whether the program will insure accurate, complete, and current reporting. A state may decide not to participate in the comprehensive data systems program and still participate in the criminal history exchange system. As of October 1972 only about half the states had submitted comprehensive data systems plans to LEAA. Although these plans contained cost estimates of state participation in the comprehensive data systems program, they did not contain cost analyses to show what costs would be required for the state to develop its state criminal history exchange system.

Although arrest and disposition reporting should improve as a result of LEAA and FBI actions, the comprehensive data systems program requires only that the states insure that mandatory reporting will be accomplished by the time the states' systems become operational. States therefore can avoid or postpone mandatory reporting by not participating in the comprehensive data systems program or by delaying participation.

REVIEW QUESTIONS

1. Which of the following personal attributes are most helpful to the systems analyst during conversion? Why?
   Intelligence
   Creativity
   Interpersonal skills
   Good with details
   Health
2. Are arguments about project benefits likely to occur in an organization? Describe the nature of some.
3. One of the conversion programs often written for large real-time systems is a system simulator. Why is this developed?
4. Why don't most organizations have their auditors review completed systems projects?
5. Why should the user sign the project report?

DISCUSSION QUESTIONS

1. Should auditors include comments about user satisfaction with the system in their report? Why?
2. Discuss when conversions should be parallel.
3. Discuss the elements of a project report for the project in Chapter 15.
4. Discuss the elements of an audit report for the project in Chapter 15.
5. Develop a list of items to include in a conversion plan for the system described in Chapter 20.

BIBLIOGRAPHY

Benjamin, James E., "Major Considerations in Systems Conversion," *Ideas for Management, 1972,* pp. 60-63.

Benoit, Paul S., "Critique Meetings Refine Systems Projects," *Journal of Systems Management,* Vol. 23, No. 7, July 1972, pp. 8-10.

Bricker, George B., "Taking the Risk out of Systems Upgrading," *Data Processing Magazine,* Vol. 12, No. 9, September 1970, pp. 27-29.

Bugby, David S., and Joseph P. Schwitter, "Conversion to Computerized Inventory Control," *DPMA Quarterly,* Vol. 2, April 1966, pp. 2-12.

Burlo, C. Russell, Jr., "The Ecology of Change in a Major Computer Conversion," *3rd CPRG Proceedings,* 1965, pp. 79-85.

Canning, Richard G. (Ed.), "Policies that Aid Computer Conversions," *EDP Analyzer,* Vol. 9, No. 2, February 1971, 14 p.

Fried, Louis, "Installing Software Systems," *Modern Data,* Vol. 6, No. 6, June 1973, pp. 50-53.

Hardy, I. Trotter, Jr., "System Implementation and Evaluation," *Journal of Systems Management,* Vol. 24, No. 12, December 1973, pp. 24-27.

Harmon, Robert L., Robert C. Aubuchon, and Donald C. Mengerson, "Planning Successful Conversions," *Ideas for Management, 1968,* pp. 69-80.

Holmes, Fenwicke W., "Auditing from the DP Manager's Viewpoint," *Journal of Systems Management,* Vol. 25, No. 3, March 1973, pp. 22-25.

Kennevan, Walter J., "ADP Conversion Planning," *DPMA Quarterly,* Vol. 1, April 1965, pp. 2-22.

Lenihan, John K., "Are the Scales Tipping Toward Reprogramming?" *Data Management,* February 1971.

Maulsby, G. F., "Planning and Implementing a Major Systems Conversion," *Data Processing Magazine,* Vol. 13, No. 9, Winter 1971, pp. 26-29.

Smalheiser, Marvin, "Mammoth DP Conversion Involves 1100 Programs," *Computerworld,* Vol. 7, No. 41, October 1973, p. 6.

Snellgrove, Olin C., "The Management Audit: Organizational Guidance System," *Journal of Systems Management,* Vol. 22, No. 12, December 1971, pp. 10-12.

Strassman, Paul A., "Strategy for the 70's—Stay Flexible with Datacomm Investments," *The Data Communications User,* March 1974, pp. 39-44.

Weiss, Harvey M., "Happiness is Installing a New Computer," *Journal of Systems Management,* Vol. 25, No. 2, February 1974, pp. 35-37.

System Control and Minor Maintenance

The writing of the final project report and the disbanding of the project team does not end the involvement of the information systems organization with the system. The system must be operated, controlled, modified when necessary and kept secure. Part VI discusses those ongoing activities of particular interest to the systems analyst.

Information systems controls are an important aspect of systems design as well as operation. Without adequate controls designed and operating, the best conceived system would soon be perceived by the user as of little value. Chapter 26 is concerned with placement of the control section in the organization, design of the control system and some audit considerations.

Systems are dynamic rather than static. Modifications must be made as conditions change, as errors are found and as improvements appear appropriate. Chapter 27 discusses the modification cycle and ways of having users make the modifications.

Few information systems operate without forms and many systems changes involve changes in the forms. Forms control is therefore, an important window into systems control and modification. Chapter 28 involves the organization, procedures and benefits of the forms control function.

The records management function described in Chapter 29 involves the storage, retrieval and disposal of the hard copy information in a system. This function like forms control, is probably best performed by specialists in the particular area, but should be a part of the information systems organization.

Chapter 30 completes Part VI with a discussion of security. The physical and people threats are described and the appropriate precautions are prescribed.

Taken together, Chapters 26 through 30 address the environment of the total installed system. Effective organization of these functions of the information systems organization contribute greatly to the design and operation of the systems developed by the project teams.

CHAPTER 26

APPLICATION OF CONTROLS

There are two reasons for controls on an information system. The first is accuracy. Inaccuracies in reports are soon discovered by the users and nullify any truth in the reports. Nothing can do more damage to the value of the information systems organization than a reputation for carelessness and inaccuracy.

The second reason for controls is fraud. Cases of fraudulent use of information systems are all too frequent. Errors and fraud can be reduced by using good control practices. This chapter discusses the control organization and practices that serve to improve the accuracy and reduce the opportunities for fraud in an information system.

THE CONTROL ORGANIZATION

The control function in practice may reside in one of several parts of the organization. It may be a user department function, it may be a part of the operations group of the information systems department, or it may be a separate function within information systems. It is usually the best practice to organize the control function as a separate information systems group for the following reasons.

The control clerk or control section should have no operational responsibility. The control section should report at a level above the one where the detailed operations decisions are made. This means that the control section would, in some organizations, report to the manager of computer operations but more often to the director of information systems. Some of the reasons for this reporting arrangement are:

1. It separates the duties of the controller and the doer. This is an important concept which will be discussed more fully in the next section.

2. The control clerk is isolated from the pressures of completing the schedule on time. This assures that even small discrepancies are corrected before reports are issued.

3. The skills required for control and operations people are quite different. The ideal control clerk has had long employment in the organization, preferably with experience in the system being controlled. They are meticulous, secure in their job, not unusually creative or adaptable, and are suspicious of accepting incorrect data. Such a person often has a personality that hinders promotion but provides the particular skills and exam-

ining mind needed in control jobs. The need for social acceptance is not as important as being accurate to the control clerk.

In addition to the control section, control is exercised by both internal and external auditors. External auditors are typically certified public accountants working for a professional firm or a government agency. Internal auditors usually have similar credentials but work for the organization. They often report organizationally to the audit committee of the board of directors. In auditing an information system, the auditors verify the accuracy of the internal controls of each of the important information systems of the organization.

SEPARATION OF DUTIES

Assume for illustration that one person in a hundred would risk making fraudulent entries in an information system. In this situation the chance of two employees agreeing to cooperate in a fraud might be one in ten thousand. Since the act of ascertaining the willingness of another to cooperate in fraud carries the substantial risk of being exposed, many possible defrauders will not communicate their intentions to another. This is the principal argument for separation of duties in the design of an information system.

In the information systems organization, separation of duties is accomplished by separating control from operations, programming from operations, and data entry from operations. Separation in an accounts receivable system is accomplished by separating the mail opening and preparation of bank deposits from cash application to the customer record. The principle is obvious but in practice it is often violated. In a one-girl office it is hard to avoid combining similar functions. For example, several years ago one of the authors rented his home to a widow with three children. Her employer was a fruit wholesaler for whom she did all of the accounting functions. Several months later the author was notified of the shocking information that the tenant had been arrested for stealing $250,000. She was accused of maintaining one set of accounts receivable records for the customer and another for her boss, and pocketing the difference. Having one person open the mail and another make the bank deposit would have made that fraud much more difficult.

In a payroll system it would seem to be appropriate for the supervisor to hand out checks to employees, yet that allows a person who originates a payment action to receive that payment directly without review. One organization had two instances in which a supervisor continued to send in reports to the Payroll Department of hours worked by an employee who had quit, and forged the employee's signature on the checks received. The supervisors were caught when an employee complained that the wages shown on the withholding statement were too high.

FILE CONTROLS

The principal function of the control section is the maintenance of controls for each file. This control is kept on a special form designed to establish continuity of the control process. Figure 26.1 is an example of a control form for an accounts receivable file.

Accounts Receivable Control Record

COLUMN	1	2	3	4	5
TITLE	PREVIOUS BALANCE	CURRENT PERIOD SALES	CASH RECEIPTS	BAD DEBT WRITEOFFS	NEW BALANCE
SOURCE	COLUMN (5) PREVIOUS PERIOD	COLUMN (4) SHIPMENTS CONTROL	SUM OF DUPLICATE DEPOSIT SLIPS	MEMO FROM TREASURER	$(1) + (2) - (3) - (4) = 5$
DATE 2/14	15,471,512.17	3,500,200.50	4,100,450.20	47,000.00	14,824,331.97
2/21	14,824,331.97				

Form 4798

FIGURE 26.1

The title of the control form describes its purpose; however, it is more often referred to as 4798 by those who work with it. The columns are numbered for referencing in the instructions. Each column is given a title that is descriptive of the amount to be entered in it. The precise source of the data for each column is described. The figures in column 5 could have been obtained as shown or could be the new balance total on the current period accounts receivable ledger. Using the form shown here the control clerk would check that each of the corresponding totals agreed with the control. An improvement to this procedure requires the clerk to enter the totals from the accounts receivable ledger and to then compare the pairs of numbers.

The systems designer, with the advice of the auditor, must decide which fields of a file to control. Normally all amount fields will be controlled. Often the quantity fields and the number of records in the file will also be controlled. Occasionally a total will be kept of a file key such as customer or employee numbers. These totals are most often made for transactions and serve to assure the accuracy of the keying operation. The typical internal control procedure in a computer installation is to deliver the reports from the printer to the control clerk who checks them against the control record. Then the reports are returned for decollating, bursting and distribution.

FINANCIAL AUDIT

The financial audit (done by the internal or external auditor, or both) is the last resort for controls for an information system. An auditor has two major functions. First, he checks that the controls are indeed operating as they were designed. This means he observes the entry of figures for the current period according to the instructions and that all controls are operative.

Second, he checks the file for errors against existing external sources. A product inventory is checked by physically counting the inventory. An accounts receivable file is checked by sending a verification statement to a customer. When certain customers such as the U. S. Government do not respond to verification requests, alternates must be found. Details of the auditor's verification procedures are described later in this chapter. The auditor checks for any significant variance in procedure, clerical accuracy and fraud. A large portion of the collusion frauds are caught by this procedure. The value of the audit is greatest when those being audited believe there is a reasonable chance that the auditors will appear shortly. Audits should be relatively frequent and irregular.

A Controlled System

The following case examines the control points designed into a payroll system (Figure 26.2) where the control section is separate from computer operations. In this example, programmers and systems analysts had no entry into the operational area after the conversion was completed. Each department supervisor reported hours worked to the cost people who used the data for the labor distribution. The Payroll Department checked time cards against the hours reported by the department supervisors and reconciled any differences. Additions and deletions of people from the payroll were originated by the Personnel Department, separating this action from the supervisor or Payroll. Time cards were prepared from a master file and counted so that unapproved and lost cards were caught. All totals of hours paid by the Payroll Department were entered in the payroll register and were checked to the labor distribution totals and any significant differences reconciled.

The control section kept records on the number of employees, gross pay, taxes, net pay and many of the deductions. The U. S. Savings Bond control included (Figure 26.3): (1) previous file total, (2) new deductions authorized, (3) canceled deductions, (4) new file total, (5) missed deductions [because of sickness, vacations, etc.], (6) expected total deductions, (7) actual deductions, (8) previous bond balance, (9) bonds purchased, (10) new expected bond balance, and, (11) new actual bond balance.

Data in columns 2, 3, and 5 were supported by transaction lists. Column $4 = 1 + 2 - 3$. Columns 7 and 11 were taken from the Payroll Register. Column $10 = 7 + 8 - 9$. By comparing columns 5

Control Points in a Payroll System

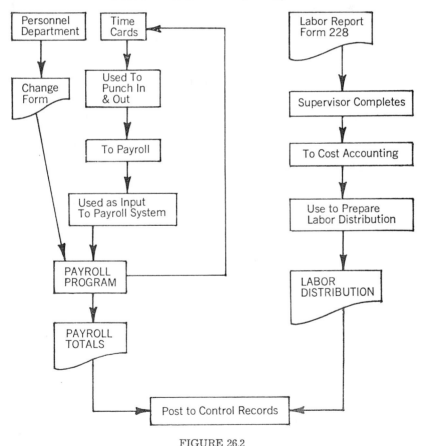

FIGURE 26.2

Savings Bond Control Record

COLUMN	1	2	3	4	5	6	7	8	9	10	11
TITLE	Previous File Total	New Deductions Authorized	Cancelled Deductions	New File Total	Missed Deductions	Expected Deductions	Actual Deductions	Previous Bond Balance	Bonds Purchased	Expected Bond Balance	Actual Bond Balance
SOURCE	Column (4) Last Week	Item 47 on Deduction Change List	Item 48 on Deduction Change List	(1) + (2) − (3)	Item 23 on Payroll Report	(4) − (5)	Item 24 on Payroll Report	Column 10 Last week	Bond Purchase List	(7) + (8) − (9)	Item 25 on Payroll Report
Date (of entries)											

Form 4799

FIGURE 26.3

and 6 or 9 and 10 it could be ascertained that the file was in balance and the deduction process was correct in total.

The time cards and changes to the master file were prepunched with appropriate codes to eliminate one source of input error.

Totals were printed at the end of the check run and checked against the control. Similarly, for the check register. For a time the system used a printer that could conceivably print a number other than the one in the record. For that reason, totals of checks in groups of 100 were made and sent to each Paymaster. The payroll clerk would then add the checks to see if they agreed with the predetermined total.

In calculating the payroll, the computer accumulated a large number of totals. These included number of employees paid, hours worked, hours paid, gross pay, FICA, federal income tax, state taxes by state, and each of one hundred optional deductions. These totals were printed at the end of the Payroll Register and represented the primary source of figures to check against control. This was also the source of the journal entries and check authorizations which disbursed the gross pay.

Auditing was done both internally and externally. The internal auditors audited each payroll unit at least once a year. Their appearance was unannounced. The auditors participated actively in the systems design. External auditors accompanied the internal auditors on infrequent occasions to monitor the quality of the internal audit program.

BATCH ENVIRONMENT AUDIT CONSIDERATIONS

Computer Control Guidelines (1970) does an excellent job of detailing the controls needed in information systems. They recommend the establishment of a control section, extensive use of edit programs and good written procedures. A discussion of some of their other recommendations follows.

Since it is easily possible to mount an incorrect tape or disk file, errors of this type can be reduced by external and internal labels on the file, computer checking of the internal labels, librarian control of all files, and good operator instructions.

Computing equipment can also make errors. The logical design of the equipment can decrease the significance of the errors by catching and correcting many of them without the necessity of aborting the run. Equipment chosen for jobs with critical control should have adequate self-checking facilities. Preventative maintenance procedures are necessary to eliminate downtime of heavily used equipment.

Certain frauds can be perpetrated by stopping program execution, modifying memory or instructions and continuing. Since frauds of this type would leave no trace other than the console log, an unburst console log would be a significant control tool. It is recommended that the log be constantly reviewed by the operations manager and any questions answered immediately.

The frequency of errors in the correction of errors is much higher than the original error-making frequency. Therefore, it is important that good error correction procedures be used, such as putting any correction through the same editing procedure that caught the error in the first place. Errors caught early in the process are much easier to correct than those caught later. The value of good edit procedures cannot be stressed enough. The edit procedure should keep track of those entry records signaled as errors to be certain that each is re-entered into the system or otherwise accounted for. This doesn't mean that each must be re-entered in the same cycle. Many systems can operate with correction during the following cycle except possibly on the last day of a fiscal period.

The traditional audit trail required by auditors is a hard copy trace of each transaction through the system. Providing such printouts in a computerized system can be quite expensive and is often eliminated. When the hard copy is eliminated the audit trail must be available through machine language records (tape, disk, etc.). The control section and the auditors are interested in the retention period of the records and the ability to develop a history.

An often discussed aspect of auditing computer systems is auditing around or through the computer. A complete hard copy audit trail allows the auditor to completely audit around the computer. Keeping some of the audit trail in machine record form may require selected printouts but still allows an audit around the computer.

Batch systems generally can be audited around the computer. Auditing through the computer is also possible in batch systems and is necessary in transaction based systems.

Batch controls are a vital part of the batch environment. The first person to handle a set of transactions (50 items, a day's receipts, etc.) should prepare a cover slip with batch identification, the number of items and amount totals. Thereafter, the batch moves as a unit and lost items are easily detected. (Figure 26.4)

Batch Control Ticket

SHIPMENTS BATCH CONTROL	
Batch No. _____ To: _____	
Date _____ From: _____	
No. of Documents _____ From: _____ To: _____	
Total Amount	
Date Received:	Received By:
Form 3174	

FIGURE 26.4

TRANSACTION SYSTEMS AUDIT CONSIDERATIONS

Entries to a transaction-based system are usually made through remote terminals. A transaction may only be a concise code accepted by the terminal or a change in the magnetic flux on a disk. Auditing transaction-based systems is more complex than auditing batch systems. Terminal access is a significant audit consideration. Who is authorized to use the terminal? What information is available through each terminal? When can the terminal be used? The systems analyst's design of the access system can add a significant amount of control.

Limiting the use of a terminal to normal office hours, changing the polling frequently and locking the terminal at night reduces the opportunities for fraud. However, restricting a terminal to only certain people also reduces the use of an expensive system.

Restricting file areas or portions of files to certain employees helps to increase confidentiality. For instance, an insurance company had an agent with a substantial Hollywood clientele. The policy files contained investigative credit reports. The employees passed along the policy numbers which contained the most sensational information until the files were restricted.

An audit trail requires special attention in a transaction-based system. The solution is usually to write a tape or disk log of all transactions including the before and after conditions of all changes to master file records. A comparison of the changed records against the log verifies the system. This method can also be used to validate the accuracy of the on-line file updating.

Test transactions are an important means of auditing through the computer. To use this method the auditor develops a set of test transactions and introduces them into the system. The system's accuracy is judged by matching the actual output with the expected results. Using this method, care must be taken to reverse the test transactions.

It is important to remember that any test is subject to the particular conditions at the time of the test. All one knows as a result of a successful test is that the equipment, operating system and other transactions competing for the resources worked correctly at that point. Important programs are tested continuously. Software testers are always seeking the improbable situation that will cause the system to fail.

Since control totals are not available at the time of input they must be developed by the application programs. The control system then must provide some external method of verifying the totals. An on-line teller system solves the problem by asking the teller to balance the transactions at the end of the day.

Unusual transactions can be identified in the systems design, selected by the program and printed on a special report for the control clerk to investigate. The best controls devised are only as good as the alertness of the control clerk. An alert clerk may have the chance to catch a case of fraud amounting to large sums once or twice in his lifetime.

Systems analysts designed and programmers wrote such precautions into an on-line program for the Dime Savings Bank in New York. The transactions of the horse-playing chief teller showed up so often on the report that the control clerk did not think them unusual, and $1,500,000 was lost.

AUDIT SOFTWARE

The large public accounting firms have written software packages to facilitate their auditing tasks. For an excellent description of the packages available, see Adams and Mullarkey (1972). The packages presently available take one or more of the client's files, manipulate the data in the file and output certain reports useful to the auditor. This assumes a static file and is a type of auditing around the computer because the result is audited—not the process. This technique is then most useful on asset files such as accounts receivable, inventory and fixed assets. The following are some of the capabilities usually included in the programs:

Arithmetic accuracy. The programs have addition, subtraction, multiplication and division functions. Addition could be used to check that the file balances to the control figures. The multiplication function could be used to check interest calculations. Certainly using a computer to perform these functions is an improvement over pounding on a desk calculator or adding machine for days at a time.

Summarizing. The ability to summarize a file by categories can be important to the auditor. For example, the accounts receivable file must be aged to review the provision for bad debts. The activity of inventory items is needed to determine what is obsolescent.

Statistical sampling. In selecting items for detailed review, it is necessary usually to stratify the file and then to statistically determine how many elements must be selected from each stratum to obtain the level of confidence needed in the accuracy of the entire file. The auditor wishes to be able to say that he is "x" per cent sure that the actual total of the file is within "y" per cent of the stated value. The auditor must be careful to select items in such a way that each item has an equal chance of being selected.

Comparing. The auditor needs to be able to compare two files to discover the differences between them. For example, by comparing two generations of the same file, one could identify the changes. The changes could then be compared to the transaction files to check the accuracy of the up-dating procedure.

Searching. The auditor needs to find certain types of items in certain files. Credit balances in account receivable files may have to be reclassified as payables, obsolete items in inventories must be eliminated, the payroll records of the payroll clerks must be individually checked, etc.

These audit packages are most often used by public accountants but are also made available for a fee to others. Several software firms have developed similar packages or suggested that their regular packages may be used in auditing.

TEST AND CONTROL

If technology were adequate to prove programs, it could replace certain of the control and audit procedures. Unfortunately, program proving is currently beyond technological capabilities except in certain very limited cases. The most likely step, short of full program proof, is testing to the point of being able to make a probability statement about the remaining errors in the program. Auditors will eventually require that the programs used in certain applications be tested so that such probabilities can be stated. The present audit techniques catch many classes of errors and fraud, but there are still many loopholes for fraud. The best way of finding such errors and fraud at present is still to manually read the programs.

THE COST OF CONTROLS

Obviously, controls cost. The addition of a check digit to the Social Security number would increase the cost of key punching that field by 11 percent, increase the length of the file and require the revision of many forms. The systems analyst must consider the gains achieved by a proposed control against the cost of implementing that control.

Whole dollar accounting is an example of the trade-off between accuracy and cost. By dropping pennies, the cost of many data operations is reduced along with the precision of the results. This example also points out one of the primary considerations a systems analyst uses in structuring a control system. The system is designed so that large errors are much less frequent than small errors. Requiring higher level approval of large expenditures is one example of this principle in action. Note that Paretian distributions (20% of the transactions involve 80% of the volume) have again influenced systems design considerations.

Unfortunately, the value of the control is not as apparent as the cost, making the decision that sets the control cost level a subjective one. Also, the auditors, users and systems analysts often have differing views on installing a certain control. The analyst will often take the position of less controls because of a belief that the existing controls are not cost-effective. If an error occurs, the first tendency is to try to find out why and a control method is proposed to catch any future errors of that type. Long-operating systems will have tighter controls than new systems.

SUMMARY

Current technology does not make it possible to prove an information system 100% accurate. It is, however, quite possible to develop controls and audit techniques that catch the most frequent errors and fraud. We have suggested certain organizational practices, control procedures and audit techniques to serve this purpose. The imposition of controls should be subject to the same cost-effectiveness analysis as other aspects of the system.

REVIEW QUESTIONS

1. What are the basic reasons for controls on an information system?
2. At what level should the control system report? Give your reasons.
3. What control functions do the auditors exercise?
4. How is separation of duties accomplished in an information system organization?
5. Why should payroll checks be given out by someone other than the supervisor?
6. What are the auditor's two major functions?
7. Name several control points in a payroll system.
8. Why are good error-correction procedures significant?
9. What kind of audit trail is available in a computerized system?
10. What controls can be applied to remote terminals?
11. How are test transactions used to audit a transaction system?
12. Tell some of the ways in which software packages may assist the auditor in his work.
13. How can one evaluate controls in relation to costs?

DISCUSSION QUESTIONS

1. In C Company the Accounts Receivable Department occasionally finds that a customer has never been billed for a shipment. This information turns up when the customer requests billing or remits for an unbilled shipment, or when goods are returned against an unbilled shipment. Describe what controls you would install to assure that copies of all shipping tickets are transmitted promptly to the Billing Department and invoiced to customers.
2. The Personnel Department of F Company found that some employees were leaving their jobs early but their time cards were being clocked out at their regular quitting times. What steps should be taken to prevent such time card irregularities?
3. The Plant Engineering Department of T Company made a practice of ordering repair jobs on machine and buildings from outside firms without the prior issuance of a purchase order. When a job was finished and priced, Plant Engineering would then request the Purchasing Department to issue a purchase order to the outside firm marked "Work Completed." Tell how this arrangement violates the concept of internal controls and how it could open the way to fraudulent practices.

BIBLIOGRAPHY

Adams, Donald L. & John F. Mullarkey, "Survey of Audit Software, A," *Journal of Accountancy*, Vol. 134 No. 3, September 1972, pp. 39-66.

Boas, Brian P., "Sample of Statistics, A," *Management Adviser*, Vol. 10 No. 3, May/June 1973, pp. 42-50.

Computer Control Guidelines, Canadian Institute of Chartered Accountants, 1970, 135 p.

Davis, Gordon B., *Auditing and EDP*, New York: AICPA, 1968.

Henderson, Reid, "Internal Control Safeguards," *Data Management*, Vol. 8 No. 9, September 1970, pp. 39-42.

Holmes, Fenwicke W., "Auditing from the DP Manager's Viewpoint," *Journal of Systems Management*, Vol. 25 No. 3, March 1973, pp. 22-25.

Hurtado, Corydon, "General Audit Techniques in Data Processing," *Data Management*, October 1970, pp. 28-31.

Jacobsen, Galen G., "Auditing Aspects of Data Processing," *Data Management*, Vol. 10 No. 7, July 1972, pp. 17-19.

Kaufman, Felix, "EDP Control Problems," *The Controller*, July 1962, pp. 364-368.

Lybrand, Ross Bros. & Montgomery, "Recognition of EDP Operational Problems," *Management Adviser*, Vol. 10 No. 1, January/February 1973, pp. 55-57.

McLaughlin, Grant E., "EDP Systems Audit," *Data Management*, Vol. 8 No. 9, September 1970, pp. 33-35.

Perritt, Roscoe D., "Impact of EDP on Auditing, The," *Data Education*, Vol. 13 No. 2, November 1972, pp. 10-23.

Porter, Thomas, "Necessity of EDP Systems Controls, The," *Data Management*, Vol. 8 No. 9, September 1970, pp. 29-32.

Rauseo, Michael J., *Management Controls for Computer Processing*, New York: American Management Association, 1970.

Smith, Leighton F., *Executive Briefing on the Control of Computers, An*, Park Ridge, Ill.: Data Processing Management Association, 1971.

Stolle, Carlton D., "Computer-Based Audits," *Management Advisor*, Vol. 8 No. 3, May/June 1971, pp. 38-43.

Thorne, Jack F., "Internal Control of Real-Time Systems," *Data Management*, Vol. 9 No. 1, January 1971, pp. 34-37.

Thorne, Jack F., "The Audit of Real-Time Systems," *Data Management*, Vol. 8 No. 5, May 1970, pp. 14-19.

Wofsey, Marvin M., "EDP Systems Controls," *Data Management*, Vol. 9 No. 9, September 1971, pp. 71-76.

CHAPTER 27

SYSTEM MAINTENANCE

Sooner or later every system devised by people needs to be changed. The major changes are the types described in other sections of this book. The minor systems changes or maintenance are the subject of this chapter. The cycle of systems design and change is described in Figure 27.1. It begins with analysis and reaches a high level when the programmers join the team. The peak is reached at cut-over time. After cut-over errors are corrected, the project team including the analysts is usually disbanded. If the analyst is not moved on to a new project, much of the analyst's time is spent in maintaining the operating system.

Maintenance is minor in the beginning and tends to increase as the system matures. Organizations change and the system must be patched to compensate for those growth changes. Soon the patches are patched until it becomes obvious that major systems changes should occur. Then a new project team starts the analysis process over again. Hopefully, the patchwork system will have been well documented to help reduce the time required in the re-evaluation of the system. The new project may only replace the deficient areas in the system and be a smaller project than the design of the original system.

PROGRAMMING CHANGES

The two most used arrangements for maintenance programming are to (1) organize maintenance as a separate group and (2) include maintenance among the responsibilities of a functional area systems and programming group. Both are good techniques with the following advantages and disadvantages.

The Separate Group

The quality of the changes made by a separate maintenance group may be lower because the group is frequently staffed with trainees or may be higher because of the attention of a supervisor specifically charged with the maintenance responsibility. The separate group is often staffed by junior programmers. Reading the existing programs may teach them the good or bad programming habits of the staff that designed the system. There are some who believe that reading a program is a more difficult skill to acquire than coding a new program to the specifications of the system. Most programmers seem to prefer the development of a new program over the modification of established programs, making job satisfaction difficult in maintenance groups.

Maintenance as Part of the Group

The major organizational purpose of the systems group assigned to a functional area is the development of new projects. Maintenance work, if it is done, tends to delay or eliminate the implementation of new projects. However, if maintenance is not done, the operating systems become increasingly dysfunctional. Figure 27.1 shows

Design and Change Cycle

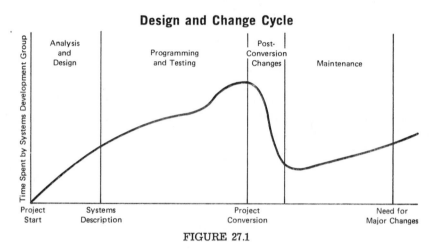

FIGURE 27.1

that all systems require maintenance at some point. As more systems are developed, more maintenance is required and if the functional systems group remains the same size, more time is devoted to maintenance and fewer hours are available for new projects.

Maintenance Reducing Techniques

The amount of time spent on revising programs is a function of the way in which the program is written. Maintenance can be minimized by Modular programming, Parameter driven programs, Interpretive programs and Decision Tables.

Modular programs are, as discussed in Chapter 23, an important simplifier of the maintenance task. Finding the place to modify a program is facilitated by the modular structure. If the modules are well conceived the maintenance programmer can limit his search for ramifications of the change throughout the system. The change normally will modify only one or two modules making it possible to simplify most of the debugging and testing of the affected modules.

Parameters are not normally in the program. By maintaining parameters as separate data sets, it is possible to change the system without a recompile. In the case of a service bureau that has separate W-2 programs for each of the ten payroll systems it processes, the writing of nine of these programs could have been avoided if the record layout of the payroll system had been a parameter in the first W-2 program to be written. Sort programs are also good examples of parameter driven programs.

Interpretive programs are less often used but can be useful. When the system designer is aware that the system is subject to frequent changes, it may be appropriate to build a program that compiles and executes the code at the time of those changes. One of the earliest of such programs was used to plan refinery runs. The relationships between the variables were dynamic and required daily revision. For this application, an interpretive program was the answer. Corporate models are often best programmed interpretively. Besides minimizing the time spent by the maintenance crew, interpretation allows the user to take the responsibility for change. The corporate models we have seen that were interpretive were used longer and more frequently.

Decision tables are, by their nature, modular so they tend to confine changes to a small number of tables. When decision table processors are used, the program can be changed by simply changing the tables and recompiling, reducing the maintenance effort.

Proponents of decision tables stress the logical neatness of the tables and suggest that system changes are more often made correctly when using them. They also suggest that the user is better able to select the necessary changes when examining the tables.

Minimum program maintenance is then relative. When the use and frequency and mode of changes are known, then the best maintenance method can be chosen.

SMALL PROGRAMMING JOBS

Data processing centers often receive requests to run small jobs. These include such jobs as preparation of sorted listings with totals from an existing data base, statistical analysis of a given data set, or perhaps the preparation of a monthly report involving a new data set with a minimum of calculation and controls. For each of these and for thousands of other cases, the programming task can be minimized by the use of one of a number of packaged programs. Three of the most frequently used programs are described.

A Query Program

This program allows a user (not a programmer necessarily) to request data be selected from a file, sorted, and listed with perhaps three levels of totals. The selection of requested information is usually possible using logical operators such as AND and OR. An example of an input of a query program is shown in Figure 27.2 and usually includes selection, sort and printing programs. This type of

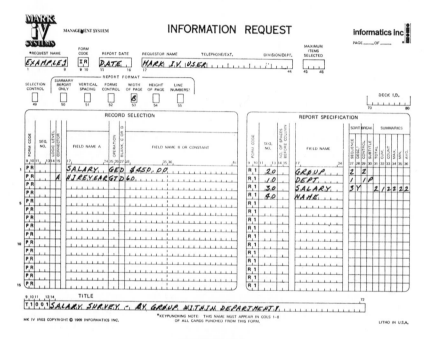

FIGURE 27.2

program is extremely useful to the data processing shop because the user typically writes the parameters that select, organize and print the data. This type of job otherwise would be given to the maintenance group. Simple query programs as well as the more general data management programs would be used for queries.

Statistical Packages

These are particularly useful in organizations where research is conducted. The packages include at least mean, standard deviation, correlation, analysis of variance and regression analysis. Some packages are much more extensive. The packages are generally classified as parameter driven programs. The user (again, not necessarily a programmer) specifies the arrangement of the data and the particular optional features of the program to be used in the processing of the data. These programs can be very useful for the same reasons the query programs are valuable: they avoid the necessity of programming each application. With substantial use of these and other packages it is necessary to provide consultants to teach the user how to use the packages and to troubleshoot the errors.

Report Program Generators (RPG)

These packages are usually a programmer's tool and allow for more elaborate selection rules and calculations and considerably more printing flexibility than the query programs. They assume the use of prior sort utilities if necessary. An RPG program can usually be written and tested in one day. Some RPGs have enough flexibility to serve as the only or principle programming language for particular computers (IBM's 360-20 for example). The training required for the skillful use of RPG is extensive enough so that only a small portion of users learn the language. The short time necessary to write an RPG program makes it an excellent tool for handling small programming jobs.

WORK SIMPLIFICATION

The basic idea behind work simplification is that every organization has many more opportunities to improve its operation than the professional systems personnel have time to investigate. The solution is to train the supervisors in a stripped down set of systems analysis and design techniques and to reward those who make improvements in their areas. Such a training program is described in Chapter 21. Organizations that implement work simplification usually find their supervisors make many worthwhile improvements. Training each new supervisor in work simplification is a worthwhile part of an executive development program. Trained supervisors are more likely to call in the systems professional for major problems and are well trained to serve as the users' representative on larger projects. The programs, however, do tend to lose some steam after the first easy improvements are made.

Those organizations that have paid little attention to their clerical procedures for many years should seriously consider the use of work simplification. The accumulation of the benefits of many small projects can have a major impact upon the productivity of an organization.

Suggestion award systems ask employees for ideas. Superiors are usually restricted from getting awards for proposing changes. The supervisor trained in work simplification is usually more receptive to suggestions and more helpful in evaluating and implementing the ideas. Thus, suggestion awards, work simplification and professional systems groups can complement each other. For those readers particularly interested in work simplification a substantial bibliography is provided at the end of the chapter.

SMALL PROJECT MANAGEMENT

The information systems group itself has many small projects to manage. While most of the techniques for managing such projects have their direct counterparts in the large project, some aspects are different. Among the differences are the analysts involved, the reports, and the implementation.

Project managers for small projects have often been forms analysts, record management analysts, trainee systems analysts, professional analysts between assignments, programmers, supervisors trained in work simplification who showed high systems interest, or systems department secretaries. They come from almost anywhere but have the ability to analyze systems.

The small project is an excellent means of training. It is also a good way of filling the slack time that some jobs have in the forms design and secretarial areas. Some people assigned to small projects will prove failures but the systems manager's experience should help him determine those persons considered competent to handle the projects.

Written reports for small projects are rare. The projects are usually simple enough to use verbal reports. The systems proposal will be given verbally to the systems manager who will add his ideas before it is presented to the supervisor involved.

Small project implementation involving some computer processing will probably use one of the packaged systems. If more extensive programming tasks are required, they will usually be assigned to a programmer analyst for completion. Small projects usually are implemented by the user with occasional assistance from other systems specialists, like the forms designer.

Small project management then, is characterized by the "get in and get out" philosophy of a good surgeon. The patient (user) is left to his own resources to heal with only occasional visits by the surgeon (analyst) to be sure the healing is proceeding as planned.

SUMMARY

Maintenance of installed systems is a necessary and important task of the systems organization. It can be productive or not depending upon the way in which it is managed. Good maintenance is dependent upon good systems design. Well designed modular systems are easier to modify. Most important, well designed systems require less maintenance.

Maintenance projects are usually small and often within the capabilities of personnel with rather limited systems expertise. This chapter suggests the use of trainees, work simplification, and other methods for getting systems improvement returns from other than the professional systems staff.

REVIEW QUESTIONS

1. Why might maintenance tend to increase with the age of the system?
2. Why do some programmers dislike program maintenance?
3. Should anticipated system maintenance be a part of the cost shown in a systems proposal? Why?
4. Develop a list of ten query programs; ten report program generators.
5. Describe the use of the logical operation of any one query language.
6. Define modular design of programs.
7. How can decision tables decrease the time to write programs?

DISCUSSION QUESTIONS

1. Discuss the relationship between the choice of programming language and maintenance staff.
2. Why is there little new literature on work simplification?
3. Given resources to acquire either a query language or implement work simplification, which would you choose for an information system? Why?
4. Discuss the causes of maintenance work.

BIBLIOGRAPHY

Burr, Larry S., "Teaching the SAVE Program," *Journal of Systems Management*, Vol. 23, No. 11, November 1972, pp. 12-17.

Canning, Richard C. (Ed.), "That Maintenance Iceberg," *EDP Analyzer*, Vol. 10, No. 10, October 1972, 13 p.

Devers, Lemuel H., "Work Simplification," *Ideas for Management, 1962*, Cleveland: Association for Systems Management.

Gay, Kermit E., "For Improvement's Sake," *Journal of Systems Management*, Vol. 21, No. 11, November 1970, pp. 32-33.

Gerding, John E., "Work Simplification," *Ideas for Management, 1961*, Cleveland: Association for Systems Management.

Graham, Ben S., Jr., "Work Simplification—It Still Pays Off," *Ideas for Management, 1969*, Cleveland: Association for Systems Management.

Larson, Herbert J., *Work Simplification*, Englewood Cliffs, New Jersey: Prentice-Hall, 1957.

Nadler, Gerald, *Work Simplification*, New York: McGraw-Hill Book Company, 1957.

Neumaier, Richard, "A Look at Work Simplification," *Ideas for Management, 1964*, Cleveland: Association for Systems Management.

Palmer, Alfred L., "Simplifying Work Simplification," *Journal of Systems Management*, Vol. 12, No. 5, September 1962.

Palmer, Alfred L., "Work Simplification—Pattern of a Successful Program," *Ideas for Management, 1963*, Cleveland: Association for Systems Management.

Public Administration Service, "Work Simplification: As Exemplified by the Work Simplification Program of the U.S. Department of the Budget," Washington, D.C. Government Printing Office, 1945.

Ross, Lynne, *Work Simplification in Food Service: Individualized Instruction*, Ames, Iowa: Iowa State University Press, 1972.

Shultis, Robert L., "A Way to Handle Small Jobs," *Journal of Systems Management*, Vol. 13, No. 3, May/June 1962.

Wallace, W. Lyle, "A Practical Approach to Work Simplification," *Ideas for Management, 1965*, Cleveland: Association for Systems Management.

Waltz, Loren E., "A Blueprint for a Work Simplification Program," *Journal of Systems Management*, Vol. 12, No. 6, November 1961.

Watson, Maynard R., "Work Simplification Program," *Journal of Systems Management*, Vol. 11, No. 1, February 1960.

CHAPTER 28

FORMS CONTROL

A Forms Control Department has three justifications for its existence in any business organization. Its first and most important justification is service—to provide the forms necessary to carry on the company's business at economical costs. The second justification is control—to eliminate unnecessary existing forms and to discourage the creation and use of unnecessary forms. The third justification is quality—to keep the forms current with timely content and responsive to conditions.

FUNCTIONS OF FORMS CONTROL

Whether it be a large department, a small unit of a larger service group, or a one-man activity, the forms control function should be a professional service unit, supported by an adequate staff and the tools necessary to carry out its objectives effectively. Its duties are closely associated with information systems, forms production, forms inventory and supply, and forms purchasing functions. Experience has shown the best control of forms is achieved by separating the forms control and forms purchasing functions. The production and supply of forms are usually under the office manager. Wherever placed, the forms control function becomes a group whose main goal is the improvement of forms and procedures.

Report Design Council

An effective and dynamic forms control function will bring the departments of a company into close and effective communication. An effective means of establishing this communication is to arrange for a coordinator or representative from each department to serve on a report design council. Ideas or policies are submitted to this body for approval or review. Problems that arise between departments can be resolved more quickly in the council. Bootleg, inactive and abnormal usage of forms can be controlled by the council's teamwork. The council can be the trainers for the use of new or complex forms. Overall, the council acts to keep paperwork costs down, to anticipate the need for changes or revisions in forms design and as a planning group for forms that affect many departments.

Effectiveness of Forms Control

Every forms control function should be able to justify its cost effec-

583

	This Month	Year-to-Date
Total Operating Costs (excluding form and printing costs)		
Form and Printing Costs		
In-house		
Vendor procured		
Total number of forms in use		
Number of forms evaluated		
Number of forms discontinued		
Number of new forms designed		
Number of forms updated		
Number of forms in process		
Number of rush jobs handled		
Backlog volume		
Number of people on staff		
Dollars saved		

tiveness to the company. Above are some measurements that should be maintained on a monthly or year-to-date basis.

From these figures a grid or matrix report can be made to highlight the cost-effectiveness of the forms control function.

In addition to the above, forms control should develop a dollar savings figure for in-house printing costs versus outside printing costs by obtaining quotations from outside printers and from the in-house facility. The annual quotations should be comparable to the in-house printing operations. Savings from the development of new form designs that reduce clerical effort or the combination of forms should also be shown.

Cost Effective Examples

When ordering forms it usually is cost-effective to combine forms of a similar size since press setup is more a function of size than of copy. For example, if one had three 8½" x 9" forms with quantities of 50,000, 50,000, and 5,000, ordering them in combination would probably result in getting the 5,000 quantity free.

Envelopes ordered in large quantities are sold at a delivered price. Combining orders to reach the minimum quantity saves the substantial shipping costs.

Changing a keypunch source document so that the form is in the same order as the card has increased keypunch productivity by 50%.

A dynamic forms control function pays particular attention to the design of forms going to the company's customers, stockholders and top management people. A poorly designed form sent to a customer or potential customer can contribute to the loss of business. A poorly designed form received by stockholders can cause adverse reaction. Well designed forms seen by top management create a good impression of the forms control section.

The forms control function must be constantly alert to new paperwork techniques that will increase operator activity, increase throughput, eliminate fatigue or reduce cost. It should keep management informed of these cost savings.

RESPONSIBILITIES OF THE
FORMS CONTROL FUNCTION

The major responsibilities of forms control functions are design, reproduction, procurement, storage, inventory and control of forms.

Design of Forms—The forms design responsibility includes the processing of all requests for new, revised or reordered forms, and the review of existing forms for possible elimination, consolidation, standardization and improvement. These responsibilities involve the analysis and design of forms, determination and provision of specifications for paper and printing processes, determination of order quantities, a forms numbering system and the ordering of printing.

1. *Forms Analysis*

This is the process of planning, or deciding WHAT should go on the form and HOW the data should be arranged. It includes consideration of the possible consolidation and standardization of existing forms and evaluation of active forms.

2. *Final Forms Design*

In companies large enough to have typesetting equipment, the forms design responsibility also includes preparation of the final art work. The forms analyst or forms design technician rules the form according to the line weights specified and then has the typist or typesetter create the type for the boxes.

3. Form Specifications

Providing specifications for forms printing is an important responsibility of forms design. This includes determination of paper stock, quantity, printing process, and all other instructions necessary to print the form.

4. Form Numbering

The form number is part of the form's identification. It provides a simple and rapid means of filing the form, and aids in its identification and control. Forms without numbers are immediately suspect as unauthorized. Quite logically, the form numbering responsibility belongs in the department responsible for the control of forms.

Reproduction and Procurement of Forms—Forms reproduction in most organizations falls into two categories: internal and external reproduction. Companies too small to support their own print shop depend on outside sources for their forms.

1. Internal Reproduction

The company print shop is responsible for reproduction of forms as specified by the forms control function. It is also expected to maintain job sheets, cost data, and mats or plates for each form it reproduces, and to destroy any plates or mats when so directed.

2. External Reproduction

Responsibility for procuring specialty and other forms specified by the forms control function which must be ordered from outside suppliers is the job of the Purchasing Department. Many companies make Purchasing responsible for determining the printing sources for all forms including the use of the company print shop.

Purchasing is also responsible for soliciting and selecting bids, negotiating contracts, final checking of proofs, receipt of the forms, return of any art work and submission of samples of the printed form.

Storage and Inventory—The Office Supply Department, or a similar unit is responsible for receiving and storing company forms, filing requisitions for form supplies, and maintaining an inventory control system to assume an adequate supply of forms at all times. When stocks reach the reorder point, it is essential that those responsible for reordering forms in the forms control function be notified promptly. If there is a major change in the usage pattern, or if internal changes are planned, the forms control group can then make adjustments of the reorder quantities.

Forms Control—Obviously, the clearance of all requests for new, revised, or reordered forms through the forms control function is essential to good control. This is an area where top management support is needed!

Control of form requests must be exercised with a good deal of common sense. For example, if the request is for a one-time use and the need is urgent, it is less costly and far more sensible to forego the time-consuming forms analysis activity and provide the forms. This should be the exception rather than the rule, and such exceptions should be few.

Control also is effected through periodic review of existing forms to verify that they are still used and necessary.

CENTRALIZED VERSUS DECENTRALIZED CONTROL

Decentralization of a forms control program depends greatly on the organizational structure of the company. In a rigidly enforced centralized arrangement, all form files are maintained in a central location and all form requests must be processed through the central unit. This affords lower operating costs but there are often time lags in processing requests from remote plant locations.

Decentralized programs are more flexible. Faster processing of form requests and the availability of forms information are important advantages which may more than offset the need for duplicate files and added personnel. Decentralized programs often result in a similar form being developed for several different parts of the organization. This reduces the economy of having one large print run since the set-up costs for printed forms are often much larger than the actual printing costs. If the company has sufficent form volumes, some forms manufacturers will assign a representative to that account to show how economies in form preparation and printing may be achieved.

FORMS CONTROL STAFF

The forms administrator must have a good knowledge of business organization and of the specific clerical operations within the company. The administrator should be thoroughly familiar with office machines and equipment, to take advantage of any savings that are possible by designing forms for specific machines, and the limitations of other machines.

The forms administrator must also know printing processes, comparative costs, paper stocks, forms construction, and the available sources of form supplies. If there are no forms designers on the staff, the forms administrators also must be expert in forms design techniques.

Although the qualifications are much the same as those of the forms administrator, the forms analyst needs especially to be expert in the technical aspects of forms work. A good working knowledge of forms analysis and design, forms production and construction, and familiarity with clerical operations, office machines and other equipment, is most important.

Records and Files

Except for certain basic forms essential to the efficient operation of any forms administration program, the number and type of records used depends upon the size of the company and the scope of its forms program. However, there is no better place to start practicing forms control than in the department responsible for this control by limiting the records and files to only those which are necessary.

The Forms Administration System

Details of the forms administration program and the responsibilities of all departments involved in this operation—the Forms Control Department, Office Supplies or Stationery Department, Purchasing, and the company Print Shop—should be clearly defined in procedures, instructions, or bulletins issued to the entire organization. Instructions also should include operating details—how to request new, revised, or reorder forms and requisition form supplies.

PROCESSING REQUESTS FOR NEW OR REVISED FORMS

Requests for new or revised forms should clear through the Forms Control Department, and a form (Figure 28.1) should be provided for this purpose. Even though this step is made clear in operating procedures there are always those who try to by-pass the forms group and order forms directly from a printer or produce their own forms on reproduction equipment.

Many companies control unauthorized forms by insisting that all forms produced on any type of equipment, within or outside the company, must clear through the Forms Control Department. Other companies go further than this and bring all duplicating equipment into one central location, in or independent of, the company print shop. Since neither the print shop nor office reproduction unit is authorized to honor unauthorized requests for forms, control is improved. Any forms produced spuriously are restricted to interdepartmental use. A more flexible approach, recommended by some forms administrators, permits duplicating equipment only in operating departments where it is required for other purposes.

To control the use of unauthorized forms, departments are asked on a regular basis to submit samples of any forms they reproduce. This approach has the following good arguments to support it:

1. Rigid control of all unauthorized forms is not worth the effort. Detailed clearance of one-shot forms by the forms

Form Requisition

To_____   Date_____19_____

From_____

Quantity_____   Name or Form No._____

Trimmed Size: height_____   width_____   Start numbering at _____

To fit Envelope: size_____   ☐ Plain ☐ Outlook   ☐ Hold type form   ☐ Have form plated

PAPER STOCK					COLORS OF INK		
COPY #	COLOR	WEIGHT	FINISH	GRADE	FRONT	BACK	NUMBERS
1							
2							
3							
4							
5							
6							
7							
8							

BINDING	PUNCHING, ETC.	HOW USED	HOW FILLED IN
☐ RULE	☐ SCORE	☐ CARD FILE	☐ PEN
☐ FOLD	☐ PERFORATE (Pin, Slot, Press)	☐ VISIBLE FILE	☐ PENCIL
☐ PAD ⎰ ____SHEETS	☐ PUNCH_____IN. HOLES	☐ LETTER FILE	☐ PICA TYPEWRITER
☐ STITCH ⎱ ____SETS	#_____ON_____IN. CENTERS	☐ VISIBLE BOOK	☐ ELITE TYPEWRITER
☐ STRING	☐ DIE CUT	☐ POST BINDER	☐ SPIRIT DUPLICATOR
☐ WIRE	☐ RULE CUT	☐ RING BINDER	☐ GELATIN DUPLICATOR
☐ GUM STRIP	☐ ROUND CORNER	☐ SPECIAL BINDER	☐ STENCIL DUPLICATOR
☐ CARBON SHEET	☐ SPECIAL SLOTTING	☐ CLIP BOARD	☐ OTHER METHODS

Miscellaneous:

Deliver to_____ Attention of_____

On or before _____ 19 ____   ☐ Wrap ☐ Carton   Single Forms
                                      ☐ Band ☐ Case   _____Sets _____to Package

Special Instructions:

Department _____

Signed _____

FIGURE 28.1

group may result in needless delay and a slowdown of the department's operations.

2. When regular systems studies are made the unauthorized forms turn up and can be dealt with.

3. By requesting samples of all forms run off in a department necessary corrective action can be taken before too much damage is done by the use of any particular form.

The usual procedure for requesting a new form is for the requesting supervisor or systems analyst to prepare a rough sketch of the desired form and submit it with the form request to the Forms Control Department. The forms analyst then checks the functional file to see if an existing form will serve the same purpose. If there is, he reviews it with the requestor and revises the existing form to include the new needs. The new form now serves two purposes.

If no similar form exists, the request goes through the forms analysis and design process. After the design is approved, a form number is assigned and entered in the form number record. The rough design is then turned over to the forms designer for preparation of the final art work.

Forms printing specifications are prepared and submitted to Purchasing. Whenever type must be set, the printer should submit proofs for approval before printing. Checking these form proofs is a very important responsibility, with the prime user or customer being asked to review and initial the proof.

NUMBERING FORMS

Forms numbering systems vary so widely it is impossible to describe them all. Their purpose is to provide quick identification and implement ordering, storing, and requisitioning. Some of the more common forms numbering techniques are:

1. Straight Numbering
    Generally considered the best, this method simply assigns numbers on a straight one-two-three basis. Numbers are easy to assign and remember. The storage problems are simplified.

2. Numbering by System
    Forms may be numbered to tie in with the systems in which they are used. This is most common where the function file is set up on a systems basis. One way to do this is to use two digits for the system, e.g., 10-Accounts Receivable, 47-Employee Benefits, 48-Payroll. Two more digits then complete the form number. For example, Payroll forms would be numbered 4801, 4802, and so on.

This system has the advantage of keeping the numbers simple and indicating at a glance the system in which the form is used.

3. Number on an Organizational Basis

Organization charts or departmental classifications may be used as the basis for forms numbering. The first digit indicates the division or major department, and the next digit the department or section. Two more digits usually suffice for the form number, e.g., 4000-Sales, 4400-Advertising, 4403-third Advertising form.

Like the systems numbering method, these numbers are easy to use and remember, but not as easy to administer as in the straight numbering method. This system can easily be obsoleted when a company goes through a re-organization that changes departmental alignments.

4. Additional Codes

Letters or numbers frequently are used before or after the form number for various other classification purposes. Actually, there is no limit to the possibilities.

Undoubtedly, there is some justification for assigning prefix codes to designate divisions of the company. Usually, identifying letters are used for this purpose and may be the first letter or the first two letters of the division's name or location, as:

E-2605	Eastern Division
LA-3162	Los Angeles Branch
W-4638	Western Division

Some companies include a suffix code with the form number to indicate the type of form construction, or one digit of the number may be used for this purpose. Retention periods for forms also are designated by letter or number, or both, as: 305-6M for six months, 4382-2Y for two years, and so on.

Quantity printed and date of order frequently are shown after the form number, as 3926-3M-6/75. The date may have some value in indicating whether the latest version of a form is being used. The quantity information should be readily available in the form folder or on the traveling requisition, which is referred to for ordering purposes.

Another practice is to show date of latest revision after the form number, or to use a numerical or alphabetic code for the purpose. Here again, the revision date has some value in quickly spotting outdated versions of a form. One way to show revisions is to add after the form number the letters "Rev." and the month and year of the revision, as: 296 Rev. 6/74. Other methods utilize a suffix letter or number, as 331-a or 5632 Rev. 2.

All of these devices, although helpful to the forms staff, can add confusion to the ordering, requisitioning, and stocking of forms. Simplicity should be a major criterion in the selection of a forms numbering system.

FORMS PROCUREMENT

Practice varies somewhat between companies, but it is generally agreed that the purchasing agent or buyer should procure all specialty forms and all other forms which cannot be reproduced economically in the company print shop. The forms analyst should sit in on discussions with the printers in case of questions or problems, and keep abreast of changes or innovations in reproduction processes, paper stocks, carbon, etc.

Beyond specialty forms procurement, there is a divergence of opinion concerning responsibility. One approach permits the print shop manager to decide which forms to print and which ones to turn over to Purchasing for outside production. Another approach is to have standards established for quantities beyond which internal reproduction is not economical. The forms group is permitted to only order directly from the company print shop within these limitations. Other orders go through Purchasing.

An important part of the forms procurement activity, and one which can effect considerable savings in forms costs, is contract buying. This is buying in quantity based on an annual contract. Bids are solicited for printing standard forms and envelopes in large quantities. For example, a contract may be negotiated for all snapset forms, all envelopes, or all tags. Quantity or contract buying sometimes poses storage problems, unless the contract calls for drop shipments to various locations or the printer agrees to do the job in installments.

When a company has many divisions, branches, or plants, quantity buying offers definite price advantages. Usually, the prices negotiated are better than those obtained by each location buying in small quantities. Even when certain large form users can obtain better prices locally than those offered in a contract, it may be necessary to insist that they purchase their forms requirements under contract. If their volume is very heavy, elimination of their requirements from the contract may mean a greater increase in the cost for all locations than the savings which that one location can effect by buying locally. Flexibility is required here.

Forms procurement also involves the consideration of processes used in printing forms. This is an important responsibility because printing results and costs hinge partly on the printing process used. Since the forms analyst is better acquainted with the equipment to be used in processing the form and the problems relating to its processing, and because he must give these factors consideration when preparing the form's specifications, he is the logical one to determine the printing process for each form.

INVENTORY CONTROL OF FORMS

Control of forms inventory is just as difficult as control of items for production. Forms must be available when needed. Conversely, over-stocking must be avoided because of possible changes or obsolescence of forms and because investment in unnecessarily large quantities of forms is undesirable. Use of the economic order quantity is appropriate here.

Forms inventory control usually is a function of office supplies, but is so closely related to the forms control function it is included here.

There are three basic methods of forms inventory control.

1. Perpetual inventory method.

This method requires a stock record for every form, and records the form's orders, receipts, issues, and balance on hand. The record shows stock position at all times, reflects usage and is a ready reference for orders placed or not placed. Where requests for balance on-hand are frequent and quantities stocked are large, the uses may more than offset the considerable amount of work necessary to keep the record current. Another advantage is that inactive forms can be easily and quickly spotted.

2. Periodic physical count method.

Physical count of forms is taken periodically and recorded on an inventory card or sheet, which may also show orders and receipts. Individual stock issues are not recorded. This method requires a minimal amount of record-keeping, but inventory counting is time consuming. Shortages may also occur between counts, but the system may be adequate where stock form quantities are small and approaching shortages quickly spotted.

3. Packaged inventory method.

A safety quantity for each form is packaged separately and labeled or tagged so that it will stand out clearly from all other packages. Placed at the bottom of the form supply, the reorder process is set in motion when that package is reached.

When quantities are too large to permit wrapping the safety

quantity in one package, large tickets may be placed between two packages at the reorder point and folded down over the lower package. A detailed record of stock issues is unnecessary with this system, yet the flagging of reorder points minimizes the possibility of shortages. This method does not reveal quickly the balance on hand or monthly usage.

Frequently, a traveling requisition is used with the packaged inventory method. This serves as a requisition for the printing or ordering of a new supply of forms, and carries a record of orders and receipts.

A small group of forms represents the greater part of total cost and common form elements appear on the greater part of forms printed. This suggests that one inventory system might be used for some forms and another system for the rest of the forms. For example, blank checks may be controlled by both quantity and check number, invoices by a perpetual inventory system and stationery by packages.

OBSOLESCENCE OF FORMS

Forms supplies or stock records should be checked every six or twelve months for inactive forms. The office supplies function is in the best position to check forms activity and report any forms which show no withdrawals in the period covered. The forms control function then checks user departments to determine whether or not the form is obsolete. It is possible that infrequent or no withdrawals over a six-month or one-year period are caused by overstocking in the user departments.

Activity can also be checked by reviewing the order record. Most forms are ordered in six-month or one-year quantities, so any form not reordered in a year should be investigated.

All forms should be reviewed with the major users once every 18 months to uncover obsolescence, need for revision or need for improvement. It is not unusual to find up to 20% obsolescence of forms.

THE FUNCTIONAL FILE

A forms control program cannot be completely effective without a functional file. It is the most important tool in forms analysis, design and control. The most common types of functional files use three categories to describe each form—subject, operation/condition, and function.

SUBJECT	OPERATION/CONDITION	FUNCTION
Automobile	Accident of	To report
Cash	Deduction of	Authorize
Employment	Inspection of	Apply for
Equipment	Inspection of	Schedule
Overtime	Allowance of	Authorize

Subject

The form's subject may be a tangible or intangible subject (machinery, illness), or a person (employee, visitor). The subject is most important in filing. Cross indexing should be used in doubtful cases.

Operation/Condition

Not every form needs an operation or condition descriptor. This descriptive connects the subject and function, and should be used only when absolutely necessary. For example, an employment application can be adequately classified without an operation or condition, but there are so many different types of cash categories that each must be clearly identified. For example:

SUBJECT	OPERATION/CONDITION	FUNCTION
Cash	Deduction of	To Authorize
Cash	Payment of	To Record
Cash	Receipt of	To Acknowledge
Cash	Receipt of	To Record

Function

The function explains what is supposed to happen to the subject or operation when the form is used. The most commonly used functions are:

Acknowledge	Claim	Order
Agree	Estimate	Record
Apply	Follow-up	Request
Authorize	Identify	Report
Cancel	Instruct	Route
Certify	Notify	Schedule

Unfortunately, the persons who classify the forms cannot always remember how they classified them, making their location difficult. For example, an overtime authorization might be classified either of two ways:

SUBJECT	OPERATION/CONDITION	FUNCTION
1. Employee	Overtime (of)	To Authorize
2. Overtime	—	To Authorize

If all forms having to do with employees are to be grouped together, the first method must be used. Otherwise the second is adequate, since "employee" is understood. When each subject, operation/condition and function are clearly defined, there will be less confusion when someone else must operate the system.

There are numerous methods of classifying forms in what are called functional files. All of the arrangements below have certain common disadvantages. When collecting similar forms for possible combination and/or standardization, there is no way of finding all the forms in the applicable category without reviewing each form folder. Forms pertaining to a particular system also can't be collected without each folder, unless it is known in advance what forms are involved. Finally, except by chance, it is impossible to spot duplications.

1. Departmental Classification

Forms are grouped according to their using departments, i.e., Accounting, Engineering, Inspection. While classifications indicate the function of the departments, they bear no relation to form functions. The major problem with this system is that many forms cross departmental lines or are general use forms.

2. Form Titles

Forms may be arranged alphabetically by title. However, where this method is used it is more likely to serve the same purpose as the numerical file.

Another grouping, based on titles, simply uses the title as a guide to the form function. It might look like this:

> Agreements
>   Employee Agreement
>   Secrecy Agreement
> Applications
>   Credit Application
>   Employment Application

This comes closer to a true functional classification, but poses many problems. Most important, a large number of forms (particularly spurious ones) have no title or the titles may be meaningless, or worse yet, misleading.

3. Types of Forms

Forms are grouped by type (envelopes, labels, snapsets, tags).

Classifications again bear no relation to the form's function. They merely describe the form construction.

4. Systems Groups

Using the major functions of business (Accounting, Finance, Marketing, Personnel, Production, etc.), approximately 40 or 50 systems groups can be classified. For example, some systems groups in the Accounting function are Accounts Payable, Accounts Receivable, Credit and Collections, and Payroll. Forms are classified according to the system in which they are used:

FORM	SYSTEMS GROUP
Employee Earnings Record	Payroll
Purchase Order	Purchasing
Employee Requisition	Personnel
Customers Invoice	Billing
Form Specifications	Forms Control

When the form's function is ignored, this classification cannot be considered a true functional file. This classification system may serve the purpose better than a functional file.

In every forms analysis activity, all related forms in the procedure must be considered and grouped together by function regardless of the different systems represented. The analyst must know in advance what forms are in each system, and can use the functional file index to find them. Similar forms would be scattered among many categories. In a systems file they would all be grouped under a title such as Employee Recruitment and no further searching would be necessary. Forms grouped by system are more likely to offer combination and standardization possibilities than forms grouped by function. For example, one can quickly find in the sales order processing system a sales order, order acknowledgment, production order, shipping notice, and invoice, which can be combined into one form set. Since each of these forms has a different function, they would be scattered throughout the functional file.

The systems file is easier to install and maintain because there are far fewer subjects (perhaps 50 systems groups) than in the functional file (250 groups), and each form needs to be classified only once under the system(s) in which it operates. The functional method considered the three classifications—subject, operation/condition, and function—which had to be defined in writing. In the systems method, only the system has to be defined. Cross-indexing to the numerical file is not necessary in the systems file if the form numbers are assigned on a systems basis.

The chief disadvantage of the systems file is that it does not permit inclusion of forms from other systems which could be combined or standardized with some of those under study. This must be weighed against the cost disadvantage of installing and maintaining the functional file.

APPLICATIONS OF THE FUNCTIONAL FILE

The two important reasons for having a functional file are for checking form requests, and the ability to analyze existing forms for combination, standardization, and/or improvement.

Checking Form Requests

When a request for a new form is received, the functional file is checked for any existing forms which serve the purpose of the requested form. If there is a similar form, the requestor is encouraged to use it.

In a request for a revised form, the form folder is checked to see if any other forms in the system will be affected by the revised form. Here's where the systems file really pays off, because all forms in each system are grouped together.

If a functional file is used, the analyst must first determine what forms are in the system. This information may be available on the original form request or data sheet in the form folder, or from tab listings. Before any form revisions can start, all other using departments must be checked to find out what effect the requested revisions may have on them.

Analyzing Existing Forms

A continuing process in any Forms Control Department is the study of existing forms for possible standardization, combination, and design improvement. The functional file aids in these studies:

1. Forms Design Improvement

Improvement in redesigning forms which can't be standardized or combined with other forms is important for the very costly and heavy usage forms. After selecting the form to be improved, the forms analysis process is used to question the form itself, each item on it, and each copy including multiple sets. When the questioning process is finished, there probably will be fewer items on the form which will require a redesign.

2. Forms Standardization

Although a form request may bring to light a need for forms standardization, this is not the only means of discovering such opportunities. The functional file will reveal many standardization possibilities. In a company where little forms standardization has been done, there might be 20 to 30 forms in a single category.

The first step in forms standardization is to determine the recurring data on all forms. Some automatically will be returned to the folder because they are unique. The challenge is to combine in a standard format all the similar data with whatever other data survives the questioning process on each form.

3. Forms Combination

Here again, the functional file pays off, because the most logical place to look for combination possibilities is in a system. Purchasing and billing forms are two of the most common form combinations. The purchase order, acknowledgement, and receiving forms can be combined into one form. In billing, the sales order, order acknowledgement, shipping order, shipping notice, packing slip (if any) and invoice copies are often combined in one set. Where production is based on the order rather than taken from stock, the production order also may be included in one set.

The advantage, in addition to the number of forms eliminated, is the reduction of clerical effort. Common data is entered on the set of forms in one operation. Using separate forms requires several different preparations of the same data.

METRICATION

For some time to come forms control will have to keep an eye on the effects of the move towards metric measure (metre) in paper sizes versus the inch measure currently in use. Paper converters can easily vary the length of a paper sheet over continuous forms press equipment to accommodate metric measure. However, paper widths on a press are not as easily adjusted. Presses are generally designed to accommodate widths of a fixed nature. These widths are of a standard nature that provide favorable press runs for the manufacturing facilities. It is doubtful that there will be any stampede towards metrication in the forms area for some time. Length yes, width perhaps. Forms designers, however, will have to accommodate both metric and unit measure in appropriate working areas of a form.

SUMMARY

The forms control function has been shown to be a part of the larger forms administration activity of an organization. The control function is essentially a systems job and is often located in the systems organization. The work done by the forms analyst is of the same type as in any other systems project. Small projects may involve only a fraction of an analyst's time, but their purpose is the same as for large projects—a more effective organization.

In large organizations people will specialize in forms control. In smaller systems groups the forms control tasks will be a part of the duties of each analyst.

The information systems manager usually has many requests to do small jobs. As was described in Chapter 27, getting the small jobs done often conflicts with efforts on major projects. One major source of talent for handling the small jobs is the forms control unit.

REVIEW QUESTIONS

1. Why should the forms control unit keep records of forms costs and savings?
2. What kinds of forms are best suited for internal reproduction? For outside printing services?
3. What are the advantages and disadvantages of tight control of forms in an organization?
4. When wouldn't one use a straight forms numbering system?
5. Why wouldn't one combine forms procurement, forms control, forms production, and forms storage in the same department?

DISCUSSION QUESTIONS

1. Discuss the reasons for and against the centralization of forms control.
2. Where the economic order quantity formula is:

$$EOQ = \sqrt{\frac{2 \times V \times O}{C \times I}}$$

   V = number of forms per year
   O = order cost
   C = cost per form
   I = inventory carrying charge

   Assume that the order cost is $15, the volume is 100,000 forms per year, each form cost $.05, and the inventory carrying cost is 20%, what is the economic order quantity?
3. Discuss the impact of multi-plant locations on the functional forms file.
4. How large must an organization be to afford forms specialists?

BIBLIOGRAPHY

Reference Books

Agnew, Peter L., and James R. Meehan, *Clerical Office Practice,* South-Western Publishing Company, Cincinnati, Ohio, 1961.

Aspley, J. C., editor, *Office Administration Handbook,* The Dartnell Corporation, Chicago, Illinois, 1967.

Birn, Serge A., Richard M. Crossan, and Ralph W. Eastwood, *Measurement and Control of Office Costs,* McGraw-Hill Book Company, Inc., New York, 1961.

Grillo, Elmer V., *Control Techniques for Office Efficiency,* McGraw-Hill Book Company, Inc., New York, 1963.

Hicks, Charles B., and Irene Place, *Office Management,* 2nd ed., Allyn and Bacon, Inc., Boston, Massachusetts, 1962.

Osteen, Carl E., *Forms Analysis,* Stamford, Office Publications, Inc., 1969.

Place, Irene, and Estelle L. Popham, *Filing and Records Management,* Prentice-Hall, Inc., Englewood Cliffs, New Jersey, 1966.

Terry, George R., *Office Management and Control,* 6th ed., Richard D. Irwin, Inc., Homewood, Illinois, 1970.

Reference Articles

Aldrich, W. S., "Using Self-Adhesives for Office Labeling and Marking," *Office,* Vol. LXVIII, September, 1968, pp. 171-173 +.

"Business Forms and Controls," *Dun's Review and Modern Industry,* Vol. LXXXVI, September, 1965, pp. 146-148 +.

"Business Systems and Forms," *Dun's Review and Modern Industry,* Vol. LXXXVIII, September, 1966, pp. 151 +.

Carey, L. C., "Quality Forms, *Journal of Systems Management,* Vol. 23 No. 6, June, 1972, pp. 28-30.

Field, David D., "Reports Control—No Longer an Enigma," *Records Management Quarterly,* July, 1968.

Floyd, H. A., "Ask Questions to Cut Forms Cost," *Supervisory Management,* Vol. XIII, August, 1968, pp. 37-39.

Kish, J. L., "Selection of Forms Papers," *Data Systems News,* Vol. IX, June 10-24, 1968, pp. 18-19.

Knox, Frank, "Forms: How to Buy and Store Them," *Administrative Management,* June, 1969.

"Label Simplifies Identification," *Administrative Management,* Vol. XXVII, August, 1968, p. 29.

Leahy, E. J., and C. A. Cameron, "Paperwork Explosion: Can We Control It?" *Nations Business,* Vol. LIII, September, 1965, pp. 102-104 +.

Marien, R., "Is Your Forms Control Program in Trouble?" *Office,* Vol. LXIV, July, 1966, pp. 88 +.

Miller, F. G., "Managing Forms," *Journal of Systems Management,* Vol. 23, No. 8, August, 1972, pp. 27-29.

"NCR Introduces Central Information File for Banks," *Management Services,* Vol. V, July, 1968, p. 10.

O'Brien, R. J., "Machine Processing Makes ISO Forms Standards Obsolete," *Office,* Vol. 70, No. 9, September, 1969, pp. 64-66.

"Packaging and Labeling Standards Speed Order Processing and Inventory Control," *Distribution Manager,* Vol. LXVII, May, 1968, pp. 37-42.

Patmore, C. W., "Forms Control," *Management Accounting,* Vol. XLVIII, April, 1967, pp. 20-22.

Peck, D., "Business Forms and Their Control," *Administrative Management,* Vol. XXVII, October, 1966, pp. 70-72 +.

Powell, D., "Why a Forms Control Program?" *Systems,* Vol. VII, July, 1966, pp. 38 +.

Staggs, E. W., "Maybe It's Your Forms," *Journal of Systems Management,* Vol. 23, No. 3, March, 1972, pp. 8-12.

Van Talge, Louise C., "Organizing a Forms Control Program," *Records Management Quarterly,* April, 1969.

Wulff, P., "Buy Better By Cutting Paperwork," *Purchasing,* Vol. LXV, July 11, 1968, pp. 56-58.

CHAPTER 29

RECORDS MANAGEMENT

The elements that cost in a typical records management operation are filing clerks, files, shelves, storage boxes, microfilm, transportation to vital storage areas, space utilization, etc. Although these costs usually total less than 1% of sales for the typical corporation, they are very substantial costs and are an important area of concern for the systems analyst.

More important than the cost of the files is the information contained in them. The availability or unavailability of vital information from files has resulted in winning or losing law suits, anti-trust cases, and consumer goodwill.

Records management includes the following activities:
1. Record creation, carbon copies, etc.
2. Forms control.
3. Reports management and control.
4. Filing and retrieval of active records.
5. Filing and retrieval of inactive records.
6. Records retention.
7. Vital records.

In previous chapters we have discussed the first three records management activities listed above. This chapter concentrates on the filing, retrieval and retention activities of records management. However, first it is important to consider the placement of the records management function within the organization.

RECORDS MANAGEMENT IN THE ORGANIZATION

Records management activities can be broadly classified as either operational or analysis. Operational tasks include filing, retrieval and retention. Analysis tasks focus on the choice of filing equipment, search techniques, retention schedules and similar activities.

In most organizations both records management functions report to the office manager although the analysis function may report to the systems manager.

In designing a system, the systems analyst must consider the filing, retrieval and retention of all the records created by the system. Since the knowledge required to design records management systems is extensive, systems analysts tend to specialize in the records management analysis function. Assigning a records analyst to the systems manager tends to reduce communications with others involved in the filing and retrieval of records. Offsetting this disadvantage is the fact that more analysis will be performed when the analyst reports to the systems manager rather than reporting to a line organization with the filing and retrieval operations involvement. This situation is routine and restricts creative planning. The benefits of better planning that result from the records analyst being assigned to the systems manager more than offset the disadvantages of poor communications.

A Files Performance Index

In a major change in its organization, The Port of New York Authority abandoned its central files operation for decentralized records keeping with centrol controls. This resulted in assigning responsibility for operating files stations, evaluating, guiding and improving the performance of technical files personnel to middle management administrators who had little or no records management background.

A problem, which was not obvious at the beginning, was how to assure management that the individual files stations were performing efficiently, that each was properly staffed, and that the new records system was serving the organization properly. The answer was to design a simple model that could measure files performance objectively.

There are three separate tasks in the design of a performance standard. First, the real purpose of an operation must be determined. Second, those elements of the operation which affect significantly the achievement of the purpose of the operation and which are capable of measurement must be found. Third, a scale must be created against which actual performance can be checked. Like the ammeter in a car, a performance standard should tell management at a glance whether a system is functioning properly or whether the system needs attention.

To convert the raw "cost per request" to a true performance index, a scale was now required. Operational data were obtained on a files installation that the National Records Management Council had rated as one of the best that it had found in the course of several years of study. This files operation, consisting of a supervisor and 12 clerks with salaries totaling $45,000, processed an average of 37,500 files requests each year for a cost per request of $1.20.

Salaries vary with organizations, geography, time and other factors. Wages must therefore be adjusted to that of a standard to obtain a universally applicable performance index. Assuming a normal distribution of salaries and duties in the control installation, the average annual salary was $3461.50. For convenience, this figure was rounded off to $3500. Now the cost of a request could be compared against an acceptable standard by the following formula:

$$\text{Cost per request} = \frac{\$3500\ P}{R}$$

where "P" is the number of full-time and part-time files personnel expressed in man-years, "R" is the number of file requests per year, and "cost per request" is the Files Performance Index (FPI).

To make this simple calculation useful under varying conditions, several refinements were introduced. First of all, the $1.20 standard denoted an excellent operation—one of the finest observed. It was necessary therefore to establish a minimum level of files performance that management should accept. Arbitrarily, it was decided that 80 percent of the basic standard should be the lower limit of performance for the Port Authority. Converting this to cost per request, the minimum level rose to $1.44 ($1.20 × 120 percent) which was rounded off to $1.45.

The next refinement attempted to take into account the difference between a central files installation and a series of decentralized files stations. The latter are small and usually contain one or two employees. In comparison to the larger unit where the problem of providing back-up personnel for fluctuating workload or absence is not so acute, the smaller files station suffers. It must either add a records clerk and increase its "cost per request" because of a higher nonproductive time or do without and reduce the quality and quantity of service it provides. Furthermore, the training of new records personnel is more critical in terms of maintaining good service in a small unit than in a large one. Taking all factors into consideration, it was estimated that the adverse effect would amount to approximately 15 percent, and an FPI for small units (up to four persons) was established between the limits of $1.35 and $1.60.

The final adjustment was concerned with numeric filing. The control installation processed material according to a subject classification system. However, the Port Authority files some material (e.g., vouchers) numerically, and a performance index for this operation had to be established. Studies have indicated that numeric files can be handled at least 25 percent faster than subject files (some claim up to 40 percent faster). On the other hand, filing and finding do not constitute the entire records operation, though in the case of numeric files, they constitute the major activity. Personal observation indicated that "file and find" was about 80 percent of the total records operation and two new Files Performance Indices were constructed (Figure 29.1). For large units filing by number alone, the FPI ranges from $0.95 to $1.20; for small units, it is $1.10 to $1.30.[1]

Standard Files Performance Index

(IN DOLLARS PER REQUEST)

LARGE FILE UNITS (5 or more clerks)		EVALUATION OF PERFORMANCE	SMALL FILE UNITS (1-4 clerks)	
Filing by Subject	Filing by Number		Filing by Subject	Filing by Number
$1.20	$0.95	EXCELLENT	$1.35	$1.10
1.45	1.20	GOOD	1.60	1.30
2.50	2.00	POOR	2.75	2.25
3.75	3.00	MAJOR PROBLEM	4.00	3.50

FIGURE 29.1

Since the FPI was devised, it has been used primarily for evaluating the need for additional staff. Similarly, an analysis of the FPI by months for several files stations can reveal seasonal fluctuations that permit the elimination of one or more positions through inter-files station transfers.

However, the FPI can also indicate that the file unit is not serving management properly, or as it wants to be served. The Files Performance Index merely shows that the files activity needs or does not need management's attention. The yardstick does not reveal what is wrong; that detail is left to the specialist to find and correct.

FILING AND RETRIEVAL OF ACTIVE RECORDS

The primary question in filing any material should be "what later

---

[1]The calculation: (80 percent of standard × 75 percent) + (20 percent of standard) or ($1.20 × .8 × .75) + ($1.20 × .2) = $0.72 + $0.24 = $0.96.

The use of electronic information retrieval systems will introduce the factors of equipment costs and maintenance into the calculation of the FPI. In addition, data processing personnel costs must be included with that for records personnel. A suggested revised equation which the writer would appreciate being tested and reported on by information retrieval managers is:

$$FPI = \frac{\$3500 \ (P_1 + P_2) + E}{R}$$

where P_1 and P_2 represent the man-years of information retrieval or records and EDP personnel respectively, and E is the annual cost of the computer and auxiliary units, including maintenance charges. This equation should permit comparing two mechanical systems or a mechanical system with a manual one.

use will be made of the material?" The following list states criteria to be considered:

1. Correspondence files confirm that a letter was mailed and the details of the letter.
2. Important corporate actions require a file documenting what actions were taken and why.
3. Insecurity has caused organizations to document every action ever taken. These are called "defensive files."
4. Recent anti-trust convictions have resulted from the use of an organization's files against itself. It seems inconceivable that organizations would file material that would convict them of criminal acts but it happened.
5. The first major records management decision, then, is whether any material should be filed at all.

As an example of the filing decision consider the handling of personal mail. One day's mail received by the author contained several conference flyers, book advertisements, periodicals, copies of letters to publishers requesting examination copies of books being considered as texts, minutes of a faculty committee meeting and student papers. None of the conferences was of interest and so was thrown out. One of the book announcements was of interest so the department secretary was asked to write a letter requesting an examination copy. The rest of the book advertisements were discarded. Periodicals were filed on shelves in the office to read later. Copies of requests for examination copies were discarded. Minutes of committees, which had been sent for information, were discarded. Student papers were graded and returned to the students. Certainly some of the material discarded or returned could have had retention value. For example, it is known that a small portion of the students cheat by copying term papers presented in a previous term. If a faculty member had a file of previous papers the evidence would be there to convict the cheating student but the frequency does not warrant keeping such files.

One of the more interesting examples of decisions not to file material is the practice of mail order houses to return all the documents relating to an order to the customer. The customer with a complaint must send in all the prior correspondence with the complaint. Operating in this fashion, the mail order house eliminates the need to keep a customer file and to retrieve individual orders from that file. The filing and retrieving problem, then, is that of the customer not that of the supplier.

A general rule is to reduce files to that minimum set likely to have value in the future. This is an easy rule to state but a difficult one to apply, for future events determine the value of current documents. Until forecasting becomes precise, people will cautiously over-file.

TYPES OF FILES

A type of common business file is shown in Figure 29.2. Since two, four and five drawer files occupy the same amount of floor space, many organizations have standardized on five drawer files. Some of

Five Drawer Files

FIGURE 29.2

the optional features of files include locks, fire protection, and extra width to accommodate legal size papers.

The horizontal file (Figure 29.3) is appropriate for frequently referenced forms and materials. Retrieval and storage are both fast. Quick reference to small files such as telephone numbers, names and addresses is accomplished by using a rotary file. Purchasing and Personnel Departments are frequent users of rotary files.

Filing systems are manufactured for special types of documents

A Horizontal File

FIGURE 29.3

such as 5 x 8 cards or Hollerith cards with the file drawers being easily removable for easy transfer to the work station. More elaborate, motorized systems are available for large files where access time is important. Generally cost and retrieval time are inversely related.

Some less expensive filing equipment is available for archival storage. The principal methods include storage boxes, shelves and microfilm. Where volume is high and retrieval is low such methods should be considered. Cost studies have shown that microfilming, where the document is destroyed, equals the cost of keeping the document in about seven years.

The best way to control unnecessary filing is to require the approval of the records analyst before additional files are purchased. File drawers have been known to contain such things as shoes, galoshes, hats, Christmas decorations, sweaters and bowling balls in addition to company documents. More often than not, an analyst is able to cull enough of the contents of the current files to make purchase of additional files unnecessary.

FILING SEQUENCE

There are many different ways in which information may be filed. The choice of file arrangement depends upon the material and retrieval methods. File sequence methods of particular interest include:

Numerical	Subject
Terminal Digit	Index
Name	Cross Reference

Numeric files are kept in ascending numeric order of the key field. That is, an invoice file might be kept in order by invoice number. An insurance policy might be kept in order by policy number. This filing method minimizes search and training time for filing clerks. However, numeric files require that the code be known before the search begins. This usually requires a name or subject cross index be kept to facilitate those retrieval requests in which the code is missing. Who hasn't experienced the displeasure of a clerk when he did not know our driver's license number, insurance policy number, bank account number, etc. The double search required accounts for the attitude of the clerk. The records analyst should consider the relative frequency of one or two stage retrievals in deciding whether to file by name or number.

Terminal Digit filing is filing by number with one difference. The last one, two or three digits of the key are transposed to the beginning before filing. This concept is somewhat similar to block sorting on unit record equipment. First the items to be filed or retrieved are sorted by blocks or terminal digits. Then the search is normal within the block of terminal digits. Most numeric filing systems add new items at the end of the file. Since 80% of the activity in the file relates to the newest 20% of the items, the file clerks find themselves stumbling over each other in the new part of the file. Also growth occurs at only one spot and decline occurs over the rest of the file, making housekeeping difficult. Large files often are arranged by terminal digit so that the activity will be dispersed over the entire filing area and to minimize the physical movement of records as a result of additions and deletions.

Names are another important filing sequence. The names used may be those of individuals, business organizations, products, titles, etc. The order of filing is alphabetical, a slower and less accurate method of manual filing and retrieval. Tests show clerks make more errors and take longer using alphabetical files. One reason for this is the many different ways of spelling a name that has the same sound (Smith, Smythe, Smyth, Smit, Smidt, Schmit, etc.). All have a similar sound but are found in different places in the file. One solution to this problem is *Soundex*, a coding system (Figure 29.4) developed by Remington Rand. This Soundex system replaces alphabetic characters with numbers. For example, Bird and Byrd are both coded B630. Soundex provides the accuracy of numeric filing without the need for a cross index. The system does require some training and thus, should be used only for large files where the training expenditure can be recovered by operating efficiencies.

File consolidation means that every name in a file does not need a separate folder. For example, a customer order file had 150 names that began with B but 28 B customers represented 85% of the orders. Individual file folders were prepared for each of the 28 with the orders for the remaining 122 placed in a B-Miscellaneous file.

This example is an application of a rule developed by experienced records analysts. *If you don't expect to enter at least twenty items in a file in a year, don't prepare a file folder.* Instead combine categories or set up a miscellaneous file. There can be Other or Miscellaneous folders either for the entire file or for subsections such as the B-Miscellaneous.

Subject files are probably the most useful but most difficult to manage of all types of files. The primary criterion for a good filing system is that the system provide pointers to all of the relevant material on the subject of immediate concern to the file user. Unfortunately, not all subjects are anticipated by the file designer. The skills of a file system designer are those of a library cataloger. All subjects of possible inquiry must be anticipated. This requires that the system design process be participative. A complete understanding of all terms used and past user file requests must be obtained by the records analyst from the file users. A general set of rules for a good subject file is:

1. No subject should have too many or too few documents.
2. It should have an index.
3. It should make liberal use of cross references.
4. It should require minimum retrieval effort for the most frequent inquiries.
5. It should minimize the need to remember the filing scheme.

A hierarchy of subjects is then needed for most schemes. There may be up to fifteen or twenty major subjects with each of these perhaps in a separate file drawer. Within each drawer perhaps twenty folders would be sufficient for the second level of the hierarchy. Rarely would more than a two-level hierarchy be needed.

SOUNDEX® FILE

All "name" records originate from handwriting or speech. When filed alphabetically, names are arranged in sequence according to exact spelling; therefore dependent upon the accurate interpretation of the spoken or handwritten name. Conversely, when filed the SOUNDEX way, varied spellings of the same name or misinterpretations of the handwriting of a name are brought together in ONE file location. The SOUNDEX coding system reduces name filing to the use of ONE alphabetic letter and a three digit code number.

With SOUNDEX the first letter of a surname or company name is NOT coded. The names are arranged alphabetically in 26 letter sections; B for Bayer; H for Harrison; S for Schneider. Within each of the 26 letter sections, SOUNDEX filing employs only six groups of consonant letters. Each of the six groups has a code number used for filing. The code number applies to each letter in its group.

SOUNDEX CODE

GROUP LETTERS AND EQUIVALENTS	CODE NUMBER
b f p v	1
c g j k q s x z	2
d t	3
l	4
m n	5
r	6

The vowels a, e, i, o, u and 3 consonants h, w, y have no number equivalent and are *not* coded. Zero (0) is used to express no consonants following first letter. Example: Day D 000, Shaw S 000 or to complete a 3 digit code number.

Bird, Burd, Berd, Byrd	"B" File section	Guide 630
Bone, Bohn, Boehne, Boan, Bohon, Bown	"B" File section	Guide 500
Dotson, Dodson, Detson, Dudson, Dadson	"D" File section	Guide 325
Hogg, Hoge, Hoag, Haag, Haug, Hooge, Hogue	"H" File section	Guide 200
Marshall, Marchall, Marschall, Merschel	"M" File section	Guide 624
Rex, Reks, Riecks, Ricks	"R" File section	Guide 200
Rhoad, Road, Roed, Rhode, Rohde, Rowd, Rood, Rude, Roat, Root	"R" File section	Guide 300
Siegel, Seagle, Segal, Sigal, Seigall, Siegle, Siegal	"S" File section	Guide 240
Schonnenschein, Sonenshein, Sonenschein Sonnenschien	"S" File section	Guide 552

FIVE SIMPLE RULES FOR CODING

Rule Nc. 1—To code a name use three digits. When no consonants or insufficient code consonants appear in a surname or organization name, add one, two or three zeros to give a three digit code.

Darlington is coded D645 (3 consonants only). Goodyear is coded G360 (add 1 zero). Levy is coded L100 (add 2 zeros). Youhey is coded Y000 (no coded consonants add 3 zeros).

Rule No. 2—Two letters *together* (double letters) are considered as one letter (single letter).

Abbott is coded A130. *Farrell* is coded F640. *Kelly* is coded K400. Ma*nn* is coded M500.

Rule No. 3—Consider any combination of two or more equivalent letters *TOGETHER* as having the same number as a single letter.

Biggs is coded B200. Jackson is coded J250. McCarthy is coded M263. Op*ff*er is coded O160.

Rule No. 4—When the first (initial) letter is immediately followed by the same letter or one or more of *its* equivalent letters (no separators) with the same code number the letters are considered one first letter and not coded.

Czerny is coded C650. *Llewellyn* is coded L450. *Scott* is coded S300. *Sczsatkal* is coded S324.

Rule No. 5—Vowels a, e, i, o, u and the consonant y are separators. Consonants having a code number when separated by vowels or y are coded individually.

Ferrara is coded F660. Ly*l*es is coded L420. McC*l*elland is coded M244. Ash*cr*oft is coded A261. G*r*eenwood is coded G653. Liverwright is coded L162.

ONE RULE FOR FILING

The records are sorted and filed alphabetically by the first letter. After coding the names, the records are sorted and filed in numeric sequence 000 to 666 for each of the 26 letters of the alphabet. The records are then arranged alphabetically between two numeric guides, by first name initial; or first name; or first name and middle initial; or the second unit of an organization name.

Remington Records Retrieval
Remington Office Systems Division Sperry Rand Corporation

FIGURE 29.4

One problem with this arrangement is that it usually results in infrequently used categories.

The specific subjects to be used for any file system are unique. As an illustration of filing speciality, consider the author's system. One file drawer is labeled "Published Papers" and contains completed papers. Another drawer is labeled "SIGCPR" and contains aspects of business related to a Special Interest Group on Computer Personnel Research. A third is labeled "Students" and contains folders for certain graduate advisees, student research projects and reference letters. These three file drawers serve to illustrate the hierarchical nature of personal files.

Index. In one of his early Perry Mason tales, Erle Stanley Gardner described a legal filing system in which each file was numbered. The index then served to decode the file. Without the index the culprit had a very difficult time finding the document of interest.

An index can have significant value even if all files are clearly identified. First the index can be an invaluable training aid to the new employee showing him what information is available and where it is located. Search of a file is certainly facilitated by a good index. As the file grows beyond the cognitive limits of the principal users, the index becomes an essential tool for daily use. In our experience the value of the index grows exponentially with number of subjects.

Cross references should exist both in the files and in the index. In the index there should be an entry for any missing item in the hierarchy giving the other location of the material. Items exist that may be filed in more than one folder. These folders should then be marked "see also _____." The index should also be marked similarly. The cross references then serve the same function as pointers in a file structure to enable the searcher to find all relevant data.

LOCATION OF FILES

Most large organizations will have three levels of files—active, semi-active, and inactive. Generally the active records are filed in the work area and the filing equipment is chosen to provide the most cost-effective access. Thus, the typical office employee has some files at the work location and others in easily accessible cabinets.

Semi-active records, such as last year's correspondence, are usually stored in a central file room. Typically the use of these records doesn't warrant the cost of prime floor space so they are often in the basement. Inactive files are often kept in even less costly space such as a warehouse. As can be seen, there is a relationship between retrieval time and storage cost.

Some organizations work from a centralized set of files, maintaining only an absolute minimum in the work area. This method does eliminate multiple copies of documents and should reduce substantially the cost of carbons and copies. Files tend to be decentralized in large organizations which suggests that a size exists where the time spent in getting to the file exceeds the cost of duplication.

Where an item is filed can influence its security. These security provisions will be discussed in the vital records section of this chapter.

FILING AND RETRIEVAL OF INACTIVE RECORDS

Organization

Inactive records are often kept away from the prime user's work area. This usually means that a separate records staff is established to care for the storage and retrieval of inactive records. This contrasts with the staffing of the active records storage and retrieval function which is usually the responsibility of the user department. The records or filing staff usually report to an office manager responsible for this area.

The responsibilities of the records staff are: filing of new and returned items, retrieval of stored data, indexing of new materials, maintenance of indexes, selection of storage media, and housekeeping of the storage area.

The records management program at the general offices of one company was arranged as shown in Figure 29.5.

One Records Management Program

Active records
    Kept in desk or in area files.
    Area files cleaned out annually and removed to basement.

Semi-active records
    Last six years kept in file cabinets in center of basement.
        Finished, well-lighted space near lunchroom and credit union.
    Older records kept on shelves in unfinished area of basement.

Inactive records
    Kept in low cost warehouse several miles from general office.

Vital records
    Where possible, duplicates were kept in other plants and offices.
    Some records kept in fire resistant safe in general office.

Grandfather records rotated to safe of a plant 150 miles away.

FIGURE 29.5

Space

The records storage area, called a Records Control Center, is usually lower-cost floor space than that given to operating departments. Despite this economy, the space used for records storage is large volume and thus fairly expensive. This has led to several space saving innovations which are discussed in the next section.

Storage Media

The most popular methods of storing inactive records are old filing cabinets, shelves and microfilm, in that order. The old filing cabinets have the advantage of being available; however, they use only about half of the floor-to-ceiling area and thus waste space.

Shelving can be easily constructed from floor to ceiling, using the space efficiently. If the storage is virtually dust-free, the records can be placed directly on the shelves. If dust is a problem, then storage boxes are used. These boxes cost about 10% of file cabinets.

Microfilm can be an attractive alternative to cabinet or shelf storage. Considerations in the use of microfilm are:

1. One roll of microfilm can contain copies of all of the records in a file drawer. Space saving potential is large.

2. Costs to prepare the document, photograph and process the film are substantial. And, unless long storage (in excess of five years) is anticipated, this cost cannot be amortized.

3. Microfilm may or may not be accepted as legal evidence. Generally it is, but exceptions do exist.

4. There is some deterioration of quality of the microfilm image with age, just as there is with paper documents. The National Microfilm Association has established national archival standards for microfilm.

5. Roll microfilm can only be accessed serially, while files of papers can be accessed randomly. Retrieval of paper records requires more physical movement.

6. If microfilm is used to reduce storage cost, then the original records must either be destroyed or placed in an even lower cost storage area. The use of microfilm for vital records is contained in a later section of this chapter.

A major area of cost reduction in the scheduling and inventorying portion of records management is the removing of non-current records from high cost office space and equipment to the records center. Let us consider an equivalent volume of records in terms of cost in a records center and cost in the office area. For example, ten 5-drawer letter-size filing cabinets of records housing some 72 cubic feet of records would occupy 60 square feet of office space. Broken down into terms of 72 cubic feet, it would cost $2.80 a year to maintain a cubic foot of records in the office based upon average office space rentals. Filing equipment would involve $1.60 amortized on a ten year basis—a total of $4.40. The same volume of records in a records center would only require 17 square feet of space—$.52 space and maintenance, $.08 filing equipment, or a total of $.60, a savings per cubic foot of $3.80. This does not include clerical costs which would also be substantially higher in an active office area.

RECORDS RETENTION

The length of time records should be kept is stated in a retention schedule. The following example describes the development of a record retention schedule.

Record Retention Case

A Fortune 500 company with some 10,000 employees in 40 different manufacturing locations had decentralized record keeping. A new comptroller and systems manager determined to make their mark by establishing a new record retention schedule.

Three approaches were used to define the types of records to be retained. First, the literature was searched for the so-called "statutes of limitations" which, by barring certain types of action after a prescribed number of years, eliminate the need to maintain the record. For example, on April 15, 1975 a 1971 income tax return filed before April 16, 1972 is no longer subject to IRS civil audit procedures or refund claims. Similar legal restrictions exist for substantial portions of the records filed by organizations. The federal government also publishes guidelines to record retention schedules.

Second, the records kept by one plant were examined in detail and all records inventoried by type.

Third, using the data gathered in the field trial, a questionnaire was prepared asking for the following data about each record filed:
Department originating
Title or name of record
Kind of copy

Stored with another record?
Order of file
Dates
Quantity
Purposes
What other copies exist?
Frequency of reference by age of record

The data gathered were analyzed. Those records involving substantial volumes of files were examined carefully while the smaller volume items were grouped together and a decision made for the group.

The first criterion was whether the record was necessary to the current operation of the business. If a record was still useful it was kept, regardless of its age. Second, the consequences for the firm of destroying each remaining record were considered. For example, the destruction of a freight bill would have made filing of a freight claim very difficult and represented a potential lost benefit. The firm could control the consequences of this loss by a regular audit of freight bills. The absence of a canceled payroll check could result in a loss of a law suit to an employee who claimed he had not been paid. The filing of a law suit by an employee was not an action that the firm could control.

Third, whatever legal restrictions existed were noted.

Fourth, and most important, the economic consequences resulting from the absence of a particular set of records were evaluated. The degree of the risk and probability that the risked event would occur were both considered.

To illustrate, a voluminous record was canceled payroll checks. These were useful for current operations until the check reconciliation was completed by the auditors. The auditors never asked for checks more than 12 months old. Since the bank microfilmed all checks before returning them, a record of the checks was always available. Federal and State Wage and Hour Laws required that payroll records be kept for four years but not the actual checks. State law required that wage claims be filed within six years. Taking all these factors into account, the decision was made to keep the checks for one year beyond the current year.

It is common to specify the record retention period in this way. This would mean that on July 15, 1975 the records on file would be all the 1974 checks plus those 1975 checks canceled and returned by July 15, 1975.

DECISION MAKING

In the previous case the decision was made by a group of people, called a Records Retention Committee. Commonly this group consists of the records analyst, a member of the legal staff and an executive from the originating department. The records analyst is usually the proponent of the shortest retention schedule. The records analyst is biased against long rows of dusty files. The lawyer usually finds possible contingencies which the others overlooked. The department executive is usually most influenced by memories of those records needed in the past and thus varies from a liberal to a conservative viewpoint. The result is usually a conservative compromise with more records being kept than the economics would justify but with reduced risks. The group's decision may call for records being destroyed sooner than the retention time specified in the statutes of limitations, but the economic considerations make such decisions entirely appropriate.

On the other hand, there are no legal reasons for keeping logs of the visitors to a plant. Yet one company that kept such a log found in a 15-year-old log the evidence to win a patent infringement suit. Often the decision is to keep the records longer than the laws would require. Retention schedules are dictated by the specific situation.

In the example of the corporation that reduced its payroll check retention to 1½ years, one plant of the corporation destroyed 17 truckloads of obsolete records. The other plants in the corporation had less spectacular actions since their retention practices had been better managed.

VITAL RECORDS

Vital records are those records necessary to continue the business after a disaster. Fire, flood, bombs and vandalism are some of the threats to the organization. Loss of just the accounts receivable file has been sufficient to close a company, so vital records protection programs are important.

Types of vital records include:
   Corporate records, charters, by-laws, etc.
   Patents
   Engineering drawings
   Accounts receivable
   Customer lists
   Physical asset list

These usually represent less than 1% of the total records volume. Once the records vital to the continuance of the organization have been determined, the records analyst must find a method of protection. If the record is duplicated elsewhere in the organization and the risk of concurrent loss is negligible, such duplication is sufficient protection. Engineering drawings usually are duplicated elsewhere and corporate records can be easily duplicated. The analyst should do this periodically, storing the duplicates in a distant safe location.

Records that are one of a kind with daily changes are difficult to protect. If that particular file is automated, protection can be achieved by the grandfather-father-son chain described in the next chapter. Otherwise microfilming once a month and storing the records in a safe or vault are the usual precautions.

There are businesses that sell cave space for storage of vital records. These firms appeared on the business scene during America's bomb shelter era. Today remote bank vaults are popular protection sites. The concern for vital records has decreased since, but it is still an important aspect of the job of the records analyst. If a company cannot continue to function because of destroyed records there are no jobs for the surviving employees. Only about 45% of companies are able to restore their business after a major disaster.

RETENTION OF MACHINE-READABLE RECORDS

Machine-readable records are different from paper records in minor retention aspects. Machine-readable records may have particular cost impacts and environmental requirements that will influence the retention schedule decision. The two principal types of these records are punched cards and magnetic tape.

Magnetic Tape

Magnetic tape technology has changed so much in recent years that many firms have tapes in their archives which are recorded at several different densities. The usual solution is to retain the old tapes and equipment, re-recording the most active records in an up-dating process and finally converting the remaining useful tapes.

The extent to which recordings on magnetic tape deteriorate with age is largely unknown. Age deterioration is more a cost problem than a lost record problem. One can copy from an old tape to a new tape at the point where deterioration is significant. The loss then is restricted to the machine time needed to make the copy and the cost of correcting the errors found at the time the copy is made. In many firms the cost of the computer time needed to duplicate tape is large enough to preclude this alternative for most tapes.

For further information on the use of magnetic tapes for archival records the interested student should read Canning (1973).

Punched Cards

A storage area for tapes and cards is usually kept at 68 degrees and 40% humidity. For punched cards, the primary archival problems are warping caused by improper temperature and/or humidity and changes in code structure. This latter problem occurs on magnetic tape as well. Use of an old file requires that the old code book be available. Where economically possible changes in codes should be made to update old card files.

SUMMARY

This chapter has described in general terms the records management function. Records management is an area for "professional" specialization and has developed its own organization—the American Records Management Association. The body of records management knowledge common to its practitioners has only been touched on here. The systems analyst may work in an organization where records management specialists exist. If so, the information in this chapter is sufficient to establish a communication link with the records analyst. The systems analyst will usually ask for advice about file storage media, organization and retention for inclusion in the design. Where such experts do not exist the systems analysts must perform as records analysts. This requires further study of the references provided.

Records are the memory of the organization just as libraries are the memory of our civilization. They are an extremely important aspect of systems design. The design of a system must include answers to where records are to be filed, in what order and for how long. This chapter has shown some of the considerations involved in those decisions.

REVIEW QUESTIONS

1. What are the pros and cons of records management as a career?
2. Compare the cost of standard and horizontal filing equipment.
3. What are some good uses of horizontal files?
4. Give five examples of files that might be organized by terminal digit.
5. Are paper files more or less secure than those kept on magnetic tape? Why?
6. Are paper files more or less private than those kept on magnetic tape? Why?
7. Develop the Soundex code for five classmates or associates. For each code develop another name that would have the same code.
8. Should invoices for the purchase of computers be kept the same length of time as invoices for magnetic tape? Why?

DISCUSSION QUESTIONS

1. Discuss a filing equipment and space policy for a company.
2. Discuss the vital records program of a typical organization.
3. Develop a records retention schedule for a company.
4. Find several places in your community where copies of vital records might be stored. Find the costs of each.

BIBLIOGRAPHY

Avedon, Don M., *Computer Output Microfilm,* National Microfilm Association, 1971, 279 p. (2nd Edition).

Bressler, Matthew F., "Care and Feeding of Punched Cards, The," *DPMA Quarterly,* Vol. 2, July 1966, pp. 30-45.

Canning, Richard G., "Long Term Retention of Data," *EDP Analyzer,* Vol. 11, No. 7, July 1973.

Cavner, J. Paul, "Systems Study of COM, A," *Journal of Systems Management,* Vol. 23 No. 9, September 1972, pp. 24-25.

Collison, Robert Lewis, *Commercial & Industrial Records Storage,* New York: J. deGraff 1969.

Connors, Richard J., "Microfilm: Past, Present and Future," *Infosystems,* Vol. 20 No. 3, March 1973, pp. 39-43.

Corporate Records Retention, New York: Controllership Institute Research Foundation.

Exelbert, Rodd S., "Commercial Records Storage and Underground Vaults," *Information & Records Management,* Vol. 5 No. 5, May 1971, pp. 16-19.

Fullman, Francis A., Jr., "Legal Aspects of Corporate Records Problems," *Information & Records Management,* Vol. 7 No. 9, October 1973, p. 67.

Grawe, Bill, "Open Letter from one C.G.M.I.S., An," *Information & Records Management,* Vol. 7, No. 2, February 1973, pp. 27-30.

Hammel, Wayne, "Computer Output Microfilm Service Bureaus," *Data Management,* Vol. 8 No. 9, September 1970, pp. 140-141.

Harmon, George H., "Throughput Myth?" *Datamation,* Vol. 16 No. 12, October 1970, p. 39.

Kish, Joseph L., Jr., "Effective COM Evaluation," *Computerworld,* Vol. 7 No. 3, January 1973, p. 44.

Macbeth, Charles, "Initiating a Records Management Program," *Journal of Systems Management,* Vol. 24 No. 8, August 1973, pp. 8-13.

Menkus, Belden, "Retention of Data . . . for the Long Term," *Datamation,* Vol. 17 No. 18, September 1971, pp. 30-32.

Mitchell, William E., *Records Retention,* New York: Ellsworth Publishing Company, 1959.

Odell, Margaret K. and Earl V. Strong, *Records Management and Filing Operations,* New York: McGraw-Hill Book Co., 1947.

Records Retention Requirements, Office of the Federal Registrar, Washington: Superintendent of Documents.

Ridge, Warren J., *Value Analysis for Better Management,* New York: American Management Association 1969.

Snyder, Paul D., "Computer Output Microfilm," *Journal of Systems Management,* Vol. 25 No. 3, March 1974, pp. 8-13.

Vital Records Microfilm Retrieval System, Government Data Systems, Vol. 2 No. 3, March/April 1972, pp. 26-27.

CHAPTER 30

SECURITY

Even a small information system represents a substantial investment for a corporation. The total direct and indirect time costs of a small information systems project budgeted for one man-year probably represent an expenditure of $50,000. An average size data file of 20,000,000 characters on one reel of magnetic tape could cost $20,000 to replace. The magnitude of the risks involved in the loss of an information system requires the analyst to carefully consider protecting the system. Figure 30.1 lists the various types of hazards and counter-actions taken to protect information systems.

Hazard	Protection
Natural disaster	Fire, earthquake, flood, etc., protection Redundancy Insurance
People—outside Bombs Electronic invasion	 Guards, access controls Cipher, password
People—inside Fraud Theft Destruction	 Controls Access, guard, employment agreement Access, guard, reinforcers

FIGURE 30.1

EXAMPLES OF SYSTEM LOSSES

The following examples demonstrate the importance of security to systems design and maintenance:

1. A 300-watt bulb in the fire-resistant ceiling of the Pentagon computer installation overheated and caused a fire in 1959. Although only a minor fire, it activated the automatic sprinkler system. The water damage to equipment and thousands of computer tapes and programs was a disaster that took a long time to replace. (Chu, 1971)

2. In 1970 a bomb was exploded outside the computer center at the University of Wisconsin. It resulted in one death plus the loss of $7,500,000 in computer equipment and an estimated 1,300,000 man-hours of data. (Morton, 1970)

3. The 1969 bombing of the computer center at Sir George Wil-

liams University in Montreal destroyed two computers. (Van Tassel, 1971)

4. A raid on the computer center of Dow Chemical Company in Midland, Michigan, in 1970 resulted in the destruction of 10,000 reels of magnetic tape. (Chu, 1971)

5. A morning earthquake in Los Angeles in 1971 shut down most of the computers in the area. Although half were operational by noon, and the remainder by the next morning, the most damage was caused by the power outage. Floating floors protected the small and third generation computers from having the most damage. (Huggins, 1971)

6. An employee in a time-sharing firm accessed the computer of another customer causing a proprietary program to be printed out on his terminal and stole the information. (Huggins, 1971)

7. An employee of the Encyclopaedia Britannica stole and sold tapes containing the Britannica's customer list to a list user. (Morton, 1970)

8. Fire destroyed two 360/50 computers, three System 3 computers, an 1130 and a 360/20 computer in IBM's Program Information Department. The fire also destroyed large quantities of programs stored on punched cards. Programs stored on magnetic tape were protected by a CO_2 system in a tape vault. The information loss was minimized by backup available from other IBM computer centers.

These examples show that security can be a complex problem in an information system. The three major security hazards are: (1) natural disasters, (2) outside people and (3) inside employees. The categories of protection to guard against these hazards are:

Site hardening
Equipment redundancy
File and data redundancy
Insurance
Physical access controls
Electronic access controls
Data controls (discussed in Chapter 26)
Ownership claims
Personnel policies

Each type of protection is discussed in this chapter. However, the determining factor in security is the degree of protection the system requires. Each method of security must be evaluated against the magnitude of loss. Figure 30.2 gives some data about the actual security practices of universities and insurance companies. Obviously, certain precautions seem much more important than others to the user.

Factors Influencing Percent of Security in Universities and Insurance Firms

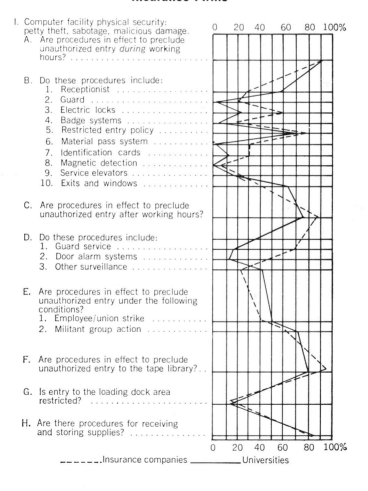

I. Computer facility physical security: petty theft, sabotage, malicious damage.
  A. Are procedures in effect to preclude unauthorized entry *during* working hours? . . . .

  B. Do these procedures include:
     1. Receptionist . . . .
     2. Guard . . . .
     3. Electric locks . . . .
     4. Badge systems . . . .
     5. Restricted entry policy . . . .
     6. Material pass system . . . .
     7. Identification cards . . . .
     8. Magnetic detection . . . .
     9. Service elevators . . . .
     10. Exits and windows . . . .

  C. Are procedures in effect to preclude unauthorized entry after working hours?

  D. Do these procedures include:
     1. Guard service . . . .
     2. Door alarm systems . . . .
     3. Other surveillance . . . .

  E. Are procedures in effect to preclude unauthorized entry under the following conditions?
     1. Employee/union strike . . . .
     2. Militant group action . . . .

  F. Are procedures in effect to preclude unauthorized entry to the tape library?. .

  G. Is entry to the loading dock area restricted? . . . .

  H. Are there procedures for receiving and storing supplies? . . . .

0   20   40   60   80   100%

_ _ _ _ _ _.Insurance companies _____Universities

FIGURE 30.2

II. Computer facility physical security: disasters

A. *Fire*—are procedures in effect to prevent or minimize damage/loss due to fire? . . . .

B. Do these procedures include:
1. Adequate fire extinguishing equipment . . . .

2. Periodic inspection of extinguishing equipment . . . .
3. Temperature deviation system . . . .
4. Smoke detection system . . . .

5. Files and programs stored in temperature/humidity controlled, fireproof way . . . .
6. Emergency power/air conditioning switches accessible . . . .
7. Periodic inspection of area beneath false floor . . . .
8. "No smoking" procedures . . . .
9. Waste receptacles fireproof . . . . . .
10. Auxiliary battery lights . . . .
11. Cleanliness and neatness . . . .
12. Personnel trained in emergency methods . . . .

C. *Water*—are procedures in effect to prevent or minimize damage/loss due to water? . . . .

D. Do these procedures include:
1. Air conditioning, sprinkling valves access. . . . .

2. Emergency equipment covers available
3. Personnel training area. . . . .

E. *Building damage*—are procedures in effect to minimize damage due to hurricane, wind, etc.? . . . .

F. *Supply power compromise*—Do overall procedures exist? . . . .

G. Do these procedures include:
1. Variable supply transformer . . . .
2. Uninterruptable power source . . . . . .
3. Standby generator . . . .
4. Backup power . . . .

H. Have arrangements been made for alternate processing at other location, in event of disaster? . . . .

I. Have the backup facilities been used or tested? . . . .

J. Does insurance coverage include damage/loss due to all the above hazards? . . . .

K. Does insurance coverage include costs of recreating files, rewriting programs, and of alternate equipment? . . . .

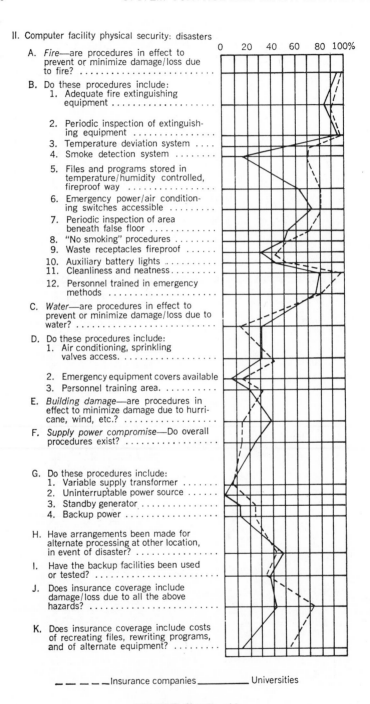

_ _ _ _ _Insurance companies_____ Universities

FIGURE 30.2 Cont'd

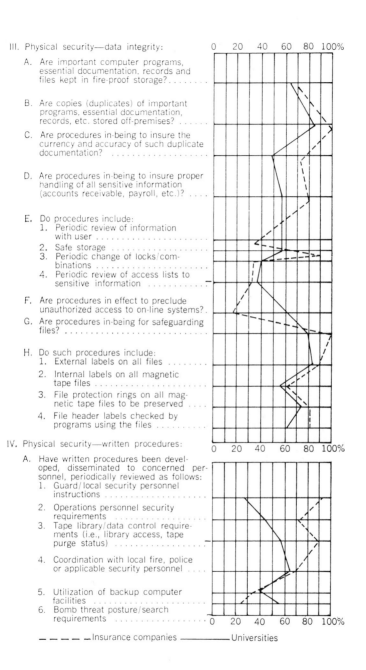

III. Physical security—data integrity:

  A. Are important computer programs, essential documentation, records and files kept in fire-proof storage? . . . .

  B. Are copies (duplicates) of important programs, essential documentation, records, etc. stored off-premises? . . . . . .

  C. Are procedures in-being to insure the currency and accuracy of such duplicate documentation? . . . .

  D. Are procedures in-being to insure proper handling of all sensitive information (accounts receivable, payroll, etc.)? . . . .

  E. Do procedures include:
    1. Periodic review of information with user . . . .
    2. Safe storage . . . .
    3. Periodic change of locks/combinations . . . .
    4. Periodic review of access lists to sensitive information . . . .

  F. Are procedures in effect to preclude unauthorized access to on-line systems?.

  G. Are procedures in-being for safeguarding files? . . . .

  H. Do such procedures include:
    1. External labels on all files . . . .
    2. Internal labels on all magnetic tape files . . . .
    3. File protection rings on all magnetic tape files to be preserved . . . .
    4. File header labels checked by programs using the files . . . .

IV. Physical security—written procedures:

  A. Have written procedures been developed, disseminated to concerned personnel, periodically reviewed as follows:
    1. Guard/local security personnel instructions . . . .
    2. Operations personnel security requirements . . . .
    3. Tape library/data control requirements (i.e., library access, tape purge status) . . . .
    4. Coordination with local fire, police or applicable security personnel . . . .
    5. Utilization of backup computer facilities . . . .
    6. Bomb threat posture/search requirements . . . .

_ _ _ _ _Insurance companies _____Universities

FIGURE 30.2 Cont'd

V. Employee security:

A. Are initial checks/background investigations accomplished on those *having
access* to the computer? . . . .

B. Are periodic follow-up security checks
accomplished? . . . .

C. Are initial security checks/background
investigations accomplished on those
working in the DP group? . . . .

D. Are periodic follow-up security checks
accomplished? . . . .

E. Have procedures been established to
evaluate DP employees' performance
in assigned functions? . . . .

F. Are employees who have been identified
as "disgruntled" assigned duties with
continued access to critical areas? . . . .

G. Are all proof & control functions performed by personnel other than machine
operators and programmers? . . . .

H. Are the functions & duties of computer
operators and programmers separate
and distinct? . . . .

I. Are operators assigned to particular
jobs or applications subject to
periodic rotation? . . . .

J. Are computer operators required to
take vacations? . . . .

K. Are DP employees separated from all
duties relating to initiation of transactions and master file changes? . . . . . .

L. Are appropriate machine operation logs
being maintained? . . . .

M. Is there an independent check of computer logs? . . . .

.N. If a computer has a typewriter console,
is there an independent check of
printouts to detect wrong intervention? . .

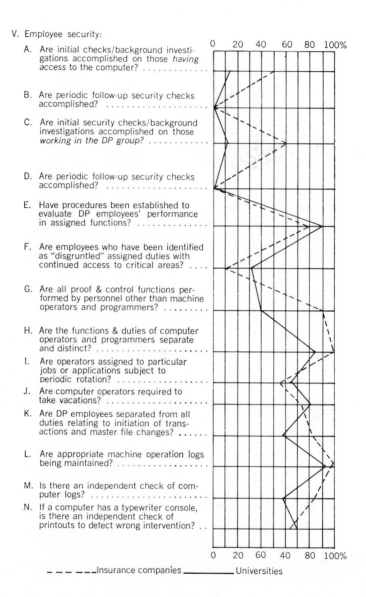

– – – – – –Insurance companies _____ Universities

FIGURE 30.2 Cont'd

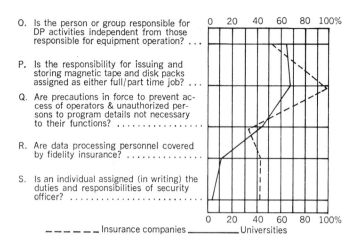

O. Is the person or group responsible for DP activities independent from those responsible for equipment operation? . . .

P. Is the responsibility for issuing and storing magnetic tape and disk packs assigned as either full/part time job? . . .

Q. Are precautions in force to prevent access of operators & unauthorized persons to program details not necessary to their functions? . . . .

R. Are data processing personnel covered by fidelity insurance? . . . .

S. Is an individual assigned (in writing) the duties and responsibilities of security officer? . . . .

– – – – – – Insurance companies ————— Universities

FIGURE 30.2 Cont'd

SITE HARDENING

Site hardening is a Defense Department term to describe the physical protections that can be used to reduce or eliminate the possible damage to an information system center. The physical location of the computer center is important to its security. Locating a computer in the basement of a frame building built in a flood plain near the San Andreas Fault illustrates some of the obvious things to avoid. Some of the important physical precautions to consider are:

1. Site location should be away from earthquake areas, flood plains, aircraft landing strips, routes of hazardous materials, centers of disruptive behavior, etc.

2. Materials used in the construction of a computer center should be as fireproof and waterproof as possible. The reduced use of glass will decrease dust and dirt particles.

3. Installation of emergency power generation equipment will prevent power interruption. The emergency power generating equipment must also be protected from potential disaster. Where emergency power equipment is not cost-effective, it may be possible to select a computer center site that is not susceptible to power failures. Certainly the local power company should be consulted on the location of a future computer center so they can warn of any impending problems.

4. Heat sensors and smoke detectors can signal an alarm and initiate a fire-fighting system. Fires in a computer center can be either electrical or paper. Thus, both regular and CO_2 fire extinguishers are needed. Sprinkler systems are contro-

versial because the damage caused by the water can be many times greater than that caused by fire. However, the sprinkler system may be essential to saving of the building.

5. Covers for equipment cabinets will reduce the water and smoke damage during a fire.

6. All shut-off switches must be clearly marked and accessible. The number of these should be minimal. Consideration should be given to a master "panic" switch.

EQUIPMENT REDUNDANCY

It has been the practice to duplicate some or all of the computing equipment for real-time systems. On-line real-time systems typically require very high reliability. It is a serious problem as well as very costly when such systems are down. An airline reservations system which is non-operative results in half-filled aircraft. A stock trading system that goes down, results in fewer trades and fewer commissions. In these cases, the need for equipment backup to keep the system in operation is obvious. Normal equipment failure, maintenance considerations and security will require that certain equipment be duplicated in all systems.

The following preventive measures can help avoid disaster in a critical computer center:

1. The organization may equip two or more substantially identical centers. Thus, if one is destroyed, priority work can be done on the other.

2. Computer suppliers may guarantee to replace equipment within a short period of time, such as 48 hours.

3. Reciprocal arrangements may be made with a similar installation of another firm. This has proven awkward in actual practice because of the difficulty in arranging priorities.

4. Stand-by arrangements may be made with commercial service bureaus. Here the priority problem can usually be solved contractually. This solution may be costly.

5. An emergency system may be designed using less expensive or otherwise available resources. For example, consider an airline with a reservations system on a large computer and with a smaller computer handling most other applications. Programs could be developed to implement a limited version of the reservations system on the smaller computer when disaster strikes the large computer.

Implementation of any solution to an emergency situation is subject to problems. The primary problem is to keep the emergency equipment as up-to-date as the on-going system. Changes in equipment in one system must be duplicated in the other. With microprogrammable hardware and complex operating systems existing at the same time, it may prove very difficult to maintain identity between systems.

When only compatibility is required of the backup facility, the emergency equipment should be tested regularly to assure that the required compatibility exists. Actual tests are more effective in uncovering problems than the examination of hardware and software specifications.

The five alternatives to an emergency situation (above) vary considerably in their cost. Not counting the costs of communication lines and equipment, two smaller computers will usually cost more than one large computer for the same work. The computer supplier may require compensation for guaranteeing that replacement equipment be available at all times. The costs for each particular situation must be examined carefully by the systems manager before deciding which redundancy arrangement is most appropriate for his organization and must be re-examined frequently. For example, reciprocal arrangements appropriate at one volume of computer use may be inappropriate when that use increases.

FILE AND DATA REDUNDANCY

More than equipment backup is needed to salvage an emergency that will completely destroy the computer center. The critical programs and files also need to be duplicated.

Programs exist in four principal forms: (1) listing and documentation; (2) source codes (usually on cards or magnetic tape); (3) object codes (in some machine readable form off the computer); and (4) object forms (usually on the computer or its peripherals). Backup programs are possible for all four forms. Let's assume that the program library is in object language form on one or more magnetic tapes. Any computer center of significant size will have a library of these programs requiring regular updates. There is a security need in such an installation for an established updating procedure. Some of the security considerations in the following paragraphs apply to updating such a system.

A copy of the program library should be protected in a safe or a location remote from the computer site. Many firms have locations where vital records of the organization are stored. Some even use caves.

There are several organizations which will store backup tape programs for a fee. Other companies use a distant branch plant or a vault of a rural commercial bank. Risks to consider in establishing a remote vital records center are fire, natural and atomic disasters. The most used scheme for protecting data files is the grandfather-father-son concept described in Figure 30.3. This system requires no duplication of computer runs but does require that additional tapes or disks be purchased. Destruction of the current master file by some disaster (or an operating error) is corrected by repeating the updating run which created the current master (son). This is produced from the previous master file (father). The most secure environments use two back-up levels (father and grandfather).

Batch system files are usually easy to protect by keeping the previous master and transaction files in a secure location. On-line transaction systems are somewhat more difficult to secure. One way of providing backup for such systems is to dump the on-line file periodically and to write a record in a batch file for each transaction. Using this procedure a special program may be necessary if the on-

---

Life of a Master Tape File

Responsibility	Action
Librarian	1. Receive a blank tape from the vendor.
Computer Operator	2. Use during the update run to record the updated master file.
Librarian	3. Hold until next scheduled update.
Computer Operator	4. Use as input during the next scheduled update run. The tape now becomes the father tape.
Computer Operator	5. Use if necessary to rerun the update. Need may occur because of errors or security incident.
Librarian	6. Hold until next father tape received. The tape now becomes the grandfather tape.
	7. Send to security area such as safe, bank vault or cave.
Security People	8. Use if necessary to rerun the update.
	9. Hold until next grandfather tape received.
	10. Mark as available for use and return to librarian.
	11. Repeat steps 2 through 10 for physical life of tape.

FIGURE 30.3

line file is destroyed. This method can also be used to audit the accuracy of the on-line program. Both the batch and transaction-based systems described here are deficient in their protection of current transactions.

The systems analyst must consider security in designing the input into the system. This may be done by keeping keypunching and data origination in a separate location, by maintaining separate source documents and by duplicating transaction files before taking them to the computer center. The designer will choose the method most applicable to his particular situation.

In the University of Wisconsin bombing described earlier, the data loss could have been avoided by the simple precaution of keeping a copy of the data deck remote from the computer center. As it was, students who lost all of their data for their Ph.D. dissertations had to share in the blame for the loss.

INSURANCE

Insurance companies are in business to protect their policy holders against financial disaster. In a computer installation, the equipment, the files and business continuation are all subject to insurance protection. The amount of insurance necessary is determined by the system's protection. For example, in a batch accounts receivable system, using the father-son security design, a lost master file could be replaced by the computer at a cost of a few hundred dollars. If no backup tapes were available but only a hard copy of the last report, then the cost of recreating the master file would be the keypunching of the entire file. A 20,000 record file might cost $20,000 to replace. If no copy of the master file were available in either machine readable or hard copy form, the firm would be out of business. The complete loss of a firm's accounts receivable files often results in business failure.

The amount of insurance needed and the resultant cost of insurance protection varies directly with the precautions taken. One must make a choice between prevention and insurance. There are situations in which insurance protection is more cost-effective than expensive preventative measures to eliminate risk. In the first of the three situations described above, the amount of the insurance would be the amount of computer time needed to process the grandfather tapes. In the second example, the insurance would cover the cost of keypunching. In the third example, the insurance would be for the value of the business.

The opportunities for employee fraud in an information system are numerous. The risks involved for the majority of employees may be well covered by a blanket bond. However, there are those in critical jobs who should be bonded for more substantial amounts. The act of bonding employees has the good effect of informing the employee that the organization considers his job to be important and the assets he handles to be valuable. Behavioral scientists generally believe that such knowledge increases job satisfaction and even improves performance.

The amount of insurance and bonding protection needed by an organization can be determined by taking an inventory of the assets of the computer center, considering the potential hazards, evaluating the costs of returning the center to operation after a disaster, and evaluating the costs of a safer system against insurance costs. The assets inventoried should include:

Hardware
Operating system programs
Application programs
Master files
Transaction and data files
Program and system documentation
Control records
Computer operating instructions
Programs and systems in process of development
People
Supplies

Values assigned will often be replacement costs, but some files have greater value than their replacement cost. The Encyclopaedia Britannica customer list mentioned earlier had a much greater value.

It is possible to buy business continuation insurance that will insure the difference between normal profit levels and the lower profits during a disaster recovery period.

PHYSICAL ACCESS CONTROLS

The purpose of physical access controls is to keep unauthorized people out of locations where they might cause a data or equipment loss. In information systems this usually involves restricting access to the computer room and to the tape and disk library. Often the company will provide guards at the entrance to the data center or will lock the doors. In either event there must be provision for those working in the center and for approved guests to have access. The duties of each information systems employee should be classified to determine which areas he is allowed to enter. Employees are given a key or badge which enables them to enter those specific areas. The tape and disk library is normally restricted to the librarian. Security for complex work schedules can be easily implemented with mini computers.

The possibility of employee theft, sabotage or other harmful acts is great enough so that some organizations have restrictions for employees who have given their termination notice. Some terminate the employee immediately while paying the salary up to the notice date. Others restrict the employee to low security areas until the termination date.

ELECTRONIC ACCESS CONTROLS

A large portion of the information systems currently being installed involves collecting and dispensing data and information from and to geographically dispersed locations. This involves using wire or microwave transmission systems. Such systems are subject to interception and wiretapping.

The organization that transmits important information must be concerned about incursions into the system. There are three basic ways in which data can be protected. It can be coded, scrambled or encrypted.

Confidential data in a record is usually coded. Accounting debits and credits are examples of data that are transmitted. Assume that each record contains just an account number, amount and sign. It is easy to recognize in a stream of pulses the pattern of the records. The limited use of numbers in accounting makes it easy to determine which field is the code and which the amount. However, going from an account number 4078 to an identification where 4078 means manufacturing costs for widgets is another matter. This requires extensive decoding and is quite costly.

Scramblers are hardware devices that transform the data being sent to a form resembling noise. The noise is unscrambled at the receiving end. These devices are used mostly for voice transmission at present.

Cryptographic techniques have long been used to keep messages secret. Software packages have been developed to apply cryptographic techniques to data transmission. The computer at one end ciphers the data and a module of a package at the other end deciphers it. This technique can be applied to all files if the security needs are great. This would mean that all disks and tapes would be ciphered but only deciphered during the application.

All data transmission, including the computer, is vulnerable to electronic eavesdropping. This is primarily because the electronics involved make the computer a weak transmitter.

"An electromagnetically secure plant is one in which the electromagnetic radiation resulting from operations such as writing data into the main memory, disk or tape, has been reduced by methods such as electromagnetic shielding of the facility and equipment, use of low-level signal equipment and power line filtering." (Peck, 1972).

A practice for systems needing a high level of security is to block or zero the computer core following each operation, shred the carbons and printer ribbons, and print garbage so that the platen loses any information it once possessed. Doubt of the capacity of the platen to provide a short term storage of printed information will be removed by an examination of a typewriter platen. It is also normal procedure to restrict a multi-programming computer to one program during highly secure runs.

Time-shared computers represent a difficult security problem for both the supplier and the user. The supplier is concerned about being paid for the use of the computer, keeping highly proprietary programs confidential and the client's information confidential. There have been breaches of security of each of the three areas. Thwarting the countering attempts to get free access to the computer is a function of the operating system of the time-shared computer. The system usually uses a password kept secure by the user. Compromise can occur by a demonstration to a client of the user, so frequent change of passwords is necessary.

One of the games played on college campuses for years has been the attempt by students to outwit the telephone company. The goal has been to get free long distance service. Despite sophisticated telephone billing techniques the system has been beaten on many occasions. The future will probably bring increasing attempts to get free computer time. The ultimate security measure may be to offer a prize to those who can break the system and reveal their methods so preventative steps can be taken.

Access use of programs must be given to time-share computer customers as part of the service they buy. The supplier allows a program to be called by the user but does not allow the program to be copied or printed by the user. A theft of one supplier's program was caught by the printer operator, who thought it peculiar to be sending a program to a customer. The printer operator was alerted to the theft because the magnitude of the printing task made printing the program on the customer's terminal unfeasible. This case shows that large programs are somewhat more secure but that there is no substitute for a vigilant operator.

Terminal security, both time-sharing and other, can be improved by locking the terminal after hours, by polling the terminal only during specified hours, by changing passwords and by use of a validation algorithm. Some algorithms are a function of a piece of user data such as birth date or social security number, date and hour of day. Ideally the terminal should never print and reveal this validation data.

OWNERSHIP CLAIMS

The insurance section of this chapter describes information systems related assets of an organization. Employees agree that some assets belong solely to the organization while other assets are shared in ownership with the employees. A third group of assets may have values not generally recognized by employees.

Equipment. The usual way of making an ownership claim on equipment is to tag it with the organization's name and an identification number. A record of the numbered tags and equipment descriptions is kept. An annual physical inventory is made and missing equipment is subject to careful investigation.

Programs present a more difficult ownership problem. They represent substantial commitments of a programmer's time. When a program is complete, many programmers feel it is "their program." If the organization wishes to claim ownership, it must be explicit in denying any claim of an individual programmer.

Company ownership of discoveries by researchers and engineers is often enforced through a patent waiver. By signing this waiver the employee admits that the product of his work belongs to the organization. The primary thrust of the form is informational since legal authorities generally state that the ownership by the organization exists whether or not a form is signed. The use of ownership claims similar to the patent waiver was slow to develop in information systems partly because employees not considered to be "creative" were developing programs. Today, information systems people are creating valuable program assets for their organizations and a form similar to the patent waiver is needed to remind the employee that the organization owns the programs.

The three methods by which an organization may protect its program assets are *patents, copyrights* and *trade secrets.* Several patents have been granted on programs by individuals working for organizations, but the patents are still subject to reversal by further court action. It is not currently clear whether patent protection will be generally available for programs. In any event, the disclosure involved for a patent makes it easily possible for another firm to use the ideas involved with little fear of infringement or of being caught if infringement occurs.

Copyright protection also involves disclosure which severely limits the effectiveness of the protection. This has more value for limiting the reproduction of written text.

Treating a program as a trade secret is the normal way of protecting programs. The program documentation might be stamped COMPANY CONFIDENTIAL or the employees required to sign an agreement to keep certain types of information confidential. If no one outside the organization knows about a program, then a copy would be purely accidental. If the program were given to others by an employee, legal recourse is available. The status of claim of a trade secret on a patentable item is currently being evaluated by the courts. It may be that treating a program as a trade secret is of limited value if the program is patentable.

Reports are certainly not patentable, so they are treated as trade secrets. The real problem is educating the staff that confidentiality is expected from them. One way to remind them is a liberal use of the words COMPANY CONFIDENTIAL on the cover or even each page of every report.

Asserting an ownership claim, while important, is not the end of the process. Violations of trade secrets must be prosecuted or the secrets may be lost. Courts have discounted claims where a previous history of non-enforcement has existed. Inaction in prosecuting is quickly communicated throughout the organization and encourages more theft.

PERSONNEL POLICIES

Ideally, the personnel selection process should reject the careless, malcontented and dishonest applicants. This process is not 100% effective. Certainly past behavior correlates with future behavior so rejecting applicants on the basis of poor recommendations or criminal records tends to reduce but not eliminate the high risk employee. The process of rejecting whole classes of applicants is subject to legal and social pressures. Discrimination on the basis of sex, race, national origin, religion and disability is generally illegal. Discrimination on the basis of a criminal record is a subject of legislative review as this is being written. The problem is that since no prediction method is 100% accurate all selection processes reject potentially good employees. While predictions relative to the group are possible and quite accurate, predictions for each individual are either 100% right or 100% wrong.

The information needed to make accurate predictions is also considered to be private by some commentators and thus, not an appropriate subject for prospective employer inquiry. With both the privacy and discrimination public policy restrictions, it is unlikely that the prospective employer will in the future be able to eliminate a substantial portion of security risks in the selection process. Also similar restrictions are likely to limit the gathering of relevant security information on current employees.

The systems analyst then must assume that any employee could be a security problem and all systems should be designed with adequate control and security.

Often the computer center employees lack company identification as well as any knowledge or appreciation of the needs for control systems as described in Chapter 26. The majority does not have a broad business background. The newer people in the data centers have usually worked only with computers and tend to be younger than others in the organization. Adequate security controls may add steps to programs, processing steps to systems, time to computer runs and the inconvenience of locked doors, but are necessary. Where control procedures interfere with effective job performance, the data processor has a conflict of values. Employee threats to the security of an information system can include deliberate circumvention of controls in order to improve job performance, as well as the more blatant fraud, negligence and deliberate damage.

Since systems can be over-controlled, control procedures should be subject to question and challenge, but not to avoidance. The following incident illustrates this situation. A payroll system had checks printed on a printer which had no read-back facility so occasionally it was possible that a character other than the signaled character could be printed. To control errors the Paymaster had to add the checks and compare them to the total. After a year of always balancing out, a young Paymaster stopped adding up the checks. Four months later another Paymaster reported four checks were each short ten cents. These checks were corrected, the bank was notified and the systems designers were gratified that the control was adequate. The next day the first Paymaster got several complaints that checks were short by ten to forty cents. He checked the addition and found that the checks were indeed wrong. But how many other wrong checks had slipped through? There was no way of knowing until the checks were returned from the bank and reconciled. Needless to say, the bank reconciliation process was a mess for six weeks and employees were led to distrust the payroll system.

Negligence and overzealousness can be corrected by establishing a strong control section, having the control section reporting to the director of information systems and indoctrinating the employees in control philosophy and procedures. Most significant is that no procedure be changed without having the security and control aspects of the change considered.

Vandalism of computers or files by a disgruntled employee is rare. Such situations can probably never be completely avoided. Their consequences can be reduced by considering file and equipment redundancy, hiring stable people, following good personnel practices, and immediately removing all terminating employees from vulnerable positions.

SUMMARY

In this chapter the importance of adequate security arrangements for a computer center and an information system has been described. After enumerating the risks, the costs of reducing the risks by the methods described in the chapter should be evaluated. By balancing risk versus protection cost the director of information systems can recommend the most appropriate security arrangements for the organization.

REVIEW QUESTIONS

1. What are some of the natural disasters that can cause problems for a computer center?
2. What are some of the threats from people outside a computer center?
3. What are some of the threats from people inside an information systems organization?
4. Explain how an organization might decide how much redundancy to permit.
5. What parameters help an analyst decide how much insurance to purchase?

DISCUSSION QUESTIONS

1. Discuss the tasks necessary for the Pentagon to take in recovering from its fire.
2. What records were assumed to exist in accomplishing the tasks above?
3. What file security measures should a profit-making, time-sharing service company take?
4. Discuss the tasks necessary to survey the security needs of a computer installation.
5. Note in Figure 30.2 that while many companies run an initial security check on their employees, few recheck them. Discuss disadvantages.
6. Describe some of the problems in protecting the current transactions in a batch information system.
7. Discuss ways to protect a partially complete program.

BIBLIOGRAPHY

Benedon, William, "Disaster Planning," *Ideas for Management*, 1971, Association for Systems Management: Cleveland, Ohio, pp. 114-141.

Bergart, Jeffrey G., Marvin Denicoff & David K. Hsiao, *An Annotated and Cross-Referenced Bibliography on Computer Security and Access Control in Computer Systems*, Ohio State: OSU-CISRC-TR72-12, 57 p.

Browne, Peter S., "Computer Security—A Survey," *Data Base*, Vol. 4 No. 3, Fall 1972, pp. 1-12.

Canning, Richard G., "Computer Fraud and Embezzlement," *EDP Analyzer*, Vol. 11 No. 9, Sept. 1973.

Canning, Richard G., "Computer Security: Backup and Recovery Methods," *EDP Analyzer*, Vol. 10 No. 1, January 1972, p. 15.

Canning, Richard G., "Security of the Computer Center," *EDP Analyzer*, Vol. 9 No. 12, December 1971, p. 13.

Canning, Richard G., "Protecting Valuable Data—Part I," *EDP Analyzer*, Vol. 11 No. 12, December 1973.

Canning, Richard G., "Protecting Valuable Data—Part II," *EDP Analyzer*, Vol. 12 No. 1, January 1974.

Chu, Albert L. C., "The Corporate Achilles Heel," *Business Automation*, Vol. 18 No. 3, February 1, 1971, pp. 32-38.

Conway, R. W., W. L. Maxwell, & H. L. Morgan, "On the Implementation of Security Measures in Information Systems," *Communications of the ACM*, Vol. 15 No. 4, April 1972, pp. 211-220.

Dickey, C. Lewis, "Securing the Computer," *Journal of Systems Management*, Vol. 23 No. 2, February 1972, pp. 8-10.

Evans, Arthur Jr., William Kantrowitz, & Edwin Weiss, "A User Identification Scheme Not Requiring Secrecy in the Computer," *Communications of the ACM*, Vol. 17 No. 8, August 1974, pp. 437-441.

"Fire Protection," *Infosystems*, Vol. 19 No. 9, September 1972, pp. 40-41.

Goode, George E., "New Developments in Data and Voice Security," *Telecommunications*, Vol. 8 No. 3, March 1974, pp. 35-38.

Greenlee, *Guide to Computer and Software Security*, AMR International, 1971.

Hamilton, *Computer Security*, Auerbach, 1973.

Hoffman, *Security and Privacy in Computer Systems*, Melville, 1973.

Holmes, Fenwicke W., "Software Security," *Journal of Systems Management*, Vol. 24 No. 9, September 1973, pp. 18-23.

Huggins, Phyllis, "Computers Show Resiliency After Earthquake," *Computerworld*, Vol. 5 No. 7, February 17, 1971 pp. 1-2.

Huggins, Phyllis, "Employee Charged in Program Theft," *Computerworld*, Vol. 5 No. 10, March 10, 1971, p. 1.

Huggins, Phyllis, "Rebuilt Fresno State DP Center Follows Tight Security," *Computerworld*, Vol. 4 No. 27 July 8, 1970, p. 8.

Jacobson, Robert, "Planning for Back-up Facilities," *Computer Services*, Vol. 2 No. 3, May/June 1970, pp. 21-29.

Katzan, Harry Jr., *Computer Data Security*, Van Nostrand, 1973.

Kennedy, J. D., "The Data Sentinel Computer Security System—A Practical Answer to Data Security Installation," *Management Review*, Vol. 1 No. 3, July 1972, pp. 7-10.

Koehn, Hank E., "Are Companies Bugged About Bugging?" *Journal of Systems Management*, Vol. 24 No. 1, January 1973, pp. 12-13.

Krauss, *SAFE—Security Audit and Field Evaluation*, AMACOM, 1972.

Lackey, R. D., "Penetration of Computer Systems," *Honeywell Computer Journal*, Vol. 8 No. 2, 1974, pp. 81-85.

Lundell, E. Drake Jr., "Big Cleanup Begins After Agnes," *Computerworld*, Vol. 6 No. 27, July 5, 1972, pp. 1-2.

Martin, James, *Security, Accuracy and Privacy in Computer Systems*, Englewood Cliffs, N.J.: Prentice-Hall, 1973.

Morton, Thomas J., "Bomb Demolishes Army Computer Complex," *Computerworld*, Vol. 4 No. 35, September 2, 1970, p. 1.

Morton, Thomas J., "Firms Sue in Mailing List Theft," *Computerworld*, Vol. 4, No. 27, July 8, 1970, p. 1.

Parker, Donn B., Susan Nycum, & S. Stephen Oura, *Computer Abuse*, Menlo Park, California, Stanford Research Institute, 1973.

Peck, Paul L., "Data Processing Safeguards," *Journal of Systems Management*, Vol. 23 No. 10, October 1972, pp. 11-17.

Recommended Good Practice for the Protection of Electronic Data Processing and Computer Controlled Industrial Processes, Factory Insurance Association, 1971.

Rittersbach, George H., "Data Processing Security: A Selected Bibliography," *Management Adviser*, Vol. 10 No. 5, September/October 1973, pp. 52-56.

Sorensen, J. L., "Common Sense in Computer Security," *Journal of Systems Management*, Vol. 23 No. 4, April 1972, pp. 12-14.

Taylor, Alan, "The Great Fraud: DP or Not DP?", *Computerworld*, Vol. 7 No. 17, April 25, 1973, pp. 1-4.

"To Catch A Thief," *Datamation*, Vol. 19 No. 2, February 1973, pp. 121-123.

Van Tassel, Dennis, *Computer Security Management*, Prentice-Hall, 1972.

Van Tassel, Dennis, "Contingency Plan for Catastrophe, A," *Datamation*, Vol. 17 No. 13, July 1, 1971, pp. 30-33.

Verba, Joseph, "Protecting Your EDP Investment," *Management Services*, Vol. 7 No. 5, September/October 1970.

Waterman, John J. Jr., "Uninterruptible Power Systems—Part I," *Modern Data*, Vol. 5 #5, May 1972, pp. 30-36.

Weissman, Clark, "Trade-Off Considerations in Security System Design," *Data Management*, Vol. 10 No. 4, April 1972, pp. 14-19.

Willoughby, Theodore C., Wayne K. Messner & Richard L. Reed, "A Search for Security," *Installation Management Review*, Vol. 2 No. 3, July 1973, pp. 6-15.

Wooldridge, Susan, Colin Corder and Claude Johnson, *Security Standards for Data Processing*, Wiley, 1973.

EPILOGUE

John Dearden of Harvard University on occasion has enumerated the attributes and abilities needed by a systems analyst. Dearden concludes that there is no way that anyone could possibly have all of the needed knowledge and characteristics. Obviously, we disagree or this book would not have been written. The one hundred thousand or more people performing the job is a testimony that the job can be done.

We agree with Dearden that the systems analyst has a difficult job, and that the analyst requires a great amount of knowledge to perform effectively. This text is an introduction to the many areas of knowledge that the analyst needs. The material provides enough information so that the junior analyst can start to work. But this text should be just the beginning of the education of the systems professional. The education should be continued by reading professional journals and books and by attending appropriate continuing education courses and programs. This is costly in time and money. Keeping up-to-date is likely to require three evenings per week of reading and as much as $500 per year for periodicals and books. The references given in this text were designed as pointers to the currently relevant literature. These should start the junior analyst's continuing education. We hope that the reader will go well beyond them in the quest of true systems knowledge.

INDEX